A HISTORY
OF MUSICAL STYLE

A History of Musical Style

by Richard L. Crocker
University of California, Berkeley

Dover Publications, Inc., New York

Published in Canada by General Publishing Company, Ltd., 30 Lesmill Road, Don Mills, Toronto, Ontario.
Published in the United Kingdom by Constable and Company, Ltd., 10 Orange Street, London WC2H 7EG.

This Dover edition, first published in 1986, is an unabridged and slightly corrected republication of the work first published by McGraw-Hill Book Company, New York, in 1966.

Manufactured in the United States of America
Dover Publications, Inc., 31 East 2nd Street, Mineola, N.Y. 11501

Library of Congress Cataloging in Publication Data

Crocker, Richard L.
  A history of musical style.

  Reprint. Originally published: New York : McGraw-Hill, 1966.
  Includes index.
  Bibliography: p. 531–554.
  1. Style, Musical. 2. Music—Performance—History. I. Title.
ML430.5.C76 1986   781'.09   85-20718
ISBN 0-486-25029-6

IN MEMORIAM

LEO SCHRADE

PREFACE

THIS BOOK TRACES THE DEVELOPMENT OF WESTERN MUSICAL style from the time of its earliest written records down to the present. Designed as a text for college music majors, it tries to tell the story of style as simply, as connectedly as possible. The book stresses the continuity of basic musical principles over long periods of history, while exploring in greater detail moments of high stylistic achievement.

Our basic ideas of what happened in music history clearly need overhauling to make them accord with the facts brought out by modern research. Traditional explanations often no longer explain the growing body of music now easily accessible in anthologies; traditional interpretations often are not reflected in the increasing—and increasingly good—performances of music from other times. In response to this need for a fresh look at music history, every effort has been made here to incorporate up-to-date interpretations where they seemed warranted, or to advance new ones where necessary.

The present text offers the college music major a continuous account of music's changing style. While all important composers are mentioned, stress is laid on those composers, and those works, that mark out the main lines of music. Seeking the reasons for stylistic change within the history of style itself (rather than in the history of men or of ideas), the account tries to show how music, growing out of its own past, has shaped its own development.

The book is so constructed that its outline should be clear even if some phases may seem rather dense. Discussion of individual topics is initiated at a

relatively low factual and conceptual level, then pursued through more sophisticated levels. By passing over some of the denser passages, any music major
should be able to follow the main line of argument, while the better student
should find enough to keep him occupied.

This book can be used as a text for several kinds of course work. The
basic account presented here can be placed in dialog with material from social
or intellectual history, from literature and the other arts, according to the
interests of the individual instructor and his students. The analytical approaches
suggested here for the various historical phases can be used as guidelines in
courses oriented more toward analysis than historical survey. Selected parts of
the book (as suggested on page 554) could be used as readings in an introductory
course. The book has proved useful to graduate students for review survey. Lists
of Selected Study Materials for each chapter are given at the back of the book
to guide the student to the all-important study of significant musical compositions.

Richard L. Crocker

ACKNOWLEDGMENTS

Colleagues of all kinds—faculty, staff, and students—of the Department of Music, University of California (Berkeley), and elsewhere have contributed ideas, materials, criticism, and encouragement. Many pairs of eyes sharper than mine have found countless errors of fact and style; many skillful hands have helped with the drudgery. The long-suffering staff of the Music Library has provided assistance at every turn.

M. Thomas, Director of the Department of Manuscripts, of the Bibliothèque nationale (Paris) graciously permitted the inclusion of materials from that library, as did also Dr. Mason, Librarian of Christ Church College, Oxford.

Copyright releases were kindly provided by Mrs. Gertrud Schoenberg, Dr. G. Francesco Malipiero, the Ministère de l'education nationale (Paris), Director Mieczyslaw Tomaszewski (for the Fryderyk Chopin Institute, Warsaw), the American Musicological Society, the Mediaeval Academy of America, the Royal Musical Association, the Trustees of Smith College, and the following publishers: Bärenreiter, Boosey & Hawkes, J. & W. Chester Ltd., Wilhelm Hansen, Jean Jobert, Möseler, Leo S. Olschki, Oxford University Press, Suvini Zerboni, Universal Edition A. G. (Vienna) and Universal Edition Ltd. (London), and Yale University Press.

Special appreciation is due to Desclee and Company, to Editions de l'Oiseau-lyre, and to Dr. Armen Carapetyan of the American Institute of Musicology for copyright releases of extensive material.

Since this book does not include full scholarly acknowledgments, perhaps a token expression of my indebtedness can find a place here—first of all to my teacher, in whose memory this book is inscribed; then to my many colleagues, both here and abroad, whose publications have made this one possible.

R.L.C.

CONTENTS

A History
of Musical Style

PART 1
CHANT 700-1150

1
BEFORE THE BEGINNING: GREGORIAN CHANT

THE HISTORY OF WESTERN MUSIC PROPERLY BEGINS NOT WITH the Greeks or Romans but with the Franks. These rough, vigorous tribes of redheaded warriors (as they are described) came down across the Rhine into what is now northern France and the Benelux region during the 200s and 300s. The Franks moved into a cultural space called Gallo-Roman, civilized for centuries under the Roman Empire, but now decaying within as fast as it was being infiltrated from without. At first it seemed as though the Frankish ascendancy was just another of the turbulent shifts in power as one tribe after another stormed across the remains of the Roman Empire. But the Franks stayed. They solidified their own position to the point where they themselves could afford to become civilized. Absorbing whatever elements of culture they encountered, they initiated a new phase of cultural synthesis. What made the Franks different from the other barbarians was not their great military aptitude but rather their even greater organizational ability. Rough and uncultured they had been, but they set up a culture that has lasted more than a thousand years.

THE FRANKS AND GREGORIAN CHANT The education of the Franks began under the Carolingians, the leading Frankish dynasty. Under Pippin III, crowned king in 751, and his son Charles the Great, or Charlemagne (ca 742–814), the Carolingians not only extended their kingship into an empire, but set in motion the process of acculturation through which Frankish energies and talents eventually found their own modes of expression. In their search for cultural values, the Carolingians turned to Rome and the Christian Church. Pagan Rome was a symbol of past greatness, of accumulated learning; as a symbol it was valued highly by the politically astute Carolingians. The Church, on the other hand, was one of the most important social realities on the European scene: it stood for order, and it stood for it in a way that obviously appealed to growing numbers of Westerners. The Carolingian political program, especially in education, came to depend largely on the institutions of the Church.

Surveying the European scene, the Carolingians saw local autonomy and variety. They found in the Roman Church, specifically in the Roman liturgy, the means best suited to producing cultural unity. And the liturgy was largely sung. Pippin III and even more Charlemagne made universal adoption of the Roman liturgy—including its chant—one of their main objectives; their efforts toward this objective were sustained from 750 to Charlemagne's death in 814. They sent to Rome for chant books and for cantors to come to teach the Frankish singers; they sent their own cantors to Rome to learn Roman chant; they not only caused these things to be done, but followed up their execution with a keen personal interest. Although the results of this interest are hard to assess at a distance of over a thousand years, it is clear that by 850 there was in use in the Frankish realm a repertory of Roman chant that had not been there a century earlier. Although the relationship of the imported Roman chant to past and future Frankish music was extremely complex, still the Roman chant set a standard of excellence and a point of departure for the Franks.

The unity we now observe in the repertory of Roman chant seems in large part due to the Franks themselves, whose unsurpassed organizational talents left their mark here as elsewhere. The Franks began by calling this chant *Gregorian,* after Pope Gregory I (ca 540–604), who was supposed to have set the repertory in order. The propriety of the term *Gregorian* has long been in dispute, beginning in the 800s, and now more than ever; but the term has stuck.

There are increasing indications, however, that even in Rome all was not pure Gregorian, that there were several repertories of chant, successive or simultaneous, that in fact the local variety prevailing throughout the West was present within the Eternal City itself. Inquiries from the North about Roman practice were sometimes put off with official double-talk or inscrutable silence by Roman authorities; Northern investigations over the century 750–850 brought back different versions of Roman chant. Things got so bad that the Franks circulated a rumor that Rome had sent North a dozen experts with specific instructions to teach a dozen different versions. The rumor is undoubtedly not true; but given the conditions it reflected, the remarkable thing is how stable the Gregorian repertory turned out to be, even with all the variants and complexities now being scrutinized by specialists.

Without a foundation of written documents, we cannot at present even outline the history of the Gregorian repertory. The earliest surviving chant books, written around 900, include variants and additional material. It is possible to penetrate backward from these earliest books a little way by studying the history of the liturgies which the chant accompanied, but even granting the relationship of music and liturgy, the historical results are not at present conducive to a clear picture.

One has to distinguish among several local rites of greater or lesser importance, including Roman, Milanese or Ambrosian, Mozarabic or Spanish (that is, Toledo), and assorted ''Gallican'' practices. The Roman rite—or at any rate, the Roman rite that came North—immediately engendered endless local variants due to errors in transmission, if not variation at the source itself. Then, as this imported Roman rite was established in various localities, it acquired in each a different set of additions and expansions. The Franks enthusiastically imitated Byzantine practices, borrowing isolated melodies with or without Greek texts. They also borrowed from the Mozarabic liturgy and probably elsewhere. Nor was all this variation purely local: crisscrossing back and forth went the lines of communication of the great monastic orders, such as the Benedictines, carrying chant versions far beyond the normal barriers of geography, language, and local government.

The most important fact to remember when dealing with these variations—and with the whole Gregorian repertory—is that by the time of our earliest chant books with written melodies (around 900) the Christian Church had been singing for a period almost half as long as its present age; furthermore, that period saw the Church's greatest growth and development. Obviously musical style did not remain static up to 900, nor is it likely that it developed in a single, well-defined direction. At most we can assume only the normal continuity of stylistic growth. Inheriting centuries of accumulated techniques and meaning, the Roman chant of the 700s was highly stylized and extremely sophisticated when, at the end of its long, intricate development, it was taken over by the Franks.

For our purposes, we can pass over the problems of the history of Gregorian chant; we need to be acquainted with it only as a block of music embedded in liturgy. The stylistic development we will be tracing (at least up to 1600) took place in the Frankish sphere of influence. For the sake of understanding that development we need to know the Roman chant only as it was known in the North, in versions resembling those now standard. We need to see the Roman, or better, the Gregorian style as the Carolingians themselves idealized it—perfect, complete, in many ways inscrutable, without a past and largely without a stylistic future.

ROMAN LITURGY One of the most orderly features of Gregorian chant is the way various styles of chant are assigned different functions in the worship service. The Gregorian repertory includes a wide range of styles; very simple chant is reserved for simple occasions, or for those portions of festive occasions where the text being sung is far more important than the music, or where both text and music merely accompany an important liturgical action. More elaborate styles are used for more festive occasions, or for those portions of the service whose function is largely musical.

A large part of the Gregorian repertory is ''service music'' in the sense that its principal purpose is to accompany or solemnify the action of worship; such music does not claim to be a complete artistic experience in itself. Only a few kinds of Gregorian chant are designed to occupy the listener's full attention, and these kinds are carefully placed in the service so that full attention may be given them. In judging and analyzing Gregorian styles, one must know the intended liturgical function of a piece.

The most important service of the Roman Church was, and is, the mass—important first for theological reasons, but important to us because music for the mass is the central part of the Gregorian repertory. Over the centuries this service, originally a simple, direct sequence of events, has been surrounded by much supplementary ritual, as naturally happens to any well-loved, oft-repeated action. For musical purposes, however, we need to know only the main outlines of the liturgical action. Furthermore, we need to concern ourselves primarily with those portions that attracted the attention of composers.

The Roman mass consists of two disparate parts, descended from two distinct services. The first part, called *synaxis* (cf. *synagogue*), consists basically of a prayer, a Scripture reading or lesson, the singing of a part of a psalm, and another lesson. The alternation of lessons and psalm singing, descended from Judaic practice, is basic to much of Christian worship. The prayer is called a *collect*, in that it is a public prayer sung by the priest on behalf of all present. The collect is sung to a simple melodic formula or *tone*, to be described shortly. It is the prayer of the day, varying from Sunday to Sunday in order to point up the significance of the great feasts, such as Christmas and Easter, and the seasons surrounding them. The first lesson, called the *epistle*, is usually taken from the Epistles of Paul in the New Testament, and the second lesson, called the *gospel*, is from one of the four Gospels. As with the collect, there is a different epistle and gospel reading for each Sunday and feast day. Epistle and gospel are sung by the priest to melodic formulas similar to those used for the collect.

synaxis of the mass (oldest elements)

> collect (prayer of the day)
> epistle (first Scripture lesson)
> gradual (singing of part of a psalm)
> gospel (second Scripture lesson)

The portion of the psalm sung by the choir between the lessons, called the *gradual,* is the main musical event of the mass. No other liturgical action goes on. The text of the gradual is very short (two verses of a psalm), unlike the texts of the lessons that surround it; the music of the gradual, however, is relatively long. By the time the Roman mass reached the Franks, the gradual had been joined by another elaborate chant, the *alleluia,* also a musical event in its own right. Both gradual and alleluia vary from day to day, in melody as well as text. Since the alleluia (Praise the Lord!) is unsuited to times of penitence, it is replaced during Lent by a psalmodic piece called a *tract,* also very elaborate. In the very joyful season after Easter, the gradual in turn is replaced by an additional alleluia, making two alleluias between the epistle and gospel. The liturgical space between the two lessons of the synaxis is thus filled with the most important music of the mass.

chants between the lessons

	or in Lent:	or after Easter:
gradual	gradual	alleluia
alleluia	tract	alleluia

Substantial additions were made over the centuries at the beginning of the synaxis. By the time the Roman mass reached the Franks it had acquired a solemn processional song for the choir called an *introit* (going-in song), consisting of verses from a psalm with a refrain or *antiphon*. (Other now-familiar additions, including *Kyrie* and *Gloria in excelsis*, were just receiving artistic definition in Carolingian times; they will be taken up later.) The introit, like the gradual and alleluia (and tract), varies in text and music from day to day. Unlike the chants between the lessons, however, the introit is, or was originally, service music, sung during the procession. More functional, the introit is less elaborate than the gradual or alleluia; but since it is for the mass, it is still festive.

The second half of the Roman mass is peculiarly Christian, performed in obedience to the Lord's command at the Last Supper to take bread and wine, bless them, and eat "in remembrance of me." This part of the mass is called the *eucharist* (from the Greek word for *blessing*); it is also called Holy Communion. Basically a series of acts ("Take . . . bless . . . eat . . ."), it offers less opportunity for purely musical display.

The chants for the eucharist are almost entirely functional, deriving their names and forms from the actions they accompany. While the bread and wine are being "taken" from the offerings of the congregation, the choir sings an *offertory*, which consisted originally of a psalm and antiphon as at the introit. As at the introit, this psalm was once sung complete; after Carolingian times it was eliminated, leaving only the antiphon.

The eucharistic blessing, or rather the beginning of it called the *preface*, is sung by the priest to an especially elaborate formula or tone. (At the end of the preface comes the *Sanctus*—but this part does not concern us now.) The main part of the blessing, called the *canon*, is said by the priest in a low voice. At the end of the canon, the eucharistic blessing is concluded with the Lord's Prayer, sung to a solemn tone. During the communion itself still another psalm and antiphon, called *communion*, were once sung complete by the choir, but in Carolingian times, this was reduced to the antiphon. (Certain now-familiar additions to the eucharist, the *Agnus Dei* in particular, will be taken up later.) Functional, like the introit, the offertory and communion changed from day to day.

mass: synaxis and eucharist (before final additions)
     introit (antiphon and psalm verse)
     collect
     epistle
     gradual (or alleluia)
     alleluia (or tract)
     gospel
     offertory (antiphon)
                   ⎧ preface—(*Sanctus*)
     prayer of blessing ⎨ canon
                   ⎩ Lord's Prayer
     communion (antiphon)

The five items, introit, gradual, alleluia, offertory, and communion, together with collect, epistle, and gospel, make up the *proper* of the mass; their texts, changing from day to day, are proper or appropriate to a particular occasion, such as Christmas or Easter. Collect, epistle, and gospel (as well as preface and the Lord's Prayer) are sung by the priest to standard tones that stay the same from day to day. Introit, gradual, alleluia, offertory, and communion are sung by the choir, each proper text having its own melody. This group of five items constitutes the central portion of the Gregorian repertory, as it came North to the Franks and as we know it today. When we speak of the *mass propers,* or of the *proper of the mass,* we mean this repertory of texts and melodies provided for the Sundays, holy days, and saints' days of the Christian year.

RECITATION FORMULAS The melodic formulas or tones for the collect, epistle, and gospel are relatively simple, being purely functional. At the same time, they may be from the oldest preserved strata—along with the more elaborate tones for preface and the Lord's Prayer—and hence furnish a convenient introduction to Gregorian chant. Even if the musical interest of these items is not so great as other types of chant, still they expose to our view tonal progressions of a remote, fascinating quality.

(Throughout this book, *tonal* will be used as an adjective for *tone,* rather than for *tonality.* Thus a *tonal progression* is a progression of tones, that is, notes or pitches; *tonal order* is an order pertaining to notes or pitches, as contrasted, say, with rhythmic order. The use of *tone* in chant to refer to a formula consisting of a few pitches may seem confusing at first, but is actually a logical and useful extension of the use of *tone* for a pitch, then for an interval. In any case *tone,* in its Latin forms, was the preferred term in the Middle Ages.)

The ancient *prayer tone* for the collect consists of only two pitches a whole tone apart. Example 1 contains the ending formula of the collect, a formula in text as well, called a *doxology* or glorification. The preceding part of

EXAMPLE I PRAYER TONE

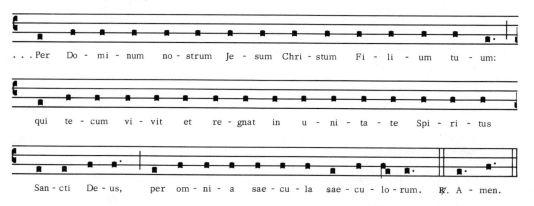

... Per Do - mi - num   no - strum Je - sum Chri - stum   Fi - li - um   tu - um:

qui te - cum vi - vit   et   re - gnat   in   u - ni - ta - te   Spi - ri - tus

San - cti De - us,   per om - ni - a sae - cu - la sae - cu - lo - rum. ℞. A - men.

(Through our Lord Jesus Christ thy Son, who liveth and reigneth with thee in the unity of the Holy Ghost, God, world without end. ℞. Amen.)

the collect, not much longer than this doxology, is sung to the same two pitches arranged in the same pattern. Most of the text is recited on the upper of the two pitches (A), the lower (G) forming inflections at beginning and end of phrases. It is by no means clear from the internal structure of this prayer tone which of the two pitches is to be the final one. This tonal ambiguity, resulting in a sense of suspension, is one of the most characteristic, appropriate, and attractive features of the Gregorian style.

The notation of Example 1 is a type developed around 1200 and still in use for modern chant books. In spite of the unfamiliar square notes, the groupings of two or more notes over a single syllable into a *neume,* and the four-line staff with movable C clef, this type of notation has proved extremely practical for chant, possessing many advantages over more modern notation. Chant is notated at whatever pitch level reduces accidentals to a minimum, with the understanding that any chant may be sung at any convenient absolute pitch. The neume over saecu-*lo*-rum represents two pitches, A, then G. The sign ℟ means *response* and is used in a number of different contexts; here it indicates the congregational response, *Amen,* to the collect.

Square notation contains no intrinsic indication of relative lengths of notes. Consequently, the rhythm of the chant has been the subject of endless discussion. The most practical solution (the one most widely accepted) is to treat each note as more or less equal in length, thinking of that length as equivalent to an eighth note of modern notation.

Certain interpretative rhythmic signs have been devised by the Benedictines of Solesmes (France), the leaders in the restoration of Gregorian chant to something approaching its original form and dignity. These signs will be used in the examples of this book. In Example 1 the dot (after tu-*um,* De-*us,* saeculo-*rum, A-men*) is one of the Solesmes interpretative signs; it means a doubling of the note it follows. Other signs are the various bars and partial bars, which are analogous to punctuation; in prayer tones and lesson tones, these correspond closely to the punctuation of the text. The double bar marks the end of a piece or a change of performer.

The central part of the eucharist, in between the offertory and communion antiphons, is governed by one basic set of prayer tones, which may be very old indeed. This part of the service begins (after the offertory) with a dialog between priest and congregation, and then continues with the preface. The dialog and invariable beginning of the preface is given in Example 2; the rest of the preface has a different text proper to important seasons, but is sung to the tone given for the opening. The rest of the great prayer of blessing is said by the priest in a low voice, while the congregation is silent. Then at the end, the Lord's Prayer (or *Pater noster*) is sung in a tone related to the preface, forming its musical conclusion.

The dialog (Example 2) proceeds by alternating a phrase for the priest, called a *versicle,* (℣) with one for the congregation, called a response (℟). The two-note neume on *vo*-biscum represents two notes, first G, then A. On *sur*-sum appears an ornamental three-note neume called *quilisma,* representing the notes A and C connected by some kind of decoration—just what we do not know; the Benedictines recommend prolonging the A slightly, then sliding easily through B to reach C.

EXAMPLE 2 *SURSUM CORDA* AND PREFACE TONE

℣. Do - mi - nus vo - bi - scum. ℟. Et cum spi - ri - tu tu - o. ℣. Sur - sum cor - da.

℟. Ha - be - mus ad Do - mi - num. ℣. Gra - ti - as a - ga - mus Do - mi - no De - o no - stro.

℟. Di - gnum et ju - stum est. Ve - re di - gnum et ju - stum est, ae - quum et sa - lu - ta - re,

nos ti - bi sem - per et u - bi - que gra - ti - as a - ge - re:

Do - mi - ne san - cte, pa - ter om - ni - po - tens, ae - ter - ne De - us:

Qui cum u - ni - ge - ni - to . . . (etc.)

(℣. **The Lord be with you.** ℟. **And with thy spirit.** ℣. **Lift up your hearts.**
℟. **We lift them up unto the Lord.** ℣. **Let us give thanks unto our Lord God.** ℟. **It
is meet and right so to do.**
**It is very meet and right, just and salutary for us at all times and in all places to
give thanks: O Lord Holy, Father Almighty, Everlasting God, who with the only
begotten . . .)**

The introductory nature of the melody for the dialog is obvious; climbing
slowly, it leads naturally into the preface. So involved is the melodic motion, so
intricate and oblique its prevailing ascent, that one is hardly aware of its narrow
limits; all takes place within the range of a fourth. This intricate kind of
motion is another of the characteristic features of Gregorian chant.

The preface tone itself (Example 2, *Vere dignum* . . .) has two elements.
The first rises to the top of the fourth G–C, reciting on C and descending to the
note below for a half cadence; this element may be repeated several times (here
only once). The other melodic element recites on B, descending eventually to A

for a full cadence. This element is not immediately repeated, but forms the conclusion to a series of statements of the first element, whereupon the whole sequence is repeated as often as necessary to intone the given text (for example, *XXXY, XXY, XXXXY* . . .). In general the last notes and neumes of each formula are fixed, while elasticity is provided by the interior of the formula, especially the *reciting notes,* C and B. The principle, then, of this preface tone is similar to that of the prayer tone in Example 1, but its structure is more elaborate.

Even though both text and music of the *Pater noster* are invariable (Example 3), it still uses formulas, which are very similar to those of the

EXAMPLE 3 PATER NOSTER

(Our Father, who art in heaven, hallowed be thy Name. Thy kingdom come; thy will be done, on earth as it is in heaven. Give us this day our daily bread; and forgive us our debts, as we forgive our debtors. And lead us not into temptation. ℞. But deliver us from evil. Amen.)

preface except that they do not press up to the top of the fourth so insistently. The half cadence is made on G, the bottom of the fourth, the full cadence on A, the note above. The balance between overall clarity of phrase and intricacy of detail, combined with the sense of suspension associated with the whole tones around the final, makes this melody the most appropriate ever written for the *Pater noster.*

Simplicity is not a reliable mark of antiquity in the Gregorian repertory. Although we do not know for certain that the tones already studied are very old, we do know that other prayer tones and lesson tones simpler than these are considerably more recent. The more recent tones (dating, say, after 1000) share a tendency to recite on a note forming the top of a half step (F or C), a position that gives the reciting note much sharper definition than in the tones we studied.

OFFICE PSALMODY The parts of the proper of the mass sung by the choir—introit, gradual, alleluia (or tract), offertory, and communion—are naturally much more complex than prayer and lesson tones. To understand them we need to examine first the way of singing psalms, *psalmody,* codified by the Roman Church. During the early centuries psalmody was the backbone of Christian services outside the mass, services that were performed by parish churches, by clergy attached to cathedrals, and by the fast-growing monasteries, where the whole psalter of 150 psalms came to be sung every week at a daily cycle of services.

These services, called *offices,* had a long, complex evolution. They came to consist in Carolingian times of a morning service (*lauds*) and an evening service (*vespers*), a very large night service (*matins*), and a series of very short services throughout the day at three-hour intervals (*prime, terce, sext, none,* and—after vespers—*compline*).

monastic daily cycle of services (offices)

        matins: 1st nocturn
                2nd nocturn
                3rd nocturn
        lauds
            prime
            terce
            sext
            none
        vespers
            compline
        _____
        matins (etc.)

Matins, lauds, and vespers all begin with the singing of several psalms, and then continue with the basic Judaic pattern of Scripture lesson followed by a sung portion of a psalm, called at matins a *responsory.* At lauds and vespers the lesson is vestigial, and instead of a responsory, a *canticle* or song from the New Testament is sung, for example, the *Magnificat.* All these items involve music of greater or lesser complexity, ranging from very simple formulas for the psalms (*psalm tones*) to elaborate settings for the responsories comparable to graduals.

On festive occasions psalms are provided with antiphons, short texts set to their own independent melodies. The text might come from the psalm itself, or from elsewhere in Scripture, or might be newly composed; the meaning of the text makes the antiphon (and, by association, the psalm) proper to the occasion. The first antiphon proper to Christmas matins, for example, goes, "The Lord said unto me, Thou art my son, this day have I begotten thee," which even though taken from an Old Testament psalm expresses the New Testament theme of Christmas. Antiphons were used in various ways to frame the singing of a psalm. Sometimes the antiphon was repeated after every psalm verse like a refrain; but the common practice after Carolingian times was and is to sing the antiphon only at beginning and end of the psalm.

Example 4 gives another antiphon from Christmas matins. The text, *Suscepimus Deus*, comes from the psalm it accompanies, Psalm 47 (Psalm 48 in the English Psalter, which has a slightly different numbering from the Latin Psalter). The asterisk after *Deus* indicates the point at which the choir starts singing; every choral piece of chant is begun by a cantor (soloist) to set the pitch. Example 4 contains two more Benedictine rhythmic signs, a small horizontal mark above or below a note, and a vertical one. The horizontal mark, called *episema* (De-*us*), prolongs its note slightly. The vertical mark, called *ictus* (sus-*cep*-), suggests a rhythmic grouping. Since chant is irregular, it cannot be counted in an unbroken succession of twos or of threes (or of multiples of two or three); if it is to be counted, the counting must be done by an irregular succession of groups of two and three. The ictus suggests places to begin a new group—where to count "one."

Antiphons are among the glories of Gregorian chant. They are typically as short as *Suscepimus Deus*, and frequently as simple, but this simplicity conceals an extraordinary degree of artistry. It is hard to imagine a more compact melody, or one with more elegance. Antiphons such as this one are so compact as to resist analysis. They obviously go up and down, sometimes returning to where they came from, as here, sometimes not, but the mysterious ingredients that make them art seem concealed under centuries of Mediterranean musical culture. Not all melody is so inscrutable; in the Frankish melodies we will soon meet, the rationale is more plainly evident.

While the purely melodic logic of the antiphon may escape us, it is possible to observe the close relationship between the melody and its text. Pieces

EXAMPLE 4   ANTIPHON (mode 8)

Su - sce - pi - mus De - us,   * mi - se - ri - cor - di - am   tu - am   in me - di - o   tem - pli tu - i.

(We wait for thy mercy, O God, in the midst of thy temple.)

of this type are called *syllabic,* since each syllable gets a note. The syntax and prosody of the text show up directly in the phrases of the music—as if this melody had been made especially for this text. In a sense it was; but it may be surprising to learn that this antiphon melody, which is so beautifully wedded to its text, belongs to a large group of antiphons, all having the same basic melody.

This basic melody is not an elastic formula like a prayer tone, but is a slightly different phenomenon called a *melody type.* It has no reciting note, but is adapted more freely to each new text, resulting each time in a closed, apparently unique melody, different in nature from the open-ended recitation formulas. There are a number of melody types among the more than one thousand antiphons of the Gregorian offices. Other examples using the same melody as *Suscepimus Deus,* as well as other melody types, can be conveniently studied in the matins service for Good Friday, one of the *Tenebrae* of Holy Week.

The overall impression of clarity made by *Suscepimus Deus* is due in large part to its brevity, something that becomes apparent upon examining larger, more complex Gregorian antiphons. *Suscepimus Deus* is not regular in the relative lengths of its phrases, or at any rate, its musical phrases depend on the text phrases, which in psalm texts are apt to be irregular. As antiphons become longer and more ornate, the irregularity of phrase shape leads easily to diffuse contours. The antiphon becomes obscure in its larger shape without necessarily losing its perfection of detail. Larger antiphons such as *Genuit puerpera, Angelus ad pastores,* or *Facta est cum angelo* (all from Christmas lauds) are characteristically Gregorian in their veiled outlines, but no less beautiful thereby.

Antiphons were designed to be part of a larger piece, the singing of a whole psalm. The psalm itself is sung to a psalm tone, selected from a set of eight such tones according to the tonal structure of the antiphon. The particular set of eight psalm tones used for simple office psalmody may be Carolingian; we will return to this problem later. But singing psalms with psalm tones of some description is an age-old custom of Christians.

The simple psalm tone that would be used in connection with *Suscepimus Deus* is given in Example 5. The selection of an antiphon to go with a particular psalm (in this case, *Suscepimus Deus* for Psalm 47 at Christmas matins) is a liturgical matter that need not concern us. But the selection of the psalm tone (in this case, the eighth) is a musical choice dictated by the nature of the antiphon melody. Like the prayer tone, the psalm tone has a reciting note (C for the eighth psalm tone) and inflections at the beginning of the first half and at the end of both halves. These two halves correspond to the two halves into which each verse of every psalm is divided, making it possible to sing any psalm to any tone.

The inflection at the beginning, called *intonation,* is sung only at the beginning of the first verse of the psalm. The inflections in the middle and at the end, the *mediant* and *final* cadences, are adapted to the accents of the text by using or omitting the notes immediately following the accent notes. The mediant cadence stays up on C and the final descends to G—a simple reinforcement of textual shape by tonal differentiation.

Each verse of the psalm would be sung to the same tone; only the first

EXAMPLE 5   EIGHTH PSALM TONE

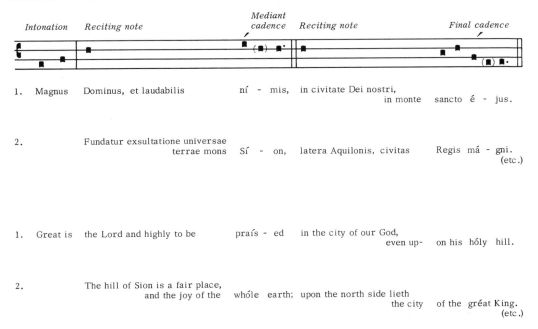

Intonation	Reciting note	Mediant cadence	Reciting note	Final cadence

1. Magnus   Dominus, et laudabilis   ní - mis,   in civitate Dei nostri,
                                                     in monte   sancto é - jus.

2.   Fundatur exsultatione universae
                              terrae mons   Sí - on,   latera Aquilonis, civitas   Regis má - gni.
                                                                                      (etc.)

1. Great is   the Lord and highly to be   praís - ed   in the city of our God,
                                                          even up-   on his hóly   hill.

2.   The hill of Sion is a fair place,
                  and the joy of the   whóle   earth; upon the north side lieth
                                                                     the city   of the gréat King.
                                                                                      (etc.)

two verses are given in Example 5. Since the psalms were inherited from the
Jews, Christians were accustomed to add the peculiarly Christian doxology
Gloria Patri ("Glory be to the Father, and to the Son, and to the Holy Ghost;
as it was in the beginning, is now, and ever shall be, world without end,
Amen") whenever using psalms in worship services. This doxology, treated as
two verses, is sung to the same tone as the psalm. Since psalm tones are abstract
formulas, they can be used for languages other than Latin. The English translation given in Example 5 is set up so that it may be sung just like the Latin.

The antiphon, *Suscepimus Deus*, would be sung before and after Psalm 47
sung to this tone. Formerly, as was mentioned, the antiphon was sung after each
verse of the psalm (hence sixteen times in all!). This meant that the end of each
verse should be smoothly modulated into the beginning of the antiphon. Although the choice of psalm tone depended on the tonal structure of the whole
antiphon, the return to the antiphon was accomplished by varying only the end
of the psalm tone, according to the first two or three notes of the antiphon.
Most psalm tones had several alternate endings, called *differences*. In the present
case the psalm tone ends on G, the same note on which the antiphon begins,
making a very clear connection. If an antiphon with a similar melody type
began on C, its psalm tone, still the eighth, might have a slightly different
cadence ending on C. Very often it was preferred not to have the psalm tone
end and the antiphon begin on the same note, but rather on different notes that
yet seemed related in context.

Psalmody was something that Christians, especially monks, did and do as a work in praise of God—at the rate of 150 psalms a week in singing monasteries. Psalmody is not intended as an artistic experience in itself, nor are the psalm tones anything other than functional, at least in the simple forms under discussion. Nonetheless, even these tones have the artistry, the stylistic polish characteristic of the whole Gregorian repertory. The inflections are simple, but they are right; they have to be, to stand up under the use they have been getting day and night for over a thousand years.

PROPERS OF THE MASS Psalmody was used at mass for those places where functional music was needed to accompany liturgical action—at the introit, offertory, and communion. Because it was the mass, both the antiphons and psalm tones were more ornate than those for the offices. Originally all of a psalm was sung (as we saw) or as much as was needed, including the *Gloria Patri;* but during or after Carolingian times the introit was cut down to the antiphon, one psalm verse, and doxology, while of the communion only the antiphon was left. The offertory blossomed out for a while in extremely florid psalm verses, sung no longer to psalm tones but to specially composed melodies. These, however, were later dropped, leaving here, too, only the antiphon.

Example 6 gives the introit *Resurrexi* for Easter Sunday, including the antiphon, one psalm verse, and doxology; the antiphon is repeated after the doxology. Antiphon and psalm tone are each distinct formal units. Not only are they different in style, but in tonal area as well, the antiphon in this case lying consistently lower than the psalm tone. The sense of departure in the psalm verse, and of return in the repeat of the antiphon, is very marked. Formal clarity at this higher level is not, however, consistently reinforced by the detail—a condition true of most larger Gregorian forms and truer as the forms get larger.

This introit is distinguished from previous examples by having frequently several notes to one syllable; such chant is called *neumatic.* (The dialog before the preface, Example 2, was mildly neumatic.) These neumes, or groups of notes, stretch the value of the syllables, giving the text a somewhat different shape than it would have in a purely syllabic chant. The text phrases are still reflected in the musical phrases, but less strongly. The neumes give more weight to musical aspects of the phrasing.

The notation is slightly more complex than previous examples. The three notes on Resurre-*xi*, written close together on the same pitch (called *tristropha*) were originally an ornament of some kind. The second group on *sum,* on the other hand, is simply the three pitches G–F–G—not the *portamento* the note shape might suggest. In general, when two notes are written close together on the same pitch (alle-*lu-*, po*su-*, allelu-*ia,* *fac-*ta) they are sung as one note twice as long. In the next to last alleluia of the antiphon, the neumes on *al-* and *lu-*, called *liquescent,* each represent the two notes G–F, but with the F sung lightly on the following liquid consonant, *l* or *i.* The ictus, as used in this piece, suggests rhythmic groupings within a neume.

The antiphon text *Resurrexi* contains three phrases, punctuated by the exclamation *alleluia!*—an exclamation found everywhere during the Eastertide liturgies. The first phrase occupies the fourth D–G, ending on E; the second

EXAMPLE 6   INTROIT (mode 4)

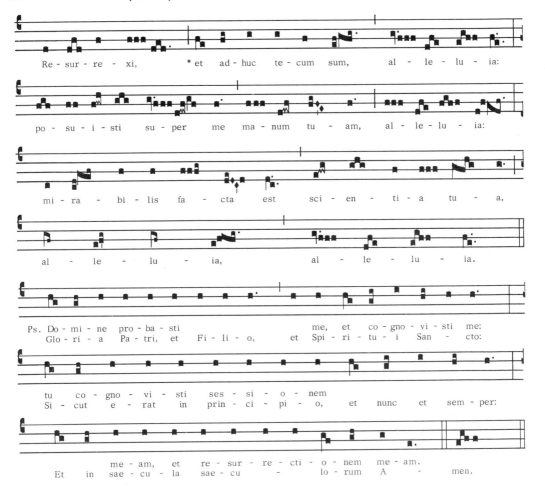

Re - sur - re - xi,   * et ad - huc te - cum sum,   al - le - lu - ia:

po - su - i - sti   su - per   me   ma - num   tu - am,   al - le - lu - ia:

mi - ra - bi - lis   fa - cta   est   sci - en - ti - a   tu - a,

al - le - lu - ia,   al - le - lu - ia.

Ps. Do - mi - ne pro - ba - sti   me, et co - gno - vi - sti me:
Glo - ri - a   Pa - tri, et   Fi - li - o,   et   Spi - ri - tu - i   San - cto:

tu   co - gno - vi - sti   ses - si - o - nem
Si - cut   e - rat   in   prin - ci - pi - o,   et   nunc   et   sem - per:

me - am,   et   re - sur - re - cti - o - nem me - am.
Et   in   sae - cu - la   sae - cu -   lo - rum   A -   men.

(I am risen, and am now with thee, alleluia; thou hast placed thy hand on me,
   alleluia; thy knowledge is made wonderful, alleluia, alleluia.
Ps. O Lord, thou hast searched me out and known me; thou knowest my downsitting
   and my uprising. Glory be . . .)

phrase occupies the fifth D–A, ending on F; the third phrase the sixth C–A,
ending on—E! Here again, there is little in the internal structure of the tune
that points toward E; but then, there is little that points to any other note either.
Swinging back and forth, the melody expands its small compass so slowly that

the mere addition of the C or the rise to the A seems in context to be a major development. The melody uses all the notes in its compass so often and in so many different ways that almost any one could be made to serve as a final, if properly prepared. The significance of the final E is better read the other way around : it bestows upon this intricate melody a stronger character than it might otherwise have. Many chants in the Gregorian repertory use the E ending, handling it in a variety of sophisticated ways.

The sophisticated character of this introit, the somber quality of its melody, may seem ill-suited to the Easter joy. This character is perhaps the most difficult, remote aspect of Gregorian chant. There are many radiant Gregorian pieces; the introit *Puer natus est nobis* (For us a child is born) for Christmas is an example easily understood as appropriate for that occasion. But for some important occasions the Gregorian repertory is apt to provide chant more evocative of deeper meaning by being less obvious in its musical style. In pieces such as *Resurrexi*, whose musical significance seems to exceed its purely functional requirements, we can learn the meaning of musical solemnity. *Resurrexi* has a quality theologians call *numinous*, or pertaining to the godhead.

Simple, functional chant is characterized by a predominantly syllabic style. Chant of higher artistic import tends to be increasingly neumatic, increasingly further away from the syllabic style. After a neume reaches five or six notes in length it is usually called a *melisma*. Melismas of up to thirty or forty notes are characteristic of graduals, alleluias, and tracts, which are described as *melismatic*, as opposed to syllabic or neumatic. Not all syllables of a chant will carry huge melismas, in fact, only a few, but those few are sufficiently impressive to distinguish melismatic chant sharply from other types.

If neumes of two or three notes stretch syllabic values, altering the textual phrase shapes, extended melismas disrupt the shape completely by the intrusion of purely musical development. Gregorian melismas, however, are inclined to be rhapsodically ornamental rather than clearly structured. They do not replace the textual phrasing with more cogent musical forms, but simply interrupt the phrasing with musical ornament; underneath, the textual phrases still operate as best they can. The musical values of melismatic chant—and they are very great—are values not of expansive structure but rather of decorative expression.

The full range of the expressive values of Gregorian chant is found only in the melismatic chants that come between epistle and gospel at mass. The gradual *A summo caelo* (Example 7) is not from one of the great popular festivals, such as Christmas or Easter, but from an equally ancient liturgy called Ember Saturday in the season of Advent, a liturgy that has not two but four lessons, each followed by a gradual. These graduals are all on the same melody type, and this type may be very old indeed. Many other graduals, including one for Christmas (*Tecum principium*, Midnight Mass) and another for Easter (*Haec dies*), use this melody type, but in an adapted form. *A summo caelo* is one of the most straightforward examples.

Graduals have two parts, each built on one verse of a psalm. The first part is called *response*, the second part, *verse*—a confusing but traditional use of this latter term merely to designate the section that alternates with the response. The response is sung by the full choir (except for the intonation up

EXAMPLE 7   GRADUAL (mode 2)

℞. A summo * cae - lo e - gres - si - o

e - jus: et oc - cur - sus e -

jus us - que ad sum - mum e - jus.

℣. Cae - li e-nar - -

- - rant glo - ri-am De - i:

et o - pe - ra ma - nu - um e - jus

an - nun - ti - at * fir - ma - men - tum.

(℞. His going out is from the uttermost part of the heaven; and his circuit unto the
end thereof.
℣. The heavens declare the glory of God; and the firmament showeth his handywork.)

to the asterisk, which, as in all Gregorian choral pieces is sung by a cantor);
the verse is sung by the cantor (except for the conclusion marked by the
asterisk after *annuntiat,* which is sung by the choir).

Originally the response was repeated after the verse, to make a large,
symmetrical form ℞ ℣ ℞; but after Carolingian times this repeat was dropped.
Like other Gregorian forms, this one stands at the end of a long development

almost entirely hidden from view. There are obvious similarities to the use of an antiphon with psalmody, but just as obvious differences. In *A summo caelo* there is a clear rounding of the verse melody to correspond to the end of the response; this happens in other gradual melodies too. In the case of this melody type, the tune for the response is very similar to the tune for the verse, tempting one to think of this melody as an extremely florid psalm tone. But the form in which this melody reaches us is so many stages removed from a recitation formula—if it is really derived from one—that it is better to think of this gradual simply as a melody type.

The response has two phrases, each divided again in two; all phrases end on the final, A, and all fill more or less the same tonal space centered on the third A–C, but extending down to F, and up to F an octave above. Each phrase, however, fills this space differently: the first starts low, and the second becomes involved in a dark modulation via a B flat; the third starts assertively on C, while the fourth starts low on F, rising through a very expressive melisma to the octave above in the convolutions already familiar to us from *Pater noster* and introit, but now expressed in a far more elaborate way. The high artistry of the gradual is reflected in its more intricate notation, involving groupings of neumes and ornamental neumes as well as a greater number of rhythmic signs added by the Benedictine editors. A melody such as *A summo caelo* requires careful working out before it makes musical sense.

If the response is difficult, the verse (*Caeli enarrant*) is more so. In this solo part the melismas get even longer and more ecstatic, completely overrunning the structural outlines of the text. It is possible, however, for a trained singer to sing the phrase on *Caeli enarrant* in one breath, endless melisma and all, producing an effect of outward sophistication and inner luminosity unique to Gregorian melismatic chant.

The verse, like the response, has two phrases, each subdivided. Here the cadences are more varied, the first being on D above A, the third on F below A. The overall design, then, is very clear—but who hears it? The interior of each phrase, rich with melismatic expression, gives no hint of what the approaching cadence will be or when it will come. Ornament, not structure, is all one hears. The infinitely subtle alternation of A with a decorated C on *De*–i is especially characteristic of this style.

Familiarity with graduals is essential to an understanding of Gregorian chant. Standing at the summit of that art, the graduals realize its loftiest aspirations, thereby defining the status of the other types and showing us how we should assess them. Not far below the graduals stand the tracts, sung immediately after the gradual in the penitential season of Lent. While there are many tracts, there are only two melody types, one ending on D, the other on G. Like the gradual melody studied, these tract melodies may be from the oldest strata of preserved chant. They tend to be less spectacular and even more sophisticated than the graduals. The G tracts are very gracious, but those on D are not easily accessible, making sense only after long acquaintance. The texts of the tracts frequently include whole psalms, sung one verse after another to basically the same set of melodic formulas; the form of the whole is $\mathbb{V}_1 \ \mathbb{V}_2 \ \mathbb{V}_3 \ldots$ instead of the form ℞ 𝕍 ℞ of graduals and responsories.

The phrases that make up the melody types found in tracts are combined in ways more varied than in the gradual melody types represented by *A summo caelo.* This more varied procedure, called *centonization,* draws upon a repertory that may include, for example, alternate opening formulas, or alternate closing formulas. Centonization permits phrases to be joined in several alternate orders. The family of graduals represented by *Viderunt omnes,* for Christmas (Third Mass), is one of the best examples of centonized melody.

The alleluia of the mass is similar to the gradual in form as well as style. Although its origins are obscure, the alleluia began probably as an ornate, perhaps melismatic, setting of the word *alleluia,* which was then made proper to a particular feast by the addition of a verse from a psalm, set to music to resemble the verse of the gradual. The alleluia, then, has the same form, ℟ ℣ ℟, as the gradual, with the word *alleluia* being the response.

Of all the chants of the Gregorian repertory, the alleluia is the only one that at present permits a reasonable guess at its stylistic development. Some alleluias, at any rate, are very different from others, and there are grounds for saying which ones are older. The type usually identified as the oldest has a modest setting of the word *alleluia,* then, on the final syllable, a melisma (later called *jubilus*) of perhaps twenty notes. The moderately melismatic verse of this oldest type is not related melodically to the alleluia. The classic example is the Alleluia *Dies sanctificatus* for Christmas, also used as a melody for other feasts, especially during the Christmas season.

Slightly later alleluias have extended melismas attached either to the word *alleluia,* or within the verse, especially at the end. The Alleluia *Ostende* for the First Sunday in Advent (also used as a melody type for other occasions) has a spectacular melisma at the end of its verse, remarkable for its tonal wandering. A still later type is represented by the Alleluia *Justus germinabit* (Example 8, for feasts of martyrs; the sign *ij* means *repeat:* after the solo intonation, the choir enters at the asterisk, first repeating *alleluia* and then going on to the jubilus). Here the melisma for the alleluia is extended, but more important, the melody for the verse is closely related to the melody for the alleluia, if not derived from it. Finally, there is an extended melisma at the end of the verse identical with that of the word *alleluia.*

Thus the form of the alleluia has been strongly rounded, making a musical AA_1A instead of the original ABA. The endings of A and A_1 are identical, the variation taking place in the middle. Sometimes this variation is expressed by a totally unrelated melisma interpolated into the middle of the verse, as in the Alleluia *Christus resurgens* (Fourth Sunday after Easter), where the word *mors* (death) has one of the mightiest of these internal, unrelated verse melismas. This most recent type of alleluia came about little by little; one can find examples with some but not all of the features mentioned.

Besides these formal changes, more subtle stylistic changes are represented by the Alleluia *Justus germinabit* (Example 8). Individual phrases possess a high degree of tonal focus. Immediately after the first asterisk, the melody makes an unmistakable half cadence on A, then a full cadence on D in a manner that not only leaves no doubt, but is preceded by a definite aura. In comparison, the older graduals seem tonally ambiguous. It should be noticed, however, that the tonal clarity of the alleluia is not a product of the large rounded form, nor does it seem to contribute to that form. The tonal clarity has

EXAMPLE 8   ALLELUIA (mode 1)

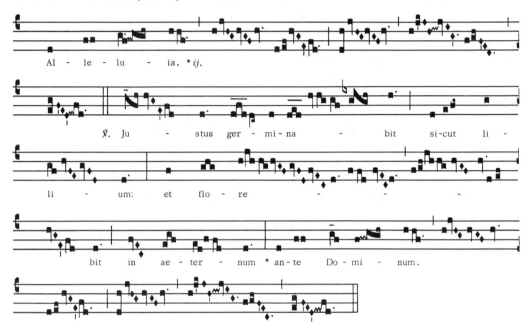

(Alleluia, alleluia. ℣. The righteous man shall spring up like the lily, and shall flourish forever before the Lord.)

to do with the way an individual phrase is constructed. The first line of the piece, for example, is so solid, so urbane, that it makes its tonal point on style alone. But the clarity within such a phrase does not have structural implications outside the phrase. In this and similar alleluias, especially the Alleluia *Justi epulentur,* and the Alleluia *Christus resurgens* already mentioned, the phrases are placed consistently on D, giving a homogeneity to the whole; but if these same clear phrases were not all grouped on the same tone, they would not by themselves give the piece unity. The Alleluia *Surrexit Dominus* (Easter Tuesday) is an interesting case—whether earlier or later is hard to say—of the same idioms used in a subtly different context.

There are indications that alleluias were among the last pieces composed for the Gregorian repertory—composed, that is, as part of a living stylistic development, for the Gregorian repertory has been expanded right up to the present by imitating the original models. But of all the chant brought North to the Franks, the alleluias seem to have been the most recent. The Alleluia *Justus germinabit,* for example, might have been composed during the mid-700s. In their effect of tonal clarity these alleluias, of all Gregorian chant, are nearest to the kind of music the Franks themselves were soon to develop. Yet even when a Frankish composer wrote an alleluia *à la grégorienne*, there was a subtle difference: the Gregorian alleluia, no matter how recent, derived its clarity from centuries of Mediterranean refinement.

CHANT THEORY Gregorian chant came North either in the minds and ears of cantors (Roman or Frankish) or in a book, called an *antiphonary* because it contained the antiphons of the mass or of the offices. That is, an antiphonary contained the texts, but since we have no Roman antiphonary from Carolingian times (only Frankish ones), we do not know whether the Roman books contained notated melodies.

Indeed, we do not know precisely what the Roman books did contain, hence the infinitely complicated controversy about the origins of Gregorian chant. It has even been suggested that the whole repertory we know as Gregorian took final form only in the North during the 700s and 800s. But the difference between this final Frankish form and whatever Roman forms stood behind it was apparently a mere difference in "editions," insignificant in comparison to the striking difference between the Gregorian repertory of mass propers (however and wherever preserved) and the indigenous Frankish chant to be taken up in the next chapter.

Our first antiphonaries are mainly Frankish from around 800; the first ones with music—also Frankish or under Frankish influence—from around 900. The antiphonary of the mass contained the proper of the mass, including introits, graduals, tracts, alleluias, offertories, and communions. It might also have contained miscellaneous items of unknown origin, possibly Roman, but more likely traditional Gallican remnants, imitations of Mozarabic or Byzantine chants, or Frankish novelties. The antiphonary of the office, much larger than that of the mass, contained antiphons and responsories. The musical notation of these earliest antiphonaries cannot be read unless one knows how the tune goes. But with the help of antiphonaries from after 1050, whose notation is clear, and allowing for the inescapable variants due to local interpretation and errors in transmission, it can be determined that these earliest antiphonaries contain basically the chants associated with the same texts in modern chant publications.

One of the first activities of Frankish musicians, after copying and learning the Gregorian repertory, was to develop systematic ways of classifying and analyzing the chant so that it could more easily be taught in monasteries and cathedral schools. Frankish theorists cast about for likely teaching aids. Aurelian of Reomé, the earliest Frankish writer on music known to us by name, relied heavily on grammatical analogies. Others ransacked the late classical theorist Boethius (ca 480–?524) and other sources of classical antiquity for theoretical tools that might be useful.

The best tool, however, was a system of chant classification described sometimes as the *four finals,* sometimes as the *eight tones* or *eight modes.* Although its origins are extremely obscure (perhaps having associations with some aspect of liturgy or calendar, such as an eight-week cycle of feasts), this system does not seem to be derived from Greek antiquity, but rather seems to have emerged as a practical means of classifying Christian chant.

In classifying chant according to the four finals, or the eight tones, the pragmatic Franks began by insisting that there were only seven notes on which a piece could begin or end—the seven notes of the diatonic system. This by itself would produce seven classes of chant. But even before the time of our earliest sources, still another basic concept had been applied to the classification of chant.

Early theorists discuss the similarities between certain of the seven notes: A is like D (they say) because from each you go down a whole step, or up a whole step, then a half step, then another whole step. At that point the similarity ceases, but in classifying the endings of chant, that much is enough—or was enough—to establish a sense of identity between chants which ended on A and those which ended on D. (This lettering system was not yet in use; but the scale to which it refers existed, and furthermore chant had been located on it—which all indicates the amount of theoretical construction that preceded our earliest theoretical sources.) Similarities could also be established between E and B and between F and C. The note G caused problems, for it corresponded exactly to no other. But going down from G was like going down from D, while going up from G was like going up from C.

In this way the seven tones of the diatonic system were reduced to four, and at some early stage these four were said to be D, E, F, and G (although they could just as well have been, say, G, A, B, and C). These were the four finals, and chants were classified according to whether they ended on the first (D), second (E), third (F), or fourth (G). To avoid confusion with another numbering soon to be introduced, we call these four finals—and the classes built upon them—by their traditional Greek numbers—*protus* (D), *deuterus* (E), *tritus* (F), and *tetrardus* (G).

It was also observed that of all chants ending on, say, D, some remained mostly above D, hanging around A a fifth above; while others went frequently below D and hung around F a third above D. Similar observations made for the other finals resulted in a systematic division of each of the four classes into two subclasses, making eight in all. The chants that dwelt on the fifth above the final were called *authentic,* the others *plagal.* Thus authentic protus dwelt on A and ended on D; plagal protus dwelt on F and also ended on D; and so for the rest.

There were, then, eight classes, called *tones* or, later, *modes.* At an early stage these eight were numbered consecutively. They were also known by names borrowed from ancient Greek music, as follows:

tone 1	protus authentic	*dorian*	final D	(high)
tone 2	protus plagal	*hypodorian*	final D	(low)
tone 3	deuterus authentic	*phrygian*	final E	(high)
tone 4	deuterus plagal	*hypophrygian*	final E	(low)
tone 5	tritus authentic	*lydian*	final F	(high)
tone 6	tritus plagal	*hypolydian*	final F	(low)
tone 7	tetrardus authentic	*mixolydian*	final G	(high)
tone 8	tetrardus plagal	*hypomixolydian*	final G	(low)

It should be pointed out that while distinction between authentic and plagal is found in the earliest sources, the means of making the distinction either are not found or occur in unsystematic and variable ways. The idea of an important nonfinal tone, such as A in tone 1, is not made particularly clear (nor is it consistently present in the music), while a firm notion of octave range, mostly absent from early chant classification, belongs to a later aspect of theory.

With the aid of this system, Frankish musicians classified the Gregorian repertory, especially the antiphons. The classification was presented in a *tonary,* a book listing all antiphons and responsories (sometimes graduals too) by tone. There were frequent doubts and arguments, by the way, about the proper final of a piece. The classification of antiphons was no idle pastime but an essential step to intelligent singing. With such classification a theorist asserted something specific about the musical nature of each piece, something that affected its internal structure or its whole character. The earliest known tonary dates from around 795; one of the largest of the early tonaries is by Regino of Prüm (ca 850–915).

Psalm tones existed in various grades; we have seen a very simple grade for office psalmody and a more elaborate one at the introit. There were other grades still more elaborate, using an increased number of neumes, more complex intonations and cadences, and even varying the reciting note from the first half of the tone to the second. The simplest grade of psalm tone, curiously enough, is the hardest to place historically. This simplest grade was not so often written down in earlier sources; because it was used for daily office psalmody it was very familiar. Familiarity does not mean fixity, however, and the system of eight simple psalm tones known to us today may be one of the last Gregorian items to receive its present form—if indeed it is Gregorian at all.

The regularity of this set of eight simple tones is one of the features which most distinguishes it from other, more elaborate sets. The fact that there are eight is in itself significant; other grades of psalm tones tend to have fewer than eight, a tendency apparent in all types of Gregorian chant and especially marked, for example, in the case of the tracts, which exist in only two tones. In contrast, the eight simple psalm tones bear a close relationship to the theoretical system of eight tones derived from the four finals (even though this relationship does not involve the final of the psalm tone itself). Psalm tones 1, 3, 5, and 7 recited (in earlier versions) on a fifth above the final of the corresponding tonal classification, while psalm tones 2, 4, 6, and possibly 8 recited a third above. More ornate plagal psalm tones, however, tended to alternate between a third and a fourth above the final, and the simple psalm tones 4 and 8 eventually settled on the fourth above, while the third psalm tone settled on the sixth above.

In this way the psalm tone was selected so as to make tonal sense coming after the antiphon. The intonation at the beginning of the psalm tone made a smooth connection between the final of the antiphon and the reciting note, while the end of the psalm tone was adjusted (as we saw) by the various endings, or differences, to match the beginning of the antiphon. In Carolingian times there were many more differences than there are now for the same eight tones, a sign that singers were more concerned then with making a smooth but not necessarily obvious connection between psalm and antiphon. A close study of these differences, as well as of the whole practice of psalmody, would give substance to our ideas about tonal relationships of that time.

The system of eight tones was a product of reason, not art; in order to adjust reason to art, theorists sometimes used more than eight tones. There was at least one other psalm tone, called *tonus peregrinus* (wandering tone). About the other tonal classes we know little except that they provided for antiphons that did not fit clearly into one of the eight tones.

It should be held firmly in mind that the theoretical system was one thing, the melodic flux of chant quite another. At one extreme stood the seven-toned diatonic system—hallowed and beautiful but not very interesting music-ally. At the other extreme was the musical intuition of the singer, who, if he thought about anything, probably thought only of tetrachords, or configurations of whole and half steps within a fourth. The system of finals and similarities mediated between these extremes as best it could. The inevitable frictions were lubricated by yet another ancient device, the variable B (B flat or B natural), which efficiently performed a number of useful operations, such as inter-changing the nature of finals C, D, and E with those of F, G, and A. In all these matters it was the Franks who were sufficiently irritated by their assimila-tion of Gregorian chant to try to find principles and order in music.

2
NEW FRANKISH
FORMS 700-1000

THE FRANKISH ASSIMILATION OF ROMAN CHANT LASTED FULLY A
century, from at least 750 until after 850. It is possible that by 750 some
Northern churches were already replacing the old local practices (about which
we know next to nothing) with Roman ones, in response to local demand. In
such cases the official acts of Pippin III merely ratified an accomplished fact.
In other Northern churches old local practices persisted in defiance of imperial
decree well past 850. But a typical up-to-date establishment, monastery or
cathedral, had by 850 probably adopted the Roman rite in its purified Northern
form, including the mass propers—introits, graduals, alleluias (or tracts),
offertories, and communions, probably also certain tones for lessons, prayers,
and psalms—and antiphons and responsories for the offices.

The Roman rite, however, had come North in such an abstract, abbrevi-
ated form that for everyday parish or monastic use it had to be extensively
supplemented. The typical Northern establishment found it necessary to surround the Roman core with a steadily increasing amount of new ritual and
chant, borrowed from near or far, adapted from the past, or just plain invented.
New ideas both for texts and music continued to come from the South, from
Milan, from Spain, from Byzantium. These importations tended, however, to be
isolated, and external in nature. The real development of Northern music depended upon the assimilation of these exotic ideas by Northerners. Paradoxical
as it may seem, the Northern thirst for outside artistic stimulation—first the

Roman chant, then other elements—was the first symptom of a strong creative urge soon to manifest itself in specifically Northern forms.

LAUDES AND MELISMAS   One of the first, most energetic Northern forms was a set of acclamations called *laudes*. One version, set down close to the year 795, is an order of acclamations specifically to greet the king, Charlemagne; other versions existed, or soon came to exist, to greet bishops upon official visits to churches or monasteries. These acclamations were modeled on imperial ceremonies, both pagan and Christian, of Rome and Byzantium; but Frankish hands fashioned a Frankish version so new it had to be specially imported *to* Rome to greet Charlemagne on his visit there in 800 to be crowned emperor.

The Frankish laudes, of whatever type, are built around a group of short, excited phrases repeated over and over in carefully controlled sequence. The central group, given in Example 9, is *Christus vincit! Christus regnat! Christus imperat!* (Christ conquers! Christ rules! Christ takes power!); this Christian war cry was repeated thrice, the threefold acclamation returning periodically to punctuate the laudes, alternating with other acclamatory phrases such as *Salus et in secula!* (Good health forever!) and *Gloria! Victoria!* which needs no translation. In between such acclamations came petitions to God, recited in melodic formulas like prayer tones. The chanting of petitions with short responses found another expression in more penitential rituals called *litanies* that became popular during the 700s, receiving definitive formulation in the North. But it was the laudes that best expressed the new Frankish aspirations.

Even though set to very simple tones, the acclamations produced a strikingly new effect, utterly different from a gradual or even a psalm tone. *Christ conquers! Christ rules! Christ takes power!*—the cry rang throughout all the new music to be taken up by Frankish musicians. True, the acclamations imitated decadent Mediterranean imperialism, but their Frankish forms injected youthful vigor into the oversophisticated art of the old world, heralding a new Western dynamism. *Gloria! Victoria! Salus et in secula!*

Among progressive developments of the late 700s, the laudes, in their militant musical and textual simplicity, represent one extreme. Another extreme is represented by various *melismas* literally tacked on here and there to other types of pieces. Melismatic writing, of course, was as old as graduals, but in the graduals and the other sophisticated forms that came North from Rome, melismas seemed to belong naturally, while the new melismas were curiously detached, leading a life of their own; they could be left out or included or shifted from one piece to another. They were, however, not radically different in style from the old art, probably representing its last stage.

Amalarius of Metz (ca 775–ca 850), one of the Carolingian authorities

EXAMPLE 9   REFRAIN FROM THE LAUDES

Chri - stus   vin - cit,   Chri - stus   re - gnat,   Chri - stus   im - pe - rat!

supervising the importation of the Roman chant, describes how Roman cantors around 800 liked to add a huge triple melisma to a responsory *In medio;* "Modern singers," Amalarius continues, transferred this triple melisma to the Christmas responsory *Descendit de caelis*. The form of these matins responsories is response–verse–end of response–*Gloria Patri*–end of response; the triple melisma (or *neume*, as Amalarius calls it) was added to the response each time it came, forming a brilliant conclusion to this rounding element. The third of the three parts of the melisma is given in Example 10.

This triplex neume was but one of many such melismas interpolated around 800 at various points in the chant, usually at the ends of phrases or sections. Nor are such melismas a peculiarly Frankish or Roman custom; found also in Mozarabic and Ambrosian (Milanese) sources, they seem to have been a symptom of a stage of development in which the old Mediterranean art forms became stereotyped and lost their inner coherence. Nevertheless these interchangeable melismas fascinated the Franks, who added them to introits, to offertory antiphons, to office responsories, and in other places, as we will see.

TROPES   Melisma and acclamation—the one diffuse to the point of formlessness, the other so compact as to be unsuited to art without the relief of more graceful contours. Substantial artistic accomplishment lay somewhere in between. Frankish musicians of the early 800s cultivated a wide variety of musical forms that combined acclamation and melisma in modified, more usable ways. Many of the new Frankish forms were associated with the recently imported Gregorian mass propers, especially with the introit.

Frankish composers wreathed the sober phrases of the Gregorian introit with flowery texts, often in acclamatory style and set to moderately neumatic music. Such an addition to the introit was called a *trope* (*tropus*). We do not know exactly what the term *trope* meant; it is doubtful whether the Carolingians themselves had a precise meaning in mind. For them a trope was basically a rhetorical flourish, introducing and elaborating upon the given Gregorian. Here are the texts of some tropes to the Easter introit *Resurrexi* studied in the previous chapter (Example 6).

Factus homo tua iussa pater moriendo peregi:
Resurrexi et adhuc tecum sum, alleluia:

EXAMPLE 10   MELISMA FOR THE RESPONSORY DESCENDIT

— ∪∪|— ∪ ∪|— ∪ ∪ |— ∪ ∪| — ∪ ∪| — —
Abstuleras miserate Manes, mihi reddita lux est:

     — |— ∪ ∪|— —|— |— ∪ ∪|— ∪
     Posuisti super me manum tuam, alleluia:

— |— ∪ ∪|— —|— |— ∪ ∪|— ∪
Plebs caecata meum nomen non novit amandum:

     Mirabilis facta est scientia tua, alleluia, alleluia.

(Having been made man, I have obeyed thy commandment, Father, in dying:
     I am risen, and am with thee, alleluia:
Thou hast graciously loosed the bonds of hell; I receive light again;
     Thou hast placed thy hand on me, alleluia:
The people, blinded, do not know my Name that they may love it:
     Thy knowledge is made wonderful, alleluia, alleluia.)

Tropes such as this are more elaborate, more artistic than the laudes, even though they sometimes tend toward the same short, ejaculatory phrases. One sign of higher artistic ambitions is the frequent imitation of classical meters, especially dactylic hexameters. The longs and shorts required for quantitative scansion are shown over the text just given. For the Carolingians, as for us, these quantities were no longer a part of the spoken language; no longer audible, they could only be looked up in ancient grammar books (hence they entailed frequent mistakes). The poetic quantities were habitually ignored in making the musical setting.

The melodic style of the tropes was modeled on the style of the related introit. Example 11 contains the music for the first section of the trope just given, sung before the beginning of the introit. Skillful as the imitation of Gregorian chant may be, one can still sense in some introit tropes the Frankish hand. Sometimes a set of tropes even seems to impose its own form upon the introit, if only by an insistent repetition of formulas.

The flowery language of the tropes—to say nothing of how they extended the length of the service—was ill-suited to the parish church; the tropes flourished in monasteries, being in fact largely a product of monastic composers. Monasteries in and around the Frankish kingdom steadily increased in wealth and influence during the 800s and 900s, becoming the leaders of Northern culture as the Carolingian political establishment declined after Charlemagne's death in 814. With a schedule of sung services lasting eight to twelve hours a day, the monasteries presented the opportunity and the overhead for musical

EXAMPLE 11 INTROIT TROPE FOR *RESURREXI*

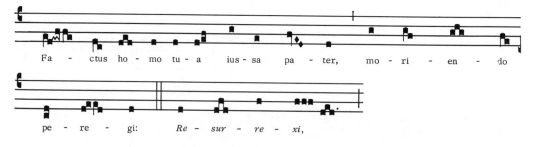

development; furthermore, they attracted the most intelligent, ambitious talent of the time. The immediate future of music was in monastic hands.

Within the monastery, tropes sometimes grew to surprising proportions. The Easter introit in particular provoked an extended trope that took a dramatic form. Beginning with the words *Quem queritis,* this trope was acted out by three monks representing the three Marys coming to the tomb at daybreak; another monk, representing the angel, sang, "Whom do ye seek?" (*Quem queritis?*). The Marys responded, "Jesus of Nazareth." The angel replied, "He is not here, He is risen, as He said." Whereupon appropriately began the Easter introit, "I am risen."

Many sets of tropes were cast in dramatic dialog for Christmas as well as for Easter. There was a tendency, however, toward lyric rather than dramatic expression as the dialogs expanded. The protagonists sometimes responded with short antiphons drawn from other parts of the service but appropriate to the dramatic trope. Eventually the expansion resulted in relatively large sacred dramas; but that takes us past 1000 and into a later development.

ACCLAMATIONS OF THE MASS In the introit tropes the distinction between the Gregorian original and the Frankish addition is very clear, since the Gregorian, both text and music, is set down once for all in the Gregorian antiphonary. In the other troped items the distinction is far from clear, simply because the items in question were not part of the Gregorian repertory, but rather were in the very process of formation. Here the creative act of composing tropes linked right on to the development of the form being troped.

These forms are *Kyrie, Gloria in excelsis, Sanctus,* and *Agnus Dei.* They are all acclamations of one sort or another, and hence close to the heart of the Frankish composer. The history of these texts is one thing; the history of their present placement in the liturgy quite another; and the history of their melodies still another. Even though the history of the texts and liturgical placement takes us back before Carolingian times, the importance of these texts for the subsequent history of music requires a brief summary.

The text of the acclamation *Sanctus* is very old, enjoying an almost aboriginal place in the liturgy.

Sanctus, Sanctus, Sanctus Dominus Deus Sabaoth!	*(Holy! Holy! Holy Lord God of hosts!*
Pleni sunt caeli et terra gloria tua!	*Heaven and earth are full of thy glory!*
Hosanna in excelsis!	*Hosanna in the highest!*
Benedictus qui venit in nomine Domini!	*Blessed is he that cometh in the Name of the Lord!*
Hosanna in excelsis!	*Hosanna in the highest!)*

Drawn ultimately from the Old Testament, this text was interpolated into what was originally *the* prayer of Holy Communion, the great thanksgiving or eucharist, from which that part of the mass receives its name. As the conclusion of the preface to this prayer, priest and people exclaim *Sanctus!* as an act of adoration.

The text of *Gloria in excelsis,* the next oldest, is a mighty hymn used near the beginning of the synaxis, first at Christmas and then on other joyful occasions. It consists of an initial quotation from Scripture (the song of the angelic host to the shepherds at Bethlehem) and a series of acclamations.

Gloria in excelsis Deo!	*(Glory be to God on high!*
Et in terra pax hominibus	*And on earth, peace to men*
bonae voluntatis!	*of good will!*
Laudamus te!	*We praise thee!*
Benedicimus te!	*We bless thee!*
Adoramus te!	*We worship thee!*
Glorificamus te!	*We glorify thee!*
Gratias agimus tibi propter	*We give thanks to thee for thy*
magnam gloriam tuam!	*great glory!*
Domine Deus, Rex caelestis,	*O Lord God, heavenly King,*
Deus Pater omnipotens!	*God the Father Almighty!*
Domine Fili unigenite	*O Lord, the only begotten Son,*
Jesu Christe!	*Jesu Christ!*
Domine Deus, Agnus Dei, Filius	*O Lord God, Lamb of God, Son of the*
Patris, qui tollis peccata mundi,	*Father, that takest away the sins of the*
miserere nobis!	*world, have mercy upon us!*
Qui tollis peccata mundi, suscipe	*Thou that takest away the sins of the world,*
deprecationem nostram!	*receive our prayer!*
Qui sedes ad dexteram Patris,	*Thou that sittest at the right hand of God*
miserere nobis!	*the Father,*
	have mercy upon us!
Quoniam tu solus sanctus,	*For thou only art holy,*
tu solus Dominus,	*thou only art the Lord,*
tu solus altissimus,	*thou only, O Jesu Christ,*
Jesu Christe,	*with the Holy Ghost,*
cum Sancto Spiritu	*art most high in the*
in gloria Dei Patris. Amen.	*glory of God the Father. Amen.)*

The acclamations *Kyrie eleison!* and *Christe eleison!* (*Lord, have mercy!* and *Christ, have mercy!*) originally came from the same imperial background as the laudes. Used in laudes, litanies, and various other ways, *Kyrie eleison* had for some time also been an acclamation at the beginning of the synaxis, right after the introit. Not until the early 800s, however, did the *Kyrie* at the beginning of the synaxis take this symmetrical form.

Kyrie eleison!	*(Lord, have mercy!*
Kyrie eleison!	*Lord, have mercy!*
Kyrie eleison!	*Lord, have mercy!*
Christe eleison!	*Christ, have mercy!*
Christe eleison!	*Christ, have mercy!*
Christe eleison!	*Christ, have mercy!*
Kyrie eleison!	*Lord, have mercy!*
Kyrie eleison!	*Lord, have mercy!*
Kyrie eleison!	*Lord, have mercy!)*

The relationship of *Kyrie* to *Gloria in excelsis* can be seen by realizing that in a Greek version of the *Gloria in excelsis* (which the Franks sometimes affected), the petitions "Have mercy upon us!" come out as *Eleison imas!* Some early versions of *Kyrie* also end *eleison imas.* Furthermore the acclamations

Kyrie eleison and *Christe eleison* occurred in connection with other phrases from the very beginning of their liturgical use (this happens naturally in the litanies and laudes). In fact, there seems to have been no stage at which the repeated acclamations *Kyrie . . . Christe . . .* existed *without* possibly including more flowery phrases in Latin.

The *Agnus Dei* was the most recent of all these acclamations, coming into general use only in the 800s to accompany the partaking of communion.

Agnus Dei,	*(O Lamb of God,*
qui tollis peccata mundi,	*that takest away the sins of the world,*
miserere nobis!	*have mercy upon us!*
Agnus Dei,	*O Lamb of God,*
qui tollis peccata mundi,	*that takest away the sins of the world,*
miserere nobis!	*have mercy upon us!*
Agnus Dei,	*O Lamb of God,*
qui tollis peccata mundi,	*that takest away the sins of the world,*
dona nobis pacem!	*grant us thy peace!)*

It was framed in three parts to match the *Kyrie,* and echoed the petitions of the *Gloria in excelsis.*

Although the *Credo* had existed for a long time as a statement of theological belief, it did not become a sung part of the mass until relatively late in the Middle Ages. Treated as another set of acclamations, it eventually came to occupy a position after the gospel on important feasts.

Credo in unum Deum, Patrem omnipotentem, factorem caeli et terrae, visibilium omnium et invisibilium.	*(I believe in one God, the Father Almighty, Maker of heaven and earth, and of all things visible and invisible.*
Et in unum Dominum Jesum Christum Filium Dei unigenitum. Et ex Patre natum ante omnia saecula. Deum de Deo, lumen de lumine, Deum verum de Deo vero. Genitum, non factum, consubstantialem Patri: per quem omnia facta sunt. Qui propter nos homines, et propter nostram salutem descendit de caelis. Et incarnatus est de Spiritu Sancto ex Maria Virgine: et homo factus est. Crucifixus etiam pro nobis sub Pontio Pilato: passus, et sepultus est. Et resurrexit tertia die, secundum Scripturas. Et ascendit in caelum: sedet ad dexteram Patris. Et iterum venturus est cum gloria judicare vivos et mortuos: cujus regni non erit finis.	*And in one Lord, Jesus Christ, the only begotten Son of God, begotten of his Father before all worlds. God of God, light of light, Very God of Very God, begotten, not made, being of one substance with the Father; by whom all things were made. Who for us men, and for our salvation, came down from heaven. And was incarnate by the Holy Ghost, of the Virgin Mary, and was made man. And was crucified also for us, under Pontius Pilate; he suffered and was buried. And the third day he rose again, according to the Scriptures. And ascended into heaven, and sitteth on the right hand of the Father. And he shall come again with glory, to judge both the quick and the dead; whose kingdom shall have no end.*
Et in Spiritum Sanctum Dominum, et vivificantem: qui ex Patre, Filioque procedit. Qui cum Patre et Filio simul adoratur, et conglorificatur: qui locutus est per Prophetas. Et unam, sanctam, catholicam	*And I believe in the Holy Ghost, the Lord and Giver of life. Who proceedeth from the Father and the Son; who with the Father and the Son together is worshiped and glorified; who spake by the*

et apostolicam Ecclesiam. Confiteor unum baptisma in remissionem peccatorum. Et expecto resurrectionem mortuorum. Et vitam venturi saeculi. Amen.

prophets. And I believe one holy, catholic, and apostolic Church. I acknowledge one baptism for the remission of sins. And I look for the resurrection of the dead. And the life of the world to come. Amen.)

At the end of the Middle Ages the five parts, *Kyrie, Gloria in excelsis, Credo, Sanctus,* and *Agnus Dei,* came to be regarded as a group called the *ordinary* (because their texts did not change from day to day like the proper). But until that time it is better to take these five parts for what they were—five separate additions to the mass.

With these added acclamations, the medieval mass now looked like this:

Synaxis	*Eucharist*
introit	offertory
Kyrie	preface
Gloria in excelsis	*Sanctus*
collect	canon
epistle	Lord's Prayer
gradual	*Agnus Dei*
alleluia	communion
gospel	
Credo	

None of these acclamations has a Gregorian melody. One of the melodies preserved for *Sanctus* may be very old, but even if it is, it is a very simple melody, suitable for congregational singing. None of these items was (before Carolingian times) for the choir, and hence none acquired an artistic setting within the Gregorian repertory. Only as they attracted the interest of Frankish composers did they become musically important; only then were their traditional congregational tunes (now lost) replaced or remodeled to acquire new artistic elaboration and significance.

In the same measure that these acclamations acquired artistic melodies, they were troped. (In fact, the earliest melodies preserved for these items occur side by side with their tropes.) It is sometimes difficult to decide what is trope and what original, so closely are trope, melody, and text intertwined. *Sanctus* and *Gloria in excelsis* were so old, of course, that textual additions were clearly recognizable as such. But since *Kyrie* had apparently always been accompanied by some kind of trope, or rhetorical expansion, it is misleading to think of an original "official" *Kyrie* distinct from a newly added trope.

Festal *Kyries* traditionally consisted of the short Greek acclamation alternating with more prolix Latin ones that changed according to the occasion, making the *Kyrie* proper to this feast or that. These Latin expansions of *Kyrie* varied with local practice from time to time and place to place. Thus the composition of new *Kyries* by the Carolingians did not change the basic shape or idea of the *Kyrie* as the composition of tropes changed the introit.

Frankish composers during the 800s wrote new melodies for *Gloria in excelsis, Sanctus,* and *Agnus Dei,* melodies mildly neumatic like introits, but inclined increasingly to reflect new developments in Western music. Many of the chant melodies we now use for these texts were written after 1000. The Frankish composer also wrote tropes for these items—new texts with their own neumatic melodies, to be interpolated into the standard texts; but here, unlike in the composition of introit tropes, a single composer could conceivably have written both a new tune for, say, a *Gloria in excelsis* and a set of tropes to go with it.

In composing *Kyries* the Frankish composer was working even closer to the growing edge of liturgical music. Writing a *Kyrie* was almost equivalent to writing a free fantasy, ending, to be sure, with the word *eleison*, but otherwise new in both text and music. Of all these items, *Kyries* most reflect new developments in style; after studying these developments we will return to a big *Kyrie* written around 900.

The bifurcation of melisma and acclamation persisted throughout the 800s in various ways. *Kyries*, for example, were for a long time written down in two forms, once with the acclamatory text and its syllabic tune and once with just the tune as if it were a melisma beginning *Kyrie* and ending *eleison*. *Kyries* were probably performed either as syllabic pieces or as melismas—possibly in both versions in line-by-line alternation.

TEXTED MELISMAS An interesting sidelight on the relationship of acclamation and melisma is provided by a Frankish practice of adding new words to an existing melisma. Obviously a function of poetic rather than strictly musical practice, such texting articulated the rambling melisma, giving it a sharper sense of form. Texting tended to affect a relatively small group of pieces that had suitable melismas. The melisma interpolated into the response *Descendit de caelis* received a number of these added texts; here is part of one text that goes syllabically under the beginning of the melisma given in Example 10 (after *immortalis* the tune of this particular text differs slightly from the tune already given):

Rex regum ab alta,	*(King of kings on high,*
Christus petens a terrestria,	*Christ, rising from earth,*
Regesque potestates, et tirranorum	*overcomes princes and potentates,*
fregit tartara;	*and the powers of hell;*
Claustra inferni virtus imperat,	*Good conquers the infernal regions,*
Chorusque angelorum proclamat:	*and the choir of angels sings:*
Sanctus Deus!	*Holy God!*
Sanctus fortis!	*Holy and Mighty!*
Sanctus et immortalis!	*Holy and Immortal!)*

Texting tended to occur in connection with relatively recent types of pieces—with melismas added to offertories, for example, but hardly ever with graduals. When texting occurred with alleluias, these tended to be more recent alleluias of the type represented in Example 8, Alleluia *Justus germinabit*. Sometimes texting took the curious form of being added to the entire verse of the alleluia, right through the existing text, like this:

Justus *et probitate dign*us germina *pacis et*	*(The righteous, worthy in honesty, will in-*
*vitae dona hereditab*it sicut lilium *et gloria*	*herit the seed of peace and the gift of life,*
rosarum: Et flore *gratiae cum lampade*	*like a lily and a wreath of roses; adorned*
lucis perpetuae fulgebit feliciter, ditatus	*with grace and with a torch of perpetual*
*munere iustitiae virtutum meritis flor*ebit in	*light he will shine, favored by fortune,*

aeternum ante Dominum, *quia Deus est* | *endowed with gifts of justice, with the re-*
omnium, qui salvat omne saeculum, qui fert | *wards of virtue he will flourish forever*
omnium subsidium, qui condolens nostrum | *before the Lord; because He is God of all,*
interitum pro nobis tribuit sui sanguinis | *He who redeems all time, who provides all*
pretium. | *aid, who having compassion on our destruc-*
| *tion gave for us his precious blood.)*

It is easy to see how such a text fits the contours of the preexisting melody. Texts were also added to the alleluia and its jubilus, making the melisma totally syllabic.

Obviously, the mere addition of a text could not bring about a radical change in style, but could only shape the existing melodic style to a slight extent. Texting was but a part of the overall Frankish reflex to the Gregorian stimulus—a way of beginning to rework old material into new shapes. An example of Frankish musical enthusiasm in the 800s is provided by the famous *Regnum* tropes: to a Frankish *Gloria* melody were added a set of tropes, and to the last trope, *Regnum,* a huge melisma; then this melisma was texted, not once but a number of times. The great energy represented by such proliferation was soon to find more cogent expression.

PROSE AND SEQUENCE Around the mid-800s Frankish musical aspirations crystallized into several large, impressive forms. Perhaps the most impressive is the form called either *sequence* or *prose* (the reason for the double name will soon be clear). The sequence, or prose, has sometimes been made difficult to understand because of the undue stress laid upon its prehistory—where it came from, rather than what it was. Basically the sequence, or prose, was a big, new, independent type of piece created around 850 by Frankish composers out of a wide variety of ingredients.

The prehistory of the prose is briefly this. In their enthusiasm for adding melismas, Frankish musicians around 800 sometimes replaced the repeat of the alleluia after the verse (not the rounding of the verse itself with a melisma similar to the jubilus) with an even more extended melisma called a *sequentia* (sequence), probably because it followed or continued the alleluia. Like other supplementary melismas, this sequence was occasionally texted; that is, a text was added syllabically to the preexisting melisma.

Then, around 850, the sequence was drastically revised in structure and increased in size, becoming sometimes ten times as long as a normal alleluia and jubilus. At this point it was ridiculous to think of the new sequence as a mere extension of the alleluia melisma. This new sequence became an independent entity, even though when notated as a melisma it was still called *sequentia,* and still began with the word *alleluia.*

This new, larger type of sequence came equipped with a special type of text called a *prosa* (prose), which was not a mere texting of a preexisting melisma, but rather a text created along with its melody—not just shaped according to that melody but shaping it in turn. Like *Kyrie,* this new musical form was for a while written down in two ways. When written as a melisma it was called *sequence,* and when written with its syllabic text it was called *prose.* But sequence and prose, tune and text, were now essential to each other, partners in a new artistic creation.

The new sequence, with its prose, was radically different from the old sequence in structure and style. The new complex of sequence and prose matched up melisma and acclamation in a synthesis that included previous Frankish achievements but went far beyond them. The sequence-prose was the first Frankish musical form that rivaled the Gregorian gradual—from which it was totally different in style. With justifiable pride the Franks maintained their new creation in its liturgical place next to the gradual and alleluia at the musical high point of the mass.

As often happens with important musical forms, the prose (the term used by the Franks for the combination of text and tune) did not grow straight out of any single line of development, but gathered up various stylistic elements. From the old sequence had come a name, a liturgical position, and the beginning word *alleluia* (when it was used)—but little else. The prose also included elements of the acclamations, both the abrupt, ejaculatory style of the laudes and the more flowery language of the tropes for introit.

Sequence and prose, tune and text, shared a distinctive structural pattern: two lines of text having the same number of syllables were sung to the same melodic phrase, so that the shape of the typical prose was $A_1A_2B_1B_2C_1C_2. \ldots$ This pattern, perhaps the most characteristic feature of the new form, was derived in part from a curiously artificial style of literary prose practiced by some Carolingians, a style making frequent use of paired phrases and even rhyme, so that the prose approached poetry (hence the term *prose* for the text of the new musical form). On the other hand, the paired phrases typical of the prose were often grouped into larger complexes in a manner reminiscent of some of the freely strophic poetry of the Carolingians. The melodies, too, participated in these larger structural groupings, and this feature became one of the most interesting and individual characteristics of the prose.

The melodic style of the new prose—and this is the crucial point—was all new. The difference between *Ecce pulcra* (Example 12), a typical example of the new prose, and the Alleluia *Justus germinabit* (Example 8) or even the melisma from *Descendit de caelis* (Example 10) accurately reflects the new Frankish style. There was no model for these soaring, energetic tunes, neither in the diffuse melismas nor in the disjunct acclamations. The only thing comparable in scope was the Gregorian gradual, but that belonged to a different era, indeed, to a different stylistic world.

Ecce pulcra, probably written a little before 900, is proper to the Feast of All Saints (November 1 in the liturgical calendar). In ecstatic phrases inspired by the Revelations of St. John, the text describes the angelic host, the white-robed martyrs, and the whole multitude of the saints standing around the heavenly throne singing eternal alleluias. Proses often begin with an isolated phrase that stands outside the usual pairing of lines; such an introduction may be very short and closely connected to the first pair (as in Example 12) or it may be longer and independent. Sometimes the introduction has only the text *alleluia*.

Whatever its text, the introduction sometimes quotes a Gregorian alleluia from the mass propers (a reminder of the function of the old sequence), identifying the liturgical occasion of the prose and enhancing its solemnity. The musical relationship to the mass alleluia, however, was purely one of association;

EXAMPLE 12 PROSE

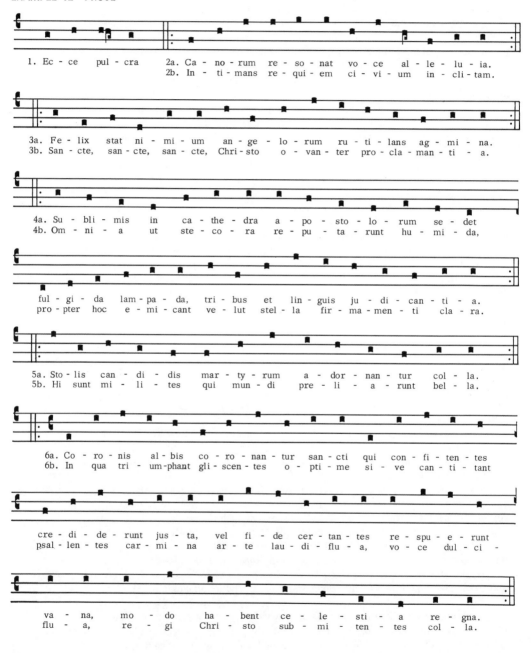

1. Ec - ce   pul - cra   2a. Ca - no - rum re - so - nat vo - ce al - le - lu - ia.
                          2b. In - ti - mans re - qui - em ci - vi - um in - cli - tam.

3a. Fe - lix stat ni - mi - um an - ge - lo - rum ru - ti - lans ag - mi - na.
3b. San - cte, san - cte, san - cte, Chri - sto o - van - ter pro - cla - man - ti - a.

4a. Su - bli - mis in ca - the - dra a - po - sto - lo - rum se - det
4b. Om - ni - a ut ste - co - ra re - pu - ta - runt hu - mi - da,

ful - gi - da lam - pa - da, tri - bus et lin - guis ju - di - can - ti - a.
pro - pter hoc e - mi - cant ve - lut stel - la fir - ma - men - ti cla - ra.

5a. Sto - lis can - di - dis mar - ty - rum a - dor - nan - tur col - la.
5b. Hi sunt mi - li - tes qui mun - di pre - li - a - runt bel - la.

6a. Co - ro - nis al - bis co - ro - nan - tur san - cti qui con - fi - ten - tes
6b. In qua tri - um - phant gli - scen - tes o - pti - me si - ve can - ti - tant

cre - di - de - runt jus - ta, vel fi - de cer - tan - tes re - spu - e - runt
psal - len - tes car - mi - na ar - te lau - di - flu - a, vo - ce dul - ci -

va - na, mo - do ha - bent ce - le - sti - a re - gna.
flu - a, re - gi Chri - sto sub - mi - ten - tes col - la.

EXAMPLE 12 (CONTINUED)

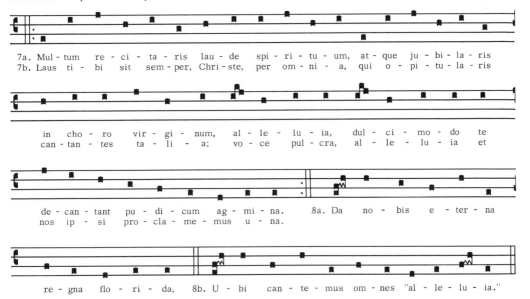

7a. Mul - tum re - ci - ta - ris lau - de spi - ri - tu - um, at - que ju - bi - la - ris
7b. Laus ti - bi sit sem - per, Chri - ste, per om - ni - a, qui o - pi - tu - la - ris

in cho - ro vir - gi - num, al - le - lu - ia, dul - ci - mo - do te
can - tan - tes ta - li - a; vo - ce pul - cra, al - le - lu - ia et

de - can - tant pu - di - cum ag - mi - na.   8a. Da no - bis e - ter - na
nos ip - si pro - cla - me - mus u - na.

re - gna flo - ri - da,   8b. U - bi can - te - mus om - nes "al - le - lu - ia."

(1. Behold how sweet
2a. the voice that sings the song, alleluia,
2b. announcing the repose of our beloved saints.
3a. Joyful stands the shining army of angels;
3b. "Holy, holy, holy," is the acclamation shouted for Christ.
4a. Lofty he sits in the seat of the apostles with blazing torch, giving judgment in
three tongues.
4b. The saints, who valued all earthly things no more than damp dung, shine like the
bright stars in the firmament.
5a. Their necks are adorned with the gleaming robes of martyrs;
5b. these are the soldiers who fought the battles of the world.
6a. With white crowns are crowned the saints who trusted in righteousness and,
fighting faithfully, rejected vanity—these only attained the kingdom of heaven,
6b. where they triumph in blazing glory, singing songs in artful melody and sweetest
voice, submitting their necks to the rule of Christ.
7a. Long shalt thou be remembered in the praises of saints, and much celebrated by
choirs of virgins, alleluia; for thee sings sweetly the holy army.
7b. Praise be to thee, O Christ, forever and always the succor of those who praise
thee; let us also sweetly proclaim an alleluia.
8a. Grant us that kingdom, forever flowering,
8b. where we may all sing "alleluia.")

it did not affect the internal musical structure of the prose. Prose introductions could also be related, in text or tune or both, to chants other than the alleluia. About half the early repertory (including *Ecce pulcra*) does not seem to be related to any chant already in existence. Most important, the introductory phrase often has a distinctly introductory character: more stereotyped and less individual than phrases that followed, the first line tended to function as an intonation.

In *Ecce pulcra* (pages 36–37), the beginning of the third couplet (*Felix stat*) obviously starts something new, moving downward with a melodic figure quite different from the first couplet. This new departure is frequent in proses, sometimes occurring in the very first couplet if the intonation is long and not connected to it (as in the prose *Nato canant omnia*). With such idioms the composer seems to announce that what follows is not mere extension of something old, but the beginning of a new piece in a new style. This type of beginning also makes the rounding at the end of the couplet more noticeable, a rounding that in *Ecce pulcra* and many others is carried out consistently.

In the fourth couplet (*Sublimis*) the melodic beginning is immediately echoed, then extended (*apostolorum—lampada*). Internal melodic repetition within the couplet is a regular feature of prose construction, a frequent way of extending phrases economically. Sometimes the internal repetition is so strong as to obscure temporarily the couplets themselves. The real couplet ending, however, is always made clear through a stereotyped cadential formula; the one used at the end of every phrase (except the last) of *Ecce pulcra* is extremely frequent throughout the whole early repertory.

Beginning at the fifth couplet (*Stolis*) the tune starts to press upward, even though returning to G for phrase endings. The upward trend is not winding and involute, as in a Gregorian gradual, but rather steps decisively from one level to the next, phrase by phrase. Couplet 6 (*Coronis*) leaps a fifth, and then confirms the higher level with two separate internal repetitions; the descent to G gains increasing sweep by being the extension of something both simple and by now familiar. This sixth couplet and the following one (*Multum*) are noticeably longer and more complex than preceding couplets. Here the rapidly gaining momentum of the piece reaches its high point with the exclamation *alleluia* in 7*a*, and again in 7*b* with *talia voce pulcra alleluia*. The eighth and last couplet, containing the petition *Da nobis*, is short and relatively simple, with neumes to slow down the motion and a slight melodic variant to end.

Ecce pulcra is not long, as early proses go; its form is extremely cogent, more than most. As in any repertory of forceful, living forms, there is much individual variation of certain basic procedures. The steady rise toward a high point in *Ecce pulcra* is a shape typical of early proses, although often there are two peaks, or even three, instead of one. For purposes of rough comparison we can represent the shape of *Ecce pulcra* schematically in the following fashion, with large numbers for the couplets and small numbers for the number of syllables:

$$1^4 \quad 2^{12}_{12} \quad 3^{16}_{16} \quad 4^{30 (= 7 + 13 + 10)}_{30} \quad 5^{14}_{14} \quad 6^{44 (= 11 + 6 + 10)}_{44} \quad 7^{42 (= 12 + 4 + 10)}_{42} \quad 8^{11}_{11}$$

Here it is easy to see a correlation between rhythmic complexity (represented by the internal structure of the couplet) and the overall melodic curve, which peaks in couplets 6 and 7. A larger prose, *Rex omnipotens* (for the Ascension), has melodic climaxes in the eighth and twelfth couplets:

$$1^{11} \; 2^{13}_{13} \; 3^{11}_{11} \; 4^{15}_{15} \; 5^{17}_{17} \; 6^{15}_{15} \; 7^{22}_{22} \; 8^{20}_{20}$$

$$9^{17}_{17} \; 10^{19}_{19} \; 11^{21}_{21} \; 12^{33\,(=13+13+7)}_{33} \; 13^{13}$$

In a few of the largest proses the overall shape is strikingly highlighted by the placement of easily recognizable, well-known acclamations, such as *Salus et victoria, illi sit et gratia, omnia per secla!* contrasting with their surroundings by their terse, rhyming texts and their melodic style, which is closer to that of the laudes. *Fulgens praeclara*, a really big prose for Easter, has a set of acclamations beginning *Rex in aeternum!* (King forever!) placed at X in this diagram:

$$1^{527}_{27} \; 2^{16}_{16} \; 3^{12}_{12} \; 4^{\;8+17+9}_{\;8+17+9}{}^{\times}$$

$$5^{22}_{22} \; 6^{23}_{23} \; 7^{14}_{14} \; 8^{\;6+19+8}_{\;6+19+7}{}^{\times}$$

$$9^{14}_{14} \; 10^{20}_{20} \; 11^{18}_{18} \; 12^{\;7+14+8}_{\;7+14+8}{}^{\times}$$

$$13^{15}_{14} \; 14^{14}_{14} \; 15^{7}$$

Fulgens praeclara is perhaps the largest of the group of early proses that seem not to be related to an alleluia—or to anything else—in their intonation. There are also some large proses that are related to an alleluia, for example *Gloriosa dies* (for St. Stephen), where the words *Gloriosa dies* replace the word *alleluia* in the intonation of the Alleluia *Beatus vir qui timet Dominum* (for saints' days). Only the intonation is borrowed, however; thereafter the melody bears no relationship to the Gregorian alleluia or its jubilus, but is independent. *Nato canant omnia*, a Christmas prose, begins with the alleluia taken directly from the Alleluia *Multifarie* (formerly for Christmas). Here, too, the rest of the prose is independent of the alleluia.

Created in the Frankish kingdom, the new prose was quick to spread elsewhere, as is shown most explicitly in a famous collection of proses prepared by Notker, monk at the abbey of St. Gall in eastern Switzerland. Notker was primarily a poet; among his other literary accomplishments he made some forty new texts for thirty-three existing sequences, providing two texts for some tunes. Of these thirty-three sequences (that is, tunes) at least half are known to be Frankish in origin. The remaining tunes may also be Frankish, but it is more likely that they were written at St. Gall or elsewhere on the eastern border of the Frankish kingdom. Alongside Notker's proses were others from Switzerland or the Rhineland. A few Frankish texts made their way eastward, while an even smaller number of Notker's texts returned to Frankish circles.

Notker's texts are considerably more learned, more polished, more "classical" than the Frankish ones; at the same time they stand further away from the excited, acclamatory language that so well expressed the new style. Notker wrote a charming preface to his *Liber hymnorum* (Book of Hymns), as he called his collection of proses. By way of explaining this new type of piece, Notker told a romantic tale (which might even be true) of how a monk, fleeing from a Norman raid on his monastery at Jumièges (west of Rouen), came to St. Gall carrying a chant book that contained some *versus ad sequentias*— presumably proses. Inspired by the idea but critical of the quality of these Frankish proses, Notker tells how he proceeded to write some of his own. While Notker's texts are indeed impressive, some of the non-Frankish melodies he used lack the lyricism as well as the form-building potential of the best Frankish ones.

Notker's proses, composed apparently in the years around 880, formed the core of a distinct repertory current for the next two or three centuries in Switzerland and the Rhineland. As often happens in peripheral areas, this repertory did not develop, but remained more or less fixed, even though it was increasingly infiltrated by the more progressive Frankish repertory in regions closer to the Frankish center.

By 900 the total repertory of proses, including Notker's, numbered perhaps seventy-five; by 1000, the total rose to several hundred. The composition of texts outpaced that of tunes, since as time went on several texts were set to the same tune. The full Frankish repertory of proses, as well as tropes, is represented in an important series of manuscripts from the Limousin, a region along the southern part of the Frankish kingdom in what is now central France; the center of musical activity in the Limousin was the famous abbey of St. Martial in the city of Limoges.

The sense of melodic clarity in the big prose is largely dependent upon its couplet structure and its cadential formulas. In the prose the Frankish composer succeeded in giving his melody a new forcefulness lacking in his previous efforts. He could not find this force in the single tones or intervals; he had to create it through simple, obvious shapes of the whole piece, such as the couplet structure with its ongoing repetition. As the shape of the piece became clear, or was made to seem clear through repetition, individual notes and intervals seemed less decorative, more functional, more directly related to the phrase in which they appeared. The descending scale toward the ends of phrases in *Ecce pulcra* (Example 12), for example, sounds different from the same scale in earlier diffuse melismas, where it would not have been reinforced by the overall structure. Composers responded to the increased sense of clarity by taking care that individual notes and intervals fell smoothly into the long line; *Ecce pulcra* is more disciplined in this respect than, say, *Fulgens praeclara*. The result was a classic phase in the development of the prose around 900.

KYRIE ELEISON A similar use of repetition raised the new *Kyrie* melodies far above the settings of *Gloria in excelsis, Sanctus,* and *Agnus Dei; Kyries* stood beside proses at the height of the new style. The earliest of the new *Kyries* may date from the period 850–900, while others were written throughout the 900s. The grandest, as well as one of the most widespread, of the early *Kyries* is

Tibi Christe supplices, that being the beginning of the Latin text set syllabically to this *Kyrie* melody (Example 13).

As we saw, *Kyries* were sometimes written down in two forms, one with all the Latin text peculiar to that setting and another with the same melody but no text except *Kyrie eleison.* Which form came first in any given case—the syllabic or the melismatic—we do not know; but the high Frankish style of the important early *Kyrie* melodies indicates that they were created at about the same time as the texts associated with them. Also like the prose, these *Kyries* may have been performed syllabically and melismatically in alternation. Such phrase-by-phrase repetition (once with the text, once without) would be in keeping with the formal repetitions characteristic of the melody itself.

The formal repetitions of the text of *Kyrie* (see page 30), standardized around 800, lent themselves well to the needs of the new musical forms. Composers exploited the ninefold shape in a variety of ways. At its simplest level, the form of *Tibi Christe supplices* is *ABA CDC EFE* (extended), a form found in other *Kyries* as well. Melodic similarities, such as those between A and B a fifth lower, or between A and E, or between the rough outlines of *ABA, CDC,* and *EFE,* serve further to pull the shape together. As in the prose, the rise toward the latter part of this *Kyrie* is obvious and effective.

Even more important than the existence of a clear shape is the force of expression that this shape bestows upon the melody: the final ascent to G, simple enough in itself, becomes in context sheer exaltation. Medieval musicians are sometimes described as not being interested in musical sound. There is, to be sure, always a gap between the ideal inside the composer's head and the reality of actual performance. And sometimes the terms in which medieval literary figures expressed musical ideals seem to us remote and unconvincing. But if we cannot profitably imagine *Tibi Christe supplices* sung by an apocalyptic choir of cherubim and seraphim, we should at least think of it as sung by a (perhaps equally remote) ideal choir of twenty-four lyric tenors, in order to hear the purely musical exaltation the composer must have had in mind.

As Frankish melody became more forceful, it acquired greater variety of expression. Two other early *Kyries, Clemens rector* (popular at St. Martial) and *Cunctipotens genitor* (sung all over Western Europe), are very different in tone from *Tibi Christe supplices.* These other *Kyries* are stern, eloquent, rich in animated gravity—the kind of melody sometimes described as "real Dorian." But the modal system has little to do, as a system, with the character of pieces such as these. In them it is the careful shaping of the whole that most affects the quality of individual pitches: their relationship to the whole becomes increasingly clear; they have greater weight, greater significance because of this relationship. The piece seems to revolve around and press toward its final, which happens to be D. Not all melodies that end on D have this quality, but only those created in a stage of high musical integration, such as took place around 900.

Kyries and proses were the most progressive accomplishments of Frankish musicians during the 800s. At the same time, European composers (not just Frankish ones) were also writing music in more traditional forms in response to expanding liturgical needs. As new saints' days and other observances were added to the liturgical calendar, propers for the mass and for the office had to

EXAMPLE 13 KYRIE

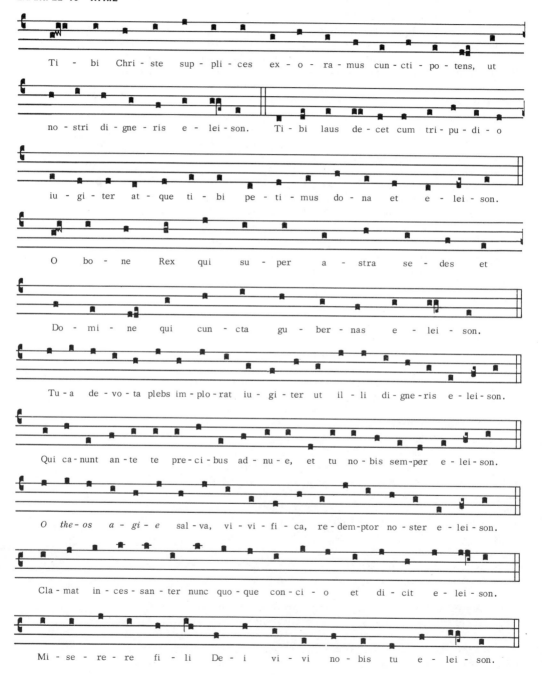

Ti - bi Chri - ste sup - pli - ces ex - o - ra - mus cun - cti - po - tens, ut

no - stri di - gne - ris e - lei - son. Ti - bi laus de - cet cum tri - pu - di - o

iu - gi - ter at - que ti - bi pe - ti - mus do - na et e - lei - son.

O bo - ne Rex qui su - per a - stra se - des et

Do - mi - ne qui cun - cta gu - ber - nas e - lei - son.

Tu - a de - vo - ta plebs im - plo - rat iu - gi - ter ut il - li di - gne - ris e - lei - son.

Qui ca - nunt an - te te pre - ci - bus ad - nu - e, et tu no - bis sem - per e - lei - son.

O the - os a - gi - e sal - va, vi - vi - fi - ca, re - dem - ptor no - ster e - lei - son.

Cla - mat in - ces - san - ter nunc quo - que con - ci - o et di - cit e - lei - son.

Mi - se - re - re fi - li De - i vi - vi no - bis tu e - lei - son.

EXAMPLE 13 (CONTINUED)

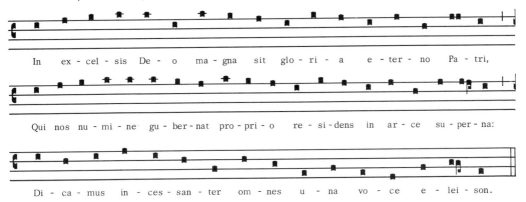

In   ex - cel - sis De - o   ma - gna   sit   glo - ri - a   e - ter - no   Pa - tri,

Qui nos nu - mi - ne gu - ber - nat pro - pri - o   re - si - dens in   ar - ce   su - per - na:

Di - ca - mus   in - ces - san - ter   om - nes   u - na   vo - ce   e - lei - son.

(To thee, Christ Almighty, we suppliants plead, that thou mayest hear us, *eleison!*
For thee is meet the praise and celebration and to thee we offer gifts and *eleison!*
O good King who sittest beyond the stars, and Lord who governest all things, *eleison!*
Thy devoted people together beg thee to have mercy, *eleison!*
Mayst thou always look with favor on us who sing with prayers before thee, *eleison!*
O Holy God, save us, give us life, our Redeemer, *eleison!*
Let the assembly now cry without ceasing and say *eleison!*
Let there be great glory on high for God, the eternal Father,
Who, dwelling in highest heaven, governs us with his own word;
Let us cry always with one voice, *eleison!*)

be adapted or composed. Composers provided new introits, new graduals—all
the items of the Roman proper, singly or in complete sets. The growth of responsories for the monastic service of matins was especially marked between 800
and 1200. Sometimes the new pieces remained purely local, but often they were
taken into the international repertory of sacred chant, largely through the
standardizing influence of the international, or supranational, monastic orders.

In musical style these neo-Gregorian pieces varied widely. Some reflected
modern styles of the new proses and related forms; others were so closely
modeled on Gregorian originals as to be indistinguishable from them. The
melody types common in Gregorian chant, for instance in graduals, make possible these authentic reproductions; even when composed in the 1900s, they may
be stylistically undetectable. Although this kind of chant is not stylistically
significant, being purely derivative, it does demonstrate something very important about medieval accomplishment. It makes clear that a good monastic
composer could be quite competent in Gregorian style and techniques. If he
wrote tropes and proses in a radically different style, it was because he wanted
to, not because he was forced to by ignorance or lack of skill. The only necessity
involved was purely artistic—the perennial necessity of doing something new
and original.

HYMN In many ways the most elegant expression of the new Frankish styles was the *hymn*. A hymn originally was a song of praise to God. In this sense the *Gloria in excelsis* was considered a hymn, even though written in prose; perhaps the most splendid Christian prose hymn is the *Te Deum* (We praise thee, O God), set to music probably in early Frankish times. Various Latin poets between 300 and 800, including St. Ambrose of Milan (340–397), the Spanish Prudentius (348–?413), and Venantius Fortunatus (ca 530–ca 600), wrote more specialized types of hymns in regular poetic forms. In spite of high artistic quality, their poems were not at that time taken up extensively by composers (as far as we know) or included in the Gregorian repertory. Eight hymns of St. Ambrose were incorporated into the Benedictine monastic offices, but what melodies these hymns used before 800 we have no specific idea.

Hymns with regular poetic structure offered Frankish monastic composers many advantages, most of all the chance to write melodies even more repetitive than those for the prose or *Kyrie*. Furthermore such hymns already had a position in the liturgy, at least in the monastic offices (but never in the mass), while the prose had to be slipped in. During the 700s and 800s many hymns must have been written. We know of several important writers of hymn texts, such as Paul the Deacon (730–799), Theodulfus (ca 760–ca 821, *All glory, laud, and honor*), and Rabanus Maurus (780–856, *Come, Holy Ghost*), eminent in church and state as well as letters.

In the hymn, as in the prose and *Kyrie*, Frankish composers of the 700s and 800s were responsible for a decisive phase of musical composition. Taking up the metrical hymn, a relatively isolated form, they gave it a musical definition so strong it still serves today. Nowhere has the medieval musical achievement been so enduring as in the hymn—not necessarily in individual tunes, although many are still in use, but in the musical concept of a hymn. While medieval hymn writers used many poetic structures, they favored far above all others the very simple one invented by St. Ambrose and so closely identified with him as to be called *Ambrosian*. This meter is still our most basic type of hymn.

Splendor paternae gloriae,	*(O splendor of God's glory bright,*
De luce lucem proferens,	*O thou that bringest light from light,*
Lux lucis et fons luminis,	*O Light of Light, light's living spring,*
Diem dies illuminans,	*O Day, all days illumining;)*

This most popular form consists of strophes each made of four lines of eight syllables. As this form was used in the 800s, the accents sometimes suggest an iambic line (x'x'x'x', where x is an unstressed and ' a stressed syllable); but usually hymns were not that regular in their accent patterns. Regularity lay rather in the number of syllables in each line, the number of lines in each strophe. This same principle held in other hymn structures: the significant factors were the number of syllables and the number of lines. The strophe was the basic structural unit.

Composers worked with this basic unit, the strophe, and its elements, syllables and lines. A hymn tune was one strophe long, being literally repeated for every succeeding strophe. The tune was constructed to reflect clearly the internal division of the strophe into lines. There was a strong cadence after the second line, dividing the tune into half, and weaker cadences at the ends of lines 1 and 3. Frequently the tune was rounded by making lines 1 and 4 similar or identical. In any case the tonal disposition of the four lines was carefully made to bring about the most cogent melody possible for the basic unit, the strophe. The conclusion of the strophe was inescapable: its shape was square.

Example 14 contains a hymn tune that may go back to the 800s. It has the same form as *Splendor paternae gloriae,* and hence may be used for that text; but it was commonly used for the text *Conditor alme siderum.* The clarity of its shape is unmistakable, in spite of the dark ending on E, which makes the tune hypophrygian, plagal deuterus, or tone 4 in the system of eight tones. A high proportion of hymns are deuterus, either plagal or authentic, as if to compensate for the clarity of their internal structure.

Very simple hymns are strictly syllabic, but most, including what seem to be some early versions, have at least a few neumes of two or three notes. More often than not these neumes are placed on weak syllables—why we do not know, but the rhythmic snap resulting from such placement is another source of relief to the obviousness intrinsic to hymns. Melodically these neumes are placed with great care, providing simple yet graceful decoration.

Frankish hymn writers handled more complex hymn forms with great skill and matching enthusiasm, as in the famous text *Pange lingua* by Venantius Fortunatus (another hymn with the same beginning, designed as a pendant to this one, is ascribed to St. Thomas Aquinas).

Pánge língua, gloriósi	*(Sing, my tongue, the glorious battle,*
láuream certáminis,	*Sing the winning of the fray;*
Et súper crúcis trophaéo	*Now above the cross, the trophy,*
dic triúmphum nóbilem:	*Sound the high triumphal lay:*
Quáliter Redémptor órbis	*Tell how Christ, the world's Redeemer,*
immolátus vícerit.	*As a victim won the day.)*

The tune commonly associated with this text in modern chant books may also be very old. This particular text is fairly regular in its accent patterns, but this is not necessarily typical.

EXAMPLE 14   HYMN (mode 4)

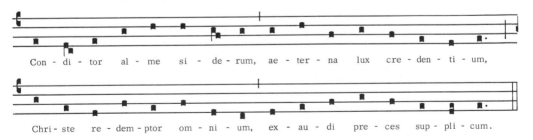

Con - di - tor al - me si - de - rum, ae - ter - na lux cre - den - ti - um,

Chri - ste re - dem - ptor om - ni - um, ex - au - di pre - ces sup - pli - cum.

(Beloved Founder of the heavens, everlasting light of believers, O Christ, Redeemer of us all, hear the prayers of thy suppliants!)

An analog of the classical sapphic meter was very popular with the Carolingians (and also afterward); it consists of three lines of eleven syllables each (subdivided 5 and 6), concluding with a short fourth line of five syllables. This form, which evoked some very imaginative solutions, can be illustrated by a famous hymn by Paul the Deacon, one that may be read either according to its classical long and short quantities or according to the word accents (the translation, however, works only with accents).

Ut quéant láxis
 resonáre fíbris
 Mira gestórum
 fámuli tuórum
 Sólve pollúti
 lábii reátum
 Sáncte Joárnes
	(See them now singing,
	     open throats resounding,
	 As best they're able,
	     deeds of thine recalling;
	 Cleanse thou of evil,
	     lips with which to praise thee,
	 Saint John our Baptist!)

A special class of processional hymns used a refrain. There would be one tune for the strophes and another for the refrain, which might be broken into two parts that recurred alternately.

$$R_a + R_b, S_1, R_a, S_2, R_b, S_3, R_a \ldots$$

(S = strophe; R_a, R_b = two halves of refrain.) The most famous processional hymn is *Salve festa dies*, also by Venantius Fortunatus (its refrain, however, is not split).

R.   *Sálve festa dies, toto venerabilis aevo*
        Qua Deus infernum vicit et astra tenet

S_1.   *Ecce renascentis testatur gratia mundi*
        Omnia cum Domino dona redisse suo

(Hail thee, Festal Day! blest day that art hallowed forever;
Day wherein God o'ercame hell and arose from the dead.
Lo, the fair beauty of earth, from the death of the winter arising,
Every good gift of the year now with its Master returns.)

This particular text is another late imitation of classical quantitative meter, but a very skillful one. The word accents may or may not correspond to long syllables; in any case they are not essential to the poetic form. Already by Venantius's time (600) the sense of classical Latin quantity had been forgotten and Venantius's use of quantitative forms was as academic as that of the Carolingians. As the sense of quantity disappeared, it left the number of syllables as the only determinant of the poetic form—the state of affairs predominant in Latin hymns from 700 to 1000.

3
VERSUS AND RELATED FORMS 1000-1150

AROUND 1000 CREATIVE MUSICAL COMPOSITION SEEMED TO PAUSE for a few decades. This was most evident in the prose: both the Notkerian and Frankish prose cycles hardened after 1000 into almost invariable repertories. During the 1000s proses in a new style gradually appeared, until by 1100 they were assembled into new cycles sharply distinct from the old ones, soon to go out of use. Similarly whole new generations of *Kyries* appeared, also new tropes to *Sanctus* and *Agnus Dei,* while older tropes to introit and *Gloria in excelsis* disappeared leaving scarcely a trace. One could almost take the year 1000 as marking a completely new style, except that the basic medium was still chant, and the stylistic novelties, while impressive, were novelties of detail within basic shapes already set up.

RHYME AND SCANSION Changes may have gone on first in kinds of music other than tropes, hymns, and proses; they are certainly easier to observe in the other kinds. While the changes affected musical style strongly, they appear equally strong in poetic techniques, which may even have led the way. The two basic poetic changes are easily stated: lines belonging together (as in a couplet) were made to rhyme, and rhyming lines of the same number of syllables were given identical stress patterns.

Fúlget díes hodiérna
Náta lúce sempitérna

The techniques of rhyme and scansion can be separated only for purposes of analysis; they belong together in a compound so perfect the poetry seems to sing all by itself. It is easy to see that if two lines are to rhyme, their terminal stress patterns, at least, must match. This matching was merely extended back from the end of the line to the beginning. Only two regular stress patterns were possible, one alternating a stressed with a single unstressed syllable:

Díes írae, díes ílla, sólvet sáeculum ín favílla

the other alternating a stressed with two unstressed syllables:

Hóra novíssima, témpora péssima súnt, vigilémus

The two basic patterns could begin and end either stressed or unstressed. This rhyming, scanning poetry danced along in a swinging rhythm that left its mark everywhere in the 1000s and 1100s. At its worst it descended to meaningless jingle, totally lacking the grandeur of the earlier, less regular styles. At its best the new rhythm generated a wealth of new strophic forms unequaled in Western history.

Musical style was directly affected by the new strophic forms, since the melodic style remained basically syllabic. Although neumes of three, four, or five notes were sometimes very frequent, they did not obscure the clearly syllabic framework underneath—at least, not until later. Hence the new shapes of the poetry became musical shapes. If the poem had simple hymnlike strophes, so did the music. Much of the new poetry, however, had more complex structures, lying in between hymns and the irregular couplets of proses. A poem might be strophic, but with long strophes containing several different lengths of lines arranged in an intricate rhyme scheme. The structure might even vary through-out the poem, making it no longer strophic. Refrains were frequent, sometimes cleverly worked into the structure of the strophe. Whatever the poetic shape, it was translated directly into musical terms through the close relationship of text and melody.

The new poetic rhythm affected music in more subtle ways. Just as the poet now exercised increasing control over the interior of the poetic line, making its stresses fall regularly every two or three syllables—even using extensive internal rhyme—so the composer made the interior of his melodic line increas-ingly related to the overall structure. The choice of cadences and ranges, the melodic direction, the placement of neumes—all were carefully controlled. Some-times the tunes were so obvious as to jingle as shamelessly as some of the poems. But the best tunes developed great melodic warmth by moving with ease and assurance through progressions so immediately perceptible as to seem old and familiar.

VERSUS One of the most important collections of the new rhythmic poetry with its new style of melodies comes from the abbey of St. Martial of Limoges, already famous for its tropes and proses. This collection (Paris, Bibliothèque nationale, MS latin 1139) is actually not one manuscript but frag-ments of several; it gives a fascinating cross section of all important stylistic novelties from around 1050 to 1150. The oldest part of the manuscript contains (among other things) about forty pieces of a type called *versus* (plural: *versus*).

The term *versus* was used throughout medieval music in a variety of meanings, both poetic and liturgical. Here it is used to designate poetic forms that are neither hymns nor proses. It is impossible to classify or define these versus further, for their only common feature is a joy in the endless possibilities of strophic form. Some poems have very short strophes, so short as to make it seem that one line with its melody is repeated throughout the entire piece. Others are extremely complex. Some have long refrains, some very short ones, for example *Gaudeamus!* One poem, a Christmas song, has a modulating refrain that starts out "In Bethlehem," then changes to "Jerusalem," then to "Artificem," and so forth.

The versus in Example 15, *Gaudeamus nova cum leticia* (designated in the manuscript as *Versus Trotter,* possibly a reference to the author), has no refrain as it is written down, but the isolated introductory line could certainly serve as one, being typical both in text and tune of refrains in this collection. The strophe is of moderate length and complexity, having two couplets followed by two concluding lines—$A_1A_2B_1B_2CD$. The tune is a marvel of concentration on the final, D, combined with differentiation between opening couplet, closing couplet, and epilog, ornamented with a simple but effective melisma. Apparently natural and spontaneous, such tunes conceal their solid foundation of art inherited from at least two centuries of chant composition.

The older sections of the St. Martial versus collection seem to be specially designed for the monastic night office of matins as it would be celebrated at St. Martial on a festive night during the Christmas season. In some versus the

EXAMPLE 15 VERSUS (refrain and first strophe)

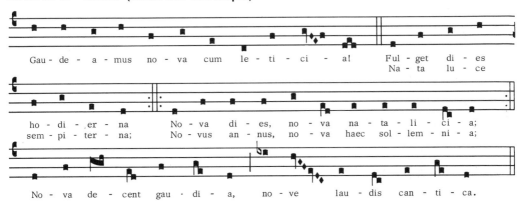

Gau - de - a - mus no - va cum le - ti - ci - a!   Ful - get di - es
                                                       Na - ta   lu - ce

ho - di - er - na   No - va di - es, no - va na - ta - li - ci - a;
sem - pi - ter - na;   No - vus an - nus, no - va haec sol - lem - ni - a;

No - va de - cent gau - di - a,   no - ve   lau - dis can - ti - ca.

(Let us rejoice with new joy!
Today shines forth, born in eternal light,
New day, new birth, new year, new festivity;
These call for new rejoicing, new songs of praise.)

first line is set to a short reciting tone terminating in a melisma—the exact form of certain short *versicles* used at matins between psalms and lessons. A big versus could appropriately be substituted on a festive occasion for a little versicle.

In addition to the versus already described, the St. Martial collection contains a group of more than fifteen *versus ad Benedicamus,* versus intended to replace a liturgical versicle that comes at the end of matins (and also vespers).

℣. *Benedicamus Domino!*　　　　　│　*(Let us bless the Lord!)*
℟. *Deo Gratias!*　　　　　　　　　│　*(Thanks be to God!)*

These *Benedicamus* versus have the words of the liturgical versicle worked in at the end, or paraphrased, or simply tacked on, so that in effect any versus could be adapted to a *Benedicamus.* Here is a *Benedicamus* versus with the liturgical words skillfully incorporated at the end of each strophe.

Vállus móntem, lápis fóntem, spína rósam speciósam édidit;
Vírga núcem, vírgo dúcem, máter fácta sed intácta rédidit;
Stélla sólem, vírgo prólem, cáro númen párit lúmen cécitas,
Et látuit quod pátuit sub servíli cárne víli déitas;
Ergo nos púro ánimo
Benedicámus dómino!
O miránda et laudánda cúius tális eternális déitas!
Nam servátur ne rumpátur in pregnántis generántis cástitas;
Reformárat, animárat páter mátrem, máter pátrem generárat;
Lux diéi, déus déi, vérbum pátris pártu mátri splénduit.
Pro séculi misérias
Redámus déo grátias!

(The valley a mountain, the rock a fountain, the thorn a beautiful rose gives forth;
The bough a nut, the Virgin a leader, the mother ever chaste remains;
The star a sun, the Virgin a Son, flesh gives birth to godhead as blindness sight,
Therefore with a pure spirit let us bless the Lord!
How wonderful and praiseworthy that eternal deity!
For she was safeguarded so that her virginity might not be lost in giving birth;
That the Father might reform and vivify the mother, she bore the Father;
Light of light, God of God, the Word of the Father shines forth in birth by the mother.
For the mercies of this world, Let us give thanks to God.)

Sometimes quoted verbatim, as here, sometimes paraphrased, the liturgical versicle has the effect of making an apparently irrelevant piece of poetry suddenly and cleverly appropriate to the liturgy.

Benedicamus versus, like other versus, often have refrains; in Example 16, the versus *Castitatis lilium* has the refrain *Fulget dies ista celebris.* Other strophes follow, and the refrain eventually changes. Here the melody has the same direct naturalness as *Gaudeamus* in Example 15. It consists of only two phrases, almost identical except that the first ends on B, the second on G. This difference in endings makes the couplet more intricate, more of a musical unit;

EXAMPLE 16 VERSUS (first strophe and refrain)

Ca - sti - ta - tis   li - li - um   ef - flo - ru - it,   qui - a   De - i

Fi - li - us   ap - pa - ru - it. ℟. Ful - get   di - es   i - sta   ce - le - bris.

(The lily of chastity has flowered forth
Because the Son of God has appeared.
℟. Let shine this festal day!)

its members are at once better differentiated and better unified. First and second endings on couplets (soon to be called *open* and *closed*) reflect the increased control over melodic detail characteristic of the new style.

EFFECTS ON OTHER FORMS The effect of the new rhymed poetry on the prose was drastic and obvious. The prose ceased to be prose and became poetry; its lines scanned; its couplets became uniform. Proses, firmly seated among the mass propers, were now different from hymns or versus chiefly in liturgical position; in style proses were still more elevated than other forms and still used the ongoing repetition without strophes. Under the pressure of the versus, however, even the prose sometimes became strophic. Proses in this new style began to appear around 1050; during the next several centuries literally thousands were written, displacing most of the old proses.

The new proses, too, finally went out of use, after being officially deleted from the mass propers by the Council of Trent in 1563. By action of that council four proses were retained for important feasts: *Victimae paschali laudes* (Praises to the paschal Victim) for Easter, *Veni sancte Spiritus* (Come, Holy Ghost) for Pentecost, *Lauda Sion* (Sion, praise) for Corpus Christi, and *Dies irae* (Day of Wrath) for the Mass for the Dead, or *Requiem*. The choice of these four was skillfully made. While none of them belongs to the old repertory, they well represent the varieties of new proses. *Victimae paschali laudes* was written in Germany by Wipo, who died in 1048; it possesses much of the songfulness of the new style, yet recalls the irregularity of the older prose. *Victimae paschali laudes* is one of very few proses with dramatic dialog, preserving something of the old introit dialog trope for Easter.

Veni sancte Spiritus, ascribed to Pope Innocent III (1160–1216), and *Lauda Sion,* whose text is ascribed to St. Thomas Aquinas (died 1274) but whose melody goes back to the early 1100s, are both excellent examples of the new French prose; both have extremely persuasive yet elevated melodies. *Lauda*

Sion is one of the largest proses, very regular in its construction, even though not strophic. It uses melodic formulas that became increasingly prevalent in the later history of the prose; the proses of Adam of Saint Victor (died 1192), the most famous composer of the later period, are mostly constructed out of formulas.

Dies irae, sometimes ascribed to Thomas of Celano (died after 1250), consists of three huge strophes and a coda, showing the full effects of the new strophic poetry and the virtual elimination of the basic features of the old prose. In addition to being literally strophic, *Dies irae* is neumatic rather than syllabic, and its diction as well as its musical character are expressively lugubrious, far from the dynamism of the 800s, echoing the Carolingian Judgment Day theme in a peculiarly personal tone.

Settings of *Kyrie, Sanctus,* and *Agnus Dei* multiplied after 1100; eventually there were over 250 *Kyrie* melodies and around 300 *Agnus Dei. Kyries,* especially, reflected in their musical technique the detailed control of the new style. The well-known *Kyrie cum jubilo* (from the 1100s?) has a melody whose flow is controlled down to the smallest unit, making a motivic analysis appropriate and revealing.

Concomitant with the clarity developed under the impact of rhyming chant was a compensating tendency toward melodic ornamentation. Toward 1100, versus not infrequently featured a heavy overlay of four- and five-note neumes. Even though these neumes never gave the versus the sense of suspension or inscrutability found in Gregorian graduals, still the neumatic overlay tended to stress musical elements over poetic ones. This tendency was especially strong in the antiphon, an older category which medieval musicians continued to cultivate.

Somewhere in between the older proses and the new rhyming, scanning, strophic poetry, with its appealing melodies, lay *votive antiphons,* antiphons of a relatively elaborate, neumatic style used for special occasions associated with the mass and offices, but not directly prescribed by them. Votive antiphons had been accumulating around the Gregorian core ever since it arrived in the Frankish kingdom; needed at first for ceremonial processions, votive antiphons eventually became an act of worship in themselves. While they could be used with a psalm, as in office psalmody, the more elaborate votive antiphons were also sung as independent compositions or followed by a versicle and collect to identify their liturgical position.

Votive antiphons were composed in great numbers after 1000. The most important are four (out of hundreds) addressed to the Virgin Mary: *Alma redemptoris mater, Ave regina caelorum, Regina caeli letare,* and *Salve regina.* These texts do not strictly scan or rhyme, but they have strongly symmetrical features typical of the prose or versus. All four antiphons are acclamations (Dear mother of our Redeemer! Hail, Queen of heaven! O Queen of heaven, rejoice! Hail, Queen!) of the elegant type cultivated in Swiss and Rhenish monasteries. These antiphons were long used on a variety of occasions as acts of devotion; eventually they were tacked on to the end of compline—one during each of the four seasons—where they now seem to be an integral part of the office.

Salve regina and *Alma redemptoris mater* both have grave, expressive melodies, more reminiscent than their texts of the new squarish shapes. Like most votive antiphons, they are mildly neumatic; but *Alma redemptoris mater* begins with one of the sweetest melismas ever written. This tune, with its distinctive beginning, was a favorite for centuries. Like the "Hail, Mary!" known at least by name to millions of Westerners, the *Alma* became for layfolk in the 1400s and 1500s one of their most meaningful liturgical acts, far exceeding the now remote, austere Gregorian propers in devotional significance.

The momentum of the new rhythmic poetry swept composers along toward huge aggregate forms. Rhyming pieces were not merely interpolated into monastic offices; they became the very substance of newly composed offices called *rhymed offices*. A poet might write rhymed antiphons, responsories, versicles—everything for a complete twenty-four-hour cycle including matins, lauds, vespers, and the small day offices. These rhymed texts would be set to new tunes or tunes adapted from existing offices. Or the new rhymed poetry and its tunes might replace some of the office texts, say, the antiphons, leaving the traditional psalms and responsories. The result in that case was an aggregate of various chant forms and styles within the ancient liturgical framework.

Along with the new techniques, and the increasing standardization they inevitably entailed, came a tendency toward dramatization. The St. Martial collection contains an extended versus titled *Lamentatio Rachelis,* the lament for the children slaughtered by Herod, with a consolation by an angel at the end. One eloquent melody is used for all the lines of the lament, another for the consolation. Such versus on dramatic topics are frequent. They are sometimes criticized for being too monotonous for drama. But the point is, they are not versified drama; rather they are dramatized verse. Any increase in intensity through drama is a gain over the effect the verse and its repeated tune would have otherwise.

Dramatized versus could take very elaborate forms. The St. Martial collection also contains the *Sponsus,* a dramatic dialog between the five foolish and the five wise virgins, waiting with their lamps for the bridegroom (*sponsus*), a figure of Christ. Strophic forms punctuated by refrains make up the structure of this new type of liturgical drama, which superseded the old prose dialogs of the Christmas and Easter introit tropes. Sometimes the old Easter dialogs were livened up with the *Victimae paschali laudes,* which had some of the feeling of the new style.

The infiltration of liturgical drama by verse came to a climax in the *Play of Daniel,* written at Beauvais probably around 1150. *Daniel* is so good it is hard to assign its success to any one element. Nonetheless, the drama consists basically of a series of versus. Even the dramatic dialog is sometimes cast in the form of a versus, while much of the dramatic substance and brilliance of the play resides in the pageantry, accompanied by high processional songs.

These songs are here called *conductus* (plural: *conductus* or *conducti*), evidently meaning a piece with which to conduct someone—the king, the queen, Daniel—on or off the scene. Some conductus in *Daniel,* for example, *Jubilemus regi nostro,* incline toward the structure of a prose, but more tend to be versus. Some versus are long and elaborate, like *Hic verus Dei, Rex tua nolo munera,*

and *Regis vasa referentes.* The versus *Congaudentes, celebremus* is apparently
a Christmas piece adapted for use in *Daniel.*

The conductus are not in themselves dramatic, but without them the
actual drama would have no foundation. *Daniel,* easily accessible, is perhaps the
best place to study the technique of the versus in all its spectacular variety.
Running like a refrain throughout the play, incidentally, is the acclamation
Rex in aeternum vive!

TROUBADOURS   The new style of poetry with its music was the font and
origin of large repertories of vernacular song that sprang up after 1100. Our
St. Martial collection contains some of the earliest Provençal lyrics. There is a
Provençal versus in the *Sponsus, Oiet virgines,* and a Provençal refrain to a
Latin versus, *Dolentas, chaitivas, trop i avem dormit!* (We poor, unfortunate
ones have slept too long!) The versus *In hoc anni circulo* has alternate lines in
Provençal. There is another Provençal lyric entitled *Tu autem,* a Latin liturgical
versicle at matins. And there is a versus addressed to the Virgin, *O Maria deu
maire e fils e paire,* sung to the tune of a famous Marian hymn, *Ave maris stella.*
All these probably date from before 1100, from the same decades that saw the
rise of the troubadours, composers of secular poems and music at the brilliant
courts of Provence.

The earliest troubadours were associated with Guillaume of Aquitaine,
Count of Poitiers (1071–1127), himself a poet; then Marcabru (active 1129–
1148), Jaufré Rudel (active 1130–1147), and especially Bernart de Ventadorn
(1145–1195) brought the Provençal lyric, the song of courtly love, to a stage of
high refinement. The extant repertory of troubadour songs, extending until
1300, includes over 270 melodies. A discussion of this and other repertories of
secular song takes us well past 1150; yet the structural principles remain those
of the versus, fully developed by that date. The Provençal pieces cited from the
St. Martial collection are only symptomatic of the relationship of the troubadour
repertory to the rhyming Latin sacred chant of the 1100s. That chant was the
basis of the art of the troubadours, who, like their monastic predecessors, were
fascinated by the endless possibilities of strophic structure. The troubadour
songs are shot through with melodic reminiscences of their sacred models.

Like the versus, troubadour songs are sometimes rendered nowadays in
long and short note values in metered rhythms. The original notation contains
no hint of any lengths or rhythms, which can be read into the music only by
trying to match up long and short notes with stressed and unstressed syllables,
roughly according to a kind of rhythm (called *modal rhythm*) that is first
known to operate in polyphonic music after 1150. We will study modal rhythm
in its proper place. It suffices here to point out that the only grounds for
assuming modal rhythm for the versus or for the troubadours before 1200 is the
poetic regularity of the texts, their alternation of stressed and unstressed
syllables.

If a line of poetry has every other syllable stressed, then it can of course
be set to alternately long and short note values. But the fact that it can does
not mean either that it should be or that it originally was. The imposition of
long and short notes sometimes produces highly convincing results; sometimes
it does not. The most that can be concluded is that some singers may on some

occasions have performed certain pieces in a swinging manner by lengthening or shortening alternate notes, but the result cannot be imputed to the original artistic conception—at least, not in chant before 1200. In any case, there was no "modal system," such as is often employed to transcribe troubadour songs, until 1250 or so. The same songs, incidentally, are also very effective without longer or shorter notes or syllables.

In fact the relative indifference of rhyming chant (sacred or secular) to long and short notes is its most important rhythmic feature. The troubadour, like the composer of versus, was working primarily with strophes and phrases. *Rhythm* in this kind of chant pertains to the disposition of phrases—most of all to their relative lengths. The relationship of these lengths is unaffected by any *consistent* lengthening of alternate notes. The regularity of stressed and unstressed syllables is, of course, an important step in the direction of regularly alternating long and short values such as will appear in modal rhythm; but these longs and shorts are in no way necessary, or even desirable, to the conception or perception of rhyming, strophic chant.

Troubadour songs were sometimes known by generic names that indicated their poetic content. One such type is the *alba* (dawn song); a famous example is *Reis glorios* by Guiraut de Bornelh (1173–1220)—in which, incidentally, there are strong reminiscences of sacred chant, including *Cunctipotens genitor*. But terms such as *alba* (and there are several others) have little to do with style or form. Even the more general terms *vers* and *canso* do not seem to specify forms. *Vers*, the French word for *versus*, was used from the beginning of the troubadour repertory to refer to a variety of forms. The Provençal term *canso* (like the north French *chanson*) was the Latin word *cantio* (song).

Troubadour forms were largely strophic, but the inner construction of strophes varied from simple hymnlike schemes to long, complex ones. On one hand, troubadours sought, and valued, individual strophic structures; on the other hand, they frequently borrowed structures already invented, setting new words to old tunes.

Italian writers after 1300 (including Dante Alighieri, 1265–1321) described troubadour forms in what is still the most useful way. Dante himself distinguished songs in which there is no repetition within the strophe, that is, no couplet, from those which do have repetition. In the latter, the music of the strophe consists of two sections; if the first is repeated, there is a couplet at the beginning (A_1A_2B); if the second, then there is a couplet at the end (AB_1B_2). If both sections are repeated $(A_1A_2B_1B_2)$, the strophe consists of two couplets.

Couplets remained one of the cornerstones of strophic structure right through the troubadour repertory and all medieval song. Troubadours favored especially a strophe that began with a couplet. Couplets at the end of the strophe were relatively rare, at least in earlier songs.

TROUVÈRES Beginning almost as early as the troubadours, the *trouvères*, their Northern counterparts, produced a repertory of song equally dependent upon the techniques of the versus. While trouvères were active at court, like the troubadours, they also frequented the bourgeois strata of the rising town culture around Paris and throughout the north of France. The trouvère repertory was much larger, running to almost two thousand melodies, and more varied in kind and quality of subject matter. Famous trouvères were Blondel de Nesle (ca 1155–?), Gace Brulé (ca 1159–after 1213), and Gautier de Coinci (1177–1236), who also applied the now highly cultivated art of secular song to sacred subjects in his *Miracles de la sainte Vierge.*

Like the troubadours, the trouvères favored strophic forms with an opening couplet. Trouvère songs were known by several names, but here again the names have no systematic relationship to structure, except for special types to be discussed later. Earlier trouvère songs, inheriting not only the experience of the versus but that of the troubadour as well, frequently have long strophes and elaborate melodies, broad in scope and rich in neumatic overlay. Without differing from the versus in principle, trouvère tonal structure tends sometimes to be more oblique, especially in the ways used to differentiate lines of a couplet by *ouvert* and *clos,* open and closed cadences for first and second endings (as in Example 17).

Trouvère production lasted right through the 1200s, contemporary with the part music to be discussed in this and the following chapter. During the late 1100s and 1200s trouvère songs showed several remarkable tendencies. Refrains, already present in the versus, became increasingly frequent in trouvère

EXAMPLE 17 TROUVERE SONG

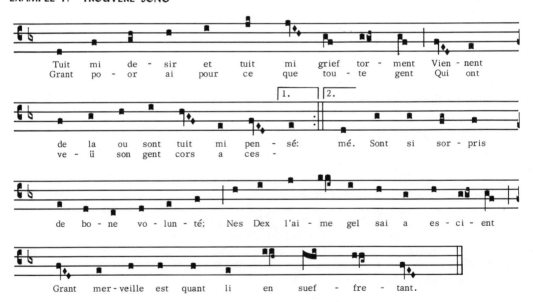

(All my longing and all my grievious pain comes from her on whom I always think . . .)

songs, but primarily as a function of the words rather than of the music. Later trouvères were apt to make the last line of each strophe of a song identical, giving that line a special poetic significance. Such refrains appeared most frequently at the end of the kind of strophe that began with a couplet. So favored was this form, usually consisting of three strophes, that it emerged around 1300 as a fixed, predominant type called *ballade*.

The term *ballade* is related to dancing, and toward the end of trouvère development such associations with dancing became frequent. We find pictures of round-dancing on the green, the dancers apparently singing as they dance. Refrain forms, of course, would be particularly appropriate for dance songs, lending themselves to performance by leader and chorus.

Other folklike elements make their appearance at the same time. We begin to find examples of the *lai*, a narrative form of poetry built like a sequence or prose. Obscure references suggest an ancient practice of rhapsody, but the examples we have belong to a late, self-conscious literary phase.

The most striking illustration of folklike tendencies is the *rondeau*, a refrain form of a particular complexity.

refrain A, refrain B
verse A (music of refrain A, new text)
refrain A
verse A' (music of refrain A, new text)
verse B' (music of refrain B, new text)
refrain A, refrain B

Originally the rondeau began with the verse A; the refrain, occurring normally after the verses, was later placed at the head of the song as well.

The principle of the rondeau goes back to the split refrain of processional hymns; but as realized in the rondeau, the refrain structure has a peculiar self-consciousness that suggests a late development. At the same time the rondeau is remarkably simple in its musical style—so simple as to seem rustic, in keeping with its pastoral texts. Clearly not reflective of a primitive stage of development, this charming rusticity seems to be a pose assumed toward the end of a development that had produced extremely sophisticated forms.

To the Northeast the trouvère repertory diffused into German-speaking lands, cultivated there by the *Minnesinger* (singers of love). To the Southeast the troubadour art strongly affected Dante and the nascent Tuscan lyric. Repertories of sacred vernacular songs called *laudi* sprang up in Italy for the devotions of layfolk. To the Southwest, across the Pyrenees, the troubadour art was reflected in another collection of vernacular, sacred songs addressed to the Virgin, the *Cantigas de Santa María*, made by Alfonso X (died 1284) of Castile and Leon.

The troubadour and trouvère repertories represent the first diffusion of chant styles and techniques into the broad realm of medieval song. The diffusion itself signaled the end of forward development in chant; the rhyming chant style of the 1100s had brought the last significant changes. From that point on, the chant was applied in ever-widening geographical and social circles, eventually becoming folksong; but it was no longer involved in the stylistic development of serious art music, a development now engaged with polyphony.

Theory and Polyphony

CHANT THEORY A major difficulty in understanding chant theorists of the period 800–1100 is in grasping the level of simplicity at which they were speaking. They were concerned with basic tonal concepts, concepts involving the relationships of a few intervals among a few notes. They were trying to conceptualize and systematize the intuitive orientations of singers, orientations which were concrete and reliable for the tonal area of, say, a fourth, but not for that of an octave. They tried to do this with the theoretical tools of antiquity, handed down either in complete, authoritative form by Boethius, or in other, more fragmentary sources.

Such tools were often ill-suited to the task; but theorists after 800 applied them with enthusiastic pragmatism. Since the music these tools originally explained was by this time totally unknown, the original meaning of the tools could be—and was—drastically altered or completely ignored. This was not a mark of the theorists' stupidity, but of their ingenious resourcefulness: their job was not to preserve intact the outmoded past but to make it meet the problems of the present. After a relatively short development of theoretical structures derived from the past, theorists by 1050 had developed entirely new structures eminently suited to the conceptualization of Western music.

We have already seen the kind of theoretical activity that preceded our earliest sources, activity resulting in the system of four finals through the similarities between D and A, E and B, F and C. Concern with these similarities, soon called the *affinities*, marked the main line of theoretical development. Several fragments known to us as the *Alia musica*, from around 900, are of great interest, but not yet sufficiently well understood to be discussed here. One of the best theorists of the 800s is Hucbald (ca 840–930) of St. Amand, in Flanders; Hucbald in his *De institutione harmonica* (*Harmonic Principles*) shows the increasing integration of theoretical tools with the realities of chant. Regino of Prüm, on the other hand, prefaced his excellent tonary with an unrelated theoretical discussion almost entirely antiquarian in nature.

The bold, ingenious author of a treatise called *Musica enchiriadis* (*Musical Handbook*, ca 900), probably also the author of the related treatise *Scolica enchiriadis* (*Scholastic Handbook*—a dialog of teacher and pupil), reasoned that these affinities were so important that they should be made the basis of the scale; that is, the scale should be rebuilt to make the affinities come out exactly rather than only approximately. The scale he made goes like this:

G A B♭ C / D E F G / A B♮ C D / E F♯ G A / B C♯

Built out of identical, disjunct tetrachords (each has the half step in the middle, and each is separated by a whole tone from the next), this scale makes D exactly like A relative to the neighboring tones—and so for the other affinities. What the author actually did was to make the four finals the basis of a single tonal unit, the fourth D–E–F–G, which alone accounted for the whole musical realm.

This imaginative, highly rigorous yet highly pragmatic, construction was apparently well known during the 900s; although pointedly ignored by one of the next great theorists, Odo (ca 1000), it was bitterly attacked by two others,

Hermannus Contractus (1013–1054) and Guido of Arezzo (ca 990–ca 1050). Odo, equally pragmatic in his own way, reasserted duplication at the octave, lack of which makes the *Musica enchiriadis* scale so unorthodox. He built octave duplication into his lettering of the scale, a lettering that became standard.

$$\Gamma \text{ A B C D E F G a } {\small\begin{matrix}\flat\\\flat\end{matrix}} \text{ c d e f g } {\small\begin{matrix}a\\a\end{matrix}}$$

Odo's A is our A; his lettering is the first (there were others) to correspond to our own. The Γ (gamma) is a note he added at the beginning of the scale. He also provided for two B's (our B flat and B natural), indicating the lower one with a round letter (b), the upper one with a square letter (♭, which eventually became the German ♮ or H). Odo based his scale—indeed his theory—on the monochord. It was he who popularized this instrument as a way of fixing and reliably demonstrating the sizes of intervals.

Guido used Odo's scale and his monochord division; he followed Odo in stressing octave duplication. Guido also stressed the affinities, like the *Musica enchiriadis*, but when it came to a conflict between affinities and octave duplication (as at the fifth notes above D and A), Guido always let octave duplication prevail. Most important, Guido developed out of this conflict a new superconcept that reconciled the two.

Starting from the relationship of finals (D–E–F–G) emphasized in the *Musica enchiriadis*, Guido expanded this unit by adding on a whole tone at either end (C–D–E–F–G–A), and then tried to make this tonal concept universal. Within this unit, eventually called a *hexachord*, one could imagine the finals of all the modes and their surrounding whole and half steps. By placing the hexachord on G (G–A–B–C–D–E) one could imagine all the same finals in their affinity a fifth higher. By placing the hexachord still higher, on C, one obtained the affinities an octave above.

Guido did not completely work out the implications of the hexachord—which is not surprising, since this was the most fruitful tonal concept developed in centuries and lasted until after 1600. Guido did, however, give the six notes the names *ut, re, mi, fa, sol, la,* which he derived from the hymn *Ut queant laxis* (see page 46), whose phrases obligingly begin on C, D, E, F, G, A. All the intervals of the hexachord were whole steps except *mi–fa,* which thus became a basic point of orientation.

Hermannus's chief interest lay in the *species,* a theoretical tool used unsystematically by his predecessors. There are three species of fourths (A–B–C–D, B–C–D–E, C–D–E–F), four of fifths, seven of octaves. Hermannus found a way of numbering and combining these species so as to express the modal system in the most economical way. Here is his construction for protus.

1st species fifth + 1st species fourth = mode 1
D–E–F–G–A   A–B–C–D

1st species fourth + 1st species fifth = mode 2
A–B–C–D   D–E–F–G–A

The three species of fourths begin, in Hermannus's system, on A, B, and

C; the four species of fifths on D, E, F, and G. The seven octave species are compounded of the fourths and fifths. This provides a way of differentiating between the octave D–D used (in Hermannus's time) to identify both tone 1 and tone 8: in tone 1, the octave D–D consists of first species fifth under first species fourth, while in tone 8 the same octave consists of fourth species of fifth (G–A–B–C–D) over first species of fourth.

Species, it should be noted, are a comprehensive way of describing tonal relationships, but not a very dynamic way: they tell nothing about the functional relationship of the tones, since these relationships change from one species to another. As Hermannus used the species, they explained the eight modes handily enough, but these modes, designed for classifying antiphons, had never had much to do with underlying tonal structure in the West, and in Hermannus's time, they were becoming more remote every day. Hermannus, too, turned eventually from species to that new concept that had only one species, the hexachord. This he perfected as he had perfected the doctrine of species.

After Hermannus there remained only to find a third position of the hexachord, on F, to build a complete tonal system whose internal functions could be easily grasped and whose external form corresponded with the realities of octave duplication. In this hexachord on F (added before 1300) the lower of Odo's two B's was a *fa*. As the concept of *fa* became generalized, the sign for the round B was applied eventually to any note of the scale, becoming the sign for a flat (b = ♭). Similarly Odo's higher B came to stand for a generalized *mi*, and its sign eventually turned into a natural (♭ = ♮). In this way tonal functions defined within the hexachord were later isolated and extracted, adhering to a single note.

EARLY POLYPHONY   Theorists give us our first firm information on Western polyphony. The *Musica enchiriadis,* around 900, gives directions how to sing in parallel with a chant, above or below at fourth, fifth, or octave, or consonant combinations of these intervals. From the performer's point of view, such singing in parallels means singing the same chant but starting a fourth, fifth, or octave away from the normal pitch. But from the listener's point of view, singing in parallels produces a series of very resonant sonorities with a single melodic profile—the profile of the original chant.

This effect would have been especially marked under the acoustical conditions, the kind of architecture, in which such singing was done. Perfect consonances such as fifth and octave (which, being sung, could be made pure rather than tempered) are, of course, essential to producing such resonance; false intervals such as augmented or diminished fifths or octaves would cause an immediate and disturbing disruption of the resonance.

Singing in parallels added nothing to the original chant except rich sonority; it introduced no new structural element. This kind of singing undoubtedly went back a long time and continued unchanged for centuries. It was in common use during the 900s, especially for the singing of modern chant such as hymns and proses.

The *Musica enchiriadis* also describes a way of singing at the fourth below, in which the added voice begins in unison with the original chant, but repeats the same pitch while the original chant ascends, until the two voices are in fourths. Proceeding in fourths until the end of the phrase, the added voice arrives at a unison in an analogous way. This use of oblique motion results in a varied series of less consonant intervals—seconds and thirds—in between the initial and final unisons and the parallel fourths.

While the increase in complexity over parallels is slight, and the artistic gain negligible, nonetheless a very important change in principle is here evident. The shape of the original melody may still guide the progression of intervals, but it is no longer the only factor in that progression. The progression of intervals, from unison through second and third to fourth, is subject to a whole new realm of considerations having to do with relative qualities of intervals, relative degrees of consonance. The resulting progression may still reinforce the phrase shape of the chant, may still be an analog of the original melody, but from this moment on it becomes increasingly an analog, not an identity as before.

Clearly the exploitation of interval progressions depended on hearing a great many experiments, both successful and otherwise. There were no rules in existence; they had to be arrived at pragmatically. Just as clearly, exploitation was maximized when the kind of motion was as far from parallel as possible. If parallel motion produced identical intervals in succession, then a varied succession of intervals must be produced by contrary motion. Between 900 and 1100 there must have been extensive, if sporadic and mutually isolated, experiments in handling contrary motion. Of these experiments but little record remains.

By far the largest collection of early polyphony is found in the *Winchester Troper* (ca 1000), an English collection of tropes and proses similar to Frankish ones of the late 900s. The Winchester Troper contains as an appendix a set of over 150 *organa* (as the manuscript calls them) to chants either in the Troper itself or readily available to its original users. According to a recent—and impressive—attempt at transcription (the original notation is exceedingly problematic), the organa seem to proceed largely in parallel motion to the original chant, with oblique or contrary motion for phrase endings. The organa are written primarily for difficult, elaborate pieces, such as alleluias (54 organa), responsories (51), and tracts (19); there are also organa for 12 proses, 12 *Kyries*, 8 *Gloria in excelsis*, and a few other kinds. The use of the term *organum* for the added voice (which is then an organum to a chant) seems to be borne out in other sources, where sometimes the added voice is called *vox organalis,* the original chant the *vox principalis.*

The theorists of the 1000s are remarkably closemouthed about polyphony. Their reluctance to describe it is frustrating, but understandable; in a period of experimentation, polyphony offered little opportunity for theorizing or systematic description. Furthermore the musical results were far from convincing. Throughout the 1000s and for most of the 1100s, polyphony was so inferior to contemporary chant in style and technique that it was hardly worth considering from an artistic point of view; it was also negligible in quantity.

Hermannus Contractus, writing around 1050, does not discuss polyphony, while Guido, around 1030, describes certain procedures of contrary motion suitable for closes or cadences. John of Afflighem (ca 1100) dismisses the subject with the barest description of contrary motion as a principle, which in itself is interesting, and strikingly reflected in the most notable collection of polyphony since the Winchester Troper, some alleluias from two Chartres manuscripts. Transcription of these pieces (still not without problems) shows a consistent use of contrary motion, with parallels now being the exception. The result is a wealth of variety in interval progressions—an embarrassment of riches, in fact; composers had learned how to produce but not yet control a varied stream of intervals. The added voice is provided only for the solo portions of the alleluia, the intonation and verse, in a note-against-note manner. It occupies the same range as the chant, the voices moving above and below each other within the space of an octave.

POLYPHONIC VERSUS From 1050 to 1250 there are several small treatises on polyphony preserved. Hardly to be described as theory, these unimposing treatises tend either to state what can be stated about polyphonic practice in very general terms or else give case-by-case enumeration of interval progressions. There are also a number of fragments, each containing a piece or part of a piece. All these, however, are overshadowed by the first real repertory of polyphony in contrary motion, a repertory transmitted once again by St. Martial. Early St. Martial polyphony comes to us from the same collection in which we found versus; indeed, these polyphonic pieces *are* versus, closely resembling the others in everything except number of voices.

Even that qualification is not absolute, since some pieces that appear to be chant in this manuscript turn up in other manuscripts to be polyphonic. In a typical case, *Noster cetus,* the text consists of a series of couplets, set to what looks like chant. But the melody over the second line of each couplet is entirely different from the melody over the first line—not unheard of, but suspicious. In another source, the same two lines of melody appear with the same couplet, but now written as a piece of two-part polyphony, sung to the first line of the couplet and then repeated for the second line. In another case, *Annus novus,* there appear to be two alternate refrains; but these two melodies are counterpoint to each other, forming one polyphonic refrain. Characteristic of these cases is strong contrary motion, and note-against-note motion in the two parts, whether syllabic or neumatic.

The most important polyphonic piece in this collection is a *Benedicamus* versus, *Exultemus,* a rhyming, scanning text that moves in the infectious rhythms of the new poetry.

Exultémus, jubilémus, intonémus cánticum
Redemptóri plasmatóri salvatóri ómnium
Hoc natáli salutári ómnis nóstra túrmula
Déum láudat síbi pláudat per etérna sáecula
Qui hódie de maríae útero progrédiens
Hómo vérus réx atque hérus in térris appáruit
Tam beátum érgo nátum cum ingénti gáudio
Conlaudántes exultántes benedicámus dómino.

(Let us exult, rejoice, give out the song
For the Redeemer, Lifegiver, Savior of all;
On this birthday of salvation let our whole troop

Praise God and applaud him forever,
Who issuing forth today from Mary's womb,
True man, King, and Master, appeared upon earth.
Therefore, such a blessed birth with great joy
Praising and rejoicing, Let us bless the Lord!)

The whole versus consists of eight lines rhymed in pairs, except for lines 5 and 6; each new line has a new melody. The lower voice, mostly syllabic, has a tune typical of chant versus—frank, appealing, firmly centered on G. The upper voice has anywhere from one to twenty notes for each syllable of the text, and hence for each note of the lower voice. Four or five notes to one of the lower voice is the most common; extended groups of fifteen or twenty notes appear at the rhyming ends of lines, in one case at the beginning of a line and in another at a strong internal rhyme.

The tune of the lower voice has no structural repeats to reflect the rhyming couplets; but the upper voice, not in itself tuneful, organizes the form through its choice of figure. The first two lines, a couplet, have similar extended ornaments on their penultimate syllables. The next two lines, another couplet, share a new closing ornament, a scale descending from F to G, very typical of St. Martial polyphonic cadences. The third pair of lines is not a couplet, and hence has no musical rhyme; instead, the strong internal rhyme (*verus . . . herus*) receives an ornament resembling the end of the first couplet. The last couplet also has different endings, since here the last line, ending with *Benedicamus Domino*, needs to be set off; it uses the descending scale of the second couplet.

The development of varied polyphonic relationships, of varying numbers of notes in one voice to each note of the other, made it possible to use these relationships for structural differentiation. Since the lower voice here is syllabic, the variation in the upper voice becomes (relative to the text) one of syllabic, neumatic, and melismatic style, and its structural principles are hence closely related to those of chant. Melismas are placed at beginnings and ends of phrases, as they often are in chant versus. In *Exultemus* a further structural differentiation is brought about by making the first couplet more neumatic, while the later lines, especially the last couplet, tend toward a syllabic style in their beginnings.

The shape of St. Martial polyphony, then, is founded upon the versus, the rhyming, scanning, strophic chant of the 1000s with its ingratiating melodies. The upper voice sometimes moves note-against-note with the lower one (which is the one that most resembles rhyming chant) and sometimes has extended melismas of up to twenty notes at cadences, on the penultimate syllable; but most often the upper voice ornaments the notes below with neumes of two, three, four, or five notes. In this prevailing neumatic style both contrary motion and consonance are treated freely, the upper voice moving through abundant dissonances and different types of motion. As with the rhyming chant, we do not know what the detailed rhythms were; but as with that chant, "rhythm" is phrase rhythm and concerns the larger structure.

A more concrete idea of these polyphonic styles can be gained from Example 18, containing portions of another polyphonic versus, *Per partum virginis* (from a slightly later St. Martial collection). This text is more intricate in structure:

EXAMPLE 18 EXCERPTS FROM A POLYPHONIC VERSUS (transcription)

    (a) Beginning

Per   par - tum vir - gi - nis   De - i   et   ho -   mi -

ni   * sunt   iun - cta fe -   -   de - ra

    (b) A terminal melisma

he   -   -   -   te - ra

EXAMPLE 18 (CONTINUED)

(c) Another transcription of (b)

he   -   -   -   -

-          -   -   -   -   te - ra

(d) A syllabic section

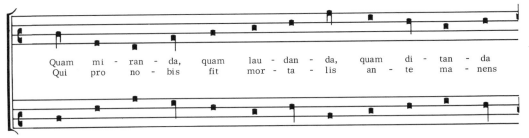

| Quam | mi – ran – da, | quam | lau – dan – da, | quam | di – tan – da |
| Qui | pro no – bis | fit | mor – ta – lis | an – te | ma – nens |

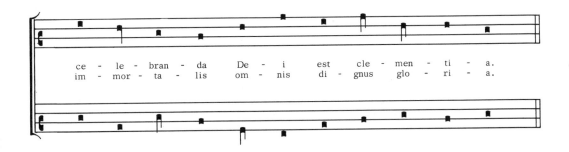

| ce – le – bran – da | De – i | est | cle – men – ti – a. |
| im – mor – ta – lis | om – nis | di – gnus | glo – ri – a. |

Per pártum vírginis
      Déi et hóminis
            sunt iúncta foédera.
Víta tribúitur
      cúlpa dilúitur
            quae claúsit hétera.

(Through virgin birth the bonds of God with man are joined. Life is given, guilt washed away that closed the womb.

Vérbum lúmen Déi Pátris
      súmpta cárne álvo mátris
            in hac díe cláruit.
Vérus Déus, vérus hómo
      est de Jésse nátus dómo
            ut prophéta dócuit.

The Word, light of God the Father, taking on flesh in the womb of the mother, this day shines forth. True God, true man, born of the house of Jesse, as the prophet fore-told.

Sub cárnis tégmine
      hómo pro hómine
            sol vérus látuit.
Félix puérpera
      quae nos et súpera
            uníre pótuit.

Under cover of flesh, made man for man, the true sun is hidden. Happy birth! that unites us with heaven above.

Quam mitánda, quam laudánda,
      quam ditánda celebránda
            Déi est cleméntia,
Qui pro nóbis sit mortális
      ánte mánens immortális
            ómni dígnus glória;
Immortális fit mortális
      sóla táctus grátia.

So highly to be admired, praised, retold, and celebrated is the mercy of God, Who for us became mortal, having been and being immortal, worthy of all glory; immortal made mortal, touched by Grace alone.)

The first couplet stresses every third syllable (with some typical varia-tion) while the second couplet (*Verbum lumen . . . Verus Deus . . .*) stresses every other syllable. The first couplet is highly neumatic, even melismatic, in the upper voice, while the second is much closer to a syllabic style, with a note-against-note relationship of the voices. Polyphony brought a whole new dimen-sion into musical texture, making the terms *syllabic* and *melismatic* more diffi-cult to use and needful of qualification. In *Per partum* the ends of both couplets have spectacular melismas in *both* voices at once, moving in strictly note-against-note polyphony, for example on *hetera* (Example 18b and c).

The fourth couplet, *Quam miranda* (Example 18d), is strictly syllabic and strictly note-against-note, also strictly in contrary motion. Both lines of the couplet are sung to the same music. This section of the piece is a distinct entity, preceded by a neumatic section and followed by an odd line in a curiously ornamented syllabic style, concluding with a grand sequential roulade.

Both in size and complexity, the St. Martial polyphonic versus represent an advanced stage of polyphonic development. There are several indications that polyphony of this type goes back well before 1100, the date of its oldest source; this polyphonic repertory is probably the product of the entire preceding century. It grew up with the new rhyming chant, from which it derived its main structural features.

OTHER POLYPHONIC FORMS   Alongside this most characteristic kind of polyphony, St. Martial sources include some interesting experiments. One versus, *Stirps Jesse,* at first glance chant, includes a lower voice that changes its pitch very slowly; this lower voice is a *Benedicamus Domino* in its liturgical form—just those words sung to a short melody. Hence the whole piece has two simultaneous texts, the *Stirps Jesse* versus in the upper voice (itself a *Benedicamus* versus) and the slow-moving *Benedicamus* below.

Three other pieces, either in later sources or added to earlier ones, also have a great disparity between the two voices. As we saw, penultimate syllables were apt to carry extended melismas; but in these three pieces this relationship persists throughout. All three are experimental in type as well as style. *Lectio libri sapientie* is the beginning of an epistle, the lower voice being a lesson tone. *Ora pro nobis* is a short versicle for St. Nicholas, the lower voice again being largely a recitation tone. The third piece is a *Benedicamus*—not a versus, but just the liturgical versicle in the lower voice, each tone sustained for great length under long melismas in the upper voice. Such "sustained-note style" (as it is sometimes called) is not typical of the St. Martial repertory; indeed, these three pieces may come from somewhere else, or be much later. At the same time, even within the standard St. Martial repertory, the usually neumatic style tended to develop in one direction toward a melismatic style and in the other toward a strictly syllabic one, the two styles being placed in clear alternation within a single piece.

Before 1150 polyphony was largely a local affair. Our picture of a dominant St. Martial "school" may be an accidental result of the way manuscripts have been preserved. We know of several flourishing musical centers during the 1100s—for example, Beauvais, where *Daniel* was produced—and at least one other repertory of polyphony of around 1140, in a manuscript from St. James in Compostela. Although in Spain, Compostela was closely linked to France, since it was one of the most important pilgrimages of the time. The manuscript is a huge set of offices in honor of St. James, patron saint of Compostela; it is called *Codex Calixtinus* because it invokes the witness of Pope Calixtus II (died 1224) to enhance the prestige of the cult of St. James. All that, however, is the result of forgery, not an uncommon event in medieval times. As a corollary, the attribution of pieces in the manuscript to various ecclesiastical dignitaries in France is also highly suspect. Nonetheless, the versus, both chant and polyphony, are in the mainstream of French development, while cultivating their own local variants.

Among some twenty pieces of polyphony, the Compostela manuscript contains one extremely interesting novelty. The manuscript includes not just versus to be inserted into matins (as in the St. Martial collection) but polyphonic settings of some of the responsories themselves. A second voice is added over the cantor's part (intonation of the response, and the verse), leaving the remainder of the response to be sung by the choir in chant. The last responsory of St. James's matins, *O adjutor,* is set in this fashion, with the same polyphony used for the verse and for the *Gloria Patri* that follows. Then at the end of the response occurs a melisma (as in *Descendit de caelis*), and that melisma is provided syllabically with a text, *Portum in ultimo da nobis iudicio.* This syllabic interpolation is set more or less in a note-against-note style, bringing to a sharper focus the structural alternation of neumatic and syllabic styles found at St. Martial and organizing them over a chant responsory.

The significance of this isolated experiment lies in its pivotal stylistic position. It comes at the end of the Frankish practice of adding texted melismas to existing pieces of traditional chant. It catches up the St. Martial practice of alternating different polyphonic styles, an alternation heretofore used in connection with a lower voice in the style of rhyming chant, but now applied to chant in the neumatic or melismatic style of the old Gregorian responsories. Looking toward the future, this Compostela polyphonic responsory can be seen as the last step before the great new polyphonic forms developed at Paris after 1160, forms built on responsories with the same alternation of styles. There was, however, no direct connection: the problems of polyphony were now not formal problems, but problems of part writing and rhythmic organization. The solution of these problems awaited a new generation and resulted in a new phase of stylistic development.

PART 2
PART MUSIC ON
A DISCANT BASIS
1150-1600

4
PARISIAN LEADERSHIP IN PART MUSIC 1150-1300

AFTER 1150 POLYPHONY BECAME THE LEADING MEDIUM OF MUSICAL development. As the result of a century of experimentation in handling contrary motion, composers now found consistent, reliable solutions to the problems of two-part composition. They learned to conceive counterpoint from the outset in interval progressions, to think two notes at a time, instead of merely erecting a series of intervals on the kind of chant melody they had so highly developed. Having made a leap in their tonal thinking from chant to polyphony, they rapidly acquired not only technical mastery of the new contrapuntal material, but also the ability to use this material in convincing artistic ways.

Successful two-part composition initiated more than a new style; it opened up a new range of possibilities. The fundamental technique of composition now became the construction of a progression of intervals, a two-part framework embodying the two principles, consonance and contrary motion. This two-part framework remained the basis of musical composition almost up to 1600, providing a foundation for textures that favored three or four voices, but could become as thick as eight or ten voices or even more. Expressed throughout a broad spectrum of rhythms, the two-part framework made possible a variety of new musical forms, forms derived to a greater or lesser extent directly from the properties of two-part writing. Two-part composition gave birth to whole new generations of musical styles that revealed themselves only in the course of a mighty procession lasting for the next four centuries.

Chant composition continued for a while, as we have already seen; a large part of the trouvère production, as well as much sacred chant, came after 1200. But such music had steadily diminishing relevance to the developing principles of musical structure. For while the new two-part music opened many doors, it also closed some. Much was gained, but also something lost—a basic fact of stylistic development.

In order to master two-part composition, the composer had to give up his mastery of one part; or better, writing for one part now became in reality writing for one "part," part of something larger. Gone forever were the conditions under which one part was the whole. The composer now referred all melody to the two-part framework of intervals he carried in his head. Gone was the freedom of a single line, the simplicity of up-and-down; gone were both the subtlety of the Gregorian melisma and the bold sweep of the big sequence. The composer of part music had less room in which to maneuver, because the desideratum of contrary motion restricted his every move. Music started down a corridor that led from bold simplicity to increasing subtlety and sophistication.

POLYPHONY FOR THE MASS   Our ignorance of the chronology of the new polyphony is only slightly less profound than of previous polyphony. We know the music only through isolated fragments or in large collections contained in manuscripts written a century or so after the music was composed. The best approach to the repertory continues to be through the large manuscript collections. One of the earliest representing the new style is *Codex Wolfenbüttel* no. 677 (known as W_1), written probably after 1250, possibly in St. Andrew's in Scotland. Codex Wolfenbüttel is fairly homogeneous, reflecting a large, stabilized polyphonic repertory, which we will deal with in some detail. But Codex Wolfenbüttel also contains an appendix (the eleventh fascicle, or section) of great interest because of its close connections with the polyphonic versus studied in the previous chapter.

If the polyphonic versus had reached by 1100 the state in which we find it at St. Martial, then it must have developed in many directions during the following century. This century was, furthermore, a time of cultural diffusion all over Europe, especially toward England, where all manner of things French poured in behind the Norman conquest (1066), although there had been no lack of contact before that time. Thus by 1200 there had been ample opportunity for musicians in England, Scotland, and Wales to become perfectly familiar with the techniques of the polyphonic versus.

The eleventh fascicle of Codex Wolfenbüttel, like the Codex Compostela, shows a determined attempt to import polyphony into the mass. This was done by taking advantage of those spots in the mass already infiltrated by medieval chant—*Kyrie*, sequence, tropes for *Gloria, Sanctus,* and *Agnus Dei,* and alleluia verses. Also like the Codex Compostela, the eleventh fascicle of Codex Wolfenbüttel provides music for a special occasion, in this case for masses for the Virgin. The repertory includes rhyming *Kyries,* rhyming alleluia verses, some on melodies associated with older, but still medieval, alleluias (such as Alleluia *Virga Jesse floruit*), and rhyming tropes to *Sanctus* and *Agnus Dei.*

All these items were set in a polyphonic style very similar to that generally prevailing in the 1100s (as at St. Martial and Compostela). The lower voice was either composed first or adapted from a recent chant; the upper voice, singing the same text at the same time as the lower voice, was apt to have from two to six notes for each note below. The upper voice could have longer ornaments, usually cadential and stereotyped, for example, a falling scale. Consonance and dissonance were handled much as in Example 18, perhaps a little more smoothly.

LEONIN'S ORGANUM   The main contents of Codex Wolfenbüttel are devoted to newer kinds of polyphony. These newer kinds were developed in Paris by the composers Leonin and Perotin, associated with the cathedral of Notre Dame that stands on an island in the Seine. The present cathedral was begun around 1160 (presumably at the moment when Leonin was working out his new musical forms) and finished during the next century. Composed and performed in and for the urban cathedral, the new music, like the old chant, was sacred because sacred worship and a sacred institution provided the best opportunities and resources. But times were changing: it was no longer the monastery, but the new complex of town and university that stood at the center of intense religious and intellectual activity. The urban cathedral now took the initiative; the monastery withdrew from the musical scene when the musical style it had created ceased to lead the way.

Leonin's new polyphony is contained in a collection called *Magnus liber organi de Gradali et Antiphonario* (The Great Book of Organum for the Gradual and the Antiphonary). In some respects the *Magnus liber,* an ambitious liturgical cycle of polyphony covering the important feasts of the whole year, rests upon and summarizes the achievements of the past; in other respects, the *Magnus liber* departs radically from previous polyphonic practice. The completion of a liturgical cycle marks the culmination of a development. The period of experimentation was over; polyphony now assumed a form sufficiently consistent to justify not only a cycle, but a cycle of great liturgical importance. The liturgical position itself, however, was relatively new to polyphony. Abandoning the rhyming, scanning, strophic versus as a basis for polyphony, Leonin turned decisively to graduals and alleluias of the mass, and the responsories of matins (which, as recent research has shown, were also used at vespers on occasion). The new liturgical position entailed using the ancient Gregorian melodies as the lower voice, the foundation of the new polyphony. This position also meant that the new polyphony was to be performed at the musical high point of the mass and of the office. As we saw, the monastic composer had inserted his most ambitious piece, the prose, directly after the alleluia. Leonin, in choosing gradual and alleluia as the basis for his new polyphony, clearly showed his intention to thrust his music into the center of the stage to contend there with the best that Gregorian and medieval chant had produced.

The arrangement of text and music in a gradual or alleluia was less distinct than in a typical versus. There were no clearly syllabic sections, as there were in a versus. Most syllables of a Gregorian gradual carried neumes of from two to six or eight notes, merging into occasional melismas of up to thirty or forty notes, which might come at any point in the piece—beginning, middle, or end, but usually somewhere in the middle. The tonal structure of a gradual was far less clear, far more diffuse than a versus melody; its phrase structure was almost imperceptible compared with the squarely syllabic phrases used for rhyming, strophic poetry. As if a gradual were not formless enough, Leonin slowed it down until it seemed to stop, making each note carry ten, twenty, thirty or more notes in the wildly rhapsodic upper voice, as in his setting of the Christmas gradual in Example 19.

Disassociated as the two voices of Leonin's polyphony may seem to be,

EXAMPLE 19   LEONIN: ORGANUM FOR THE CHRISTMAS GRADUAL

EXAMPLE 19 (CONTINUED)

(All the ends of the world have seen [the salvation of our God . . .])

they must be taken together as constituents in a new, fantastic style of melody. Compared with previous polyphony (Example 18), Leonin's upper voice was marked by greatly extended ornamentation over each single note of the lower voice, which moved now slower, now faster, filled out with varying amounts and kinds of figuration above. The functions of ornamentation and overall tonal direction are sharply divided between the two voices. Each fulfills only its own function. Yet the two voices are linked by octaves, fifths, and unisons at phrase endings in such a way that at those points, at least, the upper voice confirms the tonal plan of the chant. And sometimes the lower voice seems swept along by the patterns of the upper one. The parts belong together; they form a melody, difficult though it may be to follow its far-reaching, erratic course. Leonin's music has a strong effect even on our distant ears, its dizzy extremities seeming now, as then, deeply impressive even though bizarre.

Leonin's upper voice was not, however, the product of completely free invention, but unfolded in a series of rhetorical idioms he used over and over again throughout his *Magnus liber*. The average phrase in the upper voice was perhaps ten or twenty notes terminated by a rest. One, or several, such phrases might be set over one note of the chant below. That note might constitute a larger phrase all by itself; or several chant notes, each with one or several figural phrases in the upper voice, might go to make up the larger phrase, whose ending was clearly marked both by the choice of figure and the octave or unison between the voices.

The larger phrase was called a *clausula,* or close (compare *clause*). Successive clausulas are often distinguished from one another by their style: some are marked by repetitive figures winding around one central note; others have rapidly descending scales. Sustained notes, sometimes with dissonant appoggiaturas to an octave consonance, are used for beginnings. There is a special kind of figure used for a codetta.

One of the most striking kinds of clausula, often characterized by melodic sequences or other repetitive device, moves in a regular rhythm. It must be mentioned that the rhythmic transcription in Example 19 is not completely certain and that the uncertainty reflects the most important stylistic developmen of Leonin's time. We know that the regular type of clausula just mentioned moves in the long-short pattern (♩ ♪) given in the transcription, but we do not know how closely the other passages approximate this long-short pattern, since the original notation is not decisive in its rhythmic implications.

What must have happened, however, seems fairly clear. There must have been a time when the notes of the upper part were rhythmicized according to the soloist's discretion (Leonin's organum style leaves the singer of the upper voice free to proceed at his own rate). We know from roughly contemporary reports that the lengthening of alternate notes had taken a variety of forms other than the 2:1 (♩ ♪) ratio of the transcription, reflecting a soloist's liberties. The long-short rhythm is most convincing in clausulas that have some element of melodic repetition or sequence that supports the long-short rhythmic repetition. It is easy to imagine the soloist throwing such a melodic sequence into relief by lengthening every other note.

Once so rhythmicized, these clausulas stood out sharply against the more diffuse, irregular ones, which eventually dropped out of use. The infectious long-short rhythm, now fixed in the normal ratio 2:1, became customary for all kinds of clausulas—for all polyphony. This kind of rhythm is called *modal* (compare *module, modular*). The long-short pattern stands at the head of several generations of modal patterns: it is the first mode.

LEONIN'S DISCANT We have seen that Leonin's lower voice moves through its chant slower and faster, but we have not yet seen its fastest rate, which usually occurs only when the chant itself comes to an important melisma. Such a melisma, containing more than forty notes, comes in the verse of the gradual *Viderunt* at the word *Dominus: Notum fecit* DOMINUS *salutare suum: ante conspectum gentium revelavit justitiam suam* (The Lord hath made known his salvation; before the face of all peoples hath he shown forth his justice). Leonin's setting of the verse *Notum fecit* starts off much like Example 19; then at the melisma on *Dominus* (Example 20) the lower voice speeds up, moving almost as fast as the upper voice, which, if it goes faster, does so in the long-short pattern of modal rhythm.

It had been normal in St. Martial style for polyphonic melismas in note-against-note style to alternate with sections in which the upper voice was more neumatic with respect to the lower one. Leonin applied the same principle in his setting of the Gregorian gradual and alleluia, regularly setting chant melismas in this note-against-note style. One or sometimes two such clausulas are found in every setting of a gradual or alleluia verse, and sometimes one in the setting of the intonation of the gradual response (less often in the responsories for matins).

The note-against-note style, in which the lower voice moves as fast or almost as fast as the upper part, is called *discantus*, or discant, and the clausulas in which discant style appears are called *discant clausulas*. They usually have odd texts of one or two words, such as *Dominus*, or even a single syllable, such as *go* (from *Virgo*) since their lower voice is in each case a melisma out of a Gregorian chant. From Leonin's discant clausulas is derived the development of style for the next hundred years.

While the idea of alternating textures—organum, or sustained-note style, with discant—had antecedents at St. Martial and Compostela, there were important differences in the way Leonin applied the idea. In his organum style, Leonin's customary ratio of notes in the upper part to each note of the lower part was far greater than the St. Martial practice, which had given a general impression of a neumatic rather than melismatic relationship. Leonin's discant, on the other hand, remained relatively strict, keeping close to a note-against-note relationship. Thus in Leonin the contrast of organum and discant was sharper than before.

At the same time, the relative placement of these two styles was less clear. At St. Martial the note-against-note sections (like melismas in the versus) tended to come at obvious places such as the beginning or end of a strophe or couplet. But in Leonin's graduals and alleluias there were, naturally, neither strophes nor couplets, nor any of the structural features of rhyming chant. Since melismas had no clear position within the Gregorian forms, the discant clausulas built upon the melismas had no clear position within Leonin's organum.

EXAMPLE 20   LEONIN: DISCANT ON *DOMINUS* FOR THE CHRISTMAS GRADUAL

In the discant clausulas, the upper voice became increasingly persuasive in its impact on the listener, in its capacity to shape the notes of the chant into a new kind of melody. The longs and shorts of the upper voice, in their unvarying modal order, gave an exact sense of measure to the notes of the lower voice, which was now perceived to march along in really equal units. Rhythmic control in music reached down, in Leonin's discant, to the smallest intervals of time. Previously control had been exercised over the phrase, the verse, the strophe. Now, by making the interior of the phrase modal, the composer extended his control to every moment of the phrase as it unfolded. It should be noted that this control was developed not in connection with rhyming, scanning versus, but within melismatic discant, in a purely musical context.

Phrases were marked by simultaneous rests in both voices—rests that could now be exactly measured like the notes. (We do not always know whether Leonin's rests are equivalent to eighths or to dotted quarters, but in any case they do not interrupt the steady march of the lower voice.) These phrases were built to make polyphonic sense. Cutting up the chant in the lower voice without regard for whatever original phrasing it might have had as chant, Leonin phrased it as he thought best for two-part melody. The phrasing in *Dominus* is entirely understandable in these terms. Leonin cut his phrases into lengths of reasonable proportions and placed them in a reasonable order; yet he also took care that some kind of sense could be made of their concluding notes, since those notes and the consonances they formed with the upper voice were most apparent to the listener.

Within each phrase Leonin arranged the vertical intervals so that the succession of consonances and dissonances would shape the phrase clearly. It was the varying succession of intervals, after all, that made polyphony distinctive. The need for a variety of intervals was the reason for the basic rule of contrary motion; without that, polyphony would lapse back into overblown chant. While maintaining contrary motion, Leonin had to attend to matters that seem automatic to us after centuries of polyphonic experience. He had to preserve a basically consonant sound and keep the upper part lyric. Some of these techniques had already been worked out, but even so, the thought of controlling all these factors at once with no real models to follow brings an appreciation of Leonin's achievement.

Leonin handled vertical intervals more freely yet more effectively than did his predecessors. As is clear from *Dominus,* he had no hesitation about using dissonances, but placed them carefully. Unisons, fourths, and fifths remained the stable intervals of discant (octaves were more frequent a little later). To be lyric, however, discant needed plenty of thirds, and Leonin made extensive use of them, so much so that thirds soon came to be classed as "imperfect consonances" and numbered among the concords of discant—unisons, octaves, fifths, fourths, major and minor thirds.

As a singer and composer at the cathedral of Notre Dame in Paris, Leonin did not set out to lay the foundations of polyphonic style, but to write music for the major festivities celebrated at the church where he worked. The pieces he wrote develop a number of techniques and styles, each important by itself; but these pieces are, after all, artistic compositions in their own right that need to be grasped in their own integrity and context, no matter how bewildering the shape and how remote the context. We have to imagine the liturgy of the mass celebrated in high solemnity and sung mostly in chant (or in parallels) up to the gradual, when in place of the expected Gregorian, up stood a cantor to deliver Leonin's extraordinary flights of ornamentation over the grotesquely slow chant, breaking into animated discant at irregular intervals.

The shape of Leonin's whole piece was still the shape of the old gradual. It included the intonation of the respond, sung by a soloist in polyphony over the chant; then the continuation of the respond in chant by the choir in unison; then the verse in polyphony up to the end, where it too reverted to the choir in unison (see Example 21). Just as the alternation of chant and polyphony reproduced in its own terms—and its own incredibly distorted dimensions—the original alternation of cantor and choir, so the alternation of organum and discant reproduced the original shape of the chant in its syllabic-neumatic and melismatic portions. Leonin's gradual was still a gradual. We can see how far he went by comparing his product with what he began with.

POLYPHONIC CONDUCTUS   Meanwhile, more normal forms of polyphony were cultivated at Notre Dame in Paris, continuing the styles of St. Martial and elsewhere. These normal forms reasserted themselves strongly after 1180, now under the rhythmic influence of the new discant. The polyphonic versus, as we saw, had shared with the chant versus the structural features associated with rhyming, scanning, strophic poetry. The typical St. Martial polyphonic versus had something resembling rhyming chant in the lower voice, with an upper voice that usually placed one to six notes against each note of the lower voice, but sometimes—especially at beginning and end of strophes—moved in note-against-note counterpoint with the lower voice on an extended melisma. Versus of all types could function as processional pieces, as conductus, and this term came to be applied at Notre Dame to all polyphonic versus. As the Notre Dame repertory developed, however, the majority of polyphonic versus were no longer processional, the term *conductus* becoming largely nominal.

In the famous Wolfenbüttel Codex, which contains the Notre Dame reper-

EXAMPLE 21   LEONIN'S POLYPHONIC GRADUAL

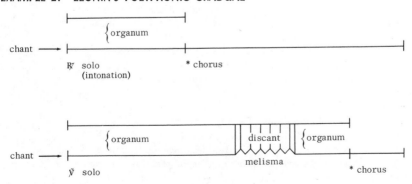

tory in its earliest preserved form, Leonin's *Magnus liber* occupies a little over 40 pages, the whole Gregorian-based repertory including the *Magnus liber* and its derivatives (to be discussed shortly) about 130 pages, while the conductus alone occupy about 180 pages. The numbers increase greatly in the next large Notre Dame manuscript, the Florence *Medicean Codex,* but the ratios change only a little, the conductus still occupying more space than the Gregorian-based pieces. Leonin's "Big Book," in other words, was much bigger in impact than in relative size; it represented not only an abnormal kind of polyphony, but a minor part of the repertory.

In the tradition of the polyphonic versus, the conductus at Notre Dame assumed a wide variety of shapes, sizes, and artistic ambitions, reflecting joy in the varieties of strophic forms. As at St. Martial, the most elaborate conductus were adorned with polyphonic melismas in note-against-note style at beginning and end of strophes, or at strategic internal points. But there was at Notre Dame a steady pressure toward purely musical thinking, a pressure perceptible in conductus in the imaginative placement of melismas. Furthermore, elaborate conductus had new music for each new strophe, even if the verse form was repeated. Less elaborate conductus had much shorter melismas routinely tacked on at the ends of verses and strophes (hence often called *caudas;* cf. *coda*) ; least elaborate conductus had no melismas, and often repeated their music for succeeding strophes.

In its early stages the rhythmic notation of conductus presents the same uncertainties as Leonin's organum. The first convincing rhythms we can make out are those of Leonin's discant, resulting in consistently long-short patterns in the note-against-note melismas, and in the syllabic sections basically equal values (dotted quarters), one for each syllable; if the upper voice has neumatic ornaments, these naturally fall into modal patterns. In elaborate conductus, however, each syllable may receive heavy ornamentation in the upper part, in melodic patterns that recall Leonin's rhapsodic organum style. Such ornamentation effectively obscures any modal pattern, and may even disrupt the steady march of syllables.

Modal rhythm makes its clearest appearance in the larger melismas, especially the great caudas typically placed at the very end of an elaborate conductus. Along with modal rhythm comes an increasing emphasis on musical construction and technique; concluding melismas are sometimes so extended as to seem the body of the piece, the adjacent syllabic portions merely episodic. The fairly large conductus *In rosa vernat lilium* has these roughly similar strophes, with melismas on the non-italicized syllables.

In *rosa vernat lilium*	*(From the rose springs up the lily,*
*Flos in flore flore*scit	*Flower in flower flourishing,*
Dum nata parit filium;	*While she who was born bears the Son;*
In *tenebris luce*scit	*In the shadows shines*
Lux sine tenebris;	*The light without darkness;*
In *carnis latebris*	*Hidden in the flesh*
*Vera dies die*scit.	*The true day dawns.*
Ex *luna solis emicat*	*Out of the moon shines*
*Radium eluce*scens;	*The sun's brightening ray.*

Mundanis solem indicat	*The moon, never waning,*
Luna numquam decrescens.	*Shows the world the sun.*
Hic sol dum lune iungitur,	*This sun, when joined with the moon,*
Venter eclipsim patitur,	*Is hidden in the womb,*
Sed est plusquam nitescens.	*But shines forth more than ever.*
In hyemali tempore	*In winter the spring*
Ver vernat ultra morem;	*Burgeons out of season;*
Dignum de digno corpore	*The mother bears*
Mater fundit odorem;	*A fragrance meet.*
O veris premium	*O prize of spring!*
Hyemis tedium	*The gloom of winter*
Ad verum fugit florem.	*Flees before the true flower.)*

At *odorem* there is a cadence; *O veris*, starting a new section, is given in Example 22. In the short syllabic sections the voices move in smooth, obvious contrary motion in and out of unisons and fifths—highly characteristic of conductus. At *florem* begins the final melisma. Both voices move in modal patterns and clear, well-directed lines. The interval progressions swing within and around the fifth G–D, with plenty of thirds facilitating the contrary motion. The melisma is in two parts (Example 22, meas. 23 to 35, 36 to 48), which

EXAMPLE 22   END OF THE CONDUCTUS IN ROSA VERNAT LILIUM

EXAMPLE 22 (CONTINUED)

sound almost identical, but look different because in the second half the voices interchange parts—another procedure frequent in conductus melismas. The drift toward an additional flat can also be found, sometimes in more pronounced form, in other conductus.

While the majority of conductus are *a 2* (for two voices), some of the largest and most impressive are *a 3*, a kind of polyphony almost unknown before the Notre Dame repertory (except in singing in parallels). There was a strong tendency, both at St. Martial and at Notre Dame, to think of writing *a 2* as a unison line that thickens to thirds, fourths, and fifths in the middle of a phrase. Accordingly, there was an equally strong tendency at Notre Dame to think of a third voice, when used, as occupying a position an octave above the lowest voice, with the second voice occupying a position a fifth above the lowest.

This is an appropriate moment to start using the terms *tenor, duplum,* and *triplum.* The tenor is the lowest voice; in Gregorian-based pieces (or pieces built on a preexisting melody), the tenor has the chant. The tenor may have received its name from the way it "hangs on" to the chant notes in Leonin's organum style. The duplum is the voice next above the tenor, and the triplum the voice above that.

The positions of fifth above the tenor for the duplum, octave for the triplum, are, of course, more ideal than real; subject to constant exception, they are regularly perceptible only at cadences. As ideal positions, however, they help us to conceive the typical polyphonic medium, pointing up the seemingly narrow range—an octave—which the polyphonic envelope tends to occupy at any given moment.

Actually this range is not so narrow. It is true that the three voices cross a good deal, but that is less a function of their ranges than of their active nature and their tendency to pursue melodic direction in forthright, energetic ways. It is also true that many pieces *a 3* are highly dissonant with much friction among the parts, but that is more a matter of the composer's inclination, and in any case is not true of all pieces *a 3*. Furthermore when the three voices resolve to the ideal, consonant positions of unison, fifth, and octave at cadences, they hardly give the impression of being crowded; on the contrary, their sound is then apt to be described by modern observers as "empty"—although that, too, is inappropriate.

Given the kinds of intervals the composer chose to work with, the texture, range, and medium of his polyphony followed naturally. During this first systematic exploration of the qualities of intervals, composers relied on the cleanest, most obvious consonances, on unison, octaves, fifths, and fourths, for stable sounds. They used these sounds to end phrases, to bring about a blending of two or three voices, a sense of repose, of sweetness. They used seconds, tritones, and sevenths in the interior of phrases for tension and excitement. They began to exploit the middling qualities of thirds and sixths, using them now in one function, now in another. A fifth had for them something of the doubling quality of an octave; a third, on the other hand, added something distinctly different, yet not dissonant. In conductus *a 3* the combination of a fifth with a third in the middle (what later ages called a *triad*) was not an infrequent sound; but it was a vibrant, unstable one—a compound, not an element.

The big conductus *a 3* are the most agreeably sonorous pieces of the whole Notre Dame repertory. In writing a conductus a composer began by writing the tenor (although some conductus make limited use of ready-made material) ; a theorist later tells us that the composer should make his tenor as beautiful as he can, and then add the other voices to it. As at St. Martial, there is little to differentiate a typical conductus tenor and a typical piece of rhyming chant; as far as the conductus was concerned, it was immaterial whether the composer wrote his own tenor or borrowed one from modern chant. In adding a second and third voice the conductus composer seemed to pay much attention to sonority, often falling into idiomatic procedures, such as those in *In rosa vernat lilium* of Example 22. Sometimes, to be sure, the voices become animated and expressive in their figuration; sometimes they engage in carefully worked out echoing of motifs through strict or free interchange of voices, but even then they fit smoothly into a sonorous whole.

Voice interchange was prominently developed in many conductus, some of which can be dated in the 1170s or 1180s, for example, *Christi miles* (*a 2*), commemorating the murder of Thomas Becket (1170). So striking is the voice interchange that it sometimes seems like a significant novelty; but it is only one of the many basic features the conductus inherited from the polyphonic versus of before 1100. The note-against-note melismas of the versus lent themselves to a variety of repetitive devices. In fact, any couplet of a St. Martial polyphonic versus (including those notated as if they were chant) could have involved voice interchange. The two singers only had to exchange parts at the end of the first line of the couplet.

The most important aspect of voice interchange was the structural repetition it entailed—two successive blocks of counterpoint that sounded almost identical. The contrapuntal considerations themselves were trivial; the only interesting aspect was the increased number of thirds that could arise out of the smooth contrary motion of two voices crisscrossing each other in the same range.

While cultivated extensively around 1200, the conductus was destined to go out of fashion a few decades later, surviving only in peripheral areas. Other forms, derived from Leonin's discant style, were to be the vehicles of progressive development. The reason the conductus failed to make essential contributions to this development seems to be its lack of engagement with the Gregorian chant tenor. While the Gregorian-based discant was in no way influenced by the intrinsic style of Gregorian chant, still, in the effort of assimilating the remote, abstract progressions of the Gregorian melisma into modern polyphony, the discant style found a stimulus to further development denied the conductus. The conductus style was comfortable: it encouraged sleek sonorities and amiable counterpoint. The Gregorian-based discant confronted the composer with an intractable piece of old chant to work around. The chant, like an irritant, seemed to provoke the composer into increasingly imaginative, if sometimes scratchy, solutions. And in some mysterious way it led the composer to a tonal cogency, a higher sense of order absent from the conductus.

PEROTIN AND DISCANT Further development of discant took place in the work of Perotin the Great, successor to Leonin, and in the works of his followers, none of whom are known to us by name. There must have been a group of composers active in Paris from 1180 to 1240 or so, either in connection

with Notre Dame or with other nearby churches. Perotin wrote a big conductus
a 3, Salvatoris hodie, one *a 2, Dum sigillum*, and others. He also wrote more
splendid versions of Leonin's organum for certain important feasts, including
settings *a 3* of Alleluia *Posui* and Alleluia *Nativitas*, for feasts of the Virgin,
and settings *a 4* (the fourth voice, called *quadruplum*, added above the triplum),
Viderunt omnes, the Christmas gradual, and *Sederunt principes*, the gradual
for the next day, St. Stephen's.

The style of Perotin's organum *a 3* is a compromise between the note-
against-note discant style found in Leonin's discant clausulas (and in conductus) and Leonin's organum style with its slow-moving tenor. When writing
two voices over the slow tenor, Perotin made them move together, note-against-
note, in modal rhythm. Triplum and duplum formed discant relative to each
other, usually making good contrary motion through consonances—a self-
contained duo. These discant duos were then placed over the tenor chant notes,
which now moved more slowly than ever (Example 23).

Perotin applied modal rhythm much more strictly than Leonin, phrase
after phrase falling into unbroken long-short repetition, which also became much
more sequential in melodic structure. Faster, less regular ornamentation tended

EXAMPLE 23   PEROTIN: FROM ORGANUS *a 3* FOR THE GRADUAL *BENEDICTA ES*

to occur at the climactic moment when the tenor changed pitch—the end of one *punctus* (= clausula) *organi* (organ point) and the beginning of another.

Seldom has there been a style so wedded to its natural habitat as Perotin's monumental organum was to the resonant interior of a French Gothic cathedral. The single tenor note has time to reverberate up and down the whole length of the church, seeming to set the very walls in sympathetic vibration. The upper voices alternately cut great dissonant swaths across the omnipresent tenor note, or, when reaching a cadential consonance, blend into the overtone structure already set up on top of the tenor. Absorbed into this great rhythm of consonance and dissonance, the modal rhythm seems mere surface animation. The elaborate polyphonic superstructure itself seems to return to the chant matrix from which it sprang.

Perotin's organum *a 3,* and even more the two mighty works *a 4,* reveal the limit of the expansive power unleashed by Leonin's new style. Perotin pressed outward as far as he could go; the organum *a 4,* impressive as it is, shows clearly that the dimensions of viable art forms had been left behind. No one else wrote organum *a 4,* and although other types of polyphony *a 4* exist, they were never so popular (during the 1200s) as their counterparts *a 2* and *a 3*—especially the latter, which became the standard medium. Perotin and his followers turned to smaller pieces with more intricate techniques.

The most significant smaller form was the discant clausula; this alone provided opportunity for full exploration of modal rhythm, on one hand, and part writing, on the other. Perotin and his followers provided several hundred discant clausulas called *substitute clausulas,* most of them designed to replace Leonin's original clausulas or each other. Substitute clausulas are written both *a 2* and *a 3,* the former being far more numerous.

Since Leonin's original discant clausulas usually occurred over a melisma in the chant, there might be five or ten substitute clausulas all on the same melisma. There seem to be several generations of substitute clausulas; at any rate, different families of clausulas (one family for each important chant melisma) seem to show a progression through similar stages of development. In Example 24 is given the beginning of some of the substitute clausulas for *Dominus,* Leonin's clausula in Example 20. All of the *Dominus* clausulas (at least fifteen, one of the largest families) use the pitches of Leonin's chant tenor. Any change in these pitches is significant, possibly a response to some need of polyphonic construction.

The rhythm of the tenor changes from clausula to clausula; the duplum is composed entirely new for each. While the technique of part writing, the handling of consonances and progressions, does not change drastically throughout the repertory of clausulas (representing musical composition roughly over the decades 1180–1220), the technique of rhythmic organization does change, reflecting progressive exploitation of the rhythmic resources opened up by Leonin's discant style.

The clausulas in Example 24 have been arranged in a presumed order of stylistic development, reconstructing the sequence in which rhythmic exploitation may have taken place. In clausula *a* the first tenor note is set off by itself; then the following three phrases are arranged to end on C (as do the next two, not shown here). These tenor phrases are made to sound even more alike by the

EXAMPLE 24   SUBSTITUTE CLAUSULAS ON *DOMINUS* FOR THE CHRISTMAS GRADUAL

EXAMPLE 24 (CONTINUED)

(e)

(f)

repetition in the duplum. As the piece progresses through its thirty-one measures, the phrases get shorter and more repetitive, finally beating out a single
fragment in the duplum over and over again. It is this intent repetition, coupled
with increasingly strict modal rhythm, that best characterizes discant development in the clausulas.

The most important step in this development—and in polyphony for two
centuries—was to give the tenor a repetitive pattern of its own. The tenor pattern in clausula *b* is the simplest and by far the most frequent in the clausula
repertory. In this clausula, as in many others from other families, the duplum
still makes many of its phrases with the tenor in Leonin's characteristic way.
Contrary motion is handled forcefully, shaping the phrases so as to emphasize
the square rhythmic shape of the tenor. The rests become, as it were, heavily
accented, so that the elision in measure 6 takes on new significance. The whole
segment falls into two measures antecedent, two measures consequent, and four
measures extension. A more sharply drawn phrase structure is hard to imagine.

It is, of course, much too sharp for our tastes; but up against Leonin's fantastic organum rhapsodies, and especially when contrasted with the formless meandering of neumatic polyphony immediately before Leonin, such phrase structure was extremely effective, carrying out the thrust of modal rhythm, indeed of the whole phrase-building tradition of several centuries.

The clausula *c* shows a more subtle realization of the same principle. The gaping rests have been partly filled in; the duplum has been shaped to give the phrase a little more grace, a little less force. At the stage represented by this clausula, composers allowed the energy of modal rhythm to blossom out into extremely attractive melodies. A new sense of lyricism was born out of the union of jig-time rhythm and smooth part writing.

Once the tenor had its own repetitive rhythms, there was only a short step from elision such as in *b* and *c* to staggering of phrases as in clausula *d*. Both voices have short phrases and many rests, but together they make up a long, repeatedly elided period. After this period, there is only one more simultaneous rest in the whole clausula. The combination of repetitive tenor pattern and staggered phrases was the most powerful technique of the 1200s and the one most to be exploited.

Clausula *e* represents one of several possible lines of development that split off from the stage marked by clausulas *b, c,* and *d*. In clausula *e* the tenor has been given a longer, more complex pattern consisting of two different elements separated by a rest. This is the most common of such compound patterns, but many others were invented, even if only for one or two pieces. In many clausulas the duplum is so arranged as to give the impression that this tenor pattern begins now with the dotted half note, now with the three dotted quarters. Manipulation of higher rhythmic levels continued to be a primary concern (as it had been in rhyming chant), but now more subtly because of the increased control of rhythmic detail.

The clausula *f* represents a very different line of development. Here is no concern for higher levels; on the contrary all attention is on detail. To begin with, the mode seems strangely out of phase. By the simple device of reversing the long and the short, composers at this stage avoided the now familiar headlong rush of modal rhythm, revealing instead a slower, more expressive rhythm—still modal, but different: this was the "second mode." It is found here in the tenor as well as in the duplum, conglutinating the texture and slowing down the progressions of intervals. The exquisite dissonances are entirely appropriate to this new kind of motion, as are also the seductive parallel thirds.

As a result of rhythmic developments within the discant clausula repertory, a system of rhythmic modes was codified around 1250. This system was described differently by different theorists. John of Garland, a relatively conservative theorist, listed Leonin's original long-short (♩ ♪) pattern as first mode; its reversal (♪ ♩) as second mode; an expanded form of the second (♩. ♪♩) as third mode; its reversal (♪ ♩♩.) as fourth mode. Then John added as fifth mode the frequent tenor rhythm of dotted quarters, and as sixth mode the continuous eighth-note motion often found in upper parts.

Franco of Cologne, writing a decade or so later, proposed John's fifth mode (dotted quarters) as first mode, on the grounds that the other modes were contained in it and logically derived from it. Franco's system reflects a growing tendency to see in the modes not the original alternation of two really different elements—long and short—but rather a mere measure or metrical grouping; since the measure (represented by Franco's first mode) was derived stylistically from the long-short pattern, it was naturally a ternary measure.

PARISIAN MOTET   Sometime after 1200, toward the end of Perotin's era, substitute clausulas were given a new text in their upper voices, a texting similar to that applied to melismas in Frankish times. The added Latin texts were related in thought to the text of the gradual or alleluia; they expanded the Gregorian text with rhetorical, metaphorical flourishes—with commentary, sung simultaneously with the Gregorian original rather than interpolated phrase by phrase into it. These texted clausulas were performed at first in place of the untexted form, as part of the polyphonic superstructure erected on top of the gradual or alleluia.

In response to this texting of the upper parts of discant clausulas, composers soon provided familiar tenor melismas with new upper parts, equipped from the start with their own specific texts. In discant *a 2*, only the duplum received a text, the tenor singing its melisma as before. In discant *a 3*, both duplum and triplum received text, and usually different texts. A large repertory of texted discant pieces sprang up, replacing the melismatic discant clausulas. The old tenors, the original Gregorian melismas, continued to be used throughout the new texted style.

The old tenors, having proved their musical usefulness, were soon taken up by secular court musicians, who set the duplum and triplum to French lyrics of courtly love instead of Latin religious devotion. A piece of discant with French texts was called a *motet;* it became common practice, however, to apply the term *motet* retroactively to pieces with Latin text as well. Similarly the term *motetus* came to be used to designate the texted duplum of either French or Latin motets. The term *triplum* continued to serve for the third voice whether texted or not. A transitional form of motet had a Latin sacred duplum and a French secular triplum, apparently representing a Latin discant *a 2* converted to a secular motet by the addition of a French triplum.

The musical effect of the added text—French or Latin—was to articulate the upper voices, throwing into relief the individual notes, which in melismatic form tended to blend together. Thus the texting of the upper parts carried out the tendencies apparent in the development of the discant clausula, tendencies toward pulling the voices apart out of their close discant relationship or out of the onrushing first mode.

The articulative effect of texting, however, made itself felt only in stages. Some of the earliest discant clausulas to be texted had identical phrasing between duplum and triplum; a single text was added to these two voices, so that they sang the same syllables at the same time. These upper voices, then, behaved just like the syllabic portions of a conductus. So close was the resemblance that the upper parts of a few motets *a 3* and *a 4* were included—without their tenors—into collections of conductus *a 2* and *a 3*, respectively, under the impression that they *were* conductus.

Trivial as this confusion may seem, it reveals a most important fact: the motet was in a certain sense a direct continuation of the conductus, and hence of the conservative, traditional form of polyphony. In between motet and conductus stood the mighty organum and the all-important developments within the discant clausula. The shape of polyphony had, in thirty or forty years, been drastically and in some ways permanently altered by Leonin and Perotin. Still, the motet represented a reflex from the fantastically extended melismas of both organum and discant clausulas to a purely syllabic style.

Even when text was written together with a new upper voice (instead of being added to a ready-made clausula), its poetic structure was inspired by the kind of phrasing developed with the discant repertory. The texts, naturally, tended to be built on rhyme; the rhyming syllables tended to come at the musical rests in the upper parts. If the phrases of an upper part were equal in length, then so were the rhyming verses of its text. But usually the musical phrases were not equal, with the result that motets' texts tended to have a variable rhythmic structure.

This was an extremely interesting development from a poetic point of view. Originally, as we saw, rhyming came about to emphasize the similarity of *equal* length lines in hymns, proses, and versus. Rhymes were extended to unequal verses as poetic structure became increasingly flexible. Now, in the motet, we find that regular verses have all but disappeared, leaving only the rhymes to mark the phrase structure inherited from the discant clausula—a phrase structure begotten by purely musical forces. The free verse of a motet might be highly convincing as poetry (as the best ones are), but convincing largely through the kind of rhythmic disposition developed within the discant clausula on the basis of modal rhythms, tenor patterns, and contrapuntal progressions.

Toward the end of the 1200s the large repertory of motets was gathered up into great anthologies. Several of these magnificent manuscripts still exist and are available for study, both in facsimile and transcription. The largest and most famous is the *Codex Montpellier,* containing around three hundred motets of various types, representing the development of motet style—that is, of polyphony—throughout the latter 1200s. Codex Montpellier is arranged in sections or fascicles, each (after the first) containing a particular type of motet; a few conductus are also included.

I   organum and discant, including works by Perotin (nos. 1–18)
II   motets *a 4* (nos. 19–35)
III motets *a 3* with Latin motetus and French triplum (nos. 36–50)
IV Latin motets *a 3* (nos. 51–72)
V   French motets *a 3* (nos. 73–177)
VI French motets *a 2* (nos. 178–252)

So far the manuscript is arranged systematically, representing a completed repertory. Two more fascicles, VII (nos. 253 to 302) and VIII (nos. 303 to 345), contain a more varied selection of motets *a 3,* representing the growing edge of the repertory toward 1300.

While many of these motets go back to discant clausulas, the greater number have new upper voices, still using, however, some of the old tenor melismas over and over again. In the earliest stages of the motet, when it was used liturgically, the choice of tenors corresponded to the liturgical cycle of graduals and alleluias. As the motet repertory developed, the motet was used more and more frequently outside the liturgy; this was obviously true of the French motet, used at court, but it was also true of the Latin motet, which tended to slip from a strict liturgical position to a looser, merely devotional or occasional one. At the same time there was a shift in the kind of tenor used for motets. On the one hand, the fragment of chant used for the tenor might come from a variety of sources other than a melisma of a gradual or alleluia. It might even come from a secular source, such as a trouvère song, resulting in a new kind of motet to be discussed later. Much more interesting musically, however, is the opposite tendency: composers tended to concentrate on a few favorite tenors from the *Magnus liber.*

The reasons for this concentration have not yet been conclusively determined. There may be obscure liturgical reasons for it, and there were certainly many associations gathered around these tenors, associations we can no longer know or appreciate. Much of the reason, however, must have to do with the musical aptitude of a tenor melody for motet construction. If we understood the musical reasons why composers favored this tenor rather than that one, we would have a powerful tool for analyzing the structure of these motets. Example 25 contains the four most popular tenors of the Codex Montpellier. All of them show the melismatic effusion typical of the Gregorian gradual, yet all—in the fragmentary form they assume *as tenors*—give an impression of tonal order

EXAMPLE 25   FAVORITE TENORS OF CODEX MONTPELLIER

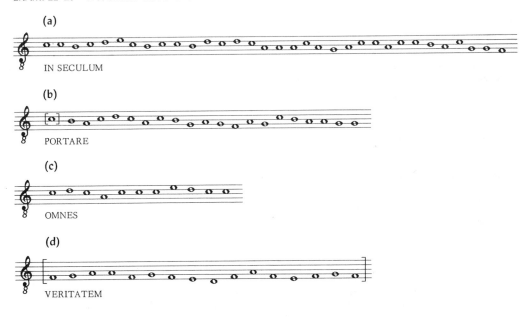

(a) IN SECULUM

(b) PORTARE

(c) OMNES

(d) VERITATEM

[ ] = varies from *Graduale romanum*

they would not have in their original setting. Each circles repeatedly through a small group of pitches, and each ends cogently on its final, not with the force- ful direction of a medieval melody, yet with the same sense of finality. It is probably in qualities such as these that we should seek the reasons for the popularity of these tenors.

It should be noted that the final of a fragmentary melisma used as a tenor may or may not be the original final of the gradual from which the melisma came (of the four given in Example 25 only two end on the final of the original chant). In other words, the old classification of four finals or eight tones makes little or no sense when applied to motets; at any rate, it made little sense then, for it was not applied to motets or to polyphony generally. The final of a tenor, and of a motet, is more usefully and appropriately referred to by its hexachord syllable. In general, motet tenors end on *ut* or *re* (or their analogs, *fa* or *sol*) but rarely on *mi* or *la*. Apparently paying no attention to the tone or mode of the tenor or of the other voices, medieval polyphonists focused their tonal attention on the overall impression of order and especially on the frame- work of vertical intervals that was erected upon the tenor.

One of the most characteristic features of motet construction after Perotin was the repetitive pattern superimposed on the tenor melody. As the motet repertory developed, composers used an ever-widening variety of rhythmic patterns in the tenor, but at the same time also favored certain most successful patterns. These are familiar to us from the discant clausula where, indeed, the basic problems of tenor construction were worked out. Other patterns were formed largely by recombining familiar elements.

It is essential to realize that the use of tenor patterns, like the use of modal rhythms, was not something forced upon the composer by any outside authority—a frequent misconception about medieval music. The motet composer elected uniformity at one level of musical structure in order to expedite indi- vidual solutions at another level. Like the composer of chant versus, the motet composer was interested in the construction of larger shapes; these larger shapes vary from piece to piece, each one in a way unique. The motet composer regularized rhythmic detail by modal rhythms and tenor patterns, just as the versus composer had regularized texts by rhyme and scansion, in order to make the larger shape more apparent and more forceful.

Individuality expressed itself frequently in the repetition of the tenor melody within a single motet. Such repetition, uncalled for by any liturgical condition, can be found in the discant repertory as well. (An extreme, but musically not very convincing example of tenor manipulation is the clausula *Nusmido*, a retrograde form of *Dominus*.) Often a tenor melody was repeated once, sometimes more often and in imaginative, irregular ways.

Upon repetition, the tenor rhythmic pattern was frequently altered, changing, for example, from fifth mode to first. If the number of notes in the tenor melody did not come out even with the rhythmic pattern, the composer might add or omit a note or two so that the repetition of the melody would start off on the same foot as the original statement. Conversely, if the melody *did* happen to start its repeat properly, and if the composer did not like it that way, he added or omitted notes so that the rhythmic pattern would cut up the melody in a way different from the first statement. The first method produced two large sections with a strong tonal resemblance, the second method two sections that might sound very different even though built on the same melody. The motet *Dieus! de chanter—Chant d'oisiaus*—IN SECULUM (Codex Montpellier no. 87) has an exact repeat of the tenor, while the motet *Liés et jolis—Je n'ai joie—* IN SECULUM (Codex Montpellier no. 102) arranges the same tenor melody so that the repeat is dislocated by one note from the first statement. (Since a voice from one motet may turn up in another, we refer to motets by quoting all three voices, beginning with the triplum and ending with the tenor in capitals.)

The greatest amount of individuality is manifested in the phrase structure of the motet. Here again the regularity of the tenor is only a means to endless variety in the relationship of phrases among the three voices. At one extreme, the composer could conceivably make the phrases in the upper voices all coincide with the rests in the tenor pattern; such a regular solution, however, is never encountered (*In salvatoris nomine—In veritate comperi*—VERITATEM, Codex Montpellier no. 57, is about as close as one comes). At the other extreme the composer can avoid all coincidence of phrase among the three voices. This extreme, too, is practically never encountered, but a great many motets approach the same effect by always having at least one voice elide every coincidence of phrase between the other two voices. Between these two extremes lie an endless number of arrangements, using coincidence or lack of it to shape the motet as a whole. Since phrase endings in the upper parts are marked by rhyme and are related to the poetic structure, individual solutions are reflected in text as well as in music. Finally, the whole phrase structure is superimposed on the handling of the tenor melody with its various possibilities of repetition, giving the composer several factors to juggle in fascinating and musically significant ways.

The oddest feature of the motet was a device called *hocket;* the word is variously spelled, sometimes in a way close to its English cognate *hiccough.* A hocket typically involves two voices, but often three. One voice sings an isolated note, while the second voice rests. Then the first voice rests while the second sings an isolated note. When this pattern is repeated in animated modal rhythms, it results in a striking texture—one that struck certain medieval observers as hopelessly ludicrous, entirely unsuited to sacred music.

Hocket proved to be extremely useful, however, persisting throughout the motet repertory of the 1200s. Some pieces (usually on the tenor IN SECULUM) are given over completely to hocketing; lacking texts in the upper parts, these hocket études may have been intended for instruments. But hocketing, as an extreme case of staggered phrasing, had its roots deep in the discant clausula, where it had been purely vocal. Hockets continued to turn up in vocal parts far into the next century.

The motet in Example 26, *Aimi! Las!—Doucement—*OMNES (Codex Montpellier no. 103) repeats the little melisma *Omnes* (from the Christmas gradual *Viderunt omnes*) five times, the first three times in dotted quarter notes, the last two speeded up in a first-mode formula. The repetition starts each time with the same note. The motetus, moving in first mode (with ornamental subdivisions, to be discussed shortly) makes clear, consonant counterpoint to the tenor and is basically synchronized with it, except for minor elisions; the motetus text has a principal rhyme *-our.* In the triplum the ornamental subdivisions have more or less eradicated the underlying first mode. The principal

EXAMPLE 26   FRENCH MOTET

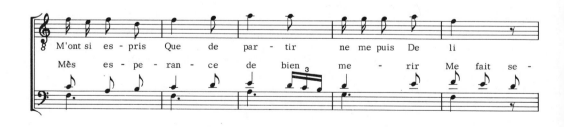

EXAMPLE 26 (CONTINUED)

Et ses trez doz re - gars m'ont o - cis, Dieus!

cours, Que nu - le do - lour Ne puis sen - tir,

m'ont o - cis, Aï - mi, aï - mi aï - mi, Dieus, aï - mi!

Mes en joi - e m'a mis a touz jours.

A join - tes mains mer-ci li pri Qu'e-le ne me mete en ou - bli;

S'en chan - te - rai par dou-cor Pour de -

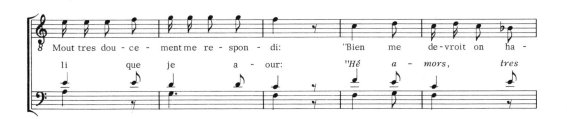

Mout tres dou - ce - ment me re - spon - di: "Bien me de-vroit on ha -

li que je a - our: "Hé a - mors, tres

EXAMPLE 26 (CONTINUED)

(Tr. Woe! Alas! Shall I so live, if my lovely will have no mercy on my torment? Her sweet figure (which I saw first) and her little mouth, her green eyes that shine so, have so taken me that I can no longer leave her. And her sweet glance has slain me— Ye gods, how it has slain me! Woe, woe, woe, O heaven, woe! With clasped hands I beg mercy, lest she forget me. So sweetly she answers, "I would indeed be hateful if I let my faithful friend die thus."
Mot. Sweetly I am held by love, and I cannot leave her, who can change my joy for sadness; my hope to merit well supports me, so that I feel no pain, but only joy forever. So I sweetly sing for her whom I adore: "Hey, love, sweetest love, I will not leave you.")

rhyme is -*i*, and the phrases are consistently staggered with respect to the lower two voices. When the upper two voices coincide in a rest (meas. 15, 27, 30, 38, and the end) they do so on an octave and a fifth, respectively, over an F in the tenor—which was not too hard to arrange, since the tenor has so many F's.

The concentration on F is striking; there are so few other notes in the tenor, and consequently so few other vertical combinations among the three voices, that the ear easily keeps track of the several possibilities. The piece is obviously on F, so much so that one might raise the artistic question, is it monotonous? It certainly would be, if the piece were much longer; but motets of this consistency are inclined to be short. They make a single tonal point, as well as a single rhythmic one, and then soon conclude. In compensation for its tonal and rhythmic consistency, the little piece is intense in its phrase complexity, to say nothing of the effect of two simultaneous texts. The last line of the motetus, (*Hé! amours,*) seems to be a quotation from a trouvère song, functioning as if it were a refrain to the motet. Such interchange between trouvère and motet repertories was common.

Example 26 is also a convenient illustration of typical contrapuntal procedures. The basic sonorities are fifths and octaves, used together at important cadences for a final sound. Almost every note of the tenor supports either that sound, or fifths or octaves separately, although thirds also appear in that position. Contrary motion is generally maintained in moving from one consonance to another. Obvious parallels such as in measures 17 to 18 are infrequent. Naturally, three voices cannot all move in contrary motion with one another; at least two must be parallel or similar. It is clear, however, that contrary motion furnishes the basic framework at any given point, parallels being a way of doubling in fifths or octaves.

Sharp dissonances, seconds and sevenths, are frequent products of contrary motion between the basic consonances, giving the motet a rich, pungent sound. As in all polyphony of the 1200s, the contrast between consonance and dissonance tends to be high: the music is more consonant as well as more dissonant than we are accustomed to. The final cadence is a representative example both of this contrast and of the variety of interval progressions cultivated throughout the century. The basic progression is fifth (G–D) to octave (F–F) outward by contrary motion; E (forming the sixth E–G) becomes an important way station between the fifth and octave. The motetus is led downward to its final fifth, C, from above, giving a strong cadential friction between its D and the E in the triplum, while reinforcing the tenor with parallel fifths. The manuscript indicates that the penultimate chord G–D–E is to be held slightly before resolving to the perfect consonance F–C–F. The result is a convincing cadence, although not one that became standardized. The form that did later become standardized has B instead of D in the motetus, which moves upward in contrary motion to the tenor and in parallel fourths with the triplum. This form is frequent in the 1200s, but only as one of several alternatives.

Both the upper voices of Example 26 illustrate, in varying degrees, the breakdown of modal rhythm into smaller ornamental values. First the longs and shorts of the original modal pattern were divided into half, producing two eighths for a quarter, or two sixteenths for an eighth. Occasionally the long, the quarter note, is subdivided into three parts, two sixteenths and an eighth; when the short, the eighth, is divided into three, however, the resulting notes are so quick as to be best represented at this stage by a triplet of sixteenths. Since syllables continue to be set to the basic modal values of quarter and eighth, the subdivisions, at least in the stage evident in the motetus of Example 26, are neumatic.

Subdivision of the modal values went hand in hand with a slackening of the tempo of motets. The headlong rush of Perotin's mighty organum and discant, retarded already by the presence of texts added syllabically to the upper parts, was further retarded by the increasing subdivision of modal values throughout the motet repertory. The retardation became especially severe when the subdivisions, at first neumatic, were themselves provided with individual syllables, as in the triplum of Example 26. What was once a long, a quarter note with one syllable, is here broken up into two sixteenths and an eighth, each with a syllable, *Aimi! las!* This particular subdivision occurs consistently throughout the piece, creating as it were a new mode; but such new modes did not have a chance to become standardized like the original six.

Up to 1260 or so, the subdivision did not proceed beyond two sixteenths for the eighth, the original short value, except for the triplet sixteenths, which remained neumatic and so fast as to be without a clearly perceptible length. Then Franco of Cologne, writing around 1260 or a little later, asserted that this short modal value (the eighth) should properly be subdivided into three equal parts rather than two. He felt, in other words, that the triplet sixteenth subdivision should become the normal one, which presupposes that by his time tempo had further slackened to the point where such triple subdivision could make musical sense. Franco went on to say that if only two notes took up the space of the short modal value, these two notes should themselves be short-long (always in that order) or ♪⌐ so as to correspond rationally to the basic triple subdivision he now postulated.

In motets that correspond to Franco's ideas (beginning in the seventh fascicle of Codex Montpellier), such subdivisions are set syllabically. The result is so intricate as to require us to change the level of our transcription—although the original notation remained consistent. At this point it is convenient to refer to the names of the original notes. Leonin's long and short had been called *longa* and *brevis,* respectively. So far we have represented the longa by a quarter note (or a dotted quarter) and the brevis by an eighth note. Now, in order to accommodate Franco's faster syllabic values (each called a *semibrevis*), we must represent the longa by a half note (or dotted half) and the brevis by a quarter note. Leonin's first mode, then, is represented in this transcription by half, quarter. The triplum of Example 26 appears in Example 27 first in its original notation, and then—in the rhythmic values Franco demands—in the two kinds of transcription. By Franco's time the tempo had slackened to the extent that his short-long semibreves sounded the way second mode had sounded twenty or thirty years before.

Once the process of subdivision and retardation had started, it urged itself onward. There was no reason to stop at a triple subdivision, particularly when the values resulting from that subdivision were now as slow as the original ones. The subtlety of composer and performer here outstripped the development of notation—as often happens. All the subdivisions were notated with the same shape, the diamond-shaped note called *semibrevis* (part of a brevis); the performer had to read these semibreves according to the composer's instructions or according to his own fancy.

The most famous composer around 1290, Petrus de Cruce, subdivided the original brevis into as many as nine semibreves, favoring subdivisions into four, five, and six semibreves. It is not clear exactly how Petrus himself wanted these various subdivisions rhythmicized (aside from the normal Franconian treatment

EXAMPLE 27 FROM THE TRIPLUM OF EXAMPLE 26

Aï - mi! las! vi - vrai je ain - si (etc.)

Aï - mi! las! vi - vrai je ain - si (etc.)

Aï - mi! las! vi - vrai je ain - si (etc.)

of two semibreves as short-long). It is known that a little later, however, four or five semibreves were performed in similar short-long pairs. Thus four semibreves might be ♪ ♪ ; five semibreves might be ♪ ♬ or alternately ♪ ♪ ♪ . The increasing subtlety of such subdivisions, called *prolations* or *manners of performance*, accurately reflects a current of overrefinement apparent in the motet toward 1300.

In the hands of Petrus himself, however, the subtlety is convincing, expressing itself through a sensitive rendition of refined texts of courtly love. As Petrus treated it, the motet became an accompanied song: the tenor, still moving in traditional patterns, moved so slowly as to be almost without rhythm; the motetus, although it had its own text, was linked **rhythmically with the** tenor rather than with the triplum, which alone seemed rhythmically animated, suavely declaiming its phrases over the accompaniment of the other two voices. Under these conditions the phrase structure of the motet literally disintegrated—but so charmingly! Treated to a series of sophisticated phrases, such as the one in Example 28 (from a motet in the style of Petrus, Codex Montpellier no. 332, *Je cuidoie—Se j'ai folement*—SOLEM), the listener has little opportunity or inclination to appreciate the larger shape. There are in Codex Montpellier two motets (*S'amours—Au renouveler*—ECCE, no. 253; *Aucun ont trouve—Lonc tans*—ANNUNTIANTES, no. 254) known to be by Petrus, and several others in a similar style. Together they represent the most modern tendencies in the motet of the late 1200s, the mainstream of music toward the end of the century.

OTHER MOTET STYLES Around Petrus de Cruce, motet style broadened to include a wide variety of styles, conveniently represented in fascicles VII and VIII of Codex Montpellier. Variety was made possible by the steadily increasing ease with which composers handled contrapuntal procedures. As contrapuntal combinations became standardized, it seemed as though composers actually sought out unusual forms for the motet. One motet for example (*Codex Bamberg* no. 92, *Je ne chant pas—Talens m'est pris*—APTATUR—OMNES) uses two traditional Notre Dame tenors that happen to fit together—or are made to fit together by manipulation of the rhythmic values.

EXAMPLE 28   FROM THE TRIPLUM OF *JE CUIDOIE—SE J'AI FOLEMENT—SOLEM*

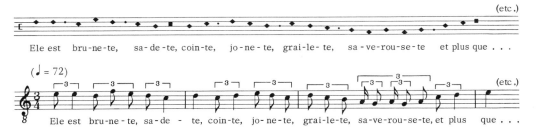

(She is dark, knowing, young, slender, fragrant, and more than any other . . .)

In the seventh fascicle of Codex Montpellier we find, after the opening two motets by Petrus de Cruce, a number of motets with tenors drawn from French secular songs, for example, *Entre Copin—Je me cuidoie*—BELE YSABELOS (no. 256), *Au cuer ai un mal—Ja ne m'en repentir*—JOLIETEMENT (no. 260), *En mai—L'autre jour*—HE, RESVELLE TOI (no. 269). Some motets have tenors such as *Chose Tassin* (Tassin's piece)—tenors apparently associated with a particular musician.

JOLIETEMENT, the tenor of Codex Montpellier no. 260, is a rondeau. The upper voices, in typical motet fashion, are staggered in their phrases relative to the tenor, so that the tenor's rondeau form is not reinforced by the upper voices and not very apparent in the motet as a whole; this tends to be true in motets using French secular tenors. But in Codex Montpellier no. 265, *Mout me fu grief—Robin maime*—PORTARE, the tenor (a Notre Dame melisma) is arranged like a rondeau and is reinforced by the motetus, whose phrases follow the tenor's closely. These two voices by themselves present a sectional structure which, even though basically uncharacteristic of motets, is a logical outgrowth of the tendencies we have already observed in tenor structure. The triplum, however, effectively clouds this structure with its irregular, staggered phrases.

French secular tenors, with or without intricate forms, are only one of several types of late motet. *Or ne sai je—Puisque d'amer*—LEYSON (Codex Montpellier no. 267) borrows its tenor from a *Kyrie*—not, in other words, a Notre Dame melisma from a Gregorian gradual or alleluia. This *Kyrie* fragment, two measures long, is cast in an unusual rhythmic pattern, and then repeated over and over again as an ostinato. Eventually the ostinato becomes slightly modified by a stammering on the first two notes several times before proceeding to the whole figure. The stammering passages are filled in with hockets in the motetus. There is no other motet exactly like this one, but a number of motets have other unique features.

A whole group of motets in the seventh fascicle of Codex Montpellier (several using *Kyrie* melodies or other novel sources for their tenors) do not superimpose a rhythmic pattern on the tenor melody, but simply state it in equal long notes, sometimes with rests after, say, every eleven notes, or irregularly, or no rests at all, robbing the tenor of its basic means of rhythmic construction and reducing it to mere tonal support for the upper voices. If this happens to coincide with a motetus of moderate pace and a fast, declamatory triplum (as in *J'ai mis—Je ne puis*—PUERORUM, no. 255), then the effect of an accompanied song, already observed in Petrus de Cruce, is that much stronger. But it is more characteristic of these motets that the three voices move at more or less the same pace, avoiding the extremely fast triplum style of Petrus.

One motet of the seventh fascicle (*Dieus! qui porroit—En grant dolour—*APTATUR, no. 278) casts its Notre Dame tenor into a rhythmic pattern of three breves and a breve rest, a binary grouping that contradicts the century-old ternary meter inherited from Leonin's modal rhythm. So strong had been the force of these modes that their ternary meter remained long after the rhythms themselves had slackened and then been diffused in fractional ornamentation. One theorist remarked late in the century that it was, of course, impossible to sing a series of "imperfect longs," that is, undotted quarter notes (in six-eight transcription) or undotted half notes (in three-four transcription). The first departures from this habitual ternary meter took a devious form, as in APTATUR, which has only breves, no longs, so that the binary meter is a grouping only, not actually a series of imperfect longs; there are, in other words, no actual syncopations over the end of a ternary measure. Other, more drastic deviations were soon to follow.

Latin motets, for a time eclipsed by French ones, became more frequent toward the end of Codex Montpellier. The Latin motets tend to be in honor of the Virgin; some of them carry the texts of votive antiphons such as *Ave Regina* or *Alma redemptoris*. One motet (no. 285) has both those texts, one in each upper voice, over a tenor melody drawn from the *Alma redemptoris*. Musically these motets tend to revive the compositional techniques of the conductus, as a form now virtually extinct.

Some motets begin with extended polyphonic melismas, with or without the exchange of voices so characteristic of the conductus. Motet construction by this time had become so facile that the amiable counterpoint previously restricted to the conductus now could be carried out over a ready-made tenor in the motet. The slick contrary motion found in conductus now turned up in pieces such as *Descendendo—Ascendendo*—DOMINO (Codex Montpellier no. 331), a motet for the Ascension of Christ; the triplum sings "God, descending to earth, becomes man," and the motetus, "God, ascending into the clouds, is raised on high."

Voice exchange is carried out systematically in Codex Montpellier no. 339, *Alle psallite ̇cum luya* (in triplum and motetus)—ALLELUYA, a novelty text featuring the insertion of words between Alle- and -luia, and a pun on *luya/lyra* (Go!—Sing with the lyre!). Upper voices alternate melismas with texted parts, while the tenor successively extends its ostinato melodic figure. Lacking the rhythmic complexities of Petrus de Cruce, and cast in rhythms almost strictly modal, this charming motet reveals the fluidity of motet construction at the end of the century.

ENGLISH POLYPHONY In all probability English composers had participated directly in the development of the Notre Dame repertory, working in Paris and writing organum, discant, and conductus indistinguishable in style from that of Perotin and his French colleagues. Two important theorists, John of Garland and another, known to scholars as Anonymous IV, were both Englishmen trained in Paris.

There seems, however, to be a distinct repertory of pieces, preserved largely in English manuscripts, that was actually written in England during the 1200s. This repertory has certain stylistic features that differentiate it from Continental polyphony, especially from the modern French motet. In general, this native English polyphony of the 1200s (and the 1300s too) stayed much closer to the techniques of the polyphonic versus than did French polyphony. While English composers in Paris might well have written up-to-date Parisian styles, composers in England, some of them still monastic, tended to retain conservative traits alongside progressive ones in often confusing combinations.

After describing the practice of the best French composers, Anonymous IV goes on to point out the slightly different practices of composers in various peripheral areas, among them "Westcuntre," that is, Western England, off toward Wales. These composers, says Anonymous IV, favored the imperfect consonances (thirds)—a trait that reflects the smooth contrary motion and rich sonorities of the old conductus (by now out of date in France), especially when linked with voice interchange.

A very important feature of English music was a reluctance to use Gregorian chant tenors. The English apparently preferred to use the more recent alleluias (as in the eleventh fascicle of Codex Wolfenbüttel) or to paraphrase a chant rather than use it literally. English composers also maintained the practice of free tenors; that is, they composed all parts afresh, as had been customary in the polyphonic versus. A small group of English pieces (as yet but dimly perceptible) suggests that English composers sometimes adapted tenors to existing counterpoint—just the reverse of Notre Dame practice, but perfectly comprehensible when we remember that the strict use of a Gregorian chant tenor was one of the most novel, most progressive features of Notre Dame style.

Some of the motets just discussed (page 103) are thought to be English. *Alle psallite cum luya* has a free tenor constructed to facilitate the voice interchange in the upper parts. Such a tenor, sometimes called *pes* (foot), might have an independent rhythmic pattern and no text, like French tenors; but the free tenor often gives itself away by the obliging manner in which it provides ideal counterpoint to the conductuslike upper parts. A pes sometimes has a repetitive melodic pattern, or one with varied repetition, as in *Alle psallite cum luya.*

When setting alleluias, which English composers did without sharp differentiation of organum and discant styles, they continued to insert rhyming versus (as in the eleventh fascicle of Codex Wolfenbüttel) in the manner of tropes before the alleluia and again before the verse. Regularly written *a 3,* these sections might have the same text in all three parts, or the same text in two upper parts over a tenor (as in the early motet), or two different but closely related texts (as in a later motet). These sections sometimes contained voice interchange, now written *a 3,* which meant that each voice had three melodic phrases instead of two, and the whole contrapuntal complex was sung three times. Voice interchange characteristically appeared as an episode in a large piece—an alleluia or a conductus; when it eventually appeared as a separate piece, it became known as a *rondellus,* in other words, a round.

Native English composers, absorbed with note-against-note counterpoint, voice interchange, and the sonorities resulting from these techniques, developed a sure, smooth kind of melody set in resonant chords—the same chords found on the Continent, but used in such a way as to impress the listener with their fullness. While the English approach to polyphony did not contribute to an overall sense of tonal order, it may have served to remind the French composers (when they came in contact with the English style) of how sweet sounds could be.

Works illustrating these English features are found primarily in a series of fragments from Worcester Cathedral—a cathedral, to be sure, therefore the appropriate setting for the new polyphony, but a cathedral off in the Westcuntre, reflecting conservative English inclinations. A few pieces contained in the Worcester fragments may go back before 1250, but most seem to fall around 1300, some well beyond that date.

The extreme case of voice interchange is the charming *Sumer is icumen in,* variously dated between 1240 and 1310, and apparently coming not from the

Westcuntre but from an abbey at Reading, in south central England. As far as rhythm and sonority are concerned, the piece could have been written any time after the big conductus of Perotin's time. Its contrapuntal technique, while unsophisticated in itself, seems to place the *Sumer* canon at a mature phase of development; but the development in question, voice interchange, is one that goes back before 1100. Stylistic details taken together, however, indicate a likely date sometime in the last half of the 1200s.

The *Sumer* canon has a tenor or pes, or rather, two tenors singing the same pes in voice interchange. This pes alternates a fifth, F–C, with a third, G–B flat, in every measure. Above the pes is another part, written once but with three more canonic entries indicated. Actually every one of the twenty-four measures of the upper part concords with F in its first half and G in its second; hence every measure can be interchanged with every other, permitting voice interchange, that is, canon, *a 24* if desired. But the instructions direct the singers to enter in succession, rather than all beginning at once as in voice interchange (and rondellus), and it is these staggered entries, later the trademark of a canon, that are the only real novelty of the piece—except possibly the fact that it can be sung as a perpetual canon, and is called a *rota* (wheel).

The step from voice interchange to canon was taken in France as well as in England, possibly about the same time. But while canonic procedures were to find steadily increasing prominence within new polyphonic styles, they were not in themselves essential or even important in the formation of those styles. The crucial factors in the next century related to large-scale tonal and rhythmic order, over which canon offered but little control. The future still belonged to the motet and what the French could do with it.

5
EXPANSION OF PART MUSIC 1300-1450

Stabilization in Motet and Song Form

DURING THE 1300s POLYPHONIC TONAL ORDER WAS BROUGHT TO A peak of efficiency. Polpyhonic forms were elevated to a highly economical relationship with the fabric of polyphony, with the intervallic framework. The materials of part writing, having been thoroughly explored during the 1200s, were now combined in more orderly ways, sacrificing some of the force and vigor of Perotin—or the charming whimsy of Petrus de Cruce—for the sake of clarity and grace. Composers stabilized the two-part framework and refined the techniques of adding a third voice. After setting the tonal foundation in order, they expanded their rhythmic shapes to an extraordinary degree. Throughout the 1300s composers gave much attention to large-scale form, with a happy combination of tonal order and rhythmic freedom.

The motet of the 1200s had been limited in its functions, whether liturgi-cal or courtly. After 1300, the motet assumed larger dimensions and greater importance. With its new sense of order, the motet acquired a new dignity; its scope became universal. It served sacred needs broader than those of the liturgy, secular needs grander and nobler than those of courtly love. It became suitable for occasions of state, royal marriages, meetings of princes. Its texts could be moral or political discourse, sometimes satire. More important, its musical worth transcended the occasions that called forth its texts. For a short time the motet became a truly independent musical achievement.

Around the motet—and eventually displacing it—developed other musical forms. The rhyming, scanning, strophic poetry of the trouvères was now set to polyphony, simultaneously becoming standardized in three most popular forms— *rondeau, virelai,* and *ballade.* Just as composers slipped easily from monophonic to polyphonic song forms, so they now wrote polyphonic settings of *Kyrie, Gloria in excelsis, Credo, Sanctus,* and *Agnus Dei,* acclamations of the mass that were still being set to chant during the 1200s. In both secular and sacred realms, polyphonic music was replacing the most recent monophonic music as if its natural consequence.

Mass music and other forms of service music were cultivated at cathedrals, as in the past. Similarly the secular song forms remained a function of courtly life. But polyphony now sprang up in courts and cathedrals far removed from Paris (the center of activity during the preceding century), especially in the brilliant cultural life at Avignon during the residency of the popes (1309–1377). Outside France, indigenous musical forms developed in northern Italy and England. In spite of these fascinating and often highly attractive peripheral repertories, the music of northern France continued to be the mainstream of musical development.

PHILIPPE DE VITRY'S MOTETS   The first task confronting composers of the early 1300s was to set in order the motet, which had gone to pieces, in a sense, at the end of the preceding century. The reconstruction of the motet was accomplished by Philippe de Vitry, (1291–1361), a brilliant figure in French intellectual life, as well as the best composer of his generation. In a series of important works dating from 1315 to the middle of the century, Philippe gave the motet a new size and shape, while remaining true to principles and possibilities that went back all the way to the substitute clausulas of Perotin.

Philippe's first motets appeared in the satirical *Roman de Fauvel,* a polemic in poetry on certain social issues of the time. Into one version of this poem were interpolated numerous musical selections, both chant and polyphony, sacred and secular, to illustrate, adorn, and relieve the lengthy *Roman.* In its mixture of chant and polyphony the musical supplement reflects the state of music around 1300—a broad base of chant of all kinds, progressively infiltrated with the new polyphonic forms. In its polyphonic selections, the supplement to the *Roman de Fauvel* reflects the motet repertory of the 1200s in all its variety. Against this background the five motets of Philippe de Vitry stand out as impressive pieces in a new style. The first half of one of these works, *Garrit gallus—In nova fert—*NEUMA, is given in Example 29. The texts of triplum and motetus attack the corruption of Enguerran de Marigni, who was "prime minister" under Philippe the Fair and Louis X of France; the "cocks" are Frenchmen (*galli*).

The first impression made by *Garrit gallus—In nova fert* (and by most of Philippe's motets) is the swinging six-eight rhythm of the upper parts. Philippe took pains to incorporate the rhythmic novelties of Petrus de Cruce while avoiding their disastrous effects upon the larger forms. The quarters and eighths of Example 29 are actually semibreves (we have changed our transcrip-

EXAMPLE 29 PHILIPPE DE VITRY: MOTET (first half)

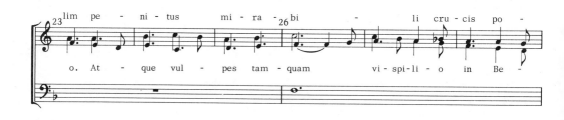

EXAMPLE 29 (CONTINUED)

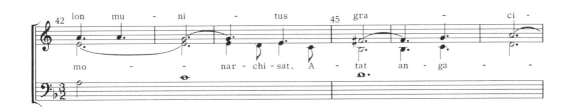

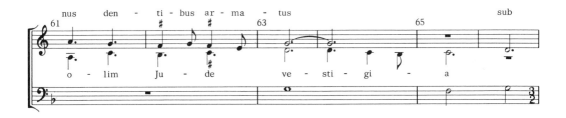

EXAMPLE 29 (CONTINUED)

(Tr. The cock chatters, weeping bitterly; the whole flock mourns, betrayed by the satrap, neglectful of his office. And the fox, like a ravaging grave-robber, waxing crafty with full consent of the lion, reigns as king. Alas, what anguish! See how Jacob's family once again flees from Pharoah! No longer able to follow the path of the ancient Jews, it mourns in the desert, tortured by hunger . . .
Mot. Once more complaint must be raised about the change in public opinion. That old dragon that great Michael once conquered with the miraculous power of the cross, lives again, now endowed with the grace of Absalon, the eloquence of Ulysses, armed with those magic teeth as a soldier in the army of Tersitis . . .)

tion ratio again), anywhere from two to six of them replacing a brevis (a dotted half note, or one measure) in the fashion of Petrus. But in Philippe's new prolation (described in a treatise called *Ars nova* that reports Philippe's teachings), these semibreves no longer move freely, or irregularly, or in the languid short-long style of Franco and Petrus. Instead they dance along in a way that, while not repetitive, has some of the momentum of modal rhythm as used long ago by Perotin.

For all their similarity to the old modal patterns, Philippe's rhythms are not modal. The real modal values, longa and brevis, are, however, still present (and are clearly apparent in the original notation), droning away in the tenor at an incredibly retarded rate. Between the new motet and the old, one of the most important differences (to which we will return) was the emergence of two distinct rhythmic levels—fast rhythms in the upper parts, slow, quasi-modal rhythms in the tenor. The tenor pattern at the beginning of Example 29 is in the third mode: the group ♩·𝅘𝅥 ♩ represents notes that would have been transcribed in Perotin as ♩. 𝅘𝅥𝅮♩♩ . In *Tribum—Quoniam secta latronum*—MERITO HAEC PATIMUR, another of Philippe's motets from the *Roman de Fauvel,* the tenor is strictly in the second mode.

Like most tenors in the 1200s, Philippe's have repetitive rhythmic patterns. In Example 29 the pattern extends through measure 25 (counting measures in the upper parts). This pattern is both longer and more complex than tenor patterns had ever been before. From Philippe's time on, motet tenors tended to assume individual patterns of unprecedented length.

The tenor pattern in Example 29 is especially complex because of its shift from three-two to two-two and back again. The two-two tenor rhythm emphatically contradicts the ternary meter, inherited from modal rhythm, that is present in the first three notes of the tenor. The second C in the tenor is, in effect, syncopated, falling over the end of a three-two bar. This would have been felt in Philippe's time as a disruption of the normal grouping in threes; there are strong indications, which we will examine more closely later, that Philippe carefully planned this particular spot so as to make the temporal displacement as convincing as he could. Tenor passages such as this one were written with red notes to signal the offending duple rhythms.

In the first half of *Garrit gallus—In nova fert* contained in Example 29 the tenor pattern appears three times; by then the tenor melody has run its course. In the second half of the motet the tenor repeats its melody in three more statements of the rhythmic pattern. Like the use of a rhythmic pattern, the repetition of the tenor melody is typical of motet procedures of the 1200s.

In *Firmissime—Adesto*—ALLELUIA BENEDICTUS, from the *Roman de Fauvel,* the tenor melody runs its course in eight statements of a pattern in longas and double longas, and then repeats the same melody in eight statements of a pattern consisting entirely of breves arranged in a duple grouping. Here, too, the altered repetition of a tenor melody is traditional, but the particular way Philippe chose to do it is novel.

In *Douce playsance—Garison selon nature*—NEUMA QUINTI TONI, a very famous motet from Philippe's later works and his only motet with French texts, the tenor has duple-rhythm inserts (as in *Garrit gallus—In nova fert*) as well as a repetition in faster note values. These accelerated repetitions are sometimes called "diminution"—not with complete accuracy, since the values of the tenor rhythm are not literally diminished in some consistent ratio, but altered in a more complex way.

While the new rhythmic shapes of Philippe's tenors are more complex, the tonal shapes tend to be more clear, more stable than before. Since the late 1200s, tenors no longer came out of the Notre Dame pool of gradual and alleluia melismas, but from a variety of sources; Philippe took advantage of this variety to select tenor melodies with especially cogent shapes. The tenor of *Garrit gallus—In nova fert* (called NEUMA because apparently taken from a set of neumes or interchangeable melismas) moves through a small group of six pitches, F up to D, with the highly directed contours of medieval chant. Because of this, and because of the slow pace of the tenor, each of these six pitches acquires a special function in the overall tonal shape of the motet.

Out of Philippe's eleven motets, eight have tenors ending on F, as in Example 29. In one of these eight, a chant originally on G has been transposed; in another, a chant has been drastically altered to keep it on F. A ninth ends on G, but since it ascends only to E (and does not descend below G), it sounds the same as those on F, which frequently have a B flat. A tenth tenor is on C, but with the motetus lying below it, cadencing on F. The eleventh tenor is on G with a persistent B flat. Except for this last, all Philippe's tenors end on a note such as C or F that has a major third above it in the scale; this note is *ut,* or *fa,* the most stable note in the hexachord. In his choice of tenors Philippe made contact with the clearest concepts of tonal order current in his time.

Internal cadences, too, are carefully placed in the tenor structure, although with this type of tenor melody and moving in these slow rhythms, almost any note can be made to sound like a convincing cadence. Still, there is a tendency in Philippe's tenors to end phrases on the first, second, third, or fifth degree, that is, on *ut, re, mi, sol,* and less often on *fa* and *la.* The cadence on *mi,* never found at this time as a final cadence but always as an internal or half cadence, has as its distinctive feature the tenor's descent through the half step *fa–mi.*

In Philippe's later motets he sometimes used a fourth voice called *contratenor,* as in *Vos qui admiramini—Gratissima—*GAUDE GLORIOSA. The contratenor works closely with the tenor, moving in the same range and the same kind of note values. Rhythmically the contratenor enters into the tenor's repetitive pattern; tonally it concords with the tenor, either above or sometimes below the tenor, in which case the contratenor changes the basic shape of the foundation of the whole motet. Adding a contratenor was one way a composer had of reinterpreting the tonal implications of a cantus firmus.

Elaborate motets *a 4* were sometimes simplified by replacing the tenor-contratenor duo with a single part called *tenor solus,* a part that consisted of the lowest notes from tenor and contratenor. Such a part provided the tonal foundation of the motet without the rhythmic interplay between the patterns in tenor and contratenor.

Even in motets *a 3* (as in Example 29) the general impression is one of greater sonority, due partly to the expansion of chords beyond the limits of an octave (outer voices frequently form tenths or twelfths) and partly to a greater refinement and sense of clarity in the spacing of chords. During the 1200s polyphony had stayed mostly within the range of an octave, since here were to be found the simplest intervals, thirds, fourths, and fifths, bounded by the simplest of all, the octave. By 1300, the possible combinations within an octave having been thoroughly explored, it became desirable to move outside the octave into larger combinations such as octave and a third, or octave and a fifth. These broad, open sonorities, mixed with the more compact, traditional sounds, gave greater variety to the texture. Philippe sometimes used the clean, telling sound of two high voices a third apart, with the tenor an octave below.

Associated with these new, more resonant sonorities was an increasing standardization both of the two-part progressions and of the way of adding a third voice. Throughout the 1200s composers had tended toward a two-part cadence formula of fifth moving outward to octave, the progression that linked the next most consonant interval (the fifth) with the most consonant one (the octave) in contrary motion. This fifth-to-octave progression was usually mediated by a sixth, and during the 1300s, this major sixth-to-octave progression, in which both voices moved stepwise in contrary motion, became so standardized as to seem to contemporary observers inevitable.

This progression existed in two forms, one in which the half step (as *mi* to *fa*) occurred in the upper part, the other in which it occurred (as *fa* to *mi*) in the lower; in each case the other part moved by a whole step (see Example 29, meas. 18 to 20, 29 to 30). During the 1300s the progression with the half step at the top was regularly used for final cadences; the progression with the half step at the bottom was reserved for internal cadences. In another type of final cadence, the two parts moved from minor third to unison, with the half step *mi* to *fa* at the bottom. Philippe used these cadential progressions frequently in the course of a motet, giving it a continuous feeling of direction.

Although these two-part progressions had been frequent in the 1200s, they had not been reinforced by a third voice in any standardized way. During the 1300s the normal way of adding the third voice in cadences was to make it approach the fifth above the tenor from the half step below. The inner voice moved in contrary motion to the tenor and in parallel fourths with the upper part (as in meas. 18 to 20 of Example 29). In this progression the third voice emphasized the direction of the two-part framework rather than obscuring it. This cadence, of particular force and clarity, became typical for polyphony *a 3* by 1350.

As clean, open chords and standard cadence formulas became common, they necessitated more frequent application of *musica ficta* (imagined notes) or the insertion of flats and sharps (which, except for B flat, were not part of the now traditional Guidonian system). Musica ficta, known since the mid-1200s, had two basic purposes. It was used to eliminate tritones, or augmented or diminished octaves, from consonant chords (fifths, octaves, twelfths, or combinations of these) when occurring in exposed positions, and to turn normally minor sixths (for example A–F) into major ones (A–F sharp), the better to move outward to an octave (G–G), or similarly—and often simultaneously—to make minor thirds into major ones (A–C sharp to G–D). Many accidentals of both kinds are provided by the manuscripts of the 1300s; many more have to be supplied, as singers of that time supplied them. The application naturally depends a great deal on context, but the principles at least are clear.

Consistent application (in so far as that is possible) of musica ficta, including that already in the original, has among other consequences a substantial increase in the number of forceful cadences within a piece. These in turn greatly increase the weight of each tenor note upon which they occur, deepening the effect of the tenor melody on the overall shape of the motet. In Example 29, musica ficta emphasizes the cadences on C (meas. 8 to 9) and on G (meas. 19 to 20, 31 to 32, 33 to 34, 59 to 63). The use of a signature of one flat in the tenor with no flat in the upper voices—a frequent procedure in the 1300s—makes F *ut,* and provides for a standard full cadence on F, the final, with a standard half cadence on A. The four tenor notes now accounted for, F, G, A, and C (*ut, re, mi, sol*), are the principal cadence points in this piece; B flat (*fa*) is not used for a cadence, and D (*la*) is handled in a special way.

The strength of these cadences lies in their stepwise contrary motion from major sixth to octave, or from major third to fifth in the inner part. This strong contrary motion was emphasized by an increasing tendency to precede it with one or more sixths or thirds in parallel motion, as in measures 17 to 20 of Example 29. Parallels—especially when exposed, as these are—are dangerous to part music, but as long as they involved the imperfect consonances, thirds and sixths, instead of perfect fifths and octaves, and as long as they resolved in strong cadences, parallels could be tolerated in the now clarified tonal shapes of polyphony.

The contrapuntal framework was expressed in relatively slow notes, explicitly in the tenor, implicitly for the most part in the upper voices. By removing the figuration from the upper voices, the underlying framework can be exposed to view; the framework of measures 1 to 20 of Example 29, expressed in three voices, is given in Example 30. While unsatisfactory as music, being stripped of lyric figuration, such a reduction gives a clearer idea of the basic chords and overall tonal shape, a shape based upon, but not identical with, the tenor melody. Here the shape first dwells upon F, rises through G to A, then again to C and D, settling back on C; then the line falls easily to rest on G. Contrary motion is usually maintained, aside from the parallels in measures 17 to 19, already discussed, and the curious consecutive fifths in measures 15 to 17, whose function remains to be seen. Example 30a can be further reduced to the guiding two-part framework, as in Example 30b.

Chords that are sustained for a measure or more, as at measures 9 to 10, 17 to 18, 43, 45, 67 to 68, are carefully spaced and positioned. Usually these

EXAMPLE 30   (a)   Reduction of the beginning of Example 29

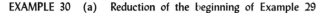
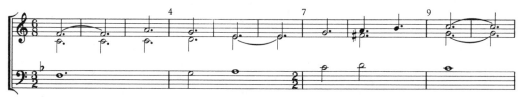

EXAMPLE 30   (b)   Reduction of (a) to two parts

chords are perfect consonances, but sometimes Philippe used a fifth with a third in the middle, or a sixth with a third in the middle, or a tenth above. These, like most of Philippe's chords, had been long in use, but Philippe, rejoicing in the vibrant quality of imperfect consonances, let them ring out unadorned by contrapuntal figuration.

Such moments, however, were the exception; usually Philippe clothed the slow framework of Example 30 with animated six-eight rhythms, facilitating the progress from one chord to the next. The figuration often led through sharp dissonances, but these, now clearly placed within the larger framework, seemed far less arbitrary than those of the 1200s. The dissonances in measures 1 to 3 of Example 29 are obvious decoration of the underlying chord F–C–F; the dissonance in measure 4 is a clear passing tone between the octave G–G and the fifth A–E; and the dissonance in measures 51 to 52 is an integral part of the long melodic curve that starts back in measure 46, then swirls up and over the climax in measure 51 on to measure 57.

The most impressive feature of Philippe's motets is the way all factors work together to produce polyphonic melody. Basic to his style is the relationship between tenor and upper parts, one note of the tenor supporting several notes above. The swinging rhythms of the upper parts animate the slow tenor, which in return groups the rhythms above it into more cogent forms. The tenor directs these rhythms into a broad tonal plan and gives them point and definition.

All this happens, not according to abstract rule, but as the result of musical decisions made specifically for each situation. For example, at measure 9 Philippe had to make audible and credible the duple rhythms he had inserted into his tenor pattern. His main problem was to avoid a strong articulation on measure 10, which would have been the beginning of the expected ternary meter.

Philippe set up the tenor so that the C in measure 7 was a false resolution of what came before; then he moved decisively in measures 7 and 8 to a standard cadence on the second C (measure 9), which could be interpreted only as a strong downbeat of the type normally found at the beginning of a ternary measure. Philippe was careful to sustain the chord through measure 10, so that nothing might contradict this strong—though displaced—downbeat, whose function was to make the ensuing duple rhythm a reality.

Even though Philippe proceeded in this pragmatic way, he soon came to favor certain solutions that helped clarify the overall shape of the motet. In measures 15 and 16 of Example 29, where those curious parallel fifths occur, the upper voices rest in alternation; the rests divide the respective voices into phrases. Naturally the rests are staggered with respect to each other and to the tenor pattern, in keeping with the traditional motet structure. Unlike the motet of the 1200s, however, the staggering is now consistent throughout the motet. From this point on, the upper voices always rest at the end of the duple-rhythm insert. Beginning in measure 32 the upper voices also rest consistently at the beginning of the insert. In other words, except for its first statement (and its last) the tenor's duple-rhythm insert is framed by the alternating rests in the upper parts. Two subtle but clearly audible factors, duple rhythm and texture, are coordinated to give a sense of periodicity to the motet's structure.

Periodicity, expressed as a synchronization of the phrase structure among the three voices, came to be a characteristic and increasingly important feature of the motet during the 1300s. Philippe eventually drew the hocket technique into the periodic structure, using this peculiar texture to signal the tenor's repetitive pattern.

Hocket is used differently in different motets; the best place to study its periodic function is in the late, very beautiful motet *Tuba sacre fidei—In arboris—*VIRGO SUM. This motet embodies the results of Philippe's search for musical order. The tenor moves through its broad tonal plan with grace and purpose; the upper parts provide smoothly animated figuration, relieved by their whimsical hockets. A disarming solo for the motetus is thrown in free before the tenor and its periodic structure get under way. Works like this remained models of motet composition throughout the greater part of the 1300s.

BETWEEN MOTET AND SONG FORM   Philippe's motets represented the most progressive tendencies in the motet up to 1350. In an important manuscript collection dating shortly after mid-century, *Codex Ivrea,* Philippe's motets occupy the place of honor. Alongside Philippe's motets, such as *Impudenter—Virtutibus—*ALMA, are motets by other composers (whose names we do not know) in styles which reflect the variety inherited from the last fascicles of Codex Montpellier. These motets may have novelty texts made up of street cries or clever lyrics; they may use voice exchange or French secular tenors cast in strophic forms. The motet repertory from 1300 to 1350, for the most part unexplored and inaccessible, is of great importance for the development of style.

Novel motet structures of the late 1200s tended to crystallize into special types of pieces after 1300; the most striking example is the *chace,* in which one voice duplicates another in strict imitation—a *canon* in later terminology.

Canonic, or literal, imitation of this type was a special case of the practice of voice exchange. Indeed, a chace could be described as a piece in which two voices consisted entirely of continuous, ongoing voice exchange.

The earliest known chace, *Talent m'est pris* (Example 31), shows clearly the connections, as well as the differences, between the chace and the old motet. In the motet *Je ne chant pas—Talens m'est pris*—APTATUR—OMNES (*Codex Bamberg* no. 92—the same motet mentioned earlier on account of its two tenors), the motetus goes, "Talent is given me that I may sing of her whom I have loved so much. . . ." The text of the chace, borrowing that of the motetus, goes, "Talent is given me that I may sing like the cuckoo, cuckoo, cuckoo. . . ." The birdcalls are the occasion for some delightful hockets. The canon is *a 3*, the voices entering at intervals of seven measures, and is perpetual.

There are four chaces in Codex Ivrea; *Se je chant*, a canon *a 3*, is the most famous. Like *Talens m'est pris*, it also has strong connections with the 1200s, but besides being much longer than *Talens m'est pris*, it is more modern rhythmically. While the popularity of the chace in France was short-lived, it was received enthusiastically outside France. German sources from the later 1300s preserve *Talens m'est pris* with two different German texts; one is *Der Sumer kumt* (Summer is coming). This, of course, recalls the English *Sumer* canon described in the previous chapter. It is difficult to be certain about the priority of one over the other, since *Talens m'est pris* may go back before 1300; but it is also not impossible that the English piece inspired the French one. In any case, the strong similarity of the two pieces involves contrapuntal procedures deeply embedded in the polyphonic tradition.

The chace was soon superseded in France by a type of piece called *virelai* that preserved the birdcalls or other naturalistic idioms while dispensing with canon, except as free, sporadic imitation. Virelais have a form built on a refrain and a couplet.

EXAMPLE 31   CHACE

* start second or third voices here

refrain

couplet (new music, new text)

epilog (music of refrain, new text)

refrain

The virelai is one of the refrain forms produced at the end of the trouvère development. In fact, the virelai (also called *chanson balladée*) was viewed in the 1300s as a special kind of ballade that had an opening couplet, then a closing couplet whose second line was textually a refrain; the refrain was sung also as an introduction to the whole song, as in the rondeau. The second and following strophes began with the couplet. Coming into favor only after 1300, the virelai was even then not very frequent, except in the works of Guillaume de Machaut (to be discussed presently), or as we find it here in connection with novelty texts. The very name *virelai* may be derived from the kind of nonsense syllables used to portray birdcalls (compare *tourelourelay*).

Codex Ivrea contains a very famous polyphonic virelai, *Or sus vous dormez trop* (Up, you sleep too long!), which has no hockets, but instead a number of special figures to reproduce the effect of birdcalls. These figures involve repeated notes or intervals, placed over a slowly moving or static tenor. Slow-moving progressions, however, not only served to support this type of figuration, but also made possible greatly expanded dimensions, which, in conjunction with the repetitions of the virelai form, give *Or sus* a stature comparable to Philippe's mature motets.

Several similar virelais, preserved in slightly later sources but reflecting mid-century styles, are easily accessible, including *Par maintes foys* (attributed to Vaillant, active ca 1370; set to a German text, *Der May,* by Oswald von Wolkenstein, ca 1377–1445), *Onques ne fut* (with hockets), *Alarme, alarme* (attributed to Grimace), and *Restoés, restoés* (with imitation, like the preceding).

Other virelais of the mid-1300s have two or even three different texts in different voices. Such polytextual construction was, of course, normal to the motet; but the prevailing trend during the 1300s was away from the motet to accompanied song—one vocal part supported by two instrumental parts. This latter medium seems so obvious for part music that it is hard to realize that it was far from obvious in the early 1300s. The approach to accompanied song was slow and devious.

When the listener of the early 1300s wanted to hear tuneful melody, he listened to the now traditional trouvère songs—pure melody, unencumbered by contrapuntal artifice. The attraction of counterpoint lay precisely in its artifice, its intricacy; three voices with two or even three different texts, in different rhythms and staggered phrasing, presented the listener with fascinating complexity. As far as the early 1300s were concerned, there must have seemed little point in making a third kind of music (accompanied song) that had neither the melodic freedom and directness of a trouvère song nor the complexity of a motet.

Some early polyphonic rondeaus by Adam de la Hale (1236–1287), a trouvère, move in very simple note-against-note style with one text in all three voices—the most traditional, most basic form of Western polyphony. These settings, however, are isolated; polyphonic settings of trouvère song forms in the early 1300s followed the traditions of the motet. The connection between the chace and the motet, in other words, was not isolated, but part of a larger trend. Exchange of texts and musical materials between motets and song forms continued through the first half of the century.

The important manuscript collection *Codex Reina,* from late in the century, still contains a number of polytextual virelais. The virelai *Ma trédol rosignol—Aluette—*ROSIGNOLIN is, as far as texture goes, a motet of the type that uses a French secular tenor; the upper voices are properly called *triplum* and *motetus.* The repetitive virelai structure has been simply superimposed on the motet texture; the tenor continues its own rhythmic and melodic repetitions straight through the couplet. Another virelai from Codex Reina, *Contre le temps et la saison—*HE MARI, MARI, has a third, instrumental part of a type to be discussed later on that marks the transition to accompanied song. These and similar pieces testify to the continuity of motet and song forms between 1290 and 1370.

LITURGICAL POLYPHONY

After 1300 composers applied polyphony to liturgical mass texts—*Kyrie, Gloria, Credo, Sanctus, Agnus Dei,* and *Ite missa est,* the dismissal. These acclamatory texts are often referred to collectively as the *ordinary* of the mass, since, unlike the mass propers, these texts do not change from day to day. But medieval chant settings of these texts, as we saw, were regularly made proper to a particular day through their tropes; polyphonic settings continued to include tropes, making the term *ordinary* misleading. There was, however, an increasing tendency (in chant as well as polyphony) to treat these items as a group. Little by little during the 1300s they were formed into musical cycles, despite their lack of liturgical interrelation.

Kyrie, Gloria, and the rest represented an important segment of medieval chant composition that continued right through the 1200s and into the 1300s. In fact, such chant settings were the principal kind of music composed for the mass, since up to 1300 polyphonic settings of these items were sporadic, and polyphonic settings of the propers were represented mainly by Leonin's *Magnus liber,* an isolated repertory. Thus when polyphonic composers after 1300 set *Kyrie, Gloria,* and the rest either singly or in cycles, they were, on the one hand, continuing the current tradition of medieval chant and, on the other, extending the realm of polyphony.

The contrapuntal procedures standardized in the motet of the later 1200s were now applied outside the motet, giving new direction to that most basic form of Western polyphony, note-against-note declamation of a single text simultaneously in all voices. For the sake of this most basic form, the whole apparatus of staggered phrasing and different rhythmic levels essential to the motet was bypassed for the time being. We saw that in the polyphonic versus and in the conductus the composer began by writing a lower voice as a good melody, and then added his counterpoint on top. A similar procedure is frequently followed in service music of the 1300s, with the result that the lowest voice, the tenor, often looks like a piece of chant. In a *Sanctus,* say, it is sometimes difficult to tell whether a composer is borrowing a recent chant *Sanctus* for a cantus firmus, or whether he is composing his own *Sanctus* melody in modern chant style as the first step in writing polyphony. In either case the musical results are essentially the same.

By relatively slow degrees, polyphonic mass music approached the high style of motets. The earliest known cycle of acclamatory mass texts set in polyphony is the *Mass of Tournai* from before 1350. Aside from the concluding versicle of the mass, *Ite missa est*, set here as a motet, and a brilliant hocket for the *Amen* of the *Gloria*, the Mass of Tournai is almost entirely in simple-note-against-note-style.

Codex Ivrea, featuring the motets of Philippe de Vitry, contains also a number of settings of these acclamatory mass texts, especially *Gloria* and *Credo*. (*Gloria* and *Credo* had been traditionally intoned by the celebrant; the choral portion, hence also the polyphonic setting, began *Et in terra* and *Patrem omnipotentem*, respectively.) Often set for two vocal parts with instrumental tenor, sometimes with a second instrumental part or contratenor, these pieces stand closer to the motet than does the Mass of Tournai. At least, they have a differentiation between vocal and instrumental parts, although the two vocal parts sing the same text, frequently at the same time.

In mass settings such as the *Credo* in Example 32, from Codex Ivrea, the contrapuntal framework tends to be far more apparent than in a motet. The two vocal parts cross only infrequently, often making parallels—thirds, fourths, fifths, or sixths. Each voice forms a simple two-part framework, with the tenor moving through the basic concords in contrary motion. Together the three voices

EXAMPLE 32   FROM A CREDO

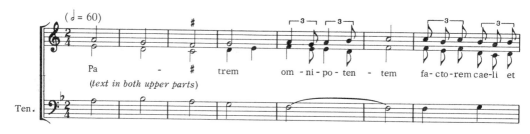

(Father Almighty, maker of heaven and earth, of all things visible and invisible.)

spell out the sonorities and progressions made standard in the motets of Philippe de Vitry and his contemporaries. Figuration in the vocal parts tends to be simple, uniform, and applied in such a way as to leave the contrapuntal framework in full view.

Long texts such as *Gloria* and *Credo* require many internal cadences; these occur in all voices simultaneously, since the tenor rarely has a motetlike pattern, and the upper parts are rarely staggered with respect to the tenor. The internal cadences fall repeatedly on the same notes in any given piece; in Example 32 they fall on A, G, or F, the final. Thus the larger tonal order is clear and simple, indeed the whole tenor moves with a narrow range firmly based on F (*ut*). Characteristic of these settings is the absence of two rhythmic levels. The tenor moves at about the same rate as the upper parts, with a minimum of figural decoration in the upper parts, little imaginative use of dissonance, and little intricacy in the relationship of figure to ground.

Simple as such mass settings were, they revealed a steady pressure toward the loftier constructions of the motet. As in the Mass of Tournai, devices such as hocket, syncopation, and sequential figuration are sometimes applied for extended phrases, although often more baldly than in a motet. Settings of *Kyrie* and especially *Sanctus* sometimes approach the level of motets; indeed, when a *Sanctus* has a troped text in the upper parts, it *is* a motet. These tropes, incidentally, tend to be relatively recent, indicating once more the continuity from chant to polyphony in mass music.

GUILLAUME DE MACHAUT   Mass composition reaches its highest level in *La Messe de Notre Dame* by Guillaume de Machaut (ca 1300–1377), most famous composer of the generation after Philippe de Vitry. Guillaume composed all types of music current at mid-century. His mass is a mixture of a simple declamatory style (*Gloria, Credo*) but with concluding hockets, and relatively elaborate motetlike settings (*Kyrie, Sanctus, Agnus, Ite missa est*).

The simple sections of Guillaume's Mass present the text in four voices simultaneously, in the style of the Mass of Tournai. The elaborate sections, however, have not only a motet texture (two vocal parts supported by tenor and contratenor) but also the rhythmic structure characteristic of motets. Tenor and contratenor, sometimes the upper parts as well, are strictly periodic, although the upper parts often coincide with the tenor in phrasing, which produces the sectional structure typical of less elaborate mass settings. The tenor of Guillaume's *Kyrie* is a chant *Kyrie* (*Cunctipotens genitor*), the tenor of *Sanctus* is a chant *Sanctus*—and so for *Agnus Dei* and *Ite missa est*. The rhythmic periods of the tenor are usually constructed so as to make sense in terms of the melodic phrasing of the chant.

Guillaume wrote twenty-three motets, most of them apparently before 1350. At any rate, Guillaume's motets seem like early works, closely modeled on those of Philippe de Vitry. Guillaume used the same kinds of tenor rhythms and tenor melodies; he also used the same swinging six-eight rhythms in the upper parts, in striking contrast to the other kinds of rhythm found outside the motet. In some cases the whole shape of a phrase or the flow of sonorities vividly recalls the motet style of Philippe; *S'il estoit—S'amours*—ET GAUDEBIT, for example, seems to look to *Tuba sacre fidei—In arboris*—VIRGO SUM for an overall concept of tenor structure as well as details of sonority. At the same time, Guillaume showed in his motets his own characteristic tendencies toward slightly twisted phrases and clouded chords. His motets initiated a phase of development, recurrent in the history of style, in which clear, established forms were overlaid with complex detail.

Guillaume favored a tenor melody—and hence a tonal structure—centered on F; but he used alternative forms to a much greater extent than Philippe, especially one ending on D (*re*), which has a minor third above. Aside from the final note, Guillaume's tenors are less clear in their internal structure, seeming to avoid confirmation of their finals. Some tenors are deliberately colored with strong accidentals, for example, F sharp in a tenor on F, as in *Qui es promesses—Ha! Fortune*—ET NON EST QUI ADJUVET.

While some of Guillaume's tenors use simple modal rhythms, others are more complex, again in seeming avoidance of Philippe's graceful clarity. Guillaume does not make much use, however, of the duple-rhythm inserts used so effectively by Philippe. Drawn, like Philippe's, from Latin chant, Guillaume's tenors are apt to have words symbolically related to the themes of the upper parts. In the motet just cited, for example, the upper parts lament the fickleness of Fortune, over the tenor text, "And there is no one who can help. . . ."

Guillaume conceived the motet basically as a vehicle of courtly love poetry rather than moral or political polemic; Guillaume's texts are mostly French, not Latin. By setting forth the themes of courtly love in refined, perhaps precious diction, Guillaume stressed one particular kind of motet at the expense of others. As if in revenge, only a few of his twenty-three motets (and usually not those dealing with courtly love) were taken into the mid-century repertory. We know most of Guillaume's motets—indeed most of his output—only through a set of manuscripts he himself compiled as his "collected works."

Guillaume did write six large Latin motets, sacred, ceremonial, or moral in nature. Three of these are *a 4*, with contratenors; four have introductions in the manner of Philippe's *Tuba sacre fidei—In arboris*—VIRGO SUM. Guillaume, characteristically embroidering on his model, makes his introduction (called *introitus*) longer and more elaborate than Philippe's. In motets *a 4*, for example, *Christe qui lux es—Veni creator Spiritus*—TRIBULATIO PROXIMA EST, all four voices participate in the introduction, entering in turn.

Guillaume's handling of tenor and contratenor in motets *a 4* is very similar to Philippe's: tenor and contratenor are both governed by a repeating pattern, involving syncopations. Such procedures are best represented by the splendid motet *Felix virgo—Inviolata genetrix*—AD TE SUSPIRAMUS, in which tenor and contratenor are each cast alternately in duple, then triple, time, but tenor's duple rhythm goes together with the contratenor's triple rhythm and vice versa.

In this motet, as in many of Guillaume's, the upper voices reinforce the periodicity of tenor (and contratenor) so consistently that each upper voice has its own repeating pattern. The resulting rhythmic structure (often called *isorhythmic*, or *with equal rhythms*) represents an extension of Philippe's principle of synchronized phrase structure to all details of rhythmic flow. It makes the motet more schematic, but not necessarily more orderly. Composers after Guillaume, pursuing isorhythm to its logical end, tended to substitute exactitude for musical cogency. Guillaume himself still treated the rhythmic detail with flexibility and imagination.

GUILLAUME'S SONG FORMS Guillaume seems to have been relatively uncommitted to the motet; in any case, his motets as a group are far less exciting than Philippe's. Guillaume's genius expressed itself with more felicity in his song forms, settings of courtly love lyrics in the strophic forms inherited from the trouvères.

In setting these song forms, Guillaume—presumably in company with other composers—made a decisive turn from the motet to accompanied song. This shift brought with it a basic revision of the nature and function of the several voices or parts. New alignments, however, came about not suddenly but by natural clarification of the old ones typical of the motet. The transition can be analyzed in three phases, although in reality, of course, it was far more complex.

The first phase involved the reduction of the two or three texts of the motet to a single text sung by a single voice, accompanied by an instrumental part. It should be noted that the traditional arrangement in versus and conductus, in which two or three voices sang the same text simultaneously, would have been a simpler solution—too simple, in fact. What the accompanied song shared with the motet was the combination of a sung part with an instrumental one.

The instrumental part of the accompanied song was called *tenor*, like the instrumental part of the motet. The vocal part of the song was not called anything in the musical sources, since texted parts were not usually labeled, even in motets. Later this vocal part was called *cantus* (song), but in range and relationship to the tenor it corresponded closely to the motetus voice, forming with the tenor the same kind of two-part framework.

In a second, transitional stage, the rhythmic patterns characteristic of motet tenors were eliminated. To be sure, this had already happened in many motets in Codex Montpellier. The tenor was soon easily assimilated to the rhythmic nature of the motetus, that is, the cantus. The effect of this aspect of transition was to replace the rhythmic structure of the motet with the rhythmic structure of a strophic form. The assimilation of tenor patterns to strophic forms can be seen in process in the polytextual virelais mentioned earlier.

In a third phase, a second instrumental part was added to the nucleus of motetus and tenor, that is, cantus and tenor. When this instrumental part lay mostly above the motetus-cantus (especially at cadences), it was naturally called *triplum,* and labeled as such since it was now instrumental, carrying no text. When it lay mostly below the motetus-cantus, in the same range as the tenor (but above the tenor in cadences), it was called *contratenor,* like the fourth voice of a motet. Of the two types, the triplum was the more traditional in function; the contratenor was a novelty in the motets of Philippe de Vitry (not found even in the *Roman de Fauvel,* 1315). Some songs had alternate triplum and contratenor; some, *a 4,* had both at once. The transition from motet texture to accompanied song *a 2,* then to accompanied song *a 3* and *a 4* is shown in this diagram; the instrumental parts, having no text, are labeled in the original sources, as indicated here by the use of quotes:

motet a 3 ——————————→ *song a 2* ——————————→ *song a 3 or a 4*
Tr (text)   + "Triplum"
Mot (text) ⎫   ⎧Mot = Can (text)   ⎧Can (text)
"Tenor"   ⎬——→   ⎨   ——→   ⎨
            ⎭   ⎩"Tenor"   ⎩"Tenor"
                                                         + "Contratenor"

(Tr = triplum, Mot = motetus, Can = cantus)

All these phases, along with many intermediate steps, can be observed in the works of Guillaume de Machaut. Three of his motets use French secular tenors; in one of these, *Lasse! comment oublieray—Se j'aim—*POURQUOY ME BAT MES MARIS? (no. 16), the tenor is built like a virelai; in another, *Trop plus est belle—Biaute paree de valour—*JE NE SUI MIE CERTEINS (no. 20), the tenor is a rondeau.

Guillaume's settings of trouvère texts include a number of monophonic lais, indistinguishable in type from those of the preceding century, although Guillaume's are cast in the new rhythms of the 1300s. Two of these lais, however, are canonic; the written melody is sung in canon *a 3* in the manner of a chace. The musical idioms, but not the texts, recall the birdcall chaces already mentioned. A third lai, *Pour ce que plus proprement* (Un lai de consolation) is *a 2*, but not canonic. Like some of the versus from the early 1100s, this lai looks like monophony but is really polyphony.

One of Guillaume's ballades, *De triste cuer—Quant vrais amans—Certes, je di* (no. 29), has three texts, one in each voice; all texts have the same refrain (*Triste et dolent . . .*), but the lowest voice seems to have been the first composed—if not a quotation from a preexisting song. This polytextual ballade, in other words, still has the texture of a motet. Another ballade is a canon *a 3, Sanz cuer—Dame par vous—Amis* (no. 17); it corresponds in type to the chace with its single text sung in staggered form by two or three voices. One more ballade, *Quant Theseus—Ne quier veoir* (no. 34), has two texts in two voices over tenor and contratenor. It is, however, not really a transitional work, but rather the outcome of a poetic exchange between Guillaume and a friend.

The first sixteen ballades by Guillaume are almost all *a 2*. Some of these have tenors whose patterns recall the motet. In ballades such as *Hélas* (no. 2), the transitional phase leading from motet to song form can be studied.

De petit po (no. 18) illustrates the last stages of transition. Tenor and cantus of this ballade were originally provided with an instrumental triplum; later an instrumental contratenor was added as an alternative to the triplum. Here (as in *De Fortune,* no. 23, and some others) the simultaneous performance of triplum and contratenor is inappropriate.

Triplum and contratenor were frequent alternatives in the 1300s. Similarly, one contratenor was sometimes replaced by another—a way of presenting an older piece in an up-to-date arrangement. Indeed, such "arranging" affected primarily those of Guillaume's works that were taken into the repertory of frequently performed pieces. *Il m'est avis* (no. 22), one of the few by Guillaume that seems intended *a 4*, also has an alternate contratenor from a later source.

A large group of eleven ballades are *a 3* with contratenor, a form that became standard not only for Guillaume but for the whole repertory. In other respects, too, as we will see, these ballades *a 3* embody standard solutions.

The rondeaus show great variety. There are two very short, apparently primitive rondeaus *a 3*. Aside from these, most of the rondeaus are *a 3,* with a contratenor in a style similar to the standard ballade. Two very beautiful rondeaus, *Rose, liz* (no. 10) and *Tant doucement* (no. 9, another repertory piece) are *a 4. Rose, liz* in particular makes a richly sonorous effect, enhanced by a tonal digression into an area marked by flats.

Ma fin est ma commencement (no. 14, My end is my beginning) has a special kind of retrograde voice exchange. This rondeau consists of an instrumental tenor, a texted cantus (which is the tenor sung backward), and a contratenor half as long as the tenor, but made full length by singing it a second time in retrograde. Since all this happens within the complex plan of the rondeau, the relationships of the parts are even more confusing. Rondeaus of this kind are few, but they turn up throughout the 1300s. Guillaume's is possibly not the first and certainly not the last.

Guillaume's virelais, like his lais, are mostly monophonic; only seven are *a 2;* only one, *Tres bonne et belle* is *a 3.* Whereas some of the ballades and rondeaus were taken into current repertory, none of the virelais were. (As we saw, the virelai as a form was not favored by other French composers, except for polytextual works or canonic, naturalistic ones.) Yet it is not at all certain that Guillaume's virelais *a 2,* simple as they may be, are early or experimental; on the contrary they present a remarkably polished, deliberately naïve appearance. Furthermore, *Tres bonne et belle* reveals a mature handling of the three-voiced medium. While the chronology of Guillaume's songs—indeed of all songs in the 1300s—remains largely in doubt, it seems clear that the simple, well-defined accompanied song was a point of arrival rather than departure.

Compared with the motet rhythms of the late 1200s, Guillaume's rhythms show, on one hand, a greater variety of meter and, on the other, more regularity of figural detail. Uniform ternary meter was replaced by several alternate meters involving both duple and triple groupings; but the whimsical variety of Petrus de Cruce gave way to a more consistent kind of rhythmic motion for any given piece. What happened was that the personal manners of performance—the prolations—proliferating around 1300 were reduced to a rational system of meters by theorists such as Johannes de Muris, active around 1320.

The new system provided for two rhythmic levels, with duple or triple groupings at each level, resulting in four meters that we can transcribe as two-four, three-four, six-eight, nine-eight—all the meters, in other words, that can be expressed as combinations of the basic rhythmic possibilities, 2 and 3. One measure in any of these meters represents a brevis; hence these measures could be combined (in motets) into larger, modal groups by the slow-moving tenor. Philippe's motets used mainly his favorite prolation, six-eight, in a duple or triple modal grouping. Song forms, however, had no slow-moving tenor, and hence rarely had a modal grouping. The brevis measures might be grouped musically, but such a grouping, subject only to the intuition of the composer, was usually not expressed overtly either in notation or in tenor pattern.

Once a composer chose a meter, he could—as far as the notation went—write rhythms as varied as those of Petrus de Cruce; but Guillaume favored a consistent set of rhythms and figural patterns in any given song. Rhythm and figuration were closely associated, since the faster rhythms were used primarily to express the figural patterns that clothed the contrapuntal framework. There is a dimly perceptible tendency for different kinds of songs, or of texts, to go with different kinds of rhythms, and for different rhythms to rise or fall in favor from one decade to the next. All that still awaits thorough investigation. In general, however, the balance of meter and rhythms accurately reflects the larger balance of musical order and freedom prevailing throughout the mid-1300s.

Song forms, as has been mentioned, lacked slow-moving tenors, and hence also the larger rhythms based upon such tenors. But song forms had their own large rhythms, the strophic forms themselves. Two of the most striking features of song forms at this time are the care with which the tonal plan is made to support the large rhythms, and the consistency with which certain tonal plans occur.

These are best studied in connection with the ballade, especially in its couplet structure. Couplets, as we saw, were an essential feature of rhyming chant; even before 1100 they were sometimes provided with ouvert and clos endings (see page 51). These first and second endings, frequent in trouvère songs, were often handled by making the ouvert a whole step higher than the clos. The two endings might be *re* and *ut* (for example, D and C) or *mi* and *re* (for example, E and D), rarely *fa* and *mi*.

Such formal principles were traditional by Guillaume's time; what is interesting in his work is their polyphonic realization. In his ballades *a 2* there is considerable variety, dependent largely upon whether the tenor of the ouvert is a whole tone, a third, a fourth, or a fifth above the clos. Sometimes Guillaume expresses the ouvert by an imperfect consonance (third or sixth), the clos by a perfect one (fifth, octave, unison)—exploiting the now clarified functions of intervals.

More decisive, however, is the standard solution eventually reached in the ballade *a 3* (with contratenor): the tenor of the ouvert is a whole tone above the clos (which is always *ut, re,* or *fa,* never *mi*). The chord on the ouvert may be perfect or imperfect, usually the former. The final of the whole piece is the same as the clos. The beginning, however, may be on some other note.

It should be noted that in the now standard contrapuntal cadence progression (see page 113) the tenor descends stepwise to its final; hence the penultimate note of this progression is the same as the tenor note in the ouvert. If the ouvert ends on a chord of a sixth, it is, in effect, pausing on the penultimate chord of a cadence. If the ouvert ends on an octave, it is, in effect, making a full cadence on a degree that previously functioned as a half cadence. In either case it is clear that the functions of chords and progressions are being used to control larger dimensions of form.

Tonal control can be observed in these and other ways throughout Guillaume's mature ballade, *Mes esperis* (no. 39, Example 33). The clos and final are on D (*re*), the ouvert on E (*mi*). These two cadences are used regularly throughout the piece; indeed, they are the only two cadences to be found. The refrain, *Se ma dame . . .* (meas. 40), is preceded by a half cadence on E with an imperfect consonance, and further marked by the absence of figuration, a chordal texture, and the rich sonority of a fifth with included third.

As in many other ballades, there is extensive rounding of the refrain to

EXAMPLE 33   GUILLAUME DE MACHAUT: BALLADE

EXAMPLE 33 (CONTINUED)

ris.   Si me con - vient

sans   cause es - tre pe - ris Par   un   re - fus

qui   en ri - ant m'a   mort, Se

ma da - me n'en fait brief - ment

l'a - - - - -

EXAMPLE 33 (CONTINUED)

(b)   Reduction of beginning of Example 33 (a)

(My hopes struggle with Nature inside my body, wherefore I am exhausted; for if Nature is defeated, my hopes cannot survive. For I will perish, without cause, because of a refusal that, smiling, kills me, unless my lady soon says "Yes".)

make it match the clos. While the overall tonal direction of the ballade is clear, Guillaume has masked it with his typically pungent sounds, achieved by passing notes and appoggiaturas in the figuration. A reduction of the opening measures is given in Example 33b.

ITALIAN SONG FORMS   Shortly after 1300 a polyphonic repertory appeared in northern Italy. This Italian repertory achieved considerable individuality by mid-century, but was then steadily absorbed into the French current toward 1400. Almost completely a secular repertory, Italian music of these decades flourished at aristocratic houses in Florence and to the north.

Connections with the French music, numerous and substantial, are apparent in the work of the first great Italian theorist, Marchettus of Padua, writing around 1320. Music from the 1330s and 1340s (contained in *Codex Rossi*) reveals the notational system described by Franco of Cologne, as well as some of the most basic features of traditional French polyphony, including the two-part framework, synchronized setting of text in two voices, alternation of syllabic and melismatic sections—all the features of the old polyphonic versus.

What makes Italian polyphony of the early 1300s seem different from French music is simply the French neglect of some of these basic features in the 1200s. French composers had taken up the motet with such enthusiasm that they almost completely leapfrogged the simpler, more traditional techniques in secular music. Simultaneously sacred composers had dropped the conductus in favor of the motet, so that the singing of text in all voices was no longer represented in the modern French repertory.

Italian composers, on the other hand, avoided the motet and everything peculiar to it—the ready-made tune in the tenor, two or more different texts with different rhythms and staggered phrases, to say nothing of the modern developments of Philippe de Vitry. Different rhythmic levels and the sense of broad tonal order associated with Philippe's tenors remained totally alien to Italians of the 1300s. They worked within the limits of the measure (the brevis), both tonally and rhythmically. This is best seen in the types of figuration they worked out, all dependent upon divisions of the brevis, in the manner of Petrus de Cruce and his generation.

Early Italian composers, such as Piero, Giovanni da Cascia, and especially Jacopo da Bologna, were associated with aristocratic circles north of the Apennines in Milan, Verona, and Padua. Giovanni also had connections with Florence, as did Gherardello. These men composed pieces called *madrigale* (*madrigals*), mostly *a 2*. Italians did not favor music *a 3*, even when, like Jacopo, they could compose in three voices with competence. The Italian art consisted mainly in gracious decoration lavishly applied on top of very simple progressions; writing *a 2* permitted full display of this brilliant art, but more voices hindered it. Example 34 contains a madrigal from Codex Rossi, typical of madrigals from the 1340s. Madrigals have a second section called *ritornello,* sometimes in a different rhythm, here set in canonic imitation.

Strict canon, curiously enough, was the one form of contrapuntal artifice that appealed to the Italians. The madrigal easily became canonic, as in Example 34. Side by side with the earliest madrigals appeared the *caccia,* Italian equivalent of the chace, typically set for two vocal parts in canon and a supporting tenor. Caccias, composed enthusiastically by Italians, included hunting cries, eventually street cries and other naturalistic noises, set in canon with devastating effect. Italian caccias frequently use Philippe's swinging six-eight, almost the only Italian manifestation of the new French rhythms.

Italian music reached its apogee of independence in Francesco Landini (ca 1335–1397), but also in his work started its inevitable return to the French orbit. Francesco, the blind Florentine, playing sweetly on his little portative organ, became a symbol of all that was most attractive and characteristic of Italian music during the 1300s. We know now that he was not the only composer of the time, but he still seems to have been the most gifted and most prolific.

Francesco apparently began with the kind of music he found in fashion— the madrigal *a 2*, with text in both voices; not all his madrigals, however, are necessarily early works. But his madrigals both *a 2* and *a 3*, together with other associated works, are remarkably few in number, thirteen in all. This includes two caccias, and two particularly isolated works that have become well known in

EXAMPLE 34 MADRIGALE

EXAMPLE 34 (CONTINUED)

me - - - i!

me - - - i!

Mo   là, vi - lan! mo là   per

Mo

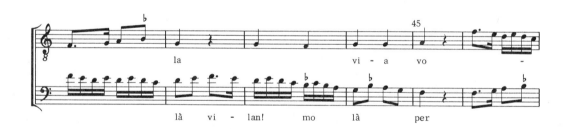

la   vi - a   vo   -

là vi - lan!   mo là   per

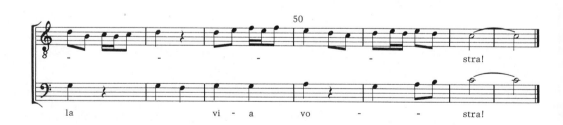

-            -   -   -   stra!

la   vi - a   vo   -   -   stra!

(Wrapped in a beautiful veil, I saw her seated, which made me cry, "Alas!" "Go on,
rascal, on your way!")

modern times, *Si dolce non sono*, a madrigal *a 3* with text in all parts and a motetlike rhythmic pattern in the tenor, and *Musica son—Gia furon—Ciascun vuoli*, an elaborate madrigal *a 3* with different text in each voice.

The weight of Francesco's production is in the ballata, a song form that became popular in Italy around 1350 or 1360. The ballata has the same form as the French virelai, namely, refrain, couplet, epilog, refrain. Francesco wrote ninety-one ballatas *a 2*, and forty-nine ballatas *a 3*. The ballatas *a 2* stand very close to the traditional Italian medium of two voices singing the same text at the same time, the upper voice elaborately figured. The widely circulated ballata *Donna, s'i' t'o fallito* (no. 1) is, except for its song form, virtually identical with the typical madrigal. There is, however, a tendency for the ballata to be simpler in texture—notably less canonic—than the madrigal.

Almost all Francesco's ballatas are for two vocal parts; but a few have instrumental tenor, and precisely these (for example, *Già ebbi libertate*, no. 34, or *Ognor mi trovo*, no. 51) show pronounced leanings toward the French style, both in the type of tenor as well as the kind of figuration employed in the upper part. They also tend to have ouvert and clos, called *verto* and *chiuso,* usually lacking in the other ballatas.

In the ballatas *a 3*, the French leanings are even more obvious and far more extensive. These ballatas *a 3* fall into three groups, according to whether one, two, or all three parts carry a text. We do not know the chronological order of composition; but it is clear that the ballatas with text in all three parts (for example, *Lasso! per mie fortuna*, no. 42) most closely resemble the Italian norm in concept and figural style, while the ballatas with text in two parts, or only in one, stand progressively closer to French models. Ballatas with text in cantus and tenor, accompanied by instrumental contratenor, can still be typically Italian, like *Cosa nulla più fe'* (no. 30); others of the same type, such as *Posto che dall'aspetto* (no. 29), look much more like Guillaume de Machaut—at least, like his ballades.

In the ballatas *a 3* with text only in cantus, accompanied by instrumental tenor and contratenor, the French influence breaks through in full force. *O fanciulla giulia* (no. 28) has the broad sweep, unhindered by seductive Italian ornament, and the clear tonal shapes so characteristic of the high French style. And Francesco's great lyric gift seems to express itself as easily in this style as in the other.

From Italy comes one of our first extensive collections of keyboard transcriptions of these song forms. *Codex Faenza,* written around 1420, includes a repertory that extends back at least to 1350. It contains some of the most celebrated pieces of the 1300s, both French and Italian, including Guillaume's ballade *Honte, paour,* an even more famous ballade, *De ce que fol pense* by P. des Moulins (ca 1350?), the virelai *Or sus vous dormez trop,* and Jacopo da Bologna's *Sotto l'imperio.* Some of the Italian pieces *a 2* seem to be merely transcribed; but some, especially the French pieces, are given in keyboard arrangements that express the basic two-part framework of the original in a new figuration suitable for the keyboard. Comparison of a vocal original with its keyboard arrangement provides a convenient means of studying the underlying structure of such a piece. Example 35a contains the beginning of Fran-

EXAMPLE 35   (a)   Landini: from a ballata

(b)   From a keyboard arrangement of (a)

(That little boy, Love . . .)

cesco's ballata *a 3, Questa fanciull'amor* (no. 6), a piece in French style; at 35b is given a keyboard arrangement of the same excerpt, taken from a source very similar to Codex Faenza.

AFTER GUILLAUME DE MACHAUT   During the 1360s the pressure toward clarity, apparent in French music throughout the century, seemed to reach a climax, producing song forms of classic shape. Less elevated and exciting than Philippe's mature motets, less expressive than Guillaume's ballades, less intricate than other ballades yet to come, these classic examples of song forms have gone largely unnoticed; yet they best represent musical achievement of the generation immediately following Guillaume.

In such pieces the two-part progressions move easily stepwise with a maximum of contrary motion, employing a nice balance of perfect consonances (fifths and octaves) with imperfect ones (thirds and sixths). Dissonances are infrequent; the three parts work smoothly together. The tonal motion is well directed, the arrival at cadences clear. The rhythmic ornament is in keeping with the shape and dimensions of the whole piece, which are moderate. Ballades and other forms of this description can be found in two famous collections from the end of the century, the Codex Reina, already mentioned, and *Codex Chantilly.*

The ballade *Gente et devis*, Example 36, has a typical tenor that descends stepwise, arriving at well-defined points of repose; these are supported by the

EXAMPLE 36 BALLADE (first half)

EXAMPLE 36 (CONTINUED)

(Sweet, pretty, noble, and wise . . .)

upper parts, which often suspend their own motion, or make a phrase, over the longer tenor notes. The contratenor is closely linked with the tenor, while the cantus places discreetly syncopated figures over the more clearly cadential progressions. The large tonal plan is orthodox, even if less clear than Philippe. The final on G (*re*) is a little darker, a little less forceful than the F final favored earlier.

It often happens, however, that classic moments such as this are abandoned as soon as reached. The most important composers after Guillaume, under obvious pressure to avoid the clarity of such pieces as *Gente et devis,* soon struck off in search of new complexities. These were of two kinds, which could appear either together or separately. The classic shapes could be obscured by twisting the underlying framework (often with musica ficta) or by the overlay of intricate rhythms.

Tonal obscurity prevailed first, appearing especially in the works of a composer we know only as Solage; he was active in the brilliant courts of southern France during the 1380s and 1390s. Sometimes he introduced unusual progressions by inflecting normal ones with sharps and flats, handled with seeming care by Guillaume, but now becoming more numerous and more erratic in their tonal function. Solage's ballade *S'aincy estoit* has some sharps sufficiently bizarre in their effect to cause difficulty in interpreting the original manuscript. Whatever the solution, it is clear that the composer is more concerned than before with inflecting the usual contrapuntal progressions in unusual ways. This is true even in the absence of puzzling ficta: the large, very beautiful *Corps femenin* (Example 37) by Solage (ca 1389) shows that unusual progressions can arise directly out of the counterpoint without extreme musica ficta—and without extreme rhythmic complexity.

Ballades such as these are sometimes called *grand ballades.* Their broad dimensions, filled with expressive melismas, are appropriate to their function as courtly dedication pieces; they can sometimes be dated almost to the day if the occasion they celebrate is known. It has been possible to date a number of ballades and motets (also used for dedications) during the late 1300s.

Names of composers are also regularly encountered, although the names given in musical manuscripts at this time are sometimes disguised, for example, by anagram; "Trebor" for "Robert" is one of the easiest. Usually but little

EXAMPLE 37   SOLAGE: FROM THE BALLADE *CORPS FEMENIN*

([Without equal], anemone of beauty.)

can be found out about the composer even when his real name is discovered. In
any case, we possess only a few pieces—sometimes only one—by many of the
composers known. Their styles, however, differ markedly; they exercized a high
degree of individuality in musical composition.

Next to Solage, the most important composers were Jacopin de Senleches
(or Selesses) and the Trebor already mentioned. The grand ballades of these
composers represent the other kind of complexity, the clouding of otherwise
straightforward progressions through syncopation and rapid figuration in ab-

normal groupings. The syncopation now typically operates with a short time interval, for example, a displacement by an eighth note when the framework is moving in quarters and halves. Such displacement has the function of anticipating or delaying one voice, blurring the contrapuntal progressions and making them spill over into one another, as in Example 38. Syncopation sometimes results in dissonances, but a consonant, if rich, sonority prevails. In any case, the framework itself proceeds frequently in a classic fashion.

Figural intricacy was brought about by the use of a *proportion*, a notational device to replace a normal note value with two faster ones, or two with three, or three with four, or other more devious replacement. The proportional figures may themselves be syncopated, leading to complexities so great as to be described by some modern observers as purely cerebral music.

It is essential to observe, however, that this complexity is nowhere near as important as it has been made out to be. In the first place, it is more apparent to the performer (or modern transcriber) than to the listener, who merely hears normal progressions through a delightful haze of ornamentation. In the second place, rhythmic complexity of the extreme kind described prevails only in a part of the total repertory (mostly in connection with ballades), in only a few works of only a few composers, for a time span of two or three decades.

In fact, the extreme examples of rhythmic complexity come from an isolated pair of renegade Italian composers, Matheus de Perusio and Antonellus da Caserta. Virtually the entire output of Matheus is represented in a single peripheral manuscript; he is not a composer of central importance. His ballades also demonstrate that this particular kind of rhythmic complexity coincided with an extreme simplicity of underlying progression. Stripped of ornament, the progression in Example 39 (from Matheus's *Le Greygnour bien*) is so routine as to be almost beneath the notice of, say, Solage.

While the craze for rhythmic complexity spent itself in the South toward 1400, the classic style of the 1360s apparently continued to be developed in the North, less spectacular but more solid, and with far greater importance for the future. At any rate, right after 1400 we find composers writing both secular and sacred pieces as if the rhythmic extravagancies of the grand ballade had never existed. Even Matheus wrote virelais and rondeaus in a simple lyric style.

Rondeaus in particular came into fashion now; their naïveté (compare Matheus's *Pour dieu vous pri*) has led some observers to imagine a basic stylistic change in the decade after 1400. But the simple rondeau represented only a surface fluctuation; much deeper lay the traditionally clear contrapuntal framework, persisting right through the most intricate rhythms Matheus could imagine for his ballades, and coming to the surface now in more recognizable form. (A French composer, Baude Cordier, wrote a sweet little rondeau, which he notated intricately in the shape of a heart.)

The decades between 1370 and 1420 have often seemed to be an age of transition. While incorrect, that impression is understandably produced by several important factors. One of the things that makes these decades seem confusing, and therefore transitional, is simply the absence of a really great composer who could make his strong stylistic identity felt in every kind of music. As we saw, composers of these decades produced (as far as we can tell) relatively little. Some of the composers were very good, but their limited output

EXAMPLE 38   TREBOR: FROM THE BALLADE *SE JULY CESAR*

("Phoebus, forward!" he carries on his crest.)

EXAMPLE 39 MATHEUS DE PERUSIO: FROM THE BALLADE *LE GREYGNOUR BIEN*

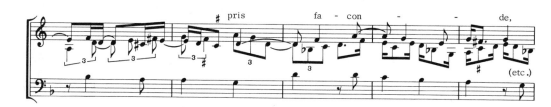

([The greatest gift . . .] was the gift of eloquence, [including therein sense and proportion].)

and lack of universality kept them from greatness. They tended to fluctuate in their personal style, unduly responding to different purposes (secular or sacred) or to different categories (motet, ballade, rondeau); the composers sometimes seem too open to influences from one another, French from Italian and vice versa. No one led the way. Nonetheless, the currents of development ran deep in France; a generally high level of technical competence and a sense of stylistic continuity—neither of which existed in Italy—is apparent in even the second-rate French composers, who awaited only new models and new standards.

Another factor giving these decades the appearance of transition is our own knowledge of the music. As long as historians could compare only Guillaume de Machaut with Guillaume Dufay (1400–1474), writing a hundred years later, they were impressed with a drastic difference in sonority between the two. Now that we are more acquainted with the repertory in between, we can see that the change in sonority was continual and not so fundamental as was once thought. During these decades there was a steady increase in the use of thirds and sixths, either enriching the intervals of the two-part framework or incorporated into the framework itself. As we saw, thirds and sixths had always been used in both ways in polyphony; now they began to outweigh the fifths and octaves. The increased frequency of imperfect consonances, however, involved no basic change in the handling of the framework, no transition from one kind of tonal organization to another.

One of the most interesting ways in which sonorities were enriched was through a new emphasis on the contratenor. From its first use in Philippe de Vitry and Guillaume de Machaut, the contratenor had passed above and below the tenor, doubling or enriching the intervals of tenor and cantus. Now the contratenor became active throughout a wider range, using wide skips to harmonize the intervals of the two-part framework in a greater variety of ways. If tenor and cantus held a fifth or octave, contratenor might supply in succession the fifth, then the third above the tenor, then the fifth below; or, by moving up and down in skips of thirds and fifths, it might supply all the concords—thirds, fifths, sixths, octaves, tenths—to a given note. If tenor and cantus held a third or sixth, the contratenor sought out the fifth or octave below, sometimes thrumming on it in a syncopated "um-pah" figure. Such contratenor idioms, which go well back into the 1300s, were apparently played on a type of slide trombone, using the natural overtones.

Example 40 contains excerpts from two contratenors, the first added to Guillaume's ballade *De petit po* in the late 1300s, the second composed by Matheus de Perusio for a ballade by Nicolas Grenon, a Northern composer active around 1400 (and later). The first contratenor, lying in this passage below the tenor, animates it with rhythmic eighths on repeated pitches. In measure 3 the contratenor harmonizes the structural sixth G–E with a C below. Grenon's tenor and cantus (Example 40b) make a clear two-part framework; Matheus set out to enrich and enliven that framework, obviously without intending to write a lyric contrapuntal line. Matheus's contratenor goes much further than the other one in the direction of reinterpreting the tonal shape provided by the two-part

EXAMPLE 40   CONTRATENORS ADDED TO BALLADES

(a)   From Guillaume de Machaut's ballade *De petit po* with a later contratenor

(b)   From Grenon's ballade *Je ne requier* with a contratenor by Matheus de Perusio

framework. Yet even Matheus does not give that framework a different meaning, but merely deflects it from its natural course.

The harmonizing contratenor brought with it new forms of old cadential progressions. The standard interval progressions of Philippe de Vitry, already varied by Guillaume de Machaut, had been further twisted by Solage's generation in ways still awaiting investigation; it was the new harmonization of these progressions, however, that decisively reshaped them. For example, contrapuntal considerations make it certain that even before 1400 the third in the penultimate chord was sometimes lowered, as in Example 41a, giving it a "blue" sound; but when the contratenor harmonized the penultimate sixth from below (Example 41b) a new cadence form was born. The behavior of the contratenor in this form—it leaps *up* an octave—shows its harmonizing, noncontrapuntal nature.

Yet another variant (Example 41c) became popular in the 1420s; here the contratenor leaped *down* to form a sonorous double octave with tenor and cantus. In addition to these modified cadences (in which the structural framework remained unaltered) other idioms were developed to allow the low-lying contratenor to harmonize two-part progressions in as sonorous a fashion as possible.

In all this development, the low, harmonizing contratenor had no effect upon the basic tonal plan, except to obscure it. It is essential to a true understanding of this music to realize that the frequent triads formed by the contratenor had no function in the tonal plan, simply because the three notes of the triad did not yet form an entity in the ear of the composer or listener. If a third or sixth between tenor and cantus functioned to form a cadence, it did so whether or not the contratenor provided a third or fifth below. If the cadences of tenor and cantus had a simple plan throughout the piece, then, of course, the triads formed by the contratenor also followed a simple plan, but through no virtue of their own. In the decades after 1400, style went through a phase of variety; the goal was not clarity of tonal plan, but joy in sonorous enrichment. Appreciation of this comes only when we hear the music not as awkward approaches to triadic progressions, but as two-part progressions smoothly harmonized.

Nicolas Grenon, whose ballade was harmonized by Matheus de Perusio, and Pierre Fontaine (ca 1380–ca 1450) are perhaps the two most important composers of a shadowy generation. Fontaine's rondeau *Sans faire de vous departir* illustrates by its classic two-part framework the unbroken continuity

EXAMPLE 41   CADENCES CA 1420

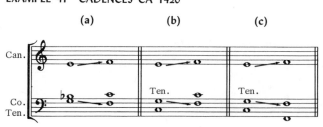

in the North between 1360 and 1420. Active in Italy was a Northern composer, Johannes de Ciconia, whose life apparently spanned the time since Guillaume de Machaut; Ciconia wrote both sacred and secular works of an elaborate cast derived from the extremists of the late 1300s and also a more lyric, if less polished kind of service music, which now adopted the song form medium of one vocal part supported by two instrumental ones.

We know by report of Martin le Franc (in his poem *Le Champion des dames*, 1440) that three composers, Tapissier, Carmen, and Cesaris, had been popular in Paris for their singing. Their few remaining works indeed reveal a preoccupation with graceful detail, which, however, seems detached from the form of their pieces and incongruous when applied to a pretentious motet such as Cesaris's *A virtutibus—Ergo beata*—BENEDICTA. Rarely used, the big motet now seemed stiff and awkward, its tenor and contratenor droning on through several long, complex repetitions. These were sometimes designated by increasingly abstruse directions or "canons" addressed to the performer, as in *Salve virgo—Vita via*—SALVE REGINA by Billart. Often completely isorhythmic, the motet had lost the marvelous integration of detail and tonal plan found in Philippe de Vitry.

French and English Developments

DUNSTABLE AND LA CONTENANCE ANGLOISE Martin le Franc's report also tells us that Tapissier, Carmen, and Cesaris were eclipsed by Guillaume Dufay (ca 1400–1474) and Gilles Binchois (ca 1400–1460), and furthermore that Dufay and Binchois learned from John Dunstable (ca 1380?–1453), adopting *la contenance angloise* (the English style).

Often discussed, the contenance angloise is perhaps hard to identify, but its import is clear, as is the leadership of Dunstable. French tradition continued to provide the substance of musical style, but the contenance angloise gave French music point and definition at a time when it suffered from too much variety, too many alternatives. Once redefined, French style—at least in the north—gained momentum rapidly, gathering up the many experiments and alternatives of the first two decades into a convincing synthesis. But for a decade or two between 1420 and 1440, English musicians in France (in the employ of English dukes on military or political adventures) illumined the Continent with one of those brief, brilliant flashes characteristic of English music.

National styles and influences, much debated, will give the student of this period difficulty unless he bears in mind these realities. Composers from northern France were the only ones with a solid past and (as it turned out) hope for the immediate future. Some of them worked in Italy; if, in deference to their patrons, they adopted in this piece or that an Italian manner, it was in imitation of a fast vanishing style which the Italians themselves—the few that still wrote anything—were abandoning as rapidly as they could master the French one. As for the English, whatever they could now give the French, they owed it to them, having got it all from France in the first place.

Dunstable gave sacred service music a dignity and eloquence that added powerful thrust to its ambitions. Purely functional music, represented most recently on the Continent by *Codex Apt,* received at Dunstable's hands an artistic definition that was the foundation of all to come. There was in principle nothing new—except artistic success. Nor was this success due to anything other than Dunstable's own ability. A collection of British music from the same period (1410–1420) called the *Old Hall* manuscript tends to the same awkward expedients as those in the sacred Continental repertory of Codex Apt; still, Old Hall has great historical interest, and also some fine music by Pycard and Leonel Power (died 1445).

Perhaps the most accessible of Dunstable's music is in his simple settings *a 3* of short devotional texts; *Quam pulchra es* is a well-known example. Part of the same reflex that produced mass music earlier in the 1300s, these devotional pieces represent the application to yet another kind of text of polyphony in its basic form. As with the mass movements, there was no resemblance to the motet, except as the composer tried to raise his work to a higher level. There was, ordinarily, no tenor cantus firmus, only one text, little or no staggering of phrases, no differentiation of rhythmic levels.

Dunstable's settings, however, did move with gracious animation, in a swinging, syncopated style that gave them artistic substance distinct from the motet while not identical with the style of secular songs. The *Sancta Maria* is an excellent example of a new kind of piece often called *song motet;* these small, devotional pieces were typically sung after a liturgical service—mass or vespers—as part of postliturgical devotions increasingly popular during the 1400s. The texts are drawn from a group of texts used for the same purpose in preceding centuries and set to chant right up until Dunstable's own time. Once again, polyphony picked up where chant left off.

Dunstable sometimes elevated his simple settings by using the familiar chant associated with the text, not as a tenor cantus firmus, but by paraphrasing the chant in the top part. *Paraphrase* technique, naturally, was a matter of personal style subject to infinite variation; it usually involved, at the very least, a new rhythm for the chant, with added ornamentation. The result looks like the cantus of a typical song (except for an indefinable difference), making identification of the tune difficult unless one happens to be familiar with it. The chant tune best loved and perhaps most frequently paraphrased was the *Alma* (see page 52). One of the perennial favorites of Western melody, the *Alma* deserved its popularity with polyphonic composers.

By coincidence, a melodic progression similar to the *Alma* is produced when the cantus is made to ascend through the basic concords, unison, third, fifth, sixth, and octave, and this cantus, in turn, is easy to fit with a descending tenor. Innumerable pieces begin this way, more than are actually paraphrases of the *Alma;* Dunstable used this idiom often, as in Example 42. When expressed in smooth syncopations and accompanied by plenty of thirds and sixths, this melodic progression may well be the contenance angloise. At any rate Johannes Tinctoris (ca 1436–1511), a theorist writing around 1475, first praised the English for inventing the new style, and then added that they never progressed beyond one tune. This seems to be the tune.

Paraphrasing chant became immensely popular in the following decades. Chant provided a melodic definition at a time when the sense of melody seemed

EXAMPLE 42   DUNSTABLE: FROM A SONG MOTET

(Blessed mother . . .)

temporarily to elude composers, but at a time when contrapuntal technique was flexible and sophisticated enough to allow a composer to work a chant into the fabric as if it belonged. Rich with centuries of artistic accomplishment often far above polyphony, chant also offered the wealth of association clustered around old, familiar melodies. Chant paraphrase was one of the principal means of giving polyphony a sacred identity.

There was still something to be gained from the tenor cantus firmus, and that something became apparent in Dunstable's mass settings. He started to group his mass pieces in pairs, a *Gloria* with a *Credo,* a *Sanctus* with an *Agnus Dei;* so did his younger contemporaries, both English and French. (Dunstable's works reach us mainly in the same manuscripts as these contemporaries, making precedence difficult to establish.) Dunstable was apparently the first to link a pair of mass pieces with a common cantus firmus in the tenor. In one case he built a *Gloria* and a *Credo* on the same cantus firmus, JESU CHRISTE FILI DEI, laid out identically in the two pieces in a pattern of diminution such as might be found in a motet.

The use of a cantus firmus in the tenor gives a mass setting something of the stature of a motet, reflecting Dunstable's general tendency toward elevation of service music. Specifically important, however, is the creation of a larger entity consisting of two pieces (for example, a *Sanctus* and an *Agnus Dei*) on the foundation of a cantus firmus. In this case, of course, either the *Sanctus* or the *Agnus Dei,* or both, had to forego its own appropriate chant as a cantus firmus. Usually both members of the pair were built on some chant other than one of the mass acclamations. Devotional antiphons or antiphons from other liturgical services (vespers, matins) were a frequent source of cantus firmi. Such a cantus firmus gave the pair of mass settings an identity based upon the associations of the chant.

While Dunstable, and others after him, took from the motet the technique of tenor cantus firmus, he did not take with it the periodic rhythms of the upper parts; these, in mass settings, remained free and irregular. And while at first composers laid out the cantus firmus with the help of repeated rhythmic pattern as in the motet, they eventually abandoned even that technique. What they wanted most from the cantus firmus was its symbolic association and the unity it gave the mass cycle. The periodic structure traditional to the motet was no longer useful; in fact, it was an obstacle.

Dunstable was perfectly able to write completely periodic structures, as he showed in his grand motet *Veni sancte Spiritus—Veni sancte Spiritus—Veni creator Spiritus—*(TUS) MENTES TUORUM (triplum has the prose text, motetus a paraphrase of the prose, contratenor the hymn text). Not only do the upper voices have repeating patterns, identical in all details, over a long, complex tenor pattern repeated in progressive diminutions; but the triplum paraphrases throughout the same hymn melody (*Veni creator*) of which a fragment forms the cantus firmus. Dunstable not only handles the technique with ease, he writes gravely expressive music, something rare in the large motet. But even in this impressive work, the most significant aspects are the rich sonorities, produced with the help of a leaping contratenor, and the lyric detail of the upper parts— effective in spite of, not because of, the isorhythmic structure.

DUFAY AND HIS CONTEMPORARIES The "smile of melody" that Dunstable and the contenance angloise brought to music touched off a series of French reactions. Around 1430 several composers, young Dufay at their head, contrived a new way to produce rich sounds, parallel thirds and sixths; these were apparently what struck their ears and what they felt to be responsible for the English success. Dufay and his followers almost certainly heard the English singers improvise these sounds, harmonizing chant melodies out of the chant book.

Throughout the 1300s there are instructions in singing parallels with chant, similar to older practices but making increasing provision for thirds in an effort to keep abreast of developments in written polyphony—in sound, even if not in art. Shortly before 1430 we hear of *faburden* as one of several English techniques of improvisation, one which produces parallel thirds below the chant (except at cadences, where the lower, faburden voice drops to a fifth below the chant) and at the same time parallel fourths above the chant, making sixths with the faburden voice below. The chord of a sixth with a third in between (what later ages designated as six-three) was common in written polyphony, as were progressions of several such chords in parallel motion approaching a cadence (see page 114). Faburden made a mannerism out of this progression, using it for a whole piece of chant. The sound is indeed "merry," as the English instructions say.

Dufay made a written equivalent of faburden, which he and other French composers called *fauxbourdon*. Paraphrasing a chant in the cantus, Dufay supplied a tenor in parallel sixths below (octaves in cadences) and directed that the contratenor should sing parallel fourths below the cantus. (Since the top two parts sang the identical tune a fourth apart, it was immaterial which of them was considered to have the chant.) Dufay used his fauxbourdon with great success in a cycle of hymn settings, in which verses were sung alternately in chant and in his paraphrased, harmonized fauxbourdon settings. The result was a happy combination of paraphrase technique with the sweet English sound, an easy way of modernizing service music.

Other composers also wrote fauxbourdon. Binchois set the whole *Te Deum* in this manner. But it was only a temporary expedient; even Dufay occasionally provided an alternate contratenor that harmonized the sixths of tenor and contratenor from below with greater artistry.

French composers now turned to chant paraphrase with enthusiasm, using it for increasing quantities of service music. Again Dufay provided excellent examples; a setting of *Alma* has the chant in the cantus throughout, sung at the beginning without any accompaniment—as if it were the intonation of the chant itself. This is an extreme case, which along with the conservative, balladelike character of the rest of the setting (it lacks the new tone of Dunstable's sacred music) suggests this to be an early work. Dufay also paraphrased the propers of the mass for St. James, which he combined with settings of the *Kyrie, Gloria,* and the rest to make a complete *Missa Sancti Jacobi.* Mass propers, both singly and in cycles, became subjects for polyphonic paraphrase.

Dufay and his contemporaries placed increasing emphasis on mass settings, turning them out in greater quantity at a higher artistic level than before. Settings of *Kyrie, Gloria,* and the rest, both singly and in pairs, now provided the nucleus for the most important manuscripts, such as the Bologna and Aosta Codices. While the French composers did not yet link their pairs with a tenor cantus firmus, they did link them in other ways, most obviously by using the same motif at the beginning for both members of a pair.

French composers also experimented with alternating solo groups (one singer on each of two parts) with chorus (several singers on each of three parts), phrase by phrase throughout a mass setting or other piece of service music. The rich, slightly fuzzy sound of a chorus was the natural medium for the rich harmonies now in fashion—as opposed to the bright, clean sounds that had so well expressed Philippe de Vitry's clear progressions. Composers matched texture with the contrast in sound between chorus and solo ensemble, using the one for agile duos, the other for more ponderous passages. Alternation of timbre and texture became an increasingly important way of articulating form.

Other experiments varied greatly from composer to composer. Guillaume Legrant, active around 1430, wrote a *Gloria* and *Credo* in very simple rhythms, but distorted the traditional contrapuntal progressions by an extraordinary use of accidentals. Binchois, on the other hand, wrote a *Credo* in which duos and trios follow each other in strong rhythmic contrasts, including some grotesquely rapid declamation. Dufay incorporated a popular song, text and all, into a *Gloria-Credo* pair. All these experiments were used later in more consistent, sophisticated ways.

CYCLIC MASS From the mass pair, composers now moved on to larger groupings of mass texts, for example, *Gloria-Credo: Sanctus-Agnus Dei,* or *Kyrie-Gloria: Sanctus-Agnus Dei,* or even all five sections in a musical unit, sometimes with paraphrase, sometimes without. Such cycles had been tried in the 1300s, as we saw, but now they began to appear more regularly and with greater purpose; no longer watered-down versions of motet or song forms, mass cycles now moved into the front rank of musical composition. Arnold de Lantins (active around 1420 and after) made a charming mass cycle *a 3.* Dufay's early cycles, like his single settings, do not seem so close to the contenance angloise. None of the French cycles at this time, however, used a tenor cantus firmus, whereas the English naturally extended the use of the cantus firmus from a pair to two pairs, setting *Gloria-Credo: Sanctus-Agnus Dei* as a cycle. (The chant *Kyries* with elaborate texts, highly regarded in England, seemed to discourage polyphonic settings of *Kyrie.*) Dunstable made such a cycle on the cantus firmus *Da gaudiorum premia,* of which only the *Credo* and *Sanctus* remain. Leonel Power made a cycle *a 3* on the *Alma.*

The creation of the mass cycle on a cantus firmus was seen as an important step, judging from the care with which Dufay followed the English example. Sometime around 1440 Dufay wrote a cyclic cantus firmus mass, *Missa Caput,* possibly using an English model (now lost). *Caput* is the word of the chant melisma used for the cantus firmus; it may well have had specific associations symbolic of the occasion for which the mass was written. Each of the sections has the cantus firmus once through, its first half in triple time, its second in duple. That, too, was an adaptation of motet technique popular with English composers; it divided each piece into two large sections, the second slightly faster in its basic tonal movement.

All these features, it is important to note, were new to mass music but traditional in the grand motet, which for years had been regularly *a 4* with a contratenor lying below the tenor for extended periods. It is useful to keep Dufay's larger motets in mind in following the development of the mass. He wrote several—great ponderous works whose graciously animated upper parts scarcely conceal the immensely deliberate tenors and contratenors. Many of these grand motets were written for ceremonial occasions in Italy. *Nuper rosarum flores*—TERRIBILIS EST LOCUS ISTE, written for the dedication of the cathedral Santa Maria del Fiore in Florence, 1436, has instead of a contratenor a second tenor singing the cantus firmus in canon at the fifth. *Ecclesie militantis—Sanctorum arbitrio—Bella canunt gentes*—ECCE NOMEN—GABRIEL, celebrating the election of a new pope in 1431, has two cantus firmi at once. Elaborate procedures such as these would have been entombed with the grand motet had they not been caught up in the new superwork, the cyclic mass.

Interesting and significant as Dufay's *Missa Caput* is, it is not artistically in the same class with Dunstable's best works nor with what seems to be Dufay's

next cyclic mass, built on the tenor of one of his own ballades, *Se la face ay pale*
(If my face is pale, the reason is love . . .). This was a curious thing, to build a
mass on a love song; we will take it up later. At the moment it is enough to
notice that in the 1440s style was in an unstable phase; many strange things had
happened, and more were to come. There were as yet very few cyclic masses in
existence—none, apparently, on a love song except this one—and almost every
new mass brought a new device. Presumably Dufay had a reason, for a mass
was now a big, important work, not to be based on mere whimsy. But the reason,
whatever it was, was not yet a general principle of mass composition.

In the *Missa Se la face ay pale* Dufay continued to apply motet techniques to the new form. The tenor cantus firmus here is written down once for
each of the five sections of the mass; but in the *Gloria* and *Credo* it is sung three
times. A canon, or verbal inscription, directs that in these sections the cantus
firmus should be sung first with all note values tripled, a second time with all
values doubled, and a third time with the values as they stand. This, of course,
is merely an elaborate way of accelerating the tenor in diminution as had regularly been done in the motet. Whenever the tenor sounds, that is, whenever the
cantus firmus is present, it is joined by the other three voices; but when the
tenor rests, there may be duos between the upper two voices, usually involving a
change of meter. Thus even if the cantus firmus is imperceptible, the textural
plan derived from it is clearly apparent to the listener.

There is a good chance that the cantus firmus will be imperceptible, since
the tenor is now mostly above the low-lying contratenor. Indeed the contratenor,
while harmonizing each note of the tenor, goes out of its way to obscure the
tonal plan of the cantus firmus. Taking up a position a fifth below the tenor
(instead of an octave) the contratenor cancels out the cantus firmus ending on
C with an insistent F, as at the end of *Kyrie*. There is tendency throughout the
mass for the low contratenor—and even the tenor—to become lyric and animated
in a manner recalling the song forms. Nevertheless, tenor and contratenor are
still basically conceived in this kind of mass music as the slow-moving foundation for the two upper parts, just as in the grand motet.

Missa Se la face ay pale was a novel achievement, but novel in format
only, not inner musical substance. The upper two parts, while lyrical in a way
unique to Dufay, fell easily into clear phrase shapes and cadences typical of his
time and dependent upon the traditional two-part framework. Only in the graceful duos (Example 43) did Dufay seem to step free from the past; but that was
due to personal mastery of line, not to any fundamental change in technique.
And even then his duos, while more polished than Dunstable's, lacked the
English warmth, the sense of flux and urgency that was to be supremely
important to the next generation.

Understanding Dufay's stylistic position begins with the fact that he was
the best composer of his time. Where his immediate predecessors, Tapissier,
Carmen, and Cesaris, had fumbled for a convincing personal style, Dufay found
a compelling lyricism all his own. Where his predecessors—and contemporaries—experimented and specialized, Dufay wrote masterworks in all categories.
He was the first universal composer since Guillaume de Machaut, the most forceful since Philippe de Vitry. Dufay did not make stylistic mistakes; he also made
no basic stylistic changes. With polish and elegance he did everything so well it

EXAMPLE 43 DUFAY: FROM MISSA *SE LA FACE AY PALE*

EXAMPLE 43 (CONTINUED)

(Blessed is he who cometh in the Name [of the Lord].)

was hard to see how, or why, it should be done again. He tended to write one of a kind, and tended, therefore, to find for each piece a special device, a reason for being. This is particularly true of his songs, in many ways the purest representation of his art. Without being progressive, each song seems to have an individuality, a real achievement at a time marked in turn by routineness and idiosyncrasy.

BINCHOIS AND OTHERS   Dufay was not the only one writing music, and while we prize Dufay's perfection, we must go to other composers to feel the rough edge of stylistic growth. Gilles Binchois, the "other" composer of Dufay's time, seems in many ways more in touch with changing musical style. Even though he wrote no mature cyclic masses, his service music betrays more contact with the English and, therefore, with the immediate future.

Binchois wrote many songs, some perhaps dull or awkward, but the best ones (for example, *Je loe amours* or *Pour prison ne pour maladie*) impressively lyric; they stand at the beginning of a flood of chansons composed during the middle decades of the century. At the side of Binchois was Hugo de Lantins (active around 1420 and after), writing excellent chansons that make extensive use of imitative entries. Imitation, which had appeared first as voice interchange, then in concentrated form in the chace, and then sporadically in whimsical songs of the mid-1300s, was now cultivated more and more seriously. Handled freely by Hugo, it tended to operate in very close time intervals, and lasted only a short time, usually at phrase beginnings. Dufay, too, did all these things; his famous rondeau, *Adieu m'amour*, has imitation among all three voices. One gets the feeling that Dufay wrote such pieces to imitate a successful technique, not to work out a new one. Dufay was also capable of writing a piece like *Mon chier amy*, different from Guillaume de Machaut only in personal inflection.

The generation after Dufay produced Walter Frye (active around 1450), who wrote three cyclic masses on sacred cantus firmi and a devotional piece that became so popular it needs to be quoted as a typical example of the mid-century song motet. Frye's *Ave regina* (Example 44) is a convenient example of the clear functions of cantus, tenor, and contratenor relative to each other at this

EXAMPLE 44   WALTER FRYE: FROM A SONG MOTET

EXAMPLE 44 (CONTINUED)

(Hail, Queen of heaven, mother of the king of angels; O Mary, flower of virgins, as
the rose, the lily . . .)

time. In many pieces (as also in Dufay's *Adieu m'amour*), tenor and cantus can
be sung as a duo without the contratenor. Often called *tenor-discant duet*
(*discant* is another name for the top voice), this duo is a complete statement of
the two-part framework of the piece.

This arrangement is not novel; it goes back to Guillaume de Machaut,
and before him all the way back to the early stages of the motet. But relative to
the immediate past—to the late 1300s—the two-part framework has in Dufay's
time been subtly modified so that it is not only structural but lyric as well. The
modifications consist in an increase in the number of thirds and sixths that are
actually included in the framework, whereas a few decades earlier the thirds
and sixths were apt to be provided by the harmonizing contratenor. These structural thirds and sixths permit more stepwise conduct of the parts as well as
more richness of sound between the two parts.

As if to ratify this subtle adjustment in the relationship of parts, the
tenor now often carries a text, the same text as the cantus but not necessarily
sung at exactly the same time. Here, too, a subtle compromise has been found
between polytextual forms such as the motet, the accompanied song, and the
primitive simultaneous declamation of text in all voices. The vocal duet with
instrumental contratenor is one of the most distinctive textures of small forms
toward 1450.

The frequency of thirds and sixths also, however, makes necessary more
progressions in parallels, or alternately, more unresolved progressions, as thirds
and sixths are led to each other rather than to fifths or octaves. The framework
becomes richer, but functionally unstable; more lyric, but less directed. The
contratenor is forced to stand apart, but in compensation it can harmonize the
sixths from below more easily than it could harmonize fifths or octaves. All this
took place within the confines of the smaller forms; when conceived as general
principles and applied on a grand scale, these techniques were to bring about a
new style.

6

FRANCO-FLEMISH MASS AND MOTET 1450-1500

AFTER 1450 MUSIC BECAME INCREASINGLY SUBTLE AND SOPHISTI-
cated. The keyword of the new style was *harmony*, in the sense of a synthesis of
varied materials in perfect balance and proportion. Out of a wide spectrum of
novelties produced in the early 1400s, composers selected those most expressive,
and then found ways to combine them into a convincing style. Four-voiced
texture, the low harmonizing contratenor, rich sonorities, choral timbre—all
these techniques, already in use, were combined after 1450 to produce a new
ideal of sound.

HARMONY AND THE NEW STYLE The treatment of three-note sonorities
was the most obvious feature of the new style. The three-note chord that we call
a *triad* was not yet an entity, but rather the result of enriching a fifth with a
third. It was still used, as in the 1300s, because of its unstable and evocative
sound. But instead of using it once in a while for a special effect, composers now
used it continually. The problem to be worked out was a technical one: composers had to find ways to make counterpoint produce this continual stream of
harmony with convincing lyricism.

Even before 1450, as we saw, traditional counterpoint was under strong
pressure from the need for rich sonority. Modern style after 1400 emphasized
the less stable elements (thirds and sixths) of the two-part framework, covering
up the more stable ones (fifths and octaves). In the traditional system of interval progressions, thirds and sixths were expected to proceed to the more con-

sonant fifths and octaves; a third or sixth that did not so proceed (if it was a basic interval of the framework) was considered unresolved. Unresolved thirds and sixths had been carefully placed in the old style to strengthen the overall shape of the framework, facilitating its progress from one resting point to the next. In the new style the unresolved thirds and sixths were often used to deflect the framework from its expected course.

Exploited in many devious ways, the traditional progressions assumed fantastic shapes between 1450 and 1500. The sounds of music became richer, while the shapes lost their clarity and direction. The two-part framework, still for a time the basis of musical composition, was treated in such a way as to become almost unrecognizable, for composers now used the old principles and techniques in the most oblique, noncommittal ways they could find. Variety, not clarity, became the distinguishing feature of polyphony.

The new ideals of sound and texture brought with them new approaches to musical form. The clear progressions of the stately old motet were now as inappropriate as the more intimate but equally clear song forms, especially the ballade. The song forms gradually withered away, the rondeau hanging on until 1500, when it, too, was generally replaced by a type of secular piece called simply *chanson* for lack of a more precise indication; none was possible from a formal point of view, since each chanson tended to have its own musical or poetic form.

The techniques characteristic of the big motet in the early 1400s—cantus-firmus tenor and strictly periodic rhythm—were rarely combined after 1450 to produce an isorhythmic motet, and then only for ceremonial purposes. But separately these techniques lived on; liberated, in a sense, from the task of controlling the musical form as it was presented to the ear, the cantus firmus became subjected to most extraordinary contortions and permutations. Deep within the sounding texture the cantus firmus was sung backward or upside down, its notes and rhythms selected and combined in ever-changing orders at the fancy of the composer. Such elaborate constructions occurred after 1450 in unprecedented frequency. They had been used before, as we saw, but had been understood only as whimsical exceptions. Now taken seriously, these constructions helped guide the composer through the maze of rich, varied harmonies out of which he would build his work.

While from within the musical form might be controlled by the most sophisticated construction, its outer shape was now much more dependent upon the composer's intuitive sense of proportion. Gross, external features of form, such as changes of texture from two voices to four, came to be more important than the tonal order of the cantus firmus. As a corollary, the rhetorical or syntactical structure of the text, rather than its poetic form, came to control the disposition of musical material.

Finally, composers turned decisively to the sacred liturgy, to the mass, finding there shapes for the new style. The cyclic mass, a creation of the preceding age, was seized by composers after 1450 as an ideal musical form. Remembering the grandeur of the motet, now no longer usable because of its too obvious structures, composers transferred its universality and grandeur to the cyclic mass. The new composer forged the five sections of the cyclic mass (*Kyrie, Gloria, Credo, Sanctus, Agnus Dei*) into a unique artistic unity, either by sophisticated manipulation of a cantus firmus or by a dimly perceptible sense of harmony and proportion. With boundless ambition, he put his personal stamp on Holy Communion.

Throughout the period 1450 to 1600 the best composers and singers came from a surprisingly small area centered roughly on Cambrai, near the Franco-Belgian border. At the great urban cathedrals of the North the new composers learned their trade as choirboys, and—after their voices changed—as regular choristers, conductors, and composers. But the style they wrote, so rich in purely musical implications, found its most characteristic setting in the ducal chapel, an ornament of courtly life on which nobility spent vast resources. A chapel was the whole religious apparatus necessary for a duke, his family, and court; it included a special priest (chaplain), acolytes, choirmaster, choir of boys and men, (originally for singing chant but now increasingly for polyphony), vestments, furnishings, and a special room or building. The last item was sometimes the most expensive, often an architectural gem decorated with priceless paintings and tapestries; but it was actually the least necessary item, and, of course, had to be left behind when the duke went traveling, while the rest of the chapel—choir included—often traveled with him. In his chapel the duke saw to it that he and the liturgy were surrounded by the best that he could afford and procure. A sumptuous cloak of varied, yet homogeneous, harmony, covering the liturgy from one end to the other, was one of the most important elements of a properly appointed chapel. In return for so glorifying the liturgy—and the duke—the cyclic mass found in the chapel a setting uniquely suited to its incredibly rich, ultrasophisticated nature.

The most famous court of the mid-1400s was that of the dukes of Burgundy, especially under Charles, who during the 1450s was prince of Charolais, then from 1467 to 1477 Charles the Bold. Many important composers and singers worked at one time or another in the Burgundian chapel. But from mid-century on, the idea of a splendid musical establishment became popular with the dukes of northern Italy—the Medici (Florence), Sforza (Milan), Gonzaga (Mantua), Este (Ferrara)—all of them rich, some of them recently so, all eager to emulate the older, more sophisticated courts of the North. All spent money lavishly to get the best music modern culture could provide. Northern musicians in residence, like Tuscan painters and poets or Spanish ironwork, became a means to glory.

DUFAY AND OCKEGHEM   One of the most striking indications of the change of style around 1450 is the difference between Dufay's earlier works and his late masses. As we saw, Dufay had written service music for the mass alongside his great ceremonial motets in the 1430s. Toward 1440 he started to write cantus-firmus masses. Dufay's *Missa Caput,* an early example, used a sacred Latin cantus firmus, while his *Missa Se la face ay pale* (around 1450), built on the tenor of a chanson, preserved the graceful cadences of the chanson style of which Dufay was master.

It is after *Missa Se la face ay pale* that a break occurs in Dufay's style. Into that break may fall an early mass by the leading composer of the younger generation, Johannes Ockeghem (ca 1420–1495). Ockeghem's *Missa L'Homme armé* is a cyclic mass based on what was to be the most famous cantus firmus of the next century. We do not know the source of the tune *L'Homme armé,* nor the significance of its text; nor do we know which is the first mass based upon it—Dufay's, Ockeghem's, or possibly an earlier work now lost.

Except for Dufay's *Se la face ay pale, L'Homme armé* is the first secular tune known to be used as the basis for a cyclic mass. It has certain structural features advantageous to this purpose (features it shares with certain virelais used as tenors in the 1300s). Moving mostly stepwise in simple shapes through well-defined areas, it falls into several very clear phrases that can easily be detached one from another. Its notes can be lengthened to make it suitable for tenor construction without destroying its basic shape. In a large work it permits a varied tonal structure, yet one that has a clear symmetry. It can be easily harmonized from below in a variety of ways. While the tune has a distinct character, it can be extensively altered—its rhythm changed, or the tones and semitones rearranged—without negating any of the other desirable features. Finally, it was identified with a text that has, and had, a mysterious reference never made entirely clear: who was the Armed Man?

Ockeghem's *Missa L'Homme armé,* possibly written in the 1450s, was to be one of two masses by him based strictly on a cantus firmus, in which the ready-made tune appeared intact in every one of the five movements. Its overall shape is comparable to its predecessor's: each of the five movements is divided into sections either by a change of texture from four voices to episodic duos or trios or by a change in meter from the broad opening triple time to faster duple time (a change typical of the old motet). The rhythm of the cantus firmus is modified from one movement to another. All these features can be found, for example, in Dufay's *Missa Se la face ay pale;* still, Ockeghem's work is distinctly novel in its basic musical fabric—novel in a way that was to be characteristic of all his works to come, and in a wider sense, characteristic of all progressive music of the last half of the century, and this in spite of the youthful appearance of the work, its lack of polish and maturity.

The novelty of Ockeghem's *Missa L'Homme armé* is subtle; the difference between it and a Dufay mass is sometimes only a difference in personal style or taste. It is interesting to compare Ockeghem's mass with the immediately preceding *Missa Se la face ay pale,* but an even more interesting comparison can be made with a mass Dufay wrote during the 1450s, presumably right after Ockeghem's, on the same cantus firmus; at any rate, the two *L'Homme armé* masses are closely related, revealing a keen rivalry between the old master and the energetic young man.

Dufay's melismatic style in the duos was, as we saw, his most successful. Ockeghem could scarcely hope to do better, but he did manage something just different enough to have its own identity. The duo for bass and tenor from *Agnus Dei II* (Example 45) shows a restless intensity unlike Dufay's animated yet basically serene style. The reasons for this difference can be grasped more easily from a comparison of four-voiced passages. In Example 46 the beginnings of *Kyrie I* are reduced to their basic sonorities (*a* and *c*), and then further reduced to the underlying two-part framework (*b* and *d*). The reduced portions each begin with a statement of the cantus firmus in the tenor; Dufay's *Kyrie* (which has four measures introductory trio before the cantus firmus enters) begins in the example at its fifth measure. The comparison of the reductions

EXAMPLE 45   OCKEGHEM: FROM *AGNUS DEI II, MISSA L'HOMME ARME*

(That takest away the sins of the world . . .)

shows how close the two works are; one is obviously based on the other, chord
for chord, at least in these opening portions. The differences, therefore, can be
taken as significant.

In general the two-part framework for the first four measures is similar,
moving from G to G, in Dufay's case, with regular contrary motion and the
usual approach through parallel sixths. Ockeghem's framework is slightly more
erratic (also more difficult to isolate from the four-voiced texture), especially
in the second measure. But when fleshing out the framework to four voices,
Ockeghem already has distorted it; Dufay's arrangement, while rich, reflects
the shape of the original framework, but Ockeghem's obscures it.

From the fifth measure on, the cantus-firmus tenor rests, and the other
three voices move more fluidly, the basic chords changing more rapidly in both
composers. While in the fifth and sixth measures the sonorities correspond
closely, the traditional two-part progressions, clearly perceptible in Dufay, are
almost impossible to isolate from Ockeghem's version. Ockeghem's seventh measure seems to have no parallel in Dufay; the progression from measure 7 to 8 is
the same as Dufay's 6 to 7 (the sixth G–B flat going to the octave A–A), but
approached by Ockeghem much more freely. In Ockeghem's measures 6 and 7
the result of his new technique can be clearly seen: the interval progressions,
wrenched from their normal course, take on strange, expressive shapes.

This comparison has involved only details of a short passage, revealing
only a very subtle difference; yet it is precisely this difference, repeated again
and again, that lies between the old style and the new. We can imagine that
Dufay heard and felt something new going on in young Ockeghem's mass;
anxious not to be left behind, he tried to imitate it in a work written especially

EXAMPLE 46   REDUCTIONS OF DUFAY, *KYRIE, MISSA L'HOMME ARME* AND OCKEGHEM, *KYRIE, MISSA L'HOMME ARME*

(a)   Dufay

(b)

(c)   Ockeghem

(d)

* = cantus firmus

to compete with Ockeghem. But the old master's ear and hand were too skilled in the old phrase shapes; he could not, or would not, distort what had taken him thirty years to control. Dufay could not spring the voices loose from the traditional rhythms and progressions of the two-part framework. He could only superimpose his perfect cantilena on top of those progressions. Young Ockeghem, with more driving energy than grace and skill, moved and shifted his parts about sometimes arbitrarily or whimsically, clouding the clear shapes of the past, overriding the demands of the traditional framework in search of the expressive and the unusual.

Dufay's last two masses, *Missa Ecce ancilla* (before 1463) and *Missa Ave regina coelorum* (after 1464) reveal a continuing effort to follow the style of the younger generation. They abound with exuberant melismas in the duos and trios, while the progressions in the four-voiced sections occasionally move in peculiar ways. Although it can hardly be said that Dufay wrote anything less than beautiful music, still there is a persistent stylistic discrepancy between the graceful phrase shapes reminiscent of his earlier style and the newer intrusions. Dufay was never at home in the new style; sometimes his attempts at the new kind of melodic effusion seem mechanical or contrived (for example, at *Qui tollis* in the *Gloria* of *Missa Ecce ancilla*) compared with Ockeghem's more fantastic but more lyrical flights. No matter how much Dufay applied rhythmic triplets or strange progressions involving accidentals—devices remembered from his youth and belonging to a still earlier age—he could not get his underlying framework moving with sufficient irregularity to make the intended effect of fantasy completely convincing.

Dufay's late style is perhaps best studied in his motet *Ave regina coelorum,* using the same cantus firmus and some of the same counterpoint as the mass by the same name. This motet, the best work of its kind in the 1450s or 1460s, is valued because of the way the suave harmonies and graceful lines fill out the symmetrical, static phrase shapes; it is a testimonial of the serene, profound order Dufay brought to music at the end of a phase of development.

OCKEGHEM'S MATURE WORKS   In the meantime the new art developed rapidly in the cyclic mass, benefiting from the standards set by Dufay but otherwise leaving him behind. Ockeghem wrote a *Missa Caput,* using the same cantus firmus as Dufay's earlier work. This, too, is perhaps an early work of Ockeghem; the conduct of the individual voices does not seem to clothe the cantus firmus with sufficiently animated figuration—as if Ockeghem's attention were focused here on the progressions of harmonies he erected on the tune placed in the bass. This curiously unfigured style or chordal texture can also be found in the *Christe* of the *Missa L'Homme armé*.

In Ockeghem's *Missa Ecce ancilla* the rivalry with Dufay can still be traced, even though Ockeghem uses an entirely different cantus firmus. Once again the beginnings of the two masses can be profitably compared. As we saw in the previous chapter, one of the first ways of unifying a mass cycle was to place at the head of each movement an emblem, a short motif insignificant in itself, but demonstrating, as it returned at the beginning of each of the five sections, that they belonged together as the work of a single composer. Hence, even though only the first measure of Ockeghem's *Missa Ecce ancilla* is identical with Dufay's, this identity, occurring as it does at that significant point, serves to relate the two works.

The selection of the cantus firmus and its treatment are of great importance for Ockeghem's development. Dufay had used two separate antiphons (*Ecce ancilla* and *Beata es*), which he distributed around each movement of the mass in such a way as to emphasize the sectional structure. In *Kyrie* and *Gloria,* for example, he used the two antiphons for the first and third sections of each movement, with a free duo or trio in between. Ockeghem, for his *Missa Ecce ancilla,* used the second half of a large chant, *Missus est angelus Gabriel.* The chant was ornate and somewhat diffuse in its overall shape; although Ockeghem used its pitches in normal order much of the time, he sometimes selected and combined isolated phrases not according to any regular scheme, but freely and differently on each presentation. Finally, the chant moves almost as fast as the other voices. The cantus firmus more and more resembles the traditionally melodic cantus—as do also the high and low contratenor. Example 47 contains

EXAMPLE 47   OCKEGHEM: *AGNUS DEI III, MISSA ECCE ANCILLA*

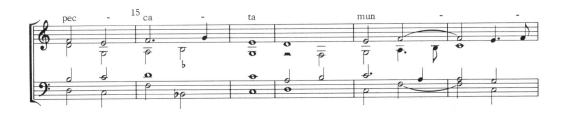

EXAMPLE 47 (CONTINUED)

(O Lamb of God, that takest away the sins of the world, grant us thy peace!)

the final *Agnus Dei* from *Missa Ecce ancilla.*

    The resulting texture consists of four very similar voices, any one of which may be the cantus firmus. This style is sometimes seen as a rapprochement between polyphony and chant, as if each of the four voices were made to sound like chant, and music was understood to be four lines of chant sounding at once. While this description offers a valuable insight into certain aspects of Ockeghem's style, it is important to remember, first, that any similarity to chant would be something new in the history of polyphony—a modern revival, not an ancient continuing tradition. In the second place, detailed studies have made it clear that while such melodic lines give the illusion of chant, it is only an illusion that vanishes upon close scrutiny. Ockeghem's lines (except for a cantus firmus) are not chant, they are polyphonic voices taking on certain shapes under the pressure of polyphonic development. In *Missa Ecce ancilla* it is not the tenor cantus firmus that sets the style for the other voices; rather, it has been selected and treated so that it will approximate them—their new melodic surge. The

tendency in Ockeghem is away from a cantus firmus that holds strictly to the
original pitches of a piece of chant, indeed, away from cantus firmus altogether.

In his masses Ockeghem fused the traditional arrangements of voices into
a new four-voiced texture. He needed, on one hand, a texture more opulent,
more solemn than that of the song motet *a 3,* on the other hand, more fluid than
that of the large cantus-firmus motet *a 4.* Abandoning the slow contratenor of
the big motet (along with its partner, the slow tenor), Ockeghem split up the
more animated contratenor of the song forms into two voices, a low contratenor
(*contratenor bassus*) and a high one (*contratenor altus*). Then he added these
two contratenors to a tenor-discant duo, the bass contratenor lying below the
tenor, the high contratenor falling more or less between tenor and cantus.

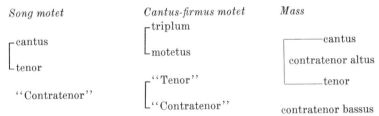

Song motet   *Cantus-firmus motet*   *Mass*

                 ┌triplum
┌cantus   └motetus   ┌——————cantus
└tenor   contratenor altus
                 ┌"Tenor"   └——————tenor
 "Contratenor"   └"Contratenor"   contratenor bassus

The essential change was in the nature of tenor and low contratenor:
both now became lyric like the cantus. The actual ranges were not sharply
defined, especially when the voices all lay low, as they often did in Ockeghem.
The naming varied considerably: either contratenor might be called by its full
name, or simply *contratenor,* or *altus* or *bassus,* respectively. The cantus, being
a texted part, was traditionally not named in musical sources. Its name now
fluctuated between *cantus* and *discantus,* and eventually *superius,* the upper
voice, a necessary term when all voices came to carry text and to be songlike.

The relation of cantus firmus to the character of the newly composed
voices is strikingly apparent in the endings of movements. Ockeghem frequently
adds to the tenor cantus firmus a free extension, the tenor moving somewhat
faster and in a very exuberant manner in which the other voices join. This type
of ending is Ockeghem's analog of the older practice of making the last cantus
firmus statement faster than preceding ones, a practice indigenous to the motet
and found in mass cycles that stand close to the motet, like *Missa Se la face ay
pale* and *Missa L'Homme armé.* Instead of making the cantus firmus go faster
for a final surge, Ockeghem would rather compose his own tenor. As he gained
skill in handling his new fluid texture, he eventually abandoned the cantus
firmus completely.

Even though Ockeghem's four voices each comes to possess a compelling
melodic nature, a life of its own, his music is basically not four independent
melodies. There are several factors in Ockeghem's texture—the frequent voice
crossings, the density, the prevailing low tessitura—which make it impossible to
discern clearly four separate melodies. What Ockeghem was really after was a
new surge to the whole progression of sonorities that made up polyphony. This
surge could most easily be set in motion in the duos; thirds and sixths could be
handled freely in duo style, and a liberal use of syncopations made it possible
to slip in and out of any too solid progression. It was easier to produce a new,

animated figuration in duo style; Dufay's duos, as we saw, often had a far more progressive effect than his four-voiced sections. The effort to make four voices move like two occupied composers throughout the last half of the century.

That Ockeghem was concerned with this problem in terms of sonority, not just individual melodies, is apparent from his continued cultivation of a special style in which the voices moved smoothly but with little independent animation. This style gradually matured, merging slightly with the duo style but gaining greater strength as the traditional two-part progressions were handled with greater subtlety. Ockeghem found ways to use the traditional cadences—ways to clothe them with counterpoint and ways to place them in the phrase structure so that they would contribute to the organization of the whole without overly articulating it (as at meas. 9, 17, 29 of Example 47). Gradually he learned to write a new kind of melody, in which four similar parts urged one another on in continual but discreet syncopations, leading smoothly from one rich chord to the next. And more and more Ockeghem found the magic effects of which this four-voice melody was capable, as at the end of Example 47.

It is extremely difficult to determine the proper placement of text in music such as that of Example 47, since the original manuscripts are indecisive. As far as composition was concerned, composers from Dufay on to 1500 seemed interested only in the distribution of large segments of text to large segments of music, for example, of the text *Agnus Dei . . . pacem* to measures 1 to 40 of Example 47. While it was important to the composer's concept to have the text sung, exactly how it was sung seems to have been less important. When they supervised performances (as they regularly did), composers may well have been particular about text placement; but what that placement was we cannot usually determine during this period. Nor can we determine how many voices were sung, how many played on instruments. Distribution of parts, like text placement and application of musica ficta, now probably varied considerably from one occasion to another. Intelligent, imaginative, flexible solutions continue to be a challenge to reconstruction of music from 1450 to 1500.

After Ockeghem's two early masses, *Caput* and *L'Homme armé*, we cannot yet determine the order in which the rest were composed. *Missa Ecce ancilla,* using a sacred chant as a cantus firmus, represented the first type of cyclic mass, the kind that stood in technique closest to the old motet; but it also demonstrated how fast and how far Ockeghem moved away from the strict form of a cantus firmus as a foundation. For various reasons, *Missa Ecce ancilla* seems not to be a late work; but we cannot place it more precisely. There seem, however, to be no other masses by Ockeghem that use a sacred cantus firmus; hence *Missa Ecce ancilla* stands at the end of that line of development in Ockeghem's work.

There is another group of Ockeghem's masses that, like Dufay's *Missa Se la face ay pale,* use a part or parts of a secular song as ready-made material. *Missa Ma maistresse,* following earlier practice, is a *Kyrie-Gloria* pair; it is built upon Ockeghem's own bergerette (one-stanza virelai), *Ma maistresse.* Without being overly short, the work tends toward the balanced phrases and sweet melody of the secular chanson, even though Ockeghem's inner surge drives the voices on in his own special way. In *Missa Au travail suis,* based on a rondeau by a composer named Barbinguant (perhaps identical with Jacobus Barbireau, died 1491, likewise obscure), the tendency toward chanson style is much stronger; sections are much shorter, phrases more concise and more songlike, the whole cast of the work less serious. It has, however, some interesting features: the movements begin with imitative entries on the material of the rondeau, sometimes antici- pating the "cantus firmus"—the line actually taken from the rondeau. Also this mass has several acclamations in chordal style. Such things are novel neither to polyphony nor to the mass nor to Ockeghem; but here he found a place for them in the midst of the new animated style, as a change of texture, a relief from the restless counterpoint. Chordal acclamations were to continue as one of the basic textural alternatives.

Ockeghem's *Missa De plus en plus,* drawing material from a rondeau by Binchois, is a much more ambitious work on the scale of *Missa Ecce ancilla.* While still permeated with songlike elements, it reaches out for the eloquence characteristic of Ockeghem's mature style. Graceful phrases like *Et unam sanctam* (Example 48a) stand beside more imaginative passages like *Pleni sunt coeli* (Example 48b). The chordal sections, as at *Osanna* (Example 48c) are apt to be more carefully made.

Why composers of this time should base the music of the mass upon secular, amorous songs is a perplexing question, one that remains without a completely satisfactory answer. But the use of ready-made material in a cyclic mass had a specific stylistic purpose, namely, to give a particular mass an identity distinct from all other masses. The use of a secular song as ready-made material has to be evaluated not in terms of the song, but rather of its function in the mass, and on the same basis with other kinds of ready-made material.

The treatment of cantus firmus throughout the 1400s is so idiosyncratic as to require a work-by-work analysis. The use of the same material by two different composers only highlights this individuality, requiring and facilitating a close comparison of their respective technical and imaginative abilities. The most important stylistic trend of the whole period is the inevitable rapproche- ment among individual styles. As each composer made music more harmonious, more perfect in blend, balance, and proportion, the more did his style resemble the next man's, until finally there was to be one perfect style. These composers lived uncomfortably close to one another and to the past. Ockeghem's handling of the traditional two-part framework is really not so different from Dufay's; he had to strain to make it as different as it is. The imaginative use of ready- made material—particularly if the material itself bore only a whimsical rela- tionship to the subject, as it did in the case of a chanson—was one way of giving a mass a personal signature.

Ockeghem's remaining masses each have such an identity, achieved each in a different way. The *Missa Fors seulement (Kyrie, Gloria, Credo)* for five voices, is based upon material from Ockeghem's own chanson, which he used here in a way far more complex than in his other chanson masses. The increase to five voices is only the outward aspect of an increase in complexity unusual for chanson masses and rivaling other, more serious types. The fifth voice is an extra bass, lying below the usual one and emphasizing the dark colors used so often by Ockeghem. An extraordinary effect occurs at the beginning of the *Qui tollis* of the *Gloria,* marking the usual division of the section into a first section in triple time and a faster one in duple time; here the low bass begins a set of imitative

EXAMPLE 48   OCKEGHEM: EXCERPTS FROM *MISSA DE PLUS EN PLUS*

(a)   From *Credo*

(b)   From *Sanctus*

(c)   From *Sanctus*

(a) (And one, holy, catholic, and apostolic [church] . . .
(b) Heaven and earth are full [of thy glory . . .])

entries rising out of the depths. Imaginative effects such as this were increasingly sought out by the best composers of Ockeghem's time. In the *Credo* the low bass moves slightly higher, the texture thins out more frequently to duos and trios, and the whole tone of the work lightens considerably.

The *Missa cuiusvis toni,* though apparently not based on ready-made material, has the character of a chanson mass, resembling *Missa Au travail suis* in dimensions and songlike cadence. Its individuality consists in the fact that it can be sung starting on "any tone you wish" (cuiusvis toni), that is, *re, mi, fa,* or *ut,* resulting in an approximation of the four finals used for old chant, or the four authentic modes called *dorian, phrygian, lydian, mixolydian.* The *Missa prolationum,* also apparently without ready-made material, is a more serious work containing some of Ockeghem's most intricate and expressive duos, as well as some intensely smoldering passages *a 4,* highly characteristic of his new style. The identity of this work, like that of *Missa cuiusvis toni,* is attached to its technical construction. Only two of the four voices are notated, the other two being in canon. The canons, furthermore, are brought about by an ingenious manipulation of the traditional system of notation (mensuration canon)—an example of how Ockeghem's generation put to serious, if obscure, use devices previously employed more playfully and more clearly.

The movements of the *Missa mi–mi* are related to each other by the use of an initial motif in the bass—two bass notes a fifth apart, each a *mi;* there seems to be no ready-made material. While the work has expressive duos, they do not rival those of *Missa prolationum* in intensity. What gives *Missa mi–mi* its very special character is that all movements end on *mi,* casting an evocative darkness over the work, and incidentally giving the *mi–mi* motif a profound significance. The endings on *mi* make the mass sound phrygian (in one source it is called "Mass in the fourth tone"). It seems to be the first mass written with such endings, paralleled, however, by darkly expressive chansons such as Ockeghem's virelai *Ma bouche rit.* Masses on *mi* with this phrygian effect soon became popular, suggesting an application of the old modal classifications— heretofore reserved for chant—to polyphony; the suggestion was soon to be taken up by theorists. Even more interesting is the implication for contrapuntal progressions: each cadence on *mi* is (by definition) reached from a sixth (*fa–re*) in which the semitone progression comes at the bottom instead of the top. This type of cadence was traditionally in an ouvert ending. Hence a mass on *mi* never really ends, a perfect expression of that magic sense of suspension found in every aspect of Ockeghem's mature style. Example 49 contains the first *Agnus Dei.*

Although chronology is largely guesswork in this period, we can probably place at least some of Ockeghem's mature masses in the 1470s, when he was approaching sixty and the end of his stylistic development. This development had taken place almost entirely in his masses. His chansons, while excellent, stand to one side, and his motets, extremely few in number, reflect the development in the mass rather than in the motet. Only one motet, *Alma redemptoris mater,* seems to reveal the full achievements of the mass. This excellent, apparently late, motet stands out among motets of the 1470s and 1480s just as Dufay's *Ave regina* does in the 1460s. The two works are very similar in certain

EXAMPLE 49 OCKEGHEM: *AGNUS DEI I, MISSA MI-MI*

EXAMPLE 49 (CONTINUED)

(O Lamb of God, that takest away the sins of the world, have mercy upon us!)

ways and can profitably be compared as examples of their composers' styles. There is, however, no direct development that leads from one to the other.

Composers active around 1475 tended to move stylistically between the extremes represented by Dufay and Ockeghem. Although he was Dufay's secretary in 1463, Regis (ca 1430–1485) sometimes inclined toward the more rhapsodic style of Ockeghem. Regis, Caron, and Faugues (all active ca 1460) all wrote masses on *L'Homme armé*. Faugues's mass placed the tune in canon—apparently the first instance of a cantus firmus used canonically in a cyclic mass. Antoine Busnois (died ca 1492) was the leading composer associated with the brilliant court of Burgundy around 1475. The taste at that court now tended to be conservative, reflecting cultural ideals of earlier decades; this conservatism is perhaps reflected in certain features of Busnois's work, especially his use of techniques associated with the old motet.

In other respects Busnois often writes a graceful, up-to-date, even progressive style. This is particularly true of his songs; here he was the leader of his generation. It was the turn now of the naïve rondeau to take on high artistic manners. In the hands of Busnois and his contemporaries, the rondeau affected imitative entries reminiscent of Hugo de Lantins, but more consistently worked out; canon, found occasionally in rondeaus, followed as the natural consequence of repeated imitative entries between tenor and cantus. The rondeau adopted the low contratenors that made the mass so richly sonorous. Finally the rondeau, less committed than the ballade to the procedures of the past, reflected more easily the new lyricism made possible by the free handling of the contrapuntal framework. Busnois's rondeau *Je ne demande* (Example 50) was sufficiently popular to become the material of chanson masses.

OBRECHT'S MASSES   Ockeghem's work opened up a whole new range of possibilities. The next generation, born 1440–1450, produced one of the most impressive rosters of first-rate composers in the history of Western music, a phenomenon at least partly due to the nature of Ockeghem's achievement. Whether or not these composers studied with him, he was in a real sense their teacher, for he provided them with models. This is true even of the oldest of the new generation, Jacob Obrecht (ca 1450–1505).

Obrecht's career, difficult to reconstruct, took him to the courts of northern Italy (Ferrara) as well as to the cathedrals of the North. His stylistic course

EXAMPLE 50 BUSNOIS: RONDEAU (first half)

EXAMPLE 50 (CONTINUED)

(I ask no social rank nor wealth . . .)

is more easy to follow; he concentrated on cyclic masses (twenty-seven, according to a recent count), and in the cyclic mass, on cantus-firmus technique. He
wrote a *Missa Caput* in obvious emulation of Ockeghem, whose model he followed closely; here Obrecht surpassed both Ockeghem and Dufay. Obrecht also
wrote a *Missa L'Homme armé*, apparently with Busnois in mind, but with the
cantus firmus altered to end on E, sounding phrygian.

Obrecht wrote several chanson masses, including *Missa Je ne demande*
(on Busnois's rondeau), *Missa Rosa playsant, Missa Forseulement, Missa Fortuna desperata* (on another Busnois song), and *Missa Malheur me bat*. There is
a tendency in these works to use more and more of the chanson model. Even
though Obrecht's starting point was a single voice of the model, used as a cantus
firmus, he soon used other voices as well, and finally two or three different
voices at once. It was only a step to working with the ready-made material as a
contrapuntal complex rather than as a source of melodic lines. This process
reaches an end point in *Missa Rosa playsant* when, in the *Pleni sunt caeli* of the
Sanctus, the polyphonic chanson is quoted in a perfectly recognizable form.
Having been made gradually aware that this mass was in some mysterious way
related to a familiar love song, the listener was finally, and abruptly, confronted
with that very song, undoubtedly to his great delight but, it is feared, also to
the distraction of his devotions.

The chanson masses, especially those on F (as are *Missa Je ne demande*
and *Missa Fortuna desperata*) are even more concise and songlike in their
phrases than Ockeghem's comparable works. Obrecht perfected a facile style
that had the depth (just barely) and the rich sonority appropriate to masses,
yet moved easily and clearly through well-defined tonal shapes and fluid scalar
figuration. Symptomatic of Obrecht's technique is his habit of rendering the
swinging lines of Ockeghem in parallel tenths, maximizing rich sound at the
expense of contrapuntal substance. But the result is seductively lyric and, furthermore, had not been done much before—which is perhaps the best excuse for
the sometimes monotonous sweetness of these chanson masses.

Missa Malheur me bat, however, is different—a cloudy, threatening work
like *Missa mi–mi*. Built on Ockeghem's rondeau, large portions of Obrecht's
mass revolve around E; but Obrecht stabilized the effect of the characteristic
half cadence by extending it to a full cadence on A at endings of sections. In
Missa Malheur me bat Obrecht essayed the high fantasy discovered by Ockeghem.

The end of the mass spins itself out over an especially ominous repeated figure in the bass, and then—to the horror of any theorist, then as now, but with complete artistic success—concludes with a long descending succession of what for convenience we can call parallel six-four chords.

Besides *Missa Malheur me bat,* some of Obrecht's best music appears in masses based on sacred models, chant or, in one case, polyphony. The *Missa Si dedero* uses a small motet by Alexander Agricola, another composer of Obrecht's generation. *Missa Salva diva parens* and *Missa Sicut spina* are on chants, but the latter, perhaps Obrecht's best work, is also related to *Missa mi–mi* and is on E.

Obrecht's main method of mass composition was to cut up the cantus firmus into segments, which he then arranged according to some objectively predetermined scheme. Combinations of several cantus firmi appear in the *Missa diversorum tenorum* and especially in the *Missa Sub tuum praesidium,* in which the chant name in the title is the real cantus firmus found throughout the mass; other chants in honor of the Virgin are added successively, as the number of voices increases from three to seven. It has been shown that Obrecht adjusted his materials to bring the number of metrical units out to the cabalistic number 888, and there is reason to believe that this was part of a comprehensive numerical plan for the whole mass. The point is, however, that the exact length of large mass sections by this time had no musically perceptible significance. In Philippe de Vitry's time, when motets were shorter and the rhythmic and tonal shape of the cantus firmus was manifest in the purely musical shape of the motet, furnishing as it did the bottom note and exact length of every underlying chord—then the length of a section made a difference. But in the late 1400s the cantus firmus no longer controlled directly either the length or the pitch of the harmonies; the other voices, including the bass, swirled around the cantus firmus; the richness of detail made the long-range plan—if there was one—musically imperceptible. Hence if a composer, for reasons of his own, chose to make the sections of a piece in the ratio 333:555, or any other set of numbers that struck his fancy, he was free to do so without affecting, for better or worse, the audible artwork.

JOSQUIN DES PRES   Obrecht's contemporaries included, besides Agricola, the eminent composers Heinrich Isaac (ca 1450–1517), Gasper van Weerbecke (ca 1445–after 1514), Loyset Compere (ca 1450–1518), Pierre de la Rue (ca 1460?–1518), Antoine Brumel (ca 1450?–after 1420), and—to pass over others simply for lack of space—Josquin Des Pres (ca 1440/1450–1521). Of those named Isaac was, next to Josquin, probably the most universal in accomplishment. Besides masses, motets, and songs in several languages, Isaac wrote a mighty cycle of mass propers called the *Choralis Constantinus.*

The cyclic mass remained the most weighty form for these composers, but they also wrote motets in greater numbers than their predecessors. Ockeghem had written very few motets; many of Obrecht's motets (of which there are perhaps two dozen) are ceremonial pieces *a 5,* with cantus firmi that carry texts different from the other parts, and some other conservative features. Josquin, on the other hand, wrote at least seventy or eighty motets. Clearly the other members of his generation had something to do with the rapid development of the motet in the 1480s and 1490s, but that story has not yet been put together. In any case, the composers listed all possessed individual styles of great persuasiveness; all of them were good, but Josquin was best. In his work we can study the last creative phase of the cyclic mass and the first of the new motet.

Josquin's masses, composed mostly during the 1480s and 1490s, reveal his mastery of the wide variety of styles and techniques developed by his predecessors and contemporaries. His *Missa L'Homme armé super voces musicales* places the cantus firmus on successively higher steps (*voces*) of the scale, thereby changing its tonal structure or mode, while the other voices return to D at the end of each section. Such manipulation shows the continuing competitive engagements with this tune among composers since Dufay and Ockeghem. Josquin's other *Missa L'Homme armé (sexti toni)* is a more lyric work, less encumbered by cantus-firmus manipulation; it is thought to be more mature. In this mass the cantus firmus behaves less like a cantus firmus, being taken up more into the contrapuntal flux. There is more imitation among all four voices as equals.

In the *Missa la sol fa re mi* the ready-made material, said to be derived from an Italian song beginning *Lascia fare a me* (Let *me* do it) is not really a cantus firmus at all, but simply a set of pitches, a subject, that recurs over and over with hypnotic persistency, treated in endlessly different ways. The mass can best be described as a fantasy; it is one of the *mi* masses, ending on E. *Missa Fortuna desperata* is a chanson mass (Busnois), but with technical developments that give it greater solemnity. *Missa Gaudeamus* is in several ways the most interesting and important of this group. It uses a sacred chant for a cantus firmus, but handles it with the freedom of a chanson mass, including much imitation *a 4;* the chant becomes more of a subject than a cantus firmus, the mass more of a fantasy.

Missa Ave maris stella (like *Missa Gaudeamus*) uses a sacred chant, a hymn, for a cantus firmus, treating it in consistent imitation *a 4* (Example 51). It is not immediately apparent, in fact, that the chant is being used as a cantus firmus and actually is "in" a single voice (the tenor), so extensively does the chant permeate the other voices and so thoroughly does the tenor take on their flowing character. Josquin here found a most elegant solution to the problem Ockeghem faced in *Missa Ecce ancilla* (and solved differently), the problem of freeing the musical flow from traditional tenor rhythms while still using a cantus firmus as a melodic symbol.

In the decades of Josquin's youth (the 1460s and 1470s) there had been two distinct types of motets—large and small. The large type was the moribund isorhythmic motet, the small type, the devotional song motet. By Josquin's time the song motet tended to have text in all voices, which were now homogeneous in melodic and rhythmic construction, at least, in the most modern examples. Ockeghem's most significant motet, *Alma redemptoris mater,* had achieved a fusion of these two types. Further development of the motet pursued this fusion in order to capitalize on the lyric flexibility of the small motet while raising it to an artistic level comparable to that previously represented by the isorhythmic motet. Composers of Josquin's generation wanted above all to be free of the progressions implied by an old-style tenor; yet they aspired to the grandeur found only in the constructions based upon such a tenor. Furthermore com-

EXAMPLE 51   JOSQUIN: *KYRIE I, MISSA AVE MARIS STELLA*

posers still—indeed, more than ever—liked to have a cantus firmus for the sake of its liturgical or devotional associations.

Josquin's seventy or eighty motets show a wide variety, partly reflecting the previous split in motet style, partly reflecting his own lively imagination and power of expression. There are huge works *a 5* and *a 6*, with cantus firmi pounding away in long notes but not sounding old-fashioned. At the other extreme there are songlike motets *a 3* and *a 4*. The use of cantus firmus does not necessarily coincide with the large motets, but it tends to.

More decisive for Josquin's use of cantus firmus is the type of text he chooses. He favors rhyming, scanning texts of the type developed after 1000 and closely related to the whole motet tradition; many of his texts, for example, are proses. It has been established that when Josquin uses a text that has its own traditional chant (usually not Gregorian but medieval in origin and style) he uses that tune one way or another, even if obscurely. But when Josquin set a text that did not have its own special tune, for instance, texts chanted to recitation formulas or especially psalm tones, then he proceeded with equal ease to compose works of comparable scope and power without a cantus firmus. Indeed, in Josquin's hands, all inherited contrapuntal techniques became plastic, flowing easily into whatever fantastic shapes he willed. It made no apparent difference to him whether he put both the *Ave Maria* and the *Pater noster,* with their tunes, into the same motet to be sung simultaneously, or whether he set the *Liber generationis Jesu Christi,* or Book of Generations (the endless "begats"), from the Gospel according to St. Matthew, in perfect lyricism of purely musical expressiveness.

His gift of fantasy transfigures even the most old-fashioned techniques: the grandiose motet *Praeter rerum seriem* uses a cantus firmus in long notes, with boiling triple-time figures in the accompanying counterpoint (Example 52). Here as elsewhere, Josquin made the detail sufficiently absorbing that the long notes of the cantus firmus have the effect of a mighty procession, rather than an endless drone. With or without a cantus firmus, Josquin sought breadth and sweep of tonal movement, by making the underlying sonorities change slowly or change in minimal ways that lacked the decisiveness—hence the triteness—of the traditional contrapuntal framework. Intricate, interesting figuration was a necessary aid to such broad tonal movement; part of Josquin's success is due to his never-failing supply of lyric ornament (Example 53).

In Josquin's masses, we saw that the cantus firmus tended to disappear in a maze of imitation as all voices became permeated with the chant subject. Imitation assumed special importance in Josquin's motets during the same decades that it appeared in his masses. There were, of course, many antecedents. Even though imitation of a cantus firmus was rare in the old motet, imitative duets preceding the entry of the cantus firmus were common in the 1400s, while imitation *a 3* had been used regularly in chansons, for example, those of Hugo de Lantins. What marked Josquin's imitation was the frequency as well as the flexibility with which he used it.

The basic problem facing Josquin was to expand and deepen the dimensions of the song motet. This type of motet might use a chant in paraphrase, but

EXAMPLE 52 JOSQUIN: FROM A MOTET

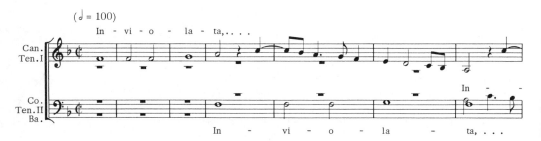

(Beyond the natural order of things . . .)

EXAMPLE 53 JOSQUIN: FROM A MOTET

(Inviolate, pure, and chaste art thou . . .)

not usually as a cantus firmus. Nor was a cantus firmus structurally desirable any more; yet the cantus firmus had been the foundation of large, impressive works. Josquin used the techniques of imitation to lend a sense of continuity to the motet. An imitative phrase seemed internally more integrated, more consistent; a succession of imitative phrases had something of the logic once provided by a cantus firmus.

Imitation was a more flexible technique than cantus firmus: it permitted not only more fluid chord progressions, but also more fluid treatment of texture. Indeed, a varied succession of textures, including but not limited to imitation, was now the basic shape of the motet. Josquin's imitative techniques are best studied in large works such as the *Liber generationis Jesu Christe* or *Planxit autem David,* David's lament for Saul and Jonathan. Here, too, one can become familiar with the style of Josquin's imitative subjects, beautifully suited to the smooth yet forceful forward motion characteristic of all his work.

For a special kind of motet, Josquin adopted the acclamations in common use throughout the 1400s. Sometimes he built most of a motet in this acclamatory style; the cycle of Passion motets, *O Domine Jesu Christe,* is synchronized declamation *a 4* almost from beginning to end. Solemnly intoned at the foot of the Cross, these devotional acclamations must have had a profound effect. Stripped of ornament as they are, the harmonies must move in ways neither too bizarre nor too traditional. Josquin's declamatory style presents an interesting study of his adaptation and harmonization of traditional two-part procedures.

Josquin's settings of psalm texts form a group apart. They may well be later than the rest; in any case they correspond more closely to motet developments after Josquin. Psalm texts were new to the motet tradition; they brought with them no specific cantus firmi, aside from the psalm tone formulas. In his psalm settings Josquin used a fluid alternation of all the textures known to him—animated figuration, short acclamations (more rapid than usual, suggesting psalmodic recitation itself), and imitation. Most important, he cultivated textures lying in between these common styles, textures that could be described either as staggered declamation or as imitation on a declamatory subject. This particular kind of imitation expressed his slow-moving sonorities in an animated, ruffled manner. More inflected subjects for imitation were often built so that they involved no real change of chords or only a very slight change.

In his best psalms Josquin included spectacular effects on the scale of his masses. The huge psalm *Caeli enarrant* begins with the broad rhythms of widely spaced imitative entries on a subject that moves only between E and F. Toward the close of the third part (Example 54) Josquin sets the text ''And I shall be cleansed from all iniquity'' to sweeping downward scales, first in thirds, then sixths, then stunning thirds and sixths together, as in fauxbourdon—but how different! This passage is followed immediately by a typical imitative passage *a 4,* the voices piling up for a normal cadence on G. The setting continues with imitative duos.

Josquin's work culminates in two late masses, *Missa Pange lingua* and *Missa De beata virgine. Missa Pange lingua* paraphrases a hymn (see page 45); appearing nowhere as a complete cantus firmus, the hymn everywhere permeates the fabric of the mass in the style of *Missa Ave maris stella.* The mass has the fluidity of Josquin's psalm settings, the brilliance and exaltation of his other

EXAMPLE 54 JOSQUIN: FROM *CAELI ENARRANT* (motet)

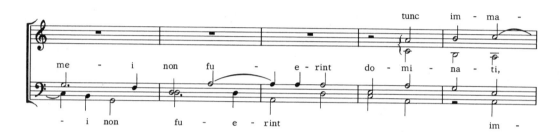

EXAMPLE 54 (CONTINUED)

(. . . [from presumptuous sins] keep thy servant, lest they get the dominion over me;
so shall I be undefiled, and innocent of the great offence. Let the words of my
mouth . . .)

masses and big cantus-firmus motets. One of the last of the phrygian masses, it
is the greatest; it may well be the greatest cyclic mass of two centuries.

The *Missa De beata virgine* paraphrases a different chant in each section—a *Kyrie* chant in the *Kyrie,* a *Gloria* chant (with one of the few surviving
tropes) in the *Gloria,* and so for the rest. This use of chant was not important
in the formative stages of the cyclic mass, since it contributed little to the cyclic
quality. But as the cantus-firmus mass receded in importance, the paraphrase
mass stepped forward. Josquin, in what is perhaps his last mass, raised the
paraphrase mass to a new level of excellence.

Josquin's secular songs, following the lead of Busnois, contain a curious
mixture of a very smooth, frequently imitative style, with elaborately hidden

canons. The canon usually involves a clearly shaped tune, presumably ready-made and well known. *Se congie prens* (*a 6*!) has such a tune in canon in two inner parts, surrounded by four voices in imitative texture. Since such tunes have distinct phrases, sometimes in a repetitive pattern (although not in one of the old song forms) the whole chanson may have an orderly design, but scarcely audible because it is cloaked in dense, expressive counterpoint.

TUNING AND TEMPERAMENT. During Josquin's maturity theoretical speculation about music went through a particularly intense phase, especially in Italy. On one hand, traditional concepts like the hexachord were given a drastically expanded interpretation, resulting in a completely chromatic tonal system. On the other hand, new applications of mathematics led eventually to a new, specific concept of harmony, which we will take up later in connection with Zarlino. But the topic that seemed to evoke the most heated debate around 1500 was tuning, that is, the proper sizes of intervals.

Up to the 1400s, Western theorists had commonly prescribed the so-called "pythagorean tuning," which called for perfect fifths and fourths (in the ratios 2:3 and 3:4, respectively), but allowed large, dissonant thirds (64:81). The size of the third as a simultaneous interval was immaterial in chant; but from 1200 on, there are signs that in actual performance of part music the sizes of thirds were being adjusted in response to their new function.

Soon after 1450 the new sizes of thirds were given theoretical definition, at first naïvely, by Bartolomé Ramos de Pareja (ca 1440–after 1491), later with more sophistication by others. Modern counterpoint, now full of thirds, needed consonant ones. It was easy enough to specify the required sizes of thirds; ratios of 4:5 (for major thirds) and 5:6 (for minor ones) produced sweet, natural, consonant intervals that made the new harmony come alive. The problem was to combine these perfect thirds into a tuning system with perfect fifths. A complete tonal system containing both types of intervals cannot be built.

Theorists around 1500, and throughout the 1500s, were concerned with various compromises. Choral music could adjust the sizes of intervals as the piece progressed, tuning up prominent chords wherever possible. (This would have entailed slight changes of pitch level within the performance of a piece.) But keyboard instruments such as organ or harpsichord, increasingly in evidence after 1450, demanded some kind of fixed tuning. The one most favored during the 1500s, and right up to the 1800s in some cases, was *meantone temperament*. It was called *meantone* because the pure third was divided in half (by temperament, not arithmetic) by a *mean* or middle tone, and *temperament* because the arithmetic ratios were *tempered,* or tampered with to produce the necessary compromise.

Besides pure thirds on most of the white notes of the keyboard, meantone temperament involved slightly flat fifths and also several false fifths and dissonant thirds on black notes. When tuned in meantone, a keyboard could approximate the sweet sonorities of a vocal ensemble. (Approximate, not reproduce.) Various multimanual keyboard instruments (based on sophisticated fractional division of the whole tone) were built during the 1500s to allow more perfect tunings. Such instruments are tangible evidence of the intensity with which musicians of this century searched for the ideal of perfect harmony.

PETRUCCI AND MUSIC PRINTING   Josquin's maturity, and that of his generation, coincided with the first successful attempts to print polyphonic music on a commercial scale. In 1501 Ottaviano Petrucci, in Venice, began issuing publications of all kinds of polyphony. Some of his publications were anthologies of sacred or secular pieces; others were collections of masses by individual composers. The first volume of masses (1502) contained five by Josquin (the first five discussed, beginning on page 173). Comparable sets by Obrecht and others followed, but Josquin was the only composer to be favored by a second and then a third set.

The development of commercial music printing eventually made a substantial impact on the social position of music; but this impact was felt slowly, and only where it was supported by other social factors—by demand, in other words. Music printing, as undertaken by Petrucci and a few other adventurers in the early 1500s, did not make the world's great music immediately available to the mass of European music lovers. There was, in the first place, no such mass market for modern polyphony, which depended upon a courtly or ecclesiastical elite for its appreciation. (Monophony in various forms continued to be the principal kind of popular music.) In the second place, the production of a printed music book was apt to be a more laborious, more expensive process than the making of a manuscript copy, a process subject to a high degree of commercial efficiency since the 1200s. Press runs were short in Petrucci's day; prices were high; a screw had to be turned by hand to make every impression. Novelty and luxury were the attraction, not availability. Material, distributors, outlets, business contacts of all kinds—these took time. It was a quarter of a century before music printing reached a substantial market and another quarter of a century before it began to affect that market.

7
DIFFUSION OF FRANCO-FLEMISH STYLE 1500-1600

After Josquin: Varied Applications

IN SPITE OF THE GREAT VARIETY OF JOSQUIN'S OUTPUT, HIS influence on the next generation was mostly in the lyric four-voiced style without cantus firmus and with imitation, found in and suitable for motets of moderate size. Josquin's big motets, with their broad designs and striking effects, profoundly impressed his younger contemporaries, but it was his lyric style that appealed to them as something to copy.

MOUTON AND THE LYRIC STYLE Josquin's sacred style was best emulated by Jean Mouton (ca 1459–1522), who seems largely responsible for interpreting and transmitting Josquin's achievement to the next generation. Mouton concentrated on motets; over a hundred are now known. In these he worked toward smoothness, placing his figuration neatly in clear, concise phrases—clear, that is, when compared with Ockeghem or the darker side of Josquin. After Josquin's expansiveness, too, there seemed to be a contraction to a more moderate style, avoiding the extremes marked out by Josquin. Underneath the now amiable exterior, however, composers continued to be fascinated with elaborate constructions, especially canon. Mouton often used canon, most impressively in a motet *a 8*, *Nesciens mater*, in which only four voices are written, the other four derived canonically.

A similarly smooth style, and even greater charm, can be found in the works of Antoine de Fevin (ca 1480–ca 1512), works full of promise if few in number. Fevin's chansons occupy a position analogous to Mouton's motets in making Josquin's style accessible to composers of the 1520s.

The intensive cultivation of the four-voiced lyric style produced several important results, first of which was an increasing detachment from the two-voiced framework. As it was harmonized progressively by the high and low contratenors, the tenor-cantus framework generated certain three-part and four-part progressions that became sufficiently current after 1500 to be considered standard. In Example 55 the traditional two-part framework is clearly apparent in tenor and cantus; but the bass, or low contratenor, whose notes are derived from a vertical harmonization of each interval of the two-part framework, is now sufficiently cogent to be thought of as the structural foundation for this progression. Once the bass, rather than the tenor, became the foundation, the upper voices could move through the harmonies in novel ways, assuming melodic shapes that would have seemed arbitrary or unreasonable before.

The integration of voices gradually effaced the traditional functions of the several voices. It became increasingly difficult to tell the contratenors from the tenor or cantus, at least in progressive works; conservative ones continued to betray how the contratenors were added on to the .tenor-discant framework. In general, however, it now makes sense to refer to the four voices as *soprano, alto, tenor,* and *bass,* terms that come down to us via Italian from the traditional Latin names we have used so far. In works for five or more voices, increasingly frequent throughout the 1500s, the extra voices were often called *quinta vox, sexta vox* (fifth voice, sixth voice), going on in that fashion as far as was needed.

Another consequence of Josquin's four-voiced style was a persistent use of imitation. There was a gradually increasing tendency after 1500 to use imitation in all four voices, also to use shorter time intervals between the imitative entries, leading eventually to a much denser style. Josquin and his contemporaries had sometimes integrated all four imitative voices sufficiently to obliterate the traditional pairing of voices—whether a pairing of two high against two low voices or of tenor and cantus against high and low contratenor. Integration of four voices on an equal basis continued to be the mark of an advanced technique. The old pairing persisted, however, especially in the pitch levels between entries, as when the tenor entered on C, imitated by the bass on F below, which was followed by soprano on C an octave above the tenor, imitated in turn on F by the alto. This typical pattern was a direct result of the older pattern of two duos, each in imitation at the fifth.

An even more important, if less concrete, result of Josquin's style was

EXAMPLE 55   HARMONIZATION *a* 4 OF A TWO-PART PROGRESSION

the complete vocalization of polyphony. For centuries polyphony had regularly involved one or two vocal lines with text over one or two instrumental lines— the motet, the song forms, much of the sacred music of the 1400s. Now, in the decades after 1500, everyone sang: music, both sacred and secular, became poly-melody. All voices were similar in style and more or less equal in importance.

It is hard to appreciate either the drastic significance of this vocalization or its artificial effect. Instead of an accompanied song cast in clearly perceptible phrases whose shapes depended upon the clear cadences of the two-part frame-work, the listener now heard four or five voices, singing the same words in stag-gered, out-of-focus rhythms and rich harmonies whose logical connection was only dimly perceptible. Where were the songs of yesteryear? The new style did well to cultivate smooth lines and, sometimes, synchronized declamation of text in compensation for its new, unusual texture.

The shift to complete vocalization was not permanent, however, nor did it take place without reactions. On one hand, there sprang up purely instru-mental forms in increasing quantity. On the other hand, the purely vocal forms were soon adapted to more traditional format of accompanied songs. Indeed, the habit of instrumental accompaniment was strong; the new vocal pieces were regularly performed in some quarters with participation of instruments, either doubling or replacing voices.

FROTTOLA, CHANSON, MADRIGAL   The older tradition of accompanied song and the new vocal style were curiously mixed in a repertory of native Italian songs popular around 1500. The Northerners employed in Italy provided their courtly patrons with the rich diet of masses and motets for which they had been hired. For secular entertainment the Northerners also provided songs, usually with French texts and in the modern, Northern style. A large repertory of these French songs was published in 1501 by Petrucci under the title *Har-monice musices odhecaton* (A Hundred Songs in Harmony). For his opus I, Petrucci obviously selected as important and popular a category of music as he could find.

It was clear, however, that some courtly Italians found the steady diet of sophisticated Northern polyphony hard to digest. From 1480, mostly in con-nection with the brilliant court of Isabella d'Este at Mantua, there was a demand for a much lighter kind of music with Italian texts—a relief from the strain of cultural uplift in the high French fashions. Isabella d'Este and her court achieved musical relaxation through the strumming and singing of Italian musicians like Marco Cara (died ca 1530) and Bartolomeo Tromboncino (died ca 1535). The songs they sang go under the generic name of *frottola*.

Both the music and poetry of the frottola repertory (preserved largely in publications by Petrucci, 1504–1514) betray the anomalies of a peripheral style. The texts are crude, both technically and in content; their low tone, how-ever, is not that of low strata of society, but rather of the most elevated strata in a posture of relaxation. Since the texts are cast regularly in strophic form, their musical settings continue the tradition (though not the particular forms) of the song forms, ballade, virelai, and rondeau. These were dying out in the North at the very moment, 1480, when their Italian counterparts were coming into fashion. In this respect the frottola group was a conservative reflex.

In texture, too, the frottola was conservative: the earliest ones were set *a 3* like the old Burgundian song, and while some frottolas could be sung in all parts, most preserved the format of one (or two) sung parts accompanied by one or two instrumental parts.

In these respects the frottola was a late phase of accompanied song. But the best frottolas (and these fell far short of Northern artistic standards) tried to reproduce some of the striking effects the Italians heard in the marvelous music of the chapel. The most effective harmonic progressions—those most easily grasped—stripped of figural artifice, were strung together to give the frottola a modern sound.

While the frottola presented old and new elements side by side, the Parisian chanson seemed to be completely modern. Chansons (the term now regularly used for all secular French polyphonic songs) were published in quantity by the first French music printer, Pierre Attaingnant (before 1500– after 1553) who began publication in 1528. The chanson repertory he printed was probably written throughout the 1520s, being dependent in style and technique upon men like Mouton and Fevin. Attaingnant's repertory was written by a number of lesser composers apparently associated with Paris; but the best chansons were written by two or three composers of more international importance, Pierre Certon (died 1572), Clement Janneqüin (died ca 1560), and especially Claudin de Sermisy (ca 1490–1562).

The new Parisian chansons of the 1520s have no fixed form. If a particular chanson has a structural repetition, that repetition is not traditional and invariable, as in the ballade or rondeau. Frequently the last line of a chanson is repeated (as in Example 56), but this is the composer's option, rather than a function of a poetic form. The song forms, in other words, disappeared in the face of a musical style that even in lighter, secular music tended to surge along in rich harmony, swinging syncopations, imitative entries, freely assuming a variety of plastic shapes.

The typical chanson was *a 4*, all parts to be sung. Compared with Ockeghem, or even Josquin, the rhythms were relatively simple, the imitative subjects easy to follow, the harmonies transparent and often close to a traditional two-part progression, yet up-to-date in their constant use of thirds and a bass that moved easily to fill out the sonority. Like the frottola, the chanson concentrated on the most effective, most obvious progressions developed by Josquin's generation. But the chanson worked these progressions into a style of incomparably greater artistry. Example 56 contains a representative chanson by Claudin.

The Italians were well aware of the superiority of the French chanson. From 1510 on, there was steady pressure in Italian courtly circles (especially at Mantua and Ferrara, in the person of Pietro Bembo, 1470–1547) for a more elevated kind of music with Italian text. Italian literary ideals were at this time higher than actual accomplishment; superior lyric poets were rare, and literary critics pressed for a return to Petrarch (1304–1374), whose sonnets and canzonas, almost two centuries old, were now taken up as ideal vehicles for Italian music.

But even with Petrarch's texts and even with the musical idioms of the French chanson, made available in Italy through publications of the 1520s.

EXAMPLE 56   CLAUDIN: CHANSON

EXAMPLE 56 (CONTINUED)

(Come, my friends, to hear my complaint;
Come hear the most desolate that ever was;
Love has driven me mad,
Yet for a false love must I die?)

native Italian composers were not able to create the longed-for Italian lyric. It took a Northerner, Philippe Verdelot (died ca 1540) to unite the modern style of the chanson with the free forms and the increasingly elegant diction of the best Italian poetry. The result was the *madrigal* (unrelated to the madrigal of the 1300s), first found in a publication of 1530, *First Book of Madrigals of Various Composers* (Rome). Verdelot's early madrigals, however, must have been composed during the 1520s. The 1530 collection also included pieces by Costanzo Festa (ca 1495–1545), whose national identity is not entirely clear but who wrote his sacred music in a modern Northern style.

All the essential features of the madrigal had to be derived from the North; these features could not be learned from the frottola—indeed, they were what distinguished the madrigal from the frottola. The madrigal was not a strophic form, but a piece of music composed especially for a particular text, tailored to its diction, its structure, eventually to its meaning. The madrigal was primarily all-vocal, printed in part books with text carefully set in each part. The madrigal used techniques of imitation in the fluid succession of various textures characteristic of modern Northern music. Most important, the madrigal had artistic ambitions. In spite of isolated frottolesque compositions, the madrigal as a form was not content with casual commonness, but matched its elevated texts with appropriately artistic music. Even the relaxation of Italian courtiers now became subject to elegant manners.

The most famous composer of early madrigals was Jacques Arcadelt (ca 1504–after 1567) who, when he wrote sacred music, did so in the amiable tone set by Mouton and predominant during the 1520s. Arcadelt's madrigals were published in large numbers during the 1530s and 1540s; *Voi ve n'andate al cielo*, and *S'infinita bellezza* are representative. Arcadelt found just the right Italian inflection for the techniques of chordal declamation or simple imitation. Smoothly sonorous Northern idioms, luminous in their all-vocal harmony, found in Arcadelt the warmth and lucidity appropriate to the new Italian lyric.

PUBLICATIONS FOR LUTE AND KEYBOARD Repertories of frottola, chanson, and madrigal owed their formation in no small measure to the initiative of a publisher. Mass and motet were still provided by composers directly to their princely employer; chansons and madrigals were, too, but soon came to be even more deeply involved in channels leading to publication. At a time when publishers were feeling their way toward potential markets, the leading houses engaged expert editors, taking aggressive steps toward the virtual creation of repertories to suit existing markets.

The publishers' initiative seems also responsible in large degree for the earliest publication of instrumental music. We know that instrumental virtuosos—especially on lute, viol, and keyboard (organ or harpsichord)—were among the most brilliant musical attractions of the Italian courts. We have, however, very few compositions by the recognized virtuosos; we know only that they either improvised, or played their own arrangements of vocal pieces such as frottolas, motets, madrigals, and especially chansons. Naturally these virtuosos kept their arrangements to themselves, the art of arrangement being intimately bound up with the player's personal style. Publication held no reward for the expert performer, whose art consisted entirely in his personal presence. The publisher, however, became interested in music for solo lute or keyboard as something he could sell to a widening audience of amateur performers. Seeking out an editor who would be willing to compose or obtain sample arrangements and "improvisations," publishers early in the 1500s put out books for lute and keyboard.

Around 1500 in Italy the lute was the favored instrument, both for experts and amateurs. Six books of lute music published by Petrucci between 1507 and 1511 represent the basic categories of instrumental music current at the time:

Lute tablature, I (1507), by Francesco Spinaccino
    21 arrangements
    17 ricercars
Lute tablature, II (1507), by Francesco Spinaccino
    33 arrangements
    10 ricercars
(*Lute tablature,* III—lost)
Lute tablature, IV (1508), by Joan Ambrósio Dalza
    13 calatas
     9 pavanes
     1 saltarello
     4 ricercars
     5 tastar de corde (4 with ricercars)
     4 arrangements
Songs with lute accompaniment, I (1509), by Francesco Bossinensis
    70 songs
    26 ricercars
Songs with lute accompaniment, II (1509), by Francesco Bossinensis
    56 songs
    20 ricercars

Tablature is the generic term for instrumental scores (including many varieties) as opposed to vocal part books. The pieces contained in these and similar publications can be grouped in two main categories, the first including pieces for solo lute, the second, functional pieces—songs and dances. The first two volumes listed, *Lute tablatures* I and II, contain solo pieces; the other volumes, mostly songs and dances. The songs of the last two volumes are almost all frottolas, and almost all taken from Petrucci's previous publications. They clearly represent an attempt to pursue a market with minimum new material. Francesco Bossinensis merely transcribed frottolas for vocal cantus, with tenor and contratenor to be played on the lute; he omitted the fourth voice if there was one.

Far more important are the arrangements of vocal pieces and the ricercars featured in the first two volumes and included in all five; these types offered the amateur a chance to imitate the virtuosos he so admired. The arrangements of motets, chansons, and frottolas are more or less faithful to the basic structure of the original, modified to a greater or lesser degree by figuration appropriate to the lute. Ricercars for lute tend to superimpose simple scalar figuration on top of a rambling series of harmonies. The meaning of the term *ricercar* (variously spelled, often *recercare*) is not clear, but the pieces so labeled are free, original compositions rather than arrangements, although sometimes a ricercar seems to be built on a subject taken from an arrangement. In any case, ricercars are sometimes paired with arrangements, sometimes (as in the last two volumes) set up to go with songs ending on the same note. A *tastar de corde* is a stylized tuning-up piece that runs rapidly over the whole instrument. Lute pieces comparable to those of Petrucci's publications can also be studied in the Capirola lute book.

Arrangements and ricercars, songs and dances—these basic categories were repeated in succeeding publications of instrumental music. Next to the lute, the keyboard seemed highly favored by solo virtuoso and amateur alike. The type of organ involved was a relatively small one appropriate to courtly entertainment, as was the harpsichord. One of the earliest printed sources of keyboard music is a publication of 1523, *Recercari, Motetti, Canzoni, composti per Marco Antonio di Bologna* (that is Marc Antonio Cavazzoni). It contains a "first ricercar," a motet *Salve virgo*, a "second ricercar," a motet *O stella maris*, followed by arrangements of four French chansons.

The motets are somewhat figural, but since the originals are not known, it is impossible to tell how much of the figuration is a result of the adaptation to keyboard. In style and placement, however, at least some of the figuration, scalar and otherwise, could have come out of sacred music by Josquin, Obrecht, or one of their contemporaries. The ricercars are much more figural than the motets; they are also more rhapsodic, tending to be open-ended in their phrase construction (as expressed in the underlying succession of harmonies).

We have so few sources of solo instrumental music from these decades that it is hard to tell whether various ricercars in different styles represent basically different types or merely reflect differences in personal approach by the composer—a significant difference in the case of the ricercar, since it stands close to improvisation. Keyboard ricercars (from a manuscript) by Giacomo Fogliano (1473–1548) are far more carefully worked out, in progression, figuration, and imitation, than those of Marc Antonio Cavazzoni. The difference seems not to be one of stylistic development or even of type (a difference of lute-type versus organ-type has been suggested), but rather of personal style, artistic taste, and skill. Only later, it seems, did these personal styles of solo keyboard music harden into universal types. The early 1500s are marked by a variety of approaches to keyboard forms, both in Italy and elsewhere, especially Germany.

Lute songs, such as those arranged for Petrucci by Francesco Bossinensis, were published throughout the century, obviously for the benefit of amateurs, since the expert could easily make his own reduction of contrapuntal settings. The expert could also easily perform another type of piece particularly in favor at the Italian courts—rhapsodic recitation of poetry over improvised instrumental accompaniment. Even before 1500 we know that Italian courtly musicians, perhaps gifted amateurs, recited lyric or epic poetry while accompanying themselves on the lute or viol. Such impromptu lyricism struck a favored compromise between the casual frottola and the elaborate chanson, possessing the spontaneity of the one and the elevated musical tone of the other.

Episodes from Ariosto's epic poem, *Orlando furioso,* were favorite subjects for the rhapsodists. We know indirectly the kind of musical formula used for recitation; later in the century we find bass formulas, for example, the *Aria di Ruggiero,* which derives its name from a popular episode in *Orlando* involving Ruggiero, one of the characters. *Aria* here means *scheme,* including the poetic form together with a melody, in this case apparently a stepwise descending line; when harmonized in the modern style, this line generates the bass we know from later sources. Such a formula would be repeated over and over, with continual variation both in tune and accompaniment, for epic recitation. Another very common recitation scheme was the *Aria di Romanesca.*

GOMBERT AND CLEMENT Parisian chanson and early madrigal—even the sacred music of Mouton and Fevin—represented a phase of relative clarity and serenity. "Relative," because when compared to the old song forms the new style was overflowing with rich complexity; but compared to the motets and chansons of Josquin, the Parisian chanson and early madrigal were a tranquil, intimate interlude. Claudin, Verdelot, Arcadelt—all avoided the high excitement as well as the dark mystery of Josquin's generation, seeking instead the perfection of the well-rounded phrase.

The generation of Northerners coming to maturity around 1530, headed by Nicolas Gombert (ca 1500–ca 1556), made musical texture strikingly dark and dense, either by finely wrought imitation or by harmonic weight, or by a combination of the two. Gombert has often been compared to Ockeghem because of the richly dark gravity of his music. In that respect the comparison is justified, but where Ockeghem soars, Gombert becomes meditative and introspective. Ockeghem's style was expanding outward, while Gombert's turned in on itself to discover the riches of contrapuntal intricacy. Gombert's style was praised around 1550 by the theorist Hermann Finck (1527–1558) as clearly novel in its concentration on subtleties of imitation and harmony. Furthermore, says Finck, Gombert happily avoided those long duets in Josquin, keeping all four voices busy most of the time.

The center of gravity in Gombert's sacred production (as in that of his contemporaries) lay in his motets. Gombert wrote at least 160 motets, *a 4* and *a 5*—twice as many as Josquin. On the other hand, Gombert wrote only ten or so masses, and those are less imaginative than his motets. Gombert also wrote some sixty chansons (Claudin wrote hundreds) which found their way into Attaingnant's voluminous collections, but contrasted there sharply with the typical Parisian chanson because of Gombert's intense, intricate style.

In Gombert's generation, masses came regularly to be built on a chanson or motet, using the whole contrapuntal complex of the model as the kernel of each of the five sections of the mass. (Later such masses were called *parody masses*, a term customary today; in Gombert's time parody masses were often titled "Mass in imitation of . . . ") The technique of parody had been long in development, as we saw; what we regard as the definitive stage is really the last stage in a process clearly operative in the chanson masses of the late 1400s.

The popularity of parody technique during the 1500s was a result not just of one factor, but of the whole development of style after Josquin—the cultivation of Josquin's lyric, four-voiced style with its emphasis on imitation and deemphasis of cantus firmus, and the shift of interest from mass to motet and chanson. As was customary since Dufay's time, cyclic masses continued to be based on some ready-made material; but now, instead of a cantus firmus, that material was logically a modern chanson or madrigal.

Gombert's motets repay the closest scrutiny, for his artistic attention was concentrated on detail, on the conduct of a point of imitation, on the expressive effect of dark, glowing sonorities. He created larger forms by artful fusion of detail. Instead of long, arching imitative duets à la Josquin, the voice pairs came closer together; in the almost continuous four-voiced texture, chords tended to change every note. The faster rate of change was reflected in the imitative subjects, using far fewer repeated notes than Josquin and favoring tortuous, serpentine shapes.

Individual phrases still approached their cadences in traditional ways, but the two-part framework (to say nothing of the four-voiced harmonization of it) was increasingly distorted for expressive purposes. The cadence, even if recognizable, was often heavily elided; one phrase flowed into the next. Variety was less important for Gombert than continuity. The previous resources of textural variety—change in number of voices, alternation of staggered and synchronized rhythms—these procedures were still there, but clouded over. The four-voiced texture was characteristically relieved by trios rather than duos. Declamatory passages failed to cut through as decisively as they did in Josquin.

Example 57 is an excerpt out of the middle of a Gombert motet; it shows a typical fluctuation among the several possible combinations of voices. The passage quoted has only two full cadences (meas. 3, 17); the formulas in measures 6 to 7, 10 to 11, 12 to 13, 14, 23 to 24, 25 to 26 are all elided or obscured. Consistently rich, the sonority is often spiked with expressive dissonances, suspended in syncopations in ways becoming standardized in Gombert's own time.

Gombert's music often presents thorny problems in the application of musica ficta. The principles of the 1300s are still clear, and still—as principles— valid; but their application is now rendered problematic by the oblique contrapuntal procedures typical of Ockeghem and Gombert. Sometimes a smooth solution seems impossible, all of the several alternatives resulting in a strong, harsh

EXAMPLE 57 GOMBERT: FROM *DOMINE PATER* (motet)

EXAMPLE 57 (CONTINUED)

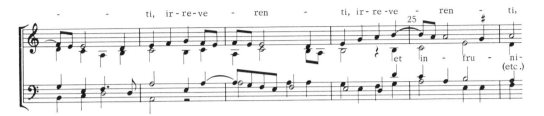

(. . . Lest the pleasures of the flesh take hold of me, and irreverence of soul [betray me])

sound. But it is evident from other passages where no ficta is involved that a certain amount of harshness is intended.

Sometimes ficta is suggested by the pattern of imitation, a consideration that becomes increasingly problematic as imitation is carried out more and more consistently. There continue to be frequent cases where the normal raising in a cadential formula cannot take place either because of the subsequent conduct of the voice in question or because of the simultaneous conduct of the other parts. There then results yet another distortion of the traditional counterpoint. Ficta in Gombert has to be solved case by case. The application of a flat to a particular note does not usually seem related to the tonal plan of the whole piece; indeed it seems to have no effect on the plan one way or another, since in general Gombert's expressive detail is so much more absorbing than the overall structure.

It is easy to see how sensitive singers, seeking an adjustment of individual notes to smooth out a passage, would drift unawares into a raising or lowering of the pitch level of the whole piece, by a tone or semitone or some more complex fraction of a tone. A similar change in pitch level could also come about as the result of singers' efforts to maintain pure fifths and at the same time pure thirds, valued around 1500 for their resonant sonority. But it is also obvious that such changes in pitch level, while perceptible to some observers, could not at that time be understood as significant either for structure or expression, for a tonal framework of a type that would make them significant was lacking.

The consistent addition of *one* flat in the middle of a piece would, of course, constitute a significant change in tonal structure; the use of such changes can be traced all the way back to chant. But the abrupt addition of, say, six flats at some point in a piece would result, in the 1500s, only in an unaccountable change of pitch level. A borderline case (one that actually shows up in a few pieces) involves the successive addition of flats in a circle of fifths extending over all or most of a piece. Each successive addition would be noticed, although the addition is usually made so smoothly that no great structural articulation results. The overall drift, however, of six successive additions would have no meaningful direction and would be perceived, if at all, only as a curiosity.

Gombert's motet texts, drawn largely from Scripture, tended toward somber subjects. While he did not go to any great lengths to underline the meaning of particular words (something that would have interrupted the very continuity he wanted), Gombert set his texts with increasing attention to prosodic detail and with a clear intent to give the text an expressive musical projection. His ideal was an overall expressiveness, brought about by heightening the purely musical intensity.

The connection between Gombert's dark music and dark texts is highlighted by an occasional setting of a brighter subject. In *Venite filii* Gombert shows he is capable of an ending that is, if not exultant, at least optimistic (Example 58). The sense of continuity, however, is still strong, obliterating the traditional cadence form at the end of this motet (meas. 6 to 7 of Example 58). The main cadence itself is rendered deceptive by the bass, while the upper voices swirl over it in novel, expressive ways.

Gombert's style was an extreme; hardly anyone else in the 1500s wrote music of such urgency. Jacob Clement (Clemens non Papa, ca 1510–1566/1568), who most nearly approached Gombert in style as well as stature, was more inclined toward the suavity of the 1520s. Clement occupied a position somewhere between Claudin and Gombert, representing, more than any other composer, the "perfect art" of the mid-century. While small in degree, the stylistic differences involved became increasingly significant as composers became acutely style-conscious.

Clement's motet style (like Gombert, he put his best efforts into motets) retained much of Gombert's expressiveness even though cast in more lucid

EXAMPLE 58   GOMBERT: FROM *VENITE FILII* (motet)

([Blessed are they] who trust in Him.)

phrase shapes. Indeed, as the phrase shapes emerged from the continuous flow of counterpoint, their expressiveness became specific rather than general; they became capable of reflecting the meaning of the particular words attached to them. The normal devices for varying texture, used before to set off one phrase from another, now acquired the capacity of highlighting a change of meaning in the text. Similarly, the motifs used for imitation, carefully shaped in Gombert, now acquired the capacity of underlining the meaning of the words they carried. This deepening in the expressive relationship of text and music came about gradually during the 1540s and 1550s.

The development of a close relationship between the music and the meaning of the words did as much for one as for the other. One can argue that in the long run what attracted composers to this kind of text expression was its capacity to articulate the musical flow. If Clement was interested in making his phrases more clear than Gombert's, then text expression was one means toward that end. This kind of text expression was born of the musical phrase; the more forcefully each musical phrase expressed its text, the more clearly the text helped delineate one phrase from the next. Eventually the successive expression of text phrases was to become a principal method of musical composition.

In Clement's motets, expression of the text was clearly evident but not obtrusive, merely enhancing the contrapuntal flow without controlling it. Clement was most absorbed by the production of rich sonorities in easy succession and with the intricacies of imitation. In his handling of imitative entries Clement showed a typical oscillation between a search for variety and for smooth harmonious blending of the parts. We have to remember that imitation was only one way of animating the basic chords and progressions. Ockeghem, Obrecht, often even Josquin, got along very well without imitation, animating their harmonies by staggering the entries or displacing rhythms.

Example 59 contains some samples of Clement's imitative techniques. The sample in 59a is not imitation at all, but merely displacement of the voices from one another. In this passage the ruffling of the texture comes as a relief to the synchronized declamation at the beginning of the phrase, which in the motet as a whole functions as a short but striking contrast to the imitative surroundings (it marks the beginning of the B section in the form *ABCB*, frequent in mid-century motets).

In Example 59b, it is difficult to say whether we are looking at highly modified imitation or a staggered chord progression. It is useful, however, to think of such passages first in terms of their underlying chords, only afterward as opportunities for imitation. The harmonic context is responsible for many of the simultaneous countersubjects as well as the doubling in thirds of imitative entries, which occurs throughout the 1500s. Procedures such as those shown in Example 59c are difficult to analyze as modified imitation but quite easy to understand as immediate harmonization of a subject.

In Example 59d, however, the emphasis is slightly changed. The imitation is more strictly, though not completely, maintained. Here it is useful to account for each deviation from strict imitation; the bass entrance, for example, maintains the rhythm of the subject, but is modified to permit a certain harmonization. In general, Clement carried through such imitative procedures more consistently than Gombert.

EXAMPLE 59   CLEMENT: SAMPLES OF IMITATIVE PROCEDURES

(a)   From *Domine clamavi* (motet)

(b)   From *Domine Deus exercituum* (motet)

(c)   From *Domine Deus exercituum*

(d)   From *Maria Magdalene* (motet)

sum . . . .

Je - sum . . .

Je - sum . . .   (etc.)

Je   -   sum . . .

(e)   From *Maria Magdalene*

($\downarrow$ = 72)

Ma - ri - a Ma - gda - le - ne, et al - te - ra Ma -

S.
A.
Q.

Ma - ri - a . . .

T.
B.

Ma -

ri - a, . . .   Ma - ri - a Ma - gda - le - ne, . . .   (Ma-

ri - a . . .

Ma - ri - a . . .

ri - a . . .)

(etc.)

(Ma - ri - a . . .)

(f)   From *Plateae tuae, Jerusalem* (motet)

($\downarrow$ = 72)

Pla - te - ae tu - ae Je - ru - sa - lem

S.
A.

Pla - te - ae tu - ae   (etc.)

T.
B.

Pla - te - (ae)

(a) (For I have provoked thy wrath . . .   (d) Jesus, whom ye seek . . .
(b) Therefore, O Lord, . . .   (e) Mary Magdalene, and the other Mary . . .
(c) O Lord God of hosts, . . .   (f) Thy high places, O Jerusalem . . .)

Example 59e is a typical motet beginning, with a pair of entries a fifth apart, followed by a similar pair, then an isolated entry in the bass on another pitch. The effect of such a series of entries is tangential: things get less clear, rather than more clear, as the series proceeds. In a few pieces one finds the type of modified imitation shown at Example 59f, where one voice begins with the leap F to A, imitated at the fourth below by a voice modified to read C to D, with subsequent changes accordingly. This kind of modification pulls the voices closer together: the fifth outlined by the first voice and the fourth outlined by the second together make up the octave C–C clearly divided by the fourth at F—a type of tonal concept much in favor in the 1500s. Furthermore, the answer C–D converges on F, instead of going off at a tangent; it prepares the third voice, which, like the first, enters on F, and which in turn links the second imitative pair more closely with the first. The sense of focus on F becomes relatively strong, stronger than it had been since the 1300s.

This specific type of modified imitation, however, is relatively rare in the 1500s, tending to occur most often in pieces on F, using the kind of subject seen here. The description by a later age of this as a "tonal" (as opposed to a "real") answer, as well as the division of all imitative answers into real and tonal, is a concept that obscures the varied, imaginative procedures of the 1500s.

WILLAERT AND CIPRIANO DE RORE Leading composers of the mid-1500s not only cultivated their own types of imitative procedures but used imitation as a whole to varying degrees. Clement used it more than Gombert. The third leading composer of the 1540s, Adrian Willaert (ca 1490–1562), used it noticeably less than Gombert, especially as he got older. Willaert, too, began in the post-Josquin motet style, preserving almost all that Josquin had done, but cultivating some features more than others. The range of possibilities represented by the post-Josquin generation can be conveniently studied in Attaingnant's thirteen books of motets (1534–1535) in which Mouton, Gombert, and Willaert appear side by side along with many others.

After holding several positions in Italy, Willaert became *maestro di capella* of the ducal chapel in Venice in 1527, when he must have been thirty-five or so. This was an important post—or became so under his direction—and through it Willaert became by 1550 perhaps the most respected Northern composer in Italy. Publications devoted entirely to his motets *a 4* and *a 5* appeared in Venice from 1539 on. Some were written in connection with secular occasions, and those which might be placed around 1530 (*Haud aliter pugnans, Victor io*) have much of the cheerful color and clear phrases typical of that time. They are imitative, but casually so; the imitative entries blossom easily into the melismatic figuration inherited from Josquin.

Other motets by Willaert, presumably from the 1530s, reveal a tendency toward gravity, for example, *Locuti sunt* (Example 60). These motets best reveal the subtle difference between Willaert and Gombert: both treat imitation as a textural animation superimposed on the harmonies, but Willaert seems even less interested in imitative consistency. Sometimes Willaert modifies imitation in a way that seems closer to the old voice pairing (Willaert was apparently older than Gombert; hence his earlier works might be less advanced in style).

On the other hand, Willaert cultivated strictly canonic procedures to a

EXAMPLE 60   WILLAERT: FROM *LOCUTI SUNT ADVERSUM ME* (motet)

(But I prayed, and thou hast heard me, O Lord . . .)

far greater extent than Gombert, who used canon rarely. Willaert often used a strict canon at the fifth between inner voices, especially in motets for five or more voices. This canon might or might not be drawn from chant; it usually involved a certain amount of imitation of the canonic subject in the other voices. The striking preservation of canon in Willaert, in the face of his tendency away from imitation, shows him emphasizing a different side of Josquin.

Willaert's mature motet style is sometimes described as "declamatory"; this is true only in a very subtle sense. Synchronized declamation is infrequent in Willaert, who used it, like everyone else, for contrast. Willaert was primarily concerned with producing a continuously staggered arrangement of voices for the sake of intensity. It is true, however, that the individual voices in Willaert tend to be more syllabic and more carefully shaped relative to the words; in this sense, more satisfying to the composer than to the listener, Willaert's music is declamatory. In his characteristic five-voiced staggered texture the niceties of declamation are not very audible. Furthermore, the declamation is often on repeated notes or stepwise figures of even value (quarter notes); under these conditions careful declamation posed no great difficulty for Willaert's contrapuntal mastery, nor did it represent any major stylistic achievement.

Willaert is often described as emphasizing harmony rather than counterpoint; this, too, needs clarification. Willaert's harmony is Gombert's harmony. In both, the two-part framework has long since been harmonized into a succession of those combinations we call *triads*—soon to be baptized as such by Gioseffe Zarlino (1517–1590), Willaert's pupil. Willaert's casual handling of imitation, his readiness to modify it or to proceed merely in staggered, nonimitative entries, may be the result of a greater concern for meticulous spacing in each harmony and meticulous conduct of the voices from one harmony to the next. In any case, such neglect of imitation greatly facilitates these harmonic considerations, especially in the handling of the bass, which in Willaert sometimes leaps around in a manner reminiscent of the old ballade contratenor.

It is clear, however, that Willaert's concern for harmony extends beyond the individual chord, or harmony, only as far as the next one, or perhaps the one beyond. There is in Willaert little connection between harmonic detail and tonal plan. The individual harmony has little to do with the tonal plan—which may, in itself, be clear and cogent, but no more so, and in no different way, than tonal plans for the preceding hundred years. And such plans are of no great interest to Willaert. He found in the sonorous relation of chord to chord the expressive potential he wanted; only at this level, perhaps involving differences too subtle for us to hear, is Willaert more "harmonic" than his contemporaries.

Meanwhile, deep within the sounding texture, Willaert's canons unfolded in extraordinary exercise of Northern artifice. Like the declamation, these canons are largely inaudible, intended for Willaert's own satisfaction or for that of his students—for the connoisseur, not the courtly amateur. At the end of Willaert's life a student supervised the editing of a collection of Willaert's motets and madrigals; the collection appeared in 1559 as *Musica nova* (New Music). Having been long in preparation, the publication represented no new style as of the date of publication. Aside from a few motets *a 4*, most used canon or a cantus firmus or both. The madrigals included in the *Musica nova* have a similarly grave character. This was the somber, reserved art of the "divine Adrian."

Toward the 1540s the madrigal manifested the same gravity already seen in the sacred music of Gombert and Willaert. Verdelot, Festa, and Arcadelt had successfully established the madrigal's popularity; it was being taken up by an increasing number of composers, both Northern and Italian. The Northerners, however, continued to lead the way, especially Cipriano de Rore (1516–1565), who in his first three books of madrigals (1542, 1544, 1548) gave Petrarch's texts the exalted, expressive settings so long awaited by Italian critics. Cipriano's settings of Petrarch culminated in the huge *Vergine bella*, eleven stanzas of Petrarch's *sestina*, addressed to the Madonna.

Building on the finely wrought style of his teacher Willaert, Cipriano achieved from the outset a style that was rich, yet free and open, relaxing

EXAMPLE 61   CIPRIANO DE RORE: FROM A MADRIGAL

(When I would be happy, I sit in the shade among the beautiful purple flowers of new-come April, and singing, I forget my lowly state, filling my heart only with thoughts of love.)

Willaert's dense texture (Example 61). The attention lavished by Willaert on text declamation thus was allowed to shine through a little more. Cipriano's madrigals seemed to be more responsive to details of phrase and meaning in the text. Cipriano also made more of contrasts from one chord to the next, exploiting, for example, the colorful shift from a major third to a minor one on the same bass. Effects of harmonic color that in Willaert were part of the continuous flow, were exposed to view by Cipriano.

Exclamations in the text could be set off by a change in harmony and texture; Cipriano's concept of contrapuntal flow allowed complete rests in all voices. Individual words could be pointed up by a particularly rich or expressive sound. On the other hand, Cipriano's sense of musical phrase and continuity kept such details carefully placed in the larger line. Although Cipriano's tonal plans are no stronger than Willaert's, his careful placement of striking detail gives his madrigals clear rhetorical shapes.

Like Clement, his contemporary, Cipriano found an equipoise of stylistic tendencies. Gardano, his Venetian publisher, summed it up in these terms: "Having given to Josquin delightful melodic invention and beautiful singing, to Mouton the true art of contrapuntal variation, and to Adrian Willaert continuity of sweet harmony, it seems that heaven wished to endow the unique Cipriano with all three at once. . . ."

LITURGICAL POLYPHONY After Josquin, a tendency toward strictly liturgical polyphony returned with renewed force. Composers looked for opportunities outside the mass for festive polyphonic settings. Chief among these was vespers, its psalms, hymns, and especially its canticle, the *Magnificat*. Festive *Magnificat* settings were made by a number of composers from Mouton on. Then the hymns traditionally sung at vespers were given polyphonic settings. Willaert published a set of vesper hymns in 1542, using a rich, contrapuntal paraphrase of the hymn tunes, sometimes in canon, the number of voices ranging from three to six.

After the hymns, composers turned to the vesper psalms. Psalm texts had been used for motets since Josquin, but not in sets destined for strictly liturgical use. In turning to vesper psalms and other liturgical categories, composers sought out distinctive styles of composition. Willaert used three such styles. The first, appearing in a publication of 1550, used large settings *a 8*, split into two semichoirs each *a 4*, called *coro spezzato* (split choir); the two semichoirs sang verses in alternation, and then joined to sing the concluding *Gloria Patri*.

Willaert's two other styles were less splendid. The simplest involved a setting *a 4* of alternate verses of the psalm; the rest, as in hymn settings, were sung in chant. Such *versi di psalmi*, which Willaert published in 1555, are set in synchronized declamation with little figural or imitative development. The third style (perhaps a promotional device of the publisher) combined a set of verses by Willaert with a dovetailing set by Jachet de Mantua (died ca 1559), forming a genial contest between the two contemporaries.

The principle of choral alternation represented in these psalms was applied extensively throughout the last half of the century in a variety of ways, after having been used experimentally since Binchois. The alternation could be carried out with two duplicate choirs, each singing its sections of text, or within one choir, by splitting up the ensemble into varying combinations of voices—as had been done with duos and trios in motets *a 4*. But whatever the application, the effect of alternation—and the underlying reason for its steadily increasing popularity—was the fresh color obtained from two distinct groups separated either in timbre or in position within the church. As with the antiphonal performance of chant (increasingly in use as the chant repertory drew to a close after 1100), alternating polyphonic choruses gave added interest to a style rapidly becoming uniform.

The declamatory style Willaert used for simple psalm settings was also very popular for other liturgical texts, especially the *Lamentations of Jeremiah* (lessons sung during Holy Week), as well as for litanies. For such texts the declamatory style seemed peculiarly appropriate, for while it was simple to the point of monotony, it rendered the liturgical texts in a manner strongly reminiscent of their chant settings, yet in the harmonies of modern music. This declamatory style had antecedents in the type of fauxbourdon practiced by Binchois; it was, as a matter of fact, called *falsobordone*. There must have been some continuous tradition now only dimly perceptible, for there is no other reason for the Italian term. Falsobordone is different from fauxbourdon precisely in its constant use of chords with a third and a fifth, rather than the third and sixth characteristic of fauxbourdon; hence there is in falsobordone no ''false bass.''

After 1550 the high Northern style was increasingly adapted for common use by being reduced to simplest terms. People wanted the sound of modern music, even if they could not afford the elaborate forms and textures requiring highly trained professional performers. Parochial churches and groups of layfolk, gathered for devotional exercises, needed music like the simple declamatory harmony used by eminent composers for vesper psalms. Less eminent, but often very competent, composers adapted the declamatory style for a wide variety of bourgeois needs, secular and sacred, Catholic and Protestant. Italian devotional meetings sang *laude*, settings for which had been provided by a Petrucci edition of 1507, born of the same stylistic reflex as the frottola. New collections appeared from 1563 on.

Protestant ideas about church music varied widely, from Luther, who encouraged regular boy choirs for the performance of music such as Josquin (Luther's ideal) to Calvin, who approved only of unison chanting of psalms, although it was agreed that the chants should be familiar tunes, not Latin psalm tones, and the psalm texts should be in vernacular versifications, rhyming, scanning, and strophic. (Extreme reformers wanted no music at all in church services; some of them, for that matter, wanted neither a church nor anything that could be called a formal service.) Luther had begun the collection of familiar tunes for congregational chanting. They were drawn from all conceivable sources, representing the full diffusion of medieval chant into all corners of European musical life.

Chant, of whatever type, had come to be associated with the large chorus (as opposed to the picked ensemble that sang polyphony as late as 1500), and the Germans called the new Lutheran chants *chorales,* even though they were now sung by the chorus-of-the-whole, that is, the congregation. The term *choraliter* (chorally) continued to be used in Germany for unison singing; the

companion term *figuraliter* (*figurally* or *in figured music*) was used for polyphony. Throughout the 1500s, Lutheran chorales, when sung by the congregation, were sung as chant; after 1600, simple settings *a 4* were provided. Trained
choirs, however, regularly sang more or less elaborate motets built on chorales
as cantus firmi, as composed, for example, by Johann Walther (1496–1570).

French Protestant music acquired simple declamatory settings *a 4* during
the 1500s. Loys Bourgeois (ca 1510–after 1560), who provided tunes for the
Genevan Psalter eventually adopted by Calvin, also made some simple settings
a 4 (1547). Two complete sets of harmonizations *a 4* for the same Psalter were
later provided by Claude Goudimel (1564 and 1565). In such settings the traditional two-part basis of composition frequently disappears; in other words,
Goudimel's harmonic procedures, even though simple, were abstracted from the
most modern counterpoint, rather than built up out of an old-fashioned method
of composition.

INSTRUMENTAL MUSIC AND PAGEANTS   Toward 1550 the high sacred
style was increasingly applied to instrumental music. Girolamo Cavazzoni, son of
Marc Antonio and pupil of Willaert, published in 1542 a collection of organ
pieces titled *Ricercars, Canzonas, Hymns, Magnificats.* The ricercars were now
usually cast in the imitative style of the modern motet, while the rhapsodic type
composed by Marc Antonio was less in evidence. Henceforth ricercars were to be
characterized by carefully worked-out contrapuntal style, often exceeding motets
in thoroughness and consistency of imitation.

In his hymns and *Magnificats* (also some organ masses published in 1543)
Girolamo followed the modern practice of alternation: he set every other line of
text, to be performed in alternation with the choir singing chant, or possibly, on
occasion, alternating organ with polyphonic choir like the psalm settings by
Willaert and Jachet. Girolamo's organ settings are in a contrapuntal style similar to motets, except for occasional figuration.

Publications for lute and keyboard, containing both arrangements and
ricercars, continued to appear throughout the century; after 1540, free, imitative pieces were sometimes called *fantasia*. Some of the most impressive works
came not from France or Italy but from Spain, as did three of the most
important treatises on instrumental music:

Diego Ortiz, *Treatise on the Ornamentation of Cadences* (1553)
Juan Bermudo, *Essay on Musical Instruments* (1549, 1555)
Tomás de Sancta Maria, *The Art of Playing Fantasias for Keyboard and
Vihuela* (1565)

Ortiz's treatise is for viol players, providing extensive examples of making
"divisions" or figural diminution on the cadential formulas derived from the
two-part framework. Bermudo's treatise is more encyclopedic, while Tomás
stresses an improvised imitative style typical of the fantasia. The vihuela was
the Spanish equivalent of the lute. One of several collections for the vihuela was
published by Miguel de Fuenllana, *Orphenica lyra* (1554); as in Italian sources,
transcriptions of vocal pieces are often paired with fantasias, occasionally on
subjects drawn from the vocal model.

The most notable product of Spanish music was the keyboard works of
Antonio de Cabezón (ca 1500–1566). Here, for once, the works of a virtuoso and

first-rate composer were made available to the public, even if only in a post-humous edition of 1578. Included were *versillos* (versicles) for intonation or alternation in psalmody, *tientos* (fantasias), *differencias* (variations), hymns, and freely ornamented transcriptions. In Cabezón's lyric handling of both figural and imitative idioms we have a sample of the persuasive instrumental style that enchanted courtly audiences but rarely got into print. A modest, but nonetheless evocative versicle is given in Example 62.

Throughout the 1500s music of one kind or another turned up with increasing frequency in connection with courtly plays and pageants. Such music at court had a long history going back several centuries. At the Banquet of the Oath of the Pheasant, held by the Burgundian court in 1454, motets and songs were included in the pageants; at one point in this most spectacular of banquets, twenty-eight performers played instruments inside a gigantic pastry. In Lorenzo de Medici's Florence of the 1480s, courtly pageants were merged with the civic

EXAMPLE 62   CABEZON: VERSICLE OF THE FOURTH TONE

celebrations in the carnival season. *Trionfi,* triumphal festivities involving songs sung from processional floats, and *canti carnascialeschi,* carnival songs, were cast in simple strophic forms.

Usually, however, courtly pageants were not part of public activities. In their natural courtly habitat, pageants were apt to involve the nobility themselves, both as actors and as dancers in the general festivities to which the pageant was a prelude. The dancing, of course, involved dance music; the pageant sometimes called for special pieces of music appropriate to the spectacle being enacted. Such pieces could be accompanied songs sung to the lute by a talented courtier. The participants were elaborately costumed and often masked—hence the generic name *masque* or *mascarade.*

Another type of courtly entertainment involved the nobility not as participants but only as spectators to a *commedia* or spoken play. Already before 1500 at the brilliant courts of Mantua and Ferrara, professional Italian musicians were singing accompanied songs in various types of dramas. Later, especially at Florence, plays came to have more elaborate musical interpolations, called *intermedii,* usually between scenes or acts.

Intermedii could be almost any kind of secular music, but toward midcentury they tended to be madrigals. As with the music for masques, the intermedii simply reflected the musical style current around them. There was no interaction of music and drama; drama did not call into being new musical shapes, nor did music call for a rebuilding of drama. The masque, in which music was in closer contact with the scenario, was not really drama, but pageant. Dramatic cogency was not expected of these courtly spectacles. What was important was an effect of charming fantasy, of enchantment, increasingly in demand at Italian courts as the sacred style deepened into somber severity, while the simpler forms lost their novelty.

After 1550: The Classic Style

The theorist Ludovico Zacconi (1555–1627) recounted a panel discussion that was supposed to have taken place in 1584 amongst a group of eminent composers and theorists, including Gioseffe Zarlino (1517–1590). They decided on a list of criteria by which to compare styles of individual composers. The list included "art, modulation, affect, texture, counterpoint, invention, good disposition." While it is difficult to reconstruct exactly what these terms referred to, it is important to note that the panelists were prepared to distinguish quite clearly among various composers on the basis of these kinds of criteria.

After 1550 the pressure toward perfect harmoniousness made musical style increasingly uniform. There were, it turned out, only two basic manifestations of the elusive quality, harmony; one was a fifth with a major third (up from the bottom) included, and the other was a fifth with a minor third included—to describe these harmonies in terms of the interval framework still current with theorists and still, to some extent, operative in actual composition. But while Zarlino treated two-part composition extensively in his *Elements of Harmony* (1558), he also described and analyzed these basic types of harmony as entities consisting each of three essential notes. Because it had three notes he called this entity a *triad* (the entities of the traditional two-part framework would be, by analogy, *dyads*). He further qualified them as *harmonic* triads because the three notes stood in a peculiarly harmonious relationship to one another. Finally he differentiated *major* from *minor* triads on the basis of the type of third occurring at the bottom.

Zarlino was ratifying the basic development of style, in the course of which almost all the sonorities of a piece had come to be these triads. Zarlino had little to say about the *progressions* of triads, since in his time the progressions were governed either by the two-part cadential formulas or by smooth conduct of the parts (both covered by the precepts of counterpoint) or were subject only to the intuition of the composer. Concerned primarily with musical variety or textual expression, the composer at this time was not inclined toward regular progressions that could be codified by theorists.

But as music came to consist of smooth successions of uniform chords, individuality of style was increasingly difficult to achieve. Subtleties of part writing, on the one hand, disposition of material into larger phrases, on the other, became critical points of difference between composers—between the best composers, that is, for the lesser ones (and the best ones in desperate moments) relied on novel or bizarre effects to give their music identity.

Once a good composer found a style, a set of tasteful but distinctive traits, he stuck to it, making it his by persistency. One of the striking features common to the leading composers after 1550 is how early in life they reached their characteristic style, which then remained perceptible even through the various "manners" of composition appropriate to different categories. Another striking feature is the technical ease with which the composers wrote huge quantities of music. Clearly they were drawing on their predecessors for the whole technical basis of style.

Finally it is striking how uniform this basis is from one composer to another, whether that composer be Philippe de Monte (1521–1603), a Northerner working in Vienna; Giovanni Pierluigi da Palestrina (1524/1525–1594), an Italian writing Northern style in Rome; Jacobus de Kerle (1532–1591), the Northerner most closely associated with the Catholic Council of Trent; Orlando di Lasso (ca 1532–1594), an international Northerner with names in three or more languages, finally located in Munich; William Byrd (1543–1623), a Catholic in Protestant England; or Tomás Luis de Victoria (1548–1611), a Spaniard writing Northern style in Italy and Spain. All these composers were sensitive to the local conditions under which they worked; all provided music in forms and manners appropriate to those conditions. All, however, spoke the now international language of Northern counterpoint, and each subtly inflected that language in a way intended to establish a personal identity.

DE MONTE Philippe de Monte possessed one of the smoothest styles in Europe. Because of this and because of the universality of his output, he might well be regarded as the embodiment of a classic style of the later 1500s. Following the pattern of Northern composers, de Monte went early to Italy, where his first book of madrigals *a 5* was published in 1555. He then occupied several positions, including one in England, finally settling in Vienna as Imperial

Choirmaster in 1568. His output included 38 masses, 319 motets, 45 chansons, 1,073 madrigals, and 144 "spiritual madrigals," devotional or meditative poetry in Italian set to madrigalesque music, a category popular in the later 1500s.

While by no means inactive in sacred categories, de Monte was especially known as a madrigal composer. He made extensive use of texts by a younger generation of Italian poets, rather than concentrating on Petrarch, whose vogue receded after 1550. Giovanni Battista Guarini (1537–1612) was the most important of the new poets; his long pastoral poem *Il Pastor fido* (1589) was to become extremely important for composers. De Monte led the way in using Guarini's texts for madrigals.

PALESTRINA Giovanni Pierluigi da Palestrina was perhaps the first Italian composer to compete successfully with the Northerners in serious music, but he did so only by writing completely in their style. Palestrina was active almost exclusively in Rome, both at the large churches and in private chapels. His publications began in 1554 and continued for the rest of the century, including madrigals, over 250 motets and related types (hymns, *Magnificats*, psalms, litanies, lamentations), but especially masses—48 published during his lifetime and 57 published after his death or recently discovered, making 105 in all.

Such an emphasis on the cyclic mass is one of several subtle ways in which Palestrina set himself off from others. De Monte was not the only one who wrote thirty or forty excellent masses, but he laid greatest stress on madrigals; and similarly with others. Palestrina was almost alone in putting his best efforts into the mass. He wrote all traditional types, beginning with *Ecce sacerdos magnus* (1554) on a sacred cantus firmus, then mainly parody masses on motets and chansons (fifty-two in all), and paraphrase masses, usually on hymn melodies (thirty-five in all). A description of all his cyclic techniques reads like a survey of the cyclic mass since its origin: the *Missa Repleatur os meum* (1570) proceeds through canons at the octave, seventh, sixth, and so forth, reminiscent of Ockeghem's *Missa prolationum;* there are two masses *L'Homme armé* (1570, 1582); the *Hexachord mass* is on an abstract subject; there are "free" masses based on no known material, reminiscent of Ockgehem's *Missa mi—mi.*

The parody masses predominate, however, as they did throughout the 1500s. But here Palestrina's choice of model is extremely interesting. With only a few exceptions, he uses motets by the post-Josquin generation active in the 1520s, or else his own motets of the 1560s and 1570s. (The exceptions include five madrigals, two by Cipriano; a motet by Josquin, the famous *Benedicta es,* often parodied; one motet by Cristóbal Morales, died 1553, the famous Spanish composer, and one by the obscure composer Jean Maillard, printed 1559; and the very popular chanson *Je suis desheritée,* which, however, comes from the same style and period as the post-Josquin motets.) Gombert, Willaert, Clement—all are avoided completely. Palestrina bypassed the whole development of the 1530s and 1540s, bypassed the dark, dense motet to reach back for the relative clarity of the 1520s. This was the style he wished to write—not literally, of course, but smoothed out, and then filled in with a deeper expression made possible by those very composers Palestrina took pains to ignore.

Palestrina's style, one of the most personal styles of the century, is paradoxically one of the most objective, precisely because he worked so hard to purge it of overly expressive turns of phrase. Purity was his obvious intent; anything that attracted undue attention was out of place. Successions of triads were severely restricted; all those striking juxtapositions and rich effects of Cipriano were almost completely absent. Limiting the kind of succession was not, however, the same thing as directing the progressions more closely. Palestrina's harmonies are not more directed than those of his contemporaries, merely less colorful. The succession of harmonies, here as elsewhere, is controlled by smooth conduct of the parts.

It was on the individual parts, therefore, that Palestrina lavished the most attention, achieving, on the one hand, a purity of line, and on the other, a contrapuntal elegance unmatched for sheer consistency. This was his style. No single element was of his own making, only his own choosing: the selection, purification, and combination were uniquely his. Of all styles in the 1500s, this was the only one that could be reduced to a cogent set of rules to be taught as the perfect art of counterpoint. Others had long used dissonances in syncopations, as in Example 63, but Palestrina was the only one who used them always in this way and no other.

Purity of technique did not result in a style without expression, at least not for Palestrina. Something about making the selection seemed to give him the power to use it expressively. For those who imitated him, however, the selection was already made, and in their hands the purity turned bland and ineffective. For Palestrina the self-imposed restrictions of technique affected merely the expressive range. He sacrificed, for example, extreme contrasts of rhythmic movement; only relatively subtle modifications of line were available to him to help set off or express a particular word or phrase of text. Palestrina's madrigals are not very effective, simply because they had to forego the extremes available to other composers. Cut off from the soaring fantasy of Ockeghem or the urgency of Gombert, Palestrina used uniform control of detail to support flowing lines unmatched in length and grace.

KERLE   Jacobus de Kerle began with the now customary publication of hymns, psalms, and *Magnificats* shortly before 1560 in Italy, and then received a very important commission. For one of the sessions of the Council of Trent an elaborate litany was written; Kerle set these *Preces speciales* to music in 1562. He used an extremely convincing blend of imitation and synchronized declama-

EXAMPLE 63   PALESTRINA'S TREATMENT OF DISSONANCE

tion, either in sharp alternation or modulating easily from one to the other, through various mixed textures. Kerle's styles in these pieces is as smooth in its way as Palestrina's, and more appealing, owing to an extremely felicitous sense of phrase combined with somewhat richer harmonic color. It is hard to form an estimate of Kerle's whole work (aside from a mass, the *Preces* seem to be his only work in modern edition), but it is clear that he stands close to de Monte in representing a classic style of the later 1500s.

LASSO   Orlando di Lasso can be considered more progressive than de Monte, Kerle, or Palestrina in that he followed out more energetically the lines of development given him by his immediate predecessors. Consequently there seems to be a greater difference between his early and late work, a greater sense of development. This development, incidentally, is difficult to study in Lasso's works because of the way they were edited. Following the *Magnum opus* edition put out by his sons in 1604, the sacred works are arbitrarily arranged in the *Collected Works* by number of voices, making chronological order laborious to reconstruct. It is easier and more fruitful to study certain sets of pieces available separately.

Lasso's first serious publication shows him completely in command of the techniques of Gombert, Willaert and Clement, as well as of a variety of musical effects. At this early stage (he was about twenty-four), he was fully engaged with the motet in its most modern form. He also became involved with more extravagant novelty of chromaticism, in a curious cycle of motets, the *Prophetiae Sibyllarum* (*Prophecies of the Sibyls*, those twelve old seers of antiquity who were supposed to have foretold the coming of Christ).

Extreme chromaticism flared up briefly during the 1550s, partly in response to the rapid development of text expression in both motet and madrigal and partly as the end product of a long drift toward increasingly abrupt juxtaposition of triads. The major-minor combinations used by Cipriano and others implied a chromatic line, but its adjacent semitones were usually not expressed in a single voice. Now, however, such implied chromaticism took explicit form. Nicola Vicentino (1511–1572), a theorist fascinated by accounts of Greek musical *genera,* tried to reproduce chromatic genera by writing lines such as E, F, F sharp, A; when used in imitation and harmonized into triads, such lines produced startling progressions, exemplified in his motet *Hierusalem convertere ad Dominum.*

Lasso and others were less extreme—and less antiquarian—yet they, too, approached chromaticism through the conduct of individual voices, that is, through the traditional control over progressions. The beginning of Lasso's *Prophetiae Sibyllarum* (Example 64) is a showcase of typical chromaticisms, with its text in dactylic hexameters:

Carmina chromatico, quae⌣audis modulata tenore

Haec sunt illa, quibus nostrae⌣olim⌣arcana salutis

Bis senae⌣intrepido cecinerunt ore sibyllae.

(The songs you hear modulated in a chromatic way are the same in which long ago the secrets of our salvation were truthfully foretold by the twice-six sibylls.)

EXAMPLE 64 LASSO: BEGINNING OF *PROPHETIAE SIBYLLARUM* (motet cycle)

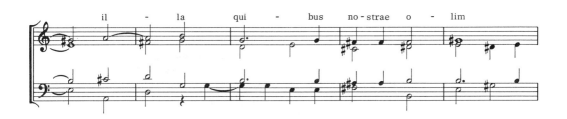

EXAMPLE 64 (CONTINUED)

Another set of Lasso's motets, the *Penitential Psalms,* written about the same time, shows a restrained, sensitive handling of the declamatory style characteristic of psalm motets, but also includes highly melismatic episodes. These excellent settings show Lasso close to the classic style, which he wrote with great mastery; but they also reveal occasionally those characteristics which were more truly his. While Lasso handled all kinds of imitative procedures with perfect ease, he inclined (like Willaert) away from persistent imitation to highly modified imitation or simply ruffled harmonies.

Lasso also emphasized declamation in the individual parts, with shorter phrases, less rhythmic variety, greater pregnancy of phrase shape than was characteristic of the classic style. Even though all these factors pertain to the structure of lines, which were usually staggered relative to each other, still the result upon the shape of the whole was significant. Lasso's style flowed less, but spoke more forcefully.

As with Willaert, the great degree to which Lasso's imitation is modified, not strict, may be associated with his desire for continuous triadic sound, which requires the bass to leap around considerably. Lasso's style is built from the top down: the upper parts were shaped in the desired way; the bass merely harmonized the structural progression already determined. The lyric bass lines of Palestrina called for more structural sixths instead of fifths between bass and upper parts, the sixth mediating from one triad to another. A melodic bass line and continuous triads tended to be mutually exclusive in this style.

As with all his contemporaries, however, Lasso's concern for triads was for the sake of harmonic color, not structure. In the measure that his style was oriented toward triads, it sacrificed overall tonal shape. Musical order still resided, for Lasso, in contrapuntal design; it was most apparent when he followed traditional contrapuntal procedures.

Lasso wrote about 50 parody masses, about 750 motets, along with perhaps 200 items of liturgical polyphony (hymns, *Magnificats,* passions, lessons) and plenty of chansons, madrigals, and German songs. An output of this magnitude suggests that the composer was not overly worried with the position of the next note to be written. The technical procedures were fully formed; composition, at the technical level, must have been almost automatic, the composer merely monitoring the quality of the fabric as it was produced.

The idea of a piece, its appropriate manner, seems to have attracted

Lasso's close attention. The number of voices, the prevailing texture—syllabic, melismatic, declamatory, imitative—shows signs of careful calculation, as well as great variety. Motets *a 5* seem to be a favored medium, as with other composers; but Lasso also wrote some well-known little motets *a 2* and some spectacular cori spezzati *a 8* (and up to *a 11*) in which the alternation of semichoirs is handled with great imagination. *Omnia tempus habent* is a famous example.

Lasso's interest seemed to incline less and less to purely musical methods of construction—canon, cantus firmus, parody—and more to an inflection of the musical flow guided by the text. His great ease of composition allowed him to underline any word or phrase in a variety of ways, which he often did. But even more than the expressive values of words, the rhetorical structure of phrases absorbed him. His contrapuntal technique, derived from Willaert, favored such structure: his short, pregnant motives permitted the loosely imitative periods to close at almost any point, there being little contrapuntal momentum that needed a melismatic flourish in which to spend itself.

Lasso's concern with phrase structure is especially apparent in comparing his early (1565) and late (1582) settings of *Nine Lessons from Job*. While the early settings are reasonably contrapuntal, the later ones (even though they borrow idioms from the earlier set) are strictly syllabic, synchronized declamation, a triad for a syllable virtually from beginning to end. Melodically the setting is highly inflected; that is, the triads change regularly from syllable to syllable, or every two or three syllables. The result is almost without tonal shape; there is no musical force present to organize the varied stream of triads. The phrase structure, however, is extremely clear and carefully made, faithfully reflecting the rhetorical shape of the text simply because it is identical with that shape.

BYRD   While it is difficult to describe the composers of this time individually, it is fairly easy to compare them. William Byrd's style, even though more consistently contrapuntal than Lasso's, is far closer to Lasso than to Palestrina, since Byrd writes forceful rhythms and dark, rich harmonies. In these respects Byrd is also close to Gombert.

Byrd was in the paradoxical position of being the best composer of sacred Latin music in England during the 1580s and 1590s, but a Catholic in a Protestant state. There was no social basis for the style he knew: Catholic music was banned, and Protestant music not yet set in its ways. It is difficult to see how Byrd could have written 100 masses, or 1,000 motets. His most important works are two books of *Sacrae cantiones* (as motets were often called) of 1589 and 1591, three masses, and two liturgical books of *Gradualia* (1605–1607), as well as a comparable quantity of service music and anthems, that is, motets, for Protestant use in English.

Among various miscellany, the *Psalmes, Sonets, and Songs of Sadnes and Pietie* of 1588 are of great interest. Byrd tells us that these were first composed as solo songs with instrumental accompaniment, and then adapted for publication in all-vocal form. Frequently of a somber, severe tone, they are comparable to the spiritual madrigals popular on the Continent. Byrd's anthems sometimes make use of the accompanied solo voice, at subsections of text where one usually reduced the number of voices, say from four to three. Liturgically such a spot was called a *verse,* and these anthems of Byrd came to be called *verse anthems.*

Byrd's *Gradualia* have a fascinating ambiguity typical of his tortured, often darkling time. To Protestant eyes the *Gradualia* is a collection of Latin motets, some appropriate to certain liturgical occasions, but in a fashion sufficiently confused to divert suspicion. But Catholic eyes, accustomed to reading a missal, can find in the *Gradualia* complete mass propers, text and music, for the principal masses of the whole church year. The *Gradualia* was apparently popular with dissembling English Catholics, and also, apparently, confiscated on occasion by the Protestant authorities.

VICTORIA   Tomás Luis de Victoria, active in Rome during the 1570s and 1580s (in 1586 he returned to Spain), followed in the footsteps of Palestrina both in career and to some extent in style. He concentrated puritanically on sacred music: his twenty masses, when in parody technique, avoid secular models (as did Palestrina); his motets include the customary service music—hymns, *Magnificats,* settings of the Passion, and other music for Holy Week, especially an excellent set of responsories *a 4* for the Tenebrae services (matins). Revealing the purity and expressiveness of his counterpoint, these settings *a 4* perhaps represent Victoria's style just as well as his larger works *a 5* and *a 6.*

Victoria was not, however, one of the mere imitators of Palestrina; rather he matched Palestrina's consistent cleanness of technique while maintaining more color and intensity of harmony, more rhythmic vigor. His particular stylistic blend sometimes produces tonal shapes more cogent than those of either Palestrina, on one hand, or of Lasso, on the other.

ITALIAN MADRIGAL AND CONCERTO TOWARD 1600   After Cipriano, leadership of the madrigal gradually passed into Italian hands. Northerners like de Monte, as we saw, still contributed heavily and significantly to the serious madrigal. Giaches de Wert (1535–1596), a Northerner active at Mantua and Ferrara during the 1570s and 1580s, was a first-rate composer with a highly polished, flexible style which he pushed increasingly in the direction of text expression. But alongside these Northern experts, Italians such as Luzzascho Luzzaschi (? 1545–1607) and Andrea Gabrieli (ca 1520–1586) began during the 1570s to produce works comparable in skill and expression.

Andrea's later madrigals show the same exploitation of alternating semi-choirs found in the cori spezzati; in madrigals this device was appropriately adapted to musical settings of poetic dialogs. Andrea also made a remarkable setting of the choruses from *Oedipus rex* (1585), to be performed as part of the staged drama in Italian translation. This is one of the few cases in the 1500s where serious drama and music are organically related; Andrea set the choruses in a declamatory style very similar to Lasso's *Lessons from Job* of 1582.

In both madrigal and motet there had been a steadily increasing tendency—without a beginning but clearly traceable before 1500—toward expression or illustration of the meaning of the text. Such expression, or better, illustration, was closely bound up with imitation: the subjects used for imitation, say, by Clement or Willaert, were constructed to fit the phonetic shape of the words they set. It was only a step to making the shape of the subject illustrate the meaning of those words. Zarlino was not being whimsical when he included under the basic concept of imitation both imitation of a musical subject and imitation of a textual subject, that is, illustration of its meaning.

Expression of text was closely associated also with the texture of motet and madrigal, especially madrigal. As the continuity typical of Willaert and Gombert gave way to a looser connection between phrases, and as the contrast from phrase to phrase increased, it was natural to use this contrast to underline the change in meaning from one text line to the next. Concomitantly, it was natural to use the changing meaning of the text to throw into relief the purely musical contrasts in texture.

Throughout the Northern art there had been a persistent habit of expressing things at two levels, one for all to hear, the other reserved to the student or connoisseur, or perhaps to the composer alone. In the works of good composers, such as Ockeghem, the public meaning was self-sufficient; the *Missa prolationum* does not depend upon perception of its canons. Almost every imaginative Northerner dealt in private meanings of one kind or another for his own amusement. Private meanings turned up in the madrigal in abundance, since the madrigal in many respects represented Northern mannerisms with Southern abandon and exaggeration. Again the best composers did not let the public meaning, consisting of the sonorous, lyric setting of the text, suffer for the sake of private meanings. If, for example, a composer used black notes over the word *night* (a device suggested by a peculiarity of notation), the result might be imperceptible to the listener, and the madrigal as a whole need not suffer musically.

The late madrigalists rejoiced in both types of text illustration, private and public, and all possible varieties in between. In the 1580s and 1590s, madrigals sometimes became a series of disjunct, contrasting phrases, almost every one illustrating its text in some musical manner, expressive or merely pictorial, naïve or sophisticated, obvious or impossibly obscure. Such madrigals caught up and reconciled all the conflicting demands made upon Italian courtly music of the 1500s. Alternating warmly expressive phrases with lighthearted ones, Northern intensity with frottolesque casualness, Italian composers tossed off sophisticated devices with charming nonchalance. One can easily imagine the delight with which expert amateurs at an Italian court archly rendered the most abstruse "madrigalism"—and the delight with which it was received. Above all, the madrigal, thus enlivened, had variety, a commodity that was becoming increasingly scarce.

The prince of the late madrigal was Luca Marenzio (1553–1599); in his works of the 1580s and 1590s the madrigal gave itself up to word painting of the most extravagant kind, yet always with musical grace and elegance, always possessing an outward shape that, while lacking tonal forcefulness, was sonorous and lyric. The madrigal *Scendi dal paradiso* has this text:

1   *Scendi dal paradiso, Venere*
    (Descend from paradise, Venus,
2   *E teco guida i pargoletti amor'*
    And bring with you your baby Cupids,
3   *Le gratie e'l riso, oltre l'usato rida*
    Let the Graces, and the laughter, more than usual, rejoice

4   *In vist' il ciel sereno, il Tebr' al mar Thirreno,*
     Beneath the sky serene, let the Tiber to the sea Tyrrhene
5   *Porti di perl'adorno invece d'acqu'il corno.*
     Bear, with pearls adorned, instead of water, his horn.
6   *El i vostri canti giungan' a le stelle, poichè l'anime belle*
     And let your songs reach to the stars, since the sweet souls
7   *D'Amarill'e di Tirsi son'unite al nodo sacro e santo*
     Of Amaryllis and Tirsi are united in the knot holy and consecrated
8   *Com'al olmo la vite, o com' al tronco l'heder' o l'acanto.*
     As to the elm the vine, or as to the trunk the ivy or acanthus.)

In line 1, the voices enter in imitation on a broadly descending subject. The Cupids (line 2) are briefly portrayed in synchronized declamation. Graces (line 3) get a little melisma, while laughter (more than usual) an unusually large melisma. The serene sky (line 4) is illustrated by placid rhythms in the four upper voices, the bass entering at the same time as the Tiber, all together then flowing smoothly and broadly to the Tyrrhenian Sea. The reader can entertain himself by discovering the rest of the madrigalisms, not neglecting the cantus-firmus manner of composition adopted at the end.

Marenzio's art was especially delightful because it was perched on the edge of an abyss. Taken too seriously, or pushed too far, these devices could easily result in something inartistic. The dangers of the madrigal became apparent in the works of Carlo Gesualdo (1560–1611). Here, contrast of phrases was sometimes extreme; rapid scale passages alternated grotesquely with slow, solemn declamation, or torturously chromatic passages in which harmonies followed one another in extraordinary ways. Yet while extreme, Gesualdo's chromaticism held no real novelty; clearly apparent in these passages was a traditional interval progression, with the result that contemporary ears found them relatively comprehensible as harmonizations of chromatic counterpoint, twisted appropriately for madrigalesque purposes. There were few complaints about Gesualdo's modernity. Gesualdo, like his contemporaries, found no structural principle within the triad.

Conglomerations of traditional forms became increasingly popular toward 1590. Against the background of the predominantly somber sacred style, the juxtaposition of various contrasting forms and styles took on great significance. Similarly, mixtures of voices and instruments became day by day more in demand. One of the most important musical events—important in terms of brilliant variety, not intrinsic musical virtue—was a great series of intermedii put on in Florence in 1589 and described in detail by Cristofano Malvezzi (1547–1597) who wrote some of them, organized the whole show, and published the music in his *Intermedi e concerti* (1591). Large instrumental ensembles, but also solo songs accompanied by instruments were featured, with brilliant soloists. Next to such spectacular aggregates, the intimate art of the madrigal was to seem pale.

Part of the effect of such productions was due to the elaborate practice of ornamenting a simple solo song with *passaggi* (passages) or *diminuzioni* (diminutions). Long cultivated (see Example 35), the practice of diminution enjoyed special popularity in the 1580s and 1590s, as reflected in a series of publications on how to do it, by:

Girolamo dalla Casa, *Il Vero modo di diminuir* (1584) (The true method of diminution)

Giovanni Luca Conforte, *Breve et facile maniera d'essercitarsi a far passaggi* (1593) (Short and easy way to practice making passages)

Giovanni Bassano, *Ricercate, passaggi, et cadentie* (1598)

Primarily intended for voice, such diminutions were paralleled on instruments—especially cornetto, viol, and keyboard.

Diminution had a very important function in style as it developed during the 1500s. Obrecht and Josquin had incorporated a great deal of figuration, largely scalar, directly into their written compositions. But as motet style deepened and darkened, there seemed less space left for ornamentation. There ceased to be a harmonic ground, distinct from the notes themselves, upon which ornamentation could be placed. All voices, including the bass, moved at about the same rate; the clear differentiation of rhythmic levels, of figure and ground, characteristic of Philippe de Vitry, had long since disappeared, but had not yet been replaced by another type of ground, implied or explicit. The style of Willaert and Lasso, when most declamatory, is least susceptible of figuration, and carried none in published form.

To some extent, then, figuration ceased to be a part of composition and became a part of performance; ornaments were superimposed by the performer where he saw fit. Certain written-out examples of ornamentation applied, say, to madrigals of Cipriano (Example 65), reveal a disturbing discrepancy between the elevated, controlled tone of the original composition and the ostentatious passage plastered on top of it.

Diminutions were regularly written into publications of keyboard music. These continued to issue from Italian printing houses in much the same categories as before. Now, however, transcriptions were largely *canzoni francese* (French chansons). Ricercars were matched by fantasias, previously found for lute or ensemble rather than keyboard. Alongside the *toccata,* now a traditional kind of piece employing sections in imitative counterpoint as well as figural sections, there sprang up the *intonazione,* a miniature toccata (the Germans

EXAMPLE 65   FROM GIROLAMO DALLA CASA'S PASSAGGI FOR CIPRIANO'S MADRIGAL *O SONNO*

(O Sleep, of the quiet, damp, [shadowy night the restful son],)

called them *praeambula*) giving the pitch for psalms or hymns. Intonations were identified by tone (or mode) and came in sets.

As before, one has to discriminate between merely expedient publications and those of first-rate keyboard composers. The best Italian of the 1580s and 1590s was Claudio Merulo (1533–1604); his toccatas reached ample proportions and made use of a variety of styles. Opening and closing sections were often figural, with brilliant passaggi superimposed on a succession of harmonies that were loosely governed by traditional procedures but spiked with suspensions. A middle section was in imitative style, or at any rate without figuration and with more lyric conduct of the voices. Sometimes this contrasting texture returns, alternating with the brilliant figural sections to make a five-part form.

In the works of Giovanni de Macque (ca 1552–1614) we meet the term *capriccio* used to describe a contrapuntal study of one or more subjects, which are usually of an abstract nature (for example, *re, fa, mi, sol*), recalling the abstract constructions found in certain cyclic masses. *Capriccio*, like *fantasia*, obviously was used first in its literal meaning, caprice; Giovanni's similar use of the term *stravaganza*—as well as his diffuse, rambling style—betray a terminal stage of development.

Sacred music for instrumental ensembles and for combinations of instruments and voices was most effectively composed by Giovanni Gabrieli (ca 1555–1612/1613), nephew of Andrea, and like him associated with San Marco in Venice. The basis of Giovanni's handling of instruments (cornetto, trombone, violin) was the coro spezzato technique, and this in turn depended upon the loosely imitative style of Willaert with its short motivic subjects. Willaert, of course, was the fountainhead of music at San Marco, and the stylistic grandfather of Giovanni. Cori spezzati turn up frequently in Giovanni's two publications of *Symphoniae sacrae* (1597 and 1615, the latter including earlier works). In the larger ones (as in some of Lasso's) a large chorus might be split into three or four semichoirs.

In some works, for example, the well-known *In ecclesiis*, Giovanni gave one choir to a solo voice and organ (as in Byrd's verse anthems), another choir to the instruments, and the remaining two choirs to vocal chorus. Such an arrangement, varied from piece to piece, produced a splendid, festive sound, echoing back and forth from various parts of the church. It made a great effect on visitors, particularly Germans; Giovanni's works were reprinted in Germany more than in Italy, and produced in the North a series of imitators.

In spite of an occasionally striking motif, Giovanni's style was not intrinsically strong. It inherited a tendency to disintegrate into fragments, a tendency now emphasized by the use of instruments. But in Giovanni's case the weakness was his strength, his principal point of stylistic importance.

The use of instruments in music went back before polyphony—in fact, as we saw, the early 1500s was one of the few times when polyphony was completely vocalized. Instrumental performance of vocal works, either supporting or replacing voices, was a perennial habit even in the 1500s, witnessed by title pages that so often specify "voices or instruments." Thus it was not simply the mixture of voices and instruments that was new, but the way in which they were now placed in opposition, accenting each other as well as blending harmoniously.

The shift was a subtle one: ensembles which blended and those which contrasted were both described as *concerted* music. *Concerto* came to be a common term for both types of ensemble, usually involving both voices and instruments; *concertato* (concerted) style became more habitual around 1600. Sacred concerted music dropped the old titles like *sacrae cantiones* and became typically *concerti ecclesiastici* (Italian) or *sacrae symphoniae* (Latin), as in Giovanni's own publications.

More important, concerto became a leading concept of style. As a musical effect, it took on the quality of a *gloria,* a sunburst of triumph, a halo of incandescent haze. Neither a uniform ensemble nor a simple antiphony, concerto was a third species, generated out of the mixture of opposed but harmoniously blending ingredients. It became the last ideal of the old art and the first of the new one to come.

FRANCE AND ENGLAND AT THE END OF THE CENTURY   Italian music in the 1590s presents a confusing, often contradictory picture, but one bursting with vitality, reflecting the enthusiasm with which a new generation of Italian musicians threw themselves into musical experiments. The results were sometimes crude, but held great potential. One does not get the same impression from French music of this period, even though many of the same techniques appeared.

The high style of chansons such as those by Gombert declined steadily in favor, being best represented by works of Lasso composed during the 1560s and 1570s. French composers included Guillaume Costeley (ca 1531–1606), and especially Claude Le Jeune (ca 1530–1600), who among numerous other works (including many lute songs) made very convincing settings of the experimental verse forms of Jean-Antoine de Baïf (1532–1589). Baïf attempted modern French analogs of classical quantitative meters; he called his poems *vers mesurée,* to be set to *musique mesurée à l'antique.* Le Jeune's *Le Printemps* reproduced these forms in lively musical rhythms by using a synchronized declamation, stripped of contrapuntal artifice. But even that was not sufficiently simple to compete with the increasing popularity of the accompanied lute song, a popularity manifested in an important publication of 1571 called *Livre d'airs de cour;* the *air de cour* tended to be strophic and chordal. France also produced a musical spectacular, the *Ballet comique de la royne* in 1581, comparable to the amalgamations of dance, solo song, vocal and instrumental ensemble put on at Italian courts with more sensational, and enduring, effect.

During the 1590s England was the scene of one of those outbursts of activity that happily punctuate the more continuous development of musical style on the Continent. This particular outburst took the form of a craze for Italian madrigals. Everyone sang "Englished" madrigals by Italian composers. Native composers composed them—and very good ones, too—even though Byrd avoided the madrigal, as being unsuited to his more serious nature.

The younger generation was headed by Thomas Weelkes (ca 1575–1623), whose excellent madrigal output came almost entirely during the late 1590s, before he settled down to extensive composition of church music. His close contemporary, John Wilbye (1574–1638), came closest of all the English madrigalists to that darker expressiveness found in the best Italian composers. In general the English madrigal was more jolly than its Italian models; the English taste was most truly represented by the lighter forms of canzonet and ballet cultivated so successfully by Thomas Morley (1557– ?1603), who popularized Italian music in England with great energy and enthusiasm.

The polyphonic madrigal, however, was even more of a passing show in England than on the Continent: English music could have gone directly from the accompanied songs that were the prototypes of Byrd's *Psalmes, Sonets, and Songs of Sadnes and Pietie* of 1588, to the *First Booke of Songes or Ayres* of John Dowland (?1563– ?1626) published in 1597. The whole madrigalesque intermezzo could have been omitted, with immeasurable loss of delight, but none of stylistic logic.

Lute songs flourished after 1600, Dowland's being by far the best, both in serious and exuberant moods. The serious ones, such as *In darkness let me dwell*, or the very famous *Flow my tears* (also called *Lachrymae*) incline to the rich, diffuse successions of harmonies of the more serious madrigal. As the lute song gets lighter, it becomes harmonically simpler and more tightly focused. Potentially this sense of focus was the way to the future, but no one in England could find that way. A hundred years later, English composers had to learn anew from the Italians the techniques of harmonic organization.

Keyboard music flourished in England, but was preserved only in manuscript collections painstakingly made by interested individuals; there were indeed no publications of keyboard music before *Parthenia, or the Maydenhead of the First Musicke that was ever printed for the Virginalls* of 1612/1613 (virginalls were the English equivalent of *cembalo* or harpsichord). The most famous manuscript collection, as well as one of the largest, is the *Fitzwilliam Virginal Book*, copied out sometime during the first two decades of the 1600s. It contains mostly dances and song transcriptions (often heavily ornamented) but also more learned fantasias, a few with abstract hexachord subjects—the kind of piece Giovanni de Macque called *capriccio*. The leading composer of this heavy, abstruse type of piece was John Bull (1563–1628), famous for his improvisations on the organ; those were probably (and hopefully) more lyric and expressive than his written compositions. Also well represented are Byrd and Giles Farnaby (ca 1565–1640).

But the best fantasia of the Fitzwilliam Book is by Jan Sweelinck (fantasia no. 217), which leads us back across the channel to Amsterdam, where Sweelinck played the organ. Sweelinck composed much sacred vocal music, including solid motets and some charming French psalms. In his keyboard works, however, Sweelinck found the beginning of the way out of the stylistic dead end that seemed to characterize the late 1500s. As Sweelinck's works come down to us in manuscripts such as the Fitzwilliam Book, they include about nineteen fantasias and ricercars, thirteen toccatas (figural and imitative), variations on Protestant chorales treated as cantus firmi, figural variations on secular tunes, as well as variations on a few dances. The fantasias are much larger than those of Merulo, and less clear in their large design, but they move with a curious inner momentum and fixity of purpose that feels very different from the diffuseness of most comparable works. Sweelinck's textures are fluid, slipping easily from imitation to various kinds of figuration; the harmonic successions are not obviously more focused than those of Merulo, yet in some inner, mysterious way Sweelinck gave his fantasias a sense of concentration, the mark of all that was truly new in the years after 1600.

PART 3
PART MUSIC ON
A TRIADIC BASIS
1600-1750

8
NEW ITALIAN DRAMATIC STYLES 1600-1650

AROUND 1600 SEVERAL MAJOR SHIFTS IN EMPHASIS COINCIDED TO give musical style a new shape. The main shift was a long-range one; long in the making, its effects are still operative today. It involved the recognition and use of harmonic triads as the basic units of musical composition. The significance of this shift is hard for us to grasp, simply because it took place: triads now seem obvious entities because they became so around 1600, whereas they were not so before.

THE NEW TRIADIC FOUNDATION   As we have seen, composers from the past several centuries thought in terms of two-note intervals; these provided the framework of music. Progressions of intervals governed the progression of the whole piece, even though intervals were enriched by the addition of one, two, three, or even more parts. Almost from the beginning of polyphony, and especially in the 1300s, the addition of a third voice tended to produce a rich sonority formed of a fifth with an included third, a sound neither perfectly consonant nor dissonant. After 1450 this sound appeared with increasing frequency, until by 1550 it accounted for the overwhelming majority of sounds in the average piece, the only other frequent sonority being a sixth with an included third.

Then, during the period 1550 to 1600, the development of musical sonority entered a critical phase. Around 1550 Zarlino gave theoretical recognition to this group of three tones—this triad—as an entity. By 1600 it was treated as an entity by most if not all progressive composers and listeners. Thus by 1600 fifths seemed empty and incomplete, whereas they had not seemed so as late as 1550. By 1600 counterpoint came to be judged, at least by the younger generation, according to whether it represented good harmony; the counterpoint was effective when it represented effective chords and chord progressions. After 1600, for the 'rest of the century, composers were increasingly preoccupied with appropriate groupings and successions of chords, groupings eventually called *keys*.

Although this change was a profound one, it was of a kind that could occur in a relatively short time, involving as it did a change of attitude toward sonority rather than a change of sonority itself. Composers after 1600, especially conservative ones, often used the same sounds in much the same way as before. The difference was in the way the sounds were regarded. Harmonies were no longer built up by adding notes to intervals; rather harmony consisted of ready-made units of triads and sixth chords—terms we may now properly use. Dissonances were understood to be projected against a standard background of triads and sixth chords. Notes were added to these chords to produce various kinds of seventh chords. Texture was enriched by doubling one or more of the three notes of the triad; these three notes now constituted the basic, irreducible minimum of sonority.

The implications of the new attitude were a long time working themselves out. At first the new attitude manifested itself in relatively simple, external ways, the most obvious being the general acceptance of the *basso continuo*. This was a bass part consisting of the lowest-sounding notes of each chord in the piece. The basso continuo was given to the player of a chord-playing instrument (lute, theorbo, harpsichord, organ), who played on each note of the bass part a triad or sixth chord according to context. In this way the basso continuo player provided the harmonic fabric of the piece, either by himself, if the only other performer was a soloist, or by doubling the counterpoint in the case of a four- or five-voiced motet.

The basso continuo is perhaps the clearest indication of the changing attitude toward musical sonority. The bass player could now be entrusted to reproduce the substance of a piece (a substance formerly provided by an enriched two-voice framework decorated by imitative polyphony) simply by placing triads and sixth chords over a series of bass notes. After 1600 almost all kinds of pieces were provided with a part for basso continuo, from accompanied solo songs to large ensembles of voices and instruments; the most frequent and obvious exception was works for solo keyboard. The basso continuo made its first appearance around 1590 in Italy.

It is essential to remember that the basso continuo is not primarily a bass *line;* instead it is a shorthand indication of a progression of *chords*. The best composers of the 1600s had in mind specific chord progressions, expressed in specific spacing, voice leading, and melodic profile, when they wrote their basses. *Realizing* a bass at a keyboard, then, is a matter of discovering for each progression the most concise, most convincing solution to voice leading and spacing. Often a solution can be found that seems so right it needs but to be stated simply, without unnecessary ornament. Indeed, the simplest realization, involving only triads and sixth chords (with occasional suspensions in cadences), and moving as stepwise as possible, is often the most effective. Simplicity does not, however, require thin texture; proper doubling within a chord is usually desirable to give substance to the harmony.

Basso continuo is sometimes called *figured bass,* since figures (for example, 6) are occasionally placed under the bass part to specify a chord (6 for sixth chord). In the 1600s, however, basses were left largely unfigured; the chords were chiefly triads, with the occurrence of sixth chords obvious from context. The bass player was guided by rules of thumb; for example, sixth chords were apt to fall over a bass note modified by an accidental, or over a *mi,* that is, a note lying below a semitone (such as E or B).

Of greatest importance is the awareness that basso continuo music consists of—is actually governed by—a stream of harmonies. This awareness is reached only by producing the harmonies over the bass at the keyboard. (Most of the examples in Part III involve a basso continuo; these have been left unrealized expressly so that the student may work them out at the keyboard, or on the guitar, which is closer to the original media than is the pianoforte.) Sufficiently standardized to be indicated by the bass alone, yet still rich, still "harmony," triads were now the sounding substance of music.

EARLY MUSIC-DRAMA AND MONODY The other major change around 1600 was less profound, not so long in the making, and much less influential for the distant future; but its short-range effects were far more spectacular. Italian composers in the decades around and after 1600 manifested increasing impatience with the intricacies of the past, increasing urgency toward a far more effective music in terms of impact on the listener. In fact, the effect on the listener became the principal if not the sole criterion for musical style. This group of composers was primarily interested in projecting music at the listener with overwhelming force. To stun the listener was the most important result; only after that was the composer concerned with the particular kind of effect and with the artistic means, the subtleties of musical technique.

The kind of effect to which the composer naturally turned, however, was provided by the past. Since 1500 musical style had sought out the pointed phrase, the clear musical gesture, underlined by some aspect of the text. This search was carried on most intensively in the madrigal, which eventually became a series of musical devices each associated with a line of text. The most thoughtful, progressive composers were increasingly drawn to the possibility of conveying the emotional meaning of the text to the listener. As these composers doubled and redoubled their efforts to make their music stun the listener, they naturally turned to the emotional aspect of the text as the best thing to project. In broader terms, however, any aspect of music could be made to stun the listener, if presented in a sufficiently startling way. The whole spectrum of musical style after 1600 was transformed by this purely musical need to make a clear, distinct, forceful impact upon the listener.

Once again the implications could not all be worked out immediately; once again the first results were external ones, the clearest being the general acceptance of a musical texture reduced to melody and bass, with a rejection of counterpoint. Even in contrapuntal texture, there was a strong tendency to write pieces in distinct sections, each section homogeneous in itself but contrasting sharply with its neighbors. Each musical device, each style, was sustained long enough to impress itself on the listener's attention—as if composers assumed that listeners, now insensitive to subtle intricacy, could only be reached by insistent, exaggerated overstatement.

These two changes manifested themselves most clearly in the works of Italian composers, especially of the generations born after 1580 and active from 1630 to 1660, for these composers were now completely cut off from the Northerners who had taught previous Italian generations. These younger men could look back on Palestrina and Marenzio as models, and on Zarlino as mentor, even though they paid little if any attention to mentor or model, but went their own way. They were Italians, writing Italian music, with its own laws, its own destiny. The rapid acceptance of the various technical changes already described depended in large part on the attitude of the new Italians.

Composers active right around 1600 were, of course, much closer to their Northern predecessors; the nearness of the powerful Northern example brought about the paradoxical results that make the decades from 1590 to 1630 so confusing. Some Italians made only minimal changes in the style they had inherited. Others rebelled violently against that past, creating in one stroke some of the basic forms and styles that were to persevere for the next century. But the extremities of these innovators prevented them from grasping the profound, subtle changes in music that really pointed toward the future. Their innovations had to do with externals, which, even though important and lasting, were in themselves unable to create a truly new, successful style. Only the most astute Italians were able to pick their way through the conflicting stylistic elements to achieve results both artistically superior in themselves and truly influential for the future. Only Claudio Monteverdi (1562–1643) and Girolamo Frescobaldi (1583–1643) managed to find just the right combination of novelty and tradition.

The innovations of Jacopo Peri (1561–1633) and Giulio Caccini (ca 1550–1610) took place during the 1590s in a Florentine academy, one of those courtly gatherings where intellectuals discussed ideas and sang madrigals. Up until 1600 the new musical ideas remained largely within the Academy, but from 1600 on, a series of four important publications made the Florentine innovations known to the musical world:

> Emilio de' Cavalieri, *La Rappresentazione di anima e di corpo* (1600)
> Jacopo Peri, *L'Euridice* (1601)
> Giulio Caccini, *L'Euridice* (1601)
> *Le Nuove musiche* (1601/1602)

The innovations of the Florentines sprang from a desire to make modern music as effective as they imagined ancient Greek music had once been. This literary desire was characteristic of the progressive tendencies within the Italian madrigal. But the Florentines, at least Peri and Caccini, did not try to write Greek music; on the contrary, they affirmed that they were trying to attain the effects Greek music had had *with the sounds of modern music*. There is little real musical novelty in Peri and Caccini: they adapted and purified the modern style of the madrigal to make it serve their literary ends.

Caccini's *Le Nuove musiche* begins with a famous preface on singing his special kind of vocal ornament. The diminutions and passaggi of the old style were used by Caccini to heighten the emotional impact of important words in the text. After the preface come two sets of compositions, first madrigals, then (after an excerpt from a music drama, *Il Rapimento di Cefalo*) a collection of *arias*. The madrigals (Example 66a) are basically what the name implies. Except for their texture (they are for solo voice and a bass part indicating the harmonies) and their ornamented style, they are shaped like typical madrigals of the declamatory type frequent in Caccini's time. In fact, if one wrote out a serious polyphonic declamatory madrigal—even as old as Cipriano da Rore—as a bass part and an ornamented melody, the result would be very similar to Caccini's madrigals. Caccini did what he said he would do: he cleared away the contrapuntal intricacy, reducing the texture to chords; he prevented indiscriminate application of passaggi by writing out the ornaments, thereby enabling the solo voice to project the text clearly with a maximum effect upon the listener.

The musical style of Caccini's arias (Example 66b) is essentially no different from that of his madrigals. The difference is primarily one of textual organization, for the arias have strophic texts, while the madrigals do not, a traditional difference going back for decades. In literary terms the strophic aria was less elevated than the free madrigal, and this in turn allowed arias to have sometimes a more frivolous subject. In response to this kind of text, some arias are lighter in tone, having a dancing bass and almost no expressive ornaments. This kind of aria, furthermore, tends to be the most obviously strophic; additional strophes were merely printed after the music. More serious arias have a slightly varied melody in each strophe over the same bass, or sometimes entirely new music written out for each strophe. Thus in Caccini's arias we find reminiscence both of the frivolous, strophic canzonetta, and the rhapsodic, improvised recitation over a strophic bass. (Caccini uses the *Aria di Romanesca* as an example in his preface.)

Like Caccini's "New Music," Peri's *L'Euridice* represents an adaptation of madrigal style to solo singing. But instead of writing separate madrigals or arias, Peri set a whole story—the story of Orfeo and Euridice—to music from beginning to end. The text, by Ottavio Rinuccini (1562–1621), was a mixture of free, madrigalesque verse and strophic forms or arias. Peri usually employed simple choral setting in chordal texture and dancelike, repetitive rhythms for the arias, while for the rest he used a continuous musical declamation like Caccini's madrigals.

This declamatory style (Example 67), later called *recitative*, responded expressively to every inflection of the text. Where the text was merely elegant, the melodic line moved only slightly, repeating the same pitch for several syllables—"speaking in harmony"; where the text was charged with emotion, this was projected to the listener by a more intense melodic shape and a stronger harmonic progression. The harmonies usually moved slowly, the voice moving much more rapidly in the stylized or expressive rhythms of poetic declamation.

The result was a musical drama—a small one, but nonetheless of great significance for the future. From this time on, poetry and music entered into a new kind of partnership. These first works were not intended to be drama of Greek or Shakespearian dimensions. Instead, they were regarded as *representations (rappresentazioni) of pastoral fables (favole pastorale)*. In the background was the music for theater or pageant (discussed in the previous chap-

EXAMPLE 66 CACCINI: FROM *LE NUOVE MUSICHE*

(a) Madrigal

(b) Aria

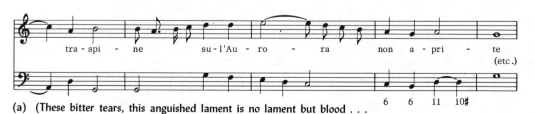

(a) (These bitter tears, this anguished lament is no lament but blood . . .
(b) Pretty little dark red roses, that through thorns do not open on the dawn . . .)

EXAMPLE 67   PERI: RECITATIVE FROM *L'EURIDICE*; Dafne Sings

EXAMPLE 67 (CONTINUED)

(Exhausted with fear and pity, my heart chills within my bosom. Wretched beauty, as though in a single moment—alas!—extinguished. A light or a flash, on a still night, can disappear swiftly, but with swifter flight does human life hasten to its fatal day.)

ter), successions of choral songs and dances in madrigalesque or canzonetta form, strung together by a loose scenario that was little more than an excuse for an extended concert. There was also the madrigal comedy, separate musical numbers whose succession was given reason by an idea or situation; the term *comedy* was freely applied to any story represented to an audience.

Peri's *L'Euridice* was similar both to the intermedii and madrigal comedy, in that it consisted of a succession of "madrigals," including the choral songs and dances typical of intermedii. But a radical shift in emphasis was now evident. Peri's chief interest lay in the madrigalesque declamation, the recitative; the *mise-en-scène* now had as its purpose the intensification of this recitative. The choral songs and dances became frames for the recitative as well as relief from its continuous, concentrated expression. The musical effect corresponds closely with the literary nature of the favola pastorale, which was not drama, but best described as "lyrical poetry in dialog."

Peri's real model, then, was the lyricism of Guarini's *Il Pastor fido*, the famous pastoral poem that had become the madrigalists' bible. Peri's intended result was a unique fusion of song and poetry, a magic combination neither literary nor musical, but lyrical—heightened poetry, words elevated above ordinary recitation by elegant language, set to harmony in such a way as to make the poetry incandescent. This ideal had been in the minds of thoughtful madrigal writers for some time, but it was Peri's single-mindedness that stripped away the usual apparatus of traditional counterpoint, expressing the ideal in the purest way.

The ideal of lyric recitative is not often realized in practice, as it is difficult to perform and requires complete comprehension by the listener of the Italian text—not merely the sense of the words, but the elegance of the poetic diction. But the ideal, and Peri's way of solving it, remained with Italian composers for more than a century. As long as they aimed at lyrical expression in their recitative (whether dialog or monolog), the recitative was successful, a valid form of musical discourse. If the dialog or monolog became dramatic, if the forward rush of action became for a moment more important than the elegance of expression, then the recitative became dangerous; it might be very exciting, but the burden now rested on the ability of the music to sustain the dramatic action, no longer on the poetical form of expression.

If, however, the recitative was used for ordinary conversational dialog, unillumined by lyrical brilliance, then it could only be ridiculous. It was used this way on purpose and with stunning effect in musical comedy; it could become so also through ineptitude or negligence on the part of librettist and composer. Recitative has often seemed ridiculous to non-Italians, either because they did not understand the spirit or the letter of the Italian original or because they knew the recitative only in translation, which, however true to the original, was never in a position to use the uniquely extravagant poetic technique that stood behind the Italian recitative.

Peri also exemplified the structural solutions most characteristic of the coming century. First, he made the recitative effective and convincing simply by making it go on for so long. Second, Peri set these long recitatives off by contrasting them with the choral songs inherited from the intermedium. The choral songs were traditionally simple, and Peri kept them that way. Since the songs were strophic, with repetitive dance rhythms set in a simple chordal style, they were at the extreme opposite end of the spectrum from the recitative. The large shape of Peri's work was made up of these two highly contrasting elements, solo recitative and choral song; only infrequently did he use forms of musical expression that lay in between these extremes. The juxtaposition of homogeneous sections, sharply contrasting each with its neighbor, was the shape of things to come.

Thus Peri was writing not a small, experimental drama, but a huge fulfillment of the old madrigal. The future destiny of his art form, however, was the music-drama. The idea of the music-drama was an exciting one; during the next decades a music-drama was a sought-after ingredient for any court occasion requiring glamorous festivities. Indeed, music-dramas usually came into existence only in connection with such festivities. The most famous took place in Rome, as indicated in this list:

Agostino Agazzari, *Eumelio* (Rome, 1606) dramma pastorale

Marco Gagliano, *La Dafne* (Mantua, 1608)

Girolamo Giacobbi, *Andromeda* (Bologna, 1610) tragedia

Domenico Belli, *Il Pianto d'Orfeo* (Florence, 1616) intermezzi

Stefano Landi, *La Morte d'Orfeo* (Rome, 1619) tragicommedia pastorale

Marco Gagliano, *Il Medoro* (Florence, 1619)

Filippo Vitali, *L'Aretusa* (Rome, 1620) favola

Domenico Mazzocchi, *La Catena d'Adone* (Rome, 1626) favola boschereccia

Marco Gagliano and Jacopo Peri, *La Flora* (Florence, 1628) favola

Stefano Landi, *Il San Alessio* (Rome, 1632) dramma musicale

Michelangelo Rossi, *Erminia sul Giordano* (Rome, 1633) dramma musicale

In general such works consist of recitative and choral strophic aggregates, the recitative typically responsible for the bulk of the work. The basic conception seems to be Peri's idea of a lyrical dialog sung in recitative. This is true even of *Il San Alessio*, a sacred subject, and one of the largest, most serious works; it is called *dramma musicale*. Even here the recitative is the chief substance and the chief problem. If the text and performance were good, the recitative could succeed; but during the 1620s we hear the word "tedious" applied to the recitative. One problem is that all recitative tends to sound alike—the paradoxical result of letting the music exactly express the text. For in expressing the text, the recitative composer drew on a rhetoric of stock phrases inherited from the declamatory madrigal. In this closed rhetoric, few new phrases were invented. There was no musical basis within the recitative for further development.

Musical development during these decades really took place outside the music-drama, in a huge, largely unexplored repertory of monody, published in Florence, Rome, and Venice by amateur and professional composers. It would be a mistake to underestimate the importance of this repertory, even though its quality is extremely uneven, its products often whimsical, bizarre, trivial, or dull. It was here that the techniques of the new style were worked out. The music-drama was the result, not the cause, of stylistic development; only the development within this monodic repertory made possible the larger, more convincing music-drama that appeared after 1640. The problem in writing music-drama was not so much one of finding a kind of music appropriate to drama, but rather of forging a successful musical style, and then finding the kind of dramatic text that would permit the most effective display of this style. The vast monodic repertory demonstrates once again that the core of the new style was lyric effusion, rather than dramatic action.

Very few examples of this monodic repertory are available in modern edition; those which are available are often not the most convincing examples. Representative composers, with their first or most representative publication, are listed here:

Severo Bonini, *Madrigali e canzonette spirituali* (Florence, 1607)
Francesco Rasi, *Vaghezza di musica* (Venice, 1608)
Sigismondo d'India, *Le Musiche* (Milan, 1609)
Marc'Antonio Negri, *Affetti amorosi* (Venice, 1608)
Antonio Cifra, *Li Scherzi* (Rome, 1613)
Claudio Saracini, *Le Musiche* (Venice, 1614)
Filippo Vitali, *Musiche* (Florence, 1617)

These publications contain a variety of short pieces for one, two, or several voices, usually with basso continuo. Such pieces may be sacred but are usually secular. Many are declamatory madrigals like those of Caccini's *Le Nuove musiche;* many others are strophic arias of varying description. The publications are sometimes titled simply "Music," sometimes have more effusive titles that say little about the type or structure of their contents but indicate accurately their intention. From 1618 on, G. Stefani in Venice edited a vast collection entitled *Affetti amorosi*.

MONTEVERDI The steps toward the fully developed music-drama can be traced most easily in the works of Monteverdi, because he, more than any other composer of his time, saw that the problems of this new form were basically musical; he also saw how to solve them. Monteverdi's thinking ran along the same line as Peri's: the most promising form of the past, the madrigal, must be transformed so as better to fulfill its inherited ideal.

Unlike Peri, however, Monteverdi did not try to accomplish this at one stroke. Instead he worked within the madrigal slowly, little by little changing its inner structure until the new style seemed to arise out of the madrigal of its own accord. Monteverdi filled in all the steps that Peri had left out. Thus Monteverdi's first opera, *La Favola d'Orfeo*, was not written until 1607, seven years after Peri's and more than fifteen years after the first experiments at the Academy in Florence. During these years Monteverdi published madrigals, five books of them, in which the inner transformation largely took place.

The madrigals of Book II (1590) show, on one hand, how close Monteverdi remained to the traditional idea of the madrigal, and on the other, his peculiar manner of twisting the madrigal into a new shape. The famous madrigal *Ecco mormorar l'onde* (Behold, the murmuring waters), having a pastoral text, uses the musical idioms customary for that mood. The piece begins and ends on F; it uses the lilting rhythms and turns of phrase characteristic of a pastoral madrigal—but with a difference. The piece is much more homogeneous than a Marenzio madrigal would have been. The pastoral mood is sustained by the increased continuity and absence of variety from one phrase of text to the next. The rhythms are all alike; the set of harmonies is very limited, and their succession is extremely smooth. Like a good madrigal, this one imitates the text, but Monteverdi chose to make the whole madrigal imitate only one idea of the text, instead of making each phrase of music imitate a different idea. The piece lacks the variety of the old style, but it has increased point, an essential feature of the new.

One other detail of *Ecco mormorar l'onde* illustrates Monteverdi's technique. At the end there is a long stepwise progression in the bass through an octave and a half, over which the upper voices repeat the same rhythmic and melodic motif in sequence. The device itself is not new; it can, for example, be found at the end of Marenzio's *Scendi dal paradiso* (page 215). To say that Monteverdi's descending bass is longer is a weak understatement. It is not merely longer; it is so much longer as to outstrip any expectation that his listener might have. It is exaggerated to the point where the traditional limits of good musical sense are far exceeded. Such exaggeration of traditional manners is Monteverdi's way of making music effective, projecting its meaning forcefully to the listener.

In Book III (1592) Monteverdi was absorbed with purely technical problems of musical organization. Here his ordering of harmonies started to acquire a purely musical focus. The opening pages of *Stracciami pur il core,* for example, are organized over a stepwise ascending bass—not used as a mannerism, as in *Ecco mormorar l'onde,* but as a purely musical device. This increased sense of focus took place in the absence of highly emotional texts.

Then in Book IV (1603) Monteverdi turned again to the intense madrigal, applying to it the sense of harmonic focus gained in Book III. He now produced madrigals of great force, even violence. They imitated the text, like the old madrigal, but the emotional effect now came from the cogency of musical expression rather than from pictorial illustration of the text—and very different from the heightened lyrical expression Peri achieved by "speaking in harmony." *Si ch'io vorrei morire,* for example, has little word painting; for the most part it declaims the text rather than illustrating it. But the declamation involves many elements of purely musical form, such as repeated rhythms, ascending and descending sequences, motivic reiterations that are really reiteration of a few, very simple chord progressions. The music has a single-mindedness that drives it far beyond the emotional capacity of the old madrigal. The piece is shocking, as befits its sensual text.

In the fifth book of madrigals (1605), the declamation is continually reinforced by musical techniques involving harmonic focus and repeated rhythms. Monteverdi seems determined to make the madrigal speak, to project its urgent message to the listener; still, however, he wrote in the traditional five-voiced texture. Peri had long since made the madrigal monodic, but Monteverdi persisted in the five-voiced counterpoint until he was sure that the sheer force of his musical expression would succeed in the absence of contrapuntal texture and the traditional intensity it provided.

Nothing but texture now separated Monteverdi's declamatory madrigal from recitative. In fact, Book V also contains six works that use the new monodic texture and the basso continuo, but here, interestingly enough, Monteverdi tended to avoid the declamatory style of recitative. Instead, he enriched the monodic style in a number of ways. The parts for solo voice and basso continuo are often ornamented with the florid passaggi or excited rhythmic figures inherited from improvisatory practice. When he did use declamatory phrases for one or two voices, he almost always set them off against phrases for the whole ensemble of five or six voices. Here Monteverdi looked within the traditional madrigal shape for some structural arrangement that would make the simple declamatory phrase more telling.

In 1607 the opportunity to write a pastoral drama in the manner of the Florentines finally presented itself, and Monteverdi responded with his *L'Orfeo, favola in musica*. The libretto by Alessandro Striggio was conceived more dramatically than the setting of the same story by Rinuccini used by Peri and Caccini; that is, Striggio placed somewhat less emphasis on the choruses of nymphs and shepherds, and, in the dialog, less emphasis on lyric elegance, with more on the heroic or pathetic pose of the principals, especially Orfeo.

The first act and the beginning of the second contain the traditional choral songs, set in the usual build-up of arias and instrumental refrains or *ritornellos*. Monteverdi used all the delicious variety of songs and dances, the varied sonorities of the huge orchestra traditionally associated with the intermedium. Then, in the middle of the second act, while Orfeo and his shepherds are rejoicing in the fields, in bursts a messenger to say that Euridice, the lovely bride of Orfeo, is dead.

The messenger sings in recitative (Example 68), so that the contrast between light-footed song and dance and somber, sustained recitative provides the musical basis for the dramatic effect of the whole act. Here Monteverdi's long preoccupation with the declamatory madrigal paid off, for his recitative is much more organized—and as a result much more telling—than Peri's.

It is significant, however, that Euridice's death (the dramatic action in this case) does not take place onstage. Instead, it is described by the messenger in a lengthy recital whose shape is not unlike an expanded madrigal. In other words, the whole art form is still one that concerns recitation and dialog, not action; or rather, the action is the action of characters speaking to one another, a feature that remains typical of music-drama for more than a century. In a sense, the action exists for the sake of poetical and musical forms; it is used to bring about circumstances so urgent as to demand the heightened expression of recitative.

Immediately after *L'Orfeo*, Monteverdi set another drama to music,

EXAMPLE 68 MONTEVERDI: RECITATIVE FROM L'ORFEO, II; Sylvia Sings

In un fio - ri - to pra - to, Con l'al - tre sue com-pa - gne,

Giù a co-lien-do fio - ri Per far ne u-na ghir-lan - da a le sue

chio - me, Quand an - gue in-si-di - o - se Ch'e - ra fra l'er-be a-sco-so Le pun-se un

piè con ve-lo-no - so den - te. Ed ec - co im-man-ti-nen-te sco-lo-

rir - si il bel vi - so, e ne suo i-lu - mi Spa - rir que lam - pi ond el - la al Sol

3 4   3

EXAMPLE 68 (CONTINUED)

fea scor - no. All' - hor noi tut-te sbi-got-ti - te e me - ste

Le fum-mo in-tor - no ri-chia-mar ten-tan-do Li spir - ti in lei smar-ri - ti con l'on-da

fre-sca e con pos-sen - ti car-mi. Ma nul - la val - se hai las - sa! Ch'el -

- la i lan-gui-di lu - mi al - quan-to a-pren-do, E te chia-man-do Or-fe-o,

Or-fe - o! Dop-po un gra - ve so-spi-ro Spi-ro fra que-ste brac-cia;

EXAMPLE 68 (CONTINUED)

ed io ri - ma - si, Pien il cor di pie-ta - de e di spa-ven - to. (etc.)

(She was in a verdant pasture, with her other companions, picking flowers to make a garland for her hair, when the insidious serpent, hidden in the grass, bit her foot with poisoned fang. And lo—at once her fair face discolored, and in her eyes that light went out that used to put the sun itself to shame. Then, all shocked and dismayed, we clustered around her trying to revive her lost sense with fresh water and potent charms. But nought availed, alas! Once she opened her drooping eyes, calling thy name, "Orfeo—Orfeo—" After a deep sigh, she expired in these arms. And I remained, my heart full of pity, and of fear.)

L'Arianna (1608). The work, unfortunately, is lost, except for a celebrated *Lamento*, an extended recitative for Arianna, left to die on a remote island. The recitative reflects a variety of thought and feeling of the text, yet maintains a remarkable continuity and homogeneity throughout. It demonstrates both the expressive power of Monteverdi's recitative, and his form-giving harmonic control. Because it was so popular, this lament was published separately from the drama; but in order to appeal to the wider audience that purchased printed music (as opposed to the small courtly audience that witnessed live productions), Monteverdi rewrote the lament as a five-voiced madrigal, externally no different from his previous declamatory madrigals of Books IV and V.

In its madrigalesque form the *Lamento* was published in Book VI (1614), along with still more declamatory madrigals, especially another lament, a *sestina, Lagrime d'amante al sepolcro dell'amata* (Tears of the lover at the tomb of the beloved; *sestina* is a poetic form), along with other madrigals. Book VI includes also the type introduced in Book V, monodic passages accompanied by basso continuo, alternating with ensemble. This type of madrigal is here described as *concertato nel clavicimbalo* (concerted with the harpsichord) or simply *concertato*—a term used increasingly after 1600 to designate the combination of contrasting musical resources, voices and instruments.

After the sixth book of madrigals, Monteverdi's output assumed a bewildering variety of forms, each work constructed on its own terms. The basic principle, however, was now clear and constant. Some single idea, drawn from the text, was impressed upon the listener as forcefully as possible, by repeated, single-minded presentation of restricted sets of chords and repetitive rhythms. Such uniformity, of course, had to be relieved if the result was to be art; relief came through changes of texture and timbre provided by concerted media and also through the figural language of the old diminutions, now composed right into the piece instead of supplied ad libitum by the performer.

The full spectrum of textural and figural combinations possible at this time can be easily surveyed in Monteverdi's *Vespers* of 1610. This work represented the application of the most modern musical techniques to sacred music. Other composers were making the same application, but none in such an extreme degree. The principles of Monteverdi's concertato style as manifested here are not so very different from those in contemporary concertos by G. Gabrieli and others, at least as far as texture goes. But Monteverdi's are more extreme, more single-minded, the sections more homogeneous, the contrast between sections sharper, the rhythmic momentum greater—all features that make Monteverdi's music more modern than Gabrieli's.

The idea of concerted music was very much in Monteverdi's mind during these years. His next book of madrigals, Book VII (1619), was entitled *Concerto. Settimo libro de madrigali a 1, 2, 3, 4, & 6 voci, con altri generi de canti,* the poetic conceit of the title being carried further in the dedicatory preface. It is important to take the term *concerto* in the general sense of "harmonious combination of varied things," without trying to attach it to any formal design or specific type of work. Each madrigal in itself is apt to be a concerto in this sense. The first, *Tempro la cetra,* has an instrumental introduction or *sinfonia,* then an ornamental monody over a vaguely strophic bass, with ritornellos in between sections, and a larger, sectional sinfonia at the end.

One of the most fruitful technical solutions of the seventh book is found in the frequent duets for two tenors over a bass, for example, *Dice la mia bellissima Licori.* That this form of monody was rapidly becoming Monteverdi's favorite was no accident: the duet of two equal voices over a bass represented the best solution to the problem of texture—a solution entirely characteristic of Monteverdi's careful course between old and new.

The old five-voiced imitative texture was now no longer useful, having neither the projective force of monody nor the splendor of the many-voiced concertato style. But the radical solutions of Peri and other monodists tended to sound barren, stripped of the interesting textures of polyphony. Monteverdi found the best of both styles in an ensemble in which two equal voices, say, two tenors, moved either in sweet thirds or in some tight imitative procedure full of friction, with the duet set off against a bass that provided the essential harmonies in the manner of a monody. The result was both projective and intricate; it rapidly became a standard form of vocal chamber music, if not of all kinds of music.

Besides projecting the text, the value of monody lay in the way the two parts, voice and bass, outlined the harmonies, throwing their profiles into relief. One must, however, guard against thinking of monody as two-voiced music. The third note that completes the triad or sixth chord is absolutely essential to the proper functioning of the two written parts. Without the firm foundation of harmony, the two written parts sound awkward and ineffective; they do not, by themselves, convey the intended sense of the music. This is another reason for the popularity of the trio. In addition to providing a more intricate top to the sound, the trio of two tenors (or sopranos) over a bass was a convenient—if partial—solution to the problem of producing a continuous stream of triads. If the two upper voices moved in parallel thirds, they tended to form with the bass something approaching a triadic texture, if only because the interval of a third was so often present.

Dice la mia bellissima Licori reveals Monteverdi's mastery of this trio style. One whole page (Example 69) is nothing but an endlessly descending step-wise bass, moving in quarter notes, under a lively alternation of eighth-note figures in the upper parts. The result is an extraordinary combination of anima-tion and smooth continuity. Technical solutions like this were necessary to make the new style work; in the years represented by the seventh book Monteverdi reached one such solution after another.

EXAMPLE 69   MONTEVERDI: FROM THE MADRIGAL *DICE LA MIA BELLISSIMA LICORI* (Book VII)

(He is a little spirit, that wanders about and flees, and cannot be caught nor touched nor seen . . .)

In this same duet, we find an alternation of sections in common time, moving in quarters and eighths, with short episodes in triple time; the latter are strangely notated in whole notes, but go much faster than their appearance suggests (probably something like six whole notes in the space of one measure of common time), tempos that would be best represented to us in three-four or six-eight. Episodes in triple time were, of course, traditional in the madrigal; but Monteverdi had not used them very much in the serious declamatory madrigal. From now on such sections appeared with increasing frequency and persuasion. The contrast they make with the common time became an increasingly important feature of musical style. Yet they are completely absent from such an effective madrigal as *Interrotte speranze,* a duet in recitative unfolding its declamation within a tightly controlled harmonic progression.

At the end of Book VII comes a variety of significant works. *Ohime dov'è il mio ben* is a set of strophic variations over one of the old basses, *Romanesca,* for a duet of two sopranos singing in highly ornamented, affective recitative—a remarkable summation of a whole era of rhapsodic effusion, and, as it turned out, one of Monteverdi's last uses of this strophic bass technique. It is followed by two *Lettere amorose* (Love letters), expressing extreme examples of that lyric pathos Peri had initiated.

These in turn are followed by two *Canzonette concertate* (Concerted canzonettas), each for two violins and basso continuo, the first for two sopranos, the second with a solo, a duet, a trio, and a concluding quartet. The first, *Chiome d'oro,* brilliantly illustrates the new spirit and technique that lead from *L'Orfeo* to the universal solutions achieved after 1640. It is built over a repeating bass figure, or rather two slightly different figures, one for the instrumental ritornello, the other for the vocal strophes. Out of this extremely repetitive scheme Monteverdi constructed a piece of the greatest charm imaginable.

It is hard to conceive anything more different from the sustained, eloquent tone of the preceding *lettere.* Almost for the first time, Monteverdi succeeded in making a kind of piece that could rival the recitative in lyrical effusion, yet be entirely different from it. The secret to this piece—and to the musical style of the next decades—lay in the repetitive bass figures moving in a dancing style; these liberated purely musical forces that could never find expression in the recitative.

Each of these pieces in the seventh book seems to be an extreme solution to a single problem; so with the last piece, *Tirsi e Clori,* a *ballo concertato con voci et instrumenti a 5* (dramatic ballet). Here the triple rhythms appear explicitly as dance music, revealing their essential nature and the new spirit they bring to the madrigal. The piece consists of an opening dialog in which Tirsi sings in triple time, while Clori answers in common-time recitative; then together they sing a duet in triple time. The dance itself starts with a slow introduction in common time, and then an extended triple time for five voices accompanied by instruments, sections of which are literally repeated. There are two interludes in common time, and a concluding *riverenza* (obeisance) in slow common time. Thus ends the seventh book, a "concerto" of madrigals "and other kinds of pieces."

In 1638 Monteverdi published an eighth book of madrigals, entitled *Madrigali guerrieri e amorosi* (Madrigals of war and love), famous for the frequent use of Monteverdi's *stile concitato* (agitated style), achieved by rapid repetition of a single chord. At first glance a striking novelty, the stile concitato actually has its roots in the battle pieces of the 1500s; in any case, Monteverdi's use of this style, as shown by the dates of several pieces in the eighth book, goes back to the 1620s. The most famous example, the *Combattimento di Tancredi e Clorinda* (Combat of Tancred and Clorinda), dates from 1624. Thus stile concitato was an extreme manifestation of the tendency of the madrigal to speak out in violent gestures; it does not, however, reflect the new forces at work in the 1630s.

During the early 1630s composers found the purely musical solution needed for the new dramatic forms. The light-footed triple-time dance rhythms became increasingly popular, both for themselves and as a contrasting element to the more ponderous recitative. In this dance style the voice and bass usually moved in more or less the same kind of rhythm; that is, the bass moved as fast as the voice, instead of much more slowly as in the recitative. This meant that melody, bass, and rhythm were all bound up together in the dancelike motion of the harmonies. It took several decades to isolate this style. It had of course been frequent in the past, either as frivolous canzonetta or as episode in a more serious madrigal or motet; but during the 1630s it was developed to the point where it could rival the power of the recitative.

The new rhythms can be observed especially in publications of monodies in Venice, beginning with Alessandro Grandi's *Cantade ed Arie* from before 1620. There were not many *cantade* in this first collection, and they were not very impressive; but the name, at least, pointed toward the future. What was needed to elevate the triple-time dances was a more characteristic, interesting rhythm, something to give point to the innocuous trochees. Around 1630, Venetian publications, especially of the composers Giovanni Pierto Berti (died 1638) and Giovanni Felice Sances (ca 1600–1679), began to exploit two dances recently imported from Spain, the *ciacona* and the *passacaglia*. Both dances were strong in exotic character; both combined Spanish *hauteur* with passion and inner fire.

It is difficult now to distinguish clearly between ciacona and passacaglia. The ciacona tends to be in major, the passacaglia in minor—but that is only a tendency, as is the use of blue, flatted thirds and sevenths in the ciacona. Dramatic composers in the 1600s sometimes used the ciacona in flagrantly seductive scenes and associated the passacaglia more with longing. Such tendencies may reflect the original character of the dances.

Both ciacona and passacaglia used repeated bass figures (which we call *basso ostinato*), much shorter and simpler than old strophic basses such as *Romanesca;* a frequent passacaglia figure consists of four descending notes, A, G, F, E. Neither the actual figure nor the way it is used is related to the character of ciacona or passacaglia or to the difference between them (as was once thought). More important is the fact that these bass figures are short enough to be immediately grasped by the ear and so simple as to define a tonal area with great clarity. Each bass figure represents a closely related group of harmonies, a set of chords that makes a key. These chords, repeated over and over in unvarying rhythm, make the sense of key continuously, inescapably present, communicating a single musical idea with great force, but at the same time freeing

EXAMPLE 70   MONTEVERDI: FROM THE CIACONA *ZEFIRO TORNA*

(Return, sweet breeze . . .)

the composer to superimpose variations in unrestrained caprice. Whether used
strictly or freely, these repetitive bass figures made their influence widely felt
in the new dramatic style.

The best examples of how ciacona and passacaglia could be adapted to
monody were provided by Monteverdi. His *Sherzi musicali, cioè arie & madrigali in stile recitativo, con una Ciaccona, a 1 & 2 voci* (1632) reflects clearly
the new interest in strophic works and triple-time rhythms. The ciacona contained in it is *Zefiro torna*, one of Monteverdi's most famous works—and rightly
so. It has an ostinato (Example 70), a bass figure derived harmonically from a
stepwise descending melodic line. The ciacona character, however, resides in the
fascinating syncopation of triple time. Over this syncopated ostinato, endlessly
repeated, two tenors compete in singing voluptuous passaggi, which now help
rather than hinder the rhythmic flow (as they were inclined to do before). There
are contrasting sections in recitative to contrast the mood of the unhappy lover
with the luminous landscape. The work is a minor miracle, exerting that magic
spell sought after by all ambitious composers of the 1600s; one of the best
ciaconas ever written, it strongly suggests a character for the original dance.

The counterpart to *Zefiro torna* is the *Lamento della ninfa* (Lament of
the Nymph), which belongs stylistically at this time, though it was not published
until 1638. In both, Monteverdi handled the technique of ostinato in an extreme
fashion to which he rarely returned, but in each, he put the stamp of success on
styles and techniques of the utmost importance for the future. While the
Lamento is not labeled *passacaglia,* its character seems to resemble one. The bass
(Example 71) has a stepwise descending figure, A–G–F–E, ostinato throughout.
Over it the nymph sings her lament in a peculiarly disassociated manner, her
phrases overlapping those of the bass—a way of handling the strict ostinato that
became standard. Three male voices, sometimes singing together, sometimes
separately, coinciding neither with bass nor with soprano, commiserate with the
nymph.

Less syncopated than the *Zefiro torna,* and stripped of passaggi, the
Lamento has the same swinging effect to its triple rhythm; it casts the same
magic spell. Here the purely musical forces of repeated harmonies and rhythms
attained a lyrical force comparable to the recitative. The animated rhythms

EXAMPLE 71   MONTEVERDI: FROM LAMENTO DELLA NINFA

(Love . . . [she said] . . . Love . . .)

could now speak out, projecting the meaning of the text to the listener. The triple time could go onstage.

KEYBOARD MUSIC AND FRESCOBALDI   The most striking kind of instrumental music in the decades after 1600 was for solo keyboard. As we saw in the preceding chapter, the keyboard had a special distinction in the late 1500s because of its ability, shared only with members of the lute family, to play all parts of a polyphonic composition. The keyboard was a "perfect" instrument, capable of reproducing all by itself the harmonic fabric of music. Since this was accomplished by a single performer, that performer was a virtuoso equal in stature to any of the other virtuosi—singers, lutenists, viol players, and others.

The virtuoso role of the player is essential in understanding music for lute or keyboard, for such music was often designed to be spectacular, to fill the listener with a sense of wonder. Figuration that looks simple and mechanical on the page would, on the proper instrument, played by a virtuoso at a properly brilliant tempo, have a spectacular effect. The art of lute or keyboard was something of a "manner," as if it were acting on a stage.

Of the many famous virtuosi of the time, Girolamo Frescobaldi (1583–1643) was the best composer. His works, published from 1608, best illustrate the various forms and styles for keyboard—*partite* (variations), *toccate, canzone alla francese, capricci, fantasie,* and *ricercari,* as well as other special types. All of these we met before; in fact, each type of piece in Frescobaldi represents a traditional style, a manner of composition. These various manners of composition are best understood as spread out over a continuum ranging from figural diminution on one end to imitative counterpoint on the other—the extremes of texture in the late 1500s.

Figural diminution involves the expression of the basic harmonic substance in fragments of scales and arpeggios. As we saw, diminution was widely practiced in the 1500s, but as improvised ornamentation of a piece, not usually written into the piece by the composer. Figural diminution typically involved very small note values—eighths, sixteenths, thirty-seconds, and even smaller. Imitative counterpoint, at the other extreme, did not use the techniques of figural diminution, nor the very small note values that went with it.

For the 1500s imitative counterpoint was a basic method of composition, a way of creating the very harmonic substance which was then subjected to figuration. But with the great reduction of counterpoint to chords that took place around 1600, imitative counterpoint became, like figural diminution, a style or manner of composition, now merely superimposed on the harmonic substance.

Awareness of counterpoint's new status is essential if we are to understand the persistence of imitative counterpoint, especially in keyboard music. In itself, imitation was not necessarily conservative or old-fashioned. It was absent from vocal music for a while because there it impeded the projection of the text. But imitative counterpoint continued in the most modern keyboard music as one extreme manner of composition, the polar opposite to figural diminution.

The clearest application of figural diminution is found in the partitas, or variations (each variation was a *parte*), which Frescobaldi and others wrote copiously over modern popular tunes or arias. The patterns of diminution were endless; furthermore they had been standardized through decades of improvisation. The art of variation lay in very subtle modification or application of these patterns, a subtlety apparent to a connoisseur of those times, but probably not to us. Like the less educated listener of those times, we hear only the extreme brilliance of each variation and the contrast from one to the next.

Besides the partitas, figural diminution was most evident in the toccatas (Example 72). In principle a toccata was a succession of harmonies expressed in a varied flow of diminution (scales and arpeggios). Here the figure could change at any time according to the whim of the composer, giving the toccata a rhapsodic structure very different from the partita, where the figure generally changed only with each repetition of the tune or aria. In fact, the toccata can be viewed as the instrumental counterpart of the recitative, dependent like the recitative on the skill and persuasion of the performer. Frescobaldi's earlier toccatas for harpsichord consist of almost nothing but figural patterns; others, for organ, could be sectional, including episodes in imitative counterpoint for contrast.

The toccata is the keyboard piece par excellence. Toccatas, of all the types mentioned, were the only kind of piece indigenous to the keyboard. Variations were just as characteristic of other virtuoso instruments (solo or in concert), while fantasias, ricercars, and canzonas, based on imitative counterpoint, were ultimately derived from vocal models of the 1500s. Furthest from the toccata is the ricercar. Frescobaldi's ricercars move in whole notes, half notes, and quarters; they have vocal subjects and vocal lines; they are somber and severe compared with the brilliant, rhapsodic toccatas. It is in the work of Frescobaldi that all these types take on their extreme distinctions—a development very characteristic of the musical style in those decades and an indication that Frescobaldi was moving parallel to Monteverdi.

In between toccata and ricercar lie the other types. The fantasia uses subjects similar to those of the ricercar, but moves from imitative counterpoint to styles of figuration similar to those of the variation. The capriccio is hard to distinguish from the fantasia, except that it is apt to use an arbitrary or whimsi-

EXAMPLE 72 FRESCOBALDI: BEGINNING OF A TOCCATA

(Freely)

cal subject, for example, the ascending scale *ut, re, mi, fa, sol, la*. If a ricercar
is a *study* or *research*, then a capriccio is a *caprice*, or *capricious fantasy*. Eventually *caprice* comes to refer to the whimsical subject itself.

Throughout these decades we see terms that once designated ideas becoming hardened into styles of composition. The capriccio and even more the
stravaganza are especially characteristic of the urge toward the unusual and
bizarre that marked the most modern composers of the early 1600s. One capriccio
in particular later became a whole style in itself: Frescobaldi's *Capriccio
pastorale*, in G major, stands at the head of a long line of pastorales.

The central form was the canzona (understood as *alla francese*), derived
from the French chanson of the early 1500s and widely cultivated as instrumental music in the late 1500s in Italy. The canzona was imitative, but in the
manner of a chanson: it started out in contrapuntal imitation, but after a few
measures tended to lapse into a figural or even chordal style. Its subjects (one
might almost say its subject, because of the strong resemblance among canzona
subjects— 𝄴 ♩ ♩♩ | ♩) were simple and jaunty; its counterpoint was easily
perceptible as harmony, and perhaps for that reason supplied the core of
ensemble instrumental style after 1650.

The canzona was not severe and sustained like the ricercar, but instead
sectional. It usually had an episode in triple time, or often two episodes, making
a five-part form. The sections might or might not be related by a common subject (the same was true of some of the fantasias and other types), but this was
not an essential feature. In its contrasting sections in different styles, the
canzona most nearly approached the shape of modern vocal compositions of the
1620s and 1630s.

Frescobaldi's publications during these decades reflected the same interest
in dances seen in Monteverdi's madrigals. Frescobaldi makes much use of the
corrente, a triple-time dance. Much more spectacular, however, is a set of *Cento
partite sopra passacagli* (a hundred variations on passacaglias), which include
sections on the corrente and ciacona as well as the passacaglia—the same exotic
dances that were making such a stir in Venetian vocal music during the early
1630s. Frescobaldi's variations are full of the blue notes, the flatted thirds
characteristic of ciacona and passacaglia, but these chromaticisms do not hinder
the reiterated bass patterns from establishing a very clear sense of tonal focus,
as in Monteverdi's ostinato works.

A sense of key is very strong in Frescobaldi's *Cento partite*, even though
the ostinato is frequently obscured by figuration or variation. According to
Frescobaldi's directions, one can play excerpts from the whole set, which, as a
matter of fact, ends in a different key than the one in which it began. The sense
of key, in other words, is stated with great force at any given moment, but does
not control the whole piece or produce a symmetrical form. In this respect
Frescobaldi's variations are representative of tonal concepts of the new music.

Actually there seem to be more than one hundred variations; but it is
easy to lose count, a fact that takes us to the very heart of the work. If played
complete, it is exceedingly long, as passacaglias and ciaconas tend to be from
this time on. The intention clearly is to go on so long that time seems to stop,
hang suspended in the magic mood created by the exotic rhythms. In works like
these Frescobaldi's genius showed most clearly what stupendous effects the new

music could achieve. Here we see that it was not novel forms or even novel styles that made the new music new, rather it was the extraordinary way of treating conventional forms and styles.

The same principle, but not the same spectacular result, is apparent in Frescobaldi's most famous collection, the *Fiori musicali* (Musical flowers) of 1635. This is a liturgical collection: it provides organ music for the mass for three occasions, a mass for Sundays, a mass for Feasts of Apostles, and a mass for the Blessed Virgin. For each mass Frescobaldi includes toccatas or canzonas for various places where incidental music is needed, and also short pieces to be played either in place of or in response to the *Kyrie* sung by the choir (another traditional way of using the organ in the liturgy).

Many of the pieces in the *Fiori musicali* are impressive because of their somber severity. Compared with the toccatas of other publications they seem restrained to the point of dullness. But severity itself was a mood—and a very important one to listeners of those decades; they were accustomed to it, and valued it in the long recitatives used increasingly for tragic characters in the music-drama. The very fact that the severity goes on for so long is one mark of its modernity in Frescobaldi. It was an extreme, and as such reflected the desire of composers to be above all impressive.

OTHER INSTRUMENTAL MUSIC   What little we know of other types of Italian instrumental music before 1650 indicates that it nowhere approached the depth and richness of Frescobaldi. Occasionally, however, it was more adventuresome, reflecting eccentric extremes one is apt to find in less astute composers. The most interesting radical composer of instrumental music is Biagio Marini (1597–1665), and his most interesting publication, even judging only from the title, is *Sonate, symphonie, canzoni, pass'emezzi, baletti, corenti, gagliarde, & ritornelli, a 1.2.3.4.5.& 6. voci, per ogni sorte d'instrumenti. Un Capriccio per sonar due violini quatro parti. Un ecco per tre violini, & alcune sonate capriciose per sonar due è tre parti con il violino solo, con altre curiose & moderne inventione.* (Op. 8, Venice, 1629).

A sonata is at this time a piece that is (mostly) played, as opposed to one that is sung; the term does not specify anything further. A symphony is a piece played by a combination of instruments—usually a larger combination; symphonies often occur as overtures to music-dramas. Canzonas, as we saw, can be written for any instrumental combination, as can the various dances. Ritornellos again usually occur in connection with vocal music, but are here published separately. A capriccio might be almost anything, but almost certainly would be a striking piece. (The adjective *capricciose* appears in this title clearly as a selling word representing a desirable feature.) An echo is the instrumental imitation of the popular echo effect of the late madrigal. The sonatas (for double and triple stops) for solo violin present the virtuoso and his stunning effects; they include several experimental imitations of the new monody, and passages significantly labeled *affetti*. The point of the publication and the repertory it represents is clearly stated in the last sentence, "other curious modern inventions"; here the term *invention* is still a general term, while later it was applied to a specific composition.

Other composers working to bring instrumental music up-to-date were

Gabriele Usper, Giovanni Battista Fontana (?-1631), Massimiliano Neri (after 1600–after 1666), Giovanni Maria Trabaci (?-1647), and Salomone Rossi (1570?–1630?). In 1637 Tarquinio Merula (ca 1595–1665) published in Venice a collection titled *Canzoni, overo sonate concertate per chiesa, e camera a 2 et a 3*, which means (taking into account Italian punctuation and the appearance of the contents), "Canzonas, or concerted sonatas, for church and chamber." There was no particular distinction, on the one hand, between canzonas and concerted sonatas, or on the other, between works for church or chamber; either type was suitable for either occasion. Merula's small quantity of extant keyboard music rivals that of Frescobaldi in quality and has greater clarity of outline and style, an indication of the prevailing direction of stylistic development toward 1650.

North of the Alps

With the shift of stylistic leadership from Northerners to Italians, the situation in Northern countries became confused. These countries turned to the new style erratically and unsystematically, interpreting what they knew of Italian novelties as best they could in terms of local stylistic conditions.

The long-range changes, the acceptance of the triad as an entity and the reduction of contrapuntal texture to melody and bass, went on at almost the same rate in all countries. In contrast, the short-range effects, the forceful definition of style, remained closely connected with Italy. Northern composers wrote music that sometimes seemed outwardly modern—dances, accompanied songs, and concerted church music. But their handling of monody, dance rhythms, and the basso continuo often sounded arbitrary and unconvincing. They composed consistently in chords but not in keys; their treatment of the harmonies lacked the focus that in Italy was associated with effective dramatic expression.

In order to produce significant results, the new style had to pass through the hands of a first-rate composer, one who possessed not merely skill and familiarity with the new techniques, but a vision of how these might be meaningfully adapted to conditions in a new country and a new language. There was only one such composer in any Northern country at this time: Heinrich Schütz (1585–1672). But for him, music in Germany would have presented the same lack of direction as in France and England during the first part of the century.

SCHUTZ AND SCHEIN: SACRED CONCERTO AND HISTORIA   It is no accident that Schütz took more trouble than anyone else to find out what was actually going on in Italy. As a youth of twenty-five, he studied in Venice with Giovanni Gabrieli, learning the splendid polychoral style for which Gabrieli was especially famous in Germany. The fruit of this phase of Schütz's Italian studies was his *Psalmen Davids* (1619), polychoral works on the grand Venetian scale. But they were only a beginning.

Like Monteverdi, his Italian counterpart, Schütz picked his way toward a radically modern style with great caution. Indeed, his *Psalmen Davids* seem conservative when compared with Johann Hermann Schein's *Opella nova* of the preceding year, 1618. The *Opella nova* (New little work) contains *Geistliche Concerten* (Sacred concertos) for three, four, and five voices together with the *Generalbass* (basso continuo), composed in the now fashionable Italian style.

Schein used the soloistic ensemble style of Monteverdi's madrigals. He combined abundant expressive passaggi, such as Caccini described, with the new device of the basso continuo. He wrote, in effect, continuo madrigals, with German chorale tunes as cantus firmi and sacred German texts. There is much that is expressive in the *Opella nova;* but it lacks the inner structure, the harmonic focus, of its models.

Schein also published, in 1617, a *Banchetto musicale* (Musical banquet), containing dances for an instrumental ensemble (pavans, gagliards, courantes, allemandes), and during the 1620s a series titled *Musica boscareccia* (Woodland music), containing basically Italian villanellas. Taken together, these publications reflect the uncertainty, widespread in Germany, about the significance of events in Italy.

Schütz, on the other hand, wrote no dances and no villanellas; like Monteverdi, he concentrated on vocal music of a serious, intense tone. The *Psalmen Davids* had represented the most serious music he thought the new style capable of in 1619. In 1625 he published an even more serious work, *Cantiones sacrae.* These were four-voiced motets, written *without* basso continuo (but the publisher added one). The *Cantiones* reflect the same concern that Monteverdi had with polyphonic imitative texture. They have all the inner fire of the new Italian style but almost none of the external mannerisms.

In 1628 Schütz went to Italy again, after explaining to his duke that it was essential for him to return to study the latest developments. Schütz was well aware of the transitional, old-fashioned features of Gabrieli's style. He also knew that the most important phase of Monteverdi's development was taking place even then, during the 1620s. This time when he went to Venice he concentrated on Monteverdi's art of the madrigal and its importance for dramatic forms. The fruit of this second Italian trip was a very important series of publications:

> *Symphoniae sacrae* I (1629)
> *Kleine geistliche Concerten* I & II (1636–1639)
> *Symphoniae sacrae* II & III (1647–1650)

The first of these sets uses Latin texts, the remainder German. They are all basically what the Italians called *concerti,* that is, pieces for a mixture of voices and instruments; *Concerten* is a Germanized form of *concerti,* while *symphoniae* is the Latin equivalent of the same term (not the same as the Italian *sinfonia*). They have to be called "sacred" (*sacrae,* or *geistliche*) because the Italian originals were secular, as in Monteverdi's later madrigals.

These sacred concertos could be small or large: they could consist of a solo voice with keyboard basso continuo, or a vocal duet with basso continuo, or a solo or duet with two obbligato violins (or oboes or trumpets) or more elaborate instrumental accompaniment—although such accompaniment is lacking in the *Kleine geistliche Concerten.* *Symphoniae sacrae III* use an ensemble of soloists alternately contrasted with and supported by a choir, which in turn may be reinforced with instruments. Although these larger concertos superficially resembled the earlier polychoral format of Gabrieli and his prolific German imitator Michael Praetorius (1571–1621), they now had the dramatic impact derived from the soloistic concerto.

In these concertos Schütz made full and effective use of the latest Italian dramatic styles, specifically those of Monteverdi. In one or two cases he simply rearranged a madrigal of Monteverdi, giving it a sacred text and making it suitable for use in Lutheran liturgy. The ciacona *Zefiro torna* became *Aber die Gerechten müssen sich freuen* (For the righteous must rejoice). He wrote a few concertos for solo voice entirely in recitative, for example *Eile mich, Gott, zu erretten* (Hasten, O God, to save me!) from *Kleine geistliche Concerten* I; Schütz labeled this concerto *in stylo oratorio*, a Latin translation of *recitativo*.

Generally, however, Schütz used the swinging triple time and the animated common time (moving in quarters and eighths) of Monteverdi's seventh book of madrigals, setting these styles in alternation with each other and with short declamatory passages. The sections were homogeneous within themselves, sharply contrasting one with another, and fitted together in a way calculated to project the emotional meaning of the text.

The passages in Example 73 are from a concerto for solo voice, two violins, and basso continuo, in two long sections, *Ich werde nicht sterben sondern leben* and *Ich danke dir Herr*. The first section begins in lively triple time—one of Schütz's more lyrical moments. Moving mostly stepwise, the bass brings about a smooth succession of triads and sixth chords, all clearly focused, during this initial phrase, on C. Succeeding phrases move into other tonal areas, almost always through the addition of a sharp that serves as the leading tone—all of this typical of the clearly defined movement in Monteverdi's most advanced pieces.

Ich werde nicht sterben continues with concertato contrast between voice and instruments, the violins repeating exactly the same material as the voice in Example 73. Then comes a dramatic change to common time for the next line of text. Alternations between voice and instruments occur progressively faster as the first part draws to a close.

A passage from the second part (*Lobe den Herrn* . . .) shows two other styles typically used by Schütz. The example begins with a strong exclamation, marked *tarde,* or slow, in the original; this exclamation, on an E-major triad, is a sharp contrast to the preceding cadence in C—a device often found in Monteverdi and other Italian madrigalists. After five measures, the slow exclamation gives way to a rapid exchange of eighth-note motives between voice and violins over an ascending scale in quarter notes, exactly the technique Monteverdi developed so highly in the seventh book of madrigals. Schütz was fond of this style and used it often for long sections of his concertos.

Schütz showed himself in these concertos capable of great stylistic variety and inventiveness. He also displayed a profoundly emotional sense of drama, of which the best example is the famous concerto *Saul, Saul* (*Symphoniae sacrae* III), using soloists, two violins, and two supporting choirs. Schütz picked as his subject the exact moment when the voice of the Lord thundered through Saul's brain on the road to Damascus: "Saul, Saul, why persecutest thou me?" Drawing on the most excited style of Monteverdi, the stile concitato, Schütz translated into musical form the abruptly rising doubts, the overwhelming accusation

EXAMPLE 73 SCHUTZ: FROM A SACRED CONCERTO (SYMPHONIAE SACRAE II)

(a)

(b)

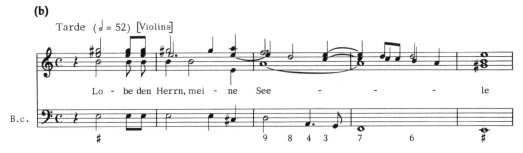

(a) (I will not die, but live . . .
(b) **Praise the Lord, O my soul, and forget not all his benefits . . .)**

echoing through Saul that brought about his startling conversion to Christ. The concerto exemplifies the combination of splendid sonorous beauty with dramatic immediacy that was characteristic of the best new music.

The new concerto tended strongly toward dramatic music; there was, in fact, only a slight difference between a large concerto, such as *Saul, Saul,* and a type of sacred music called *historia.* The historia (story) is an extended, sectional work, using distinct musical units to portray episodes in a sacred story. Schütz wrote two works entitled historia, and two others that can be included in the same category:

Tuckman

Historia der fröhlichen und siegreichen Aufferstehung unsers Erlösers und Seligmachers Jesu Christi (Story of the joyful, victorious Resurrection of our Saviour and Redeemer Jesus Christ, 1623)

Musicalische Exequien (Funeral music, 1636)

Die Sieben Worte unsers lieben Erlösers und Seligmachers Jesu Christi, so er am Stamm des Heiligen Kreutzes gesprochen (The seven last words of our dear Saviour and Redeemer Jesus Christ, as he spoke them on the wood of the Holy Cross, 1645?)

Historia der freuden- und gnadenreichen Geburt Gottes und Marien Sohnes Jesu Christi (Story of the joyful, gracious birth of the Son of God and Mary, Jesus Christ, 1664)

The *Resurrection Story,* an early work, is conservative and stylistically unimportant. The *Musicalisches Exequien* of 1636 contains three parts, each in a sense a concerto. Schütz gives in the preface very interesting directions for disposing the various choirs around the church so as to produce the most dramatic effect. An angelic choir, placed as far away as possible, intones the text, "Blessed are the dead...."

Die sieben Worte represents a stylistic high point of Schütz's dramatic music, as well as the fundamental philosophy of sacred music during the 1600s. Scenes from the Gospel were presented to the worshiper in order that he might meditate upon them, be moved by them to strongly devotional affections. Meditation upon the "Seven Last Words" became at this time a popular devotional practice. In connection with such texts, music was the means of greatly increasing the emotional impact of the text upon the worshiper, just as in the music-drama.

Schütz demonstrated, even better than the Italians, how music that represented the emotion of the lover at the tomb of the beloved could serve equally well at the foot of the Cross. Schütz's *Die sieben Worte* contains choral and instrumental movements at beginning and ending as opportunity for the worshiper's preparation and conclusion to the meditation exercise; the narrative is in recitative, while the "Seven Words" themselves are set to recitative accompanied by strings. The recitative style throughout is that elevated type characteristic of Monteverdi's mature years—lyric and expressive, even though somber.

The *Christmas Story,* published in 1664, seems to be an earlier work or, at any rate, a work in an earlier style, recalling the pastoral atmosphere of the 1620s and 1630s. It may be, however, that Schütz merely chose that style as appropriate to the pastoral nature of the subject. The work consists of narrative recitative, with intermedia, arias, or choruses depicting episodes of the story, all done in a charming manner of naïveté.

In spite of his complete assimilation of the new Italian styles, Schütz was not assimilated by them, but remained curiously detached. No other composer of the 1600s so completely mastered musical technique, and then so completely placed that technique at the service of textual projection—not by word painting, relatively unimportant in Schütz, but simply by setting each line of text to the kind of music that would most forcefully project it and its meaning into the soul of the listener.

Late in life Schütz remarked that his whole musical career had been a mistake, that he should have kept to his original plan, the study of law. This remark may have been only a reaction to the difficulties of having lived too long. Still, it tells us something important about Schütz's relation to musical style. It is hard to find his intellectual equal in the history of music; he regarded music as merely a means of communicating some higher truth. All great composers do this in some measure, but Schütz more than others. Furthermore, Schütz combined sheer musicality with these profound spiritual values in a remarkable balance. Outward style and inner idea, even though separate, were in Schütz related through a paradox supremely representative of his paradoxical generation.

Toward 1650 Schütz, now sixty-five, concerned himself more and more with spiritual values. Already in *Geistliche Chormusik* (*Sacred choral music*, 1648) Schütz abandoned concertato style and monody, reverting to a severe choral counterpoint in five, six, or seven voices. Sonorous but hardly rich, extremely skilled and smooth but not very expressive and certainly not dramatic, these works have an inner intensity neither easily comprehended nor accessible to stylistic analysis. Perhaps Schütz had in mind something of the severity of Frescobaldi's *Fiori musicali*.

In the 1660s, the last decade of his long life, Schütz wrote three more historias of a special kind, Gospel narratives of the Passion, according to Matthew, Luke, and John. Either in accordance with his own conception of what the Passion music had been in the past, or what it should be, or because of his own tendencies toward an increasingly severe style, he set the Gospel narrative in the manner of the old medieval lection tones, without a basso continuo or instrumental support of any kind. Even though the recitation was expressive, it was so in an extremely austere way, remote from the rhythmically animated operatic recitative. The narrative was interrupted only for short, powerful, but equally austere choruses, speaking the various parts of the drama—Pilate, the pharisees, the crowd. While this type of ejaculatory chorus became common in Passion music, Schütz's chant recitative remained unique.

OTHER GERMAN MUSIC Schütz was the first, and best, German composer to translate the new Italian style into German; but his compositions, especially those after 1650, had little or no effect upon stylistic development. Few of his colleagues, even his own students (to say nothing of the listener), understood fully what he was doing. The Italian style had to be watered down in order to make stylistic development possible in Germany. Of many composers who tried their hand at concertos around 1650, Andreas Hammerschmidt (1611–1675) found the best combination of accessible style and dramatic impact.

Following in the footsteps of Schütz, Hammerschmidt published from 1639 to 1653 a series of sacred concertos called *Musicalische Andachten* (Musical devotions); some were for several voices, supported by an optional chorus; others were for one or two solo voices with two violins; all used basso continuo. A slightly later series, called *Musicalischen Gespräche über die Evangelia* (Musical dialogs on the Gospels) showed the same use of Biblical text as subject of musical meditation.

Hammerschmidt's most characteristic works were *Dialogi*, "Dialogs between God and a faithful soul; collected out of biblical texts and set for 2, 3, or 4 voices with basso continuo" (1645). Often for three voices, the dialogs take place between the bass and the two upper voices moving in thirds or otherwise tightly knit together. In other words, Hammerschmidt used Monteverdi's trio style of the seventh book of madrigals to dramatize a devotional text.

As in Italy, keyboard music in Germany existed entirely apart from vocal music. The foundation for keyboard music, especially for organ, was provided throughout Germany by the numerous organs built in the late 1500s and early 1600s, as well as the numerous competent organists, skilled in playing the usual types of pieces and in improvising figural diminutions or imitative counterpoint on a given subject. This technique, expected of all professional organists, was learned through a standard vocabulary of figural patterns and imitative procedures, preserved (for example) in the works of Sweelinck, who was called the "maker of German organists."

The same vocabulary can also be seen in the endless sets of variations published in 1624 by Sweelinck's pupil, Samuel Scheidt (1587–1654), in his *Tabulatura nova*. The format of this work was indeed new, for the *tablature* was the Italian type on staves, not the old German letter tablature. The musical style, however, had little contact with new Italian music, in spite of the great variety of pieces included. Scheidt, significantly, had many students, some of them very successful as organists, but none as composers.

It is important to bear in mind that the mere act of improvisation does not of itself produce a rhapsodic, expressive flow. In the hands of an unimaginative technician, improvisation results merely in pleasant sound filling up the right amount of time. No matter how skilled they might be, German organists could not go beyond the style of the 1500s without possessing a combination of great native talent and the all-important contact with Italian style. What we will identify as rhapsodic brilliance or expressiveness in the best Northern organists was not a product of German skills inherited from Franco-Flemish tradition, but a hard-won assimilation of the new Italian techniques. It was the control of harmonies that gave point to the chord progressions and dissonances, making melody out of the endless flow of figural diminution and imitative counterpoint. This assimilation took place, in Germany, only along the borders— Vienna and Munich to the south, Hamburg to the north. The German heartland remained essentially unproductive until late in the 1600s.

Around 1650 the best Northern órganist was Heinrich Scheidemann (ca 1596–1663); active in Hamburg, Scheidemann excelled in preludes, but especially in settings of chorale tunes. These settings were a mixture of figural variations and the imitative fantasia. In Scheidemann's hands these two traditional forms became plastic: the figures flowed more easily into one another, and the forms became less rigid, when expressed in the suave harmonies of the Italian style.

9
TRENDS TOWARD CLARITY 1640-1690

MONTEVERDI'S POPPEA   At the end of his long, fruitful career, Monteverdi wrote his most fruitful work, *L'Incoronazione di Poppea* (The Coronation of Poppea), in collaboration with Francesco Busenello (1598–1659), the librettist. *Poppea* (Venice, 1642) is one of those works so full of novel artistic achievement that it required two or three generations to work out its implications. It stands at the beginning of a new phase of development in musical drama, both because of the libretto and because of the special techniques Monteverdi employed in setting it to music.

Drawn from history rather than mythology, the personages in *Poppea* are manipulated by plot intrigue into a fast-moving series of confrontations. The personages themselves are simply vehicles of strong emotional responses evoked by the confrontations. In *Poppea* the strongest emotions are Love, Ambition, and Virtue; when the drama reaches fever pitch, these emotions break out so violently that they take bodily shape onstage. In this kind of drama, passions are stronger than individuals. What is important for musical style is that it is the emotional response, not the individual's character, that is associated with musical expression.

Poppea is apparently an immoral drama in which the forces of evil win out. Nero and Poppea, having induced the suicide of the court moralist Seneca, succeed in betraying, and then exiling their respective spouses. At the end Poppea becomes Nero's bride and Rome's empress, thereby satisfying both his lust and her ambition. Upon closer inspection, however, *Poppea* is not immoral but amoral. In this realistic contest among the basic drives of Love, Ambition, and Virtue, Love (passion, not charity) is the victor, Ambition a close second, and Virtue a very poor third.

Poppea is driven by Ambition: she will be queen. Nero is driven by Love, which bids him possess Poppea at all costs. Seneca, soon disposed of, is driven by Virtue to suicide. When Ottone, driven by jealousy (and intrigue) raises his dagger over his sleeping wife Poppea, he finds that he still loves her—or rather, at that moment Love, anxious to defend its chosen vessel, the luscious Poppea, rushes out to stay the still-enchanted husband's hand. The contest between Love and Ambition is close; as late as the penultimate scene it seems that Poppea's elevation to empress will be the climactic event and Ambition the winner; but, almost as an afterthought, Nero and Poppea conclude the drama with an ostinato duet in which Love is clearly supreme.

Musically, *Poppea* represents the successful infusion into the music-drama of the techniques Monteverdi had worked out during the 1630s, especially the new, swinging, triple-time dance idioms of ciacona and passacaglia. Throughout the 1630s one can sense in Monteverdi's work the reaching out for a larger scope. This scope could only be found in music-drama, but the right one did not often present itself. Giacomo Badoaro's *Ulisses*, set by Monteverdi in 1640, was a partial solution; *Poppea*, composed immediately afterward, the complete solution.

Monteverdi's conception was still that of a drama set to continuous recitative. But the recitative had to be relieved somehow, and the new triple-time rhythms were the proper way to do it. The new intrigue drama unleashed in *Poppea*—all of a sudden—the musical forces accumulated by Monteverdi for twenty years. Never before (perhaps never again) was there such an urgent crowding of styles, erupting, boiling over, impatiently interrupting one another, fused together in the white-hot stream of musical dialog.

Poppea contains much straight recitative of Monteverdi's own expressive type. There are entire scenes in recitative; the most impressive is Ottavia's farewell to Rome (III.vii). These faithfully represent, and fulfill, Peri's old concept of music-drama. There are also some arias, strophic texts set over strophic basses, but shaped in the new rhythms, no longer in the rhapsodic, exclamatory style of the *Romanesca*. These arias, often provided with ritornellos, occupy very important positions in *Poppea*—but as special events. The body of the work is in a mixture of recitative and triple time, the mixture being constructed continuously in response to the dialog. The moment of change from recitative to triple time, or vice versa, is always carefully selected to accent the delivery of emotional language. This procedure must be studied at close range.

In a scene (III.v) toward the end of *Poppea*, Ottone has been banished, while Ottavia has been implicated in the attempted murder and is to be drowned. Nero now tells Poppea of these events and formally proposes to make her his wife and queen. This is what Poppea has been waiting to hear, for up to now she has had only blandishments, and—with her legal husband in trouble—is at the moment in a very uncertain position: she must either rise to the top, or fail utterly. Nero, for his part, is on the verge of possessing Poppea. Both are here placed in a situation bound to elicit the most intense responses. This situation requires intense musical contrast, and gives these contrasts specific emotional content.

EXAMPLE 74   MONTEVERDI: FROM *L'INCORONAZIONE DI POPPEA* III,v
Nero and Poppea sing

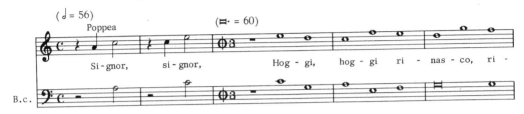

EXAMPLE 74 (CONTINUED)

ven-do, e mo-ren-do e vi-ven-do   ogn' hor t'a - do - ro.

Nero   Poppea

Non fu, non fu Dru-sil-la, no,   ch'uc-ci-der-ti ten - to.   Chi fu, chi fu il fel-lo - ne?

Nero   Poppea   Nero

Il no-stro a-mi-co Ot-to - ne.   E - gli da se?   D'Ot-ta-via fu il pen-sie - ro.

(4 ♯)

(𝅗𝅥· = 60)
Poppea

Hor hai,   hai giu-sta ca - gio - ne   di pas - sar al ri -

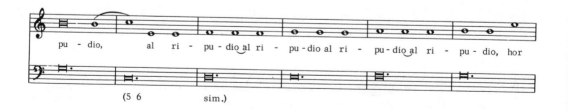

pu - dio,   al ri - pu-dio al ri - pu-dio al ri - pu-dio al ri - pu - dio, hor

(5 6   sim.)

EXAMPLE 74 (CONTINUED)

hai, hai giu-sta ca - gio-ne di pas - sar al ri - pu - dio.

(♩ = 56)
Nero

Hog-gi, co-me pro - mi - si, mia spo - sa, mia spo-sa tu sa-ra - i.

(5   6)

(♩ = 52)
Poppea

Si ca - ro dì, si ca-ro di, si ca - ro, si ca - ro, ca - ro di ve-der non spe -

(♩ = 56)
Nero

- ro   ma - i. Per il tro - no di Gio - ve, e per il mi - o,

hog - gi sa - rai, ti giu - ro, di Ro - ma im - pe - ra - tri -

EXAMPLE 74 (CONTINUED)

ce;   in pa - ro - la re-gal   te n'as - si - cu   -   ro.   In pa -

ro - la, in pa-ro - la?   In pa - ro - la re - gal.   In pa - ro - la re - gal?

In pa-ro   la re-gal, in pa-ro la re - gal,   te n'as -   si - cu - ro.

(♩. = 60)

I - do-lo del cor   mi - o,   del cor,   del cor   mi - o,   del cor,

(♩ = 60)   (♩. = 60)

del cor   mi - (i) - o,   I - do-lo del cor

EXAMPLE 74 (CONTINUED)

In the scene started in Example 74, Poppea addresses Nero formally:

Signor . . .	*My Lord . . .*

then abruptly sings, in triple time, of her anticipation of the news he brings

. . . hoggi rinasco ai primi fiori di questa nova vita; voglio che sian sospiri, sospiri che ti faccian sicuro che . . .	*. . . today I am born anew, to the first breath of this new life; I want there to be sighs, sighs to show you . . .*

So much in a swinging, agitated triple time; then, just as abruptly, in recitative:

. . . rinata per te languisco e moro, e morendo e vivendo ogn'hor t'adoro.	*. . . that reborn, for you I languish and die, and dying and living I forever adore you.*

Poppea's opening speech marks the beginning of the scene; it is followed by a short dialog:

NERO

Non fu Drusilla ne ch'ucciderti tentó.	*It was not Drusilla who tried to kill you.*

POPPEA

Chi fu il fellone?	*Who was the villain?*

NERO

Il nostro amice Ottone.	*Our friend Ottone.*

POPPEA

Egli da sé?	*All by himself?*

NERO

D'Ottavia fu il pensiero . . .	*Ottavia made the plan . . .*

Here is the crucial bit of news; Poppea responds sharply, seizing the moment to press her point:

Hor hai giusta cagione di passar al ripudio . . .	*Now you have grounds to divorce her, divorce her! divorce her! . . .*

Poppea speaks in a repetitive manner that fits exactly the style of the repetitive triple-time rhythms and the sequential harmonies that so often go with them. Then follows more dialog in recitative style. Nero announces, somewhat pompously, his intention to marry her:

Hoggi, come promisi, mia sposa tu sarai.	*Today, as I promised, my wife you shall be.*

Poppea's response again is intense, marked by an abrupt shift from G to E, and a special dotted figure used for fervent exclamations:

Si caro di veder non spero mai!	*Such a day I never hoped to see!*

Then, with as much majesty as he can summon, Nero gives his formal guarantee:

Per il trono di Giove, e per il mio, hoggi sarai, ti giuro, di Roma imperatrice; in parola regal te n'assicuro.	*By Jove's throne and mine, today you will be—I swear it—Rome's Empress; on my royal word, I affirm it!*

This is important; Poppea makes sure:

In parola?	POPPEA *Your word?*
In parola regal.	NERO *My royal word.*
In parola regal?	POPPEA *Your royal word?*
In parola regal te n'assicuro.	NERO *On my royal word, I affirm it.*

Now it is done. Rapturous with victory and close to fainting with excitement, Poppea bursts again into triple time, gulps for air, throws herself into Nero's arms, repeats her rapturous exclamation, and gives herself to Love.

Idolo del cor mio . . . idolo del cor mio, gionta e pur l'hora che del mio ben godrò.	*Idol of my heart . . . idol of my heart, now is come the time when I will delight in my love.*

Nero responds in high transport:

Non più s'interporrà noia o dimora.	*No longer shall trouble delay and interrupt us.*

and after a few bars of extremely fast, excited triple-time rhythms, the two lovers launch into an extended passacaglialike duet. The bass acts as an ostinato; the voices are now opposed, now blended, with surpassing artistry, lost in that blaze of wonder that crowned the best works of the century.

NERO & POPPEA

Cor nel petto non ho, me'l rubasti. Si, dal cor me lo rapì de' tuo' begli occhi un lucido sereno. Per te ben mio non ho più core in seno. Stringimi tra le braccia innamorate che mi trafisse—ohimè! Non interrotto havrai l'hore beate, no, no! Se ben perduta in te, in te mi troverò, e tornerò a riperdermi, ben mio, che sempre in te perduto mi troverò.	*There is no heart in my breast, you've stolen it—Yes, yes! you've stolen it with a sweet glance from your beautiful eyes— For you, my love, I no longer have a heart in my breast—Squeeze me tight in your loving arms, that wound me—oh! that blessed time will delay no more—No, no!— Lost in you I will find myself again, my love—Always lost in you, finding myself— That is what I want!)*

In a sense it is misleading to represent music-drama of the mid-1600s by *Poppea*, simply because the work is (by general acclaim) so far above other music-drama of its time, perhaps of any time. It is one of very few music-dramas in which the dramatic action emerges as most important, sweeping all other elements along with it or brushing them aside. It started out like other works of its time: drama was arranged to give occasion to lyrical music. But then the timing of musical contrast was so precisely set that the passions aroused, instead of spending themselves in lyrical moments, rebounded back on the action, driving it along by feedback in mounting excitement. The festal frame of the intermedium all but disappeared, coming only at the end to celebrate the Coronation. If the acts were not marked they would be hard to find (there are no choral dances to mark them), so hard does one scene follow on the one before. *Poppea* is often not a pretty score, any more than it is a pretty story. It is the best example of that single-mindedness that drove Monteverdi's generation to be—not beautiful—but effective.

Poppea provided the music-drama with a new type of scenario, consisting of a rapid succession of contrasting scenes, each involving one or two principals in situations constructed to evoke strong emotions. The first act, for example, confronts us with Ottone alone (a sentimental homecoming, then catastrophe), two soldiers (a comic scene), Nero's farewell from Poppea (a love scene), Poppea's confidences to her nurse (hopeful anticipation), then Ottavia's confidences with *her* nurse (grim foreboding). An intricate plot, with subplots and a multiplicity of personages, is necessary to maintain this succession of contrasting scenes. Comic roles are an obvious asset.

Equally valuable are certain special effects, keenly appreciated by librettist, composer, and audience alike, and used over and over again in the 1600s. An excellent example is Poppea's slumber scene, in which she is sung to sleep by her Nurse's lullaby. After a century of hard use, the slumber scene was often ridiculed; but in the beginning it must have been extremely expressive. There is a wondrous change that comes over a person when he passes from agitated wakefulness to sleep, a change capable of bestowing its spell on the music accompanying its dramatic representation. It was just this universal, profoundly human effect that composers sought in librettos. The student who is alert to such effects, without fretting over the absurdities of plot that elicit them, will be richly rewarded by the study of music-drama in the 1600s.

The intrigue drama immediately brought down the wrath of literary critics, as it has to the present day. Considered by themselves the librettos become admittedly impossible. Librettists rejoiced in plots heavy with intrigue; the several sets of contrasting personages pursued their interlocking destinies in a manner sufficiently intricate to baffle the most astute and intent observer. The drama regularly began in the middle of a situation already complicated by years of intrigue, described but hardly clarified in the *argomento* at the beginning of the libretto.

But all such confusion was intentional. The libretto was, after all, not intended for literary consumption; clearly displayed on the title page was the label *dramma per musica* (or some similar designation), a drama *for music*. As such the libretto did its job perfectly. For musical purposes composers were interested in clear, strong human responses, which they expressed by clear contrasts of simple musical styles—recitative and triple time. In order to inform these musical styles with human immediacy and specific emotional content, the composers depended upon the plot and the variety of situations it could produce.

Just as there was no use for cogent plots, there was no interest in the more subtle linking of human responses we call "character." Strong responses, such as the composers needed, tend to carry a person outside of the orbit of habitual behavior that constitutes character. Being "in character" would have involved a degree of response quite ineffectual next to the high passions of the music-drama.

On the contrary, being "out of character" was an effect sought after through many techniques that are sometimes hard for us to appreciate. Typical is the device of transvestiture (already present in *Poppea*), which exploits the incongruity between a person's appearance and what he feels inside. Personages regularly concealed their identity from others—sometimes from their own lovers—for extended sections of the drama, an unlikely situation but one that greatly heightened the effect of their emotional responses.

While later puritanical reforms were to continue to use transvestiture or concealed identity, they could not stomach the grotesquely comic effects common around 1650. Yet these comic effects had the same purpose of heightening a serious response, by immediate and devastating incongruity. As in *Poppea*, the most serious moments are followed by "comic relief": a comic role (a silly young page or a garrulous old nurse) echoes the serious response in musical style that, while bearing an undeniable resemblance to what has gone before, is twisted in such a way as to be indescribably ridiculous. The comic effects were not subtly modulated into the scenario, but placed where they would completely undo the dramatic tension. Although handled with consummate musical artistry, the comic effects involved not subtle, sophisticated comedy, but slapstick of the crudest sort in intentional contrast to the noble personages around them. A good example is the stutterer, whose stuttering is sometimes so severe that he cannot finish a word until after the start of the next scene, with consequently bizarre effects on the dialog.

After *Poppea*, music-drama included a complete spectrum of dramatic effects, from deep pathos, majesty, heroism, and passionate love to dalliance, insanity, parody, satire, and slapstick. These, in any combination, could appear in a single work. Anything could happen in a music-drama, and probably would, making it impossible to give a systematic topology of works during the next fifty

years. Furthermore it is impossible to see any pattern of development in terms
of plots or types of drama. There seems to be no orderly succession of types over
the decades, for the pastorale continued to exist alongside the new intrigue
drama, while plots and personages were drawn from a continuum that extended
from the historical through the hypothetical to the legendary.

CAVALLI AND OPERA IN VENICE   Since music-drama flourished primarily
at Venice during the 1640s and 1650s, those years are often called the period of
"Venetian opera," even though Italian composers from other cities were successfully cultivating similar styles at home and (especially after 1650) abroad. The
nerve center of style was not so much Venice as Monteverdi—one might say,
Poppea. The dominating figure during the 1640s, after Monteverdi's death in
1642, was his own pupil, Francesco Bruni, called Cavalli (1602–1676). The
main difference between teacher and pupil was that Monteverdi packed the
possibilities of the new style into one last work, while Cavalli spread them out
over more than forty dramatic works of various kinds.

Spurred on by Monteverdi's achievement in *Poppea*, Cavalli concentrated
on the larger aspects of construction (scenes and acts), leaving the styles of
recitative and triple-time rhythms as he found them. Although he often alternated these two styles, as in *Poppea*, he did so less intensively; his scenes tended
to become broader. He often wrote whole scenes in recitative; but he also took
care to inflect the recitative to suit different kinds of situations. In *L'Egisto*
(1643), for example, Cavalli used one kind of recitative for the endless coy
chatter of lovers, another kind for Egisto's temporary insanity. The bright
dialog chatter tended to be reserved for pastoral characters, while the historical
heroes gave occasion for the more serious, pathetic tone. Indeed, persons of
majesty tended, in Cavalli, to speak only in recitative.

Close to the old pastorale, *L'Egisto* is an interesting example of Cavalli's
large-scale thinking. The first and second acts begin with arias to set the scene.
Then follow long passages of lyrical dialog in animated recitative. As the situation becomes defined, preparing emotional responses, the stylistic contrast increases with the reappearance of arias. Finally the central personage of each act
is driven to express his or her strongest emotion; this emotion, soon dominating
the scene and the personage, takes bodily shape as an allegorical figure. Each act
concludes with an ensemble of allegorical figures singing arias, duets, and trios,
analogous to the old choral songs and dances that framed the pastorale.

Other operas of Cavalli are built differently, depending on the libretto.
The variety of large-scale plans indicates clearly how Cavalli's attention was
firmly fixed on the manipulation of musical style to produce convincing effects.
Il Gia: ne (1649) has magnificent scenes between Medea and Egeo and between
Medea and Giasone, as well as the celebrated incantation scene in which Medea
invokes the powers of hell to aid her.

Cavalli's *La Statira* (Princess of Egypt) of 1655 is a love story involving
concealed identity; it is rich in lyrical dialog, using a mixture of straight recitative with inserts in triple time, as well as common-time inserts with a moving
bass. *La Statira* also illustrates how large dramatic units were increasingly
bound up with careful placement of such inserts.

Pompeo magno of 1666, Cavalli's next-to-last work, is heroic. In spite of some exceedingly grotesque scenes involving the comic roles (including a ballet for *Gli Impazzi*, The Insane), and many amorous arias and duets, Cavalli maintained a predominantly serious tone through the impressive recitative. There are moments of high drama when Mitradate, no longer able to contain his paternal love, reveals his identity (hitherto concealed) to his own son, at great risk (II. xi). Another scene at the end (III. xix) is built on a long, descending ostinato, over which the principal personages solemnly vie for the privilege of drinking the poisoned cup.

Especially significant is a scene (III. xv) in which Pompeo, in soliloquy, is torn between love and destiny. Here these basic drives, under the appearance of allegorical figures, sing alternate duets with Pompeo, each in turn singing close parallel thirds or sixths, or answering Pompeo in imitation depending on which way his will is inclined. The alternations increase their pace as he is increasingly torn between Love and Destiny until he finally decides for Destiny. The musical rendering of the identity between the allegorical figure and the emotions of Pompeo shows us clearly how to understand such "allegories."

Heroic drama was carried on after Cavalli especially by Antonio Sartorio (ca 1620–?), whose first (or second?) opera, *Seleuco*, was staged in Venice in 1666. Perhaps his most celebrated work, one in which the heroic tone is most present and most characteristic, is *L'Adelaide* (1672), based on events and characters around the German emperor, Otto I, in 950—a medieval, "Gothic" subject. As with Cavalli, the heroic themes are increasingly surrounded by amorous songs. The heroism now takes the form of Constancy or Magnanimity, heroic affection, rather than more spectacular types of heroic action. Sartorio's techniques are largely dependent upon Cavalli and Monteverdi; his musical accomplishments are first rate.

Side by side with heroic drama (with or without comic roles) existed a lighter type of opera, cultivated especially by Pietro Andreas Ziani (ca 1620–1684). His *Annibale in Capua* (1661) was very successful, while his *La Semiramide* (1670) has been described as the outrageous climax of unnatural eroticism and concealed identity (the subject of *La Semiramide* was perhaps the most popular one of the 1600s and 1700s.) Here the comedy does not depend on slapstick, or, of course, on contrast with serious scenes (there being none) but on incongruities intrinsic to the situation itself. Nor is the music specifically comic (although there is an increasing quantity of little songs, to which we will return presently). At this stage the musical style of arias is merely effective; the meaning—comic or otherwise—depends almost completely upon the situation and the actor's projection. The same is true in some works of Giovanni Legrenzi (1626–1690) in which the comic element is strong, as in *Totila* (1677). Legrenzi also wrote high, heroic drama; his *Il Giustino* (1683) was one of the best—and best-known—works of the century. Here the neutral aria style is used for noble or passionate affections.

During the 1650s an increasing number of short, strophic songs were introduced (with apologies) into works like Ziani's *La Semiramide* but also into Cavalli's *Pompeo magno*. These songs, called *canzonettas* or *ariettas*, were in a style so popular as to be inevitably incongruous when sung by noble heroes. Unquestionably a concession to public taste, ariettas could be viewed only as a lapse from the high style of heroic drama. But far more important than a temporary weakening of dramatic conception was the eventual strengthening of the musical one; for what seemed like weakness from a dramatic point of view was the arietta's potential musical strength.

The arietta emphasized once again the purely musical aspects of rhythm and harmony, giving composers an area in which to develop increasingly sophisticated musical procedures. Such development, the most important phase of the 1600s, was possible at this time only in the music-drama, for only there was music's content sufficiently defined (by the dramatic situation) to direct the growth of expression. The interaction of dramatic situation and musical structure reached a peak in the arietta. Before the century was out, the arietta became the full-fledged aria, an intense expression of emotion and the leading musical form of its time.

CANTATA   Much of the development of the aria went on in the chamber cantata, successor to the monody so popular up to 1630. Cantatas were composed in huge quantities from the 1630s on to the end of the century. Mostly in manuscript and not yet inventoried—let alone edited—the repertory runs into the thousands. These, of course, include a wide variety of type as well as quality; to give a typical example is in a sense to misrepresent the cantata, for variety was one of its important features.

Most cantatas around 1650 were for one or two voices and basso continuo. The solo ones perhaps best represent the cantata, but the duets were extremely popular. Most cantatas employed the contrasting styles of recitative and triple time, but in all imaginable combinations. Some cantatas are nothing but recitative—studies in pathos; these, however, are relatively few. Others are nothing but ariettas, simple strophic pieces in triple time, or in common time over a moving bass, in a closed form. The great majority employ an alternation of recitative and triple time, with frequent strophic arias. Sometimes the recitative is quite brief, but often it tends to be more finely wrought than operatic recitative, which must hustle along to traverse the broad dimensions of the music-drama. The arias in the best cantatas are varied from one to the next.

Everyone composed cantatas; it is possible to name only the most eminent composers. During the middle decades of the 1600s these were Luigi Rossi (1598–1653), Giacomo Carissimi (1605–1674), Marco Marazzoli (1619–1662), Marc-Antonio Cesti (1623–1669), Mario Savioni (ca 1608–1685). Since Rossi's fame was great (he was known simply as Signor Luigi) and since it depended mostly on his cantatas, one of them should be selected as an example.

Luigi's cantata for solo voice and basso continuo, *Hor che l'oscuro manto*, is a lover's rhapsody in the free, rhymed poetry typical of the cantata. It consists of alternations of recitative and triple time (Example 75); a middle section in common time with a moving bass is called *aria*. The alternations are carefully placed so as to help project the affective delivery of the text.

a   Recitative (C) G minor—21 measures
    Hor che l'oscuro manto
    Della notte ricopre il ciel d'intorno,
    A la cruda beltà ch'adoro tanto
    Fortunato amator faccio ritorno.

(a) Now that night's dark mantle covers the sky, I return, a blessed lover, to the cruel beauty I so adore.

b   3/2, G minor—37 measures
     Sù, mio cor, con dolci accenti
     Fà che desti i vaghi rai
     Per cui perdono i tormenti
     La crudeltà che non si stanca mai.

                          (b) Up, my heart, with accents sweet awake the charming glances for which I forgive those torments that never tire.

c   Recitative (C), E-flat major—9 measures
     Amanti, o voi che siete pien' di cure e d'affanni,
     Se trovar non sapete in un guare o gentil conforto al core,
     Sempre a languir con vario stile vi condanni amore.

                          (c) Lovers, full of pain and woe, if you can't find comfort in a glance, Love condemns you to everlasting, varied tortures.

d   Aria (C), E-flat major—28 measures
     Mentre sanno influir due luci belle
     Tutto il ben che qua giù piovon le stelle;
     Da due nere pupille
     Io sol chiede un sguardo.
     Poi s'en va da infaville
     L'alma trafitta da si dolce dardo;
     Beltà che sia negl'occhi armata è forte,
     Ha saette di vita è non di morte.

                          (d) Meanwhile a sweet pair of eyes can give us all the happiness that our stars can rain on earth. From two black eyes I seek only a glance. Then from ashes springs up the soul, pierced by so sweet a dart. Beauty armed with eyes is strong; it thirsts for life, not death.

e   3, G minor—48 measures
     Godete martiri:
     Trionfi'il mio core.
     Dal regno d'amore
     Nessun si ritiri.
     Quest'alma (si) sa
     Bellezza, fierezza
     In seno no ha.

                          (e) Enjoy, sufferers; my heart shall triumph. From Love's realm no one withdraws. If this soul can have beauty, it will do without pride.

f   Recitative (C), G minor—3 measures
     Hor che lilla
     Mi rimira,
     Il mio cor
     Più non sospira;

                          (f) Now that she looks at me my heart stops sighing.

g   3, C minor to G minor—24 measures
     Ond'io pur gode se per lei tanto ardo:
     A chi si strugge e gran conforte un sguardo.

                          (g) Wherefore I still rejoice that for her I burn; for one in torment, a glance is great comfort.

Within the small dimensions of the cantata, clarity of harmonic progressions expressed itself as the sense of tonal focus we call *key*. In the more dance-like sections of the cantata (those in triple time, indicated by three-two or three, and the aria), the triadic organization is so cogent that each such section can be said to be *in* the chord on which it ends, and often begins. Even the recitatives, habitually more rhapsodic, seem to move within a key, but only in the shorter sections. Often a recitative is a transition from the key of one aria to that of the next.

SACRED MUSIC AND CARISSIMI During the 1640s and after, Italians cultivated sacred music intensively and progressively, applying the styles and tech-

EXAMPLE 75   ROSSI: FROM A CANTATA

(a)

Hor che l'os-cu-ro man — to   del-la   not-te ri-co-pre il ciel
(etc.)

(b)

Sù   mio cor,   Sù   mio cor con   dol-ci ac — cen-ti
(etc.)

(c)

A-man-ti   o   voi che sie-te pien di cu-re è d'af-fan-ni
(etc.)

(d)

Aria (♩ = 72)

Men-tre san-no in-fluir due lu-ci bel-le tut-to il ben che qua'
(etc.)

(e)

Go-de-te mar-ti-ri tri-on-fi il mio   co-re dal re-gno d'a-
(etc.)

EXAMPLE 75 (CONTINUED)

(f)

Hor che lil - la   mi ri - mi - ra
(etc.)

(g)

Ond' io pur go - de se   per lei tan - to   ar - do
(etc.)

niques of modern dramatic music according to the taste of the composer and his audience. Generally the sacred concerto seems to have been concerned primarily with concertato effects (the varied combinations of voices and instruments) while less concerned with dramatic form and intent.

Sacred liturgical music flourished at Venice in the person of Cavalli himself; his most important sacred publication was *Musiche sacre concernenti messa, salmi concertati con istromenti, inni, antifone, e sonate, a 2.3.4.5.6.8.10. e 12. voci (Sacred music containing a mass, concerted psalms with instruments, hymns, antiphons, and sonatas . . ,''* 1656). The psalms, hymns, and antiphons were for vespers, the other occasion for splendid new music besides the mass. Alessandro Grandi, as well as Giovanni Rovetta (ca 1596–1668), also wrote sacred concertato music in connection with St. Mark's in Venice during these years. Practically unknown, this repertory seems in general to reflect the same development as contemporary music-drama: a sense of harmonic and rhythmic breadth begins to replace the nervous contrasts of the preceding decades.

In Rome there had been a series of attempts at sacred dramatic music since Emilio di Cavalieri's *Rappresentazione* of 1600; the most important was Stefano Landi's *San Alessio* of 1632, a dramma musicale of large proportions. Real success came during the 1640s with the works of Giacomo Carissimi (1605–1674), active in Rome since 1630 as a prominent church musician.

Besides masses and sacred concertos (and also secular cantatas), Carissimi wrote more than fifteen larger works of a dramatic nature. Some of these were called *historia*, a traditional term already encountered in Schütz; we now call all such works *oratorio*, a term that came into common use later in the 1600s. In general, Carissimi's historias consist of a mixture of recitative with more rhythmic sections in triple time (both as episodes and in aria form) for solo, duet, or chorus; the choral portions are very large, sometimes the bulk of the work. There are also instrumental sections—ritornellos, and perhaps a sinfonia at the beginning.

Although some of Carissimi's smaller works are for solo or duet (*Tolle, sponsa* is a dialog, with one chorus *a 2* at the end), the larger oratorios differ from secular drama by the great stress placed on the chorus. Although it might be possible to see these oratorios as small monodic dramas inflated with long choruses at appropriate moments, it seems better to think of them as sacred concertos (for chorus and instruments) which have been given a new intensity by providing them with short recitatives to prepare, or set the stage, for the chorus to follow.

In any case, the procedure of the oratorio is that of the music-drama: the excited triple-time portions are given affective meaning by being placed at the moment of response to a dramatic situation. Often this elevated response is given to solo or duet, as in the *Historia di Abraham et Isaac*, where significant interpolations are made into the Biblical text to provide just the kind of emotional response needed at the crisis of the story, for example, the rhymed duet, *O felix nuncium, O dulce gaudium*, set as an aria in triple time. A psalm text, *Omnes populi laudate Dominum*, is also interpolated to provide for a massive choral response. The *Historia Divitis*, a long, rhyming text of typically medieval structure (but also very close to the type of poetry used in opera librettos) has huge choruses in swinging triple time to texts such as *Iam satis edisti, iam satis bibisti*. The celebrated lament for chorus at the end of *Jephte* is another example of the stress laid on choral expression.

Sometimes the dramatic apparatus and quantity of recitative seem to overshadow the chorus. *Daniele* has a *testo*, a narrator (called *storicus* in the Latin historia), who tells the story in recitative; but even here the choruses are of great power. The musical styles used in the choral portions closely resemble those of the most advanced sacred concertos, and both owe inspiration to Monteverdi's madrigalesque composition, the musical watershed separating the new sacred concerto from the old motet.

INSTRUMENTAL MUSIC: THE TRIO SONATA   In the sacred publication of 1656 already described, Cavalli included sonatas, works for instruments alone to be played at appropriate moments in the church service. Such sonatas became frequent after 1650, finding in that decade and the next a relatively stable form and a name, *sonata da chiesa* (church sonata). Cultivated by Legrenzi from the 1650s, such sonatas found special favor at Bologna, where the central church, San Petronio, made elaborate provision for the best modern church music. Maurizio Cazzati (ca 1620–1677), Giovanni Maria Bononcini (1642–1678), and especially Giovanni Battista Vitali (1644–1692) all contributed to church music and the sonata.

The favorite instrumental ensemble consisted of two violins and basso continuo, for this ensemble (designated *a 3*) reproduced the trio of two high, equal parts and bass developed by Monteverdi and his generation as the best way of combining intricacy of imitative counterpoint with harmonic clarity. Sonatas for solo instruments, such as keyboard or unaccompanied violin, were rare at this time. The smallest ensemble for which sonatas were usually written was violin with basso continuo, that is, *a 2*. There were also sonatas *a 4* and *a 5*, but these were less frequent than those *a 3*. Considering how perfectly the sonata *a 3* represented the basic texture of music at this time, it is not surprising that this type predominated; indeed, one wonders why there was anything else.

Furthermore, the designation *a 3* referred to the skeleton, the minimum number of parts (or part books) needed for performance. In actual sound the situation was quite different and very flexible. In the first place the basso continuo part implied harmonies that could be played in as many voices as the keyboard player had fingers if the occasion required. Then the keyboard basso continuo could be reinforced by one or more stringed instruments. Finally the whole trio sonata could be treated orchestrally: several violins could play on each of the two violin parts, and the bass reinforced in proportion. The trio, in other words, was only a structural outline.

Orchestral treatment such as this would have been especially appropriate at San Petronio, where music for great liturgical occasions was carefully planned and splendidly executed. There was a custom of engaging extra musicians for such occasions to reinforce the regular players on the simpler passages. Apparently transferred to instrumental music from vocal practice, such reinforcement occurs, for example, in a *messa concèrtata* of Cazzati (1662). The mass is scored for four voices *e suoi ripieni,* or fill-in parts; the four soloists sing throughout, while the ripieni singers sing at certain points designated in the music as *tutti.* By underlining certain phrases with a more massive sound, the tutti throws the phrase structure into sharper relief. This type of reinforcement is indigenous to concertato style; its roots go back to the beginning of the century. Like many other aspects of style, it was exploited with increasing clarity and consistency as the century progressed, becoming crystallized at the end of the century in the purely instrumental concerto.

The church sonata consisted of a series of contrasting sections—contrasting in rhythmic movement, texture, and sometimes harmonic structure. The very strong contrast between recitative and triple time was unavailable to the sonata composer, since he seldom wrote recitative. Often, however, he used short passages of unstable key and slow, indecisive rhythm to separate his larger sections. Typically placed as introductions or conclusions to larger sections, these transitional passages functioned like the recitative of the chamber cantata. Occasionally fast movements contained bizarre interruptions of one or two slow measures. For the most part, however, the sonata depended on the contrast between the large sections in common time (moving in quarters and eighths) and those in triple time, as well as on the contrast between imitative counterpoint and figural diminution, or no figuration at all.

In its sectional structure and in many other ways, especially the bright themes and easy-going counterpoint, the church sonata resembled the canzona from the first part of the century. The sonata often began with a fast imitative movement on canzonalike subjects. Sometimes, however, this fast movement was preceded by a more chordal section, perhaps marked *grave* (serious), as if a Venetian opera sinfonia had been placed before the canzona to give it more solemnity. After the, fast, imitative movement, the sonata might have several sections, some in triple time, some chordal, some imitative, usually ending with a faster movement of more dancelike rhythm. The simplest plan (the one that eventually became most typical) was a slow introduction, a fast imitative movement, a less imitative, triple-time movement that might be marked at a slower tempo, and a concluding movement in a faster rhythm.

It is important to note that the alternation was often one of rhythmic character rather than of tempo. Except for passages written in common-time half notes, the prevailing pace of these movements was relatively fast. Such tempo indications as occur should be taken in their literal meaning: *grave* means *serious*, not slow; *largo* means *broad*, not slow; *andante* has nothing to do with slow at all, but means just the opposite—*going*; only *adagio* means *slow*, but slow relative to the normally fast, lilting tempo of triple time. The dirgelike pace at which such pieces are now often played makes stylistic nonsense of them. The general tone of the church sonata was one of elegant animation or lyric breadth; only occasional contrasting passages were really slow or marked by pathos.

After 1650, as the nature of the church sonata was clarified, it was more easily distinguished from the *sonata da camera* (chamber sonata), appropriate for secular occasions. The kind of instrumental music most characteristic of secular festivity was dances. When writing a set of dances (either for dancing or for listening), a composer might include an introductory movement, called "sonata" for lack of a more specific title. Such an introduction was then called a *sonata da camera*, whence the term easily came to include the set of dances that followed.

Dances had come in sets for over a century. Several combinations had been current in the 1500s; pavan and gaillard were a common pairing. In the 1600s, as instrumental dance music came to have higher artistic ambitions, the structure of dance sets took on added importance as musical form. The dances most often used in sets—for listening, rather than for dancing—were the now traditional allemande and courante (in its several forms). To this basic pair was often added a gigue or a sarabande, the latter being the third of the exotic Spanish dances (along with ciacona and passacaglia) that leavened the new music. The grouping of dances, however, was as fluid as the sectional arrangement of the serious sonata. Each dance was usually in binary form (//:A://:B://), in which both sections, A and B, might begin and end on the same chord, or the A section might end on a closely related chord, most often the one a fifth above; this final chord, in turn, might be treated as a half cadence, or as a full cadence in the key a fifth above.

Sonatas, especially church sonatas, gave the composer an opportunity to display the manner of imitative counterpoint in a way impossible in the music-drama. As harmonic progressions became smoother and clearer toward 1680, sonata composers gave evidence of increased interest in contrapuntal complexities. In 1673 Giovanni Maria Bononcini published an instruction book, *Musico prattico*, which he intended as preparation for "the composition of songs . . . and the Art of Counterpoint" (*Arte del Contrapunto*). This was one of a long line of such treatises that went back to Zarlino, still regarded as the font of contrapuntal wisdom by Italians. The pedagogical technique was Zarlino's; the style was now adapted to the newer harmonic practice.

While Bononcini's treatise contains many examples of fugue and counterpoint, it is basically a textbook. On the other hand, Giovanni Battista Vitali's *Artificii musicali* (1689) is a purely musical collection, consisting of *Canoni in diverse maniere, contrapunti dopii, inventioni curiose, capritii e sonate* (Canons in various manners, double counterpoints, curious inventions, caprices and sonatas); the collection is arranged, however, in an order reflecting pedagogical concern. Angelo Berardi's *Documenti armonici* of 1687 is midway between a treatise and a collection of pieces: the Documents are a series of relatively elaborate illustrations of contrapuntal procedures. Like the others, Berardi rejoices in the *studii artificiosi* (artful exercises). Canon and fugue, for these writers, are another manifestation of the Italian joy in finely wrought decoration, evident throughout the 1600s.

In spite of the wealth of invention in chamber cantata and in sacred concertato music, in spite of the growing scope of instrumental music, the crowning achievement of these decades remained the music-drama. Not so varied as the cantata, nor so splendidly orchestrated as the big concerto, operatic music had the overwhelming advantage of being dramatic, of being onstage, its moods and effects accented by dramatic action and text. In the opera the tendencies toward tonal clarity came into focus, especially in the works of Marc-Antonio Cesti (1623–1669).

CESTI'S OPERATIC STYLE Cesti wrote both cantatas and operas; his first opera was *L'Orontea* (Rome, 1649), and his best—said to be one of the best of the century—*La Dori* (Florence, 1661). He is known to modern times, however, only through his *festa teatrale* (theatrical celebration), *Il Pomo d'Oro* (The Golden Apple), an incredible spectacular written for the imperial court in Vienna in 1666 (or 1667).

The work was staged on a scale, and a budget, comparable only to the most colossal film extravaganzas of the 1900s. It was the supreme example of the desire of Cesti's time to stun the spectator with too much. A careful study of the plates depicting the original stage sets (there are sixty-seven scenes), found in the modern edition, is indispensable to an understanding of opera in the 1600s. It is true that *Il Pomo* is an exception; the typical opera was not a festa teatrale, but a dramma per musica, and few were carried out on so lavish a scale. But *Il Pomo* is an exception primarily in the sense that here, for once, expense was no obstacle to realizing the ambitions of grandeur cherished by every opera composer.

Il Pomo has little of the dramatic urgency of more serious opera. In character it resembles more the *serenata,* a type of loosely dramatic pageant that is larger than a cantata but smaller than an opera, usually on an allegorical or mythological subject (similar to the old masque), written to celebrate a wedding or other courtly event. Hence *Il Pomo* is overpeopled with mythological beings as well as overburdened with stage machines. Cesti's music, however, is some of his richest, illustrating the increased variety of aria styles as well as the more intricate organization of scenes.

In Act I, scene vii, of *Il Pomo,* Paride and Ennone, lovers, meet rapturously. They exclaim in short, excited phrases, and then sing more lyrically in triple time (Example 76a and b); they repeat literally the last two-thirds of what they just sang, making a closed form, *ABCBC.* Then they engage in elegant dialog, singing in turn in recitative (Example 76c). Finally they sing together in triple time, rounding out the scene.

Even though the recitative in the middle is two pages long, it now does

EXAMPLE 76   CESTI: FROM *IL POMO D'ORO* I,vii; Paride and Ennone sing

EXAMPLE 76 (CONTINUED)

EXAMPLE 76 (translations)

(a) (O my life—O my heart—O my sweet passion . . .
(b) Ever new, always, always . . .
(c) ENNONE And where to at this hour? PARIDE To adore, in the new dawn, a ray
     of your beauty. ENN. And I will follow you, jealous of my love. PAR. And what
     do you fear? ENN. Lest to shine more brightly with the aid of these twin suns,
     your eyes, the Day steals you away from me. PAR. Far from your sweet face—
     the only joy the Day can offer me—my eyes would be without light . . .
(d) My dear delight—My joy, my love—What sweet chains bind my breast . . .)

not seem to be the substance of the musical discourse, but rather an episode
between the triple-time sections that frame it. This purely structural shift of
emphasis, characteristic of the trend after 1650, seems largely responsible for
the new importance of arias over recitative in Cesti's work. The recitative is
carefully, elegantly made; the triple-time style is not drastically different from
what it had been; but more and more opera came to be a succession of arias
rather than of recitative.

Within the aria, one distinguishing feature of Cesti's style is the suavity
of the harmonic progressions, evident throughout Example 76, but especially in
the concluding section (*Mio caro e diletto*). The triads and sixth chords now
follow in the smoothest progression imaginable. The harmonies, as usual, change
slightly slower than the rhythmic values (whole and half), but the changes are
now so clearly directed that the effect seems broader than in Monteverdi. There
is a well-prepared modulation to B minor (from D major), while the rest of the
section oscillates easily between D and A. The tone gets increasingly warm and
sweet toward the end—a *dolcezza* in which Cesti excelled.

This style is often described as *bel canto* (beautiful song), which indeed
it is; but the beauty of the melodic line derives in large part from the suavity
of the triadic progressions. It is this harmonic suavity, more than anything else,
that characterizes the development of all aspects of style toward 1680.

Another scene from *Il Pomo* (I. ix) shows a more intricate structure and
a greater variety of aria styles. Aurindo laments that Paride has stolen his
Ennone. He sings first a petulant aria in common time (Example 77a). Its form
is the very popular *ABB*, with ritornello for two flutes, and a second stanza.
In this aria the bass moves in rhythms similar to those of the voice—the feature
that distinguishes common-time arias from recitative. Except for the opening
subject (which is echoed in the ritornello) the bass moves in the long descending
scales characteristic of this style since Monteverdi's seventh book of madrigals.
The aria begins in G minor, moves soon to B-flat major, then to D minor, returning to G minor for the end. Aria and ritornello together make a clear, closed
form.

Then Aurindo plunges into E major (Example 77b) for an impassioned
recitative. This recitative is accompanied (by three viols and the "deep organ"),
a kind of recitative that becomes increasingly popular for moments of pathos.

EXAMPLE 77   CESTI: FROM IL POMO D'ORO I,ix; Aurindo sings

(a) (More unfortunate than I, no one has never been, and never will be; earth has no greater torment than to see one's loved one make another happy.

(b) It is really wretched that the joy that Fate denies me . . .

(c) Enjoy! enjoy, Paride, happy with the sweetest pleasures, while I have suffer deepest pains of Tantalus; Enjoy! . . .

(d) If the food you are blessed with fulfills your desires . . .)

It ends on a half cadence on E, as if leading to A, but the following common-time section is in C major (Example 77c). Here voice and bass imitate each other, a technical subtlety that becomes increasingly frequent toward 1700. The scene closes in triple time (Example 77d). Out of four sections, three are not recitative, and of the three, each has its own individual character, reflecting Aurindo's changing responses. The possibility of giving each aria a clearly defined character became the first concern of composers in the decades to come.

North of the Alps

By 1600 France had been the scene of continuous musical leadership for 800 years. After 1600, however, as leadership passed for a while to Italy, the relation of French music to that of its neighbors became problematic. The French (like the Germans) had not fully experienced the all-important development of the Italian madrigal—the most modern musical style just before 1600. Hence the French had little appreciation for the new Italian music of Monteverdi's generation, which was derived from the madrigal.

In the decades after 1600, secular music in France (as elsewhere) came to consist largely of songs and dances. The several kinds of songs included the *air de cour* (court song), direct descendant of the huge repertory of chansons, usually on serious or tender subjects, as well as the *air à boire* (drinking song) and *voix de ville* or *vaudeville* (street song), on less elevated subjects. Although cast in regular forms and rhythms, triadic progressions, and monodic texture, these songs had little of the excitement of Italian monody. The dances, similar to those in Italy, were often found in the same courtly setting of masque or intermedium, mixtures of dramatic pageant and festal celebration. In France these were called *ballet de cour* and *ballet mascarade;* they were especially popular from 1610 to 1630, continuing on throughout the century. Yet in France neither masque nor monody led to truly dramatic music.

The same was true across the channel in England, even though Italian monody, reaching England early in the 1600s, found the way prepared by the Elizabethan madrigal. English monody was more susceptible of the new tones of passion than the French air de cour. England, furthermore, had a rich literary tradition that produced poetry and drama even more representative of the new style. In spite of this, however, England like France suffered from the lack of a great composer, a Schütz.

As early as 1617 there was an English opera, Ben Jonson's *Lovers Made Men,* set "after the Italian manner, *stylo recitativo*" by Nicholas Lanier; but it was an isolated attempt. English composers, such as the aging John Bull (1562–1628), the Lawes brothers, Henry (1596–1662) and William (1602–1645), and John Jenkins (1592–1678), expressed themselves chiefly in fantasias and dances for instrumental ensembles (viols), or in massive sacred polyphony in the style of Orlando Gibbons (1583–1625), a versatile, gifted composer. The only sustained approach to modern dramatic style took place in the masque, the counterpart of the French ballet mascarade or Italian intermedium. The English masque, whether performed at court or in private houses, consisted of songs and dances not yet fused together in dramatic continuity. Henry Lawes's setting of *Comus* (by John Milton) is only one of many such works.

FRENCH MUSIC FOR LUTE AND KEYBOARD

FRENCH MUSIC FOR LUTE AND KEYBOARD It was in the dance that French composers eventually found forms most congenial to them. As in Italy, and Germany, too, advanced instrumental music from 1600 to 1650 was almost entirely for solo rather than ensemble—partly because only the solo composer-performer seemed able to spring free from the weight of tradition, partly because the virtuoso element of solo performance was an essential ingredient of style in the first half of the century.

For a while the most favored virtuosi were lutenists. Remarkable compositions by one such lutenist, Robert Ballard, have recently come to light. Originally published in 1611, Ballard's lute dances are exceptional in musical ability and imagination. There is nothing comparable in French publications before 1670; perhaps Ballard's dances give a glimpse of the quality of the unpublished repertory performed by virtuosi. An excerpt from a courante (Example 78) shows the sense of harmonic purpose that marks the most progressive music of the early 1600s.

Ballard's courante beautifully illustrates a style of figuration later called *style brisé* (broken style). Instead of being played as chords, the basic harmonies are expressed in a free, open texture, the notes sounded one after another in the different voices; *style brisé* lies somewhere between arpeggiation, scalar diminution, and imitative counterpoint. Very sonorous for the lute and keyboard, this style has great rhythmic charm; it produces a continuously rich, warm sound (in spite of the prevailing three-voiced texture), which when combined with expressive ornamentation of trills, mordents, and appoggiaturas is the French version—less brilliant and passionate, but more refined—of that stupefying haze designed to intoxicate the senses. Measures 13 to 24 of Example 78 are an unusually engaging example of style brisé; it is clear, however, from

EXAMPLE 78 BALLARD: SECOND HALF OF A COURANTE

EXAMPLE 78 (CONTINUED)

passages such as measures 1 to 4 that this style is only one of several, used in fluid alternation.

The most famous composer for lute was Denis Gaultier (ca 1600–1672). His works were published only at the very end of his life (*Pièces de luth,* 1669/1670), but many were circulating by 1650, the height of his fame. Some of these were collected in a splendid manuscript entitled *La Rhétorique des dieux* (the rhetoric of the gods) with elaborate illustrations and descriptions accompanying separate pieces, reflecting the literary and artistic interests of the courtly circles for which Gaultier performed and composed.

The dances in *La Rhétorique des dieux* are grouped according to a system of twelve modes. This modal system itself is mere academic ornament, irrelevant to the harmonic practice of the dances. The grouping, however, which in practice amounts to a grouping by key, is typical and important for French dances. Even more important is the sharper harmonic focus evident in each piece: the harmonies now seem much more clearly related to each other and to the one that stands at the end, an effect attained through stricter selection and smoother ordering of chords in highly directed progressions. As in Cesti's arias, each piece is really in the tone or key on which it ends.

The arrangement of dances in *La Rhétorique* seems partly for the sake of the collection and partly for performance. Under some modes we find a pavane, a courante, and a sarabande, or a prelude, an allemande, and a courante, or some other series of three or four dances. Under other modes we find a much longer series containing several of one kind of dance. Under *phrygien,* for example, there are an allemande, a sarabande, a gaillarde, a courante with double, another sarabande, a caprice, a courante, a volte, and two gigues. Under *sous-dorien,* we find a prelude, an allemande, two courantes, two gigues, and a sarabande. Such varied arrangements are typical of French dance music in the 1600s.

The allemande was more highly figured than the other dances, being older and more removed from actual dancing. It was in common time (the more modern dances were in triple time) and came to be marked *grave* (serious), especially when used as a *tombeau* in memoriam of someone. Gaultier wrote such an allemande for M. Blancrocher, a most celebrated virtuoso who died about 1655. The courante, less figured, faster, more dancelike, was still rhythmically complex, especially with syncopation over the bar line. Often several courantes were provided, also frequent *doubles* or ornamented versions.

Of the other kinds of dances, the sarabande, the third of the three Spanish imports, was the most modern. It tended to be the least figural, the most chordal, moving in a moderately fast triple time. Since *La Rhétorique* contains little identification of dances, it is often hard to determine the type of a triple-time dance. One of Gaultier's dances, nameless in *La Rhétorique,* had been labeled *ciacona* when published in 1628—the very moment when the ciacona was penetrating Italian art music.

Gaultier's most striking novelty was a type of prelude called *unmeasured.* Notated without any indication of rhythm (except for short cadential figures), such preludes were partly scalar, partly arpeggio, sometimes suggesting other figures. The performer has to determine the basic harmonic progression, building upon it a convincing rhythmic rendition. The result is not unlike one of Frescobaldi's shorter harpsichord toccatas—but in a manner distinctively French.

Jacques Champion de Chambonnières (1602?–1672?), exact contemporary of Gaultier, was his counterpart in keyboard music. Son and grandson of virtuosi, Chambonnières was one of the most brilliant performers of the mid-century and the center of a whole school of clavecinists, including Jean Henri d'Anglebert (1628–1691), Nicholas Lebégue (1630–1702) and Louis Couperin (ca 1626–1661), all important keyboard composers of the next generation. Like Gaultier, Chambonnières published only late in life, his *Pièces de clavessin* appearing in 1670. These works represent, however, the middle decades of the century.

Like Gaultier, Chambonnières does not group his dances consistently; but the *Pièces de clavessin* do reveal a pattern that probably reflects the grouping of dances in performance. The dances are grouped by key, as in Gaultier's *La Rhétorique*. Each key grouping begins with an allemande or pavane, in common time, followed by one or usually several courantes; at the end comes a sarabande, or a gigue, or some other dance or combination of dances. At the end of the *Pièces de clavessin* comes a minuet. The courantes are notated in three-four, usually in double bars (six-four) to allow for the frequent *hemiolia*, or three-two—the chief source of rhythmic charm in the courante. The sarabande is still the most modern member of the group; it still is less figured, and probably moves as fast as or faster than the courante. It is fairly free from hemiolia, moving regularly in three-four. The gigues are here consistently in triple time, often six-four.

Chambonnières also wrote a few *chaconnes* (as the ciacona was now called in France), although they were not included in his printed works. The chaconne is usually cast *en rondeau*, with a refrain that returns after each couplet, or contrasting episode ($R,C_1,R,C_2,R,C_3 \cdots R$). The refrain was often pitched low on the clavecin, producing on the typical French instrument of the 1600s a wonderfully rich sound. The triple time of the chaconne is more syncopated than that of the sarabande; the harmony tends to be more chromatic through the use of the flatted, blue notes, as in the Italian models.

The most important figure of the next generation was Louis Couperin (1626–1661), pupil of Chambonnières. His works were not published, but appeared in the same magnificent manuscript (the *Bauyn Manuscript*) with Chambonnières, arranged in the same way. Couperin wrote allemandes, courantes, and sarabandes much like his teacher; but Couperin wrote more sarabandes. In them Couperin's smooth harmonic progressions are exhibited to best effect.

A sarabande in C (Example 79) has the typical character of Couperin's sarabandes, as well as the smooth progressions moving over a stepwise bass toward clearly defined goals. The progressions give expressive shape to the traditional binary form—so expressive, in fact, as to suggest a slowing down of the sarabande tempo, without, however, depriving it of the basic movement of a triple-time dance.

Louis Couperin's sarabande illustrates a new formal principle—or rather, a new application of an old principle. The two halves of the binary dance form are distinguished from each other by being ouvert and clos. This distinction is

EXAMPLE 79   LOUIS COUPERIN: SARABANDE

often lacking in prototypes of binary form in the 1500s, or for that matter in the 1300s. Techniques for differentiating ouvert from clos endings had been developed in the 1300s in terms of interval progressions. These techniques did not, however, survive intact through the 1500s, owing to the intense exploitation of rich harmonies that tended to obliterate the two-part framework.

Precisely because of these harmonies, and their fixation around 1600, ouvert and clos could now, in the 1600s, be differentiated on a new basis—the basis of triadic harmony. At the end of the first section (Example 79), the ouvert is given by the implied triad G–B–D, which bears an open relationship to the clos on C. In this particular case neither chord is spelled out complete. But the relationship between the endings is only explicable on triadic grounds; it results from the customary use of these two chords in cadence formulas. The relationship is no longer a melodic one, as it had been in the versus, nor a two-part relationship, even though the old two-part cadential progression (B–D to C–C) is still embedded in the triadic one—visible but no longer audible.

When combined with the now clarified sense of key that governs the interior of phrases, this functional differentiation of phrase endings opened up a whole new series of possibilities. The development of musical forms, particularly in instrumental music (where there was no text to articulate the form), would be increasingly bound up with triadic relationships in the next century.

Couperin's most impressive pieces are perhaps his unmeasured preludes, now often much larger and more frequent than those of his predecessors. Couperin's preludes are sometimes sectional, with a *changement de mouvement* in the middle, just as some of Frescobaldi's toccatas have episodes in triple time or in imitative counterpoint. Couperin's unmeasured style is rhapsodic, often extremely eloquent. Example 80 is the shortest of his preludes, in a rhythmic transcription.

Unmeasured preludes were, of course, meant to be played freely; any attempt at transcription, such as that offered in Example 80, can only represent one performer's preference. The transcription should be compared with the facsimile of the original (available in a recent publication). It should also be compared with the German or Italian style of notating toccatas—which, it has been argued, should be played as freely as the French preludes. The unmeasured and measured notations, in other words, seem to stand equally far (or equally close) to something half way in between.

Couperin wrote chaconnes much like Chambonnières, but even better passacaglias, or *passecailles;* one in C has the same deep magnificence as the chaconne, while one in G minor captures the spellbinding effect of the best Italian ciaconas and passacaglias. The four-measure ostinato is repeated some forty times, although varied here and there by going up instead of down in the bass line; there is a stunning turn to G major toward the end, then an even more stunning, evocative conclusion in G minor. Such chaconnes went rather fast, in a swirling, hypnotic rhythm.

FRENCH OPERA: LULLY During the 1640s conditions both musical and political favored the reception of the new Venetian opera in Paris; Italian operas were performed beginning in 1645. They tended at first to resemble the grand ballets already popular in France: Sacrati's *La finta pazza* (The Feign'd Insane) was a festa teatrale; it was followed by Cavalli's *L'Egisto* in 1646 (Venetian premiere, 1643), which was largely pastoral with set allegorical scenes at the ends of acts; in 1647 Luigi Rossi was commissioned for an *Orfeo*.

But many French observers, particularly literary ones, were to find Italian opera objectionable. French opinion was from now on to be divided into two camps. On the one hand were professional musicians and musical connoisseurs, who appreciated the advanced style of Italian music sufficiently to accept

EXAMPLE 80 LOUIS COUPERIN: TRANSCRIPTION OF AN UNMEASURED PRELUDE

the operatic extravagances that went with it. On the other side were the literary
critics, tending to be violently pro-French and anti-Italian, reflecting a general
dissatisfaction with the peripheral role France now played in musical development, but not otherwise appreciative of basic musical values. In the absence of
other factors, the contest between these two groups was probably equal; but
other factors, primarily political, were present, resulting in the defeat and
temporary exclusion of Italian opera from Paris.

Political intrigue alone accounts for the involved history of attempts at

French opera during the 1660s. In 1659 Robert Cambert (ca 1628–1677), a very gifted French composer, collaborated with Pierre Perrin (1625–1675) to produce *La Pastorale,* described in the title as "the first French comedy in music" (as in Italian, *comédie* means simply a stage play). Another work, *Ariane et Bacchus,* was immediately projected. In 1662 the last Italian opera, Cavalli's *Ercole amante* (Hercules in Love) was performed in Paris; the work was not received favorably, but the ballets between the acts were praised.

These ballets were composed by a young Florentine who had joined the company of a traveling French nobleman as a page; Giovanni Battista Lulli (1632–1687), with the driving ambition of a Poppea, was changing himself as fast as he could into Jean-Baptiste Lully, absolute ruler of French music. During the 1650s he wrote successful ballets, like those which stole the show from Cavalli. After *Ercole amante* he moved on to the *comédie-ballet,* spoken plays with musical insertions, which he wrote in collaboration with Molière. The most famous is *Le Bourgeois gentilhomme* (1669), for which Lully contributed an overture, dances, and a variety of airs with ritornellos. A very clear idea of the subtle distinctions between French and Italian taste can be gained by comparing Lully's French airs with the parodies of Italian arias he wrote for the concluding *Ballet des Nations.*

In the meantime Cambert turned again to French opera, having obtained permission from the king to open an Academy for Opera *"ou représentations de musique en langue français."* In 1671 he produced a pastoral, *Pomone,* with Perrin; the next year, 1672, *Les peines et les plaisirs de l'amour* (pastorale héroique) with another writer, Gilbert. Both works (those fragments that remain) reveal a superior musical ability. The second work, especially, shows Cambert's excellent recitative style. His method of adapting recitative to French needs remained standard for almost a century.

What Cambert had in mind was the fluid alternation of common time and triple time characteristic of Cavalli. But in adapting this alternation for French drama, Cambert exploited it for the sake of declamation rather than for the emotional excitement it brought to Italian dialog—an entirely characteristic interpretation for a Frenchman to make at that time. For this reason, French recitative contained much more frequent triple time than Italian recitative, so frequent that the emotional effect was eliminated. Cambert's recitative is extremely lyrical, equal in elegance and tender expression to Cavalli, even if too restrained for successful projection of more extreme passions. The musical substance of Italian opera is, however, lacking; airs are infrequent, and as descendants of the air de cour, are often not very exciting.

Cambert's success was Lully's intolerable obstacle. In 1672 Lully obtained his own permission for an *Académie royale,* in which to perform works *"pareils et semblables aux Académies d'Italie."* Simultaneously, in a brilliant piece of Florentine intrigue, he ran Cambert out of business and eventually out of France. In 1673 he produced the first of his five-act dramas, *Cadmus et Hermione.* Although nominally a *tragédie-lyrique, Cadmus* still relied heavily on elements of the old pastoral: ballets and spectacles still accounted for much of the effect, if not the substance of the work.

But *Cadmus* also contained one of Lully's most reliable devices. In Act I, scene iv, there is a chaconne, a long set of ostinato variations for orchestra, culminating in a vocal trio (*Suivons l'Amour, laissons nous enflammer*), an exquisite replica of the mood of Monteverdi's *Zefiro torna*. Chaconnes and passecailles appeared regularly in Lully's tragédie-lyrique henceforth, at crucial moments in the drama.

Lully is often regarded as the champion of correct declamation of French in recitative, an impression he himself took pains to promote. Seeing that his success depended in large part on the favor of the pro-French literary circles then in ascendancy at court, he tried to make his tragédie-lyrique as similar in spirit to the spoken French drama and as distinct from Italian opera as possible.

Lully's recitative is built like Cambert's, with continual alternation of duple and triple rhythms, which, when sung fluently, serve to animate the declaimed rhythm, but without producing the sense of contrast associated with triple-time inserts in Italian recitative. Lully's recitative is as meticulous as the best Italian recitative, without being as expressive; that, however, reflects the difference in linguistic and national taste Lully was anxious to maintain. On occasion Lully's recitative rose to an heroic or pathetic height, as in Act V, scene iv, of *Armide* (1686), when Armide, defeated in her attempt to win the love of Renault, sees him finally depart (Example 81).

Armide herself is a remarkable character dear to the imagination of the 1600s. She is a warrior, invincible in battle and also possessor of magical powers, but betrayed at last to her enemy Renault by an unrecognized susceptibility. She takes him prisoner in battle, but soon becomes his prisoner in love. She uses all her magical powers to woo him, but he remains dedicated to glory ("After glory, I love you best"). This is too much for the overwrought, conflict-ridden Armide; she collapses at the end of the magnificent scene begun in Example 81, which would be equal in power to Cavalli except for Renault's inevitable alexandrians:

Trop malheureuse Armide, hélas!	*(Alas, unfortunate Armide,*
Que ton destin est deplorable,	*Your fate, so wretchedly forlorn . . .*
. . . (they urge him to hurry)	
Non! La Gloire n'ordonne pas	*No! even Glory cannot need*
Qu'un grand coeur soit impitoyable.	*Great hearts to be content with scorn!)*

Lully's greatest strength remained in the dance. The musical high point of his operas is a gigantic passecaille or chaconne, a set of variations on an ostinato, first for instruments, then with voices, with descriptive dances on stage. In *Armide*, Act V, scene ii, such a passecaille depicts the enchanted forest by which Armide hopes to ensnare Renault. To the sultry passecaille falls the job of creating atmosphere—amorous, langorous, exciting, hypnotic. Lully's melodic sense is at its best when driven on by the endless repetitions of dance rhythms over an ostinato. Expressed in the rich sonorities of a large orchestra, animated by sumptuous choreography against spectacular stage designs, with solo and chorus singing bittersweet lyrics of love, the swinging, seductive rhythms of the passecaille must have been overpowering—one of those stupefying moments that made the music-drama work.

CHARPENTIER'S SACRED MUSIC Although Lully's strong personality dominated all French music, his monopoly actually extended only over opera;

EXAMPLE 81   LULLY: FROM ARMIDE V,iv; Armide sings

(Renaud? Heaven! O deathly pain! You leave? Renaud! Demons—follow him! Fly, and stop him! —Alas! all betray me, and my powers are nil . . . Renaud! Heaven! . . .)

instrumental music, especially for keyboard, and sacred concertato music were cultivated by other composers. One of these, Marc-Antoine Charpentier (ca 1634–1704), wrote music that was in many ways more substantial than Lully's. Charpentier had studied in Rome with Carissimi and was therefore thoroughly acquainted with Italian styles and techniques. His sacred compositions, written during the last half of the century, are of three main types—*canticum, dialogus* and *historia*. The canticum and dialogus were usually smaller, and set for solo voices, corresponding in medium roughly to Schütz's "little spiritual concertos," or Hammerschmidt's dialogs. In concept, too, these smaller works are the French equivalent of Schütz and Hammerschmidt; some of Charpentier's works are titled *Méditations*.

Charpentier's historias, like Carissimi's, are larger works, with strong emphasis on chorus; three of them are on subjects also set by Carissimi (the Last Judgment, the Sacrifice of Abraham, the Judgment of Solomon), showing clearly that Charpentier was bringing Carissimi to France just as Schütz had brought Monteverdi to Germany. Charpentier's mature works, however, are several decades later than his teacher's, and hence naturally reflect the stylistic changes that had taken place in the meantime.

Charpentier's mature works frequently have descriptive *simphonies,* instrumental pieces inserted into the historia to depict action taking place in the story. Sinfonias had been a part of the sacred concerto since the early works of Schütz, but they acquired the power of description only in the Venetian opera of the 1640s and 1650s, where they accompanied dramatic action. Charpentier's mature works, for example, the exquisite canticum for Christmas, sometimes include sweet, simple songs—the French equivalent of the arietta frequent in Italian opera after 1650. But Charpentier is also capable of highly effective recitative and great choral laments equal to those of his teacher.

Charpentier maintained the sense of contrast as well as the careful construction of large scenes best exemplified by Cavalli; but his organization depended more and more on large symmetry of key plan, rather than the continuity of dramatic action. This was not merely characteristic of the oratorio as opposed to the opera; it reflected a general tendency toward stable tonal areas in all kinds of music around 1700.

FROBERGER One of the most brilliant keyboard virtuosi in all Europe was Johann Jakob Froberger (1616–1667). Remarkably well-traveled, he had been in all European countries except Spain. He was well trained in the art of Frescobaldi, and was in many respects Frescobaldi's only true successor; but he was equally at home in French dances. Not only did he know the French virtuosi intimately (like Chambonnières and Couperin, he wrote a tombeau for M. Blanchrocher, the celebrated Parisian clavecinist), but he was highly regarded by these Parisian virtuosi as their friend and equal. He was first of all a performer; his composition stemmed from his interests as a performer, consisting almost entirely of toccatas, suites, capriccios, canzonas, fantasias, and ricercars (no operas, cantatas, or sacred concertos). His composing fell mostly in the 1640s and 1650s, at his principal place of employment, the imperial court in Vienna. While still rhapsodic, Froberger's toccatas are smoother than Frescobaldi's; with fewer stunning effects, they have greater harmonic focus. Froberger's toccatas are dominated by figural diminution, with a slight reduction in the importance of imitation. The canzonas and capriccios, on the other hand, tend to be more imitative, with a corresponding reduction in the amount of purely figural sections. Of all these imitative forms, Froberger favored the capriccio, using animated subjects of considerable character.

Froberger composed some thirty sets of keyboard dances in the French manner; the earlier ones consist of allemande, courante, and sarabande. Gigues were added later, but did not assume a regular station after the sarabande until the important publication of Froberger's compositions in 1693. The sarabandes are particularly effective, with even richer, more poignant harmonies than the French ones (Example 82). Animated lyricism marks almost all of Froberger's work, yet the several lamentations—highly figured allemandes like the tombeaux of Chambonnières—have a pathos and gravity that rival Cavalli.

BUXTEHUDE AND OTHERS An appreciation of Froberger's accomplishments was apparently passed across the German heartland to the north, to

EXAMPLE 82 FROBERGER: SECOND HALF OF A SARABANDE

Hamburg, through Mathias Weckmann (1621–1674). Weckmann was one of a group of German composers that included Thomas Selle (1599–1663), Franz Tunder (1611–1667), and Christoph Bernhard (1627–1692)—earnest, competent men but untouched by the Italian glory, even though Weckmann and Bernhard were pupils of Schütz. The only composer of that group who seemed to catch fire was the erratic Johann Rosenmüller (1619–1684), active in Hamburg, and then, significantly, drawn to Venice. Rosenmüller's sacred concertos, for example, *Confitebor tibi,* are brilliant applications of the new Italian style to sacred texts.

The most impressive accomplishments in the extreme north were in organ music and organ performance, in the person of Dietrich Buxtehude (1637?–1707). Born in Denmark, and then permanently fixed in Lübeck (close to Hamburg on the Baltic), Buxtehude was to the north what Froberger was to the south. In them, and only in them, was the art of Frescobaldi brought to fulfillment.

Buxtehude also wrote excellent sacred concertos in modern style, with and without a chorale. Those with a chorale were sometimes in very simple form—as if an arietta for chorus. But chorale concertos could also assume grand proportions, as in *Herzlich lieb hab ich dich, O Herr,* where the chorale tune is set down, in expanded form, on top of the varied, sectional structure usual for the sacred concerto. This work approaches an oratorio, both in dimensions and dramatic shape; the several sections call for dramatic projection in keeping with the meaning of the text and the stylistic idioms used to accent it.

It is in Buxtehude's organ works, however, that his full brilliance shows forth—or better, explodes, so violent is the interaction of Italian drama with Northern thoroughness. At the center stand the mighty preludes, which are really toccatas, huge, sectional works using an alternation of figural and imitative textures (the term *praeludium* seems to describe the liturgical function of these toccatas as introductions to the service). The figuration becomes sheer fantasy (Example 83), exuberant beyond Frescobaldi's. Such figuration must, of course, be imagined in the brilliant sounds of Buxtehude's organ. The imitative sections, also highly colorful, are extended to great lengths, sometimes at the expense of the figural sections; these are then reduced to introduction and conclusion, framing the imitative section.

Buxtehude seems to have extrapolated from what he knew of Frescobaldi (and the earlier Froberger); exaggerating the contrasts of Frescobaldi, Buxtehude diverged from Froberger's increased smoothness and sense of harmonic refinement. Buxtehude's style reaches a climax in a passacaglia in D minor, and two ciaconas, in E minor and C minor. From the kinds of figuration Buxtehude applies (especially in the ciaconas), he seems to have had French models before him as well as Italian ones. At any rate these gigantic ostinato pieces have the same dizzy effect as the operatic passecailles and chaconnes of Lully written in the same decades.

Buxtehude's special gift was rhapsodic effusion, which expressed itself best in the toccatalike shape of his preludes. He also imposed this shape on chorales to produce the chorale fantasia. He let the chorale tune run throughout the sectional shape, unifying its sections (in much the same way that Frescobaldi, Sweelinck and others sometimes made each section of a toccata or fantasia a variation on a single subject). The presence of the chorale does not, however, impede the free flow of figuration and counterpoint.

The use of chorales is especially important in a smaller kind of piece that functioned like the old *intonazione*, that is, to introduce a sung portion of the service, in this case the congregational chorale. In these chorale intonations, or

EXAMPLE 83 BUXTEHUDE: FROM A PRAELUDIUM

(etc.)

By permission of Wilhelm Hansen, Copenhagen.

chorale preludes (as they are usually called), Buxtehude superimposed the chorale tune on the typically short intonation, treating it like a miniature toccata or fantasia. The chorale tune ran through once, usually in the top voice, but participating so actively in the figuration and imitative counterpoint that its presence was sometimes more felt than heard. Buxtehude wrote some thirty of these exquisite pieces, less magnificent than the big toccata preludes but more expressive. They are more modern in their implications than the toccata, being the counterpart of the closed aria forms, rather than the grandiose pathos scenes in recitative characteristic of Cavalli in the 1650s.

PACHELBEL AND BIBER Bracketed by Buxtehude to the north and Froberger to the south, the German heartland finally produced in Johann Pachelbel (1653–1706) a first-rate composer. Active in Erfurt and Nuremburg during the 1680s and 1690s, Pachelbel had studied in Vienna, but was also acquainted with Buxtehude's works. In 1699 he dedicated his *Hexachordum Apollinis* (figural variations) jointly to Buxtehude in Lübeck and F. T. Richter, imperial organist in Vienna.

Pachelbel wrote big toccatas like those of Buxtehude, but the rhapsodic figuration tended to harden into cooler, if still brilliant, forms. Pachelbel seemed more at home in his shorter toccatas with prominent pedal points, each ten or twenty measures long, only two or three running through a whole piece. These shorter toccatas were like intonations (a function toccatas had once had), having only one idea. In general, Pachelbel tended away from long, sectional works to shorter, homogeneous ones.

Most characteristic of Pachelbel are his numerous fugues. Some of these could be called capriccios, canzonas, or fantasias, direct descendants of Frescobaldi and Froberger; but Pachelbel's fugues usually have only one section with continuous treatment of the single subject from beginning to end. Pachelbel favored lively subjects, often with repeated sixteenth notes. The continuous treatment of such subjects brought about a uniform rhythmic motion throughout the fugue.

Pachelbel tended to write this smooth, fugal counterpoint whenever he was not writing a toccata with obviously figural ornamentation over a pedal. He used fugal style extensively for intonations. Apparently he liked these compact pieces based on strictly imitative style, for he wrote some ninety-four of them as *Magnificat* intonations for all the modes. One for hypophrygian on E (these intonations are *for* a mode but—like Gaultier's lute pieces—*in* a key) is given in Example 84. The expression of Pachelbel's great lyric gift through smooth harmonic progressions illustrated in these fugal intonations indicates a stage of development in German organ music analogous to the development of the Italian aria in Cesti.

Alongside Pachelbel's fugues, his chorale preludes were equally important models for the next generation. Of the several types Pachelbel cultivated, two are most frequent. One is a genuine prelude, an intonation for the singing of the chorale; it consists of continuous imitative treatment of the first line of the chorale. The second type begins like the first, and then proceeds to a complete statement of the chorale melody, often in the top voice in longer notes, accompanied neither by imitation nor figural patterns but by suavely animated

EXAMPLE 84   PACHELBEL: MAGNIFICAT FUGUE FOR THE FOURTH TONE

EXAMPLE 84 (CONTINUED)

chords. Here Pachelbel's sensitivity to harmony can best be studied. Two preludes on *Ach Herr, mich armen Sünder* (the "Passion" chorale) illustrate the
two types described.

Usually Pachelbel presents the chorale in merely beautiful harmonies,
without commenting musically upon its emotional significance. Sometimes, however, he writes a chorale prelude clearly descriptive of the meaning of the
chorale text. *Warum betrübst du dich, mein Herz* (Why art thou so troubled,
my soul?) expresses in its extended cadenza the dark, brooding atmosphere of
the text. This stress on the character of a particular chorale, analogous to the
growing character of arias after 1680, indicated the future development of
chorale preludes—indeed, of all German sacred music in the decades to come.

The same tendency toward character found unique expression in a set of
chamber sonatas for violin (ca 1674) by the south German virtuoso Heinrich
Biber (1644–1704). Although cast in familiar forms and styles (allemande,
courante, ciacona), each of Biber's fifteen sonatas has a strong sense of character; each is given specific content by being associated with one of the fifteen
episodes in the lives of Jesus and Mary that are included in the rosary. This
cycle of meditations on the sacred mysteries, a devotional practice that became
popular during the 1600s, infused emotional character into Biber's sonatas,
which are usually called the "Mystery" sonatas.

10
INTERNATIONAL STYLE AND NATIONAL TASTES 1680-1750

Italy

IN ITALY THE MUSIC-DRAMA CONTINUED TO BE THE SUPREME expression of musical style, and the aria the principal medium of stylistic development. As we saw, the musical style of the ariettas of the 1650s had been simple and neutral. These ariettas depended almost entirely on the situation provided by the libretto for emotional definition and dramatic effect. During the very decades when the arietta had been most in evidence (the 1650s and 1660s), the librettists were performing miracles of invention and resourcefulness in thinking up novel situations and unfathomable plots. All composers benefited from the fertile imaginations of the librettists; but the good composers were stimulated to an inventiveness of their own.

ARIA STYLES TOWARD 1700 Responding to the effect of the dramatic situation on the arietta, composers around 1680 found purely musical ways to give the arietta itself greater definition. They displayed increasing inventiveness of themes appropriate to the situation, increasing resourcefulness in working out the arietta so as to display the theme to greatest advantage. Themes became more and more distinct from one another. To say that the themes were original or individual would attribute to them qualities their inventors did not seek, for they were interested in themes only as vehicles of universal human response to specific dramatic situations. Nevertheless, aria themes became more substantial, more characteristic, more different one from another—and more appropriate to the specific occasion that evoked them.

The sharpening of the aria's character became especially noticeable in the 1680s. It is present in the works of one of the most promising composers then active, Alessandro Stradella (ca 1645–1681). Stradella, however, was the victim of intrigue and murder—so the story goes—before the age of forty; hence we possess only early works by him.

Another leading composer of the 1680s, Carlo Pallavicino (ca 1630–1688) reveals a wealth of invention for arias in his opera *La Gerusalemme liberata,* first performed in Venice in 1687. In one aria (Example 85a), the theme appears first in the ritornello for strings, and then in the voice ("Love!"). The two-note figure is spun out over a smooth harmonic progression to a cadence in the relative major, the remainder of the aria being built on the same material. Another aria (Example 85b), a reproach to a loved one ("Sweet lips, you hurt

EXAMPLE 85   PALLAVICINO: EXCERPTS FROM LA *GERUSALEMME LIBERATA*

(a)   Ritornello and aria; Tancredi sings

EXAMPLE 85 (CONTINUED)

(b) Aria; Armida sings

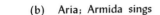

Bel lab-bro, m'of-fen-di a dir mi co - sì, m'of-fen-di, m'of-

fen-di a dir mi co-sì, m'of - fen - di, m'of-fen - di a dir mi co - sì.
(etc.)

(c) Aria; Tancredi sings

La-scia-mi in pa-ce, la-scia-mi in pa-ce, o son - no, per un mo - men-to, per un mo-men -

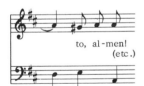

to, al-men!
(etc.)

(d) Aria; Clorinda sings

Vie-ni, vie - ni, ò Du-ce in-vit - to, vie - ni in cam-po a tri - on - far,   (etc.)

me to speak this way''), is built on a descending scale expressed in eighth-note figuration—an extremely frequent method of bass construction. By 1700 arias in common time with similar rhythms account for the majority of arias, replacing the triple time standard around 1650. Here the voice part is derived from parallel thirds with the bass, but characteristically broken up by rests.

The third aria, Example 85c, is broader and more expressive (''Let me be at peace, O Sleep, for a moment at least!''). By comparison the last aria (Example 85d, ''Come, O Leader, to the field of battle''—an invitation to the victorious general) shows how an entirely different character could be achieved when similar harmonies were set to different words in a different tempo and a different dramatic context.

As arias continued to grow in stature, a theme was often set out by the basso continuo, and then repeated by the voice. The bass now being more independent of the voice, the two could engage in counterpoint, combining the theme with itself and with counterthemes in various ways. The counterpoint was simple, to be sure; still it provided a method of spinning out the theme, so that it could permeate the whole fabric of the aria. Sometimes the voice began with a very short figure so arresting that it seemed to dominate the whole aria. Called *motto aria*, this type was cultivated especially by Legrenzi, but became frequent in all opera composers of the 1680s and 1690s.

As the aria expanded, the repetitions of theme brought repetitions of text; two or three lines of text, each several times repeated, were sufficient for relatively long arias. The strophic aria became less frequent, each strophe being by itself now quite long. Instead of strophic arias, composers now turned increasingly toward a type of aria with a single strophe, but a built-in musical repeat. The first and second halves of the text each had its own music; then the first half—text and music—was literally repeated, giving the form *ABA*. This repeat was called *da capo* (taken from the top).

By 1700 the overwhelming majority of arias was being cast in da capo form. Of hundreds, even thousands, of examples, one may be taken from the opera *Alarico* (Munich, 1687) by Agostino Steffani (1654–1728). Steffani spent much of his life in Germany (Munich and Hanover); he was one of many leading Italian composers who made Italian opera the foundation of later German music. His aria *Non sperar* (Example 86), beginning with a fine bass theme and a typically arresting motto for the voice, illustrates not only the da capo form but also its usual dimensions. It is most important to note that, even though expanded far beyond the arietta, the da capo aria was at this time relatively short, say, twenty to thirty measures in the A section and ten in the B section. It amounted in fact to a twofold statement of the basic theme (the A section) with a brief episode (the B section) in between.

The da capo aria stood at the end of a search for strong musical character; it was the most efficient musical form in which to cast an emotional response to a dramatic situation. In its original compact dimensions the da capo aria struck and held an emotional pose for just the right length of time to permit effective musical expression. The rapid adoption of the da capo form was due primarily to the elegant way in which it solved problems of musical drama.

EXAMPLE 86   STEFFANI: DA CAPO ARIA FROM ALARICO II,xv; Sabina sings

EXAMPLE 86 (CONTINUED)

io vuò mo - rir, io vuò, io vuò mo - rir.

Fine

Non pa-ven - to al Piè ca - te - ne

sa-ro un Mar-mo al - le tue Pe - ne sa-ro un A - spe al

Da Capo

tuo Lan - guir, sa-ro un A - spe sa-ro un A - spe al tuo Lan - guir.

(Hope not mercy to receive from me!
Rather than love you, I'd sooner die.
I'm not afraid to be in chains;
I'll be a statue to all your pains,
I'll be an asp for all you sigh!
Hope not! . . .)

CORELLI AND TORELLI The prevailing tendencies toward harmonic smoothness and thematic clarity, apparent in Cesti, Pallavicino, and many others, found expression also in the instrumental works of Arcangelo Corelli

(1653–1713), active in Rome from 1680 until his death. Soon acclaimed as perfect models of instrumental music, Corelli's works were presented to a European audience in an important series of publications.

While it was unheard of at this time to publish music-dramas, it was becoming increasingly popular to publish sets of instrumental pieces, usually sonatas for church or chamber. Music-dramas being designated each as a *work* (*opera*, in Italian), sets of sonatas were designated each as *opus,* the same term in Latin (for of the two types, church and chamber, the church sonatas were the more important). In publication as in other respects, Corelli expressed tradition with such elegance as to provide models for several generations:

Op. 1.   *Sonate da chiesa a 3* (12 sonatas, Rome, 1681)
Op. 2   *Sonate da camera a 3* (12 sonatas, Rome, 1685)
Op. 3   *Sonate da chiesa a 3* (12 sonatas, Rome, 1689)
Op. 4   *Sonate* (da camera) *a 3* (12 sonatas, Rome, 1694)
Op. 5   *Sonate a 2* (6 church sonatas, 6 chamber sonatas, the last a set of variations on La Follia, Rome, 1700)
Op. 6   *Concerti grossi* (8 church concertos, 4 chamber concertos, Rome, 1712?, Amsterdam, 1714)

The church sonatas *a 3* are for two violins, a violone or archlute (theorbo, or bass lute) and basso continuo for organ. The violone or archlute usually plays with the basso continuo, but sometimes has more figuration. The chamber sonatas *a 3*, on the other hand, seem to be for two violins and violone *or* basso continuo for harpsichord. They are sufficiently well made, in other words, that the three string parts alone provide the necessary harmonies; the secular dances of the chamber sonata did not, apparently, require the harmonic fullness provided by the basso continuo. The sonatas *a 2* are for solo violin and violone *or* harpsichord; here the solo violin has frequent double stops or arpeggio figuration to fill out the harmony.

Corelli's sonatas contain no particular novelty, being cast in much the same forms and styles as their predecessors, for example, sonatas by Vitali. (The elaborate ornamentation provided for a 1715 edition by an Amsterdam publisher for the violin sonatas, Op. 5, may—or may not—represent Corelli's intentions.) Corelli's sonatas tend to be longer, not by having more sections but larger ones, through the inner expansion that went on in the opera and cantata as well. While fast movements—allegro or vivace—were as fast and as frequent as before, slow movements tended to increase in size and frequency, and also went slower, judging from contemporary reports. More often than not the church sonatas began with a grave introduction, and included an adagio triple-time movement.

The style of each of Corelli's movements was smoother and clearer than before, giving a feeling of spaciousness and breadth that happily reinforced the greater length. This increased breadth came about through a careful handling of harmonic progression, both in the detail of voice leading from one chord to the next and at the higher levels of phrase and section structure.

Because the inner expansion of form was so closely linked to the poise of harmonic progression, Corelli's works clearly manifest the sense of key emerging during the 1600s. As in the Italian aria and French keyboard music, the chord on which a piece ended had increasing relevance to the chords used throughout the piece. Yet Corelli's music is more than just smoother and clearer than that of his predecessors; in his sensitive hands the church sonata became eloquent with a lyricism found before only in vocal music. This lyricism was the distinguishing feature of Corelli's style, replacing the virtuoso brilliance and whimsy of the first part of the century.

In his concertos of Op. 6 (which may go back to 1680), Corelli gave purely instrumental expression to the ripieno practice customary in the performance of larger sacred works (vocal or instrumental) throughout the century. Op. 6 has the title *Concerti grossi, con duoi violini e violoncello di concertino obligati, e duoi altri violini, viola, e basso di concerto grosso ad arbitrio, che si potranno radoppiare* (Large concertos, for two violins and cello—necessary parts that make up the concertino, and also optional parts for two more violins, viola, and bass, which may be doubled). Such concertos are basically sonatas (for church or chamber) in style, in order and number of movements, in the two violins and bass that provide the backbone of the scoring. What Corelli did in these concertos was to reinforce certain sections of the sonata with ripieno parts—still optional, it should be noticed. The words *concerto grosso* mean that these optional parts belong to the large concerted ensemble; they do not, all by themselves, constitute that ensemble, since they never play without the concertino.

From the point of view of musical style, the most important aspect of Corelli's concertos is the placement of the ripieno. Corelli exploited the contrast between the basic trio of two violins and bass, which plays all the time, and the tutti, which plays intermittently. The concertino plays in a style very similar to the sonata. The strong sound of the tutti underlines certain sections of the concertino, giving a more intense relief to the traditional phrase shapes, as can be seen in Example 87, from Op. 6, no. 1. Here the concertino begins in imitation, the ripieno adding weight to the chordal eighth notes at the end of the phrase.

Corelli's concertos show great variety in the placement of the ripieno; a different procedure is followed in almost every movement. When the texture is strictly imitative, as in a fugal movement, the phrase structure offers little opportunity for contrast. In such cases Corelli begins with the concertino, add-

EXAMPLE 87　CORELLI: FROM CONCERTO IN D, OP. 6, NO. 1

ing the tutti in successive fugal entries. Once in, the tutti usually stays in for the rest of the movement. At the other extreme of texture, certain movements, dominated throughout by driving sixteenth-note figuration in the first violin, are also played tutti throughout. The majority of movements, however, fall in between these extremes; having a more varied texture (imitative or figural), they permit more varied relationships of soli and tutti.

Although many of Corelli's concertos may have been composed fairly early in his career, they were not published until the very end of his life (or perhaps only after his death). Georg Muffat (1653–1704), an Austrian, prefaced his own collection of concertos with an account of Corelli's concertos in Rome around 1680. In any case, the ripieno practice had existed for some time and needed only to be transferred from sacred concerto to instrumental music.

It was the ripieno practice, not the contrast of tutti and soli, that was basic to the concerto; a piece for large ensemble without contrast was just as much a concerto as one with contrast. The translation *grand concert,* found in English publications of the time, probably renders the term *concerto grosso* as accurately as anything can. The term *concerto,* in general use during the 1600s for modern, serious works—and for the ensemble that played them—was now applied specifically to the most advanced kind of instrumental music, to the reinforced sonata.

In 1692 Giuseppe Torelli (ca 1650–ca 1708) published as Op. 5 a set of six sinfonias *a 3* and six concertos *a 4.* At that time *sinfonia* was roughly equivalent to *sonata;* the difference between three and four parts is not so important as Torelli's instruction to reinforce all parts in the concertos. In 1698 Torelli published *Concerti musicali,* Op. 6. These reveal a sporadic use of tutti-solo contrast, but more important, a tendency to drop the opening grave typical of Corelli's works. It was by no means a novelty to begin with a fast movement (the grave having been an addition in the first place), but in Torelli's hands the concerto began to assume a broader, simpler shape, marked—like the da capo aria—by a few large sections in a symmetrical pattern.

Torelli's last works were *Concerti grossi con una pastorale per il Santissima Natale* (Grand concertos with a pastorale for Christmas Eve), Op. 8— a set comparable to Corelli's concertos Op. 6, and, like that one, published after the composer's death in 1708. These concertos exploited tutti-solo contrast to a much greater degree. The first six concertos were for a concertino of two violins and bass, the last six for a concertino of solo violin and bass.

As the shape of each movement became less compact, statements of the theme or subject began to be separated by figural episodes. If thematic statements were given to the tutti, and the episodes to the solo violin (by no means always the case), a very clear sectional structure appeared within the movement. Torelli stressed this sectional structure by making the figural episodes neutral, contrasting with the strong sense of character in the themes.

Sometimes the solo violin had nothing but arpeggios (which Corelli used only in solo sonatas). Because of their placement, however, these long arpeggiated passages seemed filled with suspense and anticipation; they came to have the same spellbinding effect as the hypnotic chaconnes, giving the concerto, in addition, the all-important element of virtuoso brilliance. Although concertos continued to be scored for a concertino of several instruments—or no concertino at all—the concertino *a 2* for violin and bass found increasing favor, and, as the solo violin concerto, became the leading type.

SCARLATTI AND OPERA AROUND 1700 The same depth of expression, character, and lyricism that Corelli brought to sonata and concerto was manifest in the operas of Corelli's contemporary and colleague in Rome, Alessandro Scarlatti. Scarlatti was a master of opera composition; he neglected no aspect of its musical construction—certainly not the recitative, upon which he lavished attention. But his central interest lay in the aria, in working out the character of the theme in more and more elaborate musical form. Alongside his operas (perhaps as many as eighty, but more likely about fifty), he wrote almost eight hundred cantatas, whose dramatic interest is frequently slight but whose musical interest, especially in the arias, is extremely high.

Scarlatti's early operas (1679–1700) have the same features as those before him. There are numerous short arias, many in da capo form. The scenes have varied, flexible construction to reflect dramatic action. The action itself is a mixture of types ranging from comedy to pathos. In conception these works stand close to those of other composers, yet already they reveal Scarlatti's excellence in thematic invention and working out.

A variety of themes can be illustrated by arias from *La Statira* (Rome, 1690). The plot, set in ancient times, involves noble characters in a plot of intrigue and concealed identity, with themes of heroism, pathos, and love. In *Consolati, non piangere* (Console yourself), Demetrio, the rough old soldier, consoles Statira on the death of her father (Example 88a). A fine subject appears first in the basso continuo, and then is partially repeated by the voice; the rest of the aria is made out of extensions and contrapuntal treatment of this subject. The uniform but animated rhythm is characteristic of the increasingly frequent arias in common time. These rhythms are projected onto clear, simple harmonic progressions that move a little slower than the rhythms, informing them with a very clear sense of harmonic direction. The character of such a theme depends upon a fine adjustment betwen rhythmic and harmonic motion.

In *Mi consiglio col mio core* (Example 88b), Apelle, a painter, reflects on an uncertain turn of events ("I take counsel with my heart, and my heart remains in doubt.") The rhythmic figure is a chic, sweet type often found in three-eight arias—Scarlatti's equivalent of the triple time used earlier in the 1600s. The aria begins with a ritornello (not in the example) for bass and two equal instruments (oboes?), moving in thirds; the lower of the two plays the aria melody. The melodic repetitions in measures 5 to 9, especially characteristic of the taste in arias around 1700, are beautifully appropriate to the dramatic situation.

In *Se mio nume* (Example 88c), Alessandro, the emperor, is joyfully anticipating the arrival of Statira, whom he loves, in a hoped-for reconciliation. The aria is built like *Consolati*, but the character is very different. The strong harmonic frame permits the change of figuration in measure 2, where the rapid dotted rhythms seem to boil over in lyrical effusion.

Another soldier, Perinto, sings a typical comic aria, *Io no son di quei campioni tanto pazzi* (*I'm* not one of those heroes crazy for honor; I like big

EXAMPLE 88 SCARLATTI: ARIA EXCERPTS

(a) From *La Statira* I,v; Demetrio sings

Con - so - la-ti, non pian-ge-re,

con -
(etc.)

(b) From *La Statira* I,ix; Apelle sings

Mi con - si - glio   col mio   co - re

[Oboes]

ed   il   cor,   ed   il   cor   (etc.)

(c) From *La Statira* III,x; Alessandro sings

Andante (♩ = 100)

Se   mio   nu - me

6   6   6   4 3

EXAMPLE 88 (CONTINUED)

(etc.)

6   4 3

(d) From *La Statira* I,v; Perinto sings

($\bullet$ = 120)

Io   non   son   di quei cam-pio-ni tan - to   paz-zi, tan - to paz-zi, tan - to

B.c.

6   6

paz-zi per l'o - nor,
(etc.)

6

(e) From *La Santa Genuída* II,xvii; Zelone sings

A tempo giusto ($\bullet$ = 60)

[Strings]

B.c.

7   6   6   6   6   #
              5   #

EXAMPLE 88 (CONTINUED)

Que-sta   è   va-ga,   è   va-ga, ma   non mi ap-pa - ga,   (etc.)

6   4 3   6 6̸5   ♯6   ♯

(f)   From *La Teodora augusta* I,xii; Osmano sings

Largo (♩ = 60)

Se non vuoi ch'io mi la - men-ti,   ch'io mi la -
                                              (etc.)

B.c.

fat purses; I hate noise), shown in Example 88d. Over a typically animated yet neutral bass figure, the characteristic melodic repetitions are the principal means for comic effect.

From *La Santa Genuinda,* a pasticcio of 1694 to which Scarlatti contributed the second act, comes a comic aria of a different sort. This is not slapstick comedy; even though the situation in the story is not without its grisly aspects, this aria presents a sophisticated picture of a refined Italian nobleman preoccupied in the serious business of looking over the girls, who are walking by during the ritornello given in Example 88e. Zelone sings, "This one is nice—but doesn't satisfy me; that one is beautiful, but not the type to steal my heart away." Over a simple descending bass line, the ritornello unfolds in elaborate figures and harmonies, giving a true musical expression to that studied nonchalance with which a connoisseur judges feminine beauty. Arias of sharp psychological insight like this become the foundation of musical comedy later in the 1700s.

From *Teodora Augusta* (Rome, 1693) comes a magnificent aria of a more serious kind, *Se non vuoi ch'io mi lamenti* (If you do not wish me to lament, these lips will be silent), shown in Example 88f. The very expressive subject is extended in exquisite counterpoint and rich harmony. The A section of the da capo form is only seven measures long—little more than one beautifully shaped phrase; the B section is four measures longer.

This high art of the aria can be studied further in *La Rosaura* (Naples,

1690), *Rosmene* (Naples, 1688) and *Pirro e Demetrio* (Naples, 1694). In spite of his great success, Scarlatti was not the most famous opera composer of his time. Even in these earlier works he tended to seek out individual solutions of somewhat greater intricacy than that desired by the operatic audience, greater than, say, the models placed before him by Pallavicino, whom Scarlatti followed closely. Contemporaries of Scarlatti like Carlo Francesco Pollaroli (ca 1653–1722), no less skilled but less challenging, are more representative of successful opera around 1700.

While the mixture of opera types cultivated by Scarlatti is typical, there was a strong tendency in the 1690s toward comedy. As we saw, a slick, easy style had been indigenous to the arietta; it was only the labor of composers from Cesti to Scarlatti that raised the arietta to a plane where it could express pathos or other serious feeling. In a way, the elevation of the aria was artificial, an illusion created by its dramatic position and new musical interest.

During the 1680s and 1690s, even while the aria was growing in stature, it retained a smartness, especially in the works of Marc Antonio Ziani (ca 1653–1715) and the Bononcini brothers, Giovanni Battista (1670–ca 1750) and Antonio (1677–1726). In 1696 the first opera of Antonio Bononcini, *Camilla*, began an extraordinarily successful run all over Europe. *Camilla* was not comic in the sense of the slapstick still current in opera. There was one comic role (Linco) in *Camilla* with a few clever arias, but the rest of the roles, and their arias, were more serious; their subjects were love, resolve, indignation, lament.

What made *Camilla* a hit—and so important for the future—was the extreme charm and ingratiating quality of these arias. So graceful was their musical style that one could hardly become too upset about the threatening situations described in the plot. "How prettily he cries!" For all their charm these arias were not as simple as the old arietta. They made full use of the increased sense of character gained in the 1680s and 1690s. Yet their easygoing accessibility made the work as a whole not serious. *Camilla* can only be described as a sentimental comedy—a category of great importance for the coming century.

For the decade after 1700, the Bononcinis, especially Antonio, led the younger generation in the production of these sentimental comedies, consisting primarily of a succession of good songs. The serious opera, while by no means eliminated, was seen more and more as an alternative to comedy; this split in opera types was the most important development of the decade. In 1700 Scarlatti wrote *Eraclea*, a serious work but with the usual comic roles. Then for Venice in 1707 he wrote *Mitradate Eupatore*, a work in five acts instead of the usual three, with no comic parts. The plot is based on intrigue and concealed identity, but the total effect is no longer extravagant or capricious. Its accompanied recitative is extremely expressive, owing to strong harmonic effect as well as majesty and pathos in conception. The pathos aria *Cara tomba* (Beloved tomb) is a masterpiece. But serious works like this came to depend on the right librettist and the right audience—at least for Scarlatti.

In 1718 Scarlatti wrote a very fine comedy for Naples, *Il Trionfo dell'onore* (Honor triumphant). The three acts are built on a plot of intrigue, concealed identity, and love, leavened by a threatening element. The scene, however, is laid in modern times, in a familiar locale (Pisa); it is a bourgeois comedy. The characters converse in lively recitative, singing da capo arias of various kinds. They also sing charming duets, one involving a lively banter of curses. There are several very interesting arias made of short, contrasting sections. Finally, there are several ensembles, especially a quartet at the end of the second act, and another quartet (in da capo form) just before the end of the third act, preceding the *dénouement;* it catches the characters at their moment of deepest perplexity. The *dénouement* itself proceeds in recitative, followed by a slow, touching arioso in which the villain repents, and a short, concluding ensemble of relief.

The increased stature of the aria evident throughout Scarlatti's works (and those of his contemporaries) was supported by the increasingly frequent orchestral accompaniment. The da capo aria came to be regularly accompanied by a string ensemble of two violins, viola, and bass; as in the concerto, these could be doubled as desired. Such accompaniment facilitated inner expansion through concertato interplay with the voice. Usually the strings were in a rich four-part harmony, but sometimes, for special effect, they all played in unison, providing a powerful instrumental counterpart to the voice.

Whether in unison or in parts, the strings had long sections to play by themselves: large ritornellos came into fashion as ornate frames for the aria. The return of such a ritornello at the end of an aria had an effect similar to the da capo, and the so-called ritornello aria now rivaled the da capo form. As for the sinfonia used as overture, it now dropped the slow introduction, becoming (like the concerto) fast, slow, fast; the last movement could be in a dance tempo. But such opera sinfonias—even Scarlatti's—remained much less substantial than the concertos of Torelli and Vivaldi.

Some of Scarlatti's last operas, for example, *Telemaco* (Rome, 1718—the same year as *Il Trionfo dell'onore*), contain a mixture of serious and comic roles in the traditional fashion. *Telemaco* has many interesting features, including frequent use of orchestral recitative, and ensembles. Above all it reveals an expansion of musical style of fundamental importance for the next generation. The aria is increased in size, attaining a grandeur of a purely musical kind absent from previous aria styles, in spite of their wealth of other superb features. Another late opera, *Griselda* (Rome, 1721), has no comic roles. Described as "spacious," it set the tone of serious opera for the next generation.

During Scarlatti's lifetime the popularity of the *castrato,* or *evirato,* rose to its peak. Basically a boy-soprano range and timbre, but with adult power and control, the castrato voice could be extremely impressive, if not overwhelming. Even Northerners, who usually found the institution of the castrato unacceptable, were sometimes ravished by the sound. Unbelievably brilliant, the best castrato voices embodied that stunning overabundance of sound that had been the keynote of opera throughout the 1600s.

Castrati also represented other characteristics of opera of the 1600s—unnaturalness, contradiction, and complexity. Throughout the period, the solo roles were sung by men, women, and castrati, but not necessarily distributed among the singers in the most natural way. Principal roles of male or female personages alike were usually in soprano range, and hence could be sung either by castrati or women, with sometimes contradictory results. In the ever-popular story of *Semiramide* (see page 266), the title role and her son, who have an unnatural affection for each other, spend much of the story dressed in each other's clothes. The performance of either, or both, of these roles by a castrato would complicate matters considerably.

Like the spectacular stage designs and scenery, the awesome machines for transporting supernatural personages on and off the stage in unusual ways, the extravagantly costumed choreography, the hyperbolic poetry sung to glittering music and accompanied by grandly stylized poses and gestures, the castrati belonged to this kind of opera, this stupefying image of a never-never land in which human characteristics were exaggerated past belief, then exaggerated still more until they imposed belief on their own terms. It was a dangerous kind of opera; if the image flickered, the illusion collapsed, exposing the work and everyone connected with it to merciless criticism—charmingly expressed by Benedetto Marcello (1686–1739) in his *Il Teatro alla moda* (ca 1720). But opera sometimes succeeded, and then the audience was transported into a realm of musical expression unique in Western history.

VIVALDI The simultaneous infusion of character and breadth into the aria during Scarlatti's career was paralleled in instrumental music in the works of Antonio Vivaldi (ca 1678–1741). Beginning, like Corelli, with two sets of sonatas, Vivaldi proceeded immediately to more ambitious church concertos, which he published under the title *L'Estro armonico* (Harmonic raptus), Op. 3. Scored for various kinds of concertino, these important works confirmed several tendencies evident in Torelli's concertos.

Usually leaving off the slow introduction, Vivaldi began with a vigorous allegro, typically followed by a slower movement and another faster one. With this simpler, more symmetrical shape, the concerto took on a more universal character, becoming suitable for festive secular occasions as well as sacred ones. More and more such grand concertos challenged the aria as the foremost type of music.

Vivaldi's opening movements developed a new, distinctive character—dynamic, rather than lyric. Like the brilliant common-time arias of the early 1700s, these opening allegros had strongly characteristic themes set in relentless sixteenth-note rhythms that ran throughout the movement. As in Torelli, the themes, clearly announced at the beginning, were relieved by less thematic figuration. Articulated by the obvious returns of the theme, the outlines of the movement became clearer.

The sense of movement to different keys became easier to perceive, especially when a theme first stated in minor was restated in the relative major. Literal, or almost literal, restatement helped emphasize the different tonal levels of the movement. Modulation among keys became an obvious feature of musical structure. Movements that started in a major key typically moved to the dominant key, later to the relative minor, then—often abruptly—back to the tonic. The alternate keys, in other words, were the simple, obvious ones, in keeping with the goal of overall clarity.

It should be noted that the contrast of strong theme with neutral figure is not the same as the contrast of tutti with soli. The two types of contrast might be coordinated, or they might not, depending on the whim of the composer. Especially in Vivaldi, the relationship of tutti to solo passages was still fluid.

Like Corelli, Vivaldi regarded the application of ripieno to the concertino core as a way of shaping phrases and movements with ever novel results. It was, of course, natural to associate the ripieno with the theme and the solo with the figural episodes; but precisely because it was so natural, Vivaldi constantly sought out alternatives, with such brilliant success that his contemporaries considered one of his foremost qualities to be *bizarria*—a sense of the bizarre, or unusual.

Vivaldi's concertos, Op. 3, of 1709, established both his fame and the new type of concerto. Succeeding publications showed an increase in imaginative powers, culminating in the four concertos known as the *Seasons*, provided by Vivaldi with poetic programs depicted in the musical style. These concertos were published in 1725 as Op. 8—*Il Cimento dell'armonia e dell'inventione* (The contest of harmony and invention). His unpublished concertos and sonatas of all conceivable types are extremely numerous. He also wrote a substantial number of operas, reflecting an energetic career that lasted through the 1740s. His decisive works, however, remained the early concertos of 1709.

North of the Alps

PURCELL AND ENGLISH MUSIC   While England was without a Schütz for most of the century, she finally found one in Henry Purcell (1659–1695). Shortly before his untimely death, Purcell published a revealing assessment of British music in the dedication of his music for the *Prophetess, or the History of Dioclesian* (1690/1691):

> Poetry and Painting have arrived to their perfection in our own country: Music is yet but in its Nonage. . . . 'Tis now learning Italian, which is its best Master, and studying a little of the French Air to give it somewhat more of Gayety and Fashion. Thus being farther from the Sun, we are of later Growth than our Neighbour Countries, and must be content to shake off our Barbarity by degrees.

A sustained effort to "shake off Barbarity" can be traced from 1650, beginning with the publishing activities of John Playford, for example, his *Introduction to the Skill of Musick* (1654) and *Select musicall Ayres and Dialogues* (1652). There was an attempt at full-scale English opera: in 1656 William D'Avenant produced the *Siege of Rhodes*, with music by Henry Lawes (1596–1662), Henry Cooke (ca 1616–1672), and Matthew Locke (1630–1677). After 1660 there was a steadily increasing demand in England for Italian music, but in spite of the enthusiasm with which the Italian style was received, no British composer seemed willing or able to produce an indigenous version of that style in any significant quantity.

This was all the more surprising since the British seem to have had a very clear understanding of the spirit of Venetian opera in terms of their own literary drama. Although not shared by all playwrights and audiences, this understanding emerges especially in the heroic verse dramas of John Dryden (1631–1700). Dryden conceived drama as "nature wrought up to a higher pitch," and justified on that basis the use of artificial devices such as rhyme. This elevation of lyrical dialog through extravagant poetic diction is the same concept that lies behind recitative. Perhaps because this dramatic concept was identified in England with spoken drama, it was never accepted in opera; at any rate, in England the most successful operatic projects of the 1600s involved a combination of Italian arias and spoken drama. Drama sung from beginning to end in English was infrequent. During the 1680s there appeared *Venus and Adonis* by John Blow (1649-1708) and Purcell's *Dido and Aeneas,* but these are exquisite miniatures, cast in the dimensions of the early favola pastorale even though they use more modern techniques.

The composition of English music had as its point of departure after 1660 the Chapel Royal, where the "brisk and airy Prince," Charles II, caused the modern Italian style to be well represented. The Chapel flourished under the leadership of Henry Cooke: "Captain Cooke's boys"—John Blow, Matthew Locke, and Pelham Humfrey (1647-1674)—came to represent up-to-date British music. Purcell's concerted church music, written largely during his twenties, belongs in this same sphere of activity. Up to the end of his life Purcell also wrote a great deal of occasional music in modern vocal style, including the celebrated Odes for St. Cecilia's day.

Purcell's most significant work, however, took place in connection with stage dramas. Purcell's music for the stage represents the most elevated kind of music known to him. It was here that he sought most avidly to "shake off Barbarity," demonstrating in his last five years a remarkable assimilation of techniques barely established even in Italy. Between 1690 and 1695 he provided varying amounts of music for five dramas—*Dioclesian, King Arthur* (in collaboration with Dryden), *Fairy Queen, Indian Queen,* and *Tempest.* The difference in style between the first and the last of these is striking: *Dioclesian* and even *Fairy Queen* still look like Italian music of the 1660s or 1670s, but *Indian Queen* is already Pallavicino or even Scarlatti. The great motto aria *Wake! wake!* from *Indian Queen* stands as an emblem of Purcell's aspirations.

Tempest brings Purcell's most highly regarded dramatic music (even though some of it is so Italianate as to cause some British critics to question its authenticity). Examples of Purcell's now mature style are the da capo aria *Halcyon days,* the recitative and air *Great Neptune,* and the mighty *Arise, ye subterranean winds. Pretty dear youth* and *Full fathom five* anticipate the charming airs from *Camilla*—not yet written, and destined to be one of the first Italian operas produced in England(1706).

GERMAN KEYBOARD PUBLICATIONS After 1690 the three German-speaking areas—Vienna, Hamburg, and central Germany—continued to represent Northern musical activity, each in its own characteristic way. Vienna continued to be most closely associated with Italian music. Up until 1700 the court opera at Vienna was under the leadership of Antonio Draghi (ca 1635-1700), indefatigable composer of all types of dramatic music. In the years after 1700 the principal court composers were Marc Antonio Ziani, Antonio Caldara (ca 1670-1736), and especially Johann Joseph Fux (1660-1741).

Fux was remarkable in several ways, first of all because he was an Austrian who excelled at Italian opera, writing in an up-to-date style with great skill and no little sense of drama. He tended toward a heavier style than Alessandro Scarlatti, his exact contemporary, but that was characteristic even of Italians in Vienna. Fux also wrote a great deal of concertato sacred music for the imperial chapel, of which he was eventually in charge.

His most significant production, however, was a book on counterpoint in the Italian style. Toward 1720, Fux (now almost sixty) became concerned about what he called "the unrestrained insanity" of modern methods of composition; he felt that "music has become almost arbitrary and composers refuse to be bound by any rules and principles. . . ." In order to introduce a sense of order into the increasingly willful progressions of modern harmony, Fux proposed a new emphasis on the conduct of the parts, such as might be gained from an intensive study of counterpoint.

In his *Gradus ad Parnassum* (Steps to Parnassus), a "sure, new method," published in 1725, Fux summed up the revival of counterpoint initiated by Vitali, Bononcini, and Berardi. Beginning with strict counterpoint in the original sense, that is, note-against-note, Fux proceeded methodically through the traditional "species" or kinds of diminished counterpoint, coming finally to the art of canon and fugue.

German musicians continued for a while to make their most significant contributions as keyboard performers and composers, following the lead of Froberger, Buxtehude, and Pachelbel. During the 1690s there appeared a remarkable series of publications for keyboard, including the 1693 edition of Froberger's works. In these publications sets of dances were called *partite* (Italian) or *partien* (German); French editions of the same time used the term *suite*. Froberger's partitas, as presented in 1693, consisted of allemande, courante, sarabande, and gigue, an order that now became customary in Germany.

In 1697 Johann Krieger (1652–1735) published a set of six partitas, each consisting basically of allemande, courante, sarabande, gigue; then, as he says, he "filled in the spaces" with lighter French dances—bourrées, minuets, and gavottes, added on after the gigues. All were composed, continues Krieger, *"nach arieusen Manier,"* in a songlike manner. Krieger also published in 1698 a collection of preludes, ricercars, fugues, fantasies, toccatas, and a ciacona, titled *Anmuthige Clavier-Übung* (Graceful keyboard practice).

Other important composers published at this time were Johann Kuhnau (1660–1722) and Johann Kaspar Ferdinand Fischer (ca 1650–1746). In 1689 Kuhnau published at Leipzig his *Neue Clavier-Übung I* (New keyboard practice) containing seven partitas in seven major keys—C, D, E, F, G, A, and B flat. Each partita contained an allemand, sarabande, courante, and usually a gigue; in addition each partita had a prelude. In 1692, Kuhnau published part II of his *Clavier-Übung*, containing seven suites in minor keys—C, D, E, F, G, A, and B, also with preludes but less often gigues; this time Kuhnau added a sonata at the end.

This sonata was apparently the most successful feature of the publication, for in 1696 Kuhnau published his *Frische Clavier Früchte* (Fresh fruit for the keyboard) containing seven sonatas. Then in 1700 he brought out his *Musikalische Vorstellung einiger Biblischer Historien* (Musical representations of Biblical stories). These publications earned Kuhnau the title, Father of the German keyboard sonata—his being the first.

The "Biblical" sonatas (as they are called) reveal Kuhnau's attempt to raise the keyboard sonata to a new level of seriousness comparable to vocal music. In order to give the sonata more substance, Kuhnau made it programmatic like the tombeau, or like Biber's "Mystery" sonatas. Drawing upon several sources of intensity in instrumental music (especially the representational sinfonia frequent in the opera), he supplied titles and programs to the various movements of his sonatas. Kuhnau's methods are drastic, his results often grotesque, largely because the methods of musical representation appropriate to the opera seemed incongruous in the absence of the scenery, staging, and action that defined their meaning in the opera. Nevertheless his sonatas are highly entertaining and his achievement significant.

Johann Ferdinand Fischer published keyboard dances in *Les Pièces de clavessin* of 1696; his specialty, however, was best represented by a curious collection entitled *Ariadne musica,* "leading the novice organist out of a labyrinth of difficulties through twenty preludes and as many fugues, and also five ricercars on as many sacred songs from the liturgical year." This publication apparently first appeared soon after 1700. In the tradition of publishing sets of intonations for organ arranged according to modes, Fischer's set was distinguished by the systematic pairing of a prelude with a fugue, the prelude consistently figural, the fugue consistently imitative; each was homogeneous, neither was sectional; together they made a pair like a recitative and aria.

Indeed, Fischer's little preludes and fugues each have a well-defined character (whether embodied in the figurative pattern of the prelude or in the subject of the fugue) comparable to the clear character that emerged in the aria during the 1680s and 1690s. These pieces represent a significant advance in expressiveness over their predecessors, the old intonations, even though they seem unimpressive next to the staggering toccata preludes of Buxtehude; but those are really a different category of composition.

Also characteristic of Fischer's *Ariadne musica* is the increased range of keys. Fischer wrote preludes and fugues in nineteen keys, omitting C sharp and F-sharp major, B flat, E flat, and A-flat minor. (The academic modal systems of the preceding two centuries are no longer involved, even though one prelude and fugue is in E phrygian.) The use of more remote keys was in response to the purely musical need for increased tonal variety—a necessary consequence of the increased stabilization of key.

Previously musicians had found sufficient tonal contrast within the realm of keys extending from three sharps to three flats. These keys they tuned so as to be as clean, as in-tune, as possible, using as a basis the meantone temperament of the 1500s. When more keys were needed outside this realm, the keys within had to be slightly untuned so that the new ones would be acceptable. This tuning was carried out by the performer at his harpsichord (or, less conveniently, by the organ builder). Each virtuoso had his own favorite way of tuning. Called "circulating temperament" (because the inevitable out-of-tuneness was distributed around the circle of keys) or simply "good temperament," this broadening of the key realm went on progressively throughout the 1600s and 1700s. Fischer's *Ariadne musica* marks one of the last stages before closure of the circle.

SACRED CONCERTO AND CANTATA   While Kuhnau and Fischer also wrote sacred concerted music, the central figure in sacred church music was Johann Philip Krieger (1649–1725, not to be confused with his younger brother, Johann). Philip Krieger's main achievement was a lifetime output of over two thousand sacred concertos and cantatas, in the course of which Krieger reshaped the sacred concerto, with results of the greatest importance for the future.

Having spent two years in Italy studying with Rosenmüller and Rovettini in Venice, Abbatini and Pasquini in Rome (composers of greater or lesser importance, but all involved in modern Italian music), and making the acquaintance of Cavalli, Legrenzi, Ziani, and Carissimi, Krieger was fully informed on Italian stylistic development up to the 1680s; there is no reason to think he lost contact with Italy after his return to Germany. He became Kapellmeister at the court of Weissenfels in 1680, turning out a steady stream of sacred concertos during the 1690s.

Krieger's concertos are sectional works, primarily for chorus, with frequent interludes for solo voices. The sections follow one another in flexible response to the structure and meaning of the text, using contrasts of texture, key, and rhythm. The contrast of common time and triple time is still basic; in fact the shape of these works is very reminiscent of Schütz. The main difference is the greater length of Krieger's individual sections, cast in the uniform rhythmic patterns of modern Italian music, especially the common time with its omnipresent dactylic rhythms. *Uns ist ein Kind geboren, Wachet auf,* and especially *Preise Jerusalem* are superb examples of the colossal sacred concerto, the climax of almost a century's development. Sometimes, as in *Wachet auf,* a chorale is used, either as a cantus firmus or as material for melodic paraphrase, but the chorale is set down on top of the concertato style without changing its overall shape.

Then, late in the 1690s, Krieger responded more strongly to the most modern element in Italian style, the fully developed aria. In 1697 he published a collection called *Musicalischer Seelen-Friede* (Musical peace for the soul), containing twenty settings of psalm texts for solo voice, basso continuo, and one or two violins. These were, in effect, chamber cantatas in the Italian style. *Der Herr ist mein Hirt* (The Lord is my shepherd), for tenor and basso continuo with unison violins, is a curious combination of modern aria styles set down on top of the old sectional shape. The urge to write arias was clearly there, only the tradition of the German sacred concerto did not provide the proper frame.

At this very moment, Krieger apparently was urging the court poet of Weissenfels to write texts in a style and form more suitable for setting to recitatives and arias. The poet, Erdmann Neumeister (1671–1756), responded in quantity, eventually providing five cycles of texts, each sufficient for an entire church year; these, available singly from 1700 on, were then published in a collected edition of 1717 as *Fünffache Kirchen-Andachten*—''Fivefold Sacred Meditations . . . arias, cantatas, and odes for all Sundays and feast days of the year.''

Previous texts, largely psalmodic, had been too discursive for arias—especially the da capo aria—and not quite the right poetic diction for recitative. Neumeister cast his texts into sections, each designed for recitative or for aria, and often designated as such. He also included citations from psalms or from chorales; these were presented as objects of meditation, while the lyrical effusions of the recitatives and arias were the poetical result of that meditation. Neumeister's texts were *poesia per musica,* ideal foundations on which to build

German recitatives and arias. His example was immediately followed by other German court poets. "Reform" cantata texts were enthusiastically taken up by German composers in their zeal to bring German church music abruptly up-to-date.

Only one example of the new cantata by Krieger is available, *Rufet nicht die Weisheit,* but it demonstrates perfectly the new style. There is a declamatory chorus at the beginning (as a whole, therefore, this is still a concerto, not a cantata) ; then comes a large da capo aria for soprano solo, complete with furioso figure in the basso continuo, and striking exclamation for voice, all as might appear in Pallavicino or Scarlatti. This aria is followed by an instrumental recitative for bass, also in the high Italian style. Then the music of the aria is repeated to a new text (not infrequent in Italian opera), followed by an imitative chorus, a duet, and concluding chorus more in the tradition of the sacred concerto.

More consistent application of the new style of recitative and arias to the new texts appears in the work of Friedrich Wilhelm Zachow (1663–1712), cantor at Halle (near Leipzig) from 1684 on. Zachow is easily the most impressive German composer of his generation—skilled, spirited, rich in melodic invention and harmonic suavity. He wrote both cantatas (for solo voice) and concertos (including a chorus). The cantatas consist of recitatives and arias, with perhaps ritornellos for instruments, while the concertos now regularly consist of large concertato choruses separated by a series of recitatives and arias. There may be only two large choruses, at the beginning and end of a work, or there may be more in the middle. The result is a monumental build-up of contrasting styles, more static than the old concerto with its fluid interchange of textures and rhythms, but more grand, more brilliant in its final effect.

Das ist das ewige Leben contains a chorus, recitative, aria da capo, recitative, aria da capo, recitative, aria da capo, and a concluding chorus built on the chorale that has been hinted at throughout the work. *Lobe den Herrn, meine Seele* (Praise the Lord, O my soul), a psalm text with metrical interpolations, has a brilliant beginning for solo voice answered immediately by the thundering tutti. *Ruhe, Friede, Freud, und Wonne,* made of similar elements, is even more powerful; it contains a deeply pathetic recitative for bass, framed by accompanied arioso sections (marked *adagiosissimo*) with rich harmonies and eloquent exclamations for the voice (Example 89).

The quintessence of the reform cantata, its reason for being, is the core of recitatives and arias for solo voice. When there are no choral sections, then the work is properly called a cantata, the German sacred equivalent of the Italian chamber cantata. Zachow's *Ich bin sicher und erfreut,* an Easter cantata, begins with a da capo aria (two verses), followed by a recitative, a da capo aria with unison violins, a recitative, a third da capo aria, and a chorale, sung by the solo voice to the accompaniment of obbligato instrumental parts. The first recitative (Example 90) is a beautiful example of Italian recitative adapted for German text.

Actually the model for this kind of recitative would be found not in Italian opera, but in chamber cantatas or in oratorios; the Germans needed a style more dense, more finely worked than that used in the opera. German recitative becomes harmonically very rich—at least one diminished seventh chord

EXAMPLE 89 ZACHOW: ARIOSO FROM *RUHE, FRIEDE, FREUD, UND WONNE* (sacred concerto)

seems obligatory for every recitative, the other harmonies being chosen accordingly. Composers and critics of all countries thought and talked a great deal during these decades about the melodic inflection appropriate to recitative in various languages. Zachow's recitative was exemplary for German composers of his generation and the next. The proud aria that follows (Example 90), with its stirring ritornello for unison violins, is only one of the many kinds of arias that make Zachow second to none as a composer of German sacred cantatas.

HAMBURG OPERA AND HANDEL Ever since the early works of Schütz (who in 1627 had set *Dafne*, a favola pastorale) Germans had been making sporadic attempts at German opera. These attempts finally resulted in success, although a success that was short-lived and in a form not exactly anticipated. German opera depended upon a lucky combination of a gifted composer with Italian contacts and a propitious German environment. This combination was partly realized in Johann Philip Krieger at Weissenfels, beginning with his *Cecrops mit seiner drei Töchtern* (Cecrops and his three daughters) in 1688, but that was under special courtly auspices.

    In 1678 the citizens of Hamburg established a civic opera. A circle of Hamburg literati contributed librettos (including Lucas von Bostel, 1649–1716, and Christian Postel, 1658–1705), and north German composers such as Johann Theile (1646–1724), Johann Wolfgang Franck (1644–ca 1710) and especially Johann Sigismund Kusser (1660–1727) set them to music. But civic support

EXAMPLE 90 ZACHOW: RECITATIVE AND ARIA FROM *ICH BIN SICHER UND ERFREUT* (cantata)

Mein Je-sus hat nun ü-ber-wun-den, der Höllen Abgrund ist zer-stört, sein ganzes Reich und

Macht ist um-ge-kehrt, der Sa-tan selbst liegt da zu sei-nen Füssen hart ge-bun-den, sein

Hochmut, Stolz und Pracht ist nun be-zwungen, weil Je-sus in sein Reich ge-drungen.

[unison Violins]

EXAMPLE 90 (CONTINUED)

Je - sus sie - greich Ü - ber win - den (etc.)

(My Jesus has now conquered, Hell's abyss is destroyed, its whole realm and power overthrown, Satan himself lies at His feet, bound tightly, his overweening pride and pomp brought low, for Jesus has invaded his kingdom. Jesus triumphant, overcoming . . .)

was not enough; full success came only with Reinhard Keiser (1674–1739), the real hero of Hamburg opera—or better, of German opera. He was almost the only professional German composer who understood what opera had to be and how to do it. Perhaps for that reason his career was even more exciting and erratic than his librettos; a greater contrast with the plodding course of a German cantor is hard to imagine.

Keiser was active in Hamburg and the north from 1695 to 1734, with interruptions, both of a professional and personal nature. His opera *Croesus* (1710, revised 1730), one of fifty or sixty, is a heroic-pathetic work with strong comic roles. Keiser was master of the great variety of styles necessary for such an opera. His recitative is lively or expressive as needed; he uses an abundance of aria types ranging from popular ariettas to grand arias of deep pathos. There is little novelty in his work, at least when compared with its Italian models (there was nothing comparable in the history of German opera). Each aria represents a successful solution shared with other arias from other works. But as they occur in *Croesus*, these aria types reveal an impressive variety as well as propriety to the dramatic situation. Of the arias quoted in Example 91, *a* and *d* are amorous strophic ariettas; *b* and *c* are big da capo arias, the one anguished, the other a concitato, "rage" aria with full stringed accompaniment; *e* is Croesus' prayer as he is being burned at the stake, and *f* is his plea for intercession to Solon, who, at the last moment, persuades Cyrus (the potentate) graciously to pardon Croesus.

Besides the highly regarded Georg Kaspar Schürmann (ca 1670–ca 1735), Keiser had only one potential rival, a man ten years younger called Georg Friedrich Händel (1685–1759; we will call him by his German name, with the umlaut, until he settles in England). Händel had had the best possible preparation (which he later did not fail to acknowledge), having studied from the age of seven with Zachow himself, who gave Händel not only a solid grounding such as every good German should have, but also that all-important contact with Italian music. From the beginning Händel was set straight on the realities of international style.

EXAMPLE 91   KEISER: ARIA EXCERPTS FROM *CROESUS*

(a)   III, iii; Elmira sings

Fühlst du   noch der Lie-be Ker - zen,   wert-ster Prinz in   deinem   Her - zen?

[Strings without Bass]

(b)   III, v; Atis sings

[unison Strings]

El-mir!

(c)   III, v; Atis sings

[tutti]   Mich verg-nü-get die - ses   Höh - nen,   mich verg-nü-get die - ses

Höh   -   -   -   (etc.)

EXAMPLE 91 (CONTINUED)

(d) III, viii; Trigesta sings

(e) III, xii; Croesus sings

(f) III, xiii; Croesus sings

(a) (Dost thou not feel the sparks of love, most worthy Prince, in thy heart?

(c) This scorn delights me . . .

(e) O Gods! grant me mercy . . .

(f) Solon, Solon, thou wise man—Ah!)

In 1703 Händel went to Hamburg as a youth of eighteen; he worked in the opera and—when Keiser absconded in financial embarrassment—had some of his own operas produced. He also wrote a *St. John Passion*, constructed according to the usual pattern of recitative interrupted by short arioso or choral ejaculations for the mob. In 1707 Händel went to Italy. Hamburg had been only the first stop in his search of the sources of Italian style, a search that took Händel now to Venice, Rome, and Naples. Well-armed with information and presumably introductions, Händel heard and met everyone and everything of importance for Italian opera. He even gained entrance into that curious Arcadian Academy that numbered among its members Corelli and Scarlatti.

Then in 1711 Händel made a trip to London for the performance of his *Rinaldo*, one of his best works and one of the best Italian operas of its time. Like Keiser, Händel attempted no novelties; drawing fully on the classic models before him, he reproduced their shapes as clearly, as forcefully as he could. In *Rinaldo* Händel summed up two decades of Italian aria styles. He had great melodic gifts, a mastery of harmony and of the many ways, both figural and imitative, of expressing it. His attention, however, was always firmly fixed on the large effect—the character of an aria, the succession of arias and recitatives, the structure of scenes, of acts, of the whole show.

Händel knew Scarlatti well, respected his work highly, and learned much from it. Händel's own style, however, was closer to that of the Bononcini brothers. Händel's treatment of the aria marked another phase of expansion in the size of the aria, especially the da capo. This expansion took place from within: each phrase, even the instrumental ritornello (which in Scarlatti might be only three or four measures) was extended, either by sequence, or melodic spinning out, or concertato treatment. Most arias now included concerted accompaniment, the favorite form being the powerful unison strings. The interplay of voice and strings had as one of its most important functions the extension of phrases.

All of this was present in Scarlatti, as we saw, but perhaps Scarlatti's treatment was too contrapuntal, too finely wrought for Händel's purposes. In any case, he found the free-wheeling style of the Bononcinis more useful. But with German thoroughness and a sense of spaciousness he could have got only from Scarlatti, Händel turned this glib style toward a loftier expression.

FRANÇOIS COUPERIN After Lully's death in 1687, French dramatic music faltered. Without a leading opera composer, musical accomplishment manifested itself most strongly in solo keyboard music, as it often tended to do in Northern countries and as it had done in France during the 1650s. The new keyboard virtuoso-composer was François Couperin, (1668–1733), nephew of Louis Couperin, and called *le grand* to distinguish him from the several Couperins known to music. Like Purcell, François had a high esteem for Italian music, especially for Corelli, whose sonatas he emulated in early works of his own. François was active both at church and at court, writing instrumental and vocal music of various types. His best ensemble pieces are the *Concerts Royaux*, written 1714/1715 but published in 1722. It was in his keyboard works, however, that François achieved something so distinctive as to be almost inimitable.

From 1713 to 1730 François published four books of twenty-seven *ordres* or sets of dances arranged by key in the manner customary since Gaultier. The first orders (containing pieces going back before 1700) still looked like dance suites, beginning with allemandes, courantes, and sarabandes in much the same cadence and figural styles as those of Louis. There is a clear tendency, however, for these dances to use a figuration increasingly dense and expressive. This is especially noticeable in the sarabandes: *La Prude* (Order no. 2) is still simple and moderately fast, as in Louis, but *La Lugubre* (no. 3) is more turgid, while *La Dangereuse* (no. 5) seems to call for an adagio tempo. François (and others) sometimes distinguished between a sarabande and a "sarabande grave." Along-side these older dances François included a number of lighter, faster types that impressed up-to-date French observers as smart and chic.

Throughout the succeeding orders François showed a steadily increasing tendency to play upon the established character of dances, interpreting them in personal ways. He also inclined toward greater sophistication; patterns of harmony and figuration were handled with ever greater refinement, their expressive features exhibited in more and more subtle ways. In the preface to his first volume of *Pièces de clavecin* (1713), he said, "I much prefer that which touches me to that which surprises." Without moving outside the stylistic forms inherited from the 1600s, he penetrated ever more deeply into their inner nature, revealing one expressive detail after another in a seemingly endless succession of intimate character-pieces. So evocative became their character that even the titles—traditionally and whimsically attached to such pieces—seemed as though they had real significance.

EXAMPLE 92   GRAUPNER: ARIA FROM *MEIN GOTT, WARUM HAST DU MICH VERLASSEN?*
(sacred concerto)

(Ah, how sweet . . .)

GERMAN SACRED MUSIC: BACH AT WEIMAR As German sacred composers came to appreciate, after 1710, the emotional possibilities of recitative
and aria, they were confronted with the problem of the propriety of Italian
forms in the Lutheran bourgeois church. The aria had to be taught to speak
German in feeling as well as in text. Melody, harmony, figuration had to be
inflected in a manner understood by the German burgher.

Zachow had still worked within an atmosphere of innocence, using the
Italianate forms of expression in glorious unconcern. But the next generation,
whose style was formed from 1710 to 1720, had to grapple with the problem at
a deeper level. The composer who achieved the most happy combination of
Italian style with German taste in sacred music was Christoph Graupner
(1683–1760). The aria in Example 92 from the very fine concerto *Mein Gott,
warum hast du mich verlassen?* (My God, why hast thou forsaken me?), combines the breadth of an Italian largo with German harmonic depth in a remarkable blend that best expresses German sacred lyricism of the early 1700s.

As Graupner was working out his personal solution to the German cantata at Darmstadt, the assistant court musician at Weimar, Johann Sebastian
Bach (1685–1750) was struggling with similar problems. Sebastian Bach came
from a great clan of Bachs, active for generations in Thuringia (in the German
heartland) as professional musicians. Sebastian's background gave him a solid
foundation in musical craft, but at the same time made it especially difficult for
him to apprehend international style. His career was an unending struggle to
reach out beyond his provincial environment to this international style. Even
though he finally succeeded in formulating his own personal interpretation of
modern style, he did not succeed in making contact with an audience that
understood it.

Sebastian Bach began as a church organist, an intricate, demanding
trade, involving a detailed knowledge of organ management far beyond mere
performance. Bach worked at his trade with an absorption in structural detail
that was to be characteristic of all he did. He knew first the organ repertory
of central Germany, especially Pachelbel, then, in 1705, he started to reach out
for wider perspective with a trip to hear old Buxtehude (now almost seventy).
Whether from Buxtehude's playing or from his pieces, Bach caught a glimpse
of an older grandeur, the bizarre brilliance of the mid-1600s.

Both Pachelbel's clarity and Buxtehude's grandeur are perceptible in
the large organ works Bach composed in connection with his position at Weimar
(1708–1717). All the inherited possibilities, however, seemed simultaneously
available to Bach; he selected and combined them according to his fancy. Sometimes he wrote isolated fugues (to which he later added preludes). Such fugues
were usually homogeneous in subject and rhythm like Pachelbel's, although
much larger, like the brilliant fugue in D major with the concitato subject
(BWV 532).

When Bach used the term *praeludium* it was apt to mean a sectional,
rhapsodic work in the manner of Buxtehude, including an extended fugal section—in other words, a toccata, like the famous one in D minor (BWV 565).
Characteristic of Bach's cultivation of the high styles of the past is the mighty
passacaglia in C minor (BWV 582). More artful, and at the same time more
expressive, are the small chorale preludes Bach wrote during these decades.

Some of these he collected in 1723 in a set called the *Orgelbüchlein* (Little Organ Book).

In connection with his organ duties, Bach wrote several early sacred concertos, representing the sectional concerto as Krieger had found it thirty years before. *Gottes Zeit* (BWV 106), *Der Herr denket an uns* (BWV 196), and *Aus der Tiefe* (BWV 131), all presumably from 1707 and 1708, have sectional choruses typical of the old concerto, but also arias and duets. The aria *Meine Seele wartet* from *Aus der Tiefe* has a characteristic bass figure in twelve-eight, with an opening exclamation for the voice exactly like a motto aria from Scarlatti or Pallavicino. Superimposed on this purely Italian foundation is an obbligato chorale, a Lutheran symbol that Bach used in many imaginative ways.

Whether Bach wrote cantatas during the next few years we do not know; but a series of cantatas from 1714 to 1716 uses reform texts by Neumeister and especially Salomon Franck (1659–1725, court poet at Weimar) set in the new style of arias and recitatives. Some of these works are pure cantatas; that is, they consist solely of arias and recitatives with no chorus. *Mein Herze schwimmt in Blut* (BWV 199, My heart swims in blood) is an excellent example, not only of this format, but of the hyperemotional tone of the texts and the passionate arias that went with it. *Mein Herze* contains highly affective recitative (especially the first one) and a variety of arias, including a chorale with obbligato viola.

The arias of 1714 and 1715 reveal Bach's most characteristic attitude toward the forms he found around him. At this stage he was concerned with a more intense musical expression of the highly charged texts of the reform

EXAMPLE 93 BACH: ARIA EXCERPT FROM *ICH HATTE VIEL BEKÜMMERNIS* (cantata)

(Sobs, tears, sorrow, need; sobs, tears, fearful longing . . .)

cantata. He sought this heightened tension in a more dense, contorted harmonic language, clearly evident when one of Bach's arias is compared with its Italian model. A striking example (Example 93) is the aria *Seufzer, Thränen, Kummer, Not* from *Ich hatte viel Bekümmernis* (BWV 21, I was in great sorrow). Arias in twelve-eight were very frequent in Italian opera from 1700 to 1710—Scarlatti's middle years; usually very smooth, such arias were occasionally darkened by the flatted supertonic degree characteristic of the *siciliano* and overshadowed with melancholy. Bach turned this melancholy into a representation of deepest passion, mainly by a liberal application of harmonic appoggiaturas, while leaving intact the rhythmic shape of his model.

One of the most interesting developments of these works from 1715 and 1716 is the search for an alternative to the da capo aria. Bach seemed to prefer at this time an aria with a substantial ritornello at the beginning, followed by three, four, or five major sections based on similar material but progressing slowly through the text. There might or might not be rounding at the end in the voice part, but the only real repeat took place in the closing ritornello, either similar to or identical with the opening one (sometimes indicated by a *da capo* or *dal segno* but excluding a vocal repeat). The cantata *Ach, ich sehe* (BWV 162), for example, contains two arias, two recitatives, a duet, and a simple chorale, but no da capo.

Exactly why Bach turned away from the da capo aria is not completely clear; he was to write many of them later. At this time, however, the da capo aria was by no means as important in German church music as in Italian opera. Bach may have felt that his freer type of aria was more in keeping with the background of the church cantata. Or he may have been concerned with the dramatic momentum of the cantata, something that clearly preoccupied him in formulating its musical language.

HÄNDEL'S BROCKES' PASSION While Bach was laboriously assimilating Italian style in the German heartland, Händel had been getting it straight from the source, in Italy. After *Rinaldo,* Händel returned to Germany, partly to finish off his studies with the one man who might teach him something he did not already know—Steffani in Hanover.

Around 1717 Händel wrote another Passion, very different from his earlier *St. John Passion,* on a new text by the foremost Hamburg librettist, Barthold Heinrich Brockes (1680–1747). Using the Gospel narrative of the Crucifixion as a framework, Brockes interpolated poetic meditations in exactly the same way Neumeister had done for cantata texts. These interpolations gave expression to the emotional reactions of spectators confronted with the events of the Biblical story. Destined primarily for arias, the interpolations were sometimes for chorus—especially at beginning and end. Chorale texts were also used as a type of lyrical effusion different from the aria but serving the same function. Such texts were set as simple chorales by the composer.

Händel's setting of Brockes' text was his only mature contact with German sacred music, and hence the only real point of comparison with Sebastian Bach. This work reveals the same passionate intensity in its arias that is found in Bach's cantatas of 1714 to 1716. Even more important, it reveals the same adaptation of Italian styles to German taste—striking in Händel because of the completely Italian taste of his operas.

In the Brockes' Passion, Händel, avoiding the Italian joy in acting that enlivens even the most serious, most pathetic scenes of Italian opera, turned toward an earnestness more in keeping with the German burgher and also toward a warmth of sorrow found in devotional Lutheran poetry. Because Händel was more at home than Sebastian Bach in the art of effective dramatic representation, this devotional warmth is more apparent in the Brockes' Passion than in comparable works of Bach. The devotional mood had the effect, however, of keeping Händel from those heroic gestures already characteristic of his operas but found here only once, in the magnificent march to Calvary. The mood spills over into the Centurion's part, making even this secondary figure curiously heroic. The end of his recitative (Example 94), proclaiming that Jesus is the Son of God, seems in its stunning Neapolitan chord on *Sterbende* to strike a mighty pose at once Italian and Handelian.

EXAMPLE 94   HÄNDEL: RECITATIVE FROM THE BROCKES' PASSION: The centurion sings

(. . . flames, the cliff is split, mountain rock is bursting; is Jesus's death the reason? Ah, yes! I can see it in these wonders—the dying man is indeed the Son of God!)

BACH'S INSTRUMENTAL WORKS AT CÖTHEN Sebastian Bach was twenty-three when he went to Weimar in 1708, and thirty-two when he left in 1717. During those years he had developed from a skilled young organist into an ambitious composer. The cantatas showed him reaching out beyond the orbit of a German craftsman. His next job, at the court of Cöthen (1718–1722) required a different kind of music; although he presumably continued to write organ music and cantatas, his attention was now absorbed by secular instrumental forms. This meant starting anew to discover a suitable foundation as well as a path toward greater intensity. Many of the Cöthen works seem far less intense than the passionate Weimar cantatas—even allowing for the natural difference between sacred vocal works and secular instrumental ones, which might at this time be mere background pleasantry.

Cöthen saw the production of the Six Concertos with Several Instruments, which we know as the *Brandenburg Concertos*. These were written over a space of several years for Cöthen (there may have been others like them), and then collected in 1722 to be presented to the Duke of Brandenburg. An order of composition suggested by recent research is no. 3 in G, no. 6 in B flat, no. 1 in F, no. 2 in D, no. 4 in G, no. 5 in D. The Third and the Sixth are technically and structurally the simplest; they have but little solo-tutti contrast; their idiom is close to the German heart.

The First Concerto, in F, shows clearly the difference between Bach's style and Vivaldi's (whose famous Op. 3 he knew). Bach, with characteristic thoroughness, derives the material for the solo episodes from the opening tutti. The tutti theme, in other words, permeates the whole movement without relief, woven in by Bach's joy and skill in imitative counterpoint. As always, something is gained, something lost: Bach's concerto style is more intense, more continuous, but has less contrast, less variety, less clarity of phrase than Vivaldi's. Bach's concertos are an important example of a rhythmic uniformity that—far from being typical of the age—is his own personal interpretation of Italian concerto style.

Of these six concertos, only the Fourth and Fifth stand up to Vivaldi's best, and only the Fifth achieves the kind of magic effect that marks the truly successful works of that time. The Fifth Concerto is for a concertino of flute, violin, and cembalo—cembalo concertato as opposed to basso continuo. This by itself is unusual; but then the cembalo has a wondrous cadenza written out in the first movement. Here Bach exerted his special gifts in figuration to spin out a never-ending melodic flow whose effect is comparable to the best ciaconas and passacaglias of the 1600s. This was a master stroke, but of a kind and in a style that had absolutely no influence on the future of the concerto, even the concerto of Bach's own son, Philipp Emanuel.

Cöthen also saw the production of much of the solo and instrumental music of Bach we now have, including six suites for unaccompanied cello, and six sonatas for unaccompanied violin (three church sonatas and three partitas, including a big chaconne). Significantly, Bach was less attracted to trio sonatas, more to virtuoso solos. He now entered the field of harpsichord music: six suites with preludes (now called "English"), six without ("French"). The core of both sets is the sequence of old, heavily figured dances (allemande, courante, sarabande, gigue), with a selection of simpler, more modern movements (bourrée, minuet, gavotte, passepied, and others) inserted usually after the sarabande.

While these dance movements correspond in style and size to traditional models, the preludes do not. Each prelude is several times the length of a dance movement, each an extraordinary example of Bach's technique of spinning out material. For these (and other kinds of pieces) he developed a special mixture of figural and imitative procedures—the figural providing a rhythmic continuity of sixteenth-note motion, the imitative a periodic renewal of melodic interest. The running figuration was often expressed in a two-voiced texture that moved subtly through harmonies rather than stating them as chords. In this open, yet resonant, texture, Bach closely approached the mature style of François Couperin, whose works Bach came to know during these years.

On a scale comparable to these preludes, Bach wrote two important harpsichord toccatas (there had been earlier ones), one in F-sharp minor (BWV 910), consisting of a rhapsodic figural introduction, a chromatic arialike section in three-two, and two fugal sections, one in common time and one in six-eight. The other, in C minor (BWV 911), has a similar structure. Although the shape is traditional (all the way from Frescobaldi) and the styles derived from Buxtehude, on one hand, Pachelbel and Italian styles, on the other, the dimensions of these works show Bach's typical expansion of his material; furthermore they seethe with the intensity found earlier in his Weimar cantatas, but absent from the concerted works of the Cöthen concert hall.

The climax of this tendency in Bach's clavier works is the celebrated Chromatic Fantasia, which includes a recitative and fugue. There are perhaps antecedents in the fantasia cromatica going back to the early 1600s (Bach would have known such in Frescobaldi's *Fiori musicali*) and perhaps with consequents in the fantasias of his son Philipp Emanuel; but the Chromatic Fantasia stands apart from Bach's own time, even from his own work.

The most fruitful work of these years was a manuscript collection of little preludes and fugues Bach assembled under the title, *The Well-tempered Clavier,* ". . . preludes and fugues on all tones and semitones, with the major third *ut–re–mi* as well as the minor *re–mi–fa*." Many of these preludes and fugues had existed independently for several years. Bach here assembled them, consistently pairing off preludes and fugues, transposing some and writing new ones to make up a complete cycle in all twenty-four major and minor keys—in an obvious attempt to surpass similar collections, especially the *Ariadne musica* of Ferdinand Fischer.

As always, Bach strove to begin where his model left off, not hesitating to make the competition keen by using similar material. A comparison of Bach's preludes and fugues with those of Fischer is extremely valuable in understanding not merely Bach's accomplishment, but also Fischer's, for the comparison is not completely in favor of Bach. Fischer's pieces are skilled, often poetically exquisite. They are much less elaborate than Bach's, but sheer elaboration, even though it might be Bach's highest value, is not the only one in music. Furthermore, when Fischer came to the end of what he had to say, he stopped—something Bach did not always do.

Even if longer than Fischer's preludes and fugues, these of Bach's *Well-tempered Clavier* are among his more concise works. They are perhaps the most persuasive examples of the carefully worked-out style Bach was coming to regard as most important. Of all his works they contain the most lyrical effusion in the smallest space. Each is different, and each has its own character, a demonstration that instrumental music could now match arias in expression.

This difference from one prelude to the next would have been more perceptible in Bach's time than ours, owing to the kind of tuning implied by the title of the collection. Bach tuned as Fischer (and others) had tuned, using a "circulating" temperament that widened the realm of usable keys by sacrificing the purity of those in the center. Bach typically pushed the realm to its limit, to the point where there were no more keys to use. This resulted in twenty-four usable keys, but, it should be noted, not in twenty-four equal keys. The out-of-tuneness was not distributed equally among all keys; rather, those around C major were left slightly cleaner, sounding really different from those in five or six sharps or flats—but at the discretion of the performer, who could adjust the tuning as he saw fit (possibly just before playing a particular piece).

Bach also assembled another collection of small clavier pieces, which he called *praeambula* (*a 2*) or *fantasia* (*a 3*); we know them as two- and three-part Inventions. In his lengthy title (which shows that Bach had in mind not organists, but the ever-widening audience of amateurs), he gave perhaps the most concise description of his musical ideal: a "singing style," in several obbligato parts. He seemed by that to set aside the brilliant, noisy music of the grand concerto and the thumping continuo practice that went with it. Cleanness, linear clarity, seemed more and more to attract him as the best means, and lyricism as the best end. Combining the best features of traditional figuration and imitative counterpoint, the Inventions are an example of the texture that was emerging as the focus of Bach's artistic endeavor.

BACH AT LEIPZIG In 1723 Sebastian Bach left Cöthen to become cantor at Leipzig. This was an important post in German music, representing the highest level to which organists rose in their profession. But times were changing; being a cantor, even at Leipzig, no longer offered the most exciting musical prospects. Bach had to compete for the post, but his competitors were Graupner, who was already committed to the life of a cantor, and Georg Philipp Telemann (1681–1767), who had a broader career in mind and was not really interested in Leipzig. Telemann, prolific composer of all sorts of music, made contact with the international audience through the thriving opera and concert life of cosmopolitan Hamburg. Extremely skilled and well-informed, Telemann seems to have been interested more in exploiting style than in developing it; at any rate he made no significant changes in the forms he found around him.

Since neither Telemann nor Graupner took the job at Leipzig, it went to Bach—although even he was not convinced that this was a good thing. The cantorship did not mean the end of secular instrumental music of the kind Bach had pursued with such success and fulfillment at Cöthen; it did mean, however, a heavy burden of musical composition in the category of sacred music, particularly the large sacred concerto for the high service in Leipzig's big churches. With the diligence and dispatch expected of his profession, Bach set to work to assemble yearly cycles of sacred concertos.

He now settled on a more or less standard format for the sacred concerto.

The concertato element was concentrated in the opening chorus, which was often built on a chorale cantus firmus, giving it one overall character; such choruses were not divided into shorter, varied sections like the old concerto. As usual since the reform, the interior of the work was recitatives and arias. Only occasionally and for a special reason was an aria replaced by a chorus, usually singing a chorale (in the manner of an arietta). Having proved itself an effective contrasting element alongside concertato chorus and solo aria, the simple chorale was now the standard way of ending the work. The chorale made a clear emotional point, both because of its simplicity and because of its long associations with familiar congregational hymns; and, of course, its text was pure Lutheran piety.

Although Bach composed many new works, he now drew heavily on his previous works from the Weimar period. For example, the big Leipzig concerto *Ein' feste Burg* (BWV 80, *A mighty fortress*) is the Weimar cantata *Alles was von Gott* (BWV 80a) with the addition of a concertato chorus built on a chorale at the beginning, another setting of the chorale for a middle movement, and the simple chorale at the end. The celebrated Leipzig concertos, *Wie schön leuchtet der Morgenstern* (BWV 1, *How brightly shines the morning star*), *Wachet auf* (BWV 140, *Awake!*), *Herr gehe nicht ins Gericht* (BWV 105, *Lord, enter not into judgment*), and many others follow a similar plan, with or without a chorale cantus firmus in the opening movement.

There is no clearly perceptible stylistic development in the Leipzig concertos—a fact made startlingly apparent by the great discrepancy in dates scholarship has assigned to various works. It now seems that the bulk of the Leipzig concertos were composed or adapted into two annual cycles shortly after 1725, that is, during Bach's first years in his new job. Judging by what remains, his sacred output was not very large. Krieger, Graupner, and Telemann all composed much more; Telemann, whose music is admittedly much less substantial, completed twelve annual cycles of sacred concertos, besides many passions and oratorios.

The style of Bach's Leipzig works is more mature, less violent, often more amiable than the Weimar works. Certain elements, however, continued to elicit inventive solutions from Bach, for example, the integration of a chorale tune into a recitative or aria, and also the accompanied recitative, especially in company with arioso sections that permitted the flexibility of the old concerto of the 1600s, now no longer available in the static forms of chorus and aria.

Bach was usually meticulous in selecting the right musical style for the particular aria text at hand, a selection that rewards careful study. There was a tendency in the Leipzig years for the character of arias, and choruses too, to manifest itself in pictorial images. The emotional content both of text and music crystallized into images, evoking some of Bach's most grandiose passages (examples in *Erhalt uns, Herr*, BWV 126, and *Herr Jesu Christ*, BWV 127). Expressed by a variety of musical devices, these images often elicited intense figuration, brilliant passaggi, and an overwhelming extravagance by which Bach, in his own way, most closely approached the bizarre world of Italian opera.

The Leipzig period had opened with the *St. John Passion*, a work consisting largely of recitative, chorales, and short choruses as in Händel's *St. John Passion;* there are relatively few arias. The work is highly dramatic, but more because of the disposition of Biblical story (in itself highly dramatic) among the choruses and chorales than for purely musical reasons. From a stylistic point of view one of its most significant numbers is the exquisite arioso for bass, *Beträchte, meine Seel'*. Bach, like Händel, often found in the arioso a happy alternative to the now unwieldy da capo aria.

The production of sacred music at Leipzig virtually closed with the *St. Matthew Passion* of 1729, Bach's counterpart to Händel's Brockes' Passion. Much richer in meditative texts than the *St. John Passion*, the *St. Matthew* setting has a correspondingly greater number of arias. Here Bach gave the strongest expression to the devotional sentiments of the Lutheran *bourgeoisie*. The weight has been shifted from the drama of the Biblical story to the spectator's emotional reaction—what it means to him personally. The bass aria *Gebt mir meinen Jesum wieder* (Example 95, not inappropriately translated as *Give Him back—is all I ask!*) matches the sentiment with a warm, beseeching theme. The technique is Italian, the inflection unmistakably German, which is true even of the monumental chorus that opens the work.

In spite of his deep involvement with sacred music, Bach found time at Leipzig to pursue instrumental music along the path he had started at Cöthen. This path led to the wider amateur audience, who could be reached only through publication. The collections he had made at Cöthen (sonatas and suites, the *Well-tempered Clavier*, the Inventions) all pointed in this direction. True to form, Bach followed the example of his predecessors, now turning to partitas for his first publication. This was a natural choice, but probably a wrong one; the *Well-tempered Clavier* was the real, the only success Bach was to have with this wider audience in the 1700s—and that without even being published in his lifetime.

Bach published his six partitas sometime between 1726 and 1730 under the traditional title *Clavier-Übung* (Keyboard Practice). Written almost ten years later than the French or English Suites, these partitas far surpass them in length, weight, and intensity. In character they are more varied each from the other. While the core of the partita is still allemande, courante, sarabande, and (usually) gigue, each partita has a different type of prelude, called variously praeludium, sinfonia, fantasia, overture, praeambulum, and toccata, each in a different key and a different style. In following stylistic models Bach seemed

EXAMPLE 95   BACH: ARIA EXCERPT FROM ST. MATTHEW PASSION, II

now concerned to reach all important international styles, summing up several generations of keyboard practice.

The same tendency is apparent in a second part of the *Clavier-Übung*, published in 1735: it contained a seventh suite in a new key (B minor) and a different character, even though it began with a French overture similar to the partita in D major. The only other work in this *Clavier-Übung II* was a *Concerto nach Italiaenischen Gust* (Concerto in the Italian taste), a keyboard replica of a concerto grosso to balance the replica of the French orchestral overture. During the 1730s, general discussion of German music was intensely concerned with its role relative to French and Italian tastes. In this publication Bach was clearly seeking contacts on an international level.

HANDEL'S LONDON OPERA AND ORATORIO
In 1720 Händel—we should now call him Handel—having settled in England, started his London opera career in earnest in a Royal Academy, similar to those established by Perrin (Cambert's librettist) and Lully in Paris. In many ways the state of opera in London was similar to that in Paris of the 1660s: unstable, confused, subject to popular whim and personal intrigue, London opera lacked the power of a Louis XIV or a Lully to normalize the situation.

Handel mounted a long series of operas during the next two decades. He had assembled a great deal of material in his years of travel and study, including his own works as well as excerpts from the works of others that impressed him. His method of composing opera, entirely typical of his time, was spontaneous, almost improvisatory, which accounts for the widespread habit of using material already in existence.

There was no repertory of proven operas; once mounted, a work was either a failure, closing immediately, or a success, running for a few weeks. Another season, a likely work might be revived, but with some or all of the arias replaced by new ones, roles and scenes altered or rearranged. A revival was, in effect, a new work, tailored for a new set of singers and a new audience. The original version, too, was largely finished after the singers had been engaged; the composer virtually improvised the work in the few weeks of rehearsal. On top of that the singers, at least the famous ones in the leading roles, improvised the ornaments and the manner of delivery in every performance, while, of course, the continuo player improvised his part of the accompaniment over the bass.

Hence the opera was in actual performance as ephemeral as improvisation, created for an evening by singer, composer, director. Since no one could ever hear the same work twice, there was no purpose in trying to make a new work radically different. Composers like Handel composed according to the techniques of improvisation: they accumulated and assimilated a vast rhetoric of styles to suit all dramatic situations, formulas that could be applied without hesitation to the work at hand. Naturally they used the same aria types—if not actual arias—over and over again. They changed their style of composition not from one work to another, but only according to their own personal growth or that of musical style as a whole. A good composer like Handel carefully sifted the styles available to him, selecting those which, beyond being successful, were bound together by some inner affinity reflecting his own artistic identity.

While Handel was extremely interested in certain technical novelties of orchestration or aria structure, his principal level of interest was the shape of the whole work, the sequence of arias, scenes, and acts. He composed—or improvised—with arias rather than with notes or chords. How to modulate within an aria was no longer interesting; how to control the succession of keys throughout an act was an absorbing, challenging problem that related directly to the success of a work, but for which no precept save that of variety had been devised.

Probably all opera composers of the early 1700s thought in these terms, grappled with these problems, but Handel did it best. He seemed artistically at home in the rush of throwing together material from his vast store of operatic styles. The results are unequal in value; while some were successes, some were failures—and some of those deservedly so. Usually however, the mighty act of improvisation seemed to shine through in the drama itself. The Olympian disposition of huge chunks of material, the canceling, substituting, reshuffling of da capo arias each a hundred or so measures long seemed to affect the stature of Handel's heroes, towering beings who expressed themselves only in magnificent speech and grandiose gesture, characters fit to pronounce the great da capo as ordinary mortals are apt in moments of stress to repeat themselves for emphasis.

Disasters in excess of the usual kind and quantity finally ended Handel's operatic career in 1739. Stylistically committed to operatic forms, yet barred by British taste from further operatic productions, Handel cast about for some alternate format that would render acceptable the only kind of music he knew how to write. Throughout the 1600s—and the 1700s as well—vocal dramatic music had taken many forms besides opera: choral polyphony on the one hand, and monody on the other, had been dramatized in all possible degrees and combined in all conceivable mixtures to produce intermedia, masques, serenatas, cantatas, odes, anthems, sacred concertos, historias, dialogs, oratorios—as well as the innumerable classifications of music-drama that were sung, staged, and acted.

In 1718 Handel had written a masque, *Acis and Galatea;* in 1736 he set *Alexander's Feast*, an ode by Dryden on "The Power of Music"; much later, in 1750, he set the *Choice of Hercules* as an interlude, or intermedium. All this was normal, as was his cultivation of oratorio—except that the oratorio texts he now used were in English. These texts were called (besides oratorio) sacred drama, sacred story, or history; they are usually based upon incidents and personages taken from Old Testament literature. The exceptions need not disturb our basic understanding of Handel's oratorio; these exceptions include *Theodora* (1749), the story of a Christian martyr; the *Messiah* (1741), using passages from the New Testament; *Hercules* (1744), a "musical drama" on a classical subject; and *Semele* (1743), an opera performed "after the Manner of an Oratorio."

In his oratorios Handel more or less renounced the expensive staging and acting required for an opera, but retained the possibility of scenic background and minimal staging for atmosphere. He also eased the demands (and expense) of long, virtuoso singing roles; the body of an oratorio might still be solo singing, but the chorus now had a larger share. The kind of solo music, and the amount of chorus, varied greatly from one oratorio to another.

Nevertheless, Handel continued to achieve the same goals with the same means characteristic of music for over a century. The first goal was spectacular effect, achieved in the oratorio by scenery where possible and by the powerful choral sequences, often depicting magnificent festivities. Another traditional goal, lyrical effusion, was achieved in the usual forms of recitative and aria; but more and more Handel came to rely on a flexible arioso style, or on a free mixture of fragments of arias and various kinds of recitative, punctuated by choral response. In his later oratorios Handel seemed to reach back of Scarlatti to the varied dramatic structures of the 1600s.

Handel's oratorios became most dramatic when they represented human response, thus reflecting the concept of musical drama current since 1600. Through the long development we have traced, human response had come to be expressed in sustained, concentrated fashion in the da capo aria. Each response, each aria, was a basic unit; when arranged in an exciting sequence corresponding to the action of a plot, the result was musical drama. As Handel moved away from the da capo aria, these responses came in freer succession. If he treated the responses of a personage in a coherent, cumulative way, then that personage acquired dramatic identity—character. This tendency toward musical characterization, where it occurs, is an important result of stylistic development in Handel's oratorios, springing from, though not essential to, the traditional concept of musical drama.

Less spectacular, but perhaps even more artistic, was Handel's English recitative. He was one of very few composers (perhaps the only other was Purcell) who wrote convincing recitative in English, and one of very few composers during the 1700s who wrote successful recitative in any language other than Italian. Handel took special pains with the *recitativo obbligato* (orchestrally accompanied), which he placed at moments of special dramatic tension. These extraordinary pronouncements must usually be studied in context; but in *Saul* there is an apostrophe to Harmony that can be considered by itself as an example of perfect adaptation of Italian style to English taste and language (Example 96). Poetry and music that, taken separately, seem unimpressive, here combine to make each other lyric in fulfillment of Peri's original ideal.

BACH'S LAST YEARS The 1730s and 1740s were not years of professional satisfaction for Sebastian Bach at Leipzig. The outward sign was the virtual cessation of sacred concertato music. The underlying reasons had to do with personal relationships as well as the changing musical environment and Bach's attitude toward it. About 1730 Bach had occasion to be concerned more with secular music, both vocal and instrumental; in 1729 he was put in charge of the Collegium musicum founded earlier by Telemann, for which Bach wrote (presumably) an unknown quantity of instrumental music, now lost.

During the same years he also wrote secular cantatas; the most famous are the Coffee Cantata, *Schweigt stille, plaudert nicht* (BWV 211) and *Geschwinde, geschwinde, ihr wirbelnden Winde* (BWV 201), a dramma per musica on the singing contest between Phoebus and Pan. The latter work consists of fifteen numbers—a string of recitatives and arias, with opening and closing choruses. The arias continue to represent Italian types in charming German guise, even though they frequently cover up their characteristic themes

EXAMPLE 96   HANDEL: RECITATIVE FROM *SAUL* I, iv; The high priest sings

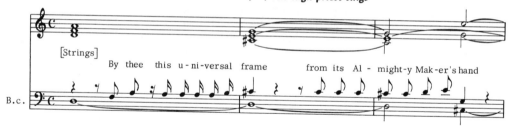

[Strings]

By thee   this u-ni-versal   frame   from its Al - might-y Mak-er's hand

B.c.

in prim-i-tive per-fec tion came,   by thee pro -duc'd   in thee con - tain'd: no soon-er did th'e-

tern-al word dispense   thy vast   myster - ious   in - fluence,   than Cha-os   his old discord ceas'd;

(etc.)

6
4

6♭

with dense, expressive counterpoint, as in the arias *Patron, patron,* and *Pan ist Meister.*

Bach preoccupied himself during these years with collecting, partly for publication and partly for his own satisfaction, his best keyboard pieces. These included three series of chorale settings of various types—*Six Chorales in Different styles* (BWV 645–650, published 1746–1750), *Eighteen Chorales* (BWV 651–668), and *Clavier-Übung III* (BWV 669–689, published 1739), containing also a huge prelude and fugue (BWV 552, *St. Anne*). Also collected during these years, presumably, were the twenty-four preludes and fugues (BWV 870–893) that make up a sequel to the *Well-tempered Clavier* (although not so designated in the surviving copies).

Toward 1747 Bach, now past sixty, was received into a scientific academy, the Mizler Society, in Leipzig. Mizler was a student of Bach's, and had in 1742, perhaps under Bach's supervision, translated Fux's treatise, *Gradus ad Parnassum*, from Latin into German. As a German organist, Bach had been intimately involved with procedures of imitative counterpoint all his life, but primarily in the way characteristic of the 1600s, that is, imitation as a textural alternative to figural patterns. The development of his own special blend of figuration with imitative procedures during the Cöthen period and after was a rapprochement of these two alternatives fixed since Frescobaldi. After 1730, however, Bach became increasingly involved with imitative procedures of a slightly different kind; canon, canonic variation, and canonic fugue now absorbed his attention as never before. Chorale preludes dating from his early years, preserved in the *Orgelbüchlein*, had already used such canonic procedures, even at that time representing a tendency different from traditional German organ counterpoint— as suggested by the Italian titles (*canone alla quinta*). The appearance of Fux's great compendium of Italian counterpoint in Leipzig in 1742 is in a way a sign of Bach's intense concern with contrapuntal artifice throughout his last years.

On the occasion of his entrance to the Mizler Society, Bach composed a set of *Canonic Variations on the Christmas Chorale Vom Himmel Hoch* (BWV 769). Earlier, around 1742, he had published a fourth volume of *Clavier-Übung*, "containing an aria and diverse variations for cembalo with two manuals" (BWV 988, *Goldberg Variations*). The aria itself (not by Bach) is like a ciacona, with the bass line of *Pur ti miro* from *Poppea*—and a hundred other ostinato arias. The ciacona, as we saw, was the one of the two dances most frequently associated with long sets of variations, usually as many as thirty or forty. Bach's set includes thirty variations, every third one of which is canonic. The canonic devices, identified in Italian terms, are expressed in a wide variety of figural patterns and styles.

In 1747, as a result of a visit to King Frederick ("the Great") of Prussia, Bach worked out a set of canonic variations on a theme provided by the king himself. These variations were published as a *Musical Offering* from Bach to the king; also included were a ricercar *a 3*, another *a 6*, and a trio sonata. The canonic inscriptions are in Latin.

In the last two years of his life, Bach busied himself with another large cycle, published immediately after his death as *Kunst der Fuge*. Its items are called *contrapunctus* or *canon*, only in two or three cases *fuga;* all are based on, or derived from, a single subject. The subject itself, as well as the order and kinds of contrapuntal device, recall the counterpoint treatises of Bononcini and Berardi, as well as Vitali's *Artifici musicali*. One could even regard the *Art of the Fugue* strictly according to its title—a treatise on fugue, consisting only of the examples (the verbal explanations being omitted), raised to a high artistic level.

The overall form of these works, much discussed in recent times, has to be considered in terms of their public presentation. No one would deny that the form of an opera is musically significant, even if that form is expressed in terms of disjunct units of arias and scenes. In the same way the form of publication of Bach's last works, the way they were presented to the public, is musically significant to a degree; but from a musical point of view we have no assurance that Bach or his audience asked any more of this form than that it present its items in an interesting variety. Since there is no text, no drama to define the overall form, that form remains in these last works subject to arbitrary judgment in description and even identification. Similar arguments apply to the Mass in B minor, even though it has a text; this work is a collection of movements composed separately over a period of years, and then adapted and assembled by Bach apparently as a presentation copy to accompany his petition for an honorary appointment.

Actually the argument about form seems irrelevant to Bach's intention in the *Canonic Variations*, the *Musical Offering*, and the *Art of the Fugue*. Bach was concerned now with texture only, contrapuntal texture exemplary of that singing style he spoke of in the preface to the Inventions. He clearly felt that music consisted essentially in maintaining this finely woven texture with no gaps, no halts or jolts, every eighth or sixteenth note expressive in every voice.

Bach clearly agreed with Fux in seeing the ultimate answer to chord progressions to lie in smooth, cogent conduct of the individual voices. Form and character were external to the creation and maintenance of this perfect texture, whose pure lyricism is apparent in every item of these last works. At a time when younger composers tended to vary the musical flow by shifts in key area or rhythmic figure, Bach persisted in canons that by their very nature minimize such articulations; one voice may change its figure and key, but the voices following must persist a short space in the old figure or key. Bach's canons have the quality of lengths cut from a perfect fabric: they begin and end, and are uniform in between.

Bach's turn toward canonic art may simply have been the total concentration of old age on one important aspect of a foregoing career. It may also have been Bach's strong conviction (as it was Fux's) about the proper course for modern music. In either case, it was a turn toward a recent Italian development, not a harking back to anything mystical, medieval, or German; traditional German organ counterpoint was something different. Bach lived and died fully engaged with the art of his own time—at least, as he understood it. Like Handel, Bach in his latter years ceased to keep up with changing style. The style both men learned and used was the Italian style of 1710. Both Bach and Handel concentrated in their later works on that aspect of Italian style that seemed important to them. For Handel this was large-scale form and character; for Bach, texture. Each persisted in his chosen direction to its extreme, so that at the end the two aspects seemed to be diametrically opposed. Yet they were both aspects of the same Italian style.

Italy and the European Scene

ITALIAN OPERA AFTER SCARLATTI   After the death of Alessandro Scarlatti (1725)—if not during his last years—Italian opera entered a new and in some respects terminal phase. Although opera itself was now a permanent fixture of European culture, with Italians its expert producers, Italian opera would soon cease to lead musical style; the leadership would soon pass to a generation of young German symphonists.

Quite apart from that, however, this phase of Italian opera was seriously truncated by the loss, within a period of six years (1730–1736) of its three most gifted, most promising composers—Francesco Conti (1682–1732), Leonardo

Vinci (1690–1730), and Giovanni Battista Pergolesi (1710–1736). Conti, the oldest, died in Vienna after an illness that made composition exceedingly difficult. Hence his last works are few, but their quality is first rate. Vinci was well launched on a brilliant career. In 1723/1724 he left Naples for the international stages of Rome and Venice, scoring major success around 1730. Pergolesi, much younger, was cut down before he had fairly started, with only a few performances in Naples (1730–1735) and one in Rome. Yet the music that he left indicates superior ability if not genius.

METASTASIAN OPERA   These composers grew up with a new kind of libretto. Under growing pressure from literary critics the opera libretto was "reformed." In its substance the new libretto was very similar to the old one: heroic, noble characters from remote times and places expressed conflicting passions, elicited by intrigue plots based on concealed identity. Aside from a slight reduction in the degree of intrigue, the principal novelty of the reform libretto was the absence of the bizarre, the spectacular, and above all the comic. Serious opera now became a distinct category.

By itself literary pressure (always present in the history of opera) would not have brought the general acceptance of the new serious opera. Indeed, the first reform libretto, *La Forza del Virtù* (The Strength of Virtue, 1693), by Domenico David (?–1698) was not eagerly sought out by composers. Only after the purely musical advantages of the new libretto had become evident did composers adopt it. At that point production of reform librettos was taken over by professional libretto makers, highly skilled in literary craft but not so concerned with the philosophy of reform as the literary intellectuals who had initiated it.

The undisputed rulers of the libretto business were Apostolo Zeno (1668–1750), who "reigned" in Vienna from 1718 to 1730 and Pietro Trapassi, called Metastasio (1698–1782), who succeeded Zeno. Alessandro Scarlatti set several of Zeno's texts, *Griselda* (1721) being a reform libretto. Metastasio, it should be noted, wrote many things besides librettos for serious opera (which he was apt to call *azione teatrale*). Serious opera was only one result—if the most important—of a general tendency to purify all forms of dramatic music by isolating them from one another.

Composers became interested in the new serious libretto because it alone permitted the expansion of the da capo aria to the grand dimensions now demanded by its development. The character of the aria, its theme, could be cast in no more effective form than that attained by Scarlatti; similarly the techniques of working out a single theme could be no more refined than they already were. But harmonic clarity and control of key areas now permitted a much larger aria, while the needs of increased musical expression demanded it. The da capo aria was now to overwhelm the spectator with a sense of grandeur by its sheer musical persistence. Its broad dimensions were to be filled up with the artful reiteration of a single strong theme. We should note that a serious libretto did not have to be set to this kind of music. It was so set because of the purely musical development of the aria. The point is, the aria could only be fulfilled in the serious, purified libretto. In a comedy the grand da capo was not believable; it could only sound ridiculous, and in fact became the object of caricature.

For Vinci, Conti, and Pergolesi, serious opera was the summit of art.

They, like the audience, rejoiced in the elegance, the sweetness, the gravity of sentiment that was Metastasio's trademark. Their dramatic imaginations were fired by the grandeur of conception, the sublimity of character, unsullied by raw comic effects. Their musical forms responded smoothly to the slow, smooth pacing of scenes. Metastasio, a professional librettist, provided composers with a perfect text form for the da capo aria: four lines for the A section, four for the B, with a nice balance of weight and reinforcement of the passion between the two couplets. The aria texts were perfectly designed to define emotional responses.

In Metastasio, opera composers found lyrical effusion dreamed of since Peri—and not just in the arias but throughout the whole libretto. Recitative now reached a state of perfect elegance; here the text was good enough in itself to elevate the recitative style to animated lyrical dialog of utmost beauty. In the last analysis, however, the result was still *musical* drama, its success dependent upon musical achievement. The burden of the drama was born by the arias, and these—with four lines of text for four pages of music—stood or fell on their musical merits.

VINCI AND CONTI   The Metastasian libretto is best illustrated by an opera of Vinci. A pupil of Scarlatti in Naples, Vinci started out writing dialect comedies—a common type of light opera after 1710. His first serious opera was performed in 1722; his last, *Artaserse,* in 1730 in Rome. *Artaserse* was one of the most famous Metastasian librettos; that is, it became famous later, for Vinci's setting was its first.

In comparing Vinci with Scarlatti, one should remember that Vinci was young, Scarlatti old. Vinci's style had the same smartness Scarlatti's had had in the 1690s, when he was a bright young composer. A direct comparison of Vinci's *Artaserse* with, say, Scarlatti's *Griselda* of 1721 illustrates a contrast of maturity and youth rather than a basic change of style.

There were, however, significant changes in Vinci's music, and the most important concerned the dimensions and scope of the aria, especially the broader harmonic rhythm that underlies these dimensions. Rhythmic figure and harmonic change, still bound fairly tightly together in Scarlatti, are now sometimes disengaged—an effect most evident in the strumming sixteenth-note patterns of the bass. Another symptom is the fact that the aria theme is no longer carried by the bass, so that bass and voice no longer are linked in animated contrapuntal dialog.

While clearly perceptible in Vinci's music, this shift in the relationship of figure and harmony had as yet only subtle effects. Eventually this shift was to result in expansion of the size of the aria; but Vinci's arias are often not much larger than Scarlatti's, the B section of a da capo aria still sometimes only eight or ten measures long. The difference between Vinci and Scarlatti might best be described as one of taste rather than style. Vinci employs many mannerisms of rhythmic or harmonic expression. Syncopations and pretty little triplets are frequent; appoggiaturas are used with great expressive effect. Harmonic digressions, chords made foreign to a key through chromatic alteration, become more prominent through being sustained longer. All such mannerisms, however, are smoothly blended into the line. Similarly the vocal coloratura, much in evidence, always has a purpose, usually in connection with an overflow of affect that gives dramatic reason to the spectacular melodic surge. Vinci's

EXAMPLE 97 VINCI: ARIA EXCERPTS FROM ARTASERSE

(a) I,i; Mandane sings

Allegro (♩ = 84)

[Strings] Con-ser-va-ti fe-de-le, pen-sa ch'io resto è peno, io re-sto, è pe-no è

B.c.   (etc.)

(b) I,vii; Semira sings

Andante (♩. = 60)

[Strings] Bramar di per-de - re per troppo af-fet-to, par-te dell' a - ni - ma nel ca-ro og-

B.c.   (etc.)

(c) From the same aria

. . . d'o-gni do - lor, Bramar di per-de-re par-te dell' ani - ma

B.c.

e il duol più

B.c.   (etc.)

(d) I,xi; Artaserse sings

Andante (♩ = 72)
[Strings]

Deh re - spi-rar la-scia-te-mi qual - che momen-to in pa - ce, qual -

B.c.

(a) (Stay faithful! Remember that I stay and suffer! . . . And think of me some-
    times . . .

(b) To wish to lose, through too much love . . .

EXAMPLE 97 (CONTINUED)

che momen - to in pa - ce   (etc.)

(d) Ah, let me breathe in peace for a moment . . .)

arias display a wide range of character. In the course of some forty arias in *Artaserse*, one is not conscious of aria types repeating themselves—or even of aria types at all. There are extremely vigorous, brilliant arias, although these tend to be the least characteristic because of their straightforward drive. The most spectacular arias occur in connection with the celebrated Metastasian similes found at the ends of acts, for example, a comparison of the hero's plight to a shipwreck on a turbulent sea.

Other arias can be sweet or sad, tender or pathetic. *Conservati fidele,* a farewell song (Example 97a) shows both the triplets and the expressive chromatic inflections. *Bramar di perdere per troppo affetto* (Example 97b), is the successor to Scarlatti's three-eight aria, in a sweet style that became the trademark of Vinci's generation. It contains a prolonged sixth chord (Example 97c), using a flatted third and flatted sixth—one of those harmonic digressions of great poignancy. *Deh, respirar lasciatemi qualche momento in pace* (Example 97d), a plea for respite at a moment of high dramatic tension, perhaps best demonstrates Vinci's persuasive lyricism.

Francesco Conti also set Metastasian librettos; *Issipile* (1732) was his last. He wrote a very fine oratorio, *Il David perseguitato* (David persecuted), in 1723 (or 1724), for the imperial court at Vienna. Made up largely of recitatives and arias (choruses were relatively infrequent), Conti's *David* can be taken both as an example of his aria style and as an Italian oratorio second to none of that time.

Conti's arias reveal the same broad range of character as Vinci's, from brilliant common time, to arch or tender three-eight. His arias (at least in the oratorio) tend to be bigger than Vinci's. The instrumental ritornellos are carefully worked out with characteristic themes set in intricate contrapuntal texture. Indeed, his concern with expressive counterpoint is one of the most striking features of Conti's work, especially in the huge choral sections that frame sections of the oratorio. Ranging from massive acclamations to heavily chromatic laments, the choruses employ strong, expressive subjects in strong but always lucid counterpoint. In workmanship and effect they are unsurpassed.

PERGOLESI Pergolesi also made a fine setting of a famous Metastasian libretto—at the age of twenty-five. His *Olimpiade* was performed in Rome in 1735, a year before his death. Here, as in Vinci, there is great variety in aria character; here, too, the most brilliant, energetic arias tend to be the least characteristic of Pergolesi himself, but they must always be included in an estimate of his musical capacity.

Pergolesi's presentation of key is as clear as Vinci's, if not more so, but— and this is the more important aspect—this clarity is used as a foil for an exploitation of contrasting elements, either abrupt changes of figuration or chromatic alterations in the harmony. This sense of contrast, almost entirely absent in Scarlatti's arias (at least at the phrase level) is perhaps the most distinguishing feature of Pergolesi. It is handled very successfully in what may be the best piece in *Olimpiade,* the duet *Ne' giorni tuoi felici* (When you are happy— remember me!) But one should also notice the somber little aria *Se cerca se dice* (Example 98a), with its startlingly furious coda. The recitative throughout *Olimpiade* is impeccable.

For Naples Pergolesi wrote dialect comedy, especially *Lo Frate 'nnamorato* (Little Brother in Love), a large, three-act comedy with extended da capo arias, again in a wide range of character. This work is another manifestation of sentimental bourgeois comedy. The traditional intrigue now unfolds in Naples itself, around everyday characters. Pergolesi's lively, mercurial style and abrupt shifts of figuration here found their most appropriate environment. Similarly his slow arias of sentiment seem more happily placed in bourgeois times than in noble antiquity.

Al grande onore sarò innalzato (Example 98b) shows the slow-moving harmonies and catchy syncopations that combine magically to produce the spirited aria at which Pergolesi excels. *Si stordisce* (Example 98c) is a very expressive larghetto (although in comic context). It begins with an ad libitum phrase for voice, after the instrumental ritornello and before the voice begins its proper theme; such ad libitum exclamations were used with great affect from 1700 on for certain kinds of arias. *Si stordisce* continues with extraordinary wealth of coloratura, but in a subdued, expressive tone.

Perhaps most characteristic of Pergolesi's style is a special kind of phrase illustrated by *Sento dire* (Example 98d) from the second part of an aria—the first part having been an extremely agitated series of short exclamations. The key turns abruptly to E flat, the voice sustains its first note over smooth progressions of the bass downward in thirds; the phrase is terminated by a fast-moving cadence. The effect is arch understatement: more must follow. The significant pause (at the fermata) is another of Pergolesi's mannerisms, one that carries much of the structural burden in his increasingly disjointed forms.

A by-product of the reform libretto and its acceptance by composers as the vehicle of strictly serious music was the isolation of the comic intermezzo. Scarlatti had still used low comic roles as integral parts of the drama, but he was virtually the last to do so. During his lifetime these comic roles assumed first a standard position at the ends of the first two acts and then a standard character to the point where they could be composed separately from the main drama, even by another composer. Now sufficiently independent to be understood as intermezzi, they were only a step away from being performed separately as short, two-act comedies, stereotyped and slapstick. This separation took place shortly after 1700; it was, in effect, merely ratified by the reform libretto.

In this as in other respects, the shift in opera types after 1700 was external; musical style developed independently and at its own rate. The music for the new serious opera, as for the independent intermezzo, was not necessarily different from what it had been before. When it was, the difference was due to

EXAMPLE 98   PERGOLESI: ARIA EXCERPTS

(a)   From *Olimpiade* II,x; Megacle sings

Se cer-ca, se di-ce: l'a - mi - co do - v'è,   do - v'è, do - v'è?

(etc.)

(b)   From *Lo Frate 'nnamorato* III,ii; Carlo sings

Al   gran - de o - no - re   sa - rò in-nal - za - to   d'im-pa-ren -

tar-mi   con voi   si - gno-re,

(etc.)

(c)   From *Lo Frate 'nnamorato* II,xi; Don Pietro sings

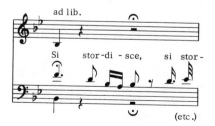

Si   stor-di - sce,   si stor-

(etc.)

EXAMPLE 98 (CONTINUED)

    (d) From *Lo Frate 'nnamorato* III,v; Ascanio sings

    (a) (One looks, one says—where is my love?
    (b) I will be elevated to great honor . . .
    (c) Let the fellow be confounded!
    (d) I hear tell . . .)   By permission of Edizioni Suvini Zerboni–Milano.

changing musical style rather than literary taste. The reform merely split apart what previously had been joined. To anticipate, neither of the two extremes so formed (serious opera and comic intermezzo) was as important for the future as the sentimental comedy that came to occupy the middle ground, for this comedy, containing musical elements of all descriptions, stood closer to the core of musical style.

Incidental to his serious opera, Pergolesi wrote comic intermezzi. One of these, *La Serva padrone* (The Maid-mistress), was received favorably in Italy and hysterically abroad; during the 1740s and later, it made its way all over Europe in many languages, remaining to the present day Pergolesi's best-known work. It deserves its success, but no more so than his other intermezzi. By itself, however, it gives only a fragmentary notion of Pergolesi's achievements and ambitions. (Most of the instrumental pieces published as Pergolesi's are not by him.)

Perhaps the best way to understand Pergolesi is through his other well-known work, the *Stabat mater,* composed at the end of his life. Here we find once more a broad range of arias of the most modern type, filled with Pergolesi's arch mannerisms. These have been the scandal of many a critic who found them unsuitable for sacred expression. Pergolesi at twenty-six was, of course, still capable of committing errors of judgment in taste. But the real reason for the lively, varied, sentimental music of the *Stabat mater* would seem to be Pergolesi's basic desire to be intensely effective. These mannerisms (not yet "music-hall" idioms) represent for him the newest way to be expressive. Side by side with such arias, the *Stabat mater* contains gestures of mighty pathos, as well as severe, impressive counterpoint. The first number (*Stabat mater dolorosa*) begins like Corelli, with chains of expressive suspensions; the truncation of phrases, however, is a mark of the difference between Corelli and Pergolesi. In the middle and at the end of the whole work come fast, driven fugues, which, along with the choruses in Conti's oratorios, are products of that ever-increasing concern for counterpoint apparent in Italian composers from 1680 on.

HASSE AND OTHERS Instead of Vinci and Pergolesi, the leading opera composers at mid-century were Johann Adolf Hasse (1699–1783) and Niccolò Jommelli (1714–1774), both equal in skill, though not in talent and imagination, to Vinci and Pergolesi. Besides being less imaginative, both Hasse and Jommelli worked primarily outside Italy, although their serious works were received favorably by Italian audiences.

Hasse was a German by birth, almost the only German opera composer to be accepted by the Italians as their equal—called *Il caro Sassone* (dear Saxon). He was the Metastasian composer par excellence, a role that surely would have gone to Vinci. (In 1730 he set *Artaserse* at the same time as Vinci.) Hasse's style, for example, in *Arminio* (1745) has Vinci's breadth and smoothness; the arias are a good deal larger than Vinci's but seem to lack Vinci's really vital, progressive strength. Hasse's music was safe for its time; he was bound to succeed in it, but not survive it.

Much the same is true of Jommelli, even though he reached out for scenes of mighty spectacle in *Fetonte* (1769). His search for heightened effects led him to exploit the now powerful orchestra; during the 1740s he developed tremolos, crescendos, and other agitated devices for increasing the excitement of serious opera. This exploitation of the orchestra, however, was by that time identified as peculiarly German, and hence alien to serious opera.

In contrast to Hasse, Pergolesi's serious operas were failures, but the significance of the failures has been overemphasized. They were the first big works of a young man in his twenties, trying to break into a business reeking with commercial cabal. He could easily have survived the effect of these early failures to become a leading composer of serious opera.

But behind all this is a more basic problem, reflected perhaps in Hasse's safe, conservative turn. Pergolesi's search for increased intensity led him into increased contrasts of figuration and harmony; indeed, this was the only path open, but it led to a disintegration of the whole idea of traditional aria structure. One could, however, only go forward or retreat; there was no standing still. Hasse retreated. It is hard to see how Pergolesi could have gone very far forward had he lived. He was using the clear tonal areas of Vinci to highlight momentary contrast; he was not yet manipulating these tonal areas at high structural levels. When Hasse left out the contrasting elements, he reduced the aria to a state of tonal boredom. Long, static tonal areas now placed an intolerable burden on the constantly reiterated theme and figuration. A completely fresh approach by a new generation, thinking in new forms, was necessary for a successful combination of tonal clarity with expressive contrast.

The personal destinies of the leading Italian composers after 1735 seem to reflect the destiny of the operatic style to which they were committed. Vinci, Conti, Pergolesi, all dead; the German Hasse the chief exponent of Italian opera, setting librettos by Metastasio, a Neapolitan who was holding court in Vienna. Vivaldi was still turning out quantities of vocal and instrumental music, but it now seemed old-fashioned in comparison with Giuseppe Tartini (1692–1770), who made the concerto speak the smart, sentimental language of Pergolesi. Toward 1750 Tartini increasingly withdrew into mysticism, and eventually went mad. Giovanni Battista Martini (1706–1784), perhaps the most brilliant mind of his generation, wrote both vocal and instrumental music, but not much and not impressive; he retreated into exhaustive, detailed studies of history and especially counterpoint. He readapted Fux in his *Demonstration, or Essay on the Practical Fundamentals of Counterpoint* (1774–1775), becoming the font of contrapuntal wisdom throughout the middle of the century—Padre Martini to several generations of young composers. Other Italians toward 1750 (Francesco Geminiani, 1687-1762, Pietro Locatelli, 1695-1764, Francesco Veracini, 1690-1750, Giuseppe Sammartini or San Martini, 1693-1750), all less than superb, mostly went to the provinces, especially Germany and England, the better to peddle what they knew of the Italian glory.

Only Domenico Scarlatti (1685-1757) stands out, not because of any great success in his own time, but because his musical instincts were so perfectly matched to stylistic conditions. Domenico, a keyboard virtuoso, entrusted his most significant expression almost entirely to harpsichord sonatas—more than five hundred of them, collected during the 1750s but perhaps written over several decades from 1730 on.

For Domenico, a sonata was basically a piece in a single rhythmic movement or tempo, like the sonatas that had introduced dance suites in the 1600s (not the sectional church sonata usually set *a 3*). This type of sonata, cast in binary form like a dance, was now expanded beyond the dimensions of an ordinary dance movement. Still, however, a sonata was too short to stand by itself; Domenico's solution was to put sonatas in pairs, the members of a pair often contrasting in character. Thus the external order of sonatas was a clear, simple outline—a pair of binary forms.

Domenico animated this order with an incredible variety of novel, bizarre, and expressive details, superimposed as decoration upon the large clear forms, just as his extraordinary harmonic effects were superimposed on the increasingly clear foundation of key. Domenico's melodic ideas often reproduce those of Pergolesi's arias; but ideas that seemed in Pergolesi basically unsuitable for the large forms of serious opera found in Domenico's intimate keyboard miniatures a perfect format.

INTERNATIONAL OPERA IN 1735   It is illuminating to list the major operatic productions (new ones) of, say, 1735, as a spot sample of the state of European music:

Rome:	Pergolesi, *Olimpiade* (Metastasio)
	Duni, *Nerone*
Naples:	Pergolesi, *Il Flaminio*
	Leo, *Demofoonte* (Metastasio)
Pesaro:	Hasse, *La Clemenza di Tito* (Metastasio)
Milan:	Giacomelli, *Cesare in Egitto*
Vienna:	Predieri, *Il Sogno di Scipione* (Metastasio)
Paris:	Rameau, *Les Indes galantes*
London:	Handel, *Ariodante*
	Alcina

Duni's *Nerone*, performed four months after Pergolesi's failure at the same theatre, was a great success; Egidio-Romoaldo Duni (1709-1775) remarked to Pergolesi, "My work, I confess, is not the equal of yours; *ma più semplice, sarà più felice* (simpler, it will be more successful)."

Pergolesi's *Il Flaminio* was a three-act comedy. *Demofoonte* was a serious work on one of the most famous Metastasian texts by the slightly older Leonardo Leo (1694-1744), a lesser opera composer who, along with Giacomelli and Predieri and many others, filled out the repertory and gave it depth. Handel's

ill-starred London operatic ventures were in their penultimate phase, repre-
sented here by two works with more old-fashioned texts based on Ariosto's
Orlando furioso. Rameau's career (like Hasse's) had just begun; Rameau's
Hippolyte et Aricie had been performed in Paris the year before, 1734.

RAMEAU AS THEORIST AND COMPOSER   Jean-Philippe Rameau (1683–
1764) came to opera relatively late; previously he had been active as a professional musician and composer, but most of all as a theorist. Rameau was the first
major theorist of the triadic epoch—that is, the first to speculate in a systematic
way on the rationale of triadic progressions. There had been little speculative
theory during the 1600s, for triadic progressions were then too new to permit
the breadth of generalization necessary for a theoretical interpretation, while contrapuntal procedures were no longer relevant to the foundation of musical style.

During the 1600s reflective musicians gradually accumulated precepts
about triadic progressions, in the form of rules for realizing the basso continuo
at the keyboard. The basic instruction book of the new style, therefore, came to
be the basso continuo manual; from it the student learned harmony and ele-
mentary composition. After 1700 basso continuo manuals came to be larger,
more systematically ordered. Francesco Gasparini's treatise of 1708, *L'Armonico
pratico al cimbalo,* is one of the earliest and best. Johann David Heinichen's
Der General-Bass in der Composition of 1728, based on Gasparini, is a huge
German encyclopedia of all aspects of musical composition—except the art of
canon and fugue.

Figured bass and counterpoint had become alternate methods of teaching
composition; they could supplement or supplant each other, depending upon the
inclination of teacher and pupil. Of the two, figured bass now represented the
core of stylistic development; counterpoint was either a superimposed ornament
or a refinement in conduct of the voices.

Neither figured bass nor counterpoint, however, offered systematic explanation of musical structure: neither was theory, but merely systematic instruction. Rameau was concerned with *why* things should be the way they were.
He sought universal reasons for the case-by-case treatment of chords as found
in the figured bass manual. His first treatise, *Treatise on Harmony Reduced to
Its Natural Principles* (1722) is basically a composition book of the basso
continuo type (like Heinichen's) but one that repeatedly reaches out for the
"natural principle" that will make sense out of the material.

The first principle Rameau used (but did not discover by himself) was
that of the partial tones produced by a vibrating string. He attempted to
demonstrate that the triad, the conventional unit of musical composition since
1600, was "natural" because its constituent tones could be found among the
natural partials. Then he went on to try to demonstrate that sixth chords could
profitably be regarded as "inversions" of triads, containing the same constituent
tones but in an "inverted" order.

While the first principle merely ratified the status of triads, the second,
that of inversions, implied a reorganization of figured bass pedagogy. Figured
bass treatises regarded triads as triads, sixth chords as sixth chords, different in
structure and function from triads. From the point of view of figured bass, there
was nothing to be gained by calling a sixth chord an "inversion" of a triad,

EXAMPLE 99   RAMEAU: ARIA EXCERPT FROM *CASTOR ET POLLUX* I,iii; Telaire sings

(Melancholy preparations, pallid torches, day darker than shadows, sorrowful stars of
  mourning;
No—I'll gaze no longer on your funereal splendor. No! no! . . .)

since over any given note in the basso continuo a triad and a sixth chord would produce quite different effects.

The difference between the two approaches is apparent from Rameau's examples, in which the basso continuo is on one line, and below it is the *basse-fondamentale*, or what was later called the *root progression*. In the more complex chords the discrepancies between figured bass doctrine and Rameau's theories became more marked. In C major, the chord that figured bass regarded as a six-five chord on the bass note F could be, for Rameau, an inversion of a seventh chord on D. Again, the various penultimate chords that in figured bass were described as $^6_5$, $^6_4_3$, and $^6_4_2$ were for Rameau successive inversions of the seventh chord on the dominant. Figured bass doctrine was interested in the different handling that these different chords required. Rameau wanted to demonstrate their similarity in order to demonstrate the reason for their similar functions.

In a series of publications that extended over the 1720s and 1730s Rameau went even further to try to derive the structure of keys and the nature of modulation from the same kind of natural phenomenon he used to justify the triad. His speculations were never completely convincing, nor completely accepted. Being theoretical speculations about music, they did not affect actual musical composition, even his own. They did, however, reflect the gradual shift of interest from chord progressions to larger tonal areas, that is, key progressions or modulations. Perception of these larger dimensions was made possible for Rameau, as for others, by the long, clear key areas developed in the da capo aria and grand concerto.

Rameau's musical compositions exemplify the thickening density of certain types of serious music after 1720—the same tendency found in Sebastian Bach. In Rameau this density did not express itself so much in imitative counterpoint as in harmony and involute figuration; but the effect is comparable. Rameau was most successful in his larger, more serious stage works, in which he emerged as the true successor to Lully.

After Lully's death French opera, freed from Lully's monopoly, had opened itself both to popular reaction and Italian influence. The first result was a return to a lighter kind of work with stronger emphasis on dance—the *opéra-ballet*. The pace setter was *L'Europe galante* (1697), with music by André Campra (1660–1744); the adjective *galante* was increasingly linked with this lighter mood in the following decades. In a preface to his *Cantates françoises* of 1708, Campra said he wished to bring to French music the "vivacity of Italian music," a character evident in his *Fêtes vénitiennes* (1710) as well as in the works of his pupil André Cardinal Destouches (1672–1749).

Thus Rameau's *Les Indes galantes* of 1735 was an opéra-ballet à la mode. Far more significant were his tragédies-lyriques—*Hippolyte et Aricie* (1734), *Castor et Pollux* (1737), and *Dardanus* (1739). Rameau admired Lully's recitative, and used it more or less intact, save for an increase in harmonic richness. His airs or arioso passages tend to be more frequent and stronger, often attaining a grandeur—either majestic, heroic, or pathetic—matched only by Handel's oratorios of the same years. In the da capo aria *Tristes apprêts* (Example 99), Telaire, at the funeral of Castor, laments the loss of her beloved. The slow harmonic pace coupled with a simplicity unusual for Rameau express a profound sentiment representative of the best of the mid-century.

PART 4
EXTENSION OF
TRIADIC FORMS
1750-1900

11
GERMAN SYMPHONY AND INTERNATIONAL OPERA 1750-1780

AFTER 1750 COMPOSERS BEGAN TO LOOK FOR A MORE VARIED, flexible style, which would provide a less stereotyped representation of human passion. Each work was to have an individual character, something to distinguish it from the now seemingly mechanical idioms of the old style. This individual character was to be expressed through a variety of rhythms, figures, and themes following one another in rapid alternation—continuing the kaleidoscopic tendencies of Pergolesi and Tartini. As variety increased, however, so did the need for larger, stronger forms that could gather up the more varied rhythms and themes into a broad but still compelling unity. Composers found their way toward these forms through a clarification and refinement of the sense of key: they brought the kind of tonal order built of triads to a peak of efficiency.

REFINEMENT IN TRIADIC STRUCTURE It is difficult to point out any single decisive factor, any novel ingredient in the change of style after 1750. Beethoven used much the same chords, for example, as Alessandro Scarlatti, but handled them differently. It was the way of using materials, not the materials themselves, that gave the new style its distinctive features. Around 1760 Philipp Emanuel Bach, in his famous *Essay on the True Art of Playing Keyboard Instruments,* spoke of the refinement of modern style. He was referring to a need for figured basses instead of the predominantly unfigured basses of the old operatic style; the older practice, resting upon a firm foundation of commonly understood progressions, had less need for specific figures, while the modern practice Philipp Emanuel had in mind made figures necessary because of more varied harmonic progressions. Even though Philipp Emanuel's own harmonic practice did not become the standard one (as we will see), his observation is still valid for the new style. That he called the new style "refined" does not mean that the old one was "crude" by comparison, only that the new solutions were more drastic, the new effects more obvious. Soon after Philipp Emanuel's time the figured bass was abandoned, in part, at least, because composers, now wishing to exercise even more refinement in the spacing of chords and the handling of inner parts, were no longer willing to entrust them to the discretion of the continuo player.

It was sometimes observed in the mid-1700s that the expressive value of a work lay largely in its "modulation," meaning the whole flux of harmonies, the tonal fabric of music. The terms *harmony, modulation,* and *melody,* or melodiousness, tended for a while to be almost identical in meaning. It was also observed that Germans were more concerned with the possibilities of harmony than French or Italian composers. After 1750 a subtle sense of harmonic modulation was the most important means to musical expression; not that other musical elements were neglected, but their effectiveness often depended upon the effectiveness of the harmony. Increased harmonic effectiveness was not, however, reached directly through richer chords and more intricate progressions but— paradoxically—through simpler chords and more efficient progressions.

This phase of development is difficult to grasp, its effect often misunderstood. The vigorous repetitions of the old style (Vivaldi, say) had made the relationships of chords within a key abundantly clear. The sense of key had been pounded into the chord until its relationship to its fellows in the key could practically be sensed in the chord itself. Progressive composers around 1750 capitalized on this infused sense of relationship, avoiding the now redundant effect of rapid transit through the essential chords of a key, by presenting chords one at a time—as it were—making each last somewhat longer than before. Each chord made a more individual contribution to the establishment of the key.

Sometimes (particularly around 1750) composers emphasized the role of a chord within a key by giving each chord a particular form: sevenths tended to be added only to the dominant triad, for example, instead of making every chord of a long sequence a seventh chord. The subdominant tended to appear only as a six-five chord, which clarified its relation to the key by avoiding any suggestion that the subdominant triad might be a tonic in its own key. All in all, composers tended to restrict the kind and number of chords used to express a key. Such clarification was only a passing phase, but a very important one for the development of style as a whole.

The purpose of this clarification was not abstract formalism, classicism, or simplicity for its own sake, but rather had to do with overall effectiveness. This is perhaps best made clear by pointing out that the infused sense of relationship is what was later called *function.* The process whereby these relationships were clarified and emphasized was the process that made harmony "functional." The function of each chord, its implied relationship to its key, became its most expressive aspect.

We can now properly apply the roman numerals (I, V, etc.) that are used to designate harmonic functions. This device was not developed until after 1800 by Gottfried Weber (the most famous harmonic theorist of the early 1800s) and the concept of function fully elaborated only by Hugo Riemann late in the 1800s. But both symbol and concept can be applied fruitfully from 1750 on, their increasing applicability reflecting the increased efficiency with which chords were being used. More efficient, however, means merely doing more with less, not necessarily doing it better. The increase in clarity of harmonic function is not to be interpreted as an approach to an absolute musical standard, an improvement over the past, but only a phase of development in which harmonic effect was sought in the long-range rather than short-range implications of a chord.

Long-range implications involved the relationships among keys and the modulation from one key to another—modulation as we now understand it. After 1750 composers exploited the relationships among keys in more refined ways. The clarification of chord functions within each key naturally led to clearer key functions, and hence to the possibility of more subtle relationships. As with chords, so with keys: first the simplest, clearest relationships, such as tonic and dominant, or minor and relative major, were emphasized, and then expanded to govern longer and longer pieces. Afterward, more remote relationships, such as tonic and mediant major (for example, C and E major), were exploited. It is important to note, however, that these more remote relationships were usually not so disjunct as certain relationships in the old style, such as the abrupt shift from a minor tonic to a minor dominant key. As in other respects, composers after 1750 sought out a middle ground in the use of tonal material.

Perhaps most important, composers now emphasized the process of getting from one key to another. This involved both the clear establishing of keys at the beginning and end of the modulation, and also the subtle exploitation of pivot-chord functions during the modulation itself. The high contrast of abruptly juxtaposed keys so characteristic of the old style was gradually replaced by the sense of transition arising from modulation. Furthermore, as keys were presented more clearly, composers made more subtle use of the whole family of secondary or applied dominants.

These dominants were handled no longer just as transitory modulations (their principal function in the old style) nor yet as an integral part of the now clarified key, but were used as a fringe area of great expressive potential, becoming one of the most characteristic traits of the new harmonic practice.

The concept of rhythm in the mid-1700s included—if not emphasized— consideration of larger phrase shapes. Here, as with chord functions, composers sought clarity as a means to greater expressivity. The regular four- and eight-bar periods that we find so square had for that time the advantage of being relatively novel, an interesting contrast to the unending rhythmic drive of Handel, for example, or the whimsical irregularities of Pergolesi. Regular phrases went hand in hand with clear keys, the one supporting the other.

The regularity was to some extent covered by a profusion of charming melodic ornament and rhythmic detail, whose expressive intensity we must not underestimate; music of the mid-1700s was neither so bland nor formalistic in its original effect as it sometimes appears to be. Later in the century, composers used such regular phrases as starting points for irregular groupings, just as they based their far-ranging modulations on well-established keys. Rhythmic structure, both large and small, eventually became extremely varied, far from the clear patterns of the past, but located halfway between the single-minded, almost unphrased continuity of the big aria and the extreme symmetry of the smaller instrumental dance forms. The mixture of regular and irregular phrases, of predictable and erratic rhythms, became the composer's principal means for an individual style.

One of the most fascinating developments of the new style was the treatment of themes. Themes with memorable melodic profiles had been essential to the full-blown aria of the early 1700s. Such themes were developed in a straightforward way in the course of the aria: their rhythmic figure was spun out to provide the rhythmic fabric of the aria, and the theme itself reappeared in various keys, perhaps slightly transformed, but generally retaining its character sufficiently to bestow uniformity upon the whole. There was, as a rule, no strongly contrasting theme or subject. Similar themes could also be found in the tuttis of concertos, there alternating with somewhat more contrasting episodes for solos.

Immediately after 1750 the most progressive composers tended to avoid striking themes. Perhaps such themes as would have suggested themselves recalled too strongly the very gestures of the old style that composers were trying to escape. As the new style developed, however, striking themes began to reappear—but now in a more variable, dynamic relationship to the movement in which they occurred. Instead of being bluntly announced at the beginning of a movement and reiterated throughout as the dominating event, themes seemed to emerge out of the stream of varied figuration as the movement proceeded. Previously the theme had given identity to the movement; now the progress of the movement helped give identity to the theme. The interchange between theme and form was a fluid one, varying from composer to composer and from work to work. Difficult to describe or understand, apart from analysis of a specific work, this interchange reveals not only the flexibility of the new style, but also the complex, delicate interdependence of structural elements that distinguished the new style from the simpler, more drastic solutions of the old.

The old style had constructed its larger forms out of sharply contrasting units (recitatives and arias, or, in instrumental music, dance movements) and the new style did the same. Here a middle ground was sought between the simple two-movement form characteristic of solo sonatas and the multimovement suites and divertimentos. Three- and four-movement forms, especially the latter, came to predominate. Uniformity of key, as in the old suite, was now avoided, but also avoided was the succession of contrasting keys typical of opera or cantata. Unified variety, refined contrast, became the guiding principles in the ordering of movements.

Four movements of varying character and tempo, only one of them in a different key, became for a while the most representative solution. The favored arrangement was fast (tonic), slow (subdominant, mediant, etc.), minuet and trio (tonic), faster (tonic). This arrangement, however, came into being in response to the needs of a particular time; later the form was modified or abandoned in favor of others.

Similarly with the internal structure of movements: shortly after 1750 we will find composers favoring a modified concerto form, superseded a decade or so later by an adaptation of the rounded binary form (sonata form)—which in its turn underwent profound modifications. Internal structure changed continually under the pressure of expressive needs; the best, most progressive composers evolved a succession of new forms out of old ones as stylistic conditions demanded.

THE NEW GERMAN SYMPHONY In 1700 progressive music had been predominantly operatic and Italian. By 1800 it was symphonic and German. In 1700 a composer wishing to write a masterpiece wrote an opera; A. Scarlatti wrote over fifty operas—not all masterpieces, perhaps, but reflecting stylistic ease and assurance. Beethoven, with extreme difficulty, wrote only *Fidelio* (1805), not universally acclaimed a success. On the other hand, Scarlatti's sinfonias, among the first in the new fast-slow-fast pattern, are not even comparable in form or content with the Beethoven symphonies directly descended from them. This shift from Italian opera to German symphony provides a guideline through the profusion of styles of the mid-1700s; among many divergent tendencies, the predominant one was the effort of German-speaking composers to make instrumental music, especially the symphony, more meaningful than it had been in the past.

This increase in the musical substance of the symphony does not, however, reflect the whole history of music from 1700 to 1800. The overall change was not from Italian sinfonia, but from Italian *opera* to German symphony. In 1750 serious opera, though almost incapable of novelty and becoming increasingly dull, still set a standard for forceful expression which the German instrumental composer tried hard to match. Operas moved people; sinfonias usually did not, being a "harmonious noise" in the words of one German critic of the time.

In seeking to move the listener, the German composer was not doing anything new, except that he did it by purely instrumental means. But he was doing something new when he tried to be original, to express *himself,* in a way that the Italian opera composer had never done because he had no desire to do so. The goal of the new German composer was the creation of an original expressive language. The symphony was chosen as the path toward this goal because, being less developed than the opera and more flexible, it could more easily be adapted to new purposes.

Concurrent with the shift from opera to symphony—and in some ways related to it—was a shift in the audience. The old opera of 1700 had, in principle at least, been supported by the courts and played to an aristocratic audience, present by invitation. Then, increasingly throughout the 1700s, opera houses were opened for public audiences. More important, however, was the growth of the public concert of instrument music, often informal, as when a rich merchant opened his house to music lovers for an evening's entertainment provided by a fluid mixture of professional and amateur musicians. By the end of the century such gatherings had begun to be institutionalized into the large public concert as we know it today.

The new symphonic composers wrote no longer specifically for church or court, nor were they employed exclusively by those institutions. Instead they addressed themselves to an international, bourgeois, concert-going audience, and were paid through the agencies of box office and publisher. These new conditions, presenting the composer with a whole new set of problems, broke Mozart, financially and spiritually; Haydn, more shrewd and businesslike, finally came to terms with them and succeeded; the blustery Beethoven dominated them.

But beyond purely personal difficulties, the new concert life gave the composer a more profound problem. No longer knowing his audience as a specific group of persons, the thoughtful composer tended to think of them in ideal terms of universal humanity, or else relied more and more on his own musical instinct (rather than on what had been commonly understood features of style) in making his musical judgments. Professional composers, as always, worked in terms inherited from their stylistic past; but for a while, especially the later 1800s, composers interpreted the past in unusually personal ways.

MANNHEIM, 1750   Around 1750 in Mannheim, where a small but dynamic court led a brilliant existence for several decades, Johann Stamitz (1717–1757) built up the court chamber orchestra into the most talked-about in Europe. While there was good opera at Mannheim, the real attraction was Stamitz's orchestral concerts. Stamitz livened up the sweet Italian sinfonia with sudden loud and soft accents; contrast of loud and soft had, of course, been basic to the old style, but Stamitz's novelty lay in his frequent, unpredictable placement of these abrupt changes, resulting in a rapid alternation of light and dark (as it was described), agitating the amiable surface of the traditional chamber style. Stamitz also developed the orchestral *crescendo*, an exciting torrent of sound reportedly capable of lifting an audience right out their seats. Stylistically the crescendo was a new, more interesting way of getting from a soft section to a loud one; here the strong contrasts of the past were replaced in the most obvious way by the new sense of transition.

Stamitz's Symphony in D (Example 100) provides a good example of this new orchestral style, as well as the forms Stamitz used. Opera symphonies usually had three movements, often fast, slow, minuet; concertos also had three—fast, slow, faster. New German symphonies wavered between these arrangements, but (like this one by Stamitz) increasingly favored a four-movement plan that included both a minuet and a fast finale.

Stamitz and his followers also favored, for their more ambitious works, a modified concerto form for the first movement. The first movement has three main sections (with no repeats), corresponding roughly to the three tuttis of the older concerto. The key plan makes the outlines clear: the first section modulates to the dominant (A), the second section to the submediant (B minor), the third begins and remains in the tonic (D). Within the first section, there is a fairly clear "solo" interlude, marked by a new figure, after a full cadence in the dominant. The second section tends to modulate continually, especially through the simple but forceful progression D major–E major–F-sharp major. Aside from the force with which such modulations are carried out, however, and a confusing use of figuration (to be discussed shortly), the overall shape of this movement is in line with the more elaborate orchestral concerto of the immediate past.

The indications *forte* and *piano* that agitate the movement from beginning to end are undoubtedly to be taken literally, not watered down by mistaken

EXAMPLE 100   STAMITZ: BEGINNING OF A SYMPHONY (reduction)

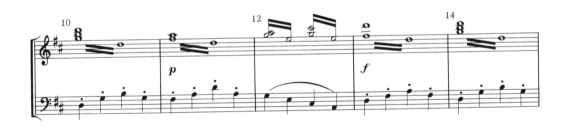

notions that all music of the time was well mannered and discreet. (Eye-witness accounts of Mannheim indicate that it was anything but discreet.) Furthermore, Stamitz probably did not have in mind those expressive swellings and fadings between *piano* and *forte* that came into fashion a few decades later (p < f);

for the time being, at least, the louds and softs in rapid alternation had their own violently expressive purpose. Gradation was reserved for the more lengthy crescendo, as in measures 5 to 8 of Example 100. This crescendo is usually supported by other elements, often a static harmony and a rising figure. Although the crescendo may be strategically placed in the form, for example, to emphasize a modulation, it just as often appears as an exciting event for its own sake, as at the beginning.

Harmony and phrase structure are militantly simple. The long opening on a D pedal is, to be sure, characteristic of the old opera symphony, the "harmonious noise" used to start the show. But these sustained harmonies now permeate the whole movement, relieved chiefly by fast-moving cadential progressions such as VI–IV$^6_5$–I$^6_4$–V^7–I. Both the sustained chords and the cadential progressions are good examples of the way familiar harmonic devices were given a new intensity through clean, forceful handling. Phrase structure, determined largely by chords and progressions and thrown into relief by orchestral texture, falls into four-bar units with remarkable persistence.

The handling of figuration, on the other hand, is anything but regular; the changes of figure are rapid, even more than in Pergolesi's style. More disturbing—intentionally so—is the way figures are related or not related to other formal features. While there is no striking theme (which would have detracted from the novel orchestral effects), the figuration used in the earlier tutti sections has just enough character to sound familiar when it returns later, but the returns are not handled with consistency, and the result is disorder, a lack of orientation in the shape as a whole. At this stage of development, however, disorder is not a defect but an asset, a way of avoiding the solidity of the old concerto ritornello. The sense of disorder goes well with the forceful harmonies and *forte-piano* effects to produce the agitation so characteristic of the new German style.

Stamitz's originality can best be measured against the symphonies of his Viennese contemporaries, Georg Christoph Wagenseil (1715–1777) and Georg Matthias Monn (1717–1750), along with a host of lesser musicians. Dependent upon the strong tradition of Italian opera in Vienna, and well acquainted with the latest developments in Italian style, the Viennese symphonists were less inclined to push forward along the lines of the Mannheimers. While they did give some of their symphonies a four-movement form and occasionally used the concerto form for the first movement, they seemed to prefer the rounded binary form as used in suite and sonata. This form was adapted to symphonic texture, however, so that the result was similar to the concerto form—except for the repeats, which continued to be an important distinction between the two types (Example 101).

In Wagenseil's symphonies, there is sometimes little tutti-solo contrast, but there is usually a change of figure to mark the dominant key. Wagenseil's figuration tends to be more lyric, more melodious than Stamitz's; there is more catchy syncopation, more tunefulness. These, however, are conservative features: they sound more like Pergolesi. Especially indicative of the Italian style are the graceful sixteenth-triplets; also conservative, but perhaps more German, are occasional expressive chromaticisms.

Wagenseil's symphonies are less representative of the new German am-

EXAMPLE 101 ROUNDED BINARY AND MODIFIED CONCERTO FORMS

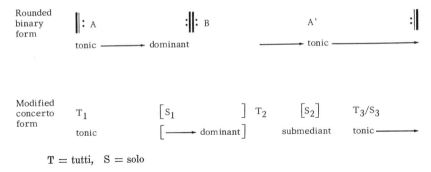

T = tutti, S = solo

bitions than those of Stamitz. (Then, too, Wagenseil and even more his Viennese colleagues seem less gifted than Stamitz.) Mannheim had the advantage of being in the Parisian sphere; even though it was a court, Mannheim was sensitive to the currents of the new bourgeois audiences of Paris and London, whose tastes were ultimately decisive for the new style and especially important in the decades immediately after 1750. Stamitz's music was not profound, not yet capable of matching the pathos of the late Italian opera. But the Mannheim orchestral dynamics, as used in this prototype of the new German symphony, made a strong impression on the new audience—much stronger than that produced by similar devices in the operas of Jommelli, who is sometimes credited with the development of these devices during the 1740s. Stamitz's symphonies are those which best correspond to the ideals expressed in J. G. Sulzer's *Allgemeine Theorie der Schönen Kunste* (General Theory of Fine Arts), an extremely popular encyclopedia current during the 1770s.

> The chamber symphony, which consists of an independent whole that does not lead on to anything else, is realized through a full-toned, brilliant, fiery style. The allegros of the best chamber symphonies contain large, bold thoughts, free handling of the texture, apparent disorder in melody and harmony, strongly marked rhythms of various kinds, powerful bass melodies and *unisoni, concertante* inner parts, free imitation, often a theme treated in fugal style, abrupt transitions and aberrations from one key to another, which are the more striking the weaker the connection; strong contrasts of *forte* and *piano,* and especially the *crescendo,* which when combined with a rising, expressive melody has the greatest effect.

PHILIPP EMANUEL BACH A more refined approach is apparent in the work of Philipp Emanuel Bach (1714–1788), in some ways the most characteristic of the new German composers, while in others set apart from them. Bach wrote no operas—did not even travel to Italy—yet through his numerous instrumental works became the most famous Bach of mid-century, in sharp contrast to his obscure father, Johann Sebastian Bach.

Early in his career, Philipp Emanuel published two important sets of keyboard sonatas, six "Prussian" sonatas (1742) and six "Würtemberg" sonatas (1744). These regularly have three movements (fast, slow, fast), the fast movements in the binary form now customary for sonatas. In the second set (1744) the binary form is often rounded, the opening section reappearing more or less intact as a recapitulation. At the same time, the style becomes more elaborate, and the effect of the whole more weighty, more expressive. Expression was Bach's foremost goal; his whole artistic career was devoted to making the slick, sweet style of late Italian opera more intensely personal. He did this by accentuating Pergolesi's tendency toward abrupt, restless phrases and varied rhythmic figures. He introduced striking harmonic changes, and generally made the melodic style so individual that its derivation from Italian models is often hard to see (Example 102).

Most important in his earlier years were his concertos for harpsichord and orchestra, of which he wrote around forty-five (and two double concertos). These concertos are not well known; only a few are available in modern edition. Clearly derived from Tartini's concepts of form and style, Philipp Emanuel's concertos are good example of the keyboard concerto at mid-century. The plan of the first movement of Philipp Emanuel's Concerto in D (Example 103) shows the typical four-tutti form.

As in the concertos examined in the previous chapter, the tutti frequently interjects short phrases, often derived from the opening theme, into the relatively abstract figuration of the long solo sections. The rounding out of the movement with an intact tutti, in full ritornello fashion, is also conservative, giving an effect of solid symmetry quite characteristic of Vivaldi but not, say, of Stamitz at his most adventurous.

At the same time, Philipp Emanuel in this concerto makes the third tutti and the following solo a clear recapitulation of the first tutti and solo, even though failing to support the recapitulation with a return to the tonic key; instead the recapitulation begins with the subdominant, thus preserving a key plan typical of the older concerto practice. (As was common in concertos, the three movements are continuous, accomplished in this work at the end of the first movement by adding a small modulating coda after the final tutti.) Experimenting with the internal structure of concerto movements, Philipp Emanuel interpreted the traditional four-tutti form in intricate and often original designs.

Of all his works, Philipp Emanuel's keyboard concertos are probably the most representative of his professional career. He also wrote symphonies, however, in the new German style. Of sixteen symphonies, only five were published in his lifetime, among them a savage work in E minor (1759), and a set of four written around 1776. Of the unpublished ones the most important are a set of six written around 1773 for a Baron von Swieten, through whom Philipp Emanuel's works were made known to Haydn and Mozart in Vienna. Few of these symphonies are available; but the Symphony in D, even though relatively late (1776), can serve as an example of Philipp Emanuel's extraordinary symphonic style.

As in Stamitz's symphonies, the first movement falls into three large sections, without repeats. Philipp Emanuel makes little effort to cloud this larger plan, the three-tutti shape being clearly perceptible. The first section has an obvious solo interlude, concluding with the more fluid alternations of tutti and solo as usual. The second section virtually reproduces the order of events in the

EXAMPLE 102   PH. EM. BACH: BEGINNING OF "PRUSSIAN" SONATA NO. 3

EXAMPLE 103   PH. EM. BACH: PLAN OF CONCERTO IN D, FIRST MOVEMENT

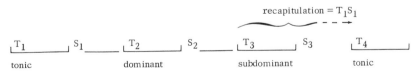

T = tutti,   S = solo

first section, the principal changes being in key; this second section cadences firmly in the submediant (B minor). This is followed by a very interesting solo section, a transition back to the dominant (A) in preparation for the recapitulation, that is, the third tutti. This is the kind of transition that is responsible for the change in the nature of the symphony. A comparison of this passage with the analogous one in Stamitz's symphony reveals the subtle differences of treatment that set off these two composers one from another. Other differences are apparent in the handling of figure and harmony.

Both Bach and Stamitz begin with extended D major, but Stamitz uses obvious chords and figures strongly centered on D, while Bach's figures are intricate and syncopated, and his harmony has started to modulate by the fourth measure (Example 104). This modulation is not directed toward the dominant, however, but seems to strike off in unpredictable directions, arriving in G by measure 15—or better, *on* G, without benefit of key-defining progressions; the sequence of triads on D, B, and G is Bach's personal interpretation of the usual spelling out of D major (in opera symphonies) by D, F sharp, and A. Then comes a shock, a diminished seventh chord on D sharp, *fortissimo*,

EXAMPLE 104   PH. EM. BACH: BEGINNING OF A SYMPHONY (reduction)

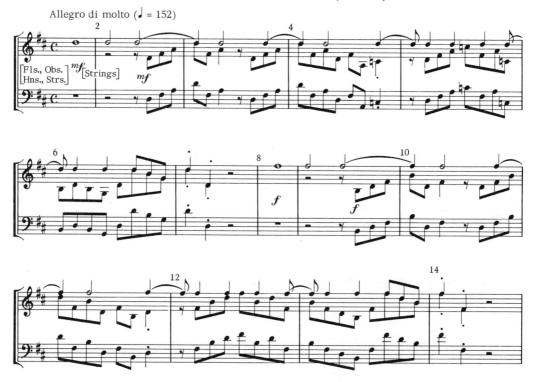

EXAMPLE 104 (CONTINUED)

followed by $^6_4$ on E, another seventh chord on A sharp, a minor triad on B, a $^{\;\;6}_{\;4}_{2}$ on A which resolves to a sixth chord in E minor, temporarily tonic.

    Curiously erratic, because so close to what might be expected, these progressions are characteristic of Bach's whole approach to style. He treats chords within the framework of figured bass practice, concentrating on the progression from one chord to the next. He does not seem so concerned with the overall direction of the phrase, with the thrust of each chord toward a long-range goal. A functional analysis, in other words, might not reveal exactly what Bach himself heard. The $^6_4$ on E would for a later generation be an arival in A minor, requiring either confirmation or subsequent modulation based on that tonic (Brahms would have moved the bass up to F, holding the A and C). But Bach understood this six-four as a subtle variation of the chord that should have appeared on that bass note, an E-minor triad, normal in the figured bass formula operating in measures 19 to 24. Bypassing the phase of tonal clarification which Stamitz exploited, Bach seemed to leap ahead directly into extreme harmonic expression without first establishing broad key areas as a basis. The irregular phrase structure of Bach's symphony, far from the four-bar regularity of Stamitz, reflects the same intense drive toward individuality. This is perhaps why Haydn and Mozart, profoundly impressed by Bach's serious goals and absorbed by his approach, could learn little from his idiosyncratic techniques. This is also why his symphonies produce an overall sense of excitement rather than a clear unfolding of form.

Beginning in 1758 Philipp Emanuel published numerous songs for voice and keyboard; the texts, by various German poets, were designed to express the devotions of the Protestant bourgeois home. Bach supplied simple, heartfelt melodies, still using the substratum of late Italian opera style, but stripping off the ornamentation. Even though these songs, *Lieder,* had German antecedents going back before 1700, still they stood near the beginning of a new tradition of German song—in a sense a protest against the more florid forms of the decadent grand aria.

Toward the end of his life, between 1779 and 1787, Bach published six sets of sonatas, rondos, and free fantasies, "for connoisseurs and music lovers." Earlier, in his treatise on keyboard performance, Bach had accepted with reservations the newfangled *pianoforte* (or *fortepiano*), which, as we will see, became popular after 1750 largely because of the Mannheimlike effects indicated in its name. For himself, Bach preferred the clavichord, which was much more intimately expressive than the robust harpsichord used for concerted music. Extremely responsive to the expressive demands of the performer, the clavichord was so intimate as to be fully effective for him alone.

In these last keyboard works, however, Bach prescribed the pianoforte on the title pages. The sonatas, still in the usual three movements, tend to have extreme key relationships—for example, a second movement in G minor between two in B minor—and in many other respects reveal Bach's continued search for original expression. Even the sonata as a form gives way to the freer rondo and especially to the fantasia, where expression reigns supreme.

It seems fruitless to try to relate the details of this expressive language to the past, or even to describe them. The essence of Bach's technique is distortion of traditional turns of phrase, or, at the most intense moments, the creation of an entirely original language. The result bears a curious resemblance to the orchestrally accompanied recitative that was the most effective part of the opera. In earlier keyboard works Bach had actually imitated recitative style, but in these last fantasias he is concerned not with style of any kind but only with expression. Perhaps the best way to understand these last works is to read the famous description of Bach playing at the keyboard: ". . . he played [at a clavichord] with little intermission, till near eleven o'clock at night. During this time, he grew so animated and *possessed,* that he not only played, but looked like one inspired. His eyes were fixed, his under lip fell, and drops of effervescence distilled from his countenance."

In a sense Philipp Emanuel's conception of music prevented him from creating a style; his intense search for original expression carried him rather in the direction of idiosyncrasy. But he brought high seriousness to music at a time when it was threatened on one side by the rowdy violence of the Mannheimers and on the other by triviality in the moribund Italian style and its derivatives.

The intense personal conviction of his music made a profound impression on his contemporaries.

Philipp Emanuel once said that his only teacher had been his father, Johann Sebastian Bach. Considering how far Johann Sebastian's music was from the style prevailing around 1750, it is in a way remarkable how modern— and how successful—Philipp Emanuel's music was. His elder brother, Wilhelm Friedemann (1710–1784), was less successful; perhaps more gifted than Philipp Emanuel, and even more inclined toward personal expression, Wilhelm Friede- mann produced some remarkable pieces but seemed unable to find the proper stylistic framework to support a steady output. Then, too, Wilhelm Friedemann tried to survive in the old *Kantorei*, the traditional institution of German church music—definitely not a proper framework for the new style. Even though this style was German, it flourished in the modern concert life of Paris and London.

ECKARD AND SCHOBERT Another composer with a strong individual bent, Johann Eckard (1735–1809), made a considerable success in Paris, where he went in 1758. Like Wilhelm Friedemann he published only a few works, some ten sonatas for keyboard; but for all their originality these pieces stood much closer to the core of style as it was developing—closer even than the sonatas of Philipp Emanuel, which they resembled. Younger and more progressive than Philipp Emanuel, Eckard apparently had the new pianoforte in mind as the preferred instrument for his first published sonatas, Op. 1 (1763). In the preface he wrote: "I tried to make the work equally useful for clavichord, clavecin [harpsichord] and forte piano. For this reason I felt it necessary to mark rather often the *doux* and the *forts*, which would have been useless if I had only clavecin in mind." Op. 2 (1764) was designated "for clavecin or forte piano." (A few years later, when more people owned the new instrument, similar publi- cations were labeled "for pianoforte or clavecin.")

Eckard's music abounds in expressive detail. His figuration is intricate, extremely varied, highly ornamental, but almost always significant rather than merely decorative. The overall feeling of urgency is increased by the dynamic marks in virtually every measure, carrying to an extreme the tendencies of both Philipp Emanuel Bach and Stamitz. There is a search for strong "character" in many movements, for example in the F-minor Sonata (Op. 1, no. 3), whose sec- ond movement, in C minor, is labeled *affetuoso*. If an E-major sonata (Op. 2, no. 12) shows clearly the derivation of Eckard's basic material from Pergolesi's generation, sonatas such as those in C (Op. 1, no. 5) or in F (Op. 2, no. 1) are full of the spirit of new German instrumental music of the 1760s.

Eckard, a keyboard virtuoso, apparently wrote only sonatas for solo key- board. Johann Christoph Schobert (1730?–1767; apparently died in his mid- thirties from eating poisonous mushrooms on a picnic), also active in Paris as a keyboard virtuoso, usually accompanied his keyboard works with strings. This practice, followed by others as well, produced a hybrid type of piece in which the keyboard was supported in a concertato texture, yet dominated the ensemble even more than in a normal keyboard concerto. If the number of stringed instru- ments was large, the result was much like a concerto; if only a single violin, then the result was the curious "sonata for keyboard with violin accompaniment''—a genre that left its mark on the violin sonatas of Mozart and even Beethoven. String accompaniments of violin and cello, or violin, viola, and cello, produced the pianoforte trio and quartet, respectively. Very popular in the decades after 1750, such combinations became the core of chamber music.

Schobert's style is less expressive than Eckard's, using far fewer dynamic markings; but the occasionally abrupt phrases, the varied figures, especially those which show Schobert developing a new ''pianistic'' technique, all manifest the new urgency of German music. Schobert was known for his use of light and shade; his keyboard style is often compared to Stamitz's orchestral style.

JOHANN CHRISTIAN BACH   The most brilliant figure of the 1760s was still another son of Bach, Johann Christian (1735–1782). After living and studying for a while with Philipp Emanuel in Berlin (1750–1754), Johann Christian left his brother—and his brother's musical world—for the charms of Italian opera. In Italy he learned the most modern opera style, exemplified in his own works such as *Artaserse* (1761, Turin). Now thoroughly Italianized, he went to London primarily as an opera composer, with *Zanaida* and *Orione* (both 1763); later works such as *Lucio Silla* (1776, Mannheim) and *Amadis des Gaules* (1779, Paris) testified to his eventual international reputation. This, however, was based not so much on his operas as on his many instrumental works, which were warmly received in London (his residence after 1763) and published in many editions on the Continent. Bach was also famous for a very successful concert series he ran in London in collaboration with Carl F. Abel (1725–1787). During the 1760s and 1770s it was he, not his elder brother, who was known as ''Bach.'' His style was taken as the ideal blend of Italian smoothness with German originality and harmonic weight; not so original and exciting as Philipp Emanuel, still Johann Christian was much more interesting than the Italians.

The most impressive of Johann Christian's works are his symphonies, including a set of *sinfonie-concertante* (sometimes called *ensemble concertos*) with concerted wind parts. Of some sixty symphonies, one in D, probably written about the same time as the one in the same key by Philipp Emanuel (1776), provides a useful comparison. With three movements (fast, slow, fast—no minuet) this work stands in some ways closer to the old opera symphony than do the symphonies of Stamitz. At the same time, Johann Christian's phrases seem less regular than Stamitz's (even if more symmetrical than those of Philipp Emanuel). After the opening unison in the first measure, the figuration works out an eight-measure phrase as two plus two plus four more subtly than Stamitz was apt to do.

Johann Christian opens on an extended D-major harmony, animated with his typically graceful figuration; but there is also a crescendo borrowed from Mannheim. The opening D pedal seems to last for a long time: the bass motion to the subdominant (meas. 14) acts as a passing decoration, as does the fast cadential progression V_3^6–I–IV^6–V^7–I. In this case the length of the static harmony seems to give increased weight to the graceful figuration.

A half cadence on the dominant chord and an abrupt move into the dominant key introduce a "solo" passage, marked as usual by a contrasting figure, dynamic level, and orchestration. Slick, routine progressions delineate A major. Then a warmer passage dwells on I^6 and V$^6_2$ in alternation (Example 105); saying it twice seems to make the difference between Italian charm and new German intensity. The effect does not last long, but we can be sure it did not go unnoticed.

Return of the tutti, rapid alternations of light and shade, and fiery figuration provide a typical ending to this first large section. The frequent neighboring chromatic tones at this point show a new kind of chromaticism; featuring expressive appoggiaturas, it is based upon an absolutely clear sense of underlying progression unmistakably oriented toward a tonic. The movement as a whole is a three-tutti concerto type (that is, without repeats). There is a simple modulation to the submediant (B minor) in the second section, followed by another of those novel, highly expressive transitions back to the tonic. Like Stamitz, Johann Christian includes in the transition a solo passage for winds, a dark touch before the brilliant tutti recapitulation.

EXAMPLE 105   J. C. BACH: FROM A SYMPHONY (reduction)

DN, 1760–1780 A Hamburg critic complained in 1766 that, except for Johann Christian Bach's name, he would have been taken for an Italian; but Hamburg was Philipp Emanuel's sphere of influence. Another critic found it necessary to defend Philipp Emanuel against the accusations of too much obscurity and asperity. Although critics' opinions are not necessarily a good guide to stylistic development—especially among the shifting tastes of the 1750s and 1760s—the opinions cited give an indication of where style was going; the path toward the future lay somewhere between the extremes represented by the two Bachs. The composer who most consistently and successfully followed this path was Joseph Haydn (1732–1809). Haydn's impressive series of a hundred-odd symphonies gives the most comprehensive, continuous picture of stylistic development from 1760 to 1780, and after.

This is all the more remarkable because during this period Haydn worked largely in relative isolation at a summer palace several carriage hours east of Vienna. In 1761 Haydn, then almost thirty, was employed as assistant music director at the court of Prince Esterhazy in Eisenstadt, near Vienna; in 1766 Haydn became music director, responsible for all musical activities and in complete charge of his own orchestra; and in the same year the prince took his court to his new summer palace, Esterhaza. Looking back on his years spent in the service of the prince, Haydn later made the famous observation, "I was cut off from the world, there was no one around to mislead and harass me, and so I was forced to become original." While Haydn's isolation was by no means complete (he was well aware of all the developments described so far), he was indeed in the advantageous position of being able to pursue his individual development, selecting and emphasizing those aspects of the new symphonic style he thought most appropriate, in relative detachment from local as well as international traditions.

Haydn's Symphony no. 1 (1759) makes use of a crescendo over the opening D pedal in the manner of Stamitz. In other respects, however, Haydn's early symphony has more of the Italian charm, more esteemed in Vienna than Mannheim dynamism—a charm especially noticeable in the slow movement of Symphony no. 1. The symphony has three movements (no minuet), concluding with the fast Italian finale.

But Haydn differed from both Bachs (and Stamitz as well) in preferring the rounded binary form, which he handled in the fashion of Wagenseil. Exceptions like Symphony no. 2 in C (1760?) usually involve special stylistic problems; the first movement of Symphony no. 2 is a three-tutti concerto form (no repeats) realized in a fashion noticeably different from Haydn's usual one. At this stage Haydn was still in doubt concerning the direction he should take. Indeed the whole symphonic situation was, as we have seen, still fluid, the experiments of the new Germans still not having made much impact on the older Italian style.

In the course of the 1760s Haydn's concept of the symphony gradually crystallized. But when, in 1761, he was hired by Prince Esterhazy, he wrote three symphonies (nos. 6, 7, 8) that showed how experimental the new tendencies were, because these three works revert to older, established practice as a guarantee that Haydn's first official appearance would be successful. They lean heavily on the idioms of the old concerto; all three employ concertante parts, passages for solo instruments that display their virtuosity against the background of the concerto grosso—in spite of the rounded binary form used for these concertante movements. French titles (*Le Matin, Le Midi,* and *Le Soir*) make them character-pieces in the French tradition. Two symphonies also have slow, overturelike introductions; no. 6 has another slow introduction to the slow movement, the introduction reappearing at the end of the movement as a recitative and aria—but without any singer. The finale of no. 8 is called *La tempesta,* in accordance with the whirlwind Italian finale. Yet all three symphonies have four movements, all have minuets.

In other words, for his inauguration Haydn imported into the symphony everything he could think of that would add weight and character, drawing almost entirely on older traditions. The result, in some ways, is new: this type of work is best described as *sinfonia concertante,* a hybrid form not extensively cultivated until a decade or so later, when it was taken up by Parisian composers. But Haydn's own development of the symphony took him in quite different directions, leaving these three symphonies isolated.

Still another arrangement used by Haydn during the early 1760s placed the slow movement, an adagio, first, followed by an allegro, minuet and trio, and finale-presto; examples are Symphony no. 5 in A (1762?), no. 11 in E flat (1763?), or no. 22 in E flat (1764—*Der Philosoph*), in which all the movements are in the same key. A change of key, often to the subdominant, but also to dominant or tonic minor or major, was regular for one of the middle movements of other arrangements. Haydn alternated throughout the 1760s between three and four movements, but more and more the minuet and trio came to be regularly included.

Throughout the 1760s Haydn produced symphonies in quick succession; by 1765 he was up to no. 31 (the numbering is not exactly chronological). After 1766 the number slackened slightly, perhaps because in his new position of authority he was also responsible for supplying operas for the theater at the new summer palace in Esterhaza. But also the symphony was acquiring more substance—not substance borrowed from older traditions, but generated out of itself, as in the works of Philipp Emanuel and Johann Christian Bach. This deeper substance is most evident in a remarkable series of symphonies in minor keys:

No. 26 (1765?)	D minor	"Lamentatione"
No. 49 (1768)	F minor	"La Passione"
No. 39 (before 1770)	G minor	
No. 44 (before 1772)	E minor	"Trauer-Symphonie"
No. 45 (1772)	F-sharp minor	"Abschieds-Symphonie"
No. 52 (1772–1774)	C minor	

The dark quality of the minor keys is exploited by a curiously relentless character, which eventually distorts the traditional style in a much more profound way than the surface agitation caused by the Mannheim dynamics. This can be seen in the opening of the "Farewell Symphony," no. 45 (Example 106). The first section of this rounded binary form still has traditional outlines. There is an opening tutti, then a modulation to relative major (A major), with somewhat different figuration (meas. 29 and on). A return of the original figure, as if in resumption of the tutti is marked by an unusual change to A minor—a striking effect. After a dark unison passage (meas. 56 to 59), the section ends softly in the minor dominant key (C-sharp minor).

The traditional shape has been distorted not only by unusual handling of the minor keys, but also by the persistent repetition of certain rhythmic patterns. With an effect very different from rhythmic repetition in the old, Vivaldi style, Haydn's rhythmic momentum threatens to obliterate his frequent four-bar antecedent and consequent phrases. This rhythmic momentum is supported by an insistence on intense harmonic progressions, with frequent sixth chords of various kinds, as well as ninth suspensions. Changing regularly in almost every bar from one unstable chord to another, the progression scarcely stops for breath from the beginning to the first repeat sign, whereupon it all comes again, followed by much the same thing a third time after the double bar—now in a major key, but that does not much relieve the intensity. The only real contrast takes place in a long solo passage with a quite new melody and texture, leading to the recapitulation.

This new momentum, which can be found as early as the D-minor Symphony of 1765, is Haydn's way of capturing the intensity brought to the symphony by Philipp Emanuel, whose E-minor Symphony, in much the same tone, dates from 1759. Haydn combined harmonic intensity with rhythmic momentum in such a way that they fill out and go beyond the phrase structure, fusing smaller phrases together into larger ones. But unlike Bach, Haydn took pains to make the new intensity support rather than destroy the form in which it unfolds, even though this meant sacrificing some of the explosive power of Philipp Emanuel's style in favor of a more cogent tonal organization. All of the chords in the first part of Haydn's Symphony no. 45 fit smoothly into their progressions, and all, no matter how striking they may be, help focus the concentration on the tonal center. The abrupt turn to tonic minor at measure 38, perhaps the most striking effect, is carefully supported by a return to the original figure so that it strengthens the overall form rather than going off at a tangent—as does the parallel passage in Philipp Emanuel's Symphony in D major.

The tone of Haydn's symphonies around 1770 represents the steady pressure within the German symphony perceptible since Stamitz; Haydn's works, responding to this pressure, are at the peak of the new German symphony. Not all symphonies of this period were in minor, however, and those in major embody the new tone just as effectively. The big Symphony in C, no. 56 (1774) applies the relentless rhythms and harmonic progressions to produce bright effects rather than dark ones, the level of intensity being the same as in the minor keys.

The inner expansion of the first movement, now very noticeable relative to earlier symphonies of Haydn, is due largely to the juggernaut treatment of harmonic progressions. This characteristic procedure usually takes place immediately after the opening of the movement; sometimes, as in the D-major Symphony no. 57 (1774), it pushes the contrasting figure that often marks arrival in the dominant key far over to the very end of the first section, right up against the repeat sign, with no room for a closing tutti. Thus the whole first

EXAMPLE 106   HAYDN: BEGINNING OF SYMPHONY NO. 45 (reduction)

EXAMPLE 106 (CONTINUED)

EXAMPLE 106 (CONTINUED)

section is taken up by dynamic expansion. This seems to be the reason for Haydn's frequently monothematic movements in which there is no contrasting subject. All is overridden by the new momentum of rhythm and harmony.

Early in his career Haydn had written many divertimentos for various small ensembles, especially for a quartet consisting of two violins, viola, and cello—not an unusual combination except that it lacked a keyboard continuo. These early works, either divertimento or sinfonia, were not associated with a specific size of performing group: one or more performers could play each part according to the desired effect. As the Germans developed their new symphonic style, they stabilized its performing medium. The most modern symphonies of Stamitz, for example, had to be played with the full Mannheim orchestra or they would not make sense (while for many less adventurous Mannheim pieces the size of the performing group was not important). As Haydn's symphonies during the 1760s acquired increased stylistic definition, they too called for a specific orchestra consisting of about five first and five second violins, two violas, two cellos, two basses. Various winds (usually oboes, bassoons, horns) were added in pairs; their choice varied from work to work.

Concomitantly Haydn worked out appropriate forms and styles for the smaller ensemble, the string quartet, which was now restricted to one player on a part. For this ensemble Haydn wrote music to be listened to for its own expressive value. In describing his works, Haydn made a sharp distinction between the early divertimentos and the string quartets Op. 9 (before 1769), Op. 17 (1771), and Op. 20 (1772). All of these quartets (there are six in each set) have four movements—fast, minuet and trio, slow, finale, usually in that order with only the slow movement in a contrasting but related key.

In the fast movements Haydn steadily expanded the rounded binary form by the continuing reflex between diversification and reintegration that had become characteristic of his approach. Slow movements, too, are often in a binary form, sometimes rounded, sometimes not. They become steadily richer with a human intensity that was indigenous to opera but had to be imported into instrumental music, sometimes via operatic styles, as in the "introduction, recitative and aria" in Op. 17, no. 5. Minuets become steadily more whimsical, occasionally grotesque (especially if played at an appropriately bright tempo); they always give evidence of Haydn's search for originality.

The first movements of the quartets in Op. 9 and Op. 17, frequently labeled *moderato*, are far more intense and absorbing than divertimentos had ever been. Op. 20 sometimes presents that somber appearance found in the symphonies of the same years. This is especially true of no. 5 in F minor, the most famous of the set. Its first movement, while carefully built and beautifully proportioned, has an inner restlessness expressed through agitated accompaniment and a tendency of the figuration to boil over, producing the same kind of onward rush found in the symphony. The minor tone is carried throughout the movement, even into the normal modulation to the relative major, turning up in expressive chromatic alterations at the end of the first section (Example 107).

The rich, passionate character of this movement best expresses the new seriousness the Germans were seeking. The remaining movements reflect the same character, each in its own way: the minuet somber, the slow movement naïvely lyrical, but with a sharply contrasting, curiously elaborate figuration

EXAMPLE 107   HAYDN: FROM STRING QUARTET OP. 20, NO. 5

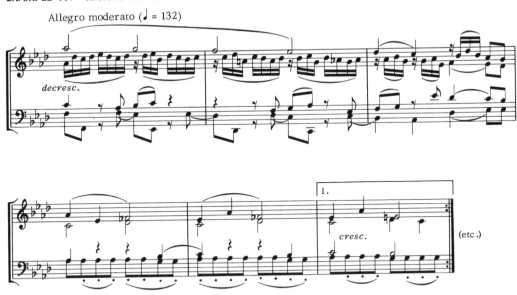

Allegro moderato (♩ = 132)

added as the movement unfolds. Most curious of all is the finale, a fugue, full of textbook contrapuntal devices (for which Haydn provides the technical labels, alla Bononcini and Padre Martini) and performed extremely fast but largely *sotto voce*. Considering the previous history of the string quartet, the effect is astonishing—as Haydn intended. There are only two other fugal finales in Op. 20, but many other movements of this set bear similar signs of Haydn's efforts to deepen musical character. Slow movements are sometimes *affettuoso e sostenuto,* or at least *adagio* or *poco adagio;* one of the nonfugal finales is *presto e scherzando,* another is *allegro molto* in G minor. Clearly the individual character of each movement was Haydn's principal concern at this time.

In spite of these brilliant quartets, and also very successful works, such as the *Missa Sanctae Caeciliae* (ca 1773) and the comedy *L'Infedeltà delusa* (1773), Haydn's continuing interest was the symphony. By 1775 Haydn had settled his mind about many aspects of the symphony besides the orchestration. The symphony now had four regular movements, fast, slow, minuet and trio, faster. While the form of slow movement varied among several treatments of binary form and variations, Haydn had found for it a new manner of grave sincerity to replace the old Italian charm. Finales, too, had become more German, that is, more dynamic, even if they did not usually employ the weighty fugal procedures of the quartets Op. 20. With these and subsequent symphonies during the 1770s Haydn was acquiring an international reputation; he was gradually being recognized as the leading composer among the new German symphonists. One of his first symphonies to become internationally famous, no. 53 in D (1775?, perhaps not the most deserving), was published in 1781 with the title "The Favourite Overture in all the parts as performed with Universal Applause at Messrs. Bach and Abel's Concerts"—reflecting the success of Haydn's appeal to the bourgeois audiences of London and Paris.

MUSICAL THEATER AFTER 1750　The forward thrust of the German symphony during the 1760s and early 1770s contrasted sharply with the confusion and hesitation on the operatic scene. Opera houses in Germany and Austria frequently experienced severe difficulties during this period; in Paris the situation was complicated beyond description by the continuing literary and political warfare among the intellectuals; only in Italy, where the ambitions of French intellectuals and German symphonists alike had little influence, was opera a going concern. And within Italy, opera now increasingly meant comedy, the high, serious style finding its best exponents in Italianized Germans, such as Hasse, or Germanized Italians, such as Jommelli (accused of being "Germanized" when he returned from Mannheim in 1769 to his native Naples).

After 1750 Italian sentimental comedy became increasingly sophisticated, involving more intricate social situations and revealing through them deeper aspects of human nature. This was due primarily to the librettos of Carlo Goldoni (1707–1793), a master literary craftsman and keen observer of those details of human existence that reveal the nature of man. The situations may seem to us artificial, because placed in a society now no longer extant; but for Goldoni that society was as real, as natural, as any other state in which man could be imagined. Analyzing with as much sympathy as satire the tragicomic disasters that befall individuals in a complex society, Goldoni furnished the composer with an ideal vehicle for the animation and sentiment required of modern music.

The Italian composers who took up Goldoni's librettos were skilled professionals, inheritors of generations of Italian dramatic know-how in stagecraft and timing. They made no attempt to break with their own musical tradition, but simply adapted the musical style they knew so well to Goldoni's librettos, which allowed them to make judicious use of both serious and comic styles of the past. Certain elements were avoided, like the orchestral recitative (except for special effects), and the grand aria, whether brilliant or somber (except for caricature).

The relationship of recitative to aria, and the concept of aria itself, was not basically different from what it had been. In comedy the composer tried to catch and fix in his aria theme the facet of human truth laid bare by Goldoni's analysis of his characters' reactions. But profiting from the stylistic developments of Pergolesi's generation, composers made their arias less static, more flexible than before.

The most interesting feature of opera was now the finale, the concluding ensemble of an act originally developed (as we saw in the previous chapter) for comic opera around 1700. Composed of a series of short, contrasting sections, the finale was especially popular in comedy, contributing both musically and dramatically to the animated atmosphere that set comedy off from serious works, whose acts were concluded with a combination of heavy-handed orchestral recitative, static arias and massive chorus in a way that, by 1750, seemed undramatic and unreal. In comedy, composers also made effective use of duets, and especially terzets, as a means of varying and animating the musical flow.

The first important comedy composer to use Goldoni's librettos was Baldassare Galuppi (1706–1785), active together with Goldoni in Venice during the 1750s (*Il Filosofo di campagna*, 1754). Nicola Piccini (1728–1800) gained his international reputation through his setting of Goldoni's *Buona figliuola* (Rome, 1760). Adapted from Richardson's immensely successful novel, *Pamela, La Buona figliuola* contained a perfect combination of pathos and comedy, suspense and sentiment. This last quality is made deeply affecting through such suave adagios as the one in Example 108, an intimate exchange in which the

EXAMPLE 108 PICCINI: FROM *LA BUONA FIGLIUOLA*, III; RITORNELLO FOR A DUET

Marchese lovingly teases the foundling Cecchina (that is, Pamela), before revealing to her that she is of noble birth and can marry him.

Comedy was well represented in Vienna by Florian Gassman (1729–1774) during the 1760s (*La Contessina,* 1770). Italian composers, both first- and second-rate, composed and exported quantities of works throughout the rest of the century. Even if facile and sometimes perfunctory, these comedies were nevertheless skilled, agile musical drama, representing at their best the most vital and certainly the most successful operatic repertory after 1750.

The situation in Paris and the cultural centers of Germany was very different, for outside Italy a variety of local conditions produced works for the musical stage of varying nature and quality, each in some way a reaction to Italian opera.

Jean Jacques Rousseau's *Le Devin du village* (1752), while embodying in its rustic scene the composer's literary program of naturalness, still uses relatively elaborate da capo arias and recitative in the Italian fashion. This, however, was atypical; French comedies, popular from mid-century on, contained music only for the arias, none for the recitatives. The net effect was to rid opera of those elements that seemed most Italian and overstylized (recitative and the grand aria), leaving a spoken drama with simple songs interpolated at appropriate moments—or a series of songs with just enough interpolated dialog to link them together, depending upon the emphasis of the particular work.

This kind of work, known in Paris as an *opéra-comique,* was cultivated during the 1760s in Paris by Egidio Romualdo Duni (1709–1775), Pierre-Alexandre Monsigny (1729–1817), and François André Danican Philidor (1726–1795; his *Tom Jones* was produced in Paris in 1765). Whether the musical style of the opéra-comique was a simplification of the Italian style (Duni was the one who succeeded where Pergolesi had failed) or a product of an amateur, self-trained hand (as in the case of Monsigny) the result was more or less the same.

With subtle differences of "national taste" perceptible more to contemporary observers than to us, the opéra-comique was duplicated in Germany by the *Singspiel,* whose librettos were often translations of French ones. Johann Adam Hiller (1728–1804) produced a series of works in Leipzig from 1766 to 1770; *Die Jagd* (1770), the most famous, is derived from an opéra-comique by Monsigny from 1762.

In singspiel, as in opéra-comique, the musical emphasis was on the short aria. Now better considered a "song" (German, *Lied*), it was treated in as simple and natural a way as possible. This involved stripping away those decorative elements that gave the late Italian style its vivacity, the underlying melodic and harmonic progressions remaining basically the same as before. Different mainly in the new effect of sincerity produced by the absence of ornament, these songs depend for their success on a naïve appeal directly to the heart. When the singspiel wanted to be forceful, it had to reintroduce Italian elements—orchestral recitative or the grand aria—or rely on dramatic rather than musical effects. Thus the singspiel, while often extremely charming, seemed to lack the intensity the new Germans were seeking.

This intensity was found temporarily in the *melodrama,* an experiment of the 1770s whose popularity gives an idea of the ambitions of German opera. The melodrama, first carried out successfully in Germany by Georg Benda

(1722–1795), eliminated the song as well as the recitative, using instead a spoken declamation against an orchestral background. As an extreme adaptation of the Italian orchestral recitative to the needs of the German stage, the melodrama was a temporary solution to a dilemma. Recitative, rarely handled convincingly in German, was inappropriate on the German stage because it sounded so artificial; but the orchestral recitative had been and still was the most intensely dramatic part of opera. If, however, the actor declaimed his German lines, instead of fitting them to Italian recitative patterns, but declaimed them over orchestral accompaniment intensified by new elements from the German symphony, then the melodrama could be modern, German, and dramatic all at once. The subject matter of Benda's most famous melodrama, *Ariadne auf Naxos* (1775), a tragic theme from Greek antiquity, indicates the difference in ambition between melodrama and singspiel.

Indeed Greek subjects often seemed to be a way for the Germans to achieve seriousness. One of the most serious attempts at German opera was *Alceste* (Weimar, 1773), a play by Christoph M. Wieland, set to music by Anton Schweitzer (1735–1787). The most impressive attempt at German opera, however, was linked with the ultrapatriotism espoused by the young German intellectuals of the 1770s, and hence drew its subject from ancient German history. *Günther von Schwarzburg*, set by Ignaz Holzbauer at Mannheim in 1778, was in serious style, with that emphasis on orchestral recitative characteristic of opera in Germany under the influence of Jommelli. As the thrust of the German symphony slackened after 1775, the opera seemed to move ahead again. Hopes were never higher in Germany for a German opera—hopes realized in part by *Alceste* and *Günther*, even if the latter embodied inherent contradictions in the patriotic exhortations sung in German to Italian-style recitative.

GLUCK Complete artistic success came to a German opera composer at this time only in a roundabout way, with results that were international rather than German. Christoph Gluck (1714–1787), a Bohemian writing Italian opera in Vienna, transformed opera during the 1760s and 1770s into a French musical tragedy that was at once international and unique. Gluck's "reform" was not a master plan; he probably had no single ideal toward which he strove for years; he was a practical man, most concerned with making the next opera a success. This accounts for the erratic succession of novel and traditional works throughout his career and reflects the current confusion in operatic taste of the public.

Gluck started as a composer of serious opera; during the 1750s, as comedy became supreme, he tried his hand at opéra-comique for the Viennese court. Then came a dramatic ballet, *Don Juan* (1761). After that, being imaginative, resourceful, and in contact with a group of literary reformers in Vienna, Gluck struck out independently of current operatic fashion. In *Orfeo* (1762) he combined the majestic choral dances of the French opera with a purified aria style from the Italian comedy to produce a new type of musical drama—or at any rate, one whose effect was sufficiently novel to attract attention. *Orfeo* is a pastoral tragedy, an alternative that gave Gluck just the opportunity he needed.

One of the most impressive elements in *Orfeo* is the very first choral dance of mourning. Act I opens with a broad ritornello and chorus in C minor, a brief recitative for Orfeo and a short dance in E flat, followed by the first ritornello and chorus; after another short recitative for Orfeo, the ritornello comes back once more. A more elaborate sequence begins Act II: first a solemn *entrée*, a chorus in C minor, and a dance for the Furies; then the chorus in C minor again, first repeating, then extending; Orfeo sings his song of entreaty, interrupted repeatedly by the Furies with cries of "No!"; then a new chorus in E-flat minor, another song by Orfeo, still another chorus in F minor, another solo, and final repetition of the F-minor chorus.

These solemn tableaux, which derive much of their effect from the choral repetitions, are descended from the huge operatic chaconnes of Lully (such as the one in *Armide* discussed in the previous chapter). Gluck, however, cast an air of solemn gravity over the whole ensemble, producing a highly individual effect. Sometimes, as in *Orfeo* (Act II), the choral ensemble embodies a gradual change of character, moving from one emotional state to another in a way quite uncharacteristic of the old Italian opera with its sharp contrasts. This kind of change—also perceptible in the luminous arioso of Act II in which Orfeo describes the Elysian fields—is perhaps the most striking feature of Gluck's new style.

Side by side with these solemn choruses come arias of great sweetness, beginning with Orfeo's first aria, *Chiamo il mio ben così*. In these arias, Gluck was following the general trend to relatively short, sweet songs. In the company of the choruses, however, these songs and duets take on an effect of naïve sincerity much more pronounced than that achieved by the singspiel in its most serious moments.

In *Alceste* (1767) Gluck, urged on by his librettist Ranieri Calzabigi (1714–1795), attempted a more sweeping reform of serious opera. In his famous preface to *Alceste*, Gluck spoke of purifying the opera of those musical elements that impeded the drama; he laid stress on "heating up the action." What is significant is that the reform, as expressed in the preface, is a purely dramatic one, linked to literary ideals, asking of music only that it get out of the way. Gluck's *musical* success, however, lay in placing intense musical effects so as to support the action instead of detracting from it. The grand aria was de-emphasized, the orchestral recitative exploited; Gluck, known as a fiery composer, made his recitative sometimes extremely dramatic through purely musical means such as rich, unstable harmonies.

In spite of all, however, Gluck's success in *Alceste* and the next "reform" opera, *Paride ed Elena* (1770), was not what he wished. Viennese taste, notoriously fickle under the best conditions, was quite unreliable during these changing decades. After 1770 Gluck conceived and carried out (with great difficulty) the idea of writing lyrical tragedy for Paris. Turning again to a Greek subject, he completed *Iphigénie en Aulide* in 1772, and had it performed in Paris in 1774—with success, partly because Gluck understood and exploited the operatic prejudices of French intellectuals, partly because he put together a very effective combination of exciting orchestral recitative, expressive arias, spectacular chorus and dance that both respected the niceties of French declamation and fulfilled the requirements of dramatic tragedy. *Orfeo* and *Alceste* were translated and produced in Paris (1774–1776); a new work, *Armide* (1776) was held up as champion of French taste in another of the interminable Parisian pamphlet wars. In 1779, at the height of success, Gluck produced another Iphigenia—*Iphigénie en Tauride,* the climax of his Parisian adventure and perhaps his finest work.

Gluck's unique achievement was to merge Italian style with French taste, making Italian *dolcezza* the legitimate successor of Lully's *tendresse.* Gluck then found how to mix the short, sweet aria in just the right proportion with highly dramatic orchestral recitative, chorus, and action to produce a work at once serious and modern. The result was far from the German opera of *Günther,* but in its synthesis of French and Italian tastes Gluck's opera achieved the international success longed for by the new Germans.

In 1778, at the same time that *Günther* was being produced at Mannheim, and Gluck was preparing for his final Parisian triumph, a national singspiel theater was opened in Vienna at the instigation of the emperor himself. The theater was a great success for several years (an indication, perhaps, that Gluck was better off in Paris). The singspiel continued to be dependent upon the opéra-comique for much of its material, but since Italian comedy was so firmly established in Vienna, having been for decades the most popular form of musical theater, the most successful Viennese singspiels resembled Italian more than Northern models. Karl Ditters von Dittersdorf (1739–1799) wrote many successful singspiels, the most famous being *Doktor und Apotheker* (1786).

Gluck's international success during the 1770s coincided with Haydn's, but a comparison shows at once how different they were. Gluck's success was due to a final reinterpretation of Italian opera—unique, inimitable, and without real immediate influence. Haydn's success was achieved through the new German symphony, for which he provided the models used by Beethoven and those who came after. Haydn also wrote operas, mainly comedies like *Lo Speziale* (1768), *L'Infedeltà delusa* (1773), *L'Incontro improviso* (1775), and *Il Mondo della luna* (1777), often using librettos descended from Goldoni. He also wrote singspiels for an elaborate marionette theater at Esterhaza, including two recently discovered works, *Philemon und Baucis* (1773) and *Vom abgebrannten Haus* (1776–1778). But no matter how charming or expressive such works may be (and they do not seem to be consistently exciting) the fact remains that Haydn's interest lay in the orchestra, not the stage. His sustained concentration on the symphony is the stylistic basis of his career and of his international reputation.

12
HAYDN AND MOZART 1770–1800

MOZART'S EARLY YEARS Wolfgang Amadeus Mozart (1756–1791) fluctuated throughout his life between symphony and opera, and within opera between Italian serious opera, comedy, and German singspiel. Mozart was born with an uncanny ability to mimic; during his early years he reproduced the sounds he heard around him, content, at least in the beginning, to work within the existing forms. What distinguished him was another inborn drive to make the result better, more musical, than his competitors.

In his early years, most of Mozart's important compositions were written for the frequent tours he made with his father; the kind of work he wrote, often the way he wrote it, depended on its intended destination. In 1765, during a trip to London, Mozart came to know, love, and admire Johann Christian Bach. Mozart wrote symphonies in Bach's style, and copied out one by Abel; these works were of the concerto type favored by German composers in Mannheim, London, and Paris. Then, two years later in Vienna, Mozart wrote symphonies using the rounded binary form and other features of the Viennese symphony. Also for Vienna, Mozart wrote comedy, *La Finta semplice,* and at the same time a charming little singspiel, *Bastien und Bastienne* (1768). During the following years he wrote two serious operas, *Mitridate, re di Ponto* (1770) and *Lucio Silla* (1772), both for Milan. Still only sixteen years old, he turned out remarkable imitations of the best efforts of adult, experienced composers, sometimes excelling them in charm, effectiveness, and musical value.

The most interesting examples of how the young Mozart reacted to influences of time and place, and also to the achievements of others, are provided by his symphonies and string quartets written between 1770 and 1773. Much of this time he spent in northern Italy, and for those tours he wrote a number of facile, melodious instrumental pieces, both symphonies and string quartets. But for Vienna, or back in Salzburg between trips, Mozart turned abruptly to symphonies in the German style, usually modeled on Haydn. Especially striking are a set of six quartets Mozart wrote in response to Haydn's String Quartets Op. 20 (1772). Mozart's quartets are entirely different in character from his Italian pieces, full of the new German seriousness; he even provided fugal finales in the manner of Haydn. And Mozart's most impressive symphony of this period is in G minor (K. 183, 1773), a brooding work that reflects not only Haydn's symphonies of the early 1770s, but in particular the character associated with the key of G minor as used by Haydn and others, for example, Johann Christian Bach. There is only one other symphony by Mozart in G minor.

During the mid-1770s there were fewer tours; now no longer a child prodigy, because no longer a child, Mozart was engaged as church musician by the archbishop of Salzburg. In connection with this post he wrote a good deal of church music—concertato masses, litanies, and also a type of sonata, a trio for two violins, bass, and organ, used in Salzburg at the gradual of the mass. He produced a continuous supply of divertimentos and serenades for various ensembles and occasions. But aside from one comedy, *La Finta giardiniera*, for Munich (1775), his activity in modern concert music took the form of concertos and sonatas. The five charming violin concertos of 1775 are fairly conservative in structure and style, but liberally supplied with modern dynamics and light and shade. Three pianoforte concertos of 1776 reflect the less serious approach of Johann Christian Bach to that category; the E-flat Concerto of 1777 (K. 271, the "Jeunehomme" Concerto written for a lady of that name) is a much more serious, interesting work.

These years saw half a dozen sonatas for pianoforte, including the famous one in D (K. 284, 1775), a faithful replica of the Mannheim orchestral style: it has the rapid alternations of light and shade, the rising line over a "trommelbass," the forceful tutti sections with thundering unisoni for bass under string tremolo. Mozart's pianoforte works are especially hard to imagine in their original stylistic meaning, because their vigor and the occasional youthful boisterousness they share with the new German style of Mannheim and Paris are often obliterated in modern performance. True, the sound of Mozart's pianoforte is now not a forceful one, but in the 1770s the pianoforte was a modern instrument whose capabilities were exploited, as we have seen, for the expressive purposes of Philipp Emanuel Bach and Johann Eckard, as well as to reproduce the startling novelties of the Mannheim orchestra.

Mozart's best works of the late 1770s were written in connection with a long tour to Mannheim and Paris, 1778–1779. In Mannheim he wrote half a dozen sonatas for pianoforte and violin that still reflect Schobert's concept of "sonata for pianoforte accompanied by violin"; but writing fifteen years later than Schobert, Mozart was able to supply a much more varied, intricate style, and along with it more equality between the two instruments. For Paris, Mozart wrote a sinfonia concertante (and in Mannheim two more), that special type of symphony with solo parts popular in Paris at the time. His most important symphonic effort, however, was the "Paris" Symphony in D (K. 297). It is in three movements, not four (the minuet is omitted), and the outer movements are cast in the concerto form without the repeats used by the Bachs and Stamitz. This was the kind of symphony the Parisian audience expected.

For the city of Schobert and Eckard, Mozart also wrote five big piano-forte sonatas (K. 310, 330, 331, 332, 333, all 1778). These still demonstrate Mozart's attachment to his stylistic surroundings, but at the same time they show that, as he grasped more clearly what was characteristic in others, he was able to express his own individuality more strongly. The A-minor Sonata (K. 310) is particularly impressive in this respect. Very different in character is the Sonata in B flat (K. 333), closer to the cantabile style of Johann Christian Bach; this sonata seems in fact to be derived from one of Bach's in G. These two works, Bach's and Mozart's, fall on either side of a crucial point for the modern listener: Bach's seems to belong still to "old music" (which the modern listener has to view in terms of an historical process), while Mozart's seems to belong to music as it is and should be. In this B-flat Sonata of Mozart, past and present seem to meet.

What Mozart brought home from this tour to Mannheim and Paris was even more important than what he took with him. In Mannheim (1778) he heard Holzbauer's *Günther von Schwarzburg*. Mozart was impressed with the work, as well he might be, but almost certainly for its music rather than its text—and probably without much concern for whether the music itself was "German." What must have been significant to him was the possibility of a large, serious dramatic piece written by a German in the German tongue, in a musical style that had international ambitions. Then in Paris Mozart was in the presence of another kind of international opera written by a German, the tragédie-lyrique of Gluck. Mozart must have been impressed by a German composer who had made good on an international operatic stage, even if in a foreign language and in a musical style that must have seemed stiff and old-fashioned to Mozart. He did not get to know Gluck's masterpiece, *Iphigénie en Tauride* (1779) until the 1781 German production in Vienna (for which Mozart attended every rehearsal). But the ideal of German opera, exemplified, on one hand, by Holzbauer, and on the other, by Gluck, certainly stood over Mozart's own operatic efforts from then on.

An interesting sidelight on Mozart's dramatic thinking at this time is provided by *Zaide* (1779), incorporating Benda's technique of melodrama (Mozart called it *melologus*), which also appears in incidental music which he wrote the same year for a play, *Thamos, König in Agypten*. But the biggest achievement of these years—indeed of Mozart's career up to that time—was the serious opera *Idomeneo* (1781). Written for the south German audience at Munich, *Idomeneo* was naturally in Italian. Now that we are gaining a better appreciation of serious opera of the 1700s, we are better able to understand and admire *Idomeneo* and see that it was one of the best such works of its time. Some aspects of this work, however, lead beyond Italian opera; influence of Gluck is sometimes pointed out. More than that, it has a musical fullness understandable only in terms of Mozart's experience with the new German symphony. It must have become apparent to Mozart that there was a certain contradiction between the traditional structure of serious opera and the new, flexible, dynamic musical language that he was learning to use with increasing freedom.

Right after the production of *Idomeneo,* Mozart moved to Vienna to make his way as a free-lance composer, a move that brought about basic changes in his whole form of life. He severed his relationship with the archbishop of Salzburg (abruptly, so the story goes). He was now a man of twenty-five, and married. He had to compete with other men, some of them almost as gifted, equally skilled, and better equipped at professional in-fighting than he. All this belongs to Mozart's story, not the story of style; what is stylistically important is that the direction in which Mozart moved after 1782 gives a decisive picture of music in that decade. In being pushed, Mozart pushed himself—and soon started to lead instead of follow. His work was, to be sure, increasingly bound up with Haydn's, but at the same time he struck out into areas left untouched by Haydn. He brought concerto and opera up to date, establishing models here as Haydn was doing in symphony and string quartet; in sum, Mozart became original.

MOZART IN VIENNA Mozart's first project in Vienna was a singspiel for the national theater. Mozart had been interested in the theater even before its opening in 1778, and was naturally attracted to it as a professional opportunity. The theater was in full swing; it seemed as though German opera, one way or the other, was going to succeed. Behind this seeming success, however, stood the reality that most of the librettos used at the national theater came from the French opéra-comique, while the prevailing musical style was close to Italian comedy. Particularly in France the comic opera included a broad range of exotic and unusual subjects—oriental, medieval, and fantastic. In *Die Entführung aus dem Serail* (1782) Mozart put together a combination of Italian and French elements in an exotic Turkish setting as the best entree into Viennese opera. Despite superb portions, however, this was not as a whole the German opera Mozart really wanted to write. Singspiel was, by itself, not the way toward a revitalized music-drama. Mozart had first to come to terms with Italian comedy, on one hand, and with the Germany symphony, on the other.

In Vienna Mozart underwent several new influences, some more fruitful than others. He was taken up by that eccentric antiquarian, Baron von Swieten, who pressed on Mozart his hobbies, the fugues of Handel and Johann Sebastian Bach, especially those of the *Well-tempered Keyboard;* the Baron actually got Mozart to write some fugues. Now it is difficult to imagine two composers more different in background, temperament, training, style, and basic conception of music than Mozart and Johann Sebastian Bach. Mozart must have regarded the fugues of Bach with the deep fascination and utter lack of comprehension of an amateur archaeologist confronted with an artifact left by a long-lost culture. At any rate (as Alfred Einstein pointed out) there are more unfinished fugues among Mozart's manuscripts than any other kind of fragment. Those which Mozart did manage to finish (as in K. 394, a Prelude and Fugue in C major, 1782) have an eerie lack of relationship both to Mozart's other works and to

Bach's as well. In his mature symphonies, quartets, and quintets Mozart is indeed contrapuntal, but this counterpoint is not Bach's counterpoint, resting on different harmonic foundations and used for different stylistic purposes.

Far more important was the influence of Philipp Emanuel Bach, which also came through the Baron and took the form of the keyboard fantasia. The most famous one in C minor (K. 475, 1785) was intended to precede the big Sonata in C minor (K. 457, 1784), forming with it an extraordinary work quite unlike anything Mozart had done before. This fantasia and one or two others, written in the rhapsodic style of Philipp Emanuel, have a forcefulness and depth of original expression whose only parallel lay in the fantasias Philipp Emanuel published between 1781 and 1787. In Bach's case, this style was the end product of a long concern for expression, going back for decades. For Mozart, it was an abrupt turn to an aspect of modern music he had not heretofore touched upon.

Since Mozart now set out to establish himself as a pianoforte virtuoso (in order to make a living), he started writing concertos again at the rate of several each season.

1782–1783			1784–1785	
K. 413	F		K. 456	B flat
K. 414	A		K. 459	F
K. 415	C		K. 466	D minor
1784 (spring)			K. 467	C
K. 449	E flat		1785–1786	
K. 450	B flat		K. 482	E flat
K. 451	D		K. 488	A
K. 453	G		K. 491	C minor

Keyboard concertos had not been taken up seriously by Haydn. Johann Christian Bach had written a number, but usually at a level below that of his symphonies and ensemble concertos. The most impressive keyboard concertos were still those of Philipp Emanuel Bach from the 1740s and 1750s. Works similar in form but for the most part less exciting were produced during the 1760s and 1770s by such composers as Benda and Dittersdorf, as well as by Mozart himself, who as a child even put concertos together out of movements by other composers for other media. The works just listed, then, represent the most serious, ambitious approach to the pianoforte concerto since Philipp Emanuel.

Mozart used basically the same plan as Philipp Emanuel, at least insofar as Philipp Emanuel had strengthened the idea of recapitulation. Mozart made the concerto much more symphonic, in the sense that he greatly enriched the orchestration, strengthened the broad sense of key and enlarged the dimensions; but all this took place within the first-movement structure more or less as found in Bach.

This movement structure (Example 109) opened with a long tutti, containing contrasting figures, and cadencing in the tonic. Then followed a longer solo section, restating and expanding some of the tutti material, adding a greater or lesser amount of new material, and including the usual tutti interjections. This first solo section was concluded in the dominant by a tutti passage (drawn

EXAMPLE 109 PLAN OF PIANO CONCERTO, FIRST MOVEMENT

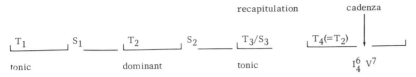

$T =$ tutti, $S =$ solo

from the opening tutti) which functioned as a "second tutti." The following
section, the "second solo," was often free or rhapsodic, sometimes based on a
previous theme, sometimes not, but marked by far-ranging modulation and
extended figural patterns for the soloist in dialog with the orchestra. With a
return to the tonic, tutti and solo together recapitulated the material of the first
tutti and first solo—a fusion of the old third tutti and third solo found already
in Philipp Emanuel—concluding with a final tutti that resembled the second
one. At the appropriate moment in this final ("fourth") tutti, the soloist provided a *cadenza* or extended ornamentation of the decisive cadential progression
I_4^6-V^7 to the tonic key. This cadenza had been improvised in Philipp Emanuel's
time (when it also appeared in slow movements), but Mozart often wrote it out.
     This plan was filled out by Mozart in a much more flexible way than the
rounded binary form in the symphony. The relationship of first solo to first
tutti, for example, was variable; also the relationship of the material in the
second solo to what went before was apt to be looser than in the corresponding
modulatory section after the repeat sign of the rounded binary. The static key
of the first tutti (it cadenced in the tonic) encouraged a greater variety both of
themes and—especially in the first solo—of abrupt episodic modulations to
remote keys.
     As for their overall form, concertos were usually in three movements,
fast, slow, fast, with the symphonic minuet and trio usually (but by no means
always) excluded. Slow movements tended to be andante rather than adagio, a
tempo more characteristic of the symphony. Finales were fast and brilliant,
often rondos or modified rondos. Thus the plan of the concerto was in fact more
conservative than that of the symphony, while its contents were brought abruptly
up-to-date: in his Viennese concertos Mozart seemed to leapfrog the step-by-step
development the symphony had gone through from 1765 to 1775, filling the old
concerto plan with the sounds of the new music in a freer, looser way. The
concertos turned out to be less cogent, but also less uniform, more individual
than the symphony. Aside from the general features described, Mozart's concertos proceed in a fascinating variety of ways, with the result that each has its
own expressive character.
     The concertos from 1782 to 1784 tend to have more formal variety in
second and third movements than the later ones: the third movement of K. 413
(F) is in *tempo di menuetto*. K. 414 (A) preserves the old-fashioned cadenza in
the slow movement, and K. 415 (C) has an adagio interlude in the finale. The

finale of K. 449 (E flat) begins in a bright allabreve, then eventually enters a dark modulation, ending with a fast six-eight section; this "finale of the finale" is not uncommon, bearing an interesting resemblance to a comic-opera finale.

The famous Concerto K. 450 (B flat) establishes its character at the outset with a chromatic passage for winds doubled in thirds—a kind of chromaticism more and more frequent in Mozart. The slow movement, while still the usual andante, has the heartfelt simplicity more typical of the symphonic adagio. In K. 453 (G) the andante is troubled by an intrusion in minor; contrasts such as this become more and more frequent. In the following Allegretto there is another contrasting passage marked by chromatic syncopations, then a Presto finale so extended as to be a fourth movement.

The concertos of the next two seasons, 1784–1785 and 1785–1786, become progressively more profound and full of character, often through the interpolation of highly contrasting elements. K. 456 (B flat) has a slow movement in G minor, an unusual procedure. This slow movement is marked *Andante un poco sostenuto,* as if to approach the solemn style of the symphony; its minor character is relieved by a section in tonic major. In K. 459 (F) an otherwise bright finale includes a startlingly learned episode in D minor made of intricate counterpoint, in which strings are doubled by winds throughout.

The next concerto, K. 466 (D minor), is demonic in a way that goes back to Haydn's "Lamentation" Symphony (no. 26, 1765); but its lyrical slow movement is called a *Romanza,* from *romance,* the current French term for sentimental song. The last concerto of the season, K. 467, begins in a very special atmosphere, somewhat solemn, somewhat festive, using a very broad, simple style Mozart reserved for works in C major. In this broad style, increasingly frequent toward the end of Mozart's life, solo figuration tends to take up more space than tutti themes, and slow-moving harmonies tend to be enlivened by decorative chromaticism rather than full-fledged modulation, although, of course, the regular structural modulations go on as usual.

The next season, 1785–1786, brought three concertos, each very different from the other. K. 482 (E flat) is in the broad style of the C-major concerto just described. K. 488 (A), a smaller work, lives in its own world; it is lyrical throughout, yet the first movement still has room for a contrasting, marchlike phrase of remarkable poignancy, first presented by strings, *piano,* toward the end of the first solo. The slow movement of this concerto is Adagio (unique among these concertos) and in F-sharp minor, a haunting siciliano. The third concerto, K. 491, is one of those C-minor works in which Mozart shows his "demonic" power, a quality that profoundly impressed his contemporaries.

HAYDN AND MOZART: STRING QUARTETS In spite of Mozart's growing originality, exemplified especially in these last three concertos, there was something still to learn from Haydn. The most important impact on Mozart during the early 1780s came from a new set of quartets Haydn published in 1781 as Op. 33. Haydn described these quartets, the first since Op. 20 (1771), as being in a "new, entirely original manner." If addressed to the uncritical amateur, then Haydn's remark might mean only that the intense seriousness of Op. 20 had been replaced by a lighter tone such as Haydn had adopted in the intervening symphonies. If, on the other hand, the remark was addressed to the connoisseur, then it might have a subtle, profound meaning concerning the most refined aspects of musical form. Mozart, often a helpful barometer of style around him, regarded these quartets of Haydn with special reverence and was moved to write six of his own, which are among his most remarkable works. Clearly there was something important about these quartets Op. 33. Indeed, in the subsequent history of quartets they represent a turning point.

The change to a lighter character apparent to the naïve amateur is far from insignificant, for this change is the outward aspect of a deeper change to a more integrated structure. The rich character, the expressive violence of the German symphony, reflected in Op. 20, gives way at this point to a more balanced, refined style. Expressive effects are achieved more economically; details count for more; outward shapes are carried out more clearly. No one ingredient is responsible, rather the way all ingredients are proportioned, harmonized, and balanced off against one another.

The compound is so perfect that perhaps it escapes analysis. Stated roughly, there seems to be an integration of the different levels of composition so that details play a greater and greater role in the unfolding of the whole, and in return the weight of the whole is brought to bear upon details, giving them an importance far beyond their intrinsic nature. The intense continuity of the early 1770s, which fused whole sections of a fast movement together in an onward rush, was relaxed after 1780 to permit clearer articulation and greater variety. High excitement was sometimes sacrificed for grace and elegance—still full of energy, but with room for other things too.

The reduction of excitement between Op. 20 and Op. 33 is startling, so much so that it is sometimes hard to see and hear the new sense of balance and integration. Op. 33 tends to sound light, even trivial, especially in those performances which patronizingly impose a largely unwarranted humorous interpretation to make up for the apparent lack of content. Haydn's succeeding quartets returned to a more substantial tone, eloquent and profound rather than violent. Example 110, from Op. 50 (six quartets written between 1784 and 1787), will more convincingly demonstrate the new manner.

Measures 1 to 16 form the first phrase, largely held together by the harmonic progression. The opening three measures define the key, D major, through the standard functions IV and V, placed in a relatively fast-moving progression tightly focused on the tonic. The remainder of the sixteen-measure phrase is more leisurely in its harmonic movement, most of it built on only two basic functions—first the tonic itself (meas. 4 to 10), relieved by $V_2^{\overset{6}{4}}$ and IV_4^6 over the pedal, both hardly more than rich passing sonorities. Then, at measure 11, the harmony shifts decisively to IV_5^6, an unstable chord with a dark quality due to a chromatic alteration, yet one whose function relative to the tonic is never in doubt. The return to tonic takes place rapidly in measures 14 and 15.

The clarity of the harmonic foundation is in sharp contrast to the variety of rhythmic and melodic figuration, changes of texture and sonority—and essential to making this variety hang together into a phrase. Each change of figure and texture has some function relative to the chord it accompanies; for example, syncopations in the second violin intensify the chromatic alteration, as does also the dynamic marking *piano*. In general the variety of detail animates the slow-

EXAMPLE 110   HAYDN: BEGINNING OF STRING QUARTET OP. 50, NO. 6

EXAMPLE 110 (CONTINUED)

EXAMPLE 110 (CONTINUED)

EXAMPLE 110 (CONTINUED)

moving harmonic foundation, preventing the ear from being bored with it or even from perceiving its slowness, while the foundation pulls the varied details together into intelligible musical discourse. In principle, nothing very new is going on, just that the variety is a little greater, the harmonic control a little greater, the onward rush a little less than in earlier works.

It is impossible to tell from these fifteen measures which of the many figures is the most important—or is going to become most important. Perhaps it is the figure over the tonic pedal in measures 4 and 5, perhaps the one repeated over the unstable subdominant function in measures 11 to 14. In measures 16 to 18 the composer tells us that it is neither of those, but rather the long note and rapid fall of the very first measure, now treated in imitation and emphasized in three different ways at once—by returning (and being the first figure to do so); by marking the close of one harmonic phrase and the beginning of another; and by now being repeated three times in as many measures, accented with a typical Mannheim *fz* (*forzando*—"forcing"). This figure starts to stand out from the stream of varied figuration as something important. Initially unnoticed, it begins to take on the weight of the large harmonic plan, and in turn to help articulate that form.

From measure 19 Haydn starts the modulation to the dominant, and abruptly drops the opening figure for a new one as intricate as it is expressive. The modulatory progression is very simple (a stepwise descent D–C$\sharp$–B–A lies underneath) so that once again harmonic directness and figural variety work together to make something both interesting and meaningful. The dominant of the dominant (E major) is reached and firmly established with a pedal and energetic figuration; then, at that difficult moment when the discourse becomes redundant, the opening figure enters once again. During measures 26 to 29 no basic harmonic motion takes place, instead V^7 of A major (dominant now become tonic) is sustained through an open network made of the main figure in imitation against a four-note chromatic group accented with another *fz*.

The new key, thus well prepared, is confirmed in measure 30; it is expressed through relatively gracious, relaxed figures set in a simple texture over symmetrical phrases and routine harmony. Like other episodes, however, this one does not last long, but soon spends itself over suave harmonic sequences, then over another IV^6 (in A), which finally becomes noteworthy by being held so long. Then, when most expected (meas. 37) the cadence in A is avoided by an abrupt fall into F major, a remote key basically unprepared (except perhaps by the dark B flat way back at the beginning).

This is a striking effect; less violent, perhaps, than certain harmonic changes in Philipp Emanuel Bach, it has a greater, more lasting impact on the shape of the piece as a whole because it is heard in the context of the long-range progression of keys. It is not merely an F-major triad after an E major with a flat seventh, but rather the interruption of a tonic-to-dominant modulation by a remote key.

Such abrupt modulations, frequently placed and handled just like this one, give us, as it were, a brief glimpse of the reverse side of a movement. The economical, restricted tonal plan of the movement around two or three sharps is greatly enriched by this sudden flip to the area of one flat. The modulatory passage (which ceases as abruptly as it began) strengthens, not weakens, the tonal plan. Furthermore the remote episode is tied securely to what has gone before through the opening figure, hammered out with *fz*. The movement so far has been "about" this theme, which is now really a *theme*, become important through its participation in all important phases of the key plan. So unified has the movement become that this section, in fact, the whole movement, can safely end with a softer, more gracious figure that is entirely new.

The purpose of analyzing a portion of one movement of one string quartet is not to show the form or the style used by Haydn and Mozart, but rather to show that form (and to some extent style) are now expressed in terms peculiar to an individual work. It now becomes less important to know that a movement is derived from a rounded binary form, more important to see how— in a given movement—figures and keys are handled relative to each other. In this purely musical sense the new style gave the composer a way of expressing himself: each work came to have an individual character, distinct from other works. This is not necessarily a better way of writing music, not an improvement over the past; it is a new and different way of using the materials of the past.

Just as the inner structure of movements in Op. 33 was more cogent while apparently less serious, so with the overall plan of the four movements. The quartets of Op. 20 had used strong finales, even driving fugues, as a way of adding weight to the end of the quartet. In Op. 33 and subsequent quartets this procedure was definitely abandoned. The center of gravity remained in the first movement, or sometimes in the slow movement. The finale reverted to its former light, bright tone, and the quartet shape as a whole seemed, on the surface at least, to be less weighty.

In reality, however, the light finale was only another symptom of a deep, inner adjustment in the distribution of weight. Haydn's purpose was to make the quartet as a whole achieve its effect in the most economical way. This involved a finale that would confirm the basic key and predominant character of the quartet, adding its own contrasting character, to be sure, but without displacing the first movement as the principal event. This is why finales after Op. 33 were fast, almost frantic, full of many small themes but no big, important ones, given to abrupt, tangential modulations while insisting more and more on the tonic of the whole quartet. Bringing the whole to a conclusion, not making a strong impression by itself, was the new function of the finale.

Haydn's Op. 33 came to Mozart at the right moment; his own maturity now enabled him to see not merely the outward gesture but the inner logic of Haydn's new style. Challenged by a style he could not so easily reproduce, Mozart wrote his own set of six quartets between 1782 and 1785, dedicating them to Haydn. Mozart's own fair copy of some of these works is unique in showing signs of great effort in composition, contrasting with his accustomed facility in putting down in final form pieces already finished in his head. The six quartets were composed in two groups, the first consisting of three quartets composed during December and January 1782–1783, in G (K. 387), D minor (K. 421) and E flat (K. 428).

These first three quartets all have themes of striking character. The bold theme of the G-major Quartet is marked by black and white contrasts in its first two phrases. The E-flat Quartet also begins boldly, using up nine of the twelve possible notes in chromatic twists and turns. The theme of the D-minor Quartet is a pathos figure, suitable for a tragic heroine. The identity of these themes is clear from the outset; they tend to be more striking than the figuration that follows, which, although extremely varied, is fused together into long phrases of ten, fifteen, even twenty or more measures by the carefully controlled tonal progressions Mozart learned from Haydn and by his own infallible sense of melody. These three quartets tend to present, especially in their opening movements, many varied, sometimes highly contrasting musical ideas.

The other three quartets proceed somewhat differently, reflecting an even greater absorption of Haydn's idiosyncrasies. Written during the winter of 1784–1785, the quartets in B flat (K. 458), A (K. 464), and C (K. 465) begin with themes that seem at first less significant but later play a much greater role in the movement as a whole. A good indication of this role is the far-reaching development that goes on at the beginning of the second section. In the A-major and C-major quartets these sections—which now can be called *development sections*—have a power and freedom supremely expressive of the aspirations of the new music. In the C-major Quartet, especially, the development of thematic material is intense, generating a whole new theme out of the old one in a way quite different from Mozart's frequent habit of beginning the second section of a binary form with a contrasting theme (as in the B-flat Quartet).

Another indication of the Haydnesque treatment of theme is the appearance of large codas at the end of the first movement (and also the last) of the quartets in B flat and C, changing the shape of these movements to *AABA'BA'C*. The big coda first appears in the B-flat Quartet, a work whose prevailing serenity hides its important structural features. The themes themselves seem trivial, but by virtue of that very quality can pervade the entire movement and become involved in the extended development that reaches a climax in the coda. The coda of the first movement of the C-major Quartet is even more exciting, with an even more original use of the initial theme. The last movement of the A-major Quartet (a movement Beethoven took the trouble to copy out by hand) is a most remarkable example of thematic concentration. The material of the opening measures turns up everywhere, yielding only for the sake of a strikingly solemn, choralelike episode. In this movement, form, theme, and character are fused together in perfect fulfillment of Haydn's techniques.

Many other features of these six quartets invite comment. All the slow movements are profound, containing utterances whose graceful gravity has no stylistic model even in Haydn. The slow movement of the A-major Quartet is a theme and variations, which show how far the new style could carry the variation form. The trios of minuets in major tend to be dark, tragic, or wistful, while the trio of the D-minor Quartet is remarkably bright, in anticipation, perhaps, of the striking turn toward D major at the very end of the finale. The C-major Quartet has a slow introduction of deep chromatic poignancy—a bonus for this quartet that already has everything. Controlled and directed by Haydn's universal forms, animated by Mozart's melodic inventiveness and keen dramatic sense, this C-major Quartet stands beside Haydn's best quartets as a model of musical integration and originality.

FROM FIGARO TO DON GIOVANNI In 1784 the national singspiel theater in Vienna closed; even this modest attempt at German opera seemed too much for the fickle Viennese audience. Italian comedy returned to its original supremacy with skilled professionals such as Giuseppe Sarti (*I Due litiganti*), Vicente Martín (*La Cosa rara*), and Giovanni Paisiello (*Il Barbiere di Siviglia*) easily capturing the public's favor. Germans might have created the new symphony, but it was extremely difficult for a German-speaking composer—even for the Austrian Mozart—to beat an Italian at his own comic game.

Composing opera was never a completely free choice in those days; much, if not all, depended on what would sell, what singers were available, what financial and managerial arrangements could be made. Mozart was as sensitive to these conditions as anyone, as was shown by his habit of composing most of an opera after it was already in rehearsal, so as better to capitalize on the abilities of the singers (or minimize their deficiencies). *Le Nozze di Figaro* (*The Marriage of Figaro*) was carefully selected by Mozart and his shrewd librettist, Lorenzo da Ponte, as likely material for a success. Coming from Beaumarchais' French comedy that was banned in Austria because of its social implications, the story was a sequel to *The Barber of Seville,* Paisiello's already successful comedy.

In setting this libretto Mozart took pains to follow the procedures of Italian comedy. The recitative was vivacious, and arias, though relatively simple, were sharply pointed toward the appropriate dramatic character. Mozart lavished great care on the ensembles, especially the long, varied finales traditional in comic opera. What differentiates Mozart's work from those of his Italian competitors is its greater musical density. His recitatives are meticulous; the arias are much more elaborate in modulation and orchestration. "The accompaniment is too full," said one amateur observer, echoing a frequent reaction that Mozart was too dissonant and confusing. The very musical qualities that appeal to us repelled the more casual elements in the Viennese audience.

Figaro is an inexhaustible supply of musical treasures; everyone finds something of special value for himself. Perhaps this is the essential nature of Mozart's achievement. Instead of appealing to all on the basis of universal types, as did the old opera, Mozart appealed to each individually through a rich variety of musical effects. He was able to do this, to raise comic opera to a new level without changing its external appearance (let alone reforming it), because he brought to it the flexibility of rhythmic figure and modulation of symphony and string quartet.

Sometimes, to be sure, Mozart's effects are indigenous to comedy—effects any good Italian composer would have produced if he could, such as the electrifying close of Figaro's *Non più andrai* at the end of Act I (*Cherubino alla vittoria!*). The intricate variety yet magic cohesiveness of the ensembles (such as the terzett *Cosa sento!* of Act I) probably lay beyond the reach of the Italians, who lacked the symphonic experience of theme-key integration. In the finale, Count and Countess step free for a moment from the net of intrigue, as the Count asks pardon of his wife. The idea was not new in comedy, but Mozart gave it an especially convincing treatment. This brief moment, rich in human truth, is made so by the placement of abruptly simple music in the midst of the usual hectic finale. The unexpected change gives the plain chords and melodies an intensity all out of keeping with their intrinsic nature. Such a procedure was native to the symphony and quartet, in which details were so placed in the larger form as to derive their power from it.

Figaro is often held up as a model of characterization, which it is; but when we look for the specific musical causes, they escape us. The melodies sung by the several characters do not really show, upon analysis, the strong individuality they seem to have in the heat of an ensemble. What really happens is of greatest importance for Mozart's concept of musical drama. The music itself is intensely and persistently interesting, expressive, compelling in its own character and individuality. The personages, exquisitely drawn in the libretto, catch and focus the intense tone of the music, giving it dramatic individuality, and getting affective substance in return. The division of labor between text and music (a division characteristic of Italian opera but less often of Northern imitations) is in principle very sharp, being hidden only by Mozart's perfect artistry. The illusion is complete—and no less effective for seeing how it is done.

Figaro was performed in the spring of 1786; it was successful, but only for a short season, being run off the stage by Martín's *Cosa rara*. Only in Prague was Mozart's success with *Figaro* complete. On the strength of that success, Mozart was commissioned to write another opera specially for Prague, which turned out to be *Don Giovanni*. In between, Mozart turned again to instrumental composition.

Now fully mature, he had tested himself against the most advanced works of Haydn and also against the best commercial products of the Italians. His previous concertos had shown a wealth of original ideas; now they became authoritative. The last three concertos, K. 503 (C, 1786), K. 537 (D, 1788), and K. 595 (B flat, 1791) are very large works, made large through a tremendous inner harmonic expansion, already begun in the concertos of 1785 in C and E flat. Here, as there, the thematic material seems to become simpler, especially if we consider only the first appearance of a theme; but the power of the expanded key plan gives these simple tunes more and more weight, so that the little march *à la Marseillaise* in the C-major Concerto, for example, eventually takes on heroic proportions.

The expansion of harmony is perhaps best studied in the string quintets, where it is combined with the greater thematic cogency characteristic of the string quartet. Mozart's quintets become especially significant when we consider the lesser interest of those quartets Mozart wrote after the famous six already discussed. In 1788 he had received a commission from the king of Prussia for six more, but for one reason or another finished only three. One other isolated quartet was written in 1786. After *Figaro* Mozart seemed to turn to the quintet as he had turned to the concerto earlier—these were forms in which he could more easily establish his independence from Haydn. In 1788 Mozart wrote two string quintets, C (K. 515) and G minor (K. 516), and rewrote an earlier wind quintet in C minor (K. 406). These, too, are large works, with a largeness made inexpressibly fuller by the increasing freedom of modulation, especially a type of transitory modulation that exploited the fringe areas of a key without actually leaving it.

A famous example is found near the beginning of the C-major Quintet. After an extremely broad opening (compare the compact, striking themes of the first three quartets dedicated to Haydn), Mozart drops abruptly into C minor, then for a moment into D-flat major (Example 111). This latter key, however, is not really established, lacking the usual cadential progression through some subdominant function. What the D-flat area really represents is not so much a short modulation as a long expansion of a single chord, the augmented sixth chord on A flat that proceeds to a six-four on G—an extremely important progression around 1800, destined to be exploited in many ways.

Mozart reveals what he is up to only by degrees. First he presents a six-four on A flat, quite unprepared; this resolves through a simple sixth chord, and can be understood as the now traditional Neapolitan sixth chord in an unusual position. Then, over a long pedal on A flat, he puts the six-four in company with a seventh chord heard as dominant to D flat. Finally, as the texture gets increasingly intricate, the dominant seventh turns into the augmented sixth chord that it really is (at least in terms of the overall harmonic curve); but now the resolution to a six-four on G, in C major, sounds as fresh as the preceding digression. In the recapitulation this digression is extended by exchanging the six-four on A flat (as if tonic in D-flat major) for a minor six-four on G sharp (as if tonic in C-sharp minor). The sleight of hand that then achieves the return to C major shows Mozart steadily exploiting the sense of transition through the more remote reaches of the triadic system.

The tangential effect of modulation in Philipp Emanuel Bach is here replaced by a broadening of the original tonic to include as actual key areas those functions previously represented by single chords. The remote episode we saw in Haydn's Quartet in D came as a contrast toward the end of a section. Here in the C-major Quintet it happens even before the work is fairly under way. The quintets contain a wealth of interesting, expressive detail; they possess each a highly individual character (especially the G minor) and together share a gravity unheard in Mozart or the new German style. More striking than all these features, however, and in large measure responsible for them, is the breadth of perspective opening up on the tonal horizon.

Don Giovanni, commissioned for Prague, was a comedy of a special kind—a maverick. The well-known story of Don Juan had been used as the basis of an extremely successful work produced in Venice early in 1787; da Ponte and Mozart pounced on it for the Prague commission. Considered by itself, the Don Juan story (The Profligate Punished) was not up to the dramatic standards of

EXAMPLE III MOZART: FROM THE STRING QUINTET IN C

sophisticated Italian comedy; but as has been said, Don Juan is the kind of show everyone disapproves of and goes often to see. As in *Figaro,* the subject of *Don Giovanni* was provoking; given intense musical support, it was bound to produce the unique impression Mozart wanted to make.

Da Ponte and Mozart worked up the simple story into operatic dimensions with two pairs of lovers (Don Ottavio and Donna Anna, and—in singspiel character—Masetto and Zerlina), a *parte seria* (Donna Elvira), and a *parte buffa* (Leporello, the servant type of the old slapstick intermezzo). Mozart handled the terzetts (for example, *Ah! Chi mi dice mai,* Act I) with an increasingly successful blend of symphonic flexibility and dramatic truth. As a musical tour de force he included a famous scene in which three orchestras play three different pieces (in different meters) all at once as accompaniment to dancing, a vocal ensemble, and a tense intrigue. Most famous, however, was the finale in which the Don, confronted by the ghost of the Commandant he killed, is dragged unrepentant down to hell.

Spectacles such as infernal scenes, earthquakes, and supernatural visitors had been standard if not essential to opera from its beginning; they went back all the way to Orpheus's trip to the underworld in the original pastoral drama. Such spectacles now contributed as much to comic relief through caricature as to dramatic excitement. But what made *Don Giovanni* such an impressive work was the musical intensity with which Mozart supported the "tragedy" of the Don. During this infernal scene the comic elements drop away, leaving the hellish fate of the Don as pure drama—an effect accomplished completely through the exciting orchestral language, the stern musical settings for the statue and the offstage chorus. So convincing was the effect that later generations had the work conclude with the Don's descent into the smoking pit, omitting the rest of the finale devoted to the traditional wrap-up of the plot. Nowadays we see that this conclusion is essential to the original conception of the work as a whole—and by no means an anticlimax.

HAYDN AND MOZART: SYMPHONIES   It was with reference to *Figaro* and *Don Giovanni* that Haydn later refused an operatic commission for Prague: how, he said, could he compete with such success? But during these same months Haydn was achieving his own success with the symphony. In 1785–1787 he wrote a set of six symphonies for Paris, as follows:

No. 82	C	("L'Ours")
No. 83	G minor	("La Poule")
No. 84	E flat	
No. 85	B flat	("La Reine")
No. 86	D	
No. 87	A	

These works were as definitive for the symphony as the Quartets Op. 33 had been for the string quartet. As with the quartets there were no striking novelties, only a deep inner balance that showed off all the usual features to best advantage. In the early 1770s Haydn's symphonies had sometimes seemed to fill their dimensions to overflowing. Later, toward 1780, the dimensions sometimes seemed too big for the musical energy. After 1785 there were no such problems, but rather a perfect matching of dimension with energy, of the individual character produced by integration of theme and key with the universal appeal required of a symphony.

For in the symphony the techniques of the string quartet acquired color and grandeur; here the new music became accessible not just to the connoisseur but to the bourgeois music lover, its new audience. In return, the procedures of the string quartet developed by Haydn enabled the symphony to speak in universal terms, valid for all men. The language spoken by the new Germans had typically been an individual language that came from the heart of the composer; Haydn in his mature symphonies made sure that the message would reach the hearts of this new, universal audience. Haydn's symphonies after 1785 climaxed and concluded his search for a new, varied representation of human passion.

Three of these six "Paris" symphonies have a slow introduction, which in itself was no novelty, but appeared now more frequently for added solemnity in large public concerts. The first movements themselves now attain striking character with a minimum of means. The actual musical materials of the D-major Symphony, for example, are not much more complex than those of the earlier D-major symphonies we studied, but even from its beginning (after the Adagio introduction) the Allegro spirituoso seems to have something significant to say. As is now often the case, the Allegro begins softly, then soon turns into a fortissimo tutti for the driving modulation to the dominant, a passage no longer allowed to overshadow the whole section, but kept in its place. The dominant key is marked first by a reappearance of the opening theme, something Haydn often did, then by an all-new theme, something he did less often. There is the usual closing tutti.

Refinement and control do not necessarily mean absence of energy: the tuttis still have plenty of thunder. But the shape of this (and other) opening sections is now eminently clear. Less complex than the analogous sections of string quartets, these symphonic forms are more colorful and forceful in their alternation of tutti with flexible solo groups, sometimes strings or winds alone, but also subtle mixtures of strings and winds.

Although slow movements can still be in binary form (no. 83), they also take other forms. The favored alternative consists of a lyrical melody in a major key, presented (often in a miniature binary form) as a closed entity, and followed by a contrasting section in tonic minor; the movement as a whole then proceeds in an alternation between these two sections, sometimes in a pattern as simple as *ABABA*, sometimes with variations, sometimes with a long, free coda (no. 82). In any case the shape of the movement involves recurring contrast of self-contained, static sections—a shape very different from the forward drive and development found in first movements.

One slow movement (no. 86), called "Capriccio," preserves something of the shape of a rounded binary, but without repeats and in a free, individual manner. Here as in the quartet, the specific shape of a given movement, and its function within the symphony of which it is a part, is more important than the shape from which it is derived. So with the Adagio to no. 87, which presents the same material twice, the first time modulating to the dominant, the second time not; in between there is a short transition using the principal theme, and at the end a coda on the same theme. The point of such a movement lies in the long, lyrical melodies, the graceful figuration of leisurely harmonies, and especially in the poignancy eventually bestowed on the principal theme, in itself almost insignificant, by its persistent reappearance throughout the movement.

Finales are often cast in rounded binary form, but here, too, there are alternatives. In no. 85 the finale is a rondo (not an uncommon solution) and in no. 87 the finale is a very interesting adaptation of a rounded binary. In this movement the binary form is "unrounded," that is, there is no recapitulation, contrary to Haydn's established handling of the binary form for over a decade. Instead, after the B section has run its full course, arriving at and establishing the tonic after a suitable lapse of time, the principal theme reappears intact at the very end as a coda. This gives the impression of a rondo—and like the rondo, serves to pull together the four movements of the symphony into a whole by making the ending, in one way or another, an especially impressive, decisive statement of a familiar theme. As in the quartet, Haydn was concerned in these symphonies more and more with the cohesiveness of the work as a whole; the whole must have shape and character, even if this meant sometimes denying individual movements the intense character they had had before.

During the summer of 1788, Mozart wrote three large symphonies, no. 39 in E flat (K. 543), no. 40 in G minor (K. 550), and no. 41 in C (K. 551). He had not shown a sustained interest in the symphony since the early 1770s, the intervening symphonies (K. 297, D—"Paris"—1778; K. 319, B flat, 1779; K. 338, C, 1780; K. 385, D—"Haffner"—1782; K. 425, C—"Linz"—1783; K. 504, D—"Prague"—1786) being for isolated occasions. Contrary to long-standing legend, it now seems probable that Mozart composed his last three symphonies for some particular occasion, possibly a subscription concert—and probable (if not certain) that they were performed before his death. It also seems reasonable to suppose that the stylistic stimulus for these three symphonies came once more from Haydn, that Haydn's "Paris" symphonies fired Mozart's symphonic imagination just as Haydn's Op. 33 had inspired Mozart to take up the string quartet again. Mozart's three symphonies have the same large dimensions, the same breadth and assurance found in Haydn's "Paris" symphonies—and only there; no other models were available.

Mozart's E-flat Symphony has an Adagio introduction, like Haydn's no. 84 in E flat; in other respects as well, especially in the character of the finale, Mozart's E flat is the most Haydnesque of the three. Mozart's G minor, like Haydn's, is demonic. Each composer wrote only two symphonies in G minor, the earlier pair around 1770. Mozart's G minor begins softly, as Haydn often did (even though not in no. 83); what is remarkable about Mozart's beginning is that the soft section goes on for so long, delaying the demonic outburst (except for a short punctuation) until the modulatory passage. A comparison with Mozart's earlier G-minor Symphony shows among other things how much more intense detail is packed into his later work. The second movement, for example, is extremely rich in expressive chromaticism and intricate figuration. The strangely wistful minuet is in a learned, contrapuntal style, orchestrated again in those curious doublings of winds and strings. The finale begins with a most ordinary tune in binary form, followed by one of the most extraordinary "juggernaut" passages he ever wrote. Such effects, along with the fantastically disordered presentation of the tune after the double bar, make Mozart's G minor a unique version of a now familiar German syndrome.

The C-major Symphony, Mozart's last, uses that solemn, festive tone noticed before in the C-major concertos. The first movement is moderate in tempo and inclined to be repetitive in its larger shape; but the detail is intricate and intense, as in the soft contrapuntal sections that alternate with the opening tuttis. The finale, too, is contrapuntal, as Haydn's sometimes were, but the counterpoint is used to intensify the texture, not control the form (as it might in a real fugue). More important, the counterpoint catches fire, ignited by the triumphant glory that springs from, then transcends, Mozart's comic style in *Figaro*.

Throughout these last three symphonies we are increasingly aware that Mozart was more than twenty years younger than Haydn. The form of the symphony, its basic conception, is Haydn's; having laid out its new proportions, Haydn seemed more and more concerned that nothing should obscure them. Much of the difference between the symphonies of Haydn and Mozart can be traced to the fact that Mozart had a model in front of him, Haydn had none. This gave Mozart the opportunity—and the obligation—to make the detail of the symphonic plan more exciting and expressive.

MOZART'S LAST WORKS After these three symphonies Mozart's output slackened somewhat. For a few months in 1789 he wrote almost nothing at all, except for the limpid clarinet quintet (for Stadler, the famous clarinetist), and the unending flow of dances, marches, occasional music that he wrote like breathing. Then came an imperial commission for a comedy, the subject, *Così fan tutte*, being specified. Da Ponte's libretto was a miracle of sophistication, and Mozart gave him music to match. The result was perfect—but perfect comedy.

By now, other possibilities were opening up in Mozart's imagination, and the ideal of a serious musical drama was always with him. The more his musical imagination and technical control grew, however, the more seldom external opportunity seemed to present itself. After *Così fan tutte* (winter, 1790), Mozart busied himself with two more profound string quintets (K. 593, D, and K. 614, E flat), the last pianoforte concerto (K. 595, B flat), and two mighty works for musical clock! (K. 594, Adagio-Allegro in F minor, and K. 608, Phantasie in F minor). With normal outlets cut off, he seemed to be entrusting his most weighty utterances to stranger and stranger media.

Then during 1791 Mozart received three major commissions, each peculiar and with peculiar results. The current fad in Viennese musical theater was the magic opera of Emmanuel Schikaneder, where singspiels using exotic or fantastic material were enlivened with magical illusions, assorted live animals, and comic stage business featuring Schikaneder himself. This resourceful manager approached Mozart at a time when Mozart had few pupils, no commissions or concerts in sight, and was plagued with domestic problems—a low point in his career. Mozart was always eager to write musical drama, but also eager to write a good one—hence choosy about librettos. Now his only opportunity was—a magic opera! It must have seemed a sorry end to a decade that had begun with *Idomeneo* and included *Figaro*. Serious German opera seemed to recede further and further from Mozart's grasp.

During the summer of 1791 Mozart and Schikaneder (or perhaps a ghost

writer named Gieseke) set to work on a fantasy using ancient Egyptian materials about a young Prince Tamino, who rescues his beloved Pamina from the
clutches of the sinister high priest Sarastro, with the aid of the Queen of the
Night, who gives Tamino a *magic flute*. The work was to be a singspiel with
simple songs and spoken dialog; the Queen of the Night was to be a *parte seria*
with grand arias. There were two trio groups, one of the Queen's Ladies and
the other of the three *genii* assigned by the Queen to guide Tamino. A *parte
buffa* was provided for Tamino's companion, Papageno the bird catcher (played
by Schikaneder). The work went forward: Mozart completed most of the first
act, composing beautiful music for this nonsensical stage business, including a
thrilling opening scene in which Tamino barely escapes from a dragon; ensembles for the Ladies; a sentimental song for Tamino; a comic song for
Papageno; a big aria for the Queen; a quintet; and two duets, a sinister one for
Pamina and the villiain Monostatos, and a sentimental one for Pamina and
Papageno.

Then something happened—just what we are not sure. In June a similar
work (*The Magic Zither*) appeared on a rival stage with great success; some
believe that Mozart and Schikaneder hastily revised their *Magic Flute* so as to
offer better competition. Indeed, the second half of *Magic Flute* is completely
inverted: Sarastro turns out to be good, the Queen evil, and instead of rescuing
Pamina, Tamino joins her in the initiation rites into the religious order of which
Sarastro is high priest. The inversion is accomplished in a highly dramatic
recitative near the beginning of the finale of Act I. In a play whose dramatic
logic was none too strong in the first place, the confusion was now complete.

It is claimed, on good grounds, that from this point on the play has to be
read as an allegory in which the Queen represented the Empress Maria Theresa,
and Sarastro's society the Freemasons, who had been persecuted by Maria
Theresa and were at that very moment under imperial ban in Austria. Now
Mozart was by this time both a desperate composer and a dedicated Freemason;
it would have been entirely in character for him to join in capitalizing on a bad
break with a daring allegory bound to arouse public interest. In any case, the
music he provided for the rest of the show, beginning with the dramatic recitative already mentioned, seems as different from that already completed as the
reasonableness of Sarastro's Day from the Queen's nefarious Night.

The curious genesis of *Magic Flute* was paralleled by the other two commissions of 1791. One, brought by a mysterious stranger, was for a Requiem
Mass. (This commission turned out later to be from a nobleman who passed off
such commissions as his own handiwork.) In deep personal trouble, depressed,
and in ill health, Mozart was startled by the commission; he eventually came to
think of it as supernatural and of the Requiem as his own, his last work. The
Requiem is full of intense, tortured music, a highly individual treatment of
texts that had for a long time summoned up solemnity and pathos. Mozart did
not live to finish it.

The third commission was outwardly what Mozart had waited years for—
an imperial summons to write a ceremonial serious opera, *La Clemenza di Tito*
(Metastasio), in honor of the coronation of the emperor as king of Bohemia in
Prague. But the text was now uninteresting, the circumstances unfavorable;
written in great haste during August of 1791, it only shows how far Mozart was

now from traditional opera, how totally inadequate the old framework was for his new musical thoughts. As late as *Idomeneo,* serious Italian opera seemed to be the path to new German music-drama. Now Mozart discovered that the path led elsewhere.

Back in Vienna *Magic Flute* was put in rehearsal, and performed on September 25. In spite of a slow reception, Schikaneder kept repeating the work, and soon it was a profound, abiding success; in a sense, Mozart's first. It is clear from his music that Mozart now attributed new and deeper significance to this erratic play. From the moment when an invisible voice cries "Back! Back!" (finale, Act I), a strange solemnity settles over the music. This recitative is infiltrated by simple yet profound phrases such as the Andante for the priest and invisible choir ("Soon, young man, or never!").

Hereafter even the most hilarious comic business takes on a new meaning, as when Monostatos and the slaves are sent marching spellbound off the stage singing *Das klinget so herrlich, das klinget so schön!* A comparison to the analogous close of Act I in *Figaro* (*Non più andrai*) shows how brilliant comedy has here been transmuted into something else. But the most impressive music is contained in Sarastro's two arias in Act II, *O Isis und Osiris,* and *In diesen Heil'gen Hallen,* in which singspiel simplicity becomes musical gravity of the most extraordinary sort.

Whatever the intended allegory—and the music tells us that allegory of some sort was intended—it seemed as though Mozart here leaped beyond textual allegory to invest dramatic music with a new kind of significance. Confronted with the fact of professional failure and the probability of death, Mozart seemed now to give up the hopeless task of following operatic fashion, of beating Paisiello and Dittersdorf and the rest at a game that no longer seemed to matter, to turn at last to a kind of musical drama that only he wanted to write. From that moment on, anything could happen, such as the eerie fugue with chorale, sung in ominous octaves by the two Armed Men at Tamino's initiation, and later the solemn march for flute (the magic flute), winds, and kettle drum; but the magic is all in the music, now, not in the flute. The motives already introduced in the first act are, of course, drawn together at the end, but no matter what their stylistic origin, all elements are illuminated from within by the new solemnity. What Haydn was doing in the symphony, Mozart now did in opera; the simplest things now acquired profound significance through careful place-ment. A new sense of unique, inner form liberated the composer from inherited, external forms.

HAYDN'S LAST WORKS At the time of Mozart's death (December 6, 1791) Haydn, now almost sixty, was in England preparing for his final triumph. No longer employed by a court but by the Universal Audience (through the concert agent Salomon), Haydn went to London to compose and conduct twelve great symphonies, those now known as the "London" symphonies, nos. 93 to 104. Aside from the regular use of slow introductions, these works contain no struc-tural novelty. They are filled with abundant musical invention, expressed with a noble simplicity which Haydn felt was appropriate to a London bourgeois audience and which corresponded to the stylistic stage Haydn himself had reached. He wrote no more symphonies after these, and it is hard to see how they would have been different if he had. Until further subtle changes took place in the relationship of tonal materials to symphonic dimensions, these dimensions could be filled in no more balanced way than Haydn now filled them.

Understanding and assessing these mature symphonies is an exercise in balancing historical against aesthetic judgment. The works are not necessarily more interesting or expressive than Haydn's earlier symphonies; in fact, they are sometimes less so, especially since they are so familiar. Nor do these later works represent a more advanced and therefore better state of music. They do represent, however, a stage of development in which the ingredients (often sharply contrasting) of the German symphony were brought into the most efficient relationship, one in which each ingredient was used just enough and no more, in which the effect of one supported the next without detracting from it—and this all the way from details such as choice of figuration to higher levels such as the balance of stable key areas against modulatory passages.

This most harmonious combination of elements meant the loss of some of those extreme effects prized by earlier symphonists. On the other hand, it produced a ''classic'' appearance that made Haydn's last symphonies the norms of future symphonic conception, whether or not these norms were observed in symphonic composition. Future generations looked back to these works; the earlier symphonies were forgotten, to be discovered only in our own time. This is why Haydn's mature symphonies were for a long time regarded as a beginning, whereas actually they stand at the end of forty years of development.

Back in Vienna in 1795, Haydn continued writing string quartets, of which the most famous set is Op. 76 (nos. 1 to 6, 1798). These are masterworks, the fruit of thirty years of development, structurally fascinating as well as profoundly expressive. Like the ''London'' symphonies, however, they present no great novelty. More significant stylistically are the large works for chorus and orchestra. Haydn took up the mass again, after a lapse of fourteen years. It is true that concertato masses had been discouraged during the 1780s by imperial decree; but it is also true that since Mozart had written very few mature masses, sacred concertato music offered an opportunity—the only one—of doing something new.

Between 1796 and 1805, when he stopped composing, Haydn wrote six masses and two oratorios. All the masses are large works that make full use of traditional concertato textures as well as the modern orchestral language born in the symphony. Unlike Haydn's earlier masses, however, the relationship of solo voice to chorus now became fluid. Solos tended to be shorter (if present at all), avoiding full-scale arias; the chorus now alternated with or accompanied the solo; especially effective use was made of the solo quartet for short, contrasting passages. With a flexibility approaching that of a Mozart comic finale, Haydn introduced light and shade into the sacred concertato style.

The concertato mass had a long history behind it. It had a traditional shape and traditional devices, which Haydn often retained. Because both the text of the mass and its musical shape were familiar to all and because modern music was symphonic in essence, Haydn was not particularly concerned with writing music that illustrated the meaning of every single phrase of text, but rather with setting the well-known text to music that was exciting, clearly shaped, and expressive in its own inner drive.

When setting *Kyrie eleison*, then, Haydn was not writing a piece about "Lord, have mercy!" nor did he write devout, prayerlike music for *Dona nobis pacem* (Grant us peace!). In both cases he needed vigorous, dynamic sections to open and close the mass. When the first *Kyrie* was preceded by a slow introduction, this was as much to convey the effect of a symphonic introduction as the sense of the words. The tempos for fast sections are probably very fast; there is no reason to slow them down in order to make the effect more "religious." When the opening *Kyrie* is dark, as in the great "Nelson" Mass (*Missa in augustiis*, D minor, 1798), the fast tempo produces great power and majesty, qualities that, like brilliance, were for Haydn entirely appropriate to sacred texts.

Haydn's masses are full also of mystery and sentiment, the latter expressed through a type of melody that seems naïve but was actually the most refined product of the new German style. There is an excellent example in the "Theresa" Mass (1799), introduced by the alto solo, *Gratias agimus;* by the time the rest of the quartet has entered, however, the naïve tune has acquired deeper substance, so that when the tenor finally presents the tune in minor, it has accumulated the kind of intensity made possible by symphonic development.

In dealing with unfamiliar texts, Haydn took pains to communicate the specific meaning of the words, as in the two oratorios, *The Creation* (1798) and *The Seasons* (1801). Both texts were translated and arranged from English sources by the ubiquitous Baron von Swieten. For Haydn the oratorio presented yet another category in which to exercise the new style; it was the way best suited to Haydn to write modern dramatic music. The new style had been forged in the symphony, where it took its most drastic, then its clearest, most balanced form. It was the symphonic experience that permitted Haydn and Mozart to reinterpret opera and oratorio in subtly new ways that gave them new life.

13
EXPANSION OF THE SYMPHONY 1800-1830

OPERA AND CHERUBINI The thrust of the German symphony could not be completely absorbed back into the stream of opera and oratorio. To some degree, at least, there now existed a gap between modern symphonic style, on the one hand, and traditional operatic forms, on the other, a gap that persisted throughout the 1800s and beyond. The cause of the gap was primarily the new sense of symphonic continuity. The driving modulations unleashed by Haydn in the interior of the symphonic movement, within the B section of the rounded binary form, eventually surged over the whole movement, obliterating the outlines of the binary form and with them the square, dancelike periods characteristic of music around 1750.

Such driving continuity was the antithesis of traditional operatic forms. The recitative could not generate this force, and the aria could not contain it; the alternation of recitative and aria as a structural principle frustrated long-range symphonic modulation. The new symphonic language could find operatic expression only in the freely developing ensembles and finales of Italian comedy (and used in its derivatives, opéra-comique and singspiel). These free structures became, indeed, increasingly popular, overwhelming the set solo numbers even in conservative opera. Still, the sense of closed phrase was strong in opera, too strong to give full scope to symphonic momentum.

As a result, musical repertory tended to split into two parts, symphony and opera, each with its own standards, its own audience. Within Germany, and to some extent in Paris, the symphony gained a new environment (symphony halls, symphony orchestras, symphonic conductors) and a relatively progressive-minded audience. But even in Paris the symphony was overshadowed by the several forms of musical theater, while in Milan and Venice Italian opera persisted as if the symphony had never been. The opera houses were civic, now, as they were elsewhere in Europe; the audiences were bourgeois. Throughout the 1800s the world of opera remained an alternative to symphonic music, a traditional, comfortable, relatively relaxed kind of musical experience.

Mozart was the only composer who was really successful in both worlds, opera and symphony. *Don Giovanni* and *Figaro* were the last real operas that partook fully of the symphony. *Così fan tutte* stood to one side of the symphonic thrust; *Magic Flute* was far beyond opera by virtue of its unique gravity. Mozart, in other words, stood at the parting of the ways. After him, most composers were either operatic composers or symphonic composers. Such gaps, however, exert a fatal fascination on imaginative minds: the man big enough to fill the gap stood to gain a unique position for himself.

Italian opera continued to be represented after 1800 by the professional comedy cultivated by Paisiello (*The Barber of Seville*), and his brilliant rival, Domenico Cimarosa (1749–1801). The subjects of their works were varied, ranging, as they always had, from sentiment to slapstick in tone, from city to rustic village in milieu. In Paris the opéra-comique, with spoken dialog and more or less elaborate sequences of songs and choruses, continued its appeal. Two very important tendencies, apparent in opéra-comique since the 1780s, came increasingly to the fore—a tendency toward romance and adventure in exotic circumstances, and ambitions of seriousness.

The opéra-comique lived in the shadow of the tragédie-lyrique, as most recently formulated by Gluck. While not numerous, successors to Gluck existed and occasionally achieved resounding success, for example, Etienne Méhul (1763–1817), and especially Gasparo Spontini (1774–1851), whose *La Vestale* (1807), on an antique subject, created the grave effects characteristic of the tragédie-lyrique since Gluck. But Spontini's tendencies toward warm bourgeois lyricism are strong, his use of ensemble progressive. In an effective scene (finale, Act I), the several principals express their different emotions simultaneously over a *sotto voce* chorus—a fluid, magical mood that owes much to the Italian ensemble technique.

The tradition of the tragédie-lyrique, then, held out a standard of seriousness, but did not of itself provide the musical or dramatic techniques for realizing that standard in terms of modern style. As so often happens, it was the more lowly form (in this case, opéra-comique) that was flexible enough to permit change. The opéra-comique was elevated to the stature of tragédie-lyrique, while preserving its own forms and techniques.

Luigi Cherubini (1760–1842), an Italian in Paris, established himself there with *Medée* (1797); far more successful, however, was his opéra-comique, *Les Deux journées* (1800), in which there is the usual amount of sentiment and adventure, but to a degree of intensity that gives the work a quasi-serious stature. More important, the intensity is not merely scenic but musical. The very first notes of the overture are arresting, and if long stretches of the ensembles and airs seem lightweight, the melodrama quoted in Example 112 may reveal an unexpected depth of sentiment.

EXAMPLE 112   CHERUBINI: MELODRAMA FROM *LES DEUX JOURNEES*, III, NO. 12

Sostenuto assai (♩ = 66)

Armand: Personne . . . il fait
une chaleur dans le creux de
cet Arbre . . . Ah! respirons
un moment.

Armand: O ma Constance!
que vas tu devenir au mi-
lieu des dangers qui t'en-
vironnent?

Armand: Veille sur elle,
O providence! je la dé-
pose dans ton sein.

EXAMPLE 112 (CONTINUED)

Armand: Mais on vient
. . . Rentrons!
(Il se cache de nouveau
dans l'arbre.)

(No one here . . . it's warm in the hollow of this tree . . . Ah! let us rest a moment.
Oh! my Constance, what is going to become of you, surrounded by such dangers!
Take care of her, Providence! I leave her to your mercy.
Someone is coming . . . Let's hide again!)

One of the most difficult aspects of reconstructing the significance of
Haydn and Mozart is the realization that warmth of musical sentiment was a
normal, if not essential, part of musical experience all around them—and independent of them. That was the way music was; what Mozart and Haydn brought
was an ennobling of that sentiment, raising it from a bourgeois level to the realm
of an aristocracy of the spirit, and also a deepening of purely musical factors to
the point where they challenged the perceptive abilities of even the most sophisticated listener. A comparison between Cherubini's melodrama quoted in Example 112 and a comparable passage from Mozart, say, the slow movement of
the B-flat Quartet (K. 458) or of the G-minor Symphony (K. 550), makes
Cherubini seem facile, less than absorbing. Yet compared with his competitors
in the Parisian opéra-comique, Cherubini merited the applause of his age for
harmonic and orchestral richness.

BEETHOVEN   Mozart had grown up with the new style, but Ludwig van
Beethoven (1770–1827) grew up entirely in it. Symphony and sonata were
mature: there was no need for Beethoven to create new forms or develop new
techniques, for Haydn had already created them and Mozart had shown how to
apply them. Beethoven was in a position to select out of the work of Haydn and
Mozart what was most forceful and effective. Furthermore Beethoven was able to
benefit from the audience's experience with the new universal forms. He could
assume that they knew how a symphony went, which allowed him—if not forced
him—to expand and modify Haydn's clear, concise shapes. At no other time in
the history of Western music has the development of style concurred so auspi-
ciously with the maturation of a gifted composer, one whose gifts were so appropriate to that particular moment; only Josquin and Perotin are comparably
placed.

Beethoven's character and early development are best revealed in his
sonatas for pianoforte. Beginning with Op. 2 (1795), his sonatas show the forceful personality that so impressed his Viennese listeners. These sonatas also show
Beethoven making use of the fully developed forms of Haydn, as he was to do

for the rest of his life. Haydn's forms permitted the release of Beethoven's energy, gave it stylistic definition.

The full force of both style and personality is apparent in the *Sonata pathétique,* Op. 13 (1798); but it is important to remember that this is a character-piece, and as such its pathos represents only one side of Beethoven's artistic personality. Haydn's forms also permitted, in fact, demanded, the portrayal of a different character in each piece, a goal Beethoven always pursued. Thus he was writing Haydn's kind of music even when he experimented with Haydn's forms—something he did most often in the pianoforte sonatas, where there were fewer models left by Haydn and Mozart, and hence more room for experiment.

The number of movements in Beethoven's sonatas varies from two to four; sometimes a single "movement" may contain contrasts of slower and faster sections, as in the *Sonata quasi una fantasia* in E flat, Op. 27, no. 1 (1801), whose first movement begins slowly but includes a fast episode; Op. 27, no. 2, also entitled *Sonata quasi una fantasia,* also begins with a slow movement, followed then by a scherzo—Beethoven's version of the grotesque Haydn minuet— and a fierce finale.

As Beethoven passed the age of thirty, however, he addressed himself more and more to larger musical forms and ideas, following Haydn more closely as he did so. Two big sonatas from 1803–1804, Op. 53 in C ("Waldstein") and *Sonata appassionata,* Op. 57 in F minor, both have symphonic character and dimensions, even if only in three movements. The broad opening of Op. 53 (Example 113) combines slow-moving harmonies and repetitive rhythms in a way that was to be typical of Beethoven's mature style.

With the Third Symphony, *Sinfonia eroica,* Op. 55, in E flat (1803–1804), Beethoven seemed to break out of Haydn's forms, particularly in the huge coda that climaxed the first movement. Actually it was the tonal control of Haydn's form that enabled Beethoven to develop the startling rhythmic momentum of this coda. The tonal forces stored up and directed by Haydn were here unleashed to produce a whole series of works like the Third Symphony—works whose driving energy seemed to open up new realms of musical expression.

The *Sinfonia eroica* marked the beginning of one of Beethoven's most fertile periods, a fertility due partly to the composer's own abundance of musical ideas, but due partly as well to the abundance of possibilities built into the

EXAMPLE 113   BEETHOVEN: BEGINNING OF PIANO SONATA OP. 53

(etc.)

symphonic style. There was so much to do, so much that Mozart had not been given time to do. The more Beethoven did, the more, it seemed, he could do. During the three years 1805 to 1807 he finished the Fourth Symphony in B flat, Op. 60, the Fourth Pianoforte Concerto in G, Op. 58, the Violin Concerto in D, Op. 61, three string quartets, Op. 59 ("Rasumovsky"), the *Coriolan* Overture, Op. 62; all this time he was working on another symphony in C minor, which when finished in 1807 as the Fifth, Op. 67, was followed closely by yet another, the Sixth in F, Op. 68.

Whether in major or minor keys, all these works share an assurance that becomes optimism, a triumphant sense of control that springs directly from Beethoven's exuberant expansion of the frame of the symphony. Musical form was for Beethoven as much as for Haydn primarily a matter of grouping a few related chords into a key, then exploiting the contrast achieved by a change of key. We saw in Haydn how the progression of chords was slowed down so that each chord might control a longer stretch of music; it was this slowing down of the underlying harmonic progression that gave the music form and direction. Beethoven now retarded chords even more, making the sense of key stronger and more secure, then pounded the key home with his characteristic rhythmic insistence. The clear, simple key plans of Haydn controlled longer and longer stretches of music—making modulation, when it came, even more effective. It was this treatment of harmony and key that enabled Beethoven to expand the symphony from within to such heroic dimensions. This process can be studied more conveniently in the string quartet, where the same broad lyricism now often replaced Haydn's intense concentration, as in the opening of the Quartet in F, Op. 59, no. 1 (Example 114).

The slowing down of harmony had another effect exactly opposite to the breadth and stability just described—an effect most apparent in the generations following Beethoven, but noticeable already in Beethoven himself. Individual chords acquired greater meaning, because the power of the key, expressed through the individual chord, endowed it with an aura of significance. Beethoven learned how to make simple triads rich and poignant by exploiting their larger implications for the key plan. The slowing down also permitted more complex chords to be more easily heard; chords which in Haydn went by too fast to be perceived by themselves were now audible, becoming the most expressive part of the chordal vocabulary. Later composers drew more and more attention to such complex chords, invested in this way with the power of the key plan and set off so as to be easily perceived. Beethoven usually kept to simple chords, always subordinating their special effect to the larger plan; still, Beethoven's harmony seems more intense than Haydn's.

The broad harmonic rhythms put an even greater premium on the nature and control of the figuration in which these harmonies were expressed. Haydn had used the simple scales, arpeggios, and graceful turns of phrase current in the 1750s (even though he gave them a new meaning); Beethoven tried to find rhythmic and melodic patterns that were increasingly original and individual. Up to 1810 he subordinated individuality to the overall effect. He wanted his pieces to drive forward with great rhythmic energy, and so used figures that— even though original—were simple. In his later works, however, he turned to more intricate patterns.

EXAMPLE 114 BEETHOVEN: BEGINNING OF STRING QUARTET OP. 59, NO. 1

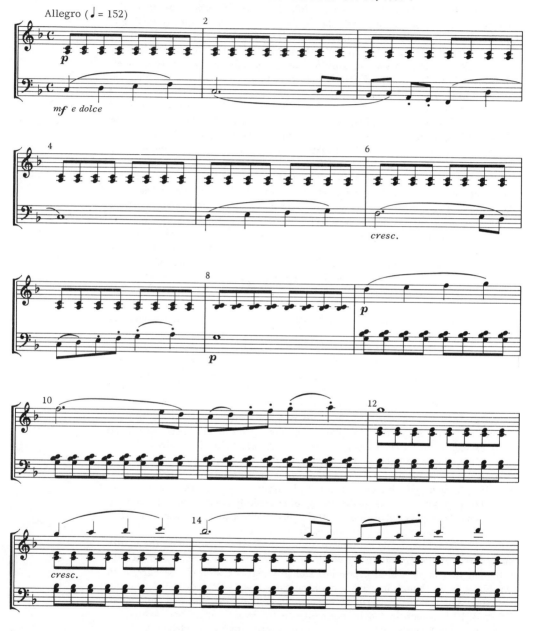

EXAMPLE 114 (CONTINUED)

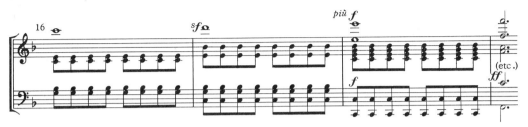

As broad areas opened up in the interior of string quartet and symphony, rhythmic patterns tended to be repeated for longer stretches of time. The result was more and more rhythmic momentum, creating an effect of dynamism and power that seemed new, even if it was only an intensification of what went on in Haydn and Mozart. Rhythmic momentum, combined with the broader tonal plan, brought about those warm surges of heroic grandeur, at once personal and universal, that were the special mark of Beethoven's style from the Third Symphony on.

Perhaps the most noticeable difference between Haydn and Beethoven (still only one of degree) lay in Beethoven's handling of themes. As Beethoven expanded the tonal plan, he paid more and more attention to working out the themes; indeed he had to, for the success of Haydn's forms depended largely on the coordination of themes with tonal plan. Themes played an increasingly important role in dramatizing the progress of a movement through its cycle of keys. In return these themes acquired more and more character from their participation in the tonal plan—not, it must be stressed, by being in themselves more complex, for if anything themes tended to get even simpler. It is easy to forget how simple the theme of the Fifth Symphony really is (Example 115). One has to imagine this first movement without its opening four measures. In the course of the first movement the thematic material of measures 5 to 8 acquires great character; but then Beethoven placed a concentrated sample of the thematic material at the very beginning, a rhetorical gesture that becomes extremely powerful when actually confirmed by the rest of the movement. The development of neutral figures into characteristic themes was first worked out by Haydn; Beethoven is here merely dramatizing this development.

Beethoven's goal was not to exalt the theme for its own sake, but to use it to sharpen the character of the movement. He made fast movements more heroic or demonic, slow movements richer and more heartfelt. Minuets, already whimsical or grotesque in Haydn, became scherzos, boisterous, driven pieces with no lingering trace of the past. But by the same logic, trios became even more naïve, genuinely rustic, equally far from courtly sophistication. These naïve trios persist through Beethoven's last works (as in the Ninth Symphony) to become a permanent feature of symphonic form.

By stressing the individual character of each movement, Beethoven deepened Haydn's universal form in the same way that he expanded its dimensions.

EXAMPLE 115   BEETHOVEN: BEGINNING OF SYMPHONY NO. 5 (reduction)

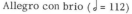

etc.

And beyond the character of the individual movement lay the overall effect of the whole symphony: the most important consideration remained the way the movements fitted together to form a unique, original unity. Beethoven's concern with the overall shape of the symphony shows up in the fusing together of the last two movements of the Fifth Symphony. Here the scherzo ends with a coda that serves also as a suspenseful introduction to the finale, which follows without a break. A similar passage is interpolated toward the end of the finale to dramatize the last return of its principal theme. Thus scherzo and finale are bound together into a larger unity—particularly important in this symphony which begins darkly, and then ends with a striking turn toward bright C major.

Beethoven interrupted work on the Fifth Symphony in order to write the Fourth in B flat, a symphony of very different character. Impressive as the Fifth Symphony is, demonic and heroic in turn, it reflects only one aspect of Beethoven's personality, only one possibility of symphonic style. The serene Fourth Symphony is just as characteristic in its own way as the symphonies that preceded and followed it. The Fourth Symphony is expanded from within in the same way as its fellows, even though its slow-moving harmonies are filled with a less urgent kind of figuration. In order to expand the scherzo to the dimensions of the other movements while retaining the rounded binary form in its original compact size, Beethoven (giving a new interpretation to an older practice) brought back the trio a second time and after it the scherzo a third time, so that the shape of the whole movement was scherzo, trio, scherzo, trio, scherzo—a solution he used again in the Seventh Symphony.

Without prejudice to the Fourth Symphony, the Fifth is clearly the most impressive work of this period in Beethoven's life, representing a high point of symphonic development. The rhythm of harmonies and keys was here brought into an optimum relationship with the detail of themes and figures, on the one hand, and with the overall shape and dimensions, on the other. The expansion had indeed been an inner one, filling the symphony with a sense of breadth and nobility but not yet extending its length unduly; the Fifth Symphony is actually not much longer than Haydn's mature works. The modulations fulfill their purpose of providing a fresh sound without becoming remote or diffuse— a problem that was to beset the symphony later.

No sooner had Beethoven finished his Fifth Symphony than he set to work on the Sixth, completed (like the Fourth) in a relatively short time. The Sixth further resembles the Fourth in being more serene than its neighbors, bearing in fact the character title *Sinfonia pastorale*. Beethoven had used such titles before, but now he went further, giving subtitles to the individual movements:

Pastoral Symphony
(expression of feeling rather than painting)

1. Awakening of joyful feeling on arrival in the country
2. Scene by the brook
3. Peasants' merrymaking
4. Storm
5. Song of thanksgiving after the storm

Since titles or "programs" were used extensively by later symphonic composers, Beethoven's use of them here calls for some observations. Programs were not a novelty in instrumental music; Haydn's own character titles stood at the end of a habit that went back at least to 1700. In his Sixth Symphony Beethoven was reintroducing such programs *after* he had shown how powerfully music could communicate without a text of any kind.

Significant here is Beethoven's hesitation about using titles at all, and his emphasis on "feeling" rather than description of nature itself—although he then proceeded to give a musical description of a thunderstorm. In terms of long-range development, it is worth noting that the symphony was the first major form that did not rely on a text as a structural outline (compare cyclic mass and opera); hence the reappearance of a text as a program is not so surprising. Finally, quite apart from Beethoven's titles, his Sixth Symphony follows Haydn's shape almost as closely as any other Beethoven symphony: first a fast movement, then a slow one, then a scherzo and trio—the return of the scherzo being cut short by, or rather for, the storm, which is interpolated before the finale. The titles merely underline the character of each movement and its function within symphonic shape; they do not replace that shape with some other.

The next two symphonies were written as a pair during 1811-1812, one energetic and one serene, like the Fifth and Sixth. The Seventh Symphony in A, Op. 92, is short on themes but long on rhythmic drive; it is one of the best examples of how Beethoven slowed down harmonies, and then filled them with energetic, repetitive rhythms. The rhythms are still simple and direct; the dance-like character they give to the whole is apt to hide the complex harmonic changes that go on beneath the surface. From this time on, Beethoven sought out unusual chord progressions and remote modulations in an effort to make the symphony ever more exciting. The rhythms of the Seventh Symphony, especially in the first and last movements, would be monotonous without the fresh chord progressions that accompany them.

Beethoven seems to have regarded the Eighth Symphony in F, Op. 93, as a favorite work—a provoking choice, for next to the energetic Seventh the Eighth Symphony seems ineffective. Upon closer inspection, this work reveals a special structural feature that (whether or not it is the feature that attracted Beethoven) is interesting in itself and important for Beethoven's further development. In the Seventh Symphony harmonies had moved in curious progressions; in the Eighth they moved in simpler progressions but in curious rhythms. The patterns of harmonic change are more intricate, as can be observed in trying to pinpoint the structural downbeats in the opening pages of the first movement, especially measures 12 to 33. The intricate harmonic rhythms are paralleled and reinforced by a new intricacy of figuration, as in Example 116. All this takes place within an overall character of stability and repose, but an acquaintance with the inner workings of this symphony will bring the kind of absorption with musical materials for their own sake that the composer himself must have experienced.

BEETHOVEN'S LAST WORKS　After 1812 Beethoven's production fell off. He no longer wrote symphonies; in fact, he avoided all the large forms. Not that he was unable to write in these forms as he had before, but having solved their problems, he seemed bored with them and anxious to find a way to carry stylistic development further. The way led through the distortion of harmony and rhythm, the involute figuration already tried in the Seventh and Eighth Symphonies, but for the time being Beethoven could not see clearly how to proceed.

In 1816 and 1817 he wrote two profound but curious pianoforte sonatas, one in A, Op. 101, the other in B flat, Op. 106 (*Hammerklavier*). The next year he made some sketches for a symphony; the year after (1819), he started work on a great mass for soloists, chorus, and orchestra. Gradually he seemed to be feeling his way toward a new phase of development. Then in 1821 and 1822 he wrote three more pianoforte sonatas—his last—using experimental shapes that recall the role the sonata had played at the beginning of his career. These sonatas interrupted work on the *Missa solemnis*, which, however, Beethoven soon finished as Op. 123 in 1822. Then he started immediately on a symphony incorporating the sketches made five years earlier.

Finished in 1824 as Op. 125 in D minor, this Ninth Symphony was fol-

EXAMPLE 116　BEETHOVEN: FROM SYMPHONY NO. 8 (reduction)

Allegro vivace e con brio (♩. = 69)

[Strings and Woodwinds]

(etc.)

lowed in rapid succession by five so-called "late" string quartets, Op. 127 in E flat, Op. 132 in A minor, Op. 130 in B flat, Op. 131 in C-sharp minor, and Op. 135 in F; these quartets, composed in this order, occupied Beethoven continuously from 1824 to 1826. Especially in the quartets, Beethoven tampered with all levels of form, from smallest detail to the arrangement of movements. Nonetheless, Beethoven's point of departure throughout three years remained the universal forms of Haydn, his goal remained Haydn's goal of a more intense, individual character for each work.

From the time of the Fifth Symphony, the development of style had tended to weaken rather than strengthen the symphonic shape. In Beethoven's Ninth Symphony the slowing down of harmony resulted in an unheard-of expansion of the size of the symphony. Each of the four movements (and each section of each movement) became much longer, making the symphony harder to grasp as an entity. Simultaneously the key plan became more diffuse, owing to Beethoven's search for fresh modulations. These were necessary for continued excitement, but they led away from strong, direct key relationships to oblique, weaker ones. The Ninth Symphony is built on the two keys D minor and B-flat major (eventually D major and B-flat major), the more obvious key relationships being avoided.

Length and diffuseness at the higher levels were paralleled by intricate fragmentation of detail. The logic of the first movement, even though still the logic of Haydn, is much harder to follow because of the great variety of figuration. Themes rarely emerge out of this boiling torrent of short, changing figures. Firmly intent on the movement's overall character, Beethoven refrained from embodying this character in any one figure.

The rounded binary form has in this piece completely disappeared, its outlines having been gradually obliterated from the time of the Third Symphony. Here are the most obvious steps in the transformation of the original dance form:

A A B B	simple binary
A A BA′ BA′	rounded binary
A A BA′ C	second repeat dropped, coda added
A B A′ C	first repeat dropped

Not only does the first repeat disappear in the Ninth Symphony, but also the clear cadences that articulated the rounded binary form are now blurred. The movement becomes continuous, with no sharp division between the *A* and *B* sections, or the *B* and *A′* sections. These sections are now identified solely by their function—the *A* section being the "exposition," *B* the "development," *A′* the "recapitulation"—since they are no longer clearly defined even by the tonal plan.

Everything about this symphony is on a vaster scale than any previous symphony. After the dark, cloudy first movement comes a demonic scherzo, a gargantuan "joke" if a joke at all, but paired with one of Beethoven's most naïve trios. The slow movement achieves its profundity in the same way as Mozart's *Magic Flute:* the simplest harmonies are presented so solemnly that they seem imbued with unutterable significance. The slow movement is virtually static, its basic harmonic motion taking place only in the remote modulations from one section to another.

section:	A	B	A'	B'	A''–A'''	Coda
key:	B flat	D	B flat	G	(G flat)	B flat

The internal structure of these sections is extremely simple, the B section being almost entirely over a single bass note.

Each of the first three movements, in other words, expresses its symphonic character, its function within the symphonic shape, so intensely that it makes sense only as a part of that shape; none of these movements could stand alone. This made structural problems acute in the finale. Should the finale provide a sharp contrast to the previous three by dispelling their intense effects with something lighter and more brilliant? Beethoven considered this solution—the usual one—having in mind a movement that eventually became the finale of the String Quartet in A minor, Op. 132. Or should the finale (for the Ninth Symphony) be powerfully triumphant, as in the other symphony in a minor key, the Fifth? This was the solution Beethoven eventually preferred, using Schiller's *Ode to Joy* sung by a chorus—a project that had intrigued him for many years. But then even more difficult problems arose. How to integrate this bright, triumphant choral finale with the three preceding movements, now that the dimensions of the symphony had been so expanded and its tonal shape made so diffuse? The simple, effective device used in the Fifth Symphony would not work here.

Beethoven's solution for the Ninth Symphony is an interesting illustration of how the symphonic form could be dramatized—quite literally, for after an abrupt introduction, the cellos, speaking in dramatic recitative, present and comment upon the themes of each of the preceding movements. Of course, the cellos cannot actually speak, but their recitative is so articulate that its meaning is perfectly clear.

Clear also is the structural significance of quoting the other three movements: this safeguards the integrity of the vast work, linking the last movement (whose theme follows immediately) directly to the preceding ones. In case the message did not get through, it is stated again, this time by a real singer declaiming in real recitative, introducing the theme of the finale in choral form. This theme, in varied form, becomes the refrain of a gigantic rondo-finale, with features of both an instrumental rondo and an operatic ensemble—the largest, most complex symphonic movement Beethoven ever wrote. The shape of the Ninth Symphony followed logically from the premise of what a symphony was and what had to be done to keep it exciting; but the Ninth Symphony stood on the threshold of tonal disorder. It was an exciting but dangerous model to hold up for the younger generation of composers.

Just as the symphony had begun, in a sense, in Haydn's string quartets, in a similar sense it ended in the last quartets of Beethoven. In these last five quartets Beethoven pursued the logic of symphonic development to its most remote consequences. Often regarded as cut off from the previous development of style, these quartets have outward shapes sometimes so different from those of Haydn, or even from those used by Beethoven himself up to that point, that it seems academic to discuss them in terms of their past. But on the other hand, the true significance of these works only becomes apparent when measured against the forms of the past. Since these works are extreme, we grasp their extremity, the lengths to which Beethoven was willing to go, only when we follow him along the path that led from Haydn.

Even though the intricate texture of these quartets is the first obstacle they present to the listener, it is their unorthodox movement plans that have provoked the most comment. For Haydn, the overall form of sonata or symphony was basically a series of contrasting movements, whose character was sufficiently varied yet sufficiently related to form a complete musical experience. Haydn's four-movement plan was the most efficient realization of this goal he could find; Beethoven was eventually willing to sacrifice some of this efficiency in favor of greater contrast and more varied character—these being Haydn's first principles.

Actually Beethoven had been adjusting the four-movement plan all his life. Slow introductions tended to infiltrate first movements, as in the *Sonata pathétique*, Op. 13, making such movements no longer one "movement" but two in alternation. Fast sections were interpolated into slow movements with the same results, as in the *Sonata quasi una fantasia*, Op. 27, no. 1. In the slow movement of the Ninth Symphony the contrast of the two themes expresses itself as an alternation of two sections, one adagio the other andante. The minuet and trio had always been treated as a sectional movement with internal contrast. Beethoven made it seem more sectional by his expansion of the form to scherzo, trio, scherzo, trio, scherzo. Recitativelike introductions to movements attracted Beethoven more and more in his later years, but the model was present already in the slow introduction to the first movement. With these realities of the development of the four-movement plan in mind, the shape of Beethoven's last quartets should appear better prepared and less mysterious.

In Op. 127 in E flat, slow introduction and first movement stand in their usual relationship. But in the next quartet, in A minor, and even more in the B-flat Quartet that followed, the slow introduction has penetrated the fast movement to a remarkable degree. In the A-minor Quartet, the real slow movement (the third) contains a contrasting faster section, while the finale is introduced by a little march.

The B-flat Quartet presents its contrasts in terms of separate movements (after the first) instead of contrasting sections within movements; thus the second movement is a relatively brief scherzo-trio, followed by a curious *Andante con moto ma non troppo/Poco scherzoso*. Here Beethoven seemed to be seeking some untouched middle ground between the character of a scherzo and that of a slow movement. This Andante is perhaps the most original, most novel of all in the late quartets. It is followed by a "German Dance" and a Cavatina (for the term, see page 433, the latter a short but extremely heartfelt slow movement. The function of the German Dance, at first glance obscure, becomes more clear when we note that it provides a fresh key (G major after movements in B-flat major, B-flat minor, D-flat major, and before E-flat major) and also a fresh naïveté normally found in the trio, which in this quartet is short and violent. The result is four shorter internal movements instead of two regular ones, but the four embody the same principles as the two. The quartet originally ended with the Great Fugue, Op. 133, which, not being well received at the first performance, was rejected by the publisher; the same audience loved the Cavatina, showing that they were judging one movement at a time. Beethoven, however, was thinking about the whole work—and in spite of its difficulties, the Great

Fugue does pull the B-flat Quartet together, making it sound more like a sonata than a suite, as it is often described.

On the score of the next quartet, in C-sharp minor, Op. 131, Beethoven wrote, "NB. Stuck together out of various odds and ends." Consisting as it does of seven sections, the work is sometimes analyzed as if Beethoven's remark was not a jest. But here, too, Beethoven carried out Haydn's principles while modifying his four-movement form. Here the slow introduction has become a very long, very poignant fugue; it is followed by the "first" movement (in D major) now much shorter and almost monothematic. The slow movement proper, a set of variations, also has an introduction, in a faster recitative character. The scherzo and trio are unmistakable, their persistent reappearance of one after the other in rotation being merely an extreme version of Beethoven's earlier handling of the scherzo. The finale, too, has a slow introduction, but is otherwise fairly regular in shape.

Like the three preceding quartets, the C-sharp minor is a unique expression of the four-movement plan, now apparently abandoned; but then this plan reappeared virtually intact in the very last quartet, Op. 135, in F. This work seems to occupy a position analogous to the Eighth Symphony; it is relatively concise and serene after the dark intensity of its predecessors. The search for character seems to have abated. Beethoven seems here once again absorbed in purely tonal problems, and delighted at their elegant solution.

In these last works Beethoven moved far out beyond the curve of development as it could be traced by his contemporaries. Succeeding composers most often took their point of departure from the Seventh Symphony or before. Occasionally they copied the external features of the Ninth Symphony, but the inner logic of the last quartets lay beyond them. Not understanding these forms, they dared not try them; and in any case Beethoven's earlier works gave them plenty to think about. Only little by little, and often on their own, did composers, following out the implications of Haydn, reproduce the stylistic development carried so far by Beethoven in his last works.

AFTER BEETHOVEN   The generation of composers after Beethoven tended to regard the strong forms created by Haydn as formalistic, unnecessarily restrictive. Consequently they viewed the changes made by Beethoven as acts of liberation. Encouraged by Beethoven's example, they proceeded to modify Haydn's forms even more. Unfortunately, however, the achievement of Beethoven presented succeeding composers with problems as well as advantages, for Beethoven had followed out the lines of development with such energy and thoroughness that there seemed but little left to do. "Who can do anything after Beethoven?" young Schubert exclaimed.

Writing a symphony became a particularly difficult problem. On one hand, each symphony had to have an individual character that would set it off from Beethoven's symphonies, while, on the other hand, the symphony, embodying the most universal forms and addressed to the widest audience, had to speak the common language more clearly than smaller, more intimate forms. In the symphony the composer had to be most individual but could least afford to be idiosyncratic. Throughout the 1800s symphonies were composed much less frequently than before, each occasioning its creator untold difficulties.

With increasing frequency composers turned toward alternate forms of expression. Often a composer would concentrate his energies on a particular alternative that seemed congenial to his special abilities, or at any rate permitted him to maintain his own identity in the face of Beethoven's accomplishment. Even more characteristic, composers tended to exercise their special abilities through inspiration, sudden insight; their first thoughts tended to be their best ones—best in the sense of most individual and convincing. While the composers might improve on their musical inspiration by working over it, the initial version tended to be the most forceful expression of their own individuality. Similarly their earlier works, products of youthful enthusiasm, were often their most successful ones. The generation of composers following Beethoven presents several examples of composers who produced brilliantly for a few short years, and then lost their inspiration—or simply died young.

SCHUBERT Franz Schubert (1797–1828) started composing songs for voice and piano as a teen-age boy; some of his best date from 1814, when he was not yet twenty. Schubert did not invent the *Lied*, or accompanied song, but he invested it with the power of the new style. Cultivated from 1750 on, the German song had at first been a protest against what was felt to be artificial bombast of the old operatic aria. Hence songs were made deliberately naïve, as "natural" and as "folklike" as possible—these being ways in which German composers could set themselves off from Italian opera. One of Schubert's songs, *Heidenröslein* (1815) was eventually taken for a genuine folk song, the highest tribute that could be accorded it. This naïveté, of course, was one of the resources of the new symphonic style. Haydn had carefully incorporated it within the structure of the symphony, reserving a place for naïve melodies in the slow movement and again in the trio. It is typical of Schubert and his generation that they did in isolated fragments what Haydn and Beethoven did within the larger framework of the symphony and string quartet.

Naïveté, however, was only one kind of character; the majority of Schubert's songs were forceful or poignant expressions of dramatic situations. *Erlkönig* (1815) is a highly dramatic setting of a folklike ballad; *Gretchen am Spinnrade* (1814) is a spinning song, a lyrical moment out of Goethe's *Faust*. These songs, more complex than the simple, strophic *Heidenröslein*, still have none of the internal variety and development of a sonata movement, being ruled by one musical idea. (Owing to the new importance attributed in the 1800s to strophic form as a typical feature of folk song, other kinds of song form came to be described by the term *durch-komponiert* or "through-composed.")

What these songs derived from the sonata was harmonic intensity, an intensity, already apparent in Beethoven, that drew its force from the key plans of the mighty symphony. In Beethoven the intensity of single chords had been subordinated to the larger structure; now, in Schubert's songs, single chords could be more fully exploited. Schubert could afford to dwell on a rich chord or on an important chord in a rich progression, without endangering the simple structure of his short pieces. The emphasis on harmony shows up in the style of the pianoforte accompaniment, which is largely responsible for the melodious effect of the simple vocal line. The introduction to *Der Wanderer* (Example 117) shows harmonic portent. This song, more complex and varied than *Erlkönig*

EXAMPLE 117   SCHUBERT: BEGINNING OF DER WANDERER (song)

(I come from distant mountains . . .)

or *Gretchen,* illustrates in each of its short sections the deepening of musical substance through harmonic effect.

As a youth Schubert also tried his hand at symphonies, but without approaching the last symphonies of Mozart, to say nothing of the tremendously expanded works of Beethoven. As Schubert turned twenty-five he tackled both string quartet and symphony on a more ambitious scale. But since he went at these forms with much the same approach he had found so successful in the song, certain problems arose even beyond the basic problem of finding something individual to say. Tone color, harmonic color—aspects of a momentary mood—pushed their way into the symphonic foreground, weakening the larger design.

Schubert wrote his first mature symphony, the B-minor ("Unfinished"), in 1822, when he was twenty-five. In the first movement a new relationship prevails between the themes and the structure of the whole; this slight change of emphasis had a profound effect on the integration of theme and key. At the beginning of Beethoven's first movements (not counting slow introductions) remarkably little happens; whatever follows is sure to heighten the excitement. The only exception is the Fifth Symphony with its portentous unison beginning. Schubert's B-minor Symphony, although very different in character from Beethoven's Fifth, begins similarly. The opening theme seems full of deep significance, the more so because this theme breaks off, its implications unconfirmed by what follows. The momentary effect is great, but the long-range accumulation of character is sacrificed. This theme (Example 118a) never becomes more characteristic than at its first appearance. The same happens to the next theme (Example 118b) and the next (Example 118c); each is so interesting in itself that

EXAMPLE 118   SCHUBERT: THEMES FROM SYMPHONY IN B MINOR

the developmental passages that follow seem dull or artificial in comparison. Only once, at the second appearance of theme *c,* is the material transfigured in extension, and that only briefly.

The character of the movement has come to reside in its themes, wonderfully lyric moments set off from each other by symphonic discourse of a more pedestrian tone. There is now a "first" theme (in this case, theme *b*), then a "bridge passage" leading to a "second" theme. Mozart had often used a contrasting theme to confirm the dominant key—a brief rallying point halfway through the A section. For Schubert (and for most symphonic composers after him) the modulation to the dominant, indeed, the whole shape of the first movement seems often to exist only for the sake of this "second" theme. In Mozart's later works, the development of themes could be more lyrical than the themes themselves; in Schubert, the theme emerges as the principal event.

The B-minor Symphony is valued for the lyricism of its themes, not for its overall form. The overall form, of course, is incomplete, lacking the last two movements. These would have been a scherzo and a finale, two vigorous, unlyrical movements. Perhaps Schubert felt that in its unfinished state the symphony better expressed its individual character; in any case it has been known ever since as the "Unfinished" Symphony.

Schubert wrote three important string quartets, in A minor, Op. 29 (1824), D minor (*Death and the Maiden,* 1826), G, Op. 161 (1826); also a famous trio for pianoforte, violin, and cello in B flat, Op. 99 (1826), and a large quintet for string quartet with an extra cello, in C, Op. 163 (1828)—all worthy successors to Mozart's mature chamber works, but all affected by the same tendency to dwell on lyric moments and rich harmonies at the expense of figuration and tonal plans. Schubert by no means avoided Beethoven's vigorous, dynamic utterances, but sometimes failed to make them come off for lack of a convincing modulation or development.

Only once, in his last Symphony in C (1828), did Schubert attempt and succeed in a work of Beethovenlike dimensions. This symphony, like Mozart's last symphonies, might fairly be regarded as one of his first, for Schubert was barely thirty. Schubert filled the wide-open spaces of the symphony with his own kind of material, reflecting a different personality; that is as it should be in symphonic style. But in spite of the differences, Schubert's Symphony in C can be placed alongside Beethoven's Seventh Symphony in A of 1812.

Schubert's most distinctive success with larger form was in the song cycle. Abandoning symphonic guidelines, Schubert used as structural module only the song—fragmentary in shape and (at least in his work) brimming over with lyric potential. Out of place in the symphony, these lyric fragments found their proper setting in the loose, balladlike sequence provided by a poetic cycle. Schubert's two cycles—*Die schöne Müllerin* (The Beautiful Miller-girl, 1823) and *Winterreise* (Winter Journey, 1827)—opened up a welcome alternative to the shape of the symphony.

14

SYMPHONIC DERIVATIVES AND OTHER MUSIC 1830-1850

INTERNATIONAL OPERA TOWARD 1830 Beethoven's work seems to us so universal, and Schubert's so typically Viennese, that it is hard to keep in mind the concurrent world of opera, as popular in Vienna as throughout the rest of Europe. Within Germany and Austria, the singspiel continued to thrive. One of the most influential elements in its development was—not *Magic Flute*—but that *dramma giocoso, Don Giovanni,* whose terrifying finale made a profound impression on the next generation. With that finale in mind, Ludwig Spohr (1784–1859), a very active composer, produced a setting of the Faust story in 1816 for Prague, where *Don Giovanni* had been such a success. Spohr was also a progressive symphonic composer; his near-continuous chromatic modulation and wealth of accompanimental figures kept his *Faust* (subtitled *romantische Oper*) at an intense musical and emotional level well above that of ordinary singspiel.

Works such as *Faust* brought increased depth to musical theater, yet fell short of Mozart and Beethoven for lack of a successful integration of theme and key. Chord for chord, Spohr is a good deal richer than Beethoven, but at higher levels of tonal organization Spohr fails to make his point.

In 1821 Carl Maria von Weber (1786–1826) produced *Der Freischütz,* a singspiel in which the element of exotic adventure has been driven to the maca-bre, through a generous admixture of old German forests, demons, and magic bullets. The work caused a sensation, even though the principles were those of the opéra-comique; and the musical means, lurid exaggerations of standard devices, do not seem to give evidence of the composer's talent for sustained musical development or dramatic timing. Musically less intense—and perhaps less convincing—than Spohr's *Faust*, and with severe dramatic faults, Weber's *Freischütz* seemed nonetheless to include the right ingredients. It was very successful, and thereafter German "romantic" opera increasingly took on sinister or demonic atmosphere. In comparison, Beethoven's *Fidelio* (Vienna, 1805, revised 1806 and 1814), often compared to Cherubini's *Les Deux journées,* seems like straight opéra-comique in German.

A list of some of the most significant, and the most successful, operas produced on international stages from 1828 to 1836 may help to suggest the backdrop against which the works of Beethoven and Schubert (as well as those of Berlioz and Schumann) must be projected.

1828	*La Muette de Portici,* Auber, text by Scribe and Delavigne	Paris
	Der Vampyr, Marschner, text by Wohlbrück	Leipzig
1829	*Guillaume Tell,* Rossini, text by Etienne de Jouy and Bis, after Schiller	Paris
1830	*Fra Diavolo,* Auber, text by Scribe	Paris
	I Capuleti e i Montecchi, Bellini, text by Romani, after Shakespeare	Venice
	Anna Bolena, Donizetti, text by Romani	Milan
1831	*La Sonnambula,* Bellini, text by Romani	Milan
	Robert-le-Diable, Meyerbeer, text by Scribe and Delavigne	Paris
	Norma, Bellini, text by Romani	Milan
1832	*L'Elisir d'amore,* Donizetti, text by Romani	Milan
1833	*Hans Heiling,* Marschner, text by Devrient	Berlin
	Lucrezia Borgia, Donizetti, text by Romani, after Victor Hugo	Milan
1835	*I Puritani di Scozia,* Bellini, text by Pepoli	Paris
	Lucia di Lammermoor, Donizetti, text by Cammarano, after Sir Walter Scott	Naples
1836	*Les Huguenots,* Meyerbeer, text by Scribe	Paris

This selected list (the number of new productions during these years is much greater, while the total number of operas produced, of course, is much greater still) gives evidence of new trends in French, German, and Italian opera. German romantic opera, represented in this list by the works of Heinrich Marschner (1795–1861), seemed to find an echo in Italy; at any rate, the operas of Gaetano Donizetti (1797–1848) and Vincenzo Bellini (1801–1835) show a steady progression from sentimental comedy to another kind of "romantic" opera.

Less macabre than the German kind, works like *I Capuleti e i Montecchi, Anna Bolena,* and *Norma* are cast in faraway times or places; Norma is a druid priestess in primeval Britain. If *L'Elisir d'amore* is still a rustic comedy alla Goldoni, it begins with a character reading from the romance of Tristan and Isolde. *La Sonnambula* (The Sleepwalker) has its unusual aspects, while *I Puritani* and *Lucia* have competing mad scenes. In *I Puritani* the heroine (Elvira) goes mad, then is revived when everything turns out all right, while

Lucia dies in insane ecstasy, imagining she is united with her lover. The texts of such works were adapted by Italian librettists, the foremost being Felice Romani (1788–1865), from Shakespeare, Victor Hugo, and Sir Walter Scott.

In characteristic Italian fashion, Donizetti and Bellini relied on the libretto to specify the time, place, and atmosphere of the dramatic action, making no effort to reflect local color in their music. The romantic English characters sang dotted martial rhythms instead of swinging triple time, but that was merely a matter of bringing operatic idioms up-to-date; similarly the harmonic idiom met international standards of richness without injecting exotic feeling into Italian opera. Voluptuous vocal ornamentation, brilliant and languishing by turns, was written out instead of being improvised as it had been for two centuries.

The most important parallel to symphonic structure took place at the upper levels of operatic organization. Formal arias virtually ceased to exist; concomitantly the number of distinct traditional sections within an act dropped from ten or fifteen to sometimes as few as two or three. Musical structure within an act was, however, far from uniform. Flexible ensembles (often with chorus) were vastly extended, often in a varied sequence of tempos and moods. Equally important, the recitative (now mostly orchestral) was shot through with arioso elements, both solo and choral. Large sections of acts might be called *scena e duetto*, the *scena* (scene) starting in recitative, with the following duet so extended and varied as to seem like a series of contrasting sections, even including more recitative. Contrasts of key, always important in operatic structure, now fell under broader systems of tonal relationships as in the symphony.

An especially interesting type of scene was called *scena e cavatina*. Derived from the age-old habit of ending a free recitative with a more cogent arioso phrase (*cavata*), the cavatina was a relatively extended lyric moment that served to bring a recitative to a sharp musical and dramatic focus. A cavatina had the regular rhythm and key sense of an aria, without a fixed repetitive form. After the cavatina, which served not to end the scene but only to focus it, came the typical succession of contrasting sections, as, for example, in scenes 2 and 3 of *Lucia di Lammermoor*, Act I. The very celebrated cavatina *Casta diva* from *Norma* is a good example of the way large-scale form and dramatic atmosphere interacted with skillfully handled detail to make a simple progression seem great melody.

Closely related to such lyric moments was their poignant recall. When Lucia goes mad, she expresses herself in the disjunct phrases used for mad scenes since the 1600s. Such scenes, however, need no longer be the bizarre exception they once were, since their musical structure, at least, was now common; the mad scene could now be the crowning glory of the work. Furthermore, Lucia's madness is poignant, not grotesque. When a vision of her lover is recalled to her—and to us—by the orchestral quotation of the theme from an earlier love duet, this particular lyric moment is elevated to a high structural and emotional level quite beyond the power of the theme itself, in a way analogous to thematic development in the symphony.

It was in Paris that a synthesis of operatic trends finally took place. Ambitions of grandeur, long latent in the opéra-comique, and plainly in evidence

since Cherubini's *Les Deux journées* were progressively realized during the
years covered in the list on page 432. *La Muette de Portici,* by Daniel Auber
(1782–1871), is a serious work by a composer otherwise known for his comedies,
such as *Fra Diavolo.* But while *La Muette de Portici* was very successful, it
cannot claim seriousness in more than intent.

The case of *Guillaume Tell,* by Gioacchino Rossini (1792–1868) is very
different. Rossini was a veteran of Italian comedy; his *Il Barbiere di Siviglia*
was so successful as to usurp completely the position of its predecessor by
Paisiello (see page 400). In Paris, Rossini turned to a superior form of opéra-
comique. Starting with a lofty historical, yet partially exotic, subject that combined adventure with sentiment and revolutionary patriotic fervor, Rossini built
up a combination of dramatic recitative, affective melodies, and large, flexible
ensembles supported by plenty of chorus. The union of Italian stagecraft and
professional music making with dramatic ideals of opéra-comique—in the process of definition and more vigorous than those of Italian opera—resulted in a
new, impressive kind of work.

The new synthesis was followed up immediately by Giacomo Meyerbeer
(1791–1864) in his *Robert-le-Diable,* and especially *Les Huguenots,* whose libretto, by the leading French writer Eugene Scribe (1791–1861), capitalized on
a high theme at once religious and political. Very impressive and extremely long,
Les Huguenots closes with a hair-raising finale as the Catholic soldiers blaze
away offstage at the Protestants besieged in a chapel; after each fusillade can be
heard brave fragments of *Ein' feste Burg* (war song of the Reformation) sung
by the decimated Protestants, until, after a final withering barrage, the principals lamenting onstage exclaim, ". . . They sing no more!" When they themselves are captured, the principals, faced with death, are caught up in an ecstatic
vision and die exultant.

Justly called *grand opera,* the new synthesis seemed to have everything;
yet it failed somehow to embody the most exciting, most progressive musical
potentialities of the age, as is evident in its failure to engage the full commit-
ment of the most imaginative, creative composers. Competent professionals such
as Rossini and Meyerbeer wrote grand opera, but during the same years a far
more gifted composer, Hector Berlioz, was dreaming of Beethoven symphonies
and of what might have come after.

BERLIOZ AND THE PROGRAM SYMPHONY Of all who dared to rival Beethoven in the symphony, none did so with greater courage and enthusiasm than
young Hector Berlioz (1803–1869)—and not without success, for Berlioz found
a way both to control the larger form and to give the symphony an individual
character. He provided the listener with a program, a poetic-dramatic text that
indicated what the various parts of the symphony meant and why they came in
the order they did. Such a device was not new, of course, having appeared in
Beethoven's Sixth Symphony (1808). Berlioz first used a program successfully
in his *Episode in the Life of an Artist,* subtitled *Symphonie fantastique.* At the
time of its first performance in 1830 (Paris), Berlioz likened the program to
"the spoken text of an opera." Here is the program in a version Berlioz made
later.

Episode in the Life of an Artist: *Symphonie fantastique* in five parts

A young musician of unhealthy sensitivity and a lively imagination drugs himself with opium in an attack of lovelorn despair. Too weak to kill him, the drug plunges him in a deep sleep, accompanied by the strangest visions, during which his sensations, feelings, and memories are transformed in his sick brain into musical ideas and images. The girl he loves becomes for him a melody, an *idée fixe* that he keeps hearing everywhere.

FIRST PART: Reveries, Passions
He remembers first that uneasiness of the soul, that emotional emptiness, that melancholy, those aimless joys that he felt before seeing his beloved; then the volcanic passion that she suddenly aroused in him, his delirious torments, his jealous rages, the return of tenderness, religious consolation.

SECOND PART: A Ball
He finds his beloved at a ball, in the midst of the tumult of a brilliant celebration.

THIRD PART: Scene in the Fields
On a summer evening in the country, he hears two shepherds sing a Swiss shepherd tune in dialog; this pastoral duet, the surroundings, the gentle rustle of the trees softly stirred by the wind, some hopeful thoughts which had lately come to mind—all combine to fill his heart with an unaccustomed calm, giving his thoughts a more cheerful color. But she appears again, his pulse quickens, sorrowful premonitions agitate him; if she should deceive him . . . ? One of the shepherds resumes his simple song, the other does not answer. The sun sets . . . sound of distant thunder . . . solitude . . . silence.

FOURTH PART: March to the Execution
He dreams that he has killed his beloved, that he is condemned to death, led to his execution. The procession advances to the sound of a march, now somber and sullen, now brilliantly solemn, in which the muffled sound of slow footsteps follows without a break the most clamorous outbursts. At the end, the *idée fixe* reappears for a moment like a last thought of love, interrupted by the fatal blow.

FIFTH PART: Dream of a Witches' Sabbath
He sees himself at a witches' sabbath, in the midst of a frightful troup of specters, sorcerers, monsters of all kinds gathered for his funeral. Strange noises, groans, outbursts of laughter, distant cries to which other cries seem to respond. The melody of the beloved appears again; but it has lost its character of shy nobility; it is now only a cheap dance tune, trivial and grotesque; it is *she* who comes to the sabbath. . . . Roars of joy at her arrival . . . she mingles in the diabolical orgy . . . funeral knell, burlesque parody of the *Dies irae*. Sabbath round-dance. Round-dance and the *Dies irae* together.

This program tries to make the character of each movement more vivid. We have seen that the logic of symphonic development from Haydn through Beethoven was to increase the individuality of each of the four movements of the basic plan. In Beethoven the character of movements reached such purely musical intensity that it began to throw off images; the listener—if he was as sensitive as Berlioz—began to see visions parading across his imagination as he listened, ". . . Huge, cloudy symbols of a high romance." In order to reproduce and intensify this effect, Berlioz (and others after him) supplied his own works with titles and programs, although usually with the disclaimer that the titles were really unnecessary, the music being sufficiently expressive in itself.

This disclaimer was actually justified by the fact that, no matter how novel or individual the program might be, the outlines of the program symphony remained basically the same as those laid down by Haydn and used by Beethoven, modified only in a degree comparable to Beethoven's own modifications of Haydn's plan. Berlioz's *Symphonie fantastique* is still a recognizable symphony with or without the program, whose chief function is to make more explicit the character regularly given each movement in the symphonic shape. The first movement ("Reveries, Passions") is the normal fast movement of Haydn's plan, preceded by a slow introduction. Berlioz lengthened the slow introduction even more than Beethoven did in his Seventh Symphony. In addition Berlioz made his introduction seem even longer by shortening the fast section that follows, so that the slow and fast sections are more nearly equal.

It is not hard to see Berlioz's reason for making such alterations. Haydn's first movement demanded the greatest control of tonal order coordinated with the greatest amount of thematic development; the one was difficult, the other (as we will soon see) preempted by the special kind of theme used by Berlioz. The first movement was the area in which competition with Beethoven was most difficult, whereas the slow introduction gave special opportunity for tone color and harmonic effect—the very thing that Berlioz, like Schubert, did best.

The second and third movements of Haydn's original plan presented no such problems. The slow movement, always static, was naturally suited to Berlioz's sensitivity for sonority and lyricism. The scherzo, being fast and rhythmic, was easiest of all—so easy that with the first movement shortened Berlioz found it desirable to include two "scherzos," one a dance and the other a march, flanking the central slow movement. In each scherzo he achieved something a little different from Beethoven; the dance was smoother, more elegant, the march brassier and grimmer.

The finale ("Dream of a Witches' Sabbath") shows Beethoven's influence and Berlioz's reaction to it most clearly, for it reproduces several features of the finale of Beethoven's Ninth Symphony. There is a violent introduction, presentation of a theme, an abrupt change to distant sounds (a bell tolls), a second, solemn theme (the *Dies irae*), which is eventually combined in counterpoint with the principal one. Models for all these features are to be found in the Ninth Symphony, which remained a storehouse of symphonic ideas not only for Berlioz but for many other composers of the 1800s.

As well as underlining the character of individual movements, the program also ensured the artistic unity of the whole, a problem that became acute when Beethoven's exuberant expansion of tonal order pushed the length of the symphony to dangerous limits. Any relaxation of tonal control now meant disaster. Berlioz sensed this, sensed also that his own control of tonal order was not the equal of Beethoven's. The program afforded him a ready kind of unity, one that would convince the listener that all did indeed belong together.

Overall unity was also achieved through the way the theme was used. In Haydn and Beethoven the theme had neither character nor importance at the beginning of a work, but acquired those qualities as the work progressed. This sense of growth and development gave the work a powerful cohesion, of which the theme became the sign. Berlioz, like Schubert (and most composers of the 1800s) took the sign for the reality, attributing to the theme the unifying force that actually belonged to the development of the whole work.

Berlioz tended to give the theme both character and importance right from the beginning. To underline its character, he gave the theme a programmatic significance. In the *Symphonie fantastique* the theme was made the image of the beloved, an *idée fixe* in the mind of the lover. Once fixed, the theme recurs in each movement, binding them—superficially at least—more tightly together. This change in the treatment of the theme brought serious complications, for if the character of the theme was fixed from the beginning, then it did not lend itself well to growth and development, thereby robbing the whole symphonic form of its most powerful lever.

Berlioz's problem (the same that confronted Schubert) becomes most apparent in the "development" section of the first movement. Little real development takes place; instead the section is soon given over to volcanic orchestral eruptions—not inappropriately, however, and not without good effect, for this kind of eruption belongs to the unstable B section. Berlioz integrated these truly symphonic effects with the rest of the movement specifically through the program rather than through thematic development or key. Another magnificent symphonic effect is found at the end of the movement, where there is an abrupt turn to a soft, dark quality, an exaggeration of Mozart's habit. This effect, too, is explained by the program (thoughts of religious consolation) but, like the volcanic "development," has its origin in symphonic style.

Since the theme does not participate in development, it becomes important through its identity in all parts of the symphony; as corollary, any changes that do take place in the theme have a special significance. Thus in the last movement the broad, lyric theme is transformed (not developed) into a grotesque dance figure, representing the witch character that the beloved assumes in the dream of the lover. Such transformation of theme later became an important feature of the symphony, closely coordinated with the program and explained by it.

Of Berlioz's later works, *Harold in Italy* (1834), a programmatic viola concerto, and to a lesser extent *Romeo and Juliet* (1840), still embody symphonic shape. *Romeo and Juliet* is described by Berlioz as a *dramatic symphony*, which means that the symphony was dramatized not only by the program but also by the addition of vocal parts, whose function was to make explicit the musical drama long ago built into the structure of the symphony. The further Berlioz went from symphony toward the forms of opera, the weaker became the result. Berlioz was no match for Meyerbeer on the dramatic stage; the strength of his program symphony lay in the symphony itself, as is best shown in his *Symphonie fantastique*, an "imaginative symphony" of great force and originality.

MENDELSSOHN The problems of German music after Beethoven, apparent first in Schubert, continued to manifest themselves in the work of two very gifted men, Felix Mendelssohn (1809–1847) and Robert Schumann (1810–1856). Mendelssohn was precocious: his musical and intellectual abilities showed up as early and as strong as those of Mozart and were cultivated by his father in as careful a fashion. Mendelssohn wrote many youthful works, including some of his most important—historically as well as artistically, for these early works (like Schubert's songs) tended to be novel in kind and style.

In 1827, at the age of eighteen, Mendelssohn published *Seven Characteristic Pieces* Op. 7. Besides revealing a provocative influence of J. S. Bach's *Well-tempered Keyboard*, these Pieces, neither sonata nor dance, were of a type soon to be extremely important with piano composers; the same is true of the fantasias and variations Mendelssohn composed both early and late in life. Mendelssohn also wrote many small character-pieces under the title, *Songs without words*—as if the accompaniment (the truly expressive part) of Schubert songs.

For some reason, perhaps his very nature, young Mendelssohn seemed not to respond to the force of Beethoven nor to the demonic side of Mozart; or if he did, he could not give such character convincing musical expression. Tender, wistful, whimsical, or spritely ideas were more congenial to him, and in treating them he was able to write music that was as convincing in its way as that of his models. His aptitude and accomplishment are especially apparent in three early overtures, *A Midsummer Night's Dream*, Op. 21 (1826), *Fingal's Cave*, Op. 26 (1830), *Meerestille und Glückliche Fahrt*, Op. 27 (1828). The first of these was a real overture to a real play; Mendelssohn later added incidental music for the rest of Shakespeare's comedy. But Beethoven's theater overtures, for example, *Egmont*, had been played separately as concert pieces—indeed, the whole German symphony was the result of a concert development of the old opera sinfonia. It was a short step, therefore, to concert development of the one-movement overture associated with spoken stage plays. Once in the concert hall, the overture, like the symphony, became autonomous; it developed its own forms, in response to its own ideas. With their literary or pictorial ideas not unlike Berlioz's programs, Mendelssohn's second and third overtures stand near the head of several generations of symphonic character-pieces.

At the age of twenty-one, Mendelssohn became engaged with the symphony itself. His three important works, the Third Symphony in A minor, Op. 56 ("Scotch"), the Fourth Symphony in A major, Op. 90 ("Italian"), and the Fifth Symphony in D minor, Op. 107 ("Reformation"), all identified by personal or programmatic meanings, were conceived between 1830 and 1833. For all their virtues these works do not carry out the thrust of Beethoven's Seventh and Eighth Symphonies (1812) nor Schubert's big C-major Symphony (1828). The comparison with Beethoven is least favorable in Mendelssohn's *Song of Praise* (usually called the Second Symphony in B flat, Op. 52, 1840), consisting of three movements and a choral finale. To write such a work placed the composer in inescapable competition with that dangerous prototype, Beethoven's Ninth; it required at the very least the strength of a Berlioz to survive such competition.

During the 1830s and 1840s Mendelssohn's capacities deepened with maturity. Striking out beyond the symphony, he infused the oratorio with new symphonic character in his *Elijah*, Op. 70 (1846–1847), conceived on a monumental scale. In the Violin Concerto, Op. 64 (1844), Mendelssohn showed unsuspected strength. Whether because of the medium, or the key (E minor), or some inner resonance, he here revealed a forcefulness hitherto largely concealed behind amiable whimsy or tenderness. The finale in particular is driven by a sense of harmonic flux and figural urgency that was the mark of the most exciting music in the 1840s.

Mendelssohn's genius was perhaps most consistently manifested not as a composer but as a conductor. He was only twenty when in 1829 he produced a performance (heavily cut) of J. S. Bach's *St. Matthew Passion,* the first performance in a hundred years. Here, too, Mendelssohn seemed to divine what was to be a significant trend. The revival of Bach, in the same tones of hushed reverence that apparently prevailed at Mendelssohn's concert, was to be a persistent feature of the 1800s. Torn loose from its own time, Bach's music came to mean almost everything to a wide variety of enthusiasts—everything, that is, except what it had originally been.

Later Mendelssohn made more orthodox contributions to the relatively new art of conducting. His direction of the Leipzig Gewandhaus symphonic concerts made that institution one of the European leaders in its field. As much as any symphony conductor of those decades, Mendelssohn gave both the post and the institution new standards of excellence and imagination.

SCHUMANN Nothing better illustrates the problems of German music after Beethoven than the career of Robert Schumann (1810–1856), perhaps the most gifted German musician of his generation. Like Schubert, Schumann's most productive years came at the beginning, when he was approaching thirty (1830–1840). His genius manifested itself in pianoforte compositions of a very special character. As he passed the age of thirty he turned his attention to the big forms, especially symphony, going on to string quartets the next year. Schubert died at thirty, Mendelssohn at thirty-six; Schumann lived on, but declined steadily. His inspiration failed him; musical composition and finally life itself became extremely burdensome. He became depressed, attempted suicide, and eventually died at forty-six. This is not to attribute his state of mental health to the development of musical style; but at a time when a composer's individual character was so closely bound up with style, and when the formulation of that style had been made so problematic by Beethoven's achievement, it is easy to understand why it took a robust or insensitive composer to survive those decades.

The same sensitivity that made it so hard for Schumann to compete with Beethoven in the symphony allowed him to excel in smaller forms. Although he, too, wrote songs, following the example of Schubert, they came later and lacked that very special surge of enthusiasm. Schumann's first, most characteristic works are for piano, his own instrument. Between the ages of twenty and thirty he poured out a steady stream of small pianoforte pieces, just as Schubert had written hundreds of songs:

Op. 1	"Abegg" Variations (1830)
Op. 2	Papillons (1831)
Op. 3	"Paganini Studies" (1832)
Op. 4	Intermezzi (1832)
Op. 5	Impromptus (1833)
Op. 6	Davidsbündlertänze (1837)
Op. 7	Toccata (1830)
Op. 8	Allegro (1831)
Op. 9	Carnaval. Scènes mignonnes sur quatre notes (1835)
Op. 10	"Paganini Studies" II (1833)
Op. 12	Fantasiestücke (1837)
Op. 13	Etudes symphoniques (1834)
Op. 15	Kinderscenen (1838)

Op. 16   Kreisleriana. Fantasien (1838)
Op. 17   Fantasie (1836)
Op. 18   Arabesque (1839)
Op. 21   Novelletten (1838)
Op. 23   Nachtstücke (1838)
Op. 26   Faschingschwank aus Wien. Fantasiebilder (1839)

Catching up forms and trends previously isolated or unimportant, Schumann concentrated on the small pianoforte piece to the point where it became central. While lesser composers even before 1800 had written such pieces, importance came only through contact with sonata and symphony; this contact, in turn, came through Beethoven. Late in life, Beethoven had written some extremely interesting works for pianoforte, including two sets of Bagatelles, Op. 119 (1822) and Op. 126 (1823). Beethoven called them "Kleinigkeiten," that is, trivia. At a stage when he was capable of the most concentrated expression imaginable, Beethoven here gave epigrammatic form to what he wanted to say, quite without reference to the external forms of sonata or symphony, but embodying their inner expressiveness. He did this also in keyboard variations. Earlier he had written two important sets, of which Op. 34 (1802) put each new variation in a new key (F–D–B flat–G–E flat–C minor–F). An extraordinary late set, the "Diabelli" Variations, Op. 120 (1819–1823), placed the epigrammatic expression of the Bagatelles into a far-ranging cyclic form very different from the form of a sonata.

The next important step in the development of the short pianoforte piece can be seen in the fate of four pieces by Schubert published as Four Impromptus, Op. 142, a title urged on Schubert by his publisher. The four pieces are Allegro moderato in F minor, Allegretto in A flat, Andante in B flat, and Allegro scherzando in F minor. It seems clear (as Schumann pointed out) that these four pieces were intended by Schubert as movements of a complete sonata. The transformation of this sonata into four "Impromptus" is a striking illustration of how the larger forms of Haydn and Beethoven could disintegrate into fragments as the character of each movement became more intense. Schubert's Impromptus mark the end of the sonata and another point of departure for the short pianoforte piece.

The word *Fantasie* appears in the list of Schumann's pianoforte pieces several times as title and subtitle, also as *Fantasie-bilder* (*Pictures in the imagination*—the same meaning as in Berlioz's *Symphonie fantastique*). This term *Fantasie* best reveals the nature of all these little pieces. Each piece has a unique character, as with Haydn and Beethoven; only now the character is so intense that it generates an image, a distinct pictorial or poetic idea. There is no longer need even for a text (as in Schubert's songs) to spell out the image.

Like Berlioz, however, Schumann supplied his pieces with titles, and for the same reason—partly to ignite the listener's imagination, partly to convince him that a particular set of images belonged together as one large piece. Schumann's pianoforte pieces came in sonata-length sets, but rather resembled Beethoven's variations, being without any trace of sonata structure, bound together only by the associations contained in their titles. Even these are sometimes so personal, intimate, or remote as to be ineffective or meaningless without explanation.

The best-known, most successful of Schumann's programmatic cycles is *Carnaval*, subtitled *Scènes mignonnes sur quatre notes*. The four notes are presented in the course of the work under the title *Sphinxes* (Example 119). The obsolete, medieval notation is part of the imaginative picture (these are the note shapes of Franco of Cologne's brevis). The four pitches are derived from Asch, the name of a town where Schumann's sweetheart lived. The whimsical melodic shapes engendered by these four notes haunt the whole *Carnaval*, binding it together like Berlioz's *idée fixe*, but in a more indefinable, mysterious way. The inner logic of composition here receded more and more into the composer's inner self.

Even the outward shape of *Carnaval* depends partly on intimate personal associations. The title refers to the traditional masked ball preceding the Lenten fast. The piece begins with an appropriate festival march; then follow waltzes in the grand manner. Beethoven's rhythmic excitement was most easily reproduced by Schubert, Berlioz, and Schumann through dance rhythms, which, as they became more intense, generated images of the glittering, glamorous festival ball, a favorite "cloudy symbol of high romance" for this generation. But Schumann, reluctant to let the rhythms run on as Beethoven did, interrupted them, twisting them in peculiar directions by remote changes of key. This erratic handling of keys helps give Schumann's style its individuality.

Carnaval continues with pieces entitled *Pierrot, Harlequin, Pantalon et Columbine*, clown types traditionally associated with the masked ball. Then come other titles whose presence involves more personal explanation. The most personal, and most characteristic, are *Eusebius* and *Florestan*, names Schumann gave to different aspects of his own personality. Eusebius was the dreamer, the meditative, introspective character, while Florestan was the extrovert—energetic, flamboyant, somewhat undirected (Example 120).

Eusebius is an excellent example of Schumann's tendencies as a composer. The phrase shape of this piece is utterly simple; interest is generated by the handling of the individual chord—its spacing, texture, figuration, the subtle way in which it suggests and then moves toward the next chord. The progression from one chord to the next now became one of the most expressive elements in music, and the actual moment of change, expressed as chromatic passing tones, became more important than the eventual arrival. Many of these chromatic progressions had been used by Haydn and Mozart, but passed over so quickly and embodied in such strong phrase shapes as to be almost imperceptible. In Schumann, the detail of progressions moved into the foreground, attracting more and more attention.

Carnaval is a set of fragments, each embodying an image. It was possible

EXAMPLE 119   SCHUMANN: "SPHINXES" FROM CARNAVAL

No. 1   No. 2   No. 3

EXAMPLE 120   SCHUMANN: "EUSEBIUS" AND "FLORESTAN" FROM CARNAVAL

(a)

(b)

to make each fragment intense enough to carry images only because the power of the symphony was packed into each, something best illustrated by the title ''Symphonic Studies,'' Op. 13. This work is a set of variations, another set of fragments for pianoforte. There is nothing symphonic about them, except for a breadth and depth of expression derived from the mighty symphony. In this sense, many of Schumann's short pieces are symphonic studies. It is their symphonic power that makes possible their ability to generate fantasy pictures.

Schumann wrote pianoforte sonatas in F-sharp minor (1835), G minor (1838) and F minor (1835). These, logically enough, tend to break into fragments. The F-minor Sonata was subtitled ''Concerto without orchestra'', another indication of Schumann's fragmentary approach to composition. His real Pianoforte Concerto, Op. 54, in A minor, started out as a fantasia for pianoforte and orchestra (1841); four years later a second movement, Romanza, and a finale were added to fill out the traditional shape of a concerto. In spite of its piece-meal genesis, this concerto remains Schumann's most successful large piece.

When he approached the symphony, problems confronted him at every turn. He came to the symphony with youthful enthusiasm and energy, and, characteristically, his first efforts were his best. In 1841 he sketched out his First Symphony in B flat in four days, and then finished it during the next four months. Immediately he started on another work which he called ''Symphonic Fantasy''; it was eventually published as Symphony no. 4 in D minor. These two symphonies are very different: one is light, the other dark. At one time Schumann considered using titles for the movements of the B-flat Symphony, in the manner of Beethoven's Pastoral Symphony; Schumann sometimes spoke of his B-flat Symphony as if it had a program, but he also remarked that these images came after the actual composition of the piece.

Both the B-flat and D-minor Symphonies are clearly symphonic in shape and structure, standing even closer to tradition than Berlioz's *Symphonie fantastique*, in spite of the fact that the movements of the D-minor Symphony are to be played without pause, making the work continuous. Schumann was clearly intent on the overall unity of the symphony, as is also evident from the way he linked the movements of the D-minor Symphony together with a common group of themes. In spite of differences in personal style, Schumann was taking the symphony in the same direction as Berlioz.

Although his approach was at once energetic and thoughtful, Schumann did not completely succeed in his symphonies, partly because he never learned to think in terms of orchestral sound. He had caught the essence of the symphony in his pianoforte pieces, but he could not do it with the orchestra. His symphonies often sag simply for lack of an effective orchestration. But the difficulties go deeper than that. His pianoforte pieces succeeded because he had developed his own personal style at the keyboard, a style unlike Beethoven or anyone else, fresh and original. When he took up the symphony he tried to write ''symphonically,'' imitating this time not the inner surge but the outward figuration; his symphonies contain page after page of mechanical figures.

Furthermore, in his pianoforte style, Schumann's own style of figuration was dense, intricate, intense—and highly effective—for short pieces, but it was too intricate, too characteristic for the wide-open spaces of the symphony. It was not plastic, could not assume a dozen different shapes in the heat of symphonic development, as Beethoven's had. The repetitions and extensions of phrase that lie behind Beethoven's development stand in Schumann painfully exposed, all the more because of the lack of effective orchestral color. Haydn had shown Mozart how to make the figuration boil over, obliterating regular phrases; Beethoven had driven these irregular phrases forward with great rhythmic momentum, sometimes giving the feeling of almost unphrased music. Suddenly in Schumann, as in Mendelssohn, regular phrases abruptly reappear, breaking up the forward momentum of the symphony.

Schumann tried to compensate for weak figuration by imbuing the symphony with the harmonic richness he used so well in his pianoforte pieces. But richness meant prominence of single chords, or intricate chord progressions. While Schumann was able to make single phrases swirl by cramming them full of exciting progressions, these eventually obscured the overall shape of the symphony; in any case the harmonic swirl could not be sustained long enough to fill a whole symphonic movement. It is interesting to compare the beginning of Schumann's Third Symphony (1849) in E flat with Beethoven's Third Symphony in the same key, a work we can be sure Schumann had ringing in his ears when he sat down to write a symphony in E flat.

The two passages in Example 121, each the first complete period of its movement, are analogous in character as well as structure and function. Beethoven's theme is simple, making the chromatic chord in measure 7 a dramatic event. Similarly the modulation beginning in measure 18 and the dissonances in measures 25 to 26 are exciting contrast. In rhythm, too, Beethoven's syncopations (as if in two-four) in measures 28 to 34 contrast with the simple beginning. Schumann, seizing on the most exciting features of Beethoven's work, filled his own progressions with chromatic elements and made the syncopations almost continuous (but with the curious result that Schumann's theme seems to move in a broad three-two meter). Schumann's theme is a stirring one, full from the beginning with the warmth that builds up gradually in Beethoven; but such a theme made writing the rest of the movement extremely problematic.

Schumann's problems with the symphony were not just personal but stylistic, shared by every composer of his generation. The symphony of the 1830s had to be more intense than Beethoven, but intensity at that time had to be achieved by more intense character—in musical terms, more chromatic harmony and more intricate figuration. These features made symphonic discourse difficult if not impossible, at least on the scale of Beethoven. Symphonies became smaller, or seemed smaller, while small pieces seemed much larger and more substantial than they really were.

CHOPIN   Fryderyk Chopin (1810–1849) solved many of the problems confronting Schumann by avoiding them, accepting the stylistic limitations of his generation. He wrote no symphonies at all, turning to the orchestra only for the sake of a few pianoforte concertos, whose orchestral parts display only Chopin's lack of interest in that medium. Chopin concentrated his efforts in pianoforte pieces, most of them small. Here, too, he avoided the dangers of large-scale form, giving his larger pieces simple, nondevelopmental forms like *ABA*, where B contained contrasting, unrelated material. His two sonatas (in B minor and B-flat minor) achieve greatness not through structural integrity but through the strong character of separate episodes. The sonata was for Chopin as for Schumann a series of episodes set into Beethoven's framework. Chopin's sonatas are exceptions in his output, for most of the time he expressed his inimitable style in the fragmentary form best suited to it.

Many of his pieces are in dance idioms—waltzes, mazurkas, polonaises; while not intended for dancing, the character (say, of the waltzes) evoked the same brilliant, glamorous atmosphere of the grand ball found also in Schumann. Quite a different atmosphere marks the nocturnes, which are dreamy and reflective. The nocturnes belong with the dances, however, in a larger class of composition often called *salon* music, music of great effectiveness but somewhat less substance, intended for an uncritical audience seeking only small doses of imaginative stimulation.

EXAMPLE 121 COMPARISON OF BEETHOVEN AND SCHUMANN

(a) Beethoven: beginning of Symphony no. 3 (reduction)

EXAMPLE 121 (CONTINUED)

(b)   Schumann: beginning of Symphony no. 3 (reduction)

EXAMPLE 121 (CONTINUED)

    Chopin's larger pieces—larger for him—are entitled *ballades* (as if songs without words), *scherzos* (as if fragments of sonatas), and two fantasias. The ballades tend to use contrasting, well-defined themes more often than Chopin's other pieces, and use them in a broader, almost symphonic fashion. Here more than anywhere, Chopin approached the breadth of symphonic style. The scherzos sometimes have the headlong drive of Beethoven's scherzos; but the connection with Beethoven is not very close, for Chopin's scherzos include more warmth and variety, making them less demonic and more complete in themselves. Then, too, the scherzos belong at least partly to the *salon*, but like the ballades they ride high, capturing the excitement of the symphony. Chopin could hear and reproduce the sense of high drama imbedded in certain harmonic progressions appropriate to certain structural points, as at the beginning of the coda of the Scherzo in C-sharp minor.

    The most concentrated expression of Chopin's style, his best character-pieces, are his Preludes, Op. 28. Here Chopin revealed both the depth and the variety of which he was capable. His book of twenty-four preludes, one in each major and minor key, is modeled in that respect on J. S. Bach's *Well-tempered Keyboard*, which Chopin studied. Like Bach's preludes, Chopin's are each built on a single musical idea. But in most respects Chopin's preludes are entirely different from Bach's, lying as they do on the other side of the symphony. Not the least difference is that Chopin's preludes lack fugues, being (so to speak) fragments of fragments.

    Beethoven had developed pianoforte style to an extraordinary degree, but—with his ear always turned toward the symphonic ideal rather than toward the capabilities of the instrument itself—had left much room for refinement, much more than he had left in the symphony. This was one of the factors that accounted for Schumann's and Chopin's ease and success in writing for the pianoforte; here there was still much to do. Both Schumann and Chopin made the pianoforte do what style demanded, but Chopin did it best, creating stylistic standards for the rest of the century. Both in writing for and in playing the pianoforte, Chopin drew from it a warm, continuous sound. Only infrequently and for special effect, did he hold chords in simple long notes; more often he kept the chord sounding and resounding by any one of a number of figures he developed specially for this purpose, conveniently illustrated from the Preludes (Example 122).

Chopin's talent for finding original "pianistic" figuration was unsurpassed in the 1800s. This figuration had the special function of making the harmonies more intense. Mozart and Beethoven, being more concerned with rhythmic drive and overall shape, had expressed their harmonies in simpler figures; Chopin, like Schumann, gave more stress to the individual chord, and hence expressed it in a more carefully wrought figure. With the use of the damper pedal (the device that allows all notes once struck to continue sounding), figures such as those in Example 122 build up great resonance, causing the pianoforte to come alive with rich, vibrant sound, fascinating in itself and ideally suited to these character-pieces.

Although Chopin was well known for such pianistic harmonies (see Schumann's parody of Chopin, intended as a tribute, in the *Carnaval*), they are only one facet of Chopin's varied style. He was also famous for an especially intricate kind of figuration used high on the keyboard in the right hand, often over very simple chords in the left (Example 122d). Such figures are sometimes brilliant, sometimes subdued, but always more involute and sophisticated than those of Beethoven. Extended passages for the right hand written in tiny grace notes (as in Example 122b) are especially characteristic, involving as they do a delicate ornamentation of a simple harmony.

The basis of Chopin's harmony was the same kind of chord used by Haydn and Beethoven, but used now in a more intricate way. As with Schumann, these harmonies either tended to result in closed, highly lyrical melodies or to become intensely absorbing each by itself. Chopin liked to build up the richness of the dominant seventh chord by adding more notes on top (as in Example 123a, meas. 4), a procedure that became popular with many composers of the 1800s. In the same example we see another trait characteristic of Chopin—remote modulation, employed now with increasing frequency as composers sought to renew the excitement gradually disappearing from the more familiar modulations.

Remote modulation was intimately associated with the chromatic passing tones we saw in Schumann. Chopin affords us even better examples, as in Example 123b, from the Fourth Prelude in E minor. All these chromatic alterations are conceived within the framework of a single phrase, beginning and ending in the key of E minor; but by moving the notes of the chords downward half step by half step Chopin has introduced foreign chords that point in some cases far away from E minor. These chords go slowly enough for their remote key implications to be apparent to the ear; in other words, the chromatic passing tones now almost result in modulation. At the same time there was a tendency for a key to be established with fewer and fewer chords, so that a single dom-

EXAMPLE 122 CHOPIN: EXCERPTS FROM THE PRELUDES

(a) No. 5

Molto allegro ($\downarrow$. = 100)

(with pedal)

(b) No. 8

Molto agitato ($\downarrow$ = 72)

(with pedal)

(c) No. 19

Vivace ($\downarrow$ = 160)

legato

(with pedal)

(d) No. 16

Presto con fuoco ($\downarrow$ = 160)

8va

(with pedal)

EXAMPLE 123 CHOPIN: EXCERPTS FROM THE PRELUDES

(a) Op. 45

inant seventh chord (like the one in meas. 4) could actually imply a key all by itself. Mozart is sometimes as chromatic as Chopin, but Mozart's chromaticisms do not usually have the effect of modulation; in slow motion, however, Mozart's progressions sometimes bear a remarkable resemblance to Chopin's.

Any attempt to make an inventory of Chopin's stylistic devices falls short of completeness because of his great ability in finding subtly new figures and harmonies—and because doing so was his principal means of stylistic identity. The Preludes, "eagle feathers," Schumann called them, are each different, each unique. Some are ingratiating, some so bitter as to be repellent, but all are original. All are fragments; each goes on as long as it interests the composer, then breaks off, having touched briefly on some musical idea whose full exposition would require symphonic dimensions. Therein lies the power of the Preludes. They, too, are symphonic studies, generating energies far too great for their tiny frame. Some of them, for want of adequate conclusion, quit with a perfunctory chord or two. One (Example 124) does not end at all, its last chord being a dominant seventh, unresolved—Chopin's way of indicating how much had been left unsaid.

LISZT'S SYMPHONIC POEMS During the 1830s and 1840s musical forms were passing through a phase of miniaturization. After Beethoven's expansion of the symphony, composers turned inward and downward to smaller, more compact forms. Beethoven had made the symphony the supreme expression of music; but in the twenty-five years since the Ninth Symphony there had been only two works that could compete with Beethoven. One was Berlioz's program symphony, while the other, Schubert's C-major Symphony, was not performed until 1839, after almost being lost altogether. What, then, could be done with the symphony as a form? Or what other kind of music could be written for the symphony orchestra, the magnificent new instrument being brought to perfection in musical centers all over Europe?

An answer to these problems was provided around 1850 by Franz Liszt (1811–1883). Like Schumann, Chopin, and Berlioz, he worked impulsively, his first efforts often being his best. It might seem from his longevity that Liszt was atypical of his generation, but, in fact, he was its most complete representative, differing largely in that he was successful in many ways while his contemporaries were successful only in their own specialty.

EXAMPLE 124 CHOPIN: END OF PRELUDE NO. 23

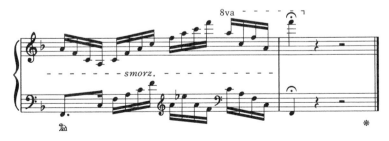

Liszt seemed to be several people all in one, or better, in turn. As a youth (1830–1840) he was a brilliant pianist, far excelling Chopin in large public performances. He wrote many songs and small pianoforte pieces; with a few exceptions these were his least substantial contributions, often only pianoforte transcriptions of other works, such as Schubert songs, for his own concert use. Then in 1848, Liszt became an orchestral conductor at Weimar; throwing himself into the situation with typical enthusiasm, he tackled the problem of the symphony. There followed a series of major symphonic works, two of them program symphonies (the *Dante Symphony* and the *Faust Symphony*), and twelve shorter works, or "symphonic poems."

Like the song and the small pianoforte piece, Liszt's symphonic poem had antecedents going back before Beethoven; but it was Beethoven's achievement in the symphony—as now interpreted by Liszt—that gave the symphonic poem new stature. Beethoven had naturally shaped his overtures (for example, *Coriolan* and *Egmont*) as he would a single movement of a symphony. We saw that Mendelssohn had written overtures directly for concert use. Instead of the overture preparing the audience for the play, the play—or whatever image might be evoked by the music's title or program—prepared the audience for the music. The concert overture was much like a Berlioz program symphony, or rather, a fragment of a program symphony, for the concert overture corresponded to a single symphonic movement in length as well as in shape and structure. In Berlioz the program provided the clue to the precise character of each section. It did not govern the internal structure of a symphonic movement, at most only explaining that structure, which sprang directly from symphonic shape.

For Liszt, at home in Paris during the 1830s, the development of style ran as much through Berlioz as through Schumann and Mendelssohn in Germany. When Liszt turned to symphonic composition he had Berlioz in his ears, and Beethoven as heard by Berlioz. Typical of his generation, Liszt composed fragments, but now fragments of the Beethoven-Berlioz symphony. He called these fragments *symphonic poems,* giving each a title and a program. The term *poem,* as Liszt used it, referred to the music, not to a literary poem that might appear on the title page as a program for the music. It was the music itself that was the poem, music being often regarded in the 1800s as capable of a more profound poetry than words. Even when the composer began with an extra-musical idea, analysis shows that he often selected, consciously or not, the kind of image for which musical style had already provided the musical expression. And the title or program only indicated the subject matter of the symphonic poem, not its inner structure, which, in Liszt anyway, remained truly symphonic.

Liszt's twelve symphonic poems have these titles:
1.   *Ce qu'on entend sur la montagne*
2.   *Tasso. Lamento e Trionfo*
3.   *Les Préludes*
4.   *Orpheus*
5.   *Prometheus*
6.   *Mazeppa*
7.   *Festklänge*
8.   *Héroïde Funèbre*

9.   *Hungaria*
10.   *Hamlet*
11.   *Hunnenschlacht*
12.   *Die Ideale*

The relationship between title, program (if there is a specific program), and music varies considerably from one work to another. Some, like *Orpheus*, have only Liszt's own explanation of the general character, placed at the beginning of the score. Others make reference to literary poems; *Die Ideale* has parts of a poem by Schiller interpolated throughout the score (but not in Schiller's original order). Similarly the length and structure of the symphonic poems vary. *Orpheus* again is a single movement, *Die Ideale* a long, sectional work like a complete symphony. *Tasso, Orpheus, Prometheus,* and *Hamlet* originated as real overtures to theater productions. *Mazeppa* began as an etude for pianoforte; *Héroïde* was part of early plans for a symphony.

Avoiding the traditional four-movement plan of the symphony, Liszt sought ways to use symphonic material in a novel format. He used literary programs to focus the image conjured up by symphonic style—to sharpen the character of individual movements, to explain to the listener the new ways in which he combined symphonic movements, and in some cases to stimulate his own creative imagination. His basic decisions, however, were made on musical grounds; the final shape of a work was determined by the same reasoning that had shaped and reshaped the symphony in Haydn, Beethoven, and Berlioz.

Mazeppa originally had a single character, that of a wildly demonic scherzo. To give this etude symphonic stature, Liszt added a triumphant martial finale, with results not unlike Beethoven's Fifth Symphony. For *Die Ideale* (the work most closely connected with a poem), Liszt again added a triumphant finale in the grand symphonic style; he called it *Apotheosis,* adding a note in the score that since he believed so strongly in the Ideal, he felt such a conclusion was preferable to Schiller's pessimistic one. Whatever Liszt's reason, the result was to pull this long work (already shaped like a symphony) together by purely musical means. As *Mazeppa* is a scherzo and finale, so *Orpheus* is a serene, sustained slow movement, and *Hamlet* is a brooding slow introduction and fast "first" movement— all derived from the symphony, all symphonic poems.

The symphonic poem that most impressed Liszt's contemporaries was *Les Préludes*. It, too, began as an overture, written for a large choral work Liszt never had performed. In order to present the overture separately, Liszt retitled it *Les Préludes, after a poem by Lamartine,* having selected Lamartine's poem as a likely program for the orphan overture. Since the connection between the overture and the poem was not very close, Liszt added his own program to the score, explaining the music but not making the connection to Lamartine much stronger. Here the music came first, the program afterward, the reference to a literary poem almost irrelevant, merely a stimulus to the listener to hear poetic images.

The music of *Les Préludes* reproduces the shape of a symphonic first movement, but with some important changes. After the introduction, a first theme is presented in C major; this same theme provides the material for the following modulatory passage—a common symphonic procedure. A contrasting theme is presented in a new key, E major (according to the same key plan

Beethoven had used in his "Waldstein" sonata, Op. 53). Actually the contrast is due to everything except the theme, which is a transformation of first one. Transformation of themes, giving them a new character and a new function, was indigenous to the symphony; Liszt made it his specialty.

As with Schubert, Liszt's themes are far more memorable than the bridge passages that connect them. After the second theme, Liszt means to increase the contrast of one phrase to the next, as Haydn and Beethoven did toward the end of the exposition. But the symphonic shape is more diffuse now, and the effect is desultory rather than more intense. The ominous beginning to a turbulent development section comes off much better. This section is identified by the return of the first theme, now placed amid unstable harmonies that foretell remote modulation. In the sequel, however, it is the outward shape of development, the chromatic eruptions, not the thematic development, that is most convincing. Like Berlioz, Liszt filled the development section with appropriate sounds but could not develop the theme. In *Les Préludes* the development section includes a pastoral episode that seems at first to alter drastically the symphonic shape. This pastoral section, however, has as its main function the anticipation of some kind of return; it is ultimately derived from the subdued transition inserted long ago before the tutti that announced the return to the tonic.

Up to this point Liszt followed the blueprint of the symphony. From here on he altered it, but in ways designed to heighten the symphonic effect—as every composer after Haydn had to alter Haydn's plan if he wanted to do something creative with the symphony. Liszt wanted *Les Préludes* to surge onward toward a big ending. He wanted only one big climax rather than the usual two (one at the recapitulation, another at the end). Anyway the means, the rationale of a big coda, thematic development, was lacking. So, from the pastoral episode at the end of the development section Liszt passed directly to the second theme (now in A major, an appropriate key for its recapitulation), and then gradually returned to the principal theme for a triumphant conclusion. Thus he avoided the formal effect of a literal recapitulation, using instead the warm feeling of recapitulation as a substitute for thematic development in the coda. The result is a different kind of symphonic form (in no way inferior as a form to the usual one) in response to the need to renew the effectiveness of symphonic style.

Liszt avoided formal aspects of symphonic style in still another way. Where Schumann had made harmonies move relatively faster, in more intricate progressions, Liszt now slowed down the harmonies again, opening the way to a broader, grander symphonic style. Liszt actually came closer to Beethoven than had Schumann or Mendelssohn, for by relaxing the more hectic harmonies of the 1840s Liszt avoided closed phrases (a major obstacle to Schumann's symphonic style) and thus recaptured the open feeling of Beethoven's harmonic progressions. There was a big difference, however, for the chords and progressions that Liszt expanded were more chromatic than Beethoven's, and when expanded brought about a more diffuse harmonic shape, giving (as in Chopin) the effect of more remote modulation. Then, instead of confirming a key by a series of chords, Liszt let the key feeling emerge out of a single sustained chord. He concentrated on single chords and the progression of one chord to the next. Certain chords, in particular the six-four chord (Example 125), became extremely poignant expressions of key all by themselves.

This concentration on the quality of a single chord had long been apparent, say, in Schumann, but Liszt did it on a much grander scale, giving his works a new, impressive tone, which we can sometimes hear shining through in Schumann, for example, in the first movement development section of the D-minor Symphony (and again at the beginning of the finale). There the sustained horn tones are full of power and mystery, but then Schumann breaks the spell with the busy, ineffective figure in the violins. Leaving aside their more mechanical features, Liszt seized upon such moments as truly expressive of symphonic grandeur.

In being so grand, Liszt ran the risk of bombast, which he did not always avoid. This was partly due to his nature as a successful showman (compare him with the impossibly shy Schumann), but partly due also to the needs of style at that moment. The symphony had to become bold again. In the treatment of figuration Liszt made the same kind of choice, for the same reasons. His use of figures is notoriously weak, which is to say he was not interested in constructing finely wrought textures for his harmonies. In Haydn and Beethoven, figure and harmonic ground were carefully integrated, but in Liszt the relation of figure to ground became tenuous and arbitrary.

Liszt shared with his contemporaries a need for highly characteristic, expressive figuration of a kind that did not adapt itself to symphonic development. These composers found their figures by inspiration; having found an appropriate figure they were reluctant to work over it for fear of losing its special character. Beethoven's workbooks show how he, on the contrary, profoundly modified the character of his figuration by working over it endlessly so that it would drive the harmonies forward; only as an end product did the figuration seem to take on character. In Liszt there is no real art of figuration. There are noble themes, but aside from these the harmonies are sustained largely through the opulence of the orchestral sound, in which the brasses, especially horns, play an increasingly important role. In this sense symphonic composition became more and more a matter of writing for symphony orchestra. Orchestration became a central discipline for the composer.

EXAMPLE 125   LISZT: FROM *LES PRELUDES* (reduction)

15
BETWEEN BRAHMS AND WAGNER: DEBUSSY 1850-1900

DURING THE SECOND HALF OF THE CENTURY THE GAP BETWEEN symphony and opera became steadily wider. But now someone stepped forward to fill that gap with a third kind of music that was neither symphony nor opera. Richard Wagner (1813–1883), profoundly critical of the shortcomings of symphony and opera alike, offered his new "music-drama" as the solution to the problems of the age.

Far from solving the stylistic split, Wagner's music-drama only brought the elements (heretofore coexisting safely in isolation) into dangerous proximity. On the one hand, the supporters of the new music-drama became engaged in acrimonious conflict with those of the symphony as revitalized by Johannes Brahms (1833–1897). On the other hand, symphony and music-drama both ran into sharper competition with various forms of traditional opera, especially as represented by Giuseppe Verdi (1813–1901). Words were exchanged and tempers flared—not the tempers of Wagner, Verdi, and Brahms, but of their self-appointed partisans.

The ensuing furor made it—and still makes it—difficult to draw an objective picture of what happened. There exist alternate interpretations of the course of music in the late 1800s, with corresponding variation in the assessment of the state of music after 1900. An attempt to trace the long line of history cannot afford to be partisan in this matter. It was a time of stylistic tension and disintegration; no one composer had a monopoly on the mainstream of development, and yet not all the composers share in it equally.

WAGNER'S MUSIC-DRAMA   Liszt had revived symphonic composition by emphasizing those aspects of the symphony that were most exciting, while avoiding stable, formal features of traditional symphonic shape. At the same time he broadened the harmonic progressions, exploiting the qualities of individual chords. More and more the feeling of symphonic shape, such as the warmth of recapitulation or the excitement of a coda, was conveyed to the listener through single chords or the progression between only two chords—fragmentary references to the long, powerful progressions in Beethoven. These stylistic developments in Liszt had a profound effect on Wagner, who, carrying them much further, brought musical style to its most important stage since Beethoven.

Wagner's musical achievement has been made especially difficult to understand because of all that Wagner himself, as well as many others, have said about it. Like many post-Beethoven composers, Wagner felt the need to explain and justify his music to the international bourgeois audience. He wrote several essays and many other communications (*Art and Revolution, The Artwork of the Future,* and *Opera and Drama,* 1849–1851) criticizing the state of music, setting forth his own artistic goals and how he intended to realize them. Wagner was expert—and unscrupulous—in representing his purposes as was most expedient. To avoid thorough confusion we must assess his musical accomplishment in stylistic terms, treating the propagandistic essays as secondary.

Wagner's mature works, especially the *Ring des Nibelungen* and *Tristan und Isolde,* are what he called music-drama. It might seem as though these works were the fulfillment of opera as written from 1750 to 1850, the solution to all the problems that had arisen from the discrepancies between traditional opera and the new symphonic style. Wagner had criticized without mercy the weaknesses and artificialities, both musical and dramatic, that made most recent operas so much less effective than the symphony. He bitterly attacked Italian opera as well as French and German forms, grand opera, opéra-comique, singspiel; he singled out, it would seem, those composers from whom he had learned most. Wagner went on to describe his own mission as an effort to make opera less artificial, more natural, more truly dramatic. But "dramatic" turned out to mean the kind of excitement he and others experienced in the high climaxes of the symphony. Rather than redeeming opera, Wagner's new music-drama was so symphonic that in many ways it seemed a fulfillment of the symphony, following the path laid out by Liszt.

Even here there was a discrepancy between what Wagner sometimes said and what he actually did. In his writings around 1850, he spoke of making the symphony articulate, able to speak words and convey ideas. He described how Beethoven, in his Ninth Symphony, caused the orchestra to burst into speech with a message for all mankind. Wagner went on to describe music-drama as the necessary consequence of Beethoven's achievement, for in music-drama the music of the symphony—heretofore dumb except for Beethoven's last work—could communicate its meaning clearly.

In his own musical compositions, however, Wagner made the music primary and the text secondary; ultimately the text merely floated on top of the rich orchestral sonorities, making their meaning more concrete but not necessarily more intense. Wagner's music-drama remained basically symphonic in the deepest sense: the text was in the end a program of the kind used by Berlioz and Liszt, to incite and guide the listener's imaginative response. Wagner himself later admitted that this had been the relation of music and text all along.

Why, then, did he write music-drama rather than symphonic poems? First, it seems, because he felt that the suggestive vagueness of his immediate predecessors was ineffective (it often was); he sought passionately to evoke an ever more concrete image. Titles and programs were not enough. There had to be singing, acting, staging, scenery, lights—everything had to be given a reason, a necessity. Wagner spelled out what his predecessors only hinted at, which accounts for the strong reactions that greeted his work. People found it either a triumphant confirmation or a tasteless overstatement. Second, Wagner clearly felt that the fragmentary pieces of his predecessors, even the symphonic poems of Liszt, did not allow sufficient scope for the expression of grandeur. It was time for music to assume a larger shape again, on the scale of Beethoven's Ninth Symphony. The symphony itself did not suit Wagner's purposes; and beside the symphony only the opera (speaking of musical forms as Wagner found them) presented the occasion for an extended musical work.

Hence Wagner had begun by writing opera—the grand. operas *Rienzi* (1842) and *Der Fliegende Holländer* (1843), then the grand romantic operas *Tannhäuser* (1845) and *Lohengrin* (1850). In these works he adopted many of the conventions of opera as practiced during the early 1800s, drawing on Weber (*Freischütz*) and Meyerbeer (*Les Huguenots*), but also Berlioz. After *Lohengrin*, however, Wagner became increasingly aware of how ineffective opera was when measured against the symphonic excitement generated by Beethoven.

Symphonies were exciting for Wagner, as for Liszt, in the amorphous slow introduction, in the lyrical "second" theme, in the eruptions of the development, in the tightening of the coda, all those places where the music seemed to catch fire and break out of the now traditional form. Because of stylistic development since Beethoven, this kind of excitement had been localized in individual harmonies. Liszt had shown how to deepen and enrich music by dwelling on these harmonies. It remained for Wagner to use the warm surge of feeling evoked by a sustained chord or a slow-breaking progression as the basis for his new music-drama. The high points of dramatic action became, for Wagner, transports of feeling brought about by harmonic effect, whose specific nature can almost always be traced back to one or the other high points of symphonic form.

Wagner himself gave a good description of the function of harmony in his music.

> If rhythm and melody are the shores at which the tonal art meets with and makes fruitful the two continents of art primevally related to it (poetry and the dance), then tone itself is the primeval fluid element, and the immeasurable expanse of this fluid is the sea of harmony. Our eye is aware only of its surface; its depth only our heart's depth comprehends. Up from its bottom, dark as night, it spreads out to its mirroring surface, bright as the sun; from the one shore radiate on it the rings of rhythm, drawn wider and wider—from the shadowy valleys of the other shore rises the longing breeze which agitates the placid surface in waves of melody, gracefully rising and falling.
>
> (from *Artwork of the Future*)

In building upon harmony in this way, Wagner sought out the hard core of stylistic development. Before his reform of opera, even before he was influenced by Liszt's harmonic practice, he had seen where this core lay. The Prelude to *Lohengrin*, considered one of his most successful pieces, is built on a single, carefully constructed progression that illustrates Wagner's effective use of harmony (Example 126). These chords are still set within a framework of key. Departing from E major (in the example) they return to E after a chromatic passage through F sharp and C sharp, their closed but wandering shape reminiscent of Schumann. Their pace, however, is different from Schumann and typical of Wagner. Each chord is an event in itself. Rhythm, not bound to jingling phrases or driven by figuration, proceeds from one chord to the next in a slow, steady pulse. We forget that the overall harmonic shape of the phrase is closed, its goal predetermined and audible in advance, for we sense a progress only chord by chord. In this characteristic kind of harmonic rhythm, Wagner found the way to renew harmony and with it musical style.

When Wagner's harmonic progressions are successful, they make even romantic opera, with all its problems, convincing; when the harmonies falter, they reveal the bombast and artificiality that endanger opera. The high point of *Lohengrin* is not the stage action or atmosphere still abundantly present in this romantic opera, but rather the moment when action stops and Lohengrin reveals his true identity in a long, sustained solo built over the harmonies of the Prelude itself (*In fernem Land . . .*, Act III). Here Wagner made effective use of a long-delayed recall, a proven device he was to use again (for example, the prize song in *Die Meistersinger*, 1867). This kind of dramatic effect is musical, depending both on the poignancy of the harmonies themselves and on their return after a long absence. Aware that his strength lay in such musical effects, Wagner turned his attention after *Lohengrin* to constructing theatrical situations and conditions that would permit him to capitalize on the power of music.

For greatest effect, Wagner gave each harmony the richest spacing, position, and orchestration he could, sustained the chord as long as he dared, and then moved to a second chord whose relationship to the first would be as exciting as possible. His purpose was to produce feeling—not vague, indefinable feeling, but a prickle on the back of the neck. He revealed to his contemporaries the last rich effects stored up within chords, effects accrued from the key plans in the symphonies of Haydn, Mozart, and Beethoven, and now spent lavishly by Wagner. This, too, made some of his contemporaries nervous, for they felt that the last, most intimate things should not be said—or else what would composers do

EXAMPLE 126 WAGNER: FROM PRELUDE TO *LOHENGRIN* (reduction)

next? Indeed, Wagner seemed to be writing the last conceivable style in music, which is a sign that he was following out the logic of stylistic development in the most progressive way.

Just as Liszt had avoided the square phrases of Schumann's symphonies by solemnifying the harmonies, so Wagner avoided the trite, jingling periods of traditional operatic arias. Operatic recitative was more difficult for Wagner to avoid, for in declaiming over sustained harmonies he was in fact coming very close to recitative. Even in his most advanced works he occasionally lapsed completely into traditional and unconvincing recitative. Everything depended upon keeping the sense of harmonic progression fluid, urgent. Toward this end he applied all his skill in orchestration, underlining important notes in the progression with short melodic fragments in an expressive orchestral color that brought out unsuspected power in a chord change.

Figuration, too, was important in animating harmonic change. Wagner had a greater command of figure than Liszt had had, and used it to make the slow rate of chord change more compelling. This he did by enhancing the power of an individual chord or by anticipating the second chord while the first was still sounding. The figuration did not, however, drive the rhythm forward over a long series of chords as it did in Beethoven. When Wagner tried to generate Beethoven's rhythmic momentum he often fell into mechanical figures or weak harmonies.

Even Wagner's poetic style (he wrote his own texts) helped urge the chords on. In his essays he made much of *Stabreim,* or alliteration of word beginnings instead of word endings, since traditional end rhyme had the same jingling effect he wished to avoid in musical phrase structure. In his musical settings of *Stabreim,* however, the principal effect of these short, alliterative lines is to bridge from one chord to the next, the alliteration highlighting the harmonic changes. Wagner's melodious recitative, his so-called "endless melody," rides supported on endless harmonic intensity.

All the details of Wagner's opera reform fell into place over this powerful harmonic foundation; but if the harmonic intensity slackened, the reforms by themselves were insufficient to hide the artificiality that still threatened his new music-drama. This danger is present throughout Wagner's grandest work, the *Ring des Nibelungen,* four mighty music-dramas forming a vast cycle of a prelude and trilogy—*Das Rheingold* (1854), *Die Walküre* (1855), *Siegfried* (begun 1856 but not finished until 1871), and *Götterdämmerung* (1874). Everything about this work (for it is one work even if it occupied Wagner for over thirty years) illustrates Wagner's unrelenting effort to make music overwhelmingly convincing.

In 1842 Wagner began working with the Norse legend of Siegfried the hero, finding in this cycle of myths the kind of material that best embodied the solemnity and mystery of romantic opera, avoiding the triviality of other types of operatic situations. The Siegfried story, being myth, evoked that depth of significance that lay behind, say, many Schubert songs, those which sounded like folk art. The importance of Wagner's treatment, however, lay in the immense scope of his conception: not a fragmentary folk song, not even one full-length drama, but four dramas, spelling out the mythical history of whole races of gods and heroes. Such was to be the final shape of the new music.

As Wagner worked with the story of Siegfried's death, the climax of the myth, he found it necessary to expand the prehistory, deepening its significance. Thus Siegfried's death takes place in *Götterdämmerung,* after having been prepared at length in the previous three dramas. The way in which Wagner led up to Siegfried's death is the exact analog of the way he achieved impressive musical effect. He made the approach to chord change so sustained that the final resolution was overpowering simply by being so long awaited. This technique of inner expansion is the basis of both Wagner's music and his drama; it is what makes them work. When the drama does *not* work (as happens here and there in the *Ring*), it is usually because the harmonies at that point lose their inner glow.

Some idea of the lengths to which Wagner expanded music can be gained from the sheer dimensions of the *Ring.* It has been argued that the four parts of the *Ring* are like the four movements of a symphony. It might, indeed, be possible to liken *Rheingold* to a slow symphonic introduction. Even if the comparison seems unbelievable (*Rheingold* lasts two hours), it is worth noting that *Rheingold's* opening E-flat major triad goes on for four minutes, setting up the extraordinarily large rhythmic pulse that is essential to Wagner's harmonic effects. As for the other "movements" of this "symphony," it is possible to see in the Ride of the Valkyrie (*Walküre,* Act III) a grandiose scherzo—a Beethoven scherzo with grim, pounding rhythms. *Götterdämmerung,* being a finale, can easily be compared (via Berlioz) to a Beethoven finale; it even has a hero's march (Rhine Journey, Prelude) like Beethoven's Ninth Symphony. But symphonic shape was not Wagner's basic aim, rather symphonic effect. What really makes the *Ring* like a symphony is not its plan but the way it uses the character of certain significant moments drawn from the symphony.

The symphony also provided Wagner with an especially effective way of using themes. The *Ring* is full of themes, usually called *leitmotifs* in this case, associated with people, things, or ideas important to the drama. Siegfried has a theme, his sword has a theme, Fate has a theme—and there are many more.

Ever since the early 1700s aria themes with ever sharper profiles participated increasingly in the emotional life of the opera. But what was available to Wagner far more than, say, to an Italian, was Beethoven's technique of handling themes in the symphony, where themes and motifs acquired power and character as nowhere else. Charged with deep significance, symphonic themes could become symbols of development deep within the work. So in the *Ring:* the themes or leitmotifs recur with or without the actual things they represent, their importance and efficacy being musical rather than strictly dramatic.

Finally, symphonic effect seems to be a source of the central idea of the *Ring,* of its musical genesis. The drama itself is resolved by Brunnhilde's immolation in the fire that destroys the whole race of gods and their glorious fortress Valhalla; but this destruction prepares the way for even greater things to come; hence the drama ends on a note of redemption. This conclusion is made dramatically credible by the music. After the tumultuous excitement of Brunnhilde's ride into the sacrificial flames, the character of the music changes, not abruptly but profoundly, to serene exaltation. This last-minute change of character is a symphonic device, one of the most thrilling developed since Beethoven. It can be found, for example, at the end of the first movement of Berlioz's *Symphonie fantastique* ("religious consolation"); in the Angelic Chorus at the end of Liszt's *Faust Symphony,* also in the Apotheosis he added at the end of *Die Ideale;* and after Wagner, but independently, at the end of Brahm's Third Symphony in F major (1878), there combined with a long-delayed recall. This "redemption" ending goes back stylistically to such works as Beethoven's F-minor String Quartet, Op. 95, and ultimately to Haydn's and Mozart's habit of concluding a vigorous section with something soft and different, thereby achieving a "characteristic" ending instead of a trite one. This last-minute change of character, tremendously expanded and provided with abundant mythical explanation and preparation, is the central, climactic idea of *Götterdämmerung* and of the whole *Ring.*

Wagner carried his conception of musical drama still further in *Tristan und Isolde,* which he composed between 1856 and 1859, interrupting work on the *Ring.* In *Tristan* the drama was conceived so as to facilitate the exploitation of luxurious harmonies and progressions. The substance of the work lies in Wagner's sensitive revelation of the qualities of harmony, the anticipations, delays, surprising but satisfying resolutions, presented to the listener in terms of unprecedented intimacy. The nature of the harmonic events is reproduced by the drama, but here, even more than in the *Ring,* the singing and acting ride on the surface of the harmonies. Even in terms of its text the drama is an inner drama. The plot, another medieval legend, is in itself unimportant, serving only to bring the two lovers, Tristan and Isolde, together in circumstances that prohibit their love. They yearn for each other. The progress of their yearning, in its most intimate aspects, provides a detailed, concrete program of the harmonic development going on in the orchestra. The climaxes are symphonic, even if the outward shape of the symphony is nowhere discernible. The last climax, another redemption ending of extraordinary power, belongs solely to the orchestra, being made possible by a release of all the energies stored up in the key plans of symphonic style.

The harmony of *Tristan* is sometimes called "atonal," meaning that there are no stable areas of key, no clear confirmation of a tonic. It is true that for Wagner a stable key is an uninteresting one. Chords that merely confirm a key already established had by Wagner's time little expressive value. But the moment of arrival at a key is another matter. This moment, this sense of arrival, is Wagner's principal harmonic resource, for in it is concentrated the whole weight of modulation. His chords either point strongly toward a key or else establish one.

What gives *Tristan* its special intensity is that keys are not established by direct routes but by indirect ones, by remote modulations. The obvious resolution of a chord is avoided in favor of an unexpected resolution—but a resolution nonetheless, one that establishes a new key. The special poignancy of such unexpected resolutions was made possible by Schumann, Chopin, and Liszt; Wagner simply slowed these chromatic progressions down to the point where each transitory moment could stand for a key. There are few new chords or progressions in *Tristan,* only more explicit use of chords and progressions which can often be found as far back as Haydn.

Wagner's harmonic effects are derivative, dependent upon a century of harmonic tradition. The opening chord of the Prelude to *Tristan* (called the *Tristan chord;* Example 127) seethes because of its several conflicting key impli-

EXAMPLE 127   WAGNER: EXCERPTS FROM TRISTAN (reduction)

(a) Prelude

Langsam und schmachtend (♪ = 72)

(b) Prelude

Zart

EXAMPLE 127 (CONTINUED)

(c)   Act III

(etc.)

(d)   Act II

(etc.)

cations. This chord and its partial resolution are repeated twice in different keys, the last time apparently preparing to cadence in E major through the repeated E sharp and F sharp; but when the cadence comes it is a clear F major (compare the similar progression in Example 110, meas. 38, and Example 123a).

Both the expectation of one resolution and the arrival of another unexpected one are essential to Wagner's music-drama. We cannot say that *Tristan* contains this or that special kind of harmony, for in *Tristan* Wagner did everything with and to harmony that could be done, neglecting no aspect of chord or progression that might yield another shiver. There are phrases almost as closed as those of Schumann, as in Example 127b. There are long, sustained chords whose key is abundantly clear, for example, further on in the Prelude, or in the passage in Example 127c. There are sequences, literal repetitions of progressions at different pitches; the most important one uses Beethovenlike chords, as in

Example 127d. The supreme climax is prepared by the most familiar progressions, written out in Example 128 in a schematic form. In Act II the resolution is interrupted by a deceptive cadence; at the end of Act III the expected resolution finally appears where the same passage is recapitulated, still using extremely familiar chords, but stressed in such a way that the effect is not trite.

Wagner's bitterest denunciations of opera had been directed at what he regarded as artificial conventions. In a comparison of Isolde's *Liebestod* with Lucia di Lammermoor's death in madness (the dramatic situations are not dissimilar), it is clear that the difference lies in the fact that Wagner succeeded in ridding his music-drama of all traces of artificiality. He did this, as he said he would, by ridding his music of the conventions of regular phrasing, as expressed in closed tonal shapes.

Both Lucia and Isolde die in ecstasy, each already experiencing union with her lover. Our reactions to the mad Lucia may range from purely musical delight to pity or wistful empathy. In Isolde's case, however, it is not she who is mad, but the everyday world. Isolde's world becomes, at the end, the real world; her ecstasy is real, for her and for us. We are persuaded of this extraordinary inversion solely by the music, specifically by the overpowering treatment of tonal modulation. Whatever may be said—and plenty has—about the ultimate truth of Wagner's vision, his greatness lies in his ability to persuade us musically, if only for a moment, that the vision is real.

AFTER WAGNER; MUSSORGSKY After Wagner, musical style tended to split apart, as was usual toward the end of a stylistic period. Now composers had to worry not just about Beethoven but about Wagner as well. Beethoven had done so much, and now it seemed that Wagner had done the rest. Whether or not composers approved of the direction taken by Wagner, whether or not they thought that his way was the way of the future, still it was clear to all that

EXAMPLE 128 WAGNER: REDUCTION FROM TRISTAN, "LIEBESNACHT" AND "LIEBESTOD"

Wagner had done something drastic to musical style, something that could not long be ignored. Even if composers like Mussorgsky, Brahms, and Verdi pretended to ignore Wagner, still they were all engaged in a desperate struggle to rival the standard of intensity that Wagner had set.

Inside Germany and Austria composers tended to work within the symphonic tradition. Bruckner, Brahms, and Mahler sought their stylistic identity back of the line drawn by Liszt and Wagner. Genuine Beethovenlike symphonies appeared from 1873 on, after an interval of half a century. Outside the German orbit the situation was more confused, with many composers (Dvořák, Tchaikovsky, Franck) following out the renewal of German symphony. More important, however, were the achievements of those peripheral composers who tried to avoid Wagner by some other route. These composers were alike only in their intense desire to be original—unique, if possible—finding some special character for their music outside the symphony or Wagnerian music-drama. The goal, special character, was, of course, old, being the same goal pursued by Haydn. Achievement of the goal, however, led these peripheral composers further and further away from the central symphonic style. Each sought in himself or in his surroundings the means to establish his stylistic identity. Local color, national traits, folk song—all were used for this purpose, with extremely diverse results in different countries and composers.

Perhaps the most characteristic, if not the only unique, composer of the 1800s was Modest Mussorgsky (1839–1881), who best represents a famous group of Russian composers dedicated to freeing Russian music from German influence. Michael Glinka (1804–1857, Berlioz's generation) and Alexander Dargomizhsky (1813–1869, Wagner's generation) had already started the search for genuine Russian character, working chiefly through opera. The next generation brought the Mighty Five—Alexander Borodin (1833–1887), César Cui (1835–1918), Mily Balakirev (1837–1910), Modest Mussorgsky (1839–1881), and Nicolas Rimsky-Korsakov (1844–1908). Of these only Mussorgsky achieved the kind of musical character that permits his work to stand up next to the Germans. Mussorgsky's stylistic connections, bypassing Wagner, led back to the German tradition through Schumann. Like Schumann, Mussorgsky composed a few masterpieces at a relatively early age, and then deteriorated and died at forty-two. In addition to a "Symphonic Fantasy," *Night on Bald Mountain* (1867), Mussorgsky wrote *Pictures at an Exhibition* (1874) for pianoforte, a work often compared to Schumann's *Carnaval*.

Mussorgsky's most ambitious, characteristic work was *Boris Godunov* (1874) a "National Folk Opera." National identity and local color were provided by folk songs, both for solo voice and for the huge mob scenes (Coronation Scene, Prologue) in which Mussorgsky presented the Russian People as the drama's true hero. Such folk elements, however, seem external when compared with the inner character of Mussorgsky's striking melodic style.

Like Wagner, Mussorgsky avoided the set forms of aria and recitative, or at any rate infused them with new dramatic urgency; like Wagner, Mussorgsky's lyrical declamation was made possible by the fluid harmonies he got from Schumann's generation. Mussorgsky's harmonic practice was more conservative than Wagner's: Mussorgsky sought novel effect not through increased chromatic modulation but rather through more diatonic means—whimsical twisting of phrases within a key, substituting one triad for the function of another. When combined with Russian-style melodies, this oblique use of harmony brought about that clouded, exotic quality that makes Mussorgsky unique.

BRUCKNER, BRAHMS, AND THE SYMPHONY

Back in Austria, a return to the symphony was already under way. The composer might be pro-Wagnerian, like Bruckner, or anti-Wagnerian, like Brahms, but in either case his model was Beethoven. The goal was a reinstatement of the symphony; not symphonic poem or symphonic drama, but symphony, with four movements, fast, slow, dance, and finale. Neither Brahms nor Bruckner had any intention of ignoring what had gone on since Beethoven. They incorporated, each in his own way, the new treatment of harmony, figuration, and orchestration developed by Schumann and Liszt. What they sought in Beethoven's symphonic form was grandeur, lacking both in Schumann's symphonies and Liszt's symphonic poems—grandeur of a kind to ensure the composer's works a place alongside the *Ring*, finally finished in 1874.

Anton Bruckner (1824–1896), an organist by trade, finished his First Symphony in 1866; death interrupted his Ninth in 1896. Aside from Masses and a *Te Deum* he wrote little else. In spite of his worship of Wagner (in 1873 he took his Third Symphony to Wagner to lay it at his feet) Bruckner's symphonic style clearly derives from late Beethoven, especially from the Ninth Symphony. The differences are those made necessary by stylistic evolution; harmonies are more ponderous, the orchestration richer. Although the traditional outline of the symphony is plainly audible, the inner logic and momentum are lacking. The movements are separate entities, fitting into the overall plan but not generating it of their own power. The relationship of figure and ground is dissolved, as was revealed when Bruckner removed from the Third Symphony some themes and motifs intended to refer to Wagner's leitmotifs, without, apparently, disrupting the intended structural effect. The symphony was now truly a form into which the composer poured whatever material struck his fancy. Bruckner's symphonies can be convincing, but only because of Beethoven—or because in some mysterious way Bruckner's own sincere conviction is communicated to the listener.

Johannes Brahms (1833–1897) led a new kind of career, different in many ways from composers of the first half of the century. He lived long, worked hard, and as he worked he learned how to improve his first inspiration. He grew up a friend and frequent visitor of Robert and Clara Schumann. As a youth he composed three grandiose, disjointed sonatas for pianoforte in the style of Schumann; but he soon settled down to more disciplined habits of composition. It is reported that he papered the walls of his room with twenty self-rejected string quartets before he made one he was willing to publish.

His early output during the 1850s and 1860s was substantial, but mainly in the smaller forms of chamber music or song. There were no symphonies, only an early concerto for pianoforte, Op. 15 (1859), another grandiose and basically unsuccessful piece. Brahms approached the symphony with infinite caution, trying out his orchestral technique in Serenades (in D, Op. 11, 1858, and A, Op. 16, 1860) and going back to Schubert and even to Haydn for models. He wrote a set of variations on a theme by Haydn (Op. 56, 1873) in two versions, one for orchestra, one for two pianofortes.

All the time he was nursing along the sketches of a symphony, keeping his ideas strictly to himself. He knew he had to write a symphony to survive. It was a necessary step to greatness, the only alternative to opera, for which he had no gift, or music-drama, for which he had no stomach. For twenty years he thought about his first symphony. "I shall never compose a symphony! You have no idea how hard it is for our kind to hear the tramp of a giant like him (Beethoven) behind us." Finally, in 1876 he did finish it—Symphony no. 1, in C minor, Op. 68. It was well received; but one person called it the "tenth symphony," and everyone saw the point. Since 1824, the date of Beethoven's Ninth, there had been no large-scale, nonprogrammatic, first-rate symphony by a German composer (except Schubert's in C major, which as we saw was little known). Another person commented on the similarity of the theme of Brahms's finale to Beethoven's *Ode to Joy.* Brahms felt the similarity so obvious as to render the comment inane, and said so.

It was laborious but not problematic to make a piece the size and shape of a symphony. The problem lay in making the size and shape convincing, avoiding the obvious discrepancies between form and harmonic content. After Liszt, harmonies were ponderous and harmonic effect momentary, accentuating the tendency of the symphony since Schubert to fall into fragments. Brahms had to make the harmonies reinforce the form, urge it forward, define its progress. To do this he had to sacrifice some of the prevalent harmonic richness so that the intoxicating quality of a chord would not blur the sense of phrase. On the other hand, to accelerate the basic harmonic rhythm would be to invite a trivial effect. Brahms arranged his chords in closed periods not unlike those of Schumann, but devoted careful attention to the avoidance of periods so clear as to jingle. It was a narrow path that Brahms trod, with the danger of too much sense of phrase, on one hand, and not enough, on the other. In his First Symphony he favored the intense, chromatic progressions used by Schumann, broadening them so as to achieve the breadth and grandeur appropriate to a symphony (Example 129). But compared with Wagner, such a phrase is stern and austere, lacking harmonic warmth. These severe qualities remained dominant in all Brahms's symphonies.

If Brahms was haunted by Beethoven's sense of form, he was haunted also by Schubert's lyricism. Brahms seemed to lie in wait for a moment when the symphonic discourse permitted an overflow of melodic and harmonic warmth, as in this passage (Example 130a) from the continuation of Example 129, and another passage (Example 130b) from the Second Symphony in D, Op. 73 (1877). Such moments, even though soon passed over, contribute much to the nostalgic quality of Brahms's symphonies—a stylistic nostalgia, a longing for the language of *Tristan,* so effective in itself but so dangerous for symphonic form.

Where Berlioz had found the outer movements of the symphony hard, Brahms now experienced difficulty with the inner ones. They had a tendency to sound alike, approaching each other in character. This was due mainly to Brahms's reluctance to write a headlong scherzo. Especially in the Third Symphony, in F, Op. 90 (1883), the slow movement is faster than usual and the Scherzo slower. In the Second Symphony the slow movement is slow enough, but the first movement is unusually lyric, again lessening the contrast among the

EXAMPLE 129 BRAHMS: FROM SYMPHONY NO. 1 (reduction)

EXAMPLE 129 (CONTINUED)

movements. It is typical of Brahms and his concern for symphonic shape that he seriously considered writing a new first movement for this Second Symphony after it was all finished! The reduction of contrast between movements, then, was not accidental but deliberate; it was indicative of how Brahms tended to move within tradition rather than trying to burst out of it, softening rather than exaggerating stylistic traits. Brahms played it safe, especially in the symphony.

Figuration was one of Brahms's major concerns. He knew that the control of figure had made symphonic form possible in Haydn, Mozart, and Beethoven. He labored long and hard to make his own figuration both functional and characteristic, with the result that in this respect he far surpassed every other composer since Beethoven. It is in this respect, too, that he most improved over the years, demonstrating in the Third Symphony and even more in the Fourth in E minor, Op. 98 (1885), an ability to make the figuration swirl along in true symphonic style.

Brahms found the way to make the figuration point up the phrase structure, getting the right figure at the right spot. This had been Haydn's art, virtually lost since Beethoven. It required little inspiration and a great deal of hard work, which suited Brahms's personality perfectly. The result was a compelling sense of melody with but few striking tunes—the very basis of symphonic style. Brahms could not always sustain the magic of melody, often because of a gray or ineffective harmony that suddenly made its figuration seem mechanical. Hence he did not completely close the gap between figure and harmonic ground that had opened up in Schubert. But when he did close it, the symphony caught fire once again, as in the high climax to the first movement of the Fourth Symphony.

Another mighty passage brings the last movement of the Fourth Sym-

EXAMPLE 130 BRAHMS: SYMPHONIC EXCERPTS (reduction)

(a) From Symphony no. 1

(b) From Symphony no. 2, second movement

phony to a close. This last movement (which follows one of Brahms's best slow movements and his only symphonic scherzo) is a set of variations, significant both in its form and genesis. Brahms always regarded variations as a potentially fruitful form, meaning one that Beethoven had not used much in symphonies. Brahms's choice of themes for variations is revealing—the Haydn variations already mentioned, an early set for pianoforte solo on a theme by Schumann, and an especially fine set, also for pianoforte, on a theme by Handel, this set being Brahms's mature substitute for a sonata. Then, in the Fourth Symphony, Brahms turned to J. S. Bach.

Bach was revered during the 1800s for the very qualities that made him inaccessible to the 1700s—contrapuntal and harmonic density. These qualities competed successfully with Wagner while avoiding Wagner's sense of luxury. At the same time, Sebastian Bach afforded Brahms a model different from and more remote than Beethoven, whose presence Brahms still felt as a burden.

In the recently published volume no. 30 of the Bach-Gesellschaft edition (Brahms was on the editorial board), he found both the idea of a set of strict variations and the theme itself, in a ciacona from Cantata no. 150 (*Nach dir, Herr, verlanget mich,* now thought not to be by Bach). It was necessary, as Brahms pointed out, to liven up the theme with a little chromaticism. This remodeled theme, eight measures long, underlies the whole finale of the Fourth Symphony. Brahms gave the eight-bar ostinato intense forward drive by an abundance of figuration. Although most of the movement is marked with that stern grandeur Brahms heard in Bach, the slow middle section contains, paradoxically, one of the most Wagnerian passages Brahms ever wrote, set in the voluptuous sound of a soft brass choir. This, however, is a lyrical episode, followed by a pseudo recapitulation and a free exciting coda superimposed on the continuing variation form, all showing that for Brahms musical drama, or at any rate epic, was still to be found in the symphony.

The symphonic achievement of Brahms, while inaccessible to much of the bourgeois audience and ridiculed by the Wagnerians, had an especially profound effect on composers, all the way from Antonin Dvořák (1841–1904; his Fifth Symphony in E minor, *From the New World,* 1893), to Anton Webern (1883–1945, most radical composer of the 1900s), for whom Brahms's tight structures were a starting point. Brahms was one of very few composers in the 1800s who put more into the symphony than he took out of it. Although like Bruckner in relying on Beethoven's framework, Brahms was unlike Bruckner because he packed this framework full once again with new, interesting detail. His work became a storehouse of figures and phrases still used after 1900. Throwing up symphonic form as a bulwark, Brahms staved off for a while the inevitable dissolution of musical style that set in after Wagner.

Just the opposite was true of Peter Ilyitch Tchaikovsky (1840–1893), whose important symphonies appeared concurrently with those of Brahms—the Fourth Symphony in F minor, Op. 36 (1877), the Fifth Symphony in E minor, Op. 64 (1888), and the Sixth Symphony in B minor, Op. 74, the *Pathétique* (1893). Often criticized, these symphonies have more merit than is allowed them, especially when seen in terms of their own stylistic circumstances. Caring little for tight structure. Tchaikovsky strove to make the symphony as effective, as characteristic as possible. He used every traditional device in the most obvious way, making for an overwhelming transport of Wagnerian intensity, but one that diminished the usefulness of these devices at an alarming rate. By the Sixth Symphony Tchaikovsky's indiscreet use of the same symphonic effects began to wear them out; it is difficult to see what kind of symphony could follow. Tchaikovsky said it straight out, and after that it could never be said again by serious, creative composers.

There is, however, a certain justification of Tchaikovsky's procedure. Symphonic style was coming to an end—Brahms could probably see that much. Why not pour out the symphony in three last heart-rending works, and put an end to it? Better that, perhaps, than encouraging nine more symphonies by Mahler, another seven by Sibelius, twelve by Shostakovitch, to say nothing of many less impressive efforts. The symphony was old in 1825; perhaps Brahms did a disservice by rejuvenating it. Whatever their relative merits, both Brahms and Tchaikovsky represent normal phases of stylistic development. Both the cautious reworking of old forms and their reckless, once-for-all consumption seem to be necessary steps in exploiting the last resources of a style.

VERDI   A special place has to be set aside for Giuseppe Verdi (1813–1901, Wagner's generation) because he himself arranged it that way. Belonging to no one phase or trend of modern (German) music, Verdi, it seemed, was always there, working away down in Milan on one good opera after another, from *Nabucco* (1842) to *Falstaff* (1893). Unlike the Germans, even Wagner (but not Brahms), Verdi lived long, worked hard and patiently, and improved as he got older. Unlike all the Germans he sought not individual character but universality, being in this respect the only composer of the 1800s to measure up to Beethoven, for Wagner and Brahms had divided Beethoven's inheritance, and public opinion, between them.

Still, Verdi sought universality within national character, that is, within Italian opera, the principal artistic embodiment of Italian national character. Verdi wrote opera because he was an Italian; he sought to come ever closer to the genius of this art form inherited from the 1800s and 1700s. In choosing a nonsymphonic form and finding in it a special, national character, Verdi was doing what Mussorgsky had done with *Boris Godunov*.

The discrepancy between intrinsic worth and historical significance is perhaps greater with Verdi than with any other major composer except J. S. Bach. Verdi chose to say what he had to say in a form and style that had only a past—no stylistic future and a debatable position in the present. At his best, Verdi spoke musical and human truths as profound as those of any man in his century. That he did so within the framework of traditional opera (capitalizing on all the potentialities of the new grand opera while mostly avoiding its weaknesses) is one of the wonders of the age. But in so far as he chose deliberate avoidance of Wagner, and of the mainstream Wagner represented, Verdi's triumph belongs to his own story, not to the story of style.

In his last works Verdi did make contact with the fluid tonal structures characteristic of the late 1800s. Although not apt to admit it, Verdi was looking for ways to rival Wagner's harmonic and orchestral opulence (Verdi once, in a rare moment, admitted his admiration for Wagner's orchestration). Verdi sought now to make his music incandescent, as Wagner had done, succeeding supremely in *Otello* (1887), but never allowing it to blur the clear dramatic gestures that were the essence of Italian opera.

STRAUSS AND MAHLER   What Tchaikovsky had done for the symphony, Richard Strauss (1864–1949) did for symphonic poem and music-drama. If Brahms had lived too close to the end of a style, Strauss lived hopelessly beyond it. Only his early symphonic poems are stylistically significant—*Don Juan* (1888), *Tod und Verklärung* (1889), *Till Eulenspiegels lustige Streiche* (1895), *Also sprach Zarathustra* (1896), and *Don Quixote* (1897). In his music-dramas, however, *Salome* (1905) and *Elektra* (1909), Strauss exploited musical sensationalism so ruthlessly that he cut away the foundation for his own further development. "Louder, louder!" cried Strauss to the orchestra at a rehearsal of *Elektra*, "I can still hear Madame Schumann-Heinck!" (the soloist). The sense of extravagance, of wasteful extremes, reflected in this anecdote marked as well the extremes of expressive dissonance and distorted modulations in his music-dramas. Yet for all the dissonance in *Salome* and *Elektra*, Strauss never became really engaged with its stylistic problems and possibilities. After *Elektra*, Strauss chose not to pursue the implications of his work up to that point.

Strauss's early symphonic poems occupied an important stylistic position as exciting, if somewhat gaudy, successors to those of Liszt, capturing the glamour sometimes omitted from the symphony because of overriding demands of form. The harmonic effect of Strauss's tone poems derives from Wagnerian transport; still, they have an energy, even a grace, of rhythmic figuration that is un-Wagnerian. These tone poems are still genuinely symphonic; like all the best program music of the 1800s, the program is secondary to the music. In *Tod und Verklärung*, perhaps the most substantial one, the literary poem came after the musical one, just as with Liszt's *Les Préludes*. Other of Strauss's tone poems, like *Don Juan*, do indeed have programs that correspond to the events in the music, but the music is always constructed independently according to symphonic style, drawing from it expressive strength.

Don Juan begins with a clear exposition of contrasting themes (here even the key plan is traditional), a development section with a long idyllic excursion as used by Brahms and Liszt, a recapitulation introduced by a heroic horn summons, and a high-riding coda that ends with a final turn toward darkness—the other side of Wagner's redemption ending.

Keys could by now be solidly established with a single, well-placed chord, and hectic modulation from one chord to the next provides much of the warmth of Strauss's style, as in Example 131a. On the other hand, long dwelling on a few clear but unresolved chords without much modulation is also used effectively. The mighty horn figure at the beginning of the recapitulation of *Don Juan* shows the power of the symphony now concentrated in a dominant pedal (Example 131b). Strauss tended to exploit the extremes of harmonic rhythm—rapid modulation, on one hand, static chords, on the other. These extremes, when combined with his energetic though unsubtle figuration and brassy orchestration, made a vigorously effective style; not the least of its virtues were drive and brevity.

Both these qualities were lacking in the symphonies of Gustav Mahler (1860–1911), the first of those symphonists already mentioned whose musical talents might have found some more congenial form of expression. An extremely sincere, sensitive personality, Mahler did indeed produce masterpieces within smaller forms. His songs and song cycles, for example, *Lieder eines fahrenden Gesellen* (1884), are rich in character, and over before Mahler's structural weaknesses become apparent.

Das Lied von der Erde (1908) for tenor, soprano, and symphony orchestra is also highly effective because it presents symphonic ideas in relatively concise fragments in connection with a text. The individual numbers of this cycle have the sharp focus of a Schubert song, the warmth and breadth of Liszt or Wagner, and something of the intricate craftmanship of Brahms. But what Mahler did best he did in brief moments. With his clear (one might say, clair-

EXAMPLE 131   STRAUSS: EXCERPTS FROM DON JUAN

(a)   Reduction

(b)   A theme

voyant) orchestration he could open up a familiar harmonic progression, revealing a hidden bit of musical expression neglected by Beethoven or even by
Wagner.

   This ability, while derived from symphonic style, was the antithesis of
large-scale structural control; yet Mahler persisted in writing symphonies,
making them larger and larger until their shape no longer bore any real musical
relationship either to the expressive fragments with which they were filled or to
the shapes of Haydn and Beethoven from which they were descended. As if in
frustration at these unresolvable contradictions of style, Mahler's musical expression tended to become convulsive, seeking to be effective through sheer

exaggeration. The extraordinarily intense, hypertense, language so produced became one of the starting points of a whole new style, but only in the hands of Mahler's admirer, Arnold Schoenberg (1874–1951), who saw that this intense language had to be dealt with objectively, abstractly, divested completely of its symphonic past. Mahler's symphonies still belong to Beethoven, even though illuminated from within by Wagner; as such they marked the end of an era.

FRENCH MUSIC AND DEBUSSY   French music after 1850, determined for the most part to ignore Wagner, was perhaps for that very reason susceptible of deep involvement with him. Since the Parisian opéra-comique was now a strongly conservative institution, its repertory tended to be anti-Wagnerian, Wagner's influence making itself felt chiefly in instrumental music. An opéra-comique *Faust* (1859) by Charles Gounod (1818–1893) became an international favorite (recitatives were added to make it "grand"), but from a Wagnerian point of view this work was blasphemy of the Faust story, holy writ of German romantic opera. A few years later Georges Bizet (1838–1875), who is said to have burned the score of his five-act, unperformed opera *Ivan le Terrible,* made a great success with *Carmen* in 1875. Bizet matched the hard realism of Mérimée's story with blatantly appealing songs. Friedrich Nietzsche, Wagner's keenest critic, could find no more telling gibe than to praise *Carmen* as the most important modern music and the best antidote to Wagnerian malaise.

Sympathetic resonance with German music appeared in the work of Camille Saint-Saëns (1835–1921), who wrote symphonic poems (*Danse macabre* and others, 1872–1877), pianoforte concertos, and cyclic symphonies. His first operatic success, the oratoriolike *Samson et Dalila,* had to be produced by Liszt in Weimar (1877) before Saint-Saëns was accepted as an opera composer in Paris. The German style was best represented in France toward 1890 by César Franck (1822–1890), whose only symphony, in D minor (1888), is as much Brahmsian as Wagnerian—a remarkable example of how German the French music had become at that time.

Claude Debussy (1862–1918), as a young man of twenty-six, underwent a heavy attack of Wagnerianism, cured eventually by his second pilgrimage in 1889 to Bayreuth, the shrine of music-drama Wagner had created. In attempting to control, define, and intensify all elements of his new music, Wagner had built his own theater, where his dramas could be performed under ideal circumstances—not performed, but "celebrated" as the central events of a quasi-religious festival in which composer and audience were reunited in a sweet artistic communion longed for by every composer of the 1800s. Reinstatement of the bond between himself and the international, anonymous audience was Wagner's greatest triumph and final goal. Confronted with its full implications, Debussy fled.

Thenceforth Debussy shrank from any musical effect that might seem to impose upon the listener, let alone overwhelm him, with the Wagnerian power Debussy found so nauseating. Debussy was faced with the same problem as every other post-Wagnerian composer: he had to rival Wagner's intensity in order to be heard at all. Debussy used Wagner's chords, progressions, orchestrations, set in motion Wagnerian transports, but then always cut them off before they threatened to engulf the listener.

Debussy's characteristic fragmentation of musical style is a direct result of using Wagnerian harmonies out of context. Debussy hinted at Wagner. He spoke with discretion and sophistication, always with impeccable taste, hardly ever raising his voice—spoke nonetheless with great sensitivity, verve, sometimes wit and sarcasm. We might discern in these qualities a Parisian character; we might say that Debussy found in this character the stylistic identity that Mussorgsky found in national folk songs. Being French was almost the only thing in which Debussy ever again became truly involved. During the First World War he became passionately concerned with the cause of France, proudly signing himself "Debussy, French musician."

Soon after reaching thirty, Debussy completed his first major work, the String Quartet (1893). It was to be his only one, just as Franck wrote only one symphony. The Quartet follows the traditional plan to a degree one might expect only in Brahms, indeed the very act of writing a string quartet might be taken as a symbolic renunciation of Wagner. Yet the harmonies of Debussy's Quartet seethe like Wagner's; there are lyrical transports that, even though disciplined in their outline, still indicate clearly their origin. The work was criticized as an "orgy of modulation." A fine work in its own right, Debussy's Quartet is not yet truly characteristic of Debussy or of French music.

The famous *Prelude to the Afternoon of a Faun* (1894) began a series of orchestral pieces that were Debussy's equivalent of the symphonic poem. The *Prelude* uses the full resources of the symphony orchestra, and, in typical fashion, has a tenuous connection to a poem by Mallarmé. Originally there was to be also an "Interlude" and a concluding "Paraphrase," but these (again, typically) were never written and the work remains a prelude, descendant from the concert overture. Like the symphonic poems of Liszt and Strauss (and also those of César Franck), Debussy's *Prelude* may or may not be internally related to the poem indicated by its title; in any case, its effectiveness is symphonic.

Stylistic maturity came with the three Nocturnes for orchestra (1893–1899). These works manifested a special character that ensured Debussy's musical identity, an identity almost as strong as Mussorgsky's (whose *Boris Godunov* Debussy came to know in 1889). The three Nocturnes each have titles: the first is *Nuages* (Clouds), the second *Fêtes* (Holiday Celebration), the third *Sirènes* (the kind that sit on rocks, seducing ships to destruction by their singing). These Nocturnes provide abundant example of Debussy's style.

Debussy is sometimes described as a harmonic innovator; most of his harmonies, however, are traditional forms or merely slight modifications of those forms. What makes Debussy's harmonies sound different from Wagner's is the speed and direction with which they move. The warmth—the very substance—of Wagner's music came from the functions of chords, the directions implied by them, whether or not these directions were actually followed out. Debussy minimized the functions of chords, concentrating instead on their sonorous quality. There were many different ways of playing down chordal functions. Sometimes Debussy used only a part of a chord, a third or a fifth, for example, in place of a whole triad (Example 132a). Other times he made the chord overrich by adding notes to it, usually in such a way as to make the chord less functional, more static, as in Example 132b.

Having constructed a chord that was both interesting and static, Debussy

EXAMPLE 132   DEBUSSY: EXCERPTS FROM *NUAGES* (reduction)

(a)

Modéré (♩ = 84)

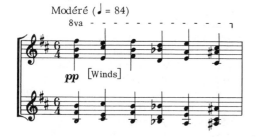

(b)

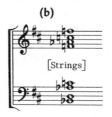

(c)

(d)

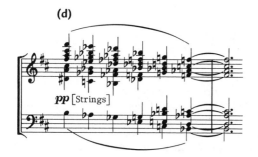

(e)

EXAMPLE 132 (CONTINUED)

(f)

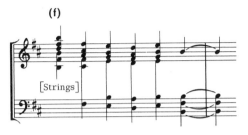

[Strings]

often let it stand still; so-called "standing chords" (Example 132c) became a specialty of Debussy's. Like Chopin's chords, Debussy's were animated from within, either by some odd but insistent rhythmic pattern or by novel orchestration. Such chords shimmered, but showed no inclination to move toward another chord. As a student of César Franck, Debussy used to infuriate the old Wagnerian by his performance in keyboard improvisation class. "Modulate, modulate!" Franck would cry, pounding on the lid of the pianoforte. "Why should I modulate? I am perfectly happy where I am," was Debussy's response. And outside of class, "César Franck is a modulating-machine."

When Debussy did move from one chord to another, the effect often bore little resemblance to traditional modulation, even to extreme Wagnerian modulation. He used chord changes to produce a fresh sound, not to heighten feeling. Hence he avoided even the indirect resolutions used by Wagner, and instead moved to a chord that had no strong functional relationship to the preceding one. He often obliterated functional relationships by moving in parallel motion, especially in motion by whole tones (Example 132d to f), thereby avoiding the leading-tone progression essential to traditional harmonic function. Wagner's harmony was dominated by the semitone; Debussy's by the whole tone, which both made the chords more bland and the progressions—or better, successions—less functional.

With the sense of key and the force of modulation virtually eliminated, musical organization often depended on minimal factors, such as orchestral timbre, or on the least hint of a motif. *Nuages* has a simple *A . . . BA'* form; on paper, at least, the A section could be understood as in B minor, the B section as in the dominant key F-sharp major, the A' section as returning to and ending in B minor. The more perceptible clues to the form, however, are the motif for English horn, and then the fresh sound of flute and harp in the B section. *Nuages* is of course a "cloudy" piece in all respects; for a comprehensive understanding of Debussy's style one must see the same techniques at work in *Fêtes* and *Sirènes,* where they produce entirely different atmospheres—*Fêtes,* rhythmic and brassy, and *Sirènes,* voluptuous. The brass band in *Fêtes* gives the curious impression of being in quotation marks; it is not a genuine product of Debussy's own style, but is borrowed for special effect.

Often called *impressionism* and related to painting, Debussy's music can with equal justification be called *symbolism* and related to poetry, especially in connection with his music-drama *Pelléas and Mélisande.* The text of *Pelléas* is a stage play by Maurice Maeterlinck, a symbolist poet. The uniquely happy marriage of music and text in this work is due to a coincidence of musical and poetic techniques. Debussy's isolation of chords, the way he concentrated on their intrinsic quality while leaving their connection to be rationalized by the listener, perfectly matches the style of Maeterlinck's text, whose characters speak in disconnected fragments, weighty with symbolic significance. In *Pelléas* Debussy wrote his own version of *Tristan*—erratic, understated, as un-Wagnerian as possible. *Pelléas* tends to sound languid; as antidote it is important to keep in mind another music-drama that occupied Debussy for many years without materializing—*The Fall of the House of Usher,* by Edgar Allan Poe. We can only imagine how Debussy would have set Poe's dark horror story.

Along with *Pelléas,* Debussy is best known for *La Mer* (1905), a large orchestral piece of symphonic dimensions. *La Mer* may even be Debussy's version of a symphony, the only kind he could have written. Debussy's small piano pieces are as original as Chopin's. *Estampes* (1903) and *Images I* (1905) and *II* (1907) best illustrate the sensuous, shimmering sound Debussy got out of the pianoforte. But here, too, we must keep in mind the more characteristic *Préludes* (1910–1913) with their many sharp sounds and odd turns of phrase.

As Debussy got older he became less dreamy; his music tended to become bright and hard, particularly in the Sonata for Violin and Pianoforte (1917), one of his last works. This Sonata seems at first prophetic of the new style of the 1900s—harsh, discontinuous, largely without a sense of key. Actually, the work only shows how Debussy was breaking up traditional style into its smallest fragments without finding a way to combine them into a new style. Many elements of the new music of the 1900s (such as the standing chord, or structure through texture) can be traced back to Debussy, but only as isolated elements, combined by Debussy only through a uniquely personal style that showed, among other things, how personal a matter style had become.

PART 5
BEYOND THE TRIAD
1900-1964

16
NEW MUSIC AFTER 1900

MUSIC OF THE 1900s OFTEN SEEMS TO US DIFFERENT FROM ALL other music. Much of the reason lies in its nearness to us. But the past, too, is near us: it is firmly embedded in our listening habits; it is manifest in our standard repertory; it is in the minds and ears of our most radical composers. In their extremes of revolt, contemporary composers betray their desire to continue certain basic procedures of Western music, while seeming not to. Music of our time looks different; but—after mid-century—nowhere near as different as it did in the 1920s.

Music of our time seems perhaps most different in the kinds of sounds it makes. Some composers have concentrated their efforts on making radically new sounds, while content to attach these sounds to relatively traditional shapes. Yet more thoughtful composers have found it more meaningful (as well as more difficult) to create really new musical shapes. These composers have also found it extremely difficult, if not impossible, to create new shapes with purely traditional sounds. At the very least, the sounds of music must change, and change again; this has always been true.

In spite of the great variety shown by music of the 1800s, it had evolved one most characteristic set of shapes, especially apparent in German symphonic style. The most exciting parts of the symphony had come to be the developmental ones, where the music surged on in ever-changing modulation, carrying the thematic material through continual transformation. These developmental shapes derived their great expressive power from their departures and especially arrivals at clear keys; but these were represented by increasingly fragmentary and momentary harmonic functions (typically a single six-four chord) until finally expression itself seemed synonymous with modulation of key and transformation of theme.

These developmental shapes, characteristic of German music, were the same ones on which Debussy had gagged. As we saw, one of his chief concerns was the frustration of the German harmonic juggernaut; he simply did not allow development to start. He interrupted the harmonic functions, still clearly present in many of his chords, by emphasizing their color, their separateness, anything that would make them static. Such procedures, at least in Debussy's hands, often led to new, unique shapes.

The choices confronting composers right after 1900 can be conveniently polarized around Wagner and Debussy. On one side lay developmental forms, based on chromatic modulation and leading to extremes of expression. Hypertense, often dissonant chordal language was draped on a long, surging line. The composers of such music were often concerned with the inner organic continuity, with the guiding expression or idea of the work at hand. These composers tended to drive forward from their Wagnerian basis as fast as possible, as if to put a safe distance between them and the past to which they were so closely connected.

On the other side lay the discontinuous forms, based upon static sonorities or interrupted progressions. Subdued in tone, or at least detached and objective, this music was less concerned with inner expression, more with qualities of sound and style. The composers of such music (for whom "organic" could be a dirty word) were in less of a hurry to leave the past. Or, having cut themselves off from Wagner and all he stood for, they enjoyed a more amiable intercourse with the pre-Wagnerian past, drawing on it for both triads and triadic forms—yet with the sense of detachment characteristic of all they did.

These two alternatives found strongest representation right at the beginning of the century; later generations found compromises. Of the two groups of composers, the radical post-Wagnerians worked in relative obscurity, while the radical post-Debussyites enjoyed fame, or at least notoriety. Each group followed its own destiny, ignoring, for the time being, the other. We will have to consider them separately.

THE INTERNATIONAL SCENE   As happens so often at the end of a style, there was a shift in the locus of composers, but this time no single locality replaced the old center, Germany. Rather, leading composers now came from the whole periphery of Germany—central Europe, Russia, Italy, France, Scandinavia, England, and the Americas. Of the four most important composers, Webern and Schoenberg were Austrian, Bartók a Hungarian, Stravinsky a Russian. Schoenberg, Bartók, and Stravinsky all fled eventually to the United States; Webern was an exile at home.

The large, bourgeois audience of the 1800s became even larger in the 1900s; it became a mass audience, consisting ultimately of anybody, anywhere. This mass audience, much of it meeting art music for the first time, experienced great difficulty in following new trends. The mass audience moved slowly; the discrepancy between its growth of comprehension and the composer's growth of creation now became so severe as to disrupt completely the normal interplay between the two. A composer often had to choose between matching his stylistic growth with the capacity of his audience, which would force a rate of development slower than ever before, and developing in a vacuum, with all the risks that entailed.

There were, however, alternatives in between. The mass audience tended to split into a number of more specialized audiences, as had already happened with opera and symphony devotees. The composer's problem lay more precisely in establishing contact with the most compatible audience. But then what was to become of the ideal of the universal language, the composer's message for all mankind? And if box office and publisher had not proved adequate support for a composer who addressed himself to the mass audience, how much less adequate for a composer who contented himself with a fragment of that audience? These and other questions have weighed upon composers down to the present.

During the 1900s the traditional forms of opera and symphony became increasingly distant from each other and increasingly fixed in repertory. Numerous other repertories appeared, each with its own audience. The lighter forms of opera engendered various kinds of musical comedy. Music for social entertainment, songs and dances, was cultivated on a scale commensurate with the rapidly expanding audience now reached through mass media. The exaltation of folk song during the 1800s led eventually to a repertory of country-style music for the modern mass market. Concerts of "early" or "pre-Bach" music became increasingly frequent. Interest in music from other times led to formal university instruction in the history of music and to books, such as this one. Interest in music from other places expressed itself in another formal discipline, ethnomusicology.

All these developments confronted the listener with an unprecedented wealth of musical experience, requiring of him an unprecedented informedness and catholicity of taste. At the same time, the wealth of experience distracted the listener's attention from the growing edge of music; it offered him alternatives to new music. The inquisitive listener could experience fresh sounds in music from other times and places, thereby escaping the challenge of the avant-garde. Progressive, avant-garde music tended, in the listener's view, to become merely one more repertory among so many; it tended, furthermore, to have its own special audience.

The account in this book must limit itself strictly to the serious, progressive repertory, primarily because this is the only one that carries out the thrust of development traced so far. But the gap between what is described here as the development of style and the actual state of music in the modern world may well be disturbing. To be sure, this discrepancy does not appear for the first time in the 1900s: a similar discrepancy existed, say, in the 1500s. The anomalies, contradictions, strange juxtapositions that we see around us are part of the reality of musical life. Still, the development of musical style seems to have been obscured by conservative competition more today than ever before.

Just as there are many audiences with many different ideas of what music is, so are there many ideas of how it got that way. Even within the relatively small area of progressive art music, there are several mutually irreconcilable interpretations of history. Some observers feel that the whole history of musical style since 1900 has been an incredible mistake, if not a disaster; others feel that the whole history of style before Webern belongs to a dark age not worth considering. (Of the two views, incidentally, the latter would be more characteristic of the centuries before 1800.) Only the long line of history can help us sort out the development of style in our time.

As the composer's relationship to the audience disintegrated, he began to establish—or reestablish—other contacts with society. After a century of proud free-lancing, composers now rediscovered some of the advantages of patronage. Anyway, it was unreasonable to expect a composer to make a living off such a motley audience as he now faced. Commissions, either from individuals or groups, became again an acceptable way of financing musical composition. Elizabeth Sprague Coolidge (1864–1953), called by Schoenberg an "ideal patron," might be singled out as one example among many. She founded a festival and a string quartet, subsidized important concerts, and commissioned works from Bartók, Prokofiev, and Stravinsky, among others. But some patrons were institutions rather than individuals. Princely prerogative of ancient times, which had often been erratic but usually had had a sharp focus, then tended to give way to bland committee taste.

A special kind of patron emerged in the United States of America. Composers frequently became teachers at universities, gaining thereby a livelihood, a position, and contact with one of the most responsive segments of the mass audience. University patronage became especially important after mid-century, sheltering almost all of a new generation of Americans with international ambitions and abilities to realize them. In Europe comparable patronage was offered by state-owned radio facilities, such as the British Broadcasting Company or German Southwest Radio (Cologne).

Public performances were often a problem to the new composer. Existing institutions, committed to traditional opera and symphony, dared confront their old audiences with new works only when goaded by fearless, imaginative conductors such as Leopold Stokowski (1882–) or Dmitri Mitropoulos (1896–1960). Early in the century modern composers banded together, agreeing, for lack of a more suitable audience, to listen to one another. Composers' leagues seized upon the idea of a festival, already current (as at Wagner's Bayreuth) in established repertories. The earliest such festivals of contemporary music took place in Donaueschingen (Germany) in 1921, Salzburg and New York in 1922. The International Society for Contemporary Music (ISCM) has continued its festivals to the present, providing premieres of some of the most important works, as well as a proving ground for young composers and a lively cross section of developing style.

MUSIC AROUND 1910 The prevailing instability of style after 1900 was apparent not so much in startling novelty as in the variety of things still possible within the tradition. This variety is made clear by a list of important performances (most of them premieres) from the 1910–1911 concert season:

September 12	Mahler: Eighth Symphony (Munich)
November 30	Bloch: *Macbeth* (Paris)
December 10	Puccini: *The Girl of the Golden West* (New York)
January 8	Schmitt: *Tragédie de Salomé* (Paris)
January 26	Strauss: *Rosenkavalier* (Dresden)

March 15	Scriabin: *Prometheus* (Moscow, Koussevitsky conducts)
April 2	Ravel: *Daphnis et Chloe,* suite I (Paris)
April 3	Sibelius: Fourth Symphony (Helingsfors)
May 22	Debussy: *Le Martyre de St.-Sébastien* (Paris)
May 24	Elgar: Second Symphony (London)
June 13	Stravinsky: *Petrouchka* (Paris, Monteux conducts)

Mahler's Eighth Symphony (". . . of a thousand") was a triumphant affirmation of symphonic form, based on themes and keys. *Macbeth,* impressive lyric drama by young Ernest Bloch (1880–1959), had the form of *Pelléas* and the dark tone of *Boris Godunov;* it struck conservative observers as totally disorganized. Not so *The Girl of the Golden West* by Giacomo Puccini (1858–1924), who along with Pietro Mascagni (1863–1945; *Cavalleria rusticana,* Rome, 1890) and Ruggiero Leoncavallo (1858–1919; *Pagliacci,* Milan, 1892) exploited the achievement of Verdi without significant advancement—as is proved by their position as rear guard in opera repertory of the 1900s.

La *Tragédie de Salomé,* "mimodrama" by Florent Schmitt (1870–1958), another impressive work, stood close to Debussy, although with brighter, harder sonorities. *Rosenkavalier* seems to mark Strauss's failure of nerve; whatever its charm, it does not belong to the story of progressive music. *Prometheus,* symphonic poem by Alexander Scriabin (1872–1915) was at least resolute in following out the logic of modulatory expression to some kind of end point. Inner idea illuminated Scriabin's rambling music with mystic enthusiasm; *Prometheus* included a special keyboard to project color analogs on a screen.

While hardly a Debussyite in any strict sense, Maurice Ravel (1875–1937) shared Debussy's discontinuous forms. Were it not for lush harmonies, *Daphnis and Chloe* would sound a lot more modern than it does. In his own elegant way, Ravel had some of the bright hardness of the next decade. The Fourth Symphony of Jean Sibelius (1865–1957), like his other six, seems to have little to do with the circumstances described in this chapter; his work is a masterly, but isolated, extension of symphonic thought and form into a personal realm. Debussy's *Le Martyre de St.-Sébastien* is one of his most inaccessible works. A relatively detached, objective set of incidental pieces to a curious drama, *Le Martyre is* far in spirit from *Pelléas.*

If Edward Elgar (1857–1934) belongs to the past, so, in a curious way, does *Petrouchka,* Russian ballet by young Igor Stravinsky (1882–); but *Petrouchka* belongs also to the present. It has the color-rich, inflated orchestral resources fashionable around 1900, especially in connection with a fantasy realm of Russian or Near Eastern fairy tales—a kind of music descended from the operatic concepts of the Russian Five, and now represented by Rimsky-Korsakov. Yet Stravinsky's harmonies in *Petrouchka* were static, his musical shapes disjunct, far more than Debussy's. And beneath the brilliant orchestral overlay, Stravinsky's chords, built in strange ways, moved in strangely insistent rhythms. *Petrouchka* already carried the imprint of a new style.

Parisians and Others; Bartók

Stravinsky was in Paris in the employ of the remarkable manager of the Russian Ballet, Sergei Diaghilev (1872–1929), who mustered the best young talent around 1900 to give a series of brilliant performances in Paris. In writing for ballet, Stravinsky, along with other young composers, found an outlet that was to be characteristic for decades. Music synchronized with other art forms—dance, poetry, or dumb show—was to elicit some of the best efforts of some of the most creative composers. These composers discovered in ballet and similar media the means to pull together their discontinuous musical shapes. A story of some kind served as substitute for the tonal line previously sustained by harmonic function.

Petrouchka presented its stylistic novelties under the guise of amiable sophistication (notwithstanding the story's dark whimsy), but Stravinsky's next ballet score, *Le Sacre du printemps* (1913), exposed the same novelties to full view. Harsh *polychords* (chords that seem to combine elements of two or more traditional chords) were reiterated relentlessly in a *unit pulse,* a rhythm of eights or quarters, say, repeated metronomically without a regular grouping. The unit pulse was usually accented at unpredictable intervals with violent, often dissonant orchestral outbursts.

The first performance of *Le Sacre,* May 29, 1913, was the scene of a riot, one whose significance has often been overemphasized. In the first place the audience's reaction was probably due as much to Nijinsky's crudely "naturalistic" choreography as to Stravinsky's music. In the second place, scandals were a perennial feature of Parisian musical life, and the Parisians were spoiling for a good one.

Particularly during those decades (1900–1920), audience reaction to musical novelty was often incommensurate with the actual degree of novelty. A seasoned critic described Ravel's *Daphnis et Chloe* (suite I) as "harmonic and polyphonic anarchy." It is clear that "anarchy" now meant not absolute musical disorder, but merely failure to confirm the familiar functions of triads and their derivatives in the delicate balance of tonal forces defined by Haydn. This refined order by now seemed natural, and deviations from it were regarded as open rebellion against nature and reasonable conformity with nature. A whole succession of well-bred, relatively harmless works was condemned, before and after 1900, by a smaller or larger portion of the audience as antimusic. And the worst was yet to come.

The years around 1910 saw the introduction of unorthodox procedures. In 1912 young Henry Cowell (1897–1965) in a concert in San Francisco, demonstrated his new "tone clusters" produced by striking the keyboard with the forearm. Charles Ives (1874–1954) worked in New England throughout the years 1900–1914 (and beyond) with novel sounds and mixtures of sounds. Like Cowell, he used tone clusters, for which he prescribed in the Concord Sonata (1909–1915) a board $14\frac{3}{4}$ inches long.

Ives combined a taste for novel sounds with realistic representation; he wrote choral music in quarter tones to reproduce the variations in pitch he heard in amateur church singing. He valued the sounds he heard around him as evocative of deep human associations, and he combined these sounds, and their associations, with texts (in songs) or with one another in free rhapsodic fashion. The sincerity and visionary breadth of his works have made them highly regarded by some observers.

Even before Ives, others were concerned with the possibilities of quarter tones and other "microtones," either constructively or coloristically. A different coloristic approach was taken by Luigi Russolo (1885-1947). Calling himself a "futurist," he produced first a manifesto, and then in 1914 a concert in Milan. His instruments were nineteen noisemakers, including "3 bumblers, 2 exploders, 3 thunderers, 3 whistlers, 2 rufflers, 2 gurglers, 1 fracasseur, 2 stridors, 1 snorer." An engaging account of the concert includes the observation that in the riot the futurists fared better than the "pastists," being better prepared for hand-to-hand combat. Clearly much of the fun has since gone out of modern concert life.

These and other novelties did not of themselves result in new shapes for music. Indeed, in some respects these experiments belong to a disintegrating phase of the old style rather than to an integration of a new one. Nonetheless, the search for novel sound has continued in some quarters down to the present, sometimes under the naïve assumption that a new sound would automatically lead to a new shape.

Stravinsky and other composers were not insensitive to such experiments. Stravinsky had a habit of waiting to hear how a new sound behaved in a real concert situation before he himself used it. Between 1914 and 1917 Stravinsky worked on *Les Noces* (*The Wedding*, choreographic scenes), sung like an oratorio by chorus and soloists, accompanied by four pianos—or better, fortes —and a large battery of percussion. Here the techniques of unit pulse and polychord are carried out in sounds that are hard, mechanistic, noiselike, recalling Russolo's intent but interpreting it more musically. The last sound of *Les Noces* illustrates Stravinsky's tendencies: basically an octave with an included second, B–C sharp–B, it can be taken as the wedding bell, a meaningful association in terms of the scene of the Russian peasant wedding. But this sound can also be regarded as an interesting, beautiful chord, wonderfully appropriate to a spot where a triad—or a real bell—would be an artistic mistake.

PARISIAN MUSIC-HALL STYLE Stravinsky was not even in the first rank of the Parisian avant-garde. A young man called Jean Cocteau (1889–1963) led the avant-garde in a denunciation of Debussy's "dampness" (as Cocteau called it). Bright, hard, brassy, commonplace—this was what music had to be to be new, real, Parisian, and above all shocking; *épater le bourgeois*, to shock the bourgeois concert goer, became a principal goal.

Cocteau, a poet, conscripted a composer named Erik Satie (1866–1925). Now Satie, left to his own devices, was a deliberate cipher. He wrote music as neutral, as close to absolute stylistic zero as it was possible to come. He did this, it seems, as his own private attempt to erase the superabundance of associations piled deep upon musical sounds. Satie seemed to recall to the ear the qualities of sound itself.

Cocteau caught up Satie for his own purposes, got him to write music for *Parade*, an offhand little show for which a young painter, Pablo Picasso (1881–) contributed the sets. Diaghilev produced *Parade* in 1917. Another riot took place. Of Satie's music, it can be said that it went on at the same time as the representation; it included commonplace song and dance idioms, such as were found in the music hall or vaudeville; it was devoid of the usual artistic pretensions. Most of all, it sounded unlike Debussy. This concept of music made sense only in terms of the whole artistic package; but it made sense.

Stravinsky again followed out a proven novelty with something more musical. In 1917–1918 he collaborated with the poet Carlo Ramuz (1878–1947) in *L'Histoire du soldat* (The Soldier's Story) a tale of our time set for dance, narration, and music. It was hard, brassy, objective music like Satie's. It was described (first by Ramuz) as a work of expediency, constructed to make possible a traveling show at a time when the deepening war made normal concert life impossible. But experts submit to expediency only when it suits their higher purposes; *L'Histoire du soldat* had an artistic validity that far outlived the wartime conditions. It became a model for the 1900s.

Much of *L'Histoire du soldat* works with the unit pulse already found in, say, *Petrouchka;* now, however, it is far more in evidence (owing to the cleaner instrumentation), as are also the polychords. The excerpt in Example 133a is representative, while Example 133b, from the Great Chorale, is a uniquely concentrated sample of Stravinsky's new harmonic technique. These chords are not full of "wrong notes" (as is sometimes said) but rather of right notes, just the notes required to give triads a new, interesting sound in a cogent context. The Great Chorale repays careful study. It is also one of several examples in *L'Histoire* of borrowing styles, a habit of Parisian composers.

After the war, concert life soon resumed its normal dimensions; but the new kind of ensemble, with its brassy, impersonal sound, now became standard for the avant-garde. Parisian music took the lead—at least, it made the most aggressive sounds, dominating the European scene for a large part of the 1920s.

One of the most energetic and skillful of the Parisians was Darius Milhaud (1892–). In 1920 Cocteau put Milhaud's music to work in a little show called *Le Boeuf sur le toit* (The Cow on the Roof—the name of a café that is the mise-en-scène). The deliberately casual construction of such plots, featuring unrelated "events," and their even more casual relationship with music ("wall-paper music," it was sometimes called) encouraged adaptation of instrumental scores to theater use, and when the original theatrical production was past, the adaptation of background music into concert suites.

In 1918 Paris first heard a jazz band; composers like Milhaud seized upon the new idioms as a welcome relief to the limited music-hall idioms already in use. One of the most attractive examples of Parisian art jazz is Milhaud's *Création du monde,* music for a Negro ballet representing the Creation. Jazz had its dark side, its blues, as well as its bright, hard one, and Milhaud's artistic adaptation of the blues added depth to the music-hall style.

Spirits were lively among postwar Parisian composers; it was art against the bourgeois world, and cameraderie among the avant-garde ran high. A casual association among Milhaud and five other composers, labeled *Les Six,* became a temporary symbol of modern music. Francis Poulenc (1899–1963) youngest of The Six, survived it to become an important composer of the next two decades, as did Milhaud.

Arthur Honegger (1892–1955), while sharing in the spirit of The Six and some of its techniques, sought and found a higher vision and a wider audience. *Le Roi David* (King David) was written first as incidental music for

EXAMPLE 133   STRAVINSKY: EXCERPTS FROM *L'HISTOIRE DU SOLDAT*

(a)   From the Introduction to the Second Part

(b)   From the Great Chorale

EXAMPLE 133 (CONTINUED)

meno f   (etc.)

seventeen instruments and percussion to a play. Then, because of its great success, it was converted into a concert work with solos, chorus, narration, and
large orchestra. Honegger's success was due to a compromise with the past, a
softening of the hard contours favored by the Parisian avant-garde. *Le Roi
David* had some of the old symphonic ecstasy in its alleluias. In accordance with
the sacred subject, Honegger adopted, in place of jazz idioms, analogous
rhythmic shapes from Bach.

Parisian music-hall style made its impact felt throughout Europe. To cite
only one of many examples, the energetic young German composer, Paul
Hindemith (1895–1964), joined in the fun with a *"1922" Suite,* Op. 26 (1922),
and an especially effective *Kleine Kammermusik* (Chamber Music for 5 Winds,
Op. 24, no. 2, 1922).

Much of the delight of the Parisian style came from the relationship, or
lack of it, between the music and what text it might accompany. The texts,
often made by such experts as Cocteau, were full of artistry in spite of their
casual appearance; they do not survive translation. The best access for the
English-speaking public to this aspect of Parisian style is a work called *Façade*
by the young Englishman William Walton (1902–), written in 1922 to accompany poems by Edith Sitwell (1887–1965). Here the absorption with sparkling
sound, the intricate interplay of text and music, the casual sophistication are
all readily apparent.

Student composers were especially attracted to Paris in the early twen-
ties. Their works appeared after 1925, at a time when the original Parisians
(Milhaud, Stravinsky, Honegger) were already doing something else. There were
some very successful operas (?) analogous to Parisian music, for example,
Jonny spielt auf (Johnny plays! Leipzig, 1927) by Ernst Krenek (1900–).
Aaron Copland (1900–) came back from Paris with a Concerto for Piano and
Orchestra (performed, 1927, with the Boston Symphony Orchestra). George
Antheil (1900–) also returned with a portfolio full of pieces that he performed
in a famous concert at Carnegie Hall on April 10, 1927, including his *Ballet
mécanique* (originally conceived as music for an abstract film of that name), for
eight pianos, a player piano, four xylophones, sound of a large airplane pro-
peller, and of a small one, a large doorbell, a small one, glockenspiel, and percussion. Virgil Thomson (1896–) wrote a soft-spoken opera, *Four Saints in
Three Acts* (Hartford, 1934) on a text by Gertrude Stein (1874–1946: they
worked on it together in Paris). When George Gershwin (1898–1937) wrote

American in Paris in 1928, it seemed like a nostalgic memorial to an intermezzo now gone by.

Honegger, always something of an outsider in Paris, had written a symphonic poem called *Pacific 231* (1924), representing a famous type of locomotive. Despite its mechanistic sounds (all produced by the orchestra), Honegger's tone poem represented another compromise with the shapes of the past. A similar, but more adventurous, use of mechanistic noises with a program appeared in the *Steel Foundry* (Moscow, 1927) by Alexander Mossolov (1900–), lively Russian composer of the twenties.

Far more advanced and sophisticated pieces were written by Edgar Varèse (1885–1965). A synthetic mind, like Stravinsky, Varèse mixed noise-makers alla Russolo with unorthodox orchestral sounds in new shapes. His *Hyperprism* (New York, 1923), for winds and percussion (including noisemakers) provides a fascinating study in form, as well as intensely intricate moments of a kind that eventually became most characteristic of music of the 1900s. *Octandre* (1924), *Intégrales* (New York, 1925), and *Ionisation* (1931), for mostly percussion, are other important works.

Varèse's chords are far from triads, his tonal structures remote from tradition. Successive musical events are pulled together by an implicit logic of textures and timbres, as in Debussy. The basic design, the long line, is expressed in minimal ways; yet the line is there, setting Varèse's music apart from lesser composers. And while the line may seem at first totally unrelated to old, familiar shapes, it can eventually be seen as sharing certain principles with them. Indeed, understanding the shape of a piece such as *Hyperprism* is one of the best ways of understanding what shape means in the symphony.

Finding one's way in the twenties could be full of hazards; few composers had a harder time than Sergei Prokofiev (1891–1953), a professional in an age afflicted with amateurishness. On an ill-starred American tour Prokofiev finally got his opera performed, *Love for Three Oranges* (Chicago, 1921). Interpreting the mechanistic Parisian sounds with his own peculiar energy and with a strong admixture of nostalgic, tuneful sentiment, Prokofiev wrote a number of successful concert works, especially sonatas and concertos for piano.

BARTÓK Béla Bartók (1881–1945) was trained in Budapest, about equally far (in terms of style) from Paris and Vienna. Impressive in his musical sincerity and sustained by profound inner conviction, Bartók made for himself a place at the very center of style during the first half century.

His early works tend to be the most rhapsodic, the most diffuse. Bartók first sought identity within the folk songs of his own people—following the example of many peripheral composers at the end of the 1800s. Then came the violent works, rebellion against not only the forms but the standards of the immediate past. *The Miraculous Mandarin,* a pantomine for dancers and orchestra, had both the blatant sensationalism of Paris and a gory emotionalism we will find at Vienna during the early 1900s. Bartók worked over the *Mandarin* several times from 1919 to 1926; even so, it was, and is, a shocker, provoking the customary scandal at early performances.

At the same time, Bartók had already started down a third path, one that eventually led to realization of what he wanted to do. He found in the string quartet an ideal medium for the intensely serious music he wanted to write— cogently expressive yet fully discursive. He valued the developmental forms of the past and sought ways to make them available to the present. The string quartet offered a special opportunity to use these forms, perhaps because it was not represented by imposing works in the immediate past, only the remote past. In many ways Bartók's six string quartets seem to be the continuation of the stylistic curve traced by Beethoven's late works, one not followed out in the 1800s.

Bartók's First String Quartet (1908), while impressive, is not yet in focus. Even so, one can see what kind of music Bartók aimed at. The slow introduction, reminiscent both of the introduction to Beethoven's Quartet in C-sharp minor, Op. 131, and of the Viennese quality often found in Brahms, has a sustained lyricism that was Bartók's ideal for the rest of his life. With the Second String Quartet (1917), Bartók achieved much greater stylistic definition; here we find many features of his mature style already formed.

As always with Bartók, the overall shape is important. The Second Quartet has a moderately fast first movement, full of varied material under close thematic control; then comes a very large scherzo and a slow movement. That concludes the quartet—a deliberate and convincing modification of traditional form.

The first movement, especially, is marked by the developmental shapes indigenous to the quartet. Bartók was steeped in chromatic modulation, a ubiquitous feature of musical style around 1900. He had by nature a lively imagination, capable of producing a wealth of musical figures. In other early works the combination of these two factors resulted in rhapsody, but in the Second Quartet they were disciplined into something more cogent.

Bartók's chromatic procedures are illustrated in Example 134a, from the opening of the Second Quartet. The accompaniment is full of dissonant intervals, mainly seconds, which serve to cloud a traditional progression Bartók might have had in mind but found too innocuous. Every traditional chord (and there are many) can be imagined in its original functional context, and every novel chord can be reduced to its traditional model—an exercise that gives insight into Bartók's lifelong search for more intense sounds.

This first phrase breaks off, having avoided the goals (but not the shape) of chromatic modulation. It is followed by another phrase that immediately starts the development of the theme, after the manner of Haydn. The originally rhapsodic melody starts to acquire thematic definition. All these procedures were normal to the string quartet; Bartók was concerned to find new sounds with which to express them. Often he comes very close to tradition, covering it up only with a few semitones. Example 134b shows the introduction of a second theme after a transition. There is a resolution to an A-major triad (meas. 3) over which the theme (viola) plays C natural, B, and G sharp. Bartók favored this friction of a simple chord with a melodic figure that did not fit.

(Bartók's quartet writing is very difficult to render in reduction, due to his frequent inversion of the instrumental ranges for the sake of subtly new sonority. These examples in reduction, designed primarily to show tonal pro-

EXAMPLE 134 BARTÓK: EXCERPTS FROM THE SECOND QUARTET

(a)

EXAMPLE 134 (CONTINUED)

EXAMPLE 134 (CONTINUED)

cedures, should be carefully compared with the score in order to understand the instrumentation.)

In due course (meas. 5) the A-major harmony moves to a sixth chord in D flat; a similarly expressive change can be found in measures 7 to 8, again discolored by the lyric line above. These and other progressions Bartók carefully salvaged from the old style. The end of Example 134b starts a long developmental passage with a turn of phrase that would be at home in Brahms. As the development proceeds, however, the freely phrased rhythms and continual frictions between the lines reveal Bartók's own style at its best. The developmental line reaches a climax in an especially sharp dissonance (Example 134c) of a kind that was to wound the ears of the mass audience for several decades.

Moments such as this were essential in directing the rhapsodic development to a sharp focus. Bartók characteristically used something very strong—often very simple—to give, as it were, the point of the discourse. Strong exclamations of several kinds can be found in this movement, particularly toward the close. These strong moments also serve to clarify the key plan, which converges on A, even though including a broad spectrum of keys. Indeed, Bartók illustrates better than anyone else the fact that the composer of the 1900s lives in a closed harmonic space, one whose limits increasingly restrict his movements. There are literally no more new keys to go to. At the beginning of the recapitulation, the introductory figure (from Example 134a) is placed in a context that alternately refers to B-flat major and E major, through the same pivotal tritone, A–E flat (D sharp).

The scherzo has the same clear focus (now on D) and the same broad sweep through other keys. Its rhythm illustrates Bartók's version of the unit pulse, handled by him with the same mechanistic insistence and frenetic drive, but grouped (even if freely) into larger, more traditional, rhythmic units.

The third movement is another kind of piece Bartók wrote often and with loving care. Extremely slow-moving harmonies, often simple, are accented with exquisitely dissonant motifs. A different effect occurs in an episode (Example 134d). These chords seem at first hearing entirely new, completely alien, as indeed they are in their sound. Yet the shape they outline is a familiar one; the whole passage can be seen as a strongly personal interpretation of a chordal pronouncement one might find in Beethoven.

Bartók's Third String Quartet (1927) takes us into new regions; here Bartók came closest to the extreme radical tendencies around him. The form of the whole quartet is furthest from tradition, consisting as it does of a Prima parte (slow), a Seconda parte (fast), Ricapitulazione della prima parte (slow), and Coda (fast); in theme and character the shape is *ABA'B'*. And while the Coda is clearly related to the Seconda parte, the Ricapitulazione is a recapitulation only through an inner logic but dimly perceptible.

Within sections, too, traditional forms are clouded over or completely eliminated. The first part consists of a series of disjunct phrases, loosely connected by motivic material. The first two phrases are chromatic and flowing; then, after a strong pronouncement in bare fifths, Bartók starts to speak the strangely broken language of our time (Example 135a). A ground is furnished

EXAMPLE 135 BARTÓK: EXCERPTS FROM THE THIRD QUARTET

(a)

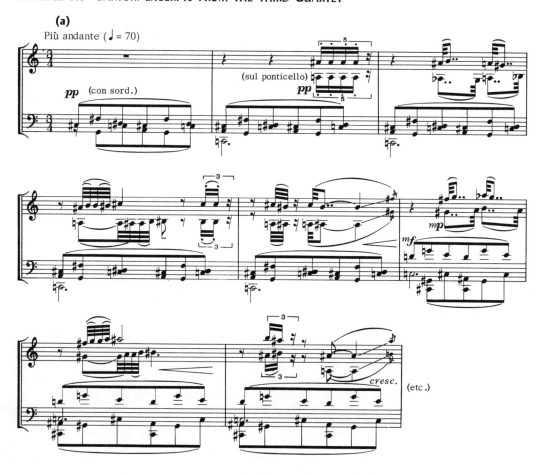

EXAMPLE 135 (CONTINUED)

(b)

by viola and cello playing the same ostinato figure a tritone apart. Since each instrument, by itself, is in a key, such devices are sometimes referred to as "polytonality"; but as Bartók uses it, the two keys (C and F sharp) can be neither distinguished nor joined into a higher tonal unity. Instead they produce a diffuse, bitter murmuring.

Over this ground comes a series of fragments, each intensely expressive, each peculiar to the new music of the 1900s. Later the intensity is relieved by broader figures in a blander tonal context; but soon this is interrupted by fortissimo polychords. Here again Bartók seeks out extreme solutions, chords representing such distant keys (E-flat minor and F major) that they refuse to support each other in any way. Nor are these polychords allowed to form relationships through voice leading, but instead are isolated by unison figures. The movement continues in a series of equally violent fragments.

The Seconda parte is, by contrast, flowing and lyric. It uses the unit pulse, grouped into freely swinging dance rhythms. These tend to be associated with fairly broad key areas, obliquely but nonetheless firmly expressed. The first melody (after a page of colorful tuning up) runs through an inversion of a V⁷ in D flat; the tonic, while never expressed, is unmistakable. A second melody, in a contrasting tonal field, is given in Example 135b. The melody begins in C major; the accompaniment consists of polychords that can be understood as C-sharp minor (with an added sixth, A) or as A major (with an added leading tone, G sharp).

C major and C-sharp minor have little in common, and insofar as they represent those keys, melody and accompaniment merely conflict. But insofar as melody and accompaniment both share in A, major or minor, they support each other in a tonal field that—no matter how obscure it may be—contrasts with the opening D-flat major. The relationship between D flat and A, stated simply, would be rich but too traditional. In order to make the relationship usable, Bartók has first stated D flat obliquely, then discolored the A major with its own tonic minor, and finally turned the A major simultaneously toward C-sharp minor, thereby setting up a competing relationship to D-flat major as another tonic minor. Such procedures, characteristic of the new composer's struggles with key, show him finding devious paths within traditional relationships, rather than breaking out beyond them.

Bartók's whole phrase includes this opening in A major-minor, a move to a related polychord centered on C, and then a strong twist through other realms back to A (meas. 8 to 9). Another such twist comes in measures 15 to 16, leading this time to the D flat and the opening melody. The remainder of the movement uses keys stated in this oblique fashion, and in spite of many hard-to-follow modulations the areas of relatively clear key seem to be balanced against one another in a way analogous to, even if not identical with, a traditional key plan.

After the Third Quartet, Bartók's attention was drawn increasingly to overall organization as a way of intensifying expression. Simultaneously both the forms and the procedures became more traditional and more developmental. The Fourth Quartet (1928) has five movements, fast, scherzo, slow, scherzo, and fast—traditional shape with an extra scherzo. The advanced shapes and textures are now concentrated in the inner movements, while the outer ones reveal a high degree of thematic development. The first movement exceeds in this respect almost every other previous string quartet, all the way back to Haydn. But what is especially characteristic of Bartók's mature works is the cyclical structure of the whole quartet, the thematic material of the first movement returning as the inevitable conclusion of the last. The violently expressive language of earlier works is now strongly framed by traditional structures.

The Fifth Quartet (1934) achieves the same cohesion with greater variety. It, too, has five movements, fast, slow, scherzo, and fast. The first movement, obviously based on traditional procedures, is an ideal place to study the oblique expression of keys and Bartók's way of moving through the tonal field. In the Sixth Quartet (1939), concern for overall structure reaches its purest form. The whole character of the work is eventually concentrated in the slow lyrical element that introduces the first three movements, and then itself becomes the fourth and final movement.

Unquestionably the most important group of quartets in the 1900s, these works gave the most convincing expression of new music. While not particularly gratifying to the mass audience, Bartók's quartets were known and respected as the work of a sincere composer. (During these same years Stravinsky was profoundly mistrusted by the mass audience, Schoenberg still unknown to it.) Bartók was even more successful with his more accessible works, especially an impressive series of concertos that were soon taken up into the repertory—in itself unusual for the 1900s. Almost all Bartók's major works were performed within a year or two of completion.

Most noteworthy are two concertos for piano and orchestra, the early one (1926) driving and mechanistic in the style of its time, the second (1931) more economical and disciplined, leading in the direction marked out by the Fourth String Quartet. A somewhat anachronistic Sonata for two pianos and percussion (1937, but with many features of Parisian music of a decade earlier) made its way better as a concerto. Perhaps most popular of all was the Music for Strings, Percussion, and Celesta (1936), which combined brilliant orchestral and percussive colors with sustained lyricism and old forms such as fugue. This work included lively rhythms, clear symphonic shapes, a broad treatment of keys, and a grand cyclic structure that left the listener with a sense of autumnal nostalgia.

Vienna: Schoenberg and Webern

The most progressive musical developments that appeared in Vienna right after 1900 had little positive effect upon the public even there, let alone in Paris and the West. Isolated concert performances of the most radical Viennese composers produced reactions of dismay and disbelief. Only in the later 1920s, as the Parisian excitement subsided, was an awareness of Viennese novelties spread abroad.

Viennese composers lived in a musical world dominated by Brahms and Mahler; Wagner and Strauss, although not personally present, made their presence felt. Important works of Mahler and Strauss were written and performed during the decades from 1890 to 1910. These works, along with a repertory of Brahms and Wagner, were the matrix of the new Viennese music.

SCHOENBERG'S EARLY WORKS The leader of the new music, Arnold

Schoenberg (1874–1951), was an admirer of Brahms and Wagner and a disciple of Mahler. Schoenberg demonstrated his affinity—better, identity—with this Viennese tradition in two early works, *Verklärte Nacht,* Op. 4 (*Transfigured Night,* 1899), and *Gurrelieder (Songs of the Dove,* 1900–1911). *Verklärte Nacht,* for string sextet, is an epitaph to the tone poem; even its date, 1899, places it at the end of an era. The poem by Richard Dehmel on which the sextet is built is perhaps questionable, but has the strong visceral character Schoenberg seemed to favor at the time. Schoenberg's music, in contrast, is exceptionally refined. It is hard to imagine a more sensitive treatment of the ecstatic modulations that had been the basis of German music since Wagner.

For Schoenberg, the style of *Verklärte Nacht* was not an end but a beginning. The developmental shapes and chromatic modulation, expressed in a fluid figural system with progressive transformation of themes—all this remained the framework of Schoenberg's art for the rest of his life. It is revealing that he worked on the huge *Gurrelieder* (whose harmonic idiom was still acceptable to conservatives) off and on during the decade of his most radical innovations.

Schoenberg had a strong (almost obsessive) sense of stylistic history and its continuity. He knew that music had to spring from its immediate past. He was convinced of the validity of his own past, of its musical concepts and techniques. He was also convinced of the necessity of developing, in logical continuity, from familiar musical ideas to new ones. When asked on one occasion if he was *the* Arnold Schoenberg, he said, "Someone had to be; no one wanted to be; so I volunteered." What set his work apart was the speed with which he traversed the development from past to future; even he, it seems, could not fully comprehend the implications of what he did.

During the years 1900 to 1912, Schoenberg pushed the old style to one extreme after another in a series of works representing the most important traditional categories as well as some new ones.

Op. 9	Chamber Symphony in E, for fifteen instruments (1906)
Op. 10	String Quartet no. 2, in F-sharp minor (1908)
Op. 11	Three Pieces for Piano (1909)
Op. 15	Song Cycle, *Das Buch der hängenden Garten* (The Book of the Hanging Gardens) by Stefan George, for voice and piano (1909)
Op. 16	Five Pieces for Orchestra (1909)
Op. 17	*Erwartung* (Expectation), monodrama for voice and orchestra (1909)
Op. 21	*Pierrot lunaire.* 21 Melodramas after Albert Giraud, for speaking voice, piano, flute (alternating with piccolo), clarinet (alternating with bass clarinet), violin (alternating with viola), cello (1912).

A comparison of this list with the previous one of the concert season 1910–1911 (page 486) will give some idea of the chasm that by now separated Schoenberg from the rest of music.

While the overall shapes of the Second Quartet are not new, the hypertense modulations frequently abandon any clear reference to a key. The mixture

EXAMPLE 136   SCHOENBERG: BEGINNING OF THE CHAMBER SYMPHONY

EXAMPLE 136 (CONTINUED)

of extreme modulation with traditional shape can be conveniently studied in the Chamber Symphony, Op. 9 (Example 136). The reduced orchestration of this work helps give it a nervous quality found also, for the same reason, in *Verklärte Nacht;* the more pointed sounds of solo instruments replace the plushy sound of the traditionally large string choirs. In spite of the tonal obscurity, the themes bear a striking resemblance to Strauss's *Don Juan,* especially the rising figure in triplets and the declaration in the strings at measures 16 to 17.

In two larger works, Schoenberg seemed driven to convulsive expression in an effort to break the relationship with the past, a relationship that so far persisted in spite of extreme modulation. While the Chamber Symphony avoided overpowering orchestral effect, the Five Pieces for Orchestra, Op. 16, exploited them to the utmost. In these, his most coloristic works, Schoenberg spoke a violently ejaculative, disjunct language in the loud movements, an abnormally static tone in the soft one—both alternatives to the usually surging development. Tonal considerations, while carefully controlled, are less in evidence, so intense is the sonority, so strong the character of each piece. When the publisher urged programmatic titles, Schoenberg succeeded in finding titles that seemed to express the character convincingly—*Premonitions, Yesteryears, Summer Morning at the Lake, Peripetia, Obbligato Recitative.* Although never made explicit, there is a strong tendency for these five pieces to suggest the outlines of a symphony.

The other convulsive work is *Erwartung,* drama for one singer; the half-hour work is to be staged and accompanied by full orchestra. In this play, one of Schoenberg's most questionable texts, a woman stumbles in mounting panic through a dark landscape at night to meet her lover. Coming suddenly upon a dead, bloody body, she finally realizes it is he. Here music is a vehicle for the expression of the woman's naked horror. This is one of the pieces that had to be written: it is the extreme form of music-drama as conceived and developed by Wagner. It is also a logical end point, the end of all purely musical means of expression. An attempt to pursue this line of development could only result in a scream of terror, the next piece sounding just the same.

In *Pierrot lunaire*, however, Schoenberg wrote a piece that was not the same. Starting with French symbolist poems instead of German expressionistic ones (although in German translation), Schoenberg set the poems for voice and instrumental ensemble in a way that revealed how traditional his previous works really were. *Pierrot* set a standard for intensity that has been rarely challenged since.

At the same time, *Pierrot* was not more convulsive than its predecessors; rather, a good deal less so, with much greater emphasis on purely musical construction. Schoenberg seemed here to step into a new phase of development, free from the past and from the need to find more and more expressive extremes. He seemed to find a new way of writing music, and with it a new approach to the text. The poetic images were sometimes reflected in the music by madrigalisms; but in general, traditional expression of inner feeling was as absent as in Satie's *Parade*. As outward sign of the new treatment of the text, the voice had to perform in a speaking manner (*Sprechstimme*), gliding through the indicated pitches rather than intoning them.

Pierrot had an intensely nervous sound, owing partly to the solo timbres used throughout. But as has often been pointed out, the instrumental lines themselves often echo traditional melodic shapes that one might find in Strauss or Mahler. The large leaps to long, expressive tones, alternating with convoluted half steps—all that was old. Yet something clearly was new, something beyond dissonance or ultrachromatic modulation (both carried to extremes in earlier works). The tonal fabric had a paradoxical combination of instability and consistency that was the work's most expressive feature and the one that put all the other features, old and new, into a meaningful relationship with each other.

At first hearing, one is inclined to ascribe the prevailing tonal fabric of *Pierrot* to mere chance, fortuitous coincidences of independent parts. Yet a little reflection will show that such consistent avoidance of familiar chords could not come about by mere chance. Of one part of *Pierrot* Schoenberg said, only half in jest, "Very strict counterpoint! Consonances only as passing tones, or on the weak beat!" Indeed, of all dimensions the aggregate sonority is the one most closely controlled and the one that makes the work really new.

Take the opening of *Pierrot* (Example 137); the first figure in the piano begins as an augmented triad (G sharp, E, C), familiar enough, except that it is

EXAMPLE 137   SCHOENBERG: BEGINNING OF *PIERROT LUNAIRE* (reduction)

completely obliterated by the rest of the figure (D, B flat, C sharp, G). The whole figure is skillfully constructed so that it may be repeated several times without referring to a key or even giving prominence to any of its constituent parts. So, too, with the accompaniment figure (F sharp, D sharp), which fails to support the first figure in any way that might suggest a familiar chord or key.

By this time nine of the twelve notes have been used; three remain—F, B, and A (ignoring the voice, whose notated pitches are not to be intoned precisely). The question is, what comes next? Many of the notes already used would constitute a breach of consistency: A flat and F sharp would function as resolutions (the A flat, for instance, as tonic to the leading tone G, the last note of the piano's figure). Some of the other notes already used would be less objectionable, but in general, they are less useful at this point than those not yet used. Of those, the B natural would almost amount to a tonic of the whole complex, especially if played below the C sharp. The F, on the other hand, would seem to maintain the delicate imbalance of that complex; so also the A. Either one would do, but Schoenberg chose the A.

This process of selecting tones, raised to a general principle, is the most important novelty of *Pierrot* and the foundation of the Viennese style. Each figure is constructed to negate traditional implications of its parts. Each successive note occupies a unique position, not confirming a traditional progression—or, if it does, that progression must be contradicted by some other element in the piece at that moment. (See the cello, meas. 34, a clear approach and resolution to B.) Through this process, notes acquire individual significance, instead of being merged into conventional groups (triads and their derivatives).

This finding of the right note was an extension of chromatic modulation as practiced since Haydn and Mozart. Composers of the 1800s had sought just the key that would sound fresh and unexpected, yet would, in retrospect, seem logical (for instance, a key an altered third away from the tonic of a major key). Schoenberg now sought notes, not keys, that would have the same property. He maximized Wagner's technique of emphasizing a note in a chord or a voice in a progression, seeking new tone qualities through new contexts.

Pierrot obviously presents us with more than one note at a time; we still have to reckon with chords. The point is, these chords are neither traditional nor accidental. Rather, they are ad hoc constructions, each specially made to provide an appropriate sonority for a particular spot in a unique form. As chords, they have to satisfy two negative conditions. They must not sound like traditional harmonies (triads and their derivatives)—or, if they do, they must not function traditionally. Second, they must not sound too simple (octaves, say, or fifths). Both a diminished seventh chord and a bare fifth would be out of place, the one being too familiar (even though complex), the other too clear. Chords, like notes, must now be chosen to avoid any kind of tonal confirmation. A balance of all twelve tones must be maintained.

The result was a diffusion of tonal relationships. Instead of high contrast among highly concentrated centers of tonal order, Schoenberg achieved lesser contrasts among each of the twelve tones taken individually. In Schoenberg's music the sense of tonal focus we call *key* is diffused to the point where it may be imperceptible for most or all of a work. Obviously, there is a continuum between the presence and absence of perceptible key. The absence of key is commonly called "atonality," but the term is undesirable and should be discouraged, simply because it corresponds to no clearly definable state, but only to the progressive elimination of references to key. *Pierrot* demonstrated that it was possible to write cogent music with very few references to key.

WEBERN'S EARLY WORKS   Working closely with Schoenberg during these years was Anton Webern (1883–1945). Since he began in Brahms, rather than in Wagner, Webern's course was not identical to Schoenberg's but ran parallel to it. Webern followed out Schoenberg's principles to different results.

In 1909, Webern wrote a set of Five Pieces for String Quartet, Op. 5, without question the most remarkable pieces of the decade. Under the pressure of Webern's search for more intense expression, music took on shapes that seemed totally alien to the few representatives of the larger audience who heard them. There was nothing in the Viennese past to prepare the ear for Webern's music. Like Schoenberg, Webern moved logically from old to new; but here the move was so swift that even now the developmental curve is hard to trace. Pupil outstripped master: Webern's Op. 5 was written at the time of Schoenberg's Chamber Symphony and Five Pieces for Orchestra—before *Petrouchka* and Mahler's Eighth Symphony.

The Five Pieces, Op. 5, are compact in dimensions, almost gestic in their forcefulness. Their harmonic language is rich, pungent with multiple dissonances. Each of the Five Pieces has a strong character, remarkably different from the others. The first consists of many disjunct elements—a type of organization much more characteristic of Webern than of Schoenberg. In this early work, the disjunct, varied elements are still bound together thematically. The third Piece and also the fifth have the character of a dance; at least, they have continuous rhythms of one kind or another. In the third Piece the rhythm takes the form of an ostinato, or a unit pulse. This device, like all others, seems reserved by Webern for a particular piece; not used as elements of a stylistic system (as they were at Paris), such devices were for Webern unique means of expression.

The pieces with rhythmic continuity seem to be the most accessible, also the most conservative. The disjunct or transitional pieces are the most progressive and the most characteristic of Webern. The second Piece, beautifully lyric, is given complete in Example 138.

This piece does not have the sophisticated sense of suspension of *Pierrot*. While it is not in a key, it has many soft spots—repetitions of tones, octave doublings, leading tones, and other tonal conjunctions that refer to keys. The little point of imitation in measure 4, for example, has a strong aura of V^7 in A flat. Yet Webern has such a keen ear for sonority (the chords really scratch, even with only a few notes) that the passing references to key cannot undo the tension.

In 1913 (the year after *Pierrot*), Webern wrote a set of Bagatelles for string quartet, Op. 9, and Five Pieces for Orchestra, Op. 10. The Bagatelles, like the Five Pieces, Op. 5, give us a glimpse into the abyss; they belong to the same expressive realm, and hence to music before *Pierrot*. Op. 10, on the other hand,

EXAMPLE 138   WEBERN: SECOND OF FIVE PIECES FOR STRING QUARTET, OP. 5

By permission of Universal Edition, Vienna.

shares in the musical advances of *Pierrot*. Freed from the inner pressure of emotional hypertension, Webern's music suddenly became more flexible, more responsive to basic structures already favored but not fully realized.

Even Op. 10 has old pieces alongside new ones. The long, static, central piece is frankly coloristic. The last piece, however, is properly disjunct, while the next to last, transitional in function, is one of the short ones—twenty seconds in a recorded performance.

Paradoxically, as the pieces get shorter, they seem more profound. Phrases become extremely compact, even cryptic, while taking upon themselves broad structural responsibilities. So elliptical is the whole construction that an analysis must enlist in advance the utmost sympathy.

The first piece, one of moderate length, is given complete in Example 139. (A piano reduction is here admittedly inadequate, so important is the factor of timbre.) After an introduction (B,C,B, upbeat and meas. 1) and a solo for glockenspiel (meas. 2), flute and clarinet unfold a soaring melodic development over a chordal accompaniment and a pedal trill (meas. 3 to 6); there is also a cello obbligato, *dolcissimo* (meas. 6, C, D). At the end of measure 6, the melodic development is punctuated by the brass, then cello and violin carry the melody to its climax, this time over a flutter-tongued flute accompaniment. Under the violin's final note, harp and trumpet start a cadential formula, and after a rhapsodic cadenza for harp (meas. 10 to 11), flute, trumpet, and celesta conclude the cadence.

Such an analysis is not apt to be immediately convincing, first, because it presupposes entry into Webern's new dimensions of musical structure, and second, because it depends to a large extent on personal interpretation. If the analysis seems far-fetched, that is because it is so; yet no more than any other. That is the way the music is. Webern's capacity to attract, and resist, various analytical approaches seems greater than that of any other composer of the 1900s. Each analysis leaves a residue of the piece beyond reach; successive attempts at analysis only strengthen the conviction that there is some mysterious inner meaning. The piece does not merely confound the observer, it seems to be urgently telling him something he needs to know. Of all modern composers Webern has perhaps the most profound spiritual message for our time—the message most for our time.

SCHOENBERG'S NEW METHOD   As long as Schoenberg looked within the realm of expression for ways to control his music, he did not seem to find an answer that was valid beyond a single work. Only when he looked at the form of what he was doing did he find an answer, a purely technical one that made continued composition in the new style possible.

Schoenberg had long felt the need to avoid repetition of pitches within a figure or a succession of chords; *Pierrot* has frequent instances of the use of many or most of the twelve chromatic tones before repetition of a tone. Schoenberg finally saw that this tendency toward nonrepetition could be stated as a method: all twelve tones should be used before returning to any one. Rigorous application of this method meant that a single order of twelve tones should be

EXAMPLE 139   WEBERN: FIRST OF FIVE PIECES FOR ORCHESTRA, OP. 10

Sehr ruhig und zart (♩ = ca 50)

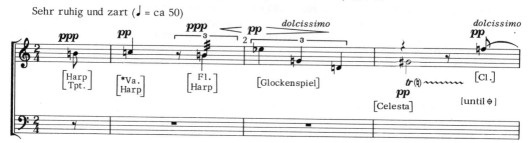

* = harmonic

repeated over and over, to guarantee that no single tone would be emphasized through a repetition more frequent than that of its neighbors.

Schoenberg came upon this method sometime in the early twenties (summer of 1921, according to one report), while working on what was to be the Serenade, Op. 24, and the Suite for Piano, Op. 25. He had not composed much since *Pierrot;* indeed, what he had achieved in *Pierrot* seemed to elude him when he tried to do it again. This occasionally happens to a composer; he writes, almost automatically, a work that solves basic technical problems, and then has to wait, sometimes for years, to discover consciously what it was that he did so that he can do it again.

The Serenade, Op. 24 (for clarinet, bass clarinet, mandolin, guitar, violin, viola, cello, and baritone voice singing a sonnet of Petrarch in the fourth movement), continues the format of *Pierrot*, which is also the format of *L'Histoire du soldat* and other important works of the twenties—a small, intense instrumental ensemble playing a series of relatively compact, disjunct forms and sections. The Serenade includes a march (with clear references to the music-hall style) and a minuet. There is a set of variations built on a theme that uses an eleven-note series.

Characteristically, Schoenberg at first tried to use the technique of a twelve-tone series as if it were something expressive, as if it were a theme. But while theme and variations was a form favored by Schoenberg in connection with a twelve-tone series, he rarely used a single twelve-tone series as a theme in itself. In fact, successive variations were usually set off from each other not on the basis of twelve-tone technique but rather by changes of figure, texture, or timbre.

The Piano Suite is often used to illustrate Schoenberg's twelve-tone technique, partly because he himself so used it in his famous lecture "Composition with Twelve Tones" (1941). Schoenberg's complete title is important: "Method of Composing with Twelve Tones Which Are Related Only with One Another." When Schoenberg saw that what he had developed was a method, not a kind of theme, then he could use the method to facilitate composition.

First a suitable series of twelve tones has to be preselected. If such a series is to realize its basic purpose, it must avoid outlining a triad or triadic derivative; it must avoid suggesting a triadic progression; it must avoid in even more subtle ways any feeling of tonal focus. The series itself must maintain the sense of tonal diffusion. This is not easy; many of the large number of possible series are stylistically undesirable. The series basic to the Piano Suite appears complete in the top line at the beginning (Example 140).

Such a series, once preselected, can be used repeatedly, taking the notes in order for as long as the piece needed to go on. But a greater variety of notes can be obtained, without seriously jeopardizing the principle of nonrepetition, by using the basic series of twelve notes in several different ways, simultaneously or successively.

There are forty-eight possible forms of a given series—a basic form, with its retrograde, inversion, and retrograde inversion, at a basic pitch and eleven possible transpositions. Which form and which pitch are basic is usually arbitrary. These forty-eight forms, together with unlimited octave transposition, give the composer an ample source of tonal material while preserving guidelines to

EXAMPLE 140 SCHOENBERG: BEGINNING OF PIANO SUITE

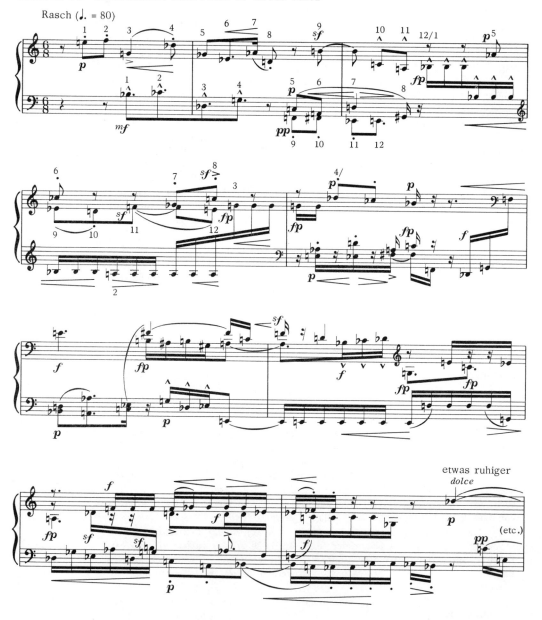

the nonrepetition of individual tones or traditional groups of tones. Considerable care has to be exercised, however, in manipulating the various forms of the row; an unchecked leading-tone progression or an exposed fifth can trap the unwary composer in a key.

Schoenberg once predicted that skill in handling these forms would eventually come to be required of all composition students. Whether or not that prediction has been fulfilled, twelve-tone technique has been widely used and even more widely discussed. In view of the many varying, even conflicting, interpretations that have been put on the technique since Schoenberg's first use of it, it is important here to emphasize its original, essential function in terms of stylistic development.

Twelve-tone technique was only a means, a method—as Schoenberg said— of carrying out a higher principle, the nonconfirmation of a tonal focus traditionally achieved through triads and their derivatives. Twelve-tone technique made it easier to compose while avoiding keys, made it possible to reproduce the style of *Pierrot* systematically and consciously, made it possible to select the next note without going laboriously through all twelve. The composer had only to reach into the series for the next note, and then drop it into place. He still, however, had to monitor the result for flaws, soft spots that might betray a familiar chord or key. But the composer's attention was largely freed from tonal considerations of that type; he could now concentrate upon melodic character, choice of figure, texture, timbre, overall shape. These dimensions were as yet subject only to the composer's intuition.

The importance of Schoenberg's Serenade and Suite for twelve-tone technique has sometimes overshadowed their integrity as pieces of music. Furthermore, they are both relatively inaccessible pieces, lacking the whimsy of *Pierrot* as well as the expressive warmth of previous pieces. Both Suite and Serenade tend to be compact, businesslike, uncompromising; they bristle with dissonance and brusque phrases. This might reflect only Schoenberg's involvement with a new method and its concentrated application. Yet the direction taken in these works corresponds closely to that of Parisian composers of the same years: in both East and West, 1925 saw a consolidation of gains made by previous experiment.

Following this consolidation came a phase of leisurely expansion. After 1925 Schoenberg and even Webern wrote long, elaborate compositions, not only for chamber ensembles, but for symphony orchestra. The expansion now was not in terms of symphonic shape—at least, not symphonic key plans—but rather depended upon the twelve-tone technique and the large quantities of keyless fabric it could turn out.

Schoenberg's more leisurely style is best studied in the Third String Quartet, Op. 30 (1927). Here the twelve-tone technique became either very complex or very free; just which, it is hard to say. For one thing, successive repetitions of a given twelve-tone series assume forms other than the forty-eight standard forms already described. "Permutation" of series according to a logic now plain, now enigmatic, seems to be at work. Then too, Schoenberg seems here to treat the twelve tones as a group, a "set," rather than as a series. He breaks the twelve-tone set down into several subsets (as he had already done in the

Piano Suite, Example 140), using these as units without worrying about the order of tones within each unit.

The first pages of the Third String Quartet are built on a five-note ostinato, one of those skillfully constructed figures that refuses to define a key no matter how many times it is repeated. Yet this ostinato (and here is an important feature emerging out of twelve-tone music) clearly defines a place in the twelve-tone field. The difference between this type of place and the type we call key is merely that a key can be designated by a single tone (or key on the keyboard), the root of its tonic triad, whereas the place of the ostinato in the Third String Quartet can only be designated by naming all its pitches—G, E, D sharp, A, C, five notes "related only one with another."

Once established, this ostinato starts to shift its locus, by exchanging one note of the five for a new one. The process is exactly comparable to modulation from one key to another, except that since keys are never stated, the motion itself cannot be designated as a traditional modulation but only as an ad hoc one, from this set of notes to that.

Schoenberg seems to have envisaged a time when the violent extremes of the early twenties would drop away, leaving him free to use, without reference to traditional functions, the old sounds he loved so well. Dissonance, in other words, was in some ways only a device to cancel out references to a key. When key had ceased to exist, consonances could again be used freely; furthermore, when keys ceased to exist, many dissonances would no longer have the argumentative effect they had within a key, and hence could be enjoyed for their own sonorous value.

The sense of key has been remarkably obstinate; several times pronounced dead, it continues to exist in devious ways. Yet in the slow movement of his Third String Quartet, Schoenberg gave us a remarkable glimpse into a keyless future—but also into a distant Viennese past. This Adagio (Example 141) is of a type that goes back to Mozart, while its chords go back further than that. Yet there is no key, or at any rate no key that lasts longer than a single chord. The whole passage is strictly controlled by a twelve-tone series related to the one used in the first movement.

After 1930, Schoenberg's music became more somber. After the amiable Third String Quartet came the much weightier Fourth, Op. 37 (1936). Composed through consistent application of the twelve-tone method—one of the classic examples, in fact, of that method—the Fourth Quartet stands even closer to tradition in outward format. As explosive extremes diminished, there was revealed a remarkably conservative sense of rhythm. The theme, for example, in spite of its serious nature, is square, even pedestrian, in its rhythmic gait. What faster movements tend to lose in impressiveness is, however, regained by the slow ones; the Largo, with its powerful unison statements of the twelve-tone series, is one of Schoenberg's gravest utterances.

This return to traditional format of the immediate past (not to be confused with forms of the remote past used in the twenties) set the tone for Schoenberg's more significant later works, among them *Moses und Aron*. A unique opera, it is an opera nonetheless, one whose subject was peculiarly suited to Schoenberg's own serious, rigorous, prophetic nature. One of his most colorful

EXAMPLE 141   SCHOENBERG: BEGINNING OF SECOND MOVEMENT, STRING QUARTET NO.3

mature works, the Variations for Orchestra, Op. 31, was finished in 1928. In 1936 he wrote a Concerto for Violin and Orchestra, Op. 36, and on the next to last day of December, 1942, he finished a Concerto for Piano and Orchestra, Op. 42. A String Trio, Op. 45 (not finished until 1946), combines a fluid, but nonetheless consistent, application of twelve-tone technique with the fullness of old age.

     WEBERN'S LATER WORKS   Webern readily adopted, and adapted, Schoenberg's twelve-tone method for his own stylistic purposes. By nature a less discursive composer than Schoenberg, Webern seemed to emphasize the static rather than the dynamic aspects of twelve-tone composition—the aspect of set as opposed to series. The sense of being in a segment of the twelve-tone field, or of being in all of it, was stronger with Webern than the sense of moving through that field.

     Schoenberg's serene Third String Quartet (1927) is matched by two works of Webern, the Symphony, Op. 21 (1928), and a Quartet for violin, clarinet, saxophone, and piano, Op. 22 (1930). Particularly in the first movement of the Symphony Webern achieved a sense of tonal suspension that has provided a classic model for succeeding composers. While the Symphony has only two movements (like Schubert's "Unfinished"), it makes striking use of traditional forms, if only as format. The first movement is even in binary form, with repeats. The inner logic, as in Schoenberg, is provided by whatever intuitive direction the composer gives to the twelve-tone material.

The A section of the binary form is perhaps the most serene passage in Webern; it is, in effect, a single standing chord. Each note is found in only one register: D is always a ledger line below the bass clef, G always the bottom line of bass clef, and so for the others (except that there are two E flats, one on each side of middle C). The chord is D–G–C–E flat–F–A flat–A–B flat–C sharp–E flat–F sharp–B–E. The chord itself is a peculiar construction, having a clear sense of location but not defining a key. This is not easy to do; many, if not most, aggregate chords have oblique references to familiar chords or functions, and hence to keys.

The chord is never sounded all at once as a chord. Webern expresses the chord in a texture that is disassociated even for him. Each instrument sounds only a few notes at a time, contributing isolated touches to the overall sonority— as if a huge gong were kept resounding by discreet taps on various parts of its surface. Here Webern resolved musical texture into tiny particles, and then integrated them mysteriously into a perfect whole.

The rhythmic order is a reflection of the tonal one. The opening of the A section moves in strict four-four meter, predominantly in quarter notes. This overall regularity, however, is found in no one part, only in the totality, which does not, curiously enough, sound like four-four. Beating time to this passage, while learning where the notes actually sound, will give insight into a new rhythmic realm, different—or at least seemingly so—from the old one.

Within this static whole, serial construction is carried out with remarkable consistency. All the tones (in the A section) are derived from two simultaneous statements of the series, each accompanied by its inversion, and followed by its retrograde—a construction often described as a *double canon*. After the double bar, the procedure, and character, of the work change; here can be found Webern's most remarkable demonstration of the expressive power of single notes, or of simple intervallic relationships between notes. There is no room in this music for the heroic surges of Beethoven or the luxurious modulations of Wagner, only for the profundity of things very small and very still.

Webern's other mature works include a Concerto for Nine Instruments, Op. 24 (1934), a String Quartet, Op. 28 (1938), Variations for Orchestra, Op. 30 (1940), and two cantatas, Op. 29 (1940) and Op. 31 (1943). Seldom has a composer written more serious music or spoken more seriously of the meaning of art and life; seldom has a composer's work seemed at first so whimsical, or his death (by accidental shooting during wartime occupation) so devoid of meaning.

BERG The new Viennese style of Schoenberg and Webern was first known to and accepted by the larger audience through another Schoenberg pupil, Alban Berg (1885–1935). Berg's appeal was partly due to a skillful compromise between twelve-tone music and the expressive shapes (with their key references) of traditional music. His music drama *Wozzeck* (Berlin, 1925), perhaps the most significant such work of the 1900s, is, on one hand, a stream of relentlessly emotional music, and on the other hand, a succession of serial constructions. The two really seem to have nothing to do with each other: inner

form and outward effect exist on two different levels. Berg, whose total output
was very small, also left an important *Lyric Suite* for string quartet (1926),
including a musical reference to Tristan, and an equally important Violin
Concerto (1935).

Toward a Common Practice

SYMPHONY IN THE THIRTIES   Meanwhile, in the concert world a revival
of the symphony was well under way. While the later works of Webern, totally
unknown, had no effect upon the concert world, still the fact that Webern wrote
a symphony (of whatever kind) was strangely symptomatic of trends in the
thirties.

The new music often gained entry into the concert hall via a concerto; a
modern composer might be unwelcome, but he might have friends who were
soloists and who could get concertos played. One has only to recall the concertos
of Schoenberg, Berg, and Bartók to get a picture of modern concert music in the
thirties. Stravinsky, too, cultivated the concerto; but Stravinsky entered the
concert hall primarily on the basis of his *Symphony of Psalms* (1930), symbol of
a new phase in new music and of a temporary truce with the mass audience.

Written for a large symphony orchestra and amateur choral ensemble, the
Symphony of Psalms tends toward rich, somber, slow-moving sonorities—the
antithesis of the music-hall style, but apparently regarded by Stravinsky as now
appropriate to symphony hall. Only the absence of the strings might recall the
more pointed sounds of the twenties; but the chorus makes up for the strings.

Structurally the work is far from a symphony. Still in evidence is
Stravinsky's use of homogeneous sections each built on a polychord and animated by a unit pulse, each giving way abruptly to the next. The first movement
is all prelude, reminding us how nondevelopmental, even nonthematic Stravinsky
really is (especially in comparison with Bartók). On the other hand, Stravinsky's great skill with figuration is well represented. Very simple figures, close to
the diatonic tradition, serve as vehicles for new phrase shapes. Economy and
refinement continue to mark Stravinsky's handling of musical materials.

So too with tonal order: the first movement moves in a field of C major,
but obliquely expressed in the weaker form of E minor. Frictional polychords do
their work unobtrusively, often consisting of two chords as closely related as a
tonic triad in E minor and I^6 in C major.

The second movement, a fugue, seems different from Bach fugues only in
the shape of the subject, which bears Stravinsky's subtle melodic stamp, and in
certain obscure harmonic involutions that ensue. So firmly are these placed in
the overall shape that it will be hard to recall, later, what dark sounds Stravinsky was making in 1930.

The third and final movement is the work's center of gravity. In spite of
the frequently bland sound, the structure is still unsymphonic, still representative of the new music—static, disjunct, nondevelopmental, curiously ordered.
The psalmodic text tells of all the ways to praise the Lord, and after Stravinsky
has presented all the usual ways (including the music hall as well as some
solemn alleluias), he turns at the end to a dead-slow ostinato, F–B flat–E flat,

over which the chorus and orchestra move—or better, stand still—in mystic exaltation. Only when a shift in tonal level takes place do we realize how firmly fixed we were around E flat.

The nature of the harmonic field is here peculiarly appropriate to the work's stylistic function. This last movement is in C major-minor, the minor being represented by an entire key structure erected on the note E flat. This relationship of a third (favored for rich modulation in the 1800s) makes for rich, but not sharp, polychords. Opulent solemnity arises naturally out of these novel—but not too novel—tonal combinations. Yet the effect is due not just to key structures, but to Stravinsky's extreme care with details of figure and orchestration.

Stravinsky was obviously not setting a trend but following one. By 1930 other erstwhile radicals were coming to terms with traditional concert-hall needs, while still other composers, who by training and conviction had never thought in terms of anything else, by now had had time to come to terms a little with modern music.

The catalog of neosymphonic composers is large, but their works (including many masterpieces) present few problems of analysis in terms of modern style. The tone of the thirties was one of stylistic nostalgia, or at least reflection. Parisian rebels like Milhaud, as well as more compromising spirits like Honegger, now wrote symphonies. Bloch, veteran of the new music almost from 1900, might well be characterized by his symphonic poem, *Voice in the Wilderness* (1936).

Perhaps most remarkable was the transformation of Hindemith. One of the wild ones of the twenties, Hindemith had written as late as 1929 a bizarre opera, *Neues vom Tage* (Top of the News), with typewriters, women in bathtubs, and similar "events." That was in 1929; the next opera, *Mathis der Maler* (Matheus the Painter), was a different story—inner religious vision, expressed in richly symbolic, emotional music. Cast into symphonic shape in 1934, *Mathis* provided a thoroughly conservative musical experience, its chromatic modulations barely touched by new styles of figuration or rhythmic shape. Heir to the German symphonic tradition, Hindemith became one of its last, if most distinguished, custodians.

Symphony and symphonic forms found special favor with Russian composers. Prokofiev, another veteran of the twenties, found reason to write a Third Symphony as early as 1928. Dmitri Shostakovitch (1906–) had been a symphonist all along. After a bold fling at progressive opera (*Lady Macbeth of the Mzensk District,* Moscow, 1934), Shostakovitch was led back to more disciplined symphonic expression in his Fifth Symphony (1937), Sixth (1939), and Seventh (1941). These still made sense to Western mass audiences, while the Eighth through Eleventh have strained even their credulity. But by Russian standards of the thirties (the lively Mossolov was in the distant past), Shostakovitch was dangerously avant-garde. The intrepid Nicolas Miaskovsky (1881–1950) outstripped Shostakovitch and other modern symphonists, with an output of twenty-four symphonies.

In Italy, symphonic expression was represented with a characteristic sense of color and visual image. Ottorino Respighi (1879–1936) and Gian Francesco Malipiero (1882–) brought to this admittedly conservative phase of development an elegance as well as a humanity much needed in the 1900s. Much the same can be said of the Latin American composers Heitor Villa-Lobos (1887–1959) and Carlos Chavez (1899–).

English-speaking composers, while unable to match the Russian effort, put out a still respectable quantity of symphonies. Arnold Bax (1883–1953) wrote seven, and Ralph Vaughan Williams (1872–1958) six, including the highly regarded Fourth Symphony in F minor (1935); but this composer would probably prefer to be remembered for his many more intimate works. In the United States, the symphonic effort included Roy Harris (1898–), writing three big symphonies in 1934, 1936, and 1939; and Walter Piston (1894–), whose First Symphony appeared in 1938. Aaron Copland turned from his polished Parisian style to a very serious set of Variations for Piano (1930), and then later a Third Symphony (1946). His popular ballet (and concert suite), *Appalachian Spring* (1944), is ripe with the nostalgia that was the keynote of symphony in the thirties.

These composers wrote much more than symphonies, yet their symphonic output best defines their stylistic position. As the fortunes of the symphony climbed in the United States, those of the avant-garde diminished, identified as they were with European experiment. By a devious, but logical process, symphony had become since the late 1800s a vehicle of nationalism. Composers who now wrote symphonies, especially with local color added, could get them performed. The public had heard just enough of the young men back from Paris in 1927 to know they wanted no more of that.

In spite of many creditable works of the thirties, the most revealing examples continued to be those of Stravinsky—perhaps because he was something of an outsider to the whole episode. In 1940 he wrote a *Symphony in C* (that is, C expressed obliquely as E), a real four-movement symphony. The closer Stravinsky got to traditional forms, however, the easier it was to see how novel his basic musical language was. A nondevelopmental composer with a horror of germinal motivic construction, Stravinsky here wrote a work that seemed to use both theme and development. Yet there was something not quite right about the way the theme persisted over its static harmony, something not quite symphonic about the way the "development" was abruptly cut off or turned in a new direction. But Stravinsky was right; it was the symphony that was now wrong. The new music was simply not symphonic, any more than it was developmental. Stravinsky's *Symphony in C* transcends the concert hall, as *L'Histoire du soldat* transcends the music hall. Like the most representative new music, this "symphony" is rich in musical moments, arranged in a largely arbitrary order.

INTO THE TWELVE-TONE FIELD   After fifteen years' involvement with the symphony, Stravinsky returned in 1948 to ballet with *Orpheus,* one of his richest works, perhaps his greatest. In addition to its intrinsic worth, *Orpheus* occupied an important position in musical development of the 1900s. As things turned out, it was the concert hall—not the music hall—that had been the scene of an int rmezzo; *Orpheus* showed that the intermezzo was over. Picking up the threads from the twenties, music now seemed to press forward to do what it had to do.

Yet while reinstating all the basic structural features of music in the twenties, *Orpheus* included something from the intervening thirties. Something about the symphony was worth saving, and that something, a tone more than a style, was reflected in the dark orchestral sonorities of *Orpheus*. The process of stylistic compromise with the past now began in earnest.

While *Orpheus* bridged two worlds, it left out a third, that of Schoenberg and Webern. *Orpheus* had a few obscure places, to be sure—obscure harmonically and contrapuntally, as in the interlude in the second tableau, obscure rhythmically in the following dance of the Bacchantes, with its strange patterns that went far beyond the unit pulse from which they sprang. Still, the work as a whole was framed by a C through E harmonic field at the beginning, and a blues I^7 at the end.

All around Stravinsky, currents were running deeper than he himself cared to go at the moment. Progressive segments of the larger audience, having been exposed in the concert hall to the possibility of a serious modern music, gradually became aware of the seriousness of composers as radical as Schoenberg. Then came the surprising discovery that a few composers, hitherto unknown (or if known, known only as eccentric) had been composing serious, progressive music advanced in style and high in quality all along.

In the United States, such a composer was Wallingford Riegger (1885–1961). Toward 1950 Riegger finally got some public recognition for his Second Symphony (1945). Strong, cogent, exciting music, it moved with authority through a twelve-tone field, with a long, lyric line that could make sense out of sharply disparate sonorities. Riegger's Symphony showed what an American composer could do when fully engaged with Western style. But Riegger had been doing it since the early thirties; both the larger audience and its leaders, dreaming of a great American symphony, had had a different idea of what that symphony should look like.

Roger Sessions (1896–) had also taken up the challenge of Schoenberg, without sounding like him, without even using the same technique. In his Second Symphony (1946) Sessions showed the same grasp of the twelve-tone field, the same sense of line found in Riegger. Sessions, too, had been at it for two decades; his music probably represents the most sustained effort by an American composer in the first half of the century to find and follow a central line of stylistic development.

During the fifties, an increasing number of composers in the United States set their hands to the task of writing modern music. It varied in style along a broad front, perhaps best represented by a number of string quartets written around 1950, including works by Irving Fine (1914–1962), Leon Kirchner (1919–), and Andrew Imbrie (1921–), as well as other composers. The most impressive, or at any rate, most respected quartet was by Elliot Carter (1908–). More inclined to rhapsody than rigor, Carter's First Quartet (1951) is a large work, convincing through the vivid phraseology and elevated tone. A Second Quartet (1959) was equally esteemed. While not necessarily serial, Carter (like most composers of the fifties) habitually moved through the twelve-tone field in such a mercurial fashion as to seem keyless to older ears. Perhaps the greatest lyric gift in this group of composers belongs to Ben Weber (1916–), whose music is distinguished by sure control of the twelve-tone field and great artistry of detail.

Taken altogether, the works of these and other composers in the United States during the fifties compared favorably with similar music being produced on the European continent. During these years, American composers became at last completely involved with Western style, rather than with American—or European—fashions. Composers in the United States could now speak the Western musical language with an accent as good as or sometimes even a little better than many Europeans. From this point on, it makes as little sense to distinguish a separate group of American composers as to distinguish Stravinsky, Bartók, Schoenberg, and Webern on the basis of their nationality.

A few composers, however (and for the moment more Europeans than Americans), moved swiftly in the early fifties to establish Webern, rather than Schoenberg, as the model of really new music. There was more to this promotion of Webern than cynical modishness, however strong that factor may have been. In some very basic way that we are only gradually coming to understand, Webern—of all composers of the first half of the century—best represents a common style of our time. This is not to say that his style *is* the common style; what it is will be clear only in the future. But precisely because this common style was not, and is not, clear, someone had to serve as its focal point. Webern, far more reticent than Schoenberg, had never volunteered; he was drafted.

An appreciation of the static, timeless quality of Webern was brought to Paris (!) primarily through Olivier Messiaen (1908–). A student of Messiaen's, Pierre Boulez (1925–), turned out to be one of the most skilled, most challenging composers to appear since 1950.

An energetic writer, the young Boulez heralded the promotion of Webern with an article entitled "Schoenberg Is Dead!" (1952). Boulez's most impressive work, *Le Marteau sans maître*, is often compared to *Pierrot lunaire*, whose format it follows. Yet the sounds are perhaps more colorful than Schoenberg, and their presentation more static. On the other hand, Boulez seems more varied, more full of exquisite detail than Webern, something apparent in the first section, *Before "L'Artisanat furieux,"* as well as the seventh, *After "L'Artisanat furieux."* The sixth section, *Bourreaux de solitude,* has the slower pace of Webern's symphony.

The approach to the text in *Le Marteau* is more oblique than in either Schoenberg or Webern—even though the text is usually intoned on pitches instead of half-spoken as in Schoenberg's *Sprechstimme*. Boulez surrounds selections from the original poems with instrumental "commentaries," preludes, and postludes, arranging the whole in a persistently confusing order. The various sections of *Le Marteau* differ markedly in style. The second section, *Commentary I on "Bourreaux de solitude,"* has a repetitive movement such as Webern sometimes used; other sections are much more irregular, held together only by that ineluctable sense of rhythmic continuity more and more in evidence in the fifties.

Boulez also emphasizes the structural aspects of Webern; he is attracted by the possibility of artistically controlling all aspects of a complex, detailed musical fabric. Boulez and other Messiaen students (it seems odd to call them Parisian, but perhaps they share an objectivity with the music-hall style of the twenties) have serialized other factors besides tone, such as rhythm or timbre. Here the basic purpose is the same as in serial treatment of pitch: serialization facilitates the choice of the next sound so as to avoid confirmation of a traditional pattern. There is, however, an important difference, for the number of tones is traditionally limited to twelve, while there is no such limit on rhythmic or timbral elements.

The significance of the twelve-tone limit is not immediately apparent— especially not to an ear accustomed to the much narrower limits of triad and key. But in the absence of triad and key, the ear can become more aware of the broader limit of twelve tones. Indeed, the fact of a twelve-tone limit seems more important than the ordering of the twelve tones in a series. Or to put it differently, the negative function of the series (avoiding triads and keys) is a more important formal element than whatever positive function the series might have as a theme, say, or as a tonal plan.

Serial ordering of rhythm or timbre, however, involves no such limit. Under these conditions the serial order might conceivably contribute to the audible form in a more positive way. In any case, there was a tendency in the fifties to regard a series less as a device for avoiding old patterns and more as a positive factor for organizing new ones—less of a method, more of a principle. Whether serialization (of any element) really has the structural properties claimed for it is one of the most intriguing aspects of stylistic development in the sixties.

The art of Webern and the technique of total serialization were best represented in the United States by Milton Babbitt (1916–), with compositions throughout the fifties and beyond. During the early fifties Babbitt was most effective as a teacher and theorist of serial techniques; artistic results of his activity became especially evident in the next generation.

The early fifties also saw rapid development of electronic music, in association with the composers just mentioned. The spectrum of electronic techniques is broad. "Real" sounds, recorded on tape, can be combined by playing them faster or slower, forward or backward, cut and spliced according to the composer's wishes. Or sounds may be completely synthesized in the laboratory, then combined, by means of increasingly sophisticated electronic equipment. There is no theoretical limit on the variety of sounds that can be produced; hence the nature of the instrument, in this case, is largely irrelevant to questions of style.

One of the important features of electronic media is the ability to produce an unlimited number of gradations in pitch. This places serialization of pitch on a common basis with serialization of timbre and rhythm—and for some composers the great advantage of electronic music is its aptitude for total serialization. In the first electronic pieces, however, the ability to produce unlimited variation in pitch did not seem to produce basically new structures, but rather analogs of those already current in the 1900s.

Similar observations can be made about the unlimited timbral resources of electronic media. Electronic composers that tend in the direction of noise-makers also approximate traditional structures of timbre and texture. This kind of electronic music tends to be less progressive than that using defined pitch; reminiscent of Russolo, it is often far less sophisticated than Varèse. Most striking is the persistent tendency of early electronic music in the fifties to sound like out-of-focus Webern. This situation can, of course, change overnight: it takes only (but at least) one really successful work to open up new possibilities.

An awareness of Webern came to Italy through Luigi Dallapiccola (1904–). In 1941 Dallapiccola had completed his *Canti di prigionia* (Songs of Captivity), rich in timbral color in a way that recalls Italian music earlier in the century. While treating serial techniques with a certain nonchalance and avoiding the more tightly drawn aspects of Webern, Dallapiccola infused his twelve-tone music with that sense—also habitual with Italians—of humane civilization.

The younger Italian generation, while in some respects living in a different world, continued to see Webern in somewhat the same way Dallapiccola saw him. In the works of Bruno Maderna (1920–), Luigi Nono (1924–), and Luciano Berio (1925–), the inner construction may or may not be rigorous; but the effect is usually colorful and sometimes radiant. Once past 1950, these composers were at home in international style.

ORDER AND CHANCE   High serialization would have been clear and easy to understand by itself; but it coexisted—even in the work of a single composer—with a kind of music called *aleatory* (*alea*, "chance"), in which one or more factors of organization were deliberately left uncontrolled by the composer. The composer might provide a number of short fragments, which the performer might perform in one of several optional orders, or in any order he pleased, or in an order given by an arbitrary chance factor, such as the throw of dice. The compositions of Karlheinz Stockhausen (1928–) in the fifties, ranged from electronic pieces, whose composition and performance were identical (being fixed once for all on a tape), to a variety of aleatory pieces whose composition would vary with each performance. Stockhausen's work, although characterized more by industry and facility than musical imagination, is a convenient catalog of serial and aleatory devices.

More extreme application of aleatory procedures can be found in the works of John Cage (1912–), active throughout the fifties. Cage's interest in aleatory procedures stemmed from his perennial interest in new sounds. The listener's attention could just as well be awakened by old sounds in a new order as by new sounds in an old one. Cage's compositions may consist of a set of abstract directions—dots or lines on transparent sheets to be superimposed in any desired way, from which can be derived instrumental parts for any number of any kinds of instruments.

Often regarded as trivial, such pieces are symptomatic of important stylistic facts. It is true that insofar as "chance" or "random" procedures (the terms are loosely used) are not ordered by some human agency, insofar as their results are totally unique and irreproducible, they do not belong to the history of style. And since their success depends largely on the personal persuasion of the performer, they do not lend themselves to objective description. But as a negation of traditional stylistic patterns, a deliberate way of unordering what has been traditionally ordered, aleatory procedures are an important aspect of music in our time.

Furthermore, it has been demonstrated that carefully structured aleatory pieces are different from sloppy ones—and that the difference is perceptible to merely sensitive (not indoctrinated) ears, which can also tell good serial music from bad and can spot wrong notes in post-Webern music. Good aleatory music, of whatever kind, seems to share with good serial music certain basic features of organization. Confirmation and clarity must be avoided; diffusion must be maintained. Within twelve-tone space, sophisticated techniques of serialization are actually necessary to maintain this diffusion. Outside the realm of twelve tones, and especially in dealing with noise, such techniques are often more trouble than they are worth, since cruder ways of diffusing the material work just as well. Unorthodox sounds (for example, a human voice saying whatever comes into the speaker's mind) will sufficiently distract the listener's attention from minor defects in form; but a crude ordering technique applied, say, to a twelve-tone piece in two linear parts, for normal piano, would very soon result in inacceptable simplicities of form and texture.

In other words, the factors being ordered in "totally" ordered music, or specifically unordered in aleatory music, are probably not the most important structural determinants involved. As a corollary, the year-by-year changes in avant-garde techniques during the fifties might well have been a frantic response to an intuition that the factors being manipulated with such virtuosity were irrelevant, or at least superficial. It may be pointed out that composers of the past have frequently used unpredictable orders and have frequently exploited the effects of unusual sounds within what now seem to be traditional orders. The most important element—or at any rate the one most apparent to an historian— seems to be that of keeping audible experience interesting by the avoidance of traditional expectations. Such avoidance seems now to be a prime structural consideration; in a real sense, it is a kind of order.

In any case, younger composers on all sides were at least annoyed when Stravinsky started writing alla Webern in the late fifties. They were annoyed because Stravinsky, a dealer in styles, listened only to the outside of Webern and then made a fairly true reproduction of what he heard. Stravinsky's actions, discounting the inner reasons so volubly articulated by younger composers, emphasized in effect the stylistic continuum as a more important determinant of musical shape.

A CLASSIC STYLE?   It took Stravinsky several tries to learn how to move in twelve-tone space. His progress is reflected in *Agon* (1952–1957), an abstract ballet about a dance contest—the shape of new music, without the story. A short episode (as if a tribute to Webern) from the end of *Agon* provides a compact example of a refined, classic twelve-tone style (Example 142). Characteristic of this style is gracious lyricism; a thin, high texture with certain bell-like qualities; widely leaping parts that insist upon sevenths and ninths (both in line and counterpoint) without, however, seeming particularly dissonant; and a leisurely progression through the twelve-tone field. Serialists may object, however, that the piece is in G major.

The main lines of development in the 1900s were by now clear. Schoenberg and Webern had been right all along—or, at any rate, more right than Sibelius or Hindemith. Furthermore Schoenberg, and especially Webern, had been right back in 1913. Was the Parisian experience, the whole output of Stravinsky up to *Agon*, the whole output of Bartók (except as it could be interpreted as twelve-tone music)—was all this a lie, a timid expedient, a cynical

EXAMPLE 142   STRAVINSKY: FROM AGON

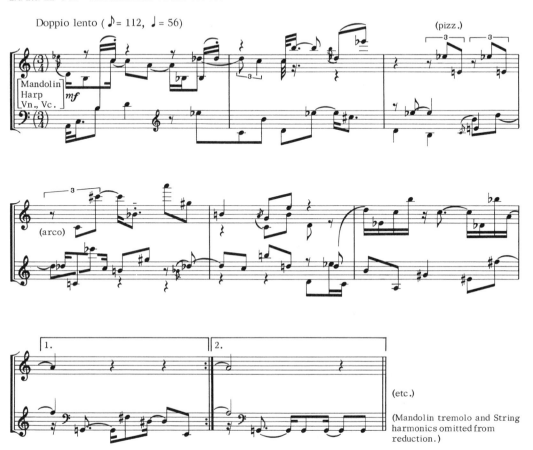

© 1957 by Boosey & Hawkes Inc. Reprinted by permission.

compromise with the mass audience? To say "yes" would be to miss one of the basic features of stylistic development.

Musical materials have to be "used up," their potential fully exploited, before style can move ahead on the long line of history. As in a development section by Beethoven, the material already introduced has to be shredded down to its constituent fibers, all its meaning extracted, before new material will seem meaningful.

Schoenberg and Webern had moved in the right direction, but too fast— not just too fast for the audience, but too fast for the nature of the stylistic material. There was still much to be done with triads, and Stravinsky showed what to do; there was still room to move within broadly dissonant expressions of key, and Bartók showed how. Until these and other things were done, the novelties of Schoenberg and Webern could only seem arbitrary and isolated. But once these things were done definitively, then the prior achievement of Schoenberg and Webern made further delay impossible. Music must move beyond the triad into a twelve-tone space.

That these things had to be was simply a matter of historical continuity. Tonal order, using triads, had reached a state of high concentration in Beethoven; it became increasingly diffused throughout the 1800s. Violent as they were, Schoenberg and Webern did not, and could not, destroy triadic tonal order—did not, because it was deteriorating at a steady rate quite independently of their efforts; could not, because the same steady rate permitted functional harmonic references to survive both of them.

For the time being, no commonly accepted form of tonal order would replace that previously provided by triads and their relationships. Only the twelve-tone space itself would serve as a common tonal order. Previously tonal order had radiated outward (insofar as we can speak of these things in spatial metaphor) from a core of closely related triads to the limits of the twelve-tone space—as from the center of a sphere out to the surface. Now tonal order was provided only by the surface itself and by whatever ad hoc order a composer might use to give meaning to a particular piece. Motion through the twelve-tone space was largely a matter of personal style; indeed, personal style was largely the manner in which one moved.

Music around 1960 is represented by a generation of skilled, sophisticated composers. Their works show practically none of the explosive violence, the incongruous extremes so frequent in the early 1900s. The styles cultivated by these composers are refined and well bred; as a complex, these styles (less and less incompatible) have all the makings of a classic style of the 1900s.

It is possible here to mention only a few examples of composers that seem (at the time of writing) to represent the spectrum of interests pursued by this generation. Mel Powell (1923–) writes both serial and electronic music with great charm and a smooth finish; of the serialists he is probably the least committed to a serial mystique and least likely to sound too static. Mario Davidovsky (1932–) is one of the most convincing composers of electronic music. Luigi Nono, like his colleagues of the fifties, has continued to compose actively; his powerful *Intolleranza 1960* fused a variety of techniques into a spectacle in the high Italian tradition. Lukas Foss (1922–) has worked out successful means of improvising twelve-tone music with an instrumental ensemble.

The counterpoise of tradition is now represented by composers who have long been at ease in the twelve-tone field; they write serially when they feel like it, but emphasize less disjunct, more rigorously developmental forms. A *Little Symphony* by Alexander Goehr (1932–) is an accessible example. Roger Sessions profoundly impressed a Berlin audience in 1964 with his opera *Montezuma,* a work that seemed to fulfill aspirations of seriousness in the sixties.

At this point the past becomes present, and history—that is, the writing of it—must pause, waiting for the present to become past.

SELECTED
STUDY
MATERIAL

INTRODUCTORY NOTE

"Where do I go to look at his music?" By way of an answer, the following lists of Selected Study Materials are intended as guides to modern publications of music.

For composers mentioned in the text the lists include complete or critical editions of their works, or, failing that, representative works published separately. References are given for specific works mentioned in the text—except when no modern edition exists; or when the work is a musical example, in which case its source is given in the lists of Sources of Musical Examples; or when the work is easily found in a collected edition cited under the composer's name.

Also included are occasional books and articles, usually in English, dealing with musical repertories and selected exclusively on the basis of their accessibility and usefulness to the college music major. The few foreign-language items represent especially relevant material not otherwise available.

Biographies are not regularly included (see the note on page 550). Four modern encyclopedias are now generally available for biographical and bibliographical data.

Die Musik in Geschichte und Gegenwart (MGG), ed. F. Blume (Kassel 1949–)

Encyclopédie de la musique, ed. F. Michel, F. Lesure, and V. Fedorov (Paris 1958)

Enciclopedia della musica, ed. C. Sartori (Milan 1963–)

Grove's Dictionary of Music and Musicians, 5th edition, ed. E. Blom (London 1954)

MGG has been used as a standard for composers' dates; MGG also contains for each composer the most recent authoritative list of works (both in their original state and in modern editions) as well as recent bibliography. Similar information can be found in *Grove's Dictionary.*

At the beginning of most sections, in a paragraph headed General, are listed standard surveys or other useful books, and, for earlier chapters, editions including several composers. Certain bibliographical tools are included here, not for their technical usefulness to historians but rather for the picture they give of musical repertory. A few biographies are mentioned for their valuable discussions of style.

Short titles in Selected Study Materials are given complete under the preceding heading, General. Abbreviations are listed in the table on page 530.

Metronome marks on the musical examples represent the author's preference and are intended only as rough guides to the basic nature of the music.

ABBREVIATIONS

AfMW   *Archiv für Musikwis-senschaft*

AM   *Annales musicologiques*

BWV   Bach Werke - Verzeich-nis = W. Schmieder, *Thematisch - systemati-sches Verzeichnis der musikalischen Werken von Johann Sebastian Bach* (Leipzig 1950)

CM   *Collegium musicum*, ed. L. Schrade, Yale Uni-versity (New Haven 1955–)

CMI   *I Classici musicali itali-ana*. Fondazione Euge-nio Bravi (Milan 1941–)

CMM   *Corpus mensurabilis musicae*, ed. A. Cara-petyan, American Insti-tute of Musicology (Rome 1947–)

DDT   *Denkmäler deutscher Tonkunst.* Series 1 (Leipzig 1892–). Series 2 = *Denkmäler der Tonkunst in Bayern* (Leipzig 1900–)

DM   *Documenta musicolo-gica*, ed. Internationale Gesellschaft für Musik-wissenschaft (Kassel 1951–)

DTOe   *Denkmäler der Ton-kunst in Oesterreich*, ed. G. Adler (Vienna 1894–)

GMB   *Geschichte der Musik im Beispielen*, ed. A. Scher-ing (Leipzig 1931)

HAM   *Historical Anthology of Music*, ed. A. T. Davison and W. Apel (Cam-bridge, Mass. 1949–)

IMAMI   *Istituzioni e monumenti dell'arte musicale ital-iana* (Milan 1931)

JAMS   *Journal of the Ameri-can Musicological So-ciety*

JMT   *Journal of Music Theory*

K   Köchel = *Chronolo-gisch-thematisches Ver-zeichnis sämtlicher Ton-werke Wolfgang Amadé Mozarts*, 6th edition, ed. F. Giegling, A. Wein-mann, G. Sievers (Wies-baden 1964)

MB   *Musica Britannica*, ed. A. Lewis, Royal Musi-cal Association (London 1951–)

MD   *Musica disciplina*

MF   *Die Musikforschung*

MGG   *Die Musik im Geschichte und Gegenwart*, ed. F. Blume (Kassel 1949–)

MM   *Masterpieces of Music before 1750*, ed. C. Par-rish and J. F. Ohl (New York 1951)

MMB   *Monumenta musicae bel-gicae*, ed. J. Watelet, Vereeniging voor Mu-ziekgeschiedenis te Ant-werpen (Antwerp 1932)

MMRF   *Les Maîtres musiciens de la renaissance fran-çaise*, ed. H. Expert (Paris 1895–1908)

MPI   *Monumenta polyphonica italica*, ed. Pontificum Institutum Musicae Sac-rae (Rome 1930–)

MQ   *Musical Quarterly*

MRM   *Monuments of Renais-sance Music*, ed. E. Low-insky, University of Chi-cago (Chicago 1964–)

MS   *Musicological Studies*, ed. L. Dittmer, Insti-tute of Medieval Music (Brooklyn 1959–)

MSD   *Musicological Studies and Documents*, ed. A. Carapetyan, American Institute of Musicology (Rome 1957–)

NOHM   *The New Oxford His-tory of Music*, ed. J. A. Westrup (London 1957–)

PAM   *Publikationen älterer Musik*, ed. Th. Kroyer, Deutscher Musikgesell-schaft (Leipzig 1926–)

PAPTM   *Publikationen älterer praktischer und theore-tischer Musik - Werke*, ed. R. Eitner, Gesell-schaft für Musikfor-schung (Leipzig 1869–)

SCMA   *Smith College Music Archives* (Northampton 1935–)

Strunk SR   *Source Readings in Mu-sic History from Classi-cal Antiquity through the Romantic Era*, ed. W. O. Strunk (New York 1950)

vfMW   *Vierteljahrschrift für Musikwissenschaft*

SOURCES OF MUSICAL EXAMPLES

CHAPTER 1

All the examples listed here are taken from *The Liber usualis, with Introduction and Rubrics in English,* edited by the Benedictines of Solesmes, Desclée Company, Printers to the Holy See and the Sacred Congregation of Rites, Tournai (Belgium) and New York, 1959. Copyright 1956 by Desclée & Co., Tournai (Belgium).

Ex. 1. Prayer tone: *Liber usualis,* The Common Tones of the Mass: Ancient Tones ad libitum, (a) Solemn Tone (p. 100).

Ex. 2. *Sursum corda* and preface tone: *Liber usualis,* The Common Tones of the Mass (p. 109).

Ex. 4. Antiphon *Suscepimus: Liber usualis,* Christmas matins, 2nd nocturn (p. 378).

Ex. 5. Psalm tone: as for Ex. 4; see also *Liber usualis,* The Ordinary Chants of the Office: The Tones of the Psalms (pp. 112–117).

Ex. 6. Introit *Resurrexi: Liber usualis,* Easter Sunday (p. 777).

Ex. 7. Gradual *A summo caelo: Liber usualis,* Saturday in Ember Week of Advent (p. 343).

Ex. 8. Alleluia *Justus germinabit: Liber usualis,* Common of Doctors (p. 1192).

Translations of liturgical texts have been adapted from the *Book of Common Prayer* or the King James Bible.

CHAPTER 2

Ex. 9. Refrain from the laudes, *Christus vincit.* Paris, Bibliothèque nationale MS fonds latin 1118, fol. 38r.

Ex. 10. Melisma for the responsory *Descendit de caelis* (part). *Le Codex F 160 de la Bibliothèque de la Cathèdrale de Worcester. Antiphonaire monastique (XIIIe Siècle)* (vol. XII of the *Paléographie musicale,* Paris 1925) p. 31.

Ex. 11. Introit trope *Factus homo* for *Resurrexi.* Paris, Bibliothèque nationale MS fonds latin 1118, fol. 41v.

Ex. 12. Prose *Ecce pulcra.* Paris, Bibliothèque nationale MSS fonds latin 1118, fol. 237v; 1240, fol. 56r; 1132, fol. 126v.

Ex. 13. *Kyrie Tibi Christe supplices. Paris,* Bibliothèque nationale MSS fonds latin 1084, fol. 90v, 92r; 1118, fol. 12r.

Ex. 14. Hymn *Conditor alme.* B. Stäblein, *Hymnen (I). Die mittelalterlichen Hymnenmelodien des Abendlandes. Monumenta monodica medii aevi,* herausgegeben im Auftrag des Instituts für Musikforschung Regensburg mit Unterstützung der Musikgeschichtlichen Kommission, Band I. Bärenreiter-Verlag Kassel und Basel, 1956. Alle Rechte vorbehalten, 1956, p. 255.

The translations of *Splendor paternae gloriae* (p. 44), *Pange lingua* (p. 45), and *Salve festa dies* (p. 46), are taken from the following sources:

O Splendour of God's Glory Bright: By Robert Bridges from *The Yattendon Hymnal* by permission of Oxford University Press.

Sing My Tongue the Glorious Battle: Translated by Percy Dearmer. From *The English Hymnal* by permission of Oxford University Press.

Hail Thee Festival Day: Translated by M. R. Bell. From *The English Hymnal* by permission of Oxford University Press.

Translations of liturgical texts have been adapted from the *Book of Common Prayer* or the King James Bible. Other translations are by the author.

CHAPTER 3

Ex. 15. Versus *Gaudeamus.* Paris, Bibliothèque nationale MS fonds latin 1139, fol. 37v.

Ex. 16. Versus *Castitatis lilium.* Paris, Bibliothèque nationale MS fonds latin 1139, fol. 42r.

Ex. 17. Trouvère song *Tuit mi desir.* Chansonnier de l'Arsenal (Paris, Bibl. de l'Arsenal MS 5198, p. 51).

Ex. 18. Polyphonic versus *Per partum.* Paris, Bibliothèque nationale MS fonds latin 3549, fol. 150v. Cf. facsimile in MGG, "Saint-Martial."

Prosula *Rex regum* (p. 33). Paris, Bibliothèque nationale MS fonds latin 1118, fol. 118v.

Versus *Radix Jesse* (p. 49). Paris, Bibliothèque nationale MS fonds latin 1139, fol. 46v.

Versus *Vallus montem* (p. 50). Paris, Bibliothèque nationale MS fonds latin 1139, fol. 42v.

CHAPTER 4

Ex. 19. Leonin: *Viderunt omnes* (organum for the Christmas gradual). W. G. Waite, *The Rhythm of Twelfth-Century Polyphony. Yale Studies in the History of Music*, no. 2 (New Haven: Yale University Press 1954), pp. 67–68 of the transcription. Copyright 1954 by Yale University Press.

Ex. 20. Leonin: discant on *Dominus* for the Christmas gradual. Codex Wolfenbüttel 677, fol. 21 (Ludwig, *Repertorium*, Dominus no. 1; see Selected Study Materials, Chapter 4, General).

Ex. 22. End of the conductus *In rosa vernat lilium*. Codex Wolfenbüttel 677, fol. 116–118.

Ex. 23. Perotin: from organum *a3* for the gradual *Benedictus es*. Codex Wolfenbüttel 677, fol. 59.

Ex. 24. Substitute discant clausulas on *Dominus* for the Christmas gradual. (a) through (e): Codex Wolfenbüttel 677, fol. 43–43v; (f): Codex Florence Bibl. Med.-Laur. pl. 29.1, fol. 149v. Ludwig, *Repertorium*, *Dominus* nos. 3(e), 4(b), 5(d), 6(c), 7(a), 11(f).

Ex. 25. Favorite tenors of Codex Montpellier. Based on Y. Rokseth, *Polyphonies du treizième siècle* (Paris 1936), vol. 4, pp. 152–157.

Ex. 26. *Ai mi! las! — Doucement*—OMNES (French motet). Y. Rokseth, *Polyphonies du treizième siècle*, vol. 2 (Paris: Editions de L'Oiseau-lyre 1936) pp. 204–205. Copyright 1936 by Louise B. M. Dyer.

Ex. 27. From the triplum of Ex. 26. (a) original notation, Codex Montpellier, fol. 143v (b) in Franco's interpretation, first transcription (c) in Franco's interpretation, second transcription

Ex. 28. From the triplum of *Je cuidoie—Se j'ai*—SOLEM (motet). Codex Montpellier, fol. 382v.

CHAPTER 5

Ex. 29. Philippe de Vitry: *Garrit gallus — In nova fert —* NEUMA (Latin motet, first half). L. Schrade, *Polyphonic Music of the Fourteenth Century*, vol. 1 (Monaco: Editions de L'Oiseau-lyre 1956), pp. 68–69. Copyright 1956 by Louise B. M. Dyer and J. B. Hanson.

Ex. 31. *Talent m'est pris* (chace). Codex Ivrea, fol. 51v.

Ex. 32. *Patrem omnipotentem* (from a *Credo*). H. Stäblein-Harder, *Fourteenth-Century Mass Music in France. Corpus mensurabilis musicae* 29 (Rome: American Institute of Musicology 1962), p. 80. Copyright 1962 by Armen Carapetyan.

Ex. 33. Guillaume de Machaut: *Mes esperis* (ballade). L. Schrade, *Polyphonic Music of the Fourteenth Century: The Works of Guillaume de Machaut*, vol. 3 (Monaco: Editions de L'Oiseau-lyre 1956), pp. 134–135. Copyright

1956 by Louise B. M. Dyer and J. B. Hanson.

Ex. 34. *Involta d'un bel velo* (madrigale). N. Pirrotta, *The Music of Fourteenth-Century Italy. Corpus mensurabilis musicae* 8 (Rome: American Institute of Musicology 1960), vol. 2, pp. 31–32, no. 21. Copyright 1960 by Armen Carapetyan.

Ex. 35. (a) Francesco Landini: from *Questa fanciull'amor* (ballata). L. Schrade, *Polyphonic Music of the Fourteenth Century: The Works of Francesco Landini*, vol. 4 (Monaco: Editions de L'Oiseau-lyre 1958), p. 116. Copyright 1958 by Louise B. M. Dyer and J. B. Hanson. (b) from a keyboard arrangement of Landini's *Questa fanciull' amor*. Codex Reina (Paris: Bibl. nat. MS fonds français nouv. acq. 6771), fol. 85.

Ex. 36. *Gente et devis* (ballade, first half). Codex Reina (Paris: Bibl. nat. MS fonds français nouv. acq. 6771), fol. 56v.

Ex. 37, 38, 39 from W. Apel, *French Secular Music of the Late Fourteenth Century* (Cambridge, Mass.: Mediaeval Academy of America 1950). Copyright 1950 by the Mediaeval Academy of America. Ex. 37, Solage: from *Corps femenin* (ballade), pp. 47*–48*. Ex. 38, Trebor: from *Se July Cesar* (ballade), p. 76*. Ex. 39, Matheus de Perusio: from *Le Greygnour bien* (ballade), p. 1*.

Ex. 40. (a) Guillaume de Machaut: from *De petit po* (ballade), with a later contratenor.

L. Schrade, *Polyphonic Music of the Fourteenth Century: The Works of Guillaume de Machaut,* vol. 3 (Monaco: Editions de L'Oiseau-lyre 1956), p. 90. Copyright 1956 by Louise B. M. Dyer and J. B. Hanson.

(b) Grenon: from *Je ne requier* (ballade) with contratenor by Matheus de Perusio.

J. Marix, *Les Musiciens de la Cour de Bourgogne au XVe siècle* (Paris: Editions de L'Oiseau-lyre 1937), p. 1. Copyright 1937 by Louise B. M. Dyer.

Ex. 42. Dunstable: from *Beata Maria* (song motet).

M. F. Bukofzer, *John Dunstable, Complete Works. Musica Brittanica,* vol. 8 (London: Royal Musical Association 1953), p. 110.

Ex. 43. Dufay: *Benedictus* from *Missa Se la face ay pale.*

H. Besseler, *Guglielmi Dufay opera omnia. Corpus mensurabilis musicae* 1 (Rome: American Institute of Musicology 1951), vol. 3, pp. 26–27. Copyright 1951 by Armen Carapetyan.

Ex. 44. Walter Frye: from *Ave regina* (song motet).

S. W. Kenney, *Collected Works. Corpus mensurabilis musicae* 19 (Rome: American Institute of Musicology 1960), pp. 8–9. Copyright 1960 by Armen Carapetyan.

CHAPTER 6

Ex. 45, 47, 48, 49 from D. Plama-nac, *Johannes Ockeghem, Collected Works,* 2nd corrected ed. (American Musicological Society 1959). Copyright 1959 by American Musicological Society.

Ex. 45, from *Agnus Dei II, Missa L'Homme armé,* vol. 1, p. 114.

Ex. 47, *Agnus Dei III, Missa Ecce ancilla,* vol. 1, p. 98.

Ex. 48, excerpts from *Missa De plus en plus,* vol. 1.

(a) from *Credo,* p. 68
(b) from *Sanctus,* p. 71
(c) from *Sanctus,* p. 72

Ex. 49, *Agnus Dei I* from *Missa mi–mi,* vol. 2, pp. 17–18.

Ex. 46. Reductions of Dufay, *Kyrie, Missa L'Homme armé,* and Ockeghem, *Kyrie, Missa L'Homme armé.*

For Dufay's *Kyrie* see HAM no. 66; for Ockeghem's *Kyrie,* HAM no. 73.

Ex. 50. Busnois: *Je ne demande* (rondeau, first half).

H. Hewitt, *Harmonice Musices Odhecaton A* (Cambridge, Mass.: Mediaeval Academy of America 1942), p. 311. Copyright 1942 by the Mediaeval Academy of America.

Ex. 51, 52, 53, 54 from A. Smijers, *Josquin Des Pres, Werken* (Leipzig and Amsterdam: Vereeniging voor Nederlandsche Muziekgeschiednis 1935–1955).

Ex. 51, *Kyrie I* from *Missa Ave maris stella,* vol. 15, p. 1.

Ex. 52, from *Praeter rerum seriem,* vol. 18, motet no. 33, p. 21.

Ex. 53, from *Inviolata,* integra, et casta es,* vol. 21, motet no. 42, p. 111.

Ex. 54, from *Caeli enarrant,* vol. 39, motet no. 61, pp. 157–159.

CHAPTER 7

Ex. 56. Claudin: *Tous mes amis* (chanson).

Courtesy of Prof. Daniel Heartz, University of California (Berkeley).

Ex. 57 and 58 from J. Schmidt-Görg, *Nicolai Gombert opera omnia. Corpus mensurabilis musicae* 6 (Rome: American Institute of Musicology 1961), vol. 5. Copyright 1961 by Armen Carapetyan.

Ex. 57, from *Domine Pater* (motet), p. 2.

Ex. 58, from *Venite filii* (motet), p. 15.

Ex. 59. Clement: samples of imitative procedures.

K. Ph. Bernet Kempers, *Jacobus Clemens non Papa, opera omnia* (Rome: American Institute of Musicology 1957), vol. 9. Copyright 1957 by Armen Carapetyan.

(a) p. 49
(b) p. 96
(c) p. 92
(d) p. 19
(e) p. 16
(f) vol. 3, p. 7

Ex. 60. Willaert: from *Locuti sunt adversum me* (motet).

H. Zenck, *Adriani Willaert opera omnia. Corpus mensurabilis musicae* 3 (Rome: American Institute of Musicology 1950), vol. 3, p. 86. Copyright 1950 by Armen Carapetyan.

Ex. 61. Cipriano de Rore: from

Quando lieta sperai (madrigal).

B. Meier, *Cipriani Rore opera omnia. Corpus mensurabilis musicae* 14 (Rome: American Institute of Musicology 1961), vol. 3, p. 34. Copyright 1961 by Armen Carapetyan.

Ex. 62.   Cabezón: versicle of the fourth tone.
F. Pedrell, *Hispaniae schola musica sacra*, vol. 3 (Barcelona 1895), p. 25.

Ex. 64.   Lasso: from *Prophetiae Sibyllarum*.
From Friedrich Blume, *Das Chorwerk*, vol. 48, ed. Joachim Therstappen (Wolfenbüttel and Zürich: Möseler Verlag 1937), p. 5. Copyright 1937 Möseler Verlag.

Ex. 65.   From Girolamo dalla Casa's passaggi for Cipriano's madrigal *O Sonno*.
G. P. Smith, *The Madrigals of Cipriano de Rore. Smith College Music Archives*, vol. 6 (Northampton: Smith College 1943), p. 106, meas. 1–6. Copyright 1943 by the Trustees of Smith College.
Il vero modo di diminuir . . . di Girolamo dalla Casa (Venice: A. Gardano 1584), fol. 32v.

CHAPTER 8

Ex. 66.   Caccini: from *Le Nuove musiche*.
(Florence: Marescotti 1601), p. 2 (a), p. 36 (b).

Ex. 67.   Peri: recitative from *L'Euridice*.
(Florence: Marescotti 1600), pp. 12–13.

Ex. 68, 69, 70, 71 from G. F. Malipiero, *Tutte le opere di Claudio Monteverdi*

(Asolo 1928–1930). Copyright by G. Francesco Malipiero.

Ex. 68, recitativo from *L'Orfeo* II, vol. 11, pp. 59–61. Cf. facs. ed. A. Sandberger (Augsburg: B. Filser 1927), pp. 37–38.

Ex. 69, from *Dice la mia bellissima Licori* (madrigal), vol. 7, p. 59.

Ex. 70, beginning of *Zefiro torna* (ciacona), vol. 9, p. 9.

Ex. 71, beginning of *Lamento della ninfa*, vol. 8:2, p. 288.

Ex. 72.   Frescobaldi: beginning of a toccata.
P. Pidoux, *Girolamo Frescobaldi, Orgel - und Klavierwerke*, vol. 3, *Das erste Buch der Toccaten, Partiten usw. 1637* (Kassel: Bärenreiter Verlag 1953), p. 28. Copyright 1953 by Bärenreiter Verlag.

Ex. 73.   Schütz: from *Ich werde nicht sterben* (*Symphoniae sacrae* II). Ph. Spitta, *Sämtliche Werke*, vol. 7 (Leipzig 1888), pp. 34, 40.

CHAPTER 9

Ex. 74.   Monteverdi: from *L'Incoronazione di Poppea*, III.
G. F. Malipiero, *Tutte le opere di Claudio Monteverdi*, vol. 13 (Asolo 1931), pp. 217–222. Copyright 1931 by G. Francesco Malipiero.
Cf. facs. ed. G. Benvenuti, Venice, Biblioteca nazionale di San Marco, MS IT. Cl. 4, no. 439 (Milan: Fratelli Bocca 1938), 91v–93v.

Ex. 75.   Rossi: excerpts from *Hor che l'oscuro manto* (cantata). Oxford, Christ Church College MS Mus. 946, fol. 47–52v.

Ex. 76.   Cesti: from *Il Pomo d'oro* I, vii.
DTOe Bd. 3:2 (1896), pp. 86–90.

Ex. 77.   Cesti: from *Il Pomo d'oro* I, ix.
DTOe 3:2 (1896), pp. 96–98.

Ex. 78.   Ballard: second half of a courante.
A. Souris and S. Spycket, *Robert Ballard, Premier livre (1611). Collection Le Choeur des Muses* (Paris: Edition du Centre National de la Recherche Scientifique 1963), pp. 58–60. Copyright 1963 by Centre National de la Recherche Scientifique.

Ex. 79.   Louis Couperin: sarabande.
P. Brunold, *Louis Couperin, Oeuvres complètes* (Paris: Editions de L'Oiseau-lyre 1936), p. 32. Copyright 1936 by Louise B. M. Dyer.

Ex. 80.   Louis Couperin: transcription of an unmeasured prelude. Paris, Bibliothèque nationale, MS Rés. Vm⁷ 674, fol. 12v. Cf. facsimile, MGG, "Bauyn MS."

Ex. 81.   Lully: from *Armide* V, vi. (Paris: C. Ballard 1686), p. 252.

Ex. 82.   Froberger: second half of a sarabande.
G. Adler, *Werke*, DTOe Jg. 6:2 (Bd. 13) (1903), p. 50.

Ex. 83.   Buxtehude: from a praeludium.
J. Hedar, *Dietrich Buxtehude, Sämtliche Orgel-*

werke, vol. 2 (Copenhagen: W. Hansen 1952), p. 27. Copyright 1952 by Wilhelm Hansen.

Ex. 84. Pachelbel: *Magnificat* fugue for the fourth tone. H. Botstiber and M. Seiffert, *94 Compositionen*, DTOe Jg. 8:2 (1901), p. 52.

CHAPTER 10

Ex. 85. Pallavicino: excerpts from *La Gerusalemme liberata*. H. Abert, DDT series 1, Bd. 55 (1916), pp. 33–34 (a), 79 (b), 166 (c), 60 (d).

Ex. 86. Steffani: *Non sperar* (da capo aria) from *Alarico* II, xv. H. Riemann, *Ausgewählte Werke*, DDT series 2, Jg. 11, Bd. 2 (1911), pp. 113–114.

Ex. 87. Corelli: from Concerto in D, Op. 6 no. 1. F. Chrysander, *Les Oeuvres de Arcangelo Corelli*, vol. 4 (London 1890), p. 13.

Ex. 88. Scarlatti: aria excerpts. A. Lorenz, *Alessandro Scarlatti's Jugendoper*, vol. 2 (Augsburg: B. Filser 1927), nos. 212 (a), 216 (b), 234 (c), 290 (d), 243 (e), 239 (f).

Ex. 89. Zachow: from *Ruhe, Friede, Freud, und Wonne* (sacred concerto). M. Seiffert, *Gesammelte Werke*, DDT series 1, Bd. 21–22 (1905), p. 56.

Ex. 90. Zachow: from *Ich bin sicher und erfreut* (cantata). M. Seiffert, *Gesammelte Werke*, DDT series 1, Bd. 21–22 (1905), pp. 262–263.

Ex. 91. Keiser: aria excerpts from *Croesus*. M. Schneider, DDT series 1, Bd. 37–38 (1912), pp. 160 (a), 167 (b), 172 (c), 187 (d), 202 (e), 211 (f).

Ex. 92. Graupner: from *Mein Gott, warum hast du mich verlassen* (sacred concerto). F. Noack, *Ausgewählte Kantaten*, DDT series 1, Bd. 51–52 (1926), p. 48.

Ex. 93. Bach: aria excerpt from *Ich hatte viel Bekümmernis* (cantata). *Werke*, Bach - Gesellschaft, vol. 5:1, p. 14 (Kirchencantate no. 21).

Ex. 94. Händel: recitative from the Brockes' Passion. F. Chrysander, *Werke*, vol. 15 (Leipzig 1863), pp. 145–146.

Ex. 95. Bach: aria excerpt from *St. Matthew Passion* II. *Werke*, Bach-Gesellschaft, vol. 4, p. 178.

Ex. 96. Händel: recitative from *Saul* I, iv. F. Chrysander, *Werke*, vol. 13 (Leipzig 1862), pp. 271–272.

Ex. 97. Vinci: aria excerpts from *Artaserse*. Berkeley, University of California, Music Library, MS 138, fol. 15v (a), 42 (b), 43v (c), 54v (d).

Ex. 98. Pergolesi: aria excerpts. M. Zanon, *Olimpiade*, Associazione dei Musicologi Italiani (Florence 1915), p. 154 (a). E. Gerelli, *Lo Frate 'nnammorato* (Milan: Edizioni Suvini Zerboni 1961), pp. 367–368 (b), p. 264 (c), p. 397 (d). Copyright 1961 by Edizioni Suvini Zerboni.

Ex. 99. Rameau: aria excerpt from *Castor et Pollux* I, iii. C. Saint-Saëns, *Oeuvres complètes*, vol. 8 (Paris 1903), pp. 73–75.

CHAPTER 11

Ex. 100. Stamitz: beginning of a symphony (reduction). H. Riemann, *Sinfonien der Pfalzbayerischen Schule*, DDT series 2, Jg. 7:2 (1906), p. 55.

Ex. 102. Philipp Emanuel Bach: beginning of "Prussian" Sonata no. 3. R. Steglich, *C. Ph. Em. Bach, Die Preussischen Sonaten für Klavier*, vol. 1 (Hannover: Nagel 1927), p. 14. Copyright 1927 by Nagels Verlag.

Ex. 104. Ph. Em. Bach: beginning of a symphony (reduction). *4 Orchester - Sinfonien*, nach der Königliche Bibliothek zu Berlin befindlichen Original - Handschrift des Componisten (Leipzig 1860).

Ex. 105. J. C. Bach: from a symphony (reduction). A. Einstein, *Sinfonia D dur*, Op. 18 no. 4 (Leipzig: Eulenberg 1934), p. 4.

Ex. 106. Haydn: beginning of Symphony no. 45 (reduction). (Leipzig: Eulenberg), pp. 1–6.

Ex. 107. Haydn: from String Quartet Op. 20 no. 5. (London: Eulenberg), p. 3.

Ex. 108. Piccini: from *La Buona figliuola* III, ritornello for a duet. G. Benvenuti, *I Classici musicali italiani*, vol. 7 (Milan 1942), p. 326.

Ex. 138. Webern: second of Five Pieces for String Quartet, Op. 5 (Vienna: Universal Edition 1922), p. 6. Copyright 1922 by Universal Edition.

Ex. 139. Webern: first of Five Pieces for Orchestra, Op. 10 (Vienna: Universal Edition 1951), pp. 1–2. Copyright 1923 by Universal Edition.

Ex. 140. Schoenberg: beginning of Piano Suite, Op. 25 (Vienna: Universal Edition 1925), p. 4. Copyright by Gertrud Schoenberg.

Ex. 141. Schoenberg: beginning of third movement, String Quartet no. 3, Op. 30 (Vienna: Universal Edition 1927), p. 24. Copyright by Gertrud Schoenberg.

Ex. 142. Stravinsky: from *Agon* (New York: Boosey & Hawkes 1957), p. 73.

SELECTED STUDY MATERIALS

PART I Chant 700–1150
CHAPTER I BEFORE THE
BEGINNING: GREGORIAN CHANT

GENERAL

Gregorian chant is best studied to-day in the chant books of the Roman Catholic Church, in the editions made by the Benedictines of Solesmes (France), especially these three volumes:

Graduale sacrosanctae romanae ecclesiae de tempore et de sanctis SS. D. N. Pii X Pontificis Maximi jussu restitutum et editum ad exemplar editionis typicae concinnatum et rhythmicis signis a Solesmensibus monachis diligenter ornatum (Desclée et Socii, Paris 1924) = *Graduale*.

Antiphonale monasticum pro diurnis horis juxta Rr. Dd. Abbatum congregationum confoederatarum ordinis Sancti Benedicti a Solesmensibus monachis restitutum (Desclée et Socii, Paris 1934) = *Antiphonale*.

The *Liber usualis, with introduction and Rubrics in English,* edited by the Benedictines of Solesmes (Desclée Company, Tournai 1959).

The *Graduale* contains the mass propers. The *Antiphonale* contains psalm tones, canticle tones, and antiphons for the monastic offices—except matins, whose music is not published in a modern, critical edition. The *Liber usualis* (available in several successive editions, the recent ones having paginations slightly different from older versions) contains the chant most commonly used in parish churches—some, but not all of the mass propers, interspersed with some but not all of the music from certain offices. It is not the most convenient source for either mass or office, but does contain other material, especially

some of the antiphons and responsories from matins, not otherwise easily accessible.

Chants mentioned in the text can be found in the *Liber usualis* as follows:

Alleluia *Christus resurgens:* p. 827
Alleluia *Dies sanctificatus:* p. 409
Alleluia *Justi epulentur:* p. 1168
Alleluia *Ostende:* p. 320
Alleluia *Surrexit Dominus:* p. 790
Angelus ad pastores (antiphon): p. 397
Facta est cum angelo (antiphon): p. 398
Genuit puerpera (antiphon): p. 396
Haec dies (gradual): p. 778
Psalm tones: pp. 112–117
Puer natus est (introit): p. 408
Tecum principium (gradual): p. 393
Tenebrae: pp. 626–660, 688–719, 752–776 c.

The standard work in English is W. Apel, *Gregorian Chant* (Bloomington 1958). P. Wagner's *Introduction to the Gregorian Melodies. Part I: Origin and Development of the Forms of the Liturgical Chant up to the End of the Middle Ages* (trans. A. Orme and E. G. P. Wyatt, Plainsong and Mediaeval Music Society 1907) is an English translation of the first volume of an authoritative three-volume work in German. A more analytic approach is taken in P. Ferretti, *Esthétique grégorienne* (Paris 1938). H. Anglés, *Gregorian Chant,* NOHM vol. 2, 92–127 is an authoritative summary. More specialized treatment of specific subjects is given in MGG under the articles Alleluia, Antiphon, Communio, Graduale, Introitus, Psalm, all by B. Stäblein. Current historical studies appear in *Etudes grégoriennes* (Paris 1954–). Facsimile editions of the most important chant manuscripts are con-

tained in the *Paléographie musicale* (Solesmes 1889–).

CHAPTER 2 NEW FRANKISH FORMS 700–1000

GENERAL

Except for the melodies of *Kyrie, Gloria in excelsis, Sanctus,* and *Agnus Dei* preserved in the *Liber usualis* and *Graduale romanum,* and the volume of hymns in the *Monumenta monodica medii aevi* cited under Hymns, there are no substantial modern collections of the music discussed in this chapter and the next; neither are there any general stylistic or historical descriptions that take into account the results of recent research.

The most accessible account is J. Handschin, *Trope, Sequence, and Conductus,* NOHM vol. 2, 128–174. B. Stäblein, *Die Unterlegnung von Texten unter Melismen. Tropus, Sequenz und andere Formen,* in Report of the Eighth Congress of the International Musicological Society, ed. J. Larue (New York 1961), vol. 1, 12–29, summarizes much recent investigation. The *Analecta hymnica,* ed. G. M. Dreves and Cl. Blume, 55 vols. (Leipzig 1886–1922), is an extremely valuable collection of texts (no music) of various kinds of medieval chant.

* * *

Agnus Dei: melodies in *Liber usualis,* pp. 16–94; trope texts in *Analecta hymnica,* vol. 47, pp. 373–405. MGG (Stäblein).

Alleluia *Justus germinabit*—texting: text from *Analecta hymnica,* vol. 49, pp. 260–261.

Fulgens praeclara (prose): J. Hesbert, *Le Prosaire de la Sainte-Chapelle. Monumenta musicae sacrae* 1 (Macon 1952), p. 23 of the facsimile. On acclamations in proses, see B. Stäblein, *Zur Früh-geschichte der Sequenz*, AfMW 18 (1961), 1–33.

Gloria in excelsis: melodies in *Liber usualis*, pp. 16–92; *Gloria XV*, p. 57, and *Gloria* ad. lib. IV, p. 91 (which still has some melismas) are sometimes said to be pre-Gregorian. Example of a *Gloria*-trope in Handschin, *Trope, Sequence, and Conductus*, NOHM vol. 2, p. 168. Trope texts in *Analecta hymnica*, vol. 47, pp. 219–299. MGG (Stäblein).

Hymns: various melodies in *Liber usualis* and *Antiphonale; Monumenta monodica medii aevi I: Hymnen (I)*, ed. B. Stäblein (Kassel 1956); *Historical Companion to Hymns, Ancient and Modern*, ed. M. Frost (London 1962). R. E. Messenger, *The Medieval Latin Hymn* (Washington, D.C. 1953). MGG (Stäblein).

Kyrie: melodies in *Liber usualis* (melismatic form only), pp. 16–86, including *Tibi Christe supplices* (as *Te Christe rex*, ad. lib. VI p. 83), *Clemens rector* (ad. lib. I p. 79), and *Cunctipotens* (IV p. 25). The version *Omnipotens genitor* is a mere scribal variant of *Cunctipotens*, and neither version was written by Tutilo of St. Gall, sometimes given as author. Trope texts in *Analecta hymnica*, vol. 47, pp. 45–216. M. Melnicki, *Das einstimmige Kyrie des lateinischen Mittelalters* (Munich 1954). MGG (Stäblein).

Laudes: E. H. Kantorowicz, *Laudes regiae: A Study in Liturgical Acclamations and Medieval Ruler Worship* (Berkeley 1946). One version of the text in W. H. Frere, *The Winchester Troper. Henry Bradshaw Society*, vol. 8 (London 1894), p. 174.

Litanies: examples in the *Liber usualis*, Holy Saturday, p. 776V–FF, and Rogation Days, p. 835.

Melismas: J. Handschin, *Trope, Sequence, and Conductus*, NOHM vol. 2, pp. 141–146.

Nato canant omnia (prose): F. Tack, *Gregorian Chant. Anthology of Music (Das Musikwerk)*, vol. 18 (Cologne 1960), no. 52.

Notker (ca 840–912): A. Schubiger, *Die Sängerschule St. Gallens vom achten bis zwölften Jahrhundert* (Einsiedeln 1858). B. Stäblein, *Notkeriana*, AfMW 19 (1962), 84–99.

Pange lingua (hymn): *Analecta hymnica*, vol. 50, p. 71.

Prose (sequence): texts in *Analecta hymnica*, vols. 7 and 53; some melodies in A. Hughes, *Anglo-French Sequelae* edited from the papers of the late Dr. Henry Marriott Bannister (London 1934); examples in Handschin, *Trope, Sequence, Conductus*, NOHM vol. 2, pp. 154, 156, and in W. Apel, *Gregorian Chant*, p. 452. (*See also* Notker.) B. Stäblein, *Zur Frühgeschichte der Sequenz*, AfMW 18 (1961), 1–33; MGG, "Sequenz."

Quem queritis (introit trope dialog): W. L. Smoldon, *Liturgical Drama*, NOHM vol. 2, 175–219; *The Music of the Medieval Church Drama*, MQ 48 (1962), 476–497.

Regnum-tropes: texts in *Analecta hymnica*, vol. 47, pp. 282–299.

Rex omnipotens (prose): J. Hesbert, *Le Prosaire de la Sainte-Chapelle. Monumenta musica sacrae 1* (Macon 1952), p. 43 of the facsimile.

Salve festa dies (hymn): text in *Analecta hymnica*, vol. 50, p. 79.

Sanctus: melodies in *Liber usualis*, pp. 18–93; the beginning of *Sanctus XVIII* (p. 63) may be old, or may preserve an old congregational acclamation; see also *Sanctus I* (p. 18) and *Sanctus VI* (p. 33). Trope texts in *Analecta hymnica*, vol. 47, pp. 303–369. MGG (Thannabaur).

Sequence: *see* Prose.

Splendor paternae gloriae (hymn): text in *Analecta hymnica*, vol. 50, p. 11.

Te Deum laudamus: Liber usualis, p. 1832.

Tropes: texts in *Analecta hymnica*, vol. 49; examples in Handschin, *Trope, Sequence, and Conductus*, NOHM vol. 2, p. 167. R. Weakland, *The Beginnings of Troping*, MQ 44 (1958), 477–488. P. Evans, *Some Reflections on the Origins of the Trope*, JAMS 14 (1961), 119–130. W. H. Frere, *The Winchester Troper. Henry Bradshaw Society*, vol. 8 (London 1894).

Ut queant laxis (hymn): text in *Analecta hymnica*, vol. 50, p. 120; melody in *Liber usualis*, St. John Baptist (June 24), p. 1504.

CHAPTER 3 VERSUS AND RELATED FORMS 1000–1150

Rhyming Chant

GENERAL

As in Chapter 2, there are no recent general accounts of the music of this period. Of the works cited in Chapter 2, the *Analecta hymnica* and J. Handschin, *Trope, Sequence, and Conductus*, NOHM vol. 2, 128–174, are useful here.

*   *   *

Cantigas de Santa Maria: ed. H. Anglés, *La musica de las Cantigas de Santa María. Biblioteca Central de la diputación de Barcelona, publicacions de la sección de musica*, vol. 15:2, vol. 18–19 (Barcelona 1943). J. A. Westrup, *Medieval Song*, NOHM vol. 2, 220–269.

Daniel (Play of): ed. W. L. Smoldon, *The Play of Daniel* (London 1960); in a metered version, ed. N. Greenberg, *The Play of Daniel* (New York 1959). W. L. Smoldon, *Liturgical Drama*, NOHM vol. 2, 175–219.

Dies irae (prose): *Liber usualis*, Mass for the Dead, p. 1810.

Kyrie cum jubilo: Liber usualis, IX, p. 40.

Lauda Sion (prose): *Liber usualis*, Corpus Christi, p. 945.

Laudi: ed. F. Liuzzi, *La Lauda e i primordi della melodia italiana* (Rome 1935).

Minnesinger: *see* Troubadour.

Prose: J. Hesbert, *Le Prosaire de la Sainte-Chapelle. Monumenta musicae sacrae* 1 (Macon 1952); E. Misset, P. Aubry, *Les Proses d'Adam de Saint-Victor* (Paris 1900).

Rhymed Offices: H. Villetard, *Office de Pierre de Corbeil* (Paris 1907); *Office de St. Savinien et de St. Potentien* (Paris 1956).

Sponsus (liturgical drama): examples in W. L. Smoldon, *Liturgical Drama*, NOHM vol. 2, 175–219.

Troubadour: examples in F. Gennrich, *Troubadours, Trouvères, Minne- und Meistergesang. Das Musikwerk*, vol. 2 (Köln 1951). F. Gennrich, *Der musikalische Nachlass der Troubadours. Summa musicae medii aevi*, vols. 3–4 (Darmstadt 1958). J. A. Westrup, *Medieval Song*, NOHM vol. 2, 220–269. R. H. Perrin, *Some Notes on Troubadour Melodic Types*, JAMS 9 (1956), 12–18.

Trouvère: *Le Chansonnier Cangé*, facs. ed. and transcription by J. Beck, *Corpus cantilenarum medii aevi*, series 1, 2 vols. (Philadelphia 1927). *Le Chansonnier de l'Arsenal*, facs. ed. and transcription by P. Aubry (Paris 1909). *See also* Troubadour. F. Gennrich, *Der altfranzösische Rondeau und Virelai im 12. und 13. Jahrhundert. Summa musicae medii aevi*, vol. 10 (Langen bei Frankfurt 1963). G. Reaney, *Concerning the Origins of the Rondeau, Virelai, and Ballade Forms*, MD 6 (1952), 155–166.

Veni Sancte Spiritus (prose): *Liber usualis*, Pentecost, p. 880.

Versus: example in Handschin, *Trope, Sequence, and Conductus*, NOHM vol. 2, p. 173.

Victimae paschali laudes (prose): *Liber usualis*, Easter, p. 780.

Votive antiphons: the four Marian antiphons, *Alma redemptoris mater, Ave regina caelorum, Regina caeli, Salve regina*, are in the *Liber usualis*, Sundays at Compline, pp. 273–276. There are two versions: the ornate melodies just cited are the original ones; the "Simple Tones" (pp. 277–279) are later, some of them apparently written after 1600. The original melodies for *Alma redemptoris mater* and *Salve regina*, formerly ascribed to Hermannus Contractus, seem not to be by him.

Theory and Polyphony 1000–1150

GENERAL

So far there is no satisfactory account of theory during this period, although the major theorists are available; a few treatises have been translated into English. H. E. Wooldridge, *The Polyphonic Period*, in the *Oxford History of Music*, vol. 1 (Oxford 1901), pp. 45–101, even though old, is still the best account in English for the polyphony of the 1000s. Several polyphonic pieces from the St. Martial repertory have recently been published, although no complete edition is yet available.

*　　*　　*

Chartres polyphony: F. Ludwig, *Die geistliche nichtliturgische, weltliche einstimmige und die mehrstimmige Musik des Mittelalters*, in *Handbuch der Musik-geschichte*, ed. G. Adler, vol. 1 (2nd ed., Berlin 1930), pp. 174–175. HAM no. 26c.

Codex Calixtinus: music ed. P. Wagner, *Die Gesänge der Jakobsliturgie zu Santiago de Compostela* (Freiburg in der Schweiz 1931); G. Prado and W. M. Whitehill, *Liber Sancti Jacobi* (Santiago de Compostela 1944). H. Anglés, *Die Mehrstimmigkeit des Calixtinus von Compostela und seine Rhythmik*, in *Festschrift Heinrich Besseler* (Leipzig 1961), 91–100. HAM nos. 27b, 28b.

Hermannus Contractus (1013–1054): trans. L. Ellinwood, *Musica Hermanni Contracti* (Rochester 1936).

Hucbald (ca 840–915): R. Weakland, *Hucbald as Musician and Theorist*, MQ 42 (1956), 66–84; *The Compositions of Hucbald*, in *Etudes grégoriennes* 3 (1959), 155–162.

Jubilemus, exultemus (versus): facs. in C. Parrish, *The Notation of Medieval Music* (New York 1957), pl. 21.

Musica enchiriadis—Scolica enchiriadis: part trans. Strunk, SR, 126–138.

Odo: *Dialog on Music*, part trans. Strunk, SR, 103–116. Odo is no longer to be identified with Odo of Cluny (died 942) but probably wrote a century later; see H. Oesch, *Guido von Arezzo* (Bern 1954).

St. Martial polyphony: W. Apel, *Bermerkungen zu den Organa von St. Martial*, in *Miscelánea en homenaje a Mons. Higinio Anglés* (Barcelona 1958), vol. 1, 61–70; J. Marshall, *Hidden Polyphony in a Manuscript from St. Martial de Limoges*, JAMS 15 (1962), 131–144; L. Treitler, *The Polyphony of St. Martial*, JAMS 17 (1964), 29–42. HAM no. 27a.

Winchester Troper, polyphony: A.

Machabey, *Remarques sur le Winchester Troper,* in *Festschrift Heinrich Besseler* (Leipzig 1961), pp. 67–90.

PART II Part Music on a Discant Basis 1150–1600
CHAPTER 4 PARISIAN LEADERSHIP IN PART MUSIC 1150–1300

GENERAL

The most basic discussions of the materials of this chapter are contained in a group of technical studies, largely in German; the principal study is by F. Ludwig, *Repertorium organorum recentioris et motetorum vetustissimi stili* (Halle 1910; 2nd ed. by L. Dittmer, MS vol. 7, 1964). Ludwig's work was supported and complemented by a number of studies by J. Handschin (listed in *In memoriam Jacques Handschin,* ed. H. Anglès et al., Strasbourg 1962, pp. 4–8). The music itself is becoming available in modern editions only slowly— the central source, the Florence Medicean Codex, being in its ensemble not much more accessible than it was in 1910. In separate categories, however, much of the music can now be studied.

Codex Wolfenbüttel 677 (W₁)
   facsimile: J. H. Baxter, *An Old St. Andrews Music Book* (London 1931).
   Leonin's *Magnus liber:* ed. W. G. Waite, *The Rhythm of Twelfth Century Polyphony. Yale Studies in the History of Music,* vol. 2 (New Haven 1954).
Codex Florence Medicea, Pluteus 29.1 (F)
   organa *a 3* and *a 4* (from W₁ and F): ed. H. Husmann, *Die drei- und vierstimmigen Notre-Dame Organa,* PAM vol. 11 (1940).
   conductus: J. E. Knapp, *Thirty-*

five Conductus for Two and Three Voices from the Notre-Dame Repertory, CM 6 (1965).
Codex Wolfenbüttel 1099 (W₂)
   facsimile: L. Dittmer, *Facsimile Reproduction of the Manuscript Wolfenbüttel 1099 (1206). Publications of Mediaeval Musical Manuscripts,* no. 2 (Brooklyn 1960).
The following sources are published complete in facsimile, transcription, and commentary:
Codex Las Huelgas (Hu)
   H. Anglès, *El Còdex Musical de Las Huelgas, Biblioteca de Catalunya. Publicacions del Departament de Musica,* 6, 3 vols. (Barcelona 1931).
Codex Bamberg (Ba)
   P. Aubry, *Cent motets du XIIIe siècle,* 3 vols. (Paris 1908).
Codex Montpellier (Mo)
   Y. Rokseth, *Polyphonies du XIIIe siècle,* 3 vols. (Paris 1935–1939).

*   *   *

Alle psallite cum luya (motet): HAM no. 33.
Codex Wolfenbüttel: J. Handschin, *A Monument of English Mediaeval Polyphony,* in *Musical Times* 73 (1932), 510–513; 74 (1933), 697–704. HAM no. 37.
Conductus: M. F. Bukofzer, *Interrelations between Conductus and Clausula,* AM 1 (1953), 65–103. MGG (Handschin).
Discant clausula: HAM nos. 28d, 28e, 28h, 30.
English polyphony: F. Ll. Harrison, *Music in Medieval Britain* (2nd ed., London 1963).
   H. Tischler, *English Traits in the Early 13th Century Motet,* MQ 30 (1944), 458–476.
   E. H. Sanders, *Peripheral Polyphony of the 13th Century,* JAMS 17 (1964), 261–287.
   L. Dittmer, *The Worcester Fragments,* MSD vol. 2 (1957).

HAM no. 57.
Franco of Cologne: Strunk, SR, 139–159.
Hocket: Separate compositions in Codex Bamberg, nos. 102–108. Codex Montpellier, no. 73. HAM no. 32e.
Magnus liber: *See* General, Codex Wolfenbüttel 677.
Motet: *See* General, Codex Bamberg, Codex Montpellier. G. Reichert, *Wechselbeziehungen zwischen musikalischer und textlicher Struktur in der Motette des 13. Jahrhunderts,* in *In memoriam Jacques Handschin,* ed. H. Anglès et al. (Strasbourg 1962), pp. 151–169. HAM nos. 28f, 28g, 28h, 28i, 32a–d.
Leonin: *See* General, Codex Wolfenbüttel 677.
Organum: HAM nos. 28c, 29, 31. *See also* Leonin, Perotin.
Perotin: organa *a 3* and *a 4* ed. H. Husmann, *Die drei- und vierstimmigen Notre-Dame Organa,* PAM vol. 11 (1940): Alleluia *Nativitas,* p. 86; Alleluia *Posui,* p. 104; *Sederunt,* p. 29; *Viderunt,* p. 10.
Petrus de Cruce: HAM nos. 34, 35.
Sumer is icumen in: HAM no. 42.

CHAPTER 5 EXPANSION OF PART MUSIC 1300–1450

GENERAL

The music discussed in this chapter is at last becoming available in several important editions, some still in progress.

L. Schrade, *Polyphonic Music of the Fourteenth Century,* 4 vols. (Monaco 1956–1958):
   vol. 1. *Roman de Fauvel; Philippe de Vitry; French Mass Cycles*
   vols. 2 and 3. *Works of Guillaume de Machaut*
   vol. 4. *Works of Francesco Landini*

N. Pirrotta, *The Music of Four-*

teenth-Century Italy, CMM 8 (1954).

H. Stäblein-Harder, *Fourteenth-Century Mass Music in France*, CMM 29 (1962).

R. Hoppin, *The Cypriot-French Repertory of the Manuscript Torino, Biblioteca Nazionale J.II.9*, CMM 21, 4 vols. (1960).

W. Apel, *French Secular Music of the Late Fourteenth Century* (Cambridge, Mass. 1950).

G. Reaney, *Early Fifteenth-Century Music*, CMM 11 (1955–).

Ch. Van Den Borren, *Polyphonia sacra; a Continental Miscellany of the Fifteenth Century* (London 1931; reprinted University Park 1963).

J. Stainer, *Early Bodleian music. Dufay and his Contemporaries* (London 1898).

J. Marix, *Les Musiciens de la Cour de Bourgogne au XVe siècle* (Paris 1937).

There is no recent comprehensive survey of music in the 1300s; some of the most basic, even preliminary matters are being discussed in current technical articles, such as U. Günther, *Datierbare Balladen des späten 14. Jahrhunderts*, I, MD 15 (1961), 39–61; K. von Fischer, *On the Technique, Origin, and Evolution of Italian Trecento Music*, MQ 47 (1961), 41–57; S. W. Kenney, *"English Discant" and Discant in England*, MQ 45 (1959), 26–48; R. L. Crocker, *Discant, Counterpoint, and Harmony*, JAMS 15 (1962), 1–21. A summary of the period after Guillaume de Machaut can be found in G. Reese, *Music in the Renaissance* (New York 1954), which becomes especially valuable from Dufay on. M. F. Bukofzer, *Studies in Medieval and Renaissance Music* (New York 1950), contains many interesting discussions on special topics. E. H. Sparks, *Cantus Firmus in Mass and Motet, 1420–1520* (Berkeley 1963)

is particularly useful for the Old Hall Manuscript and subsequent Continental service music. F. Ll. Harrison, *Music in Medieval Britain* (2nd ed., London 1963) continues to be the authority for England.

NB: Medieval composers are referred to here by their proper first names when their family or place name is preceded by some form of *de*. Look for Guillaume de Machaut under Guillaume.

Stabilization in Motet and Song form

Bologna: see Jacopo.

Caccia: W. T. Marrocco, *Fourteenth-Century Italian Cacce* (2nd rev. ed., Cambridge, Mass. 1961).

Chace: N. Pirrotta, *Per l'origine e la storia della "caccia" e del "madrigale" trecentesco*, in *Rivista musicali italiana* 48 (1946), 305–323. Chasse, MGG (Besseler).

Ciconia, Johannes (ca 1335–1411): S. Clercx, *Johannes Ciconia, un musicien liégeois et son temps, vers 1335–1411* (Brussels 1960). HAM no. 55.

Codex Apt: A. Gastoué, *Le Manuscrit de musique du Trésor d'Apt, XIVe–XVe siècle. Publications de la Société française de musicologie*, series 1, vol. 10 (Paris 1936).

Codex Faenza: facs. ed. A. Carapetyan, *An Early Fifteenth-Century Italian Source of Keyboard Music*, MSD vol. 10 (1961).

D. Plamenac, *Keyboard Music of the 14th Century in Codex Faenza 117*, JAMS 4 (1951), 179–201.

Codex Rossi: N. Pirrotta, *The Music of Fourteenth-Century Italy*, CMM 8, vol. 2, pp. 15–45.

Contre le temps (virelai-motet): W. Apel, *French Secular Music*, no. 64.

Cordier, Baude: works ed. G. Reaney, *Early Fifteenth-Century Music*, CMM 11, vol. 1. HAM no. 48.

De ce que fols pense (ballade) by P. des Moulins: E. Droz et G. Thibault, *Poètes et musiciens du XVe siècle. Documents artistiques du XVe siècle*, vol. 1 (Paris 1924).

Fontaine, Pierre: *Sans faire de vous departie* (rondeau): J. Marix, *Les musiciens de la Cour de Bourgogne*, p. 14.

Gherardello: works ed. N. Pirrotta, *The Music of Fourteenth-Century Italy*, CMM 8, vol. 1. HAM no. 52.

Giovanni da Cascia (Johannes de Florentia): works ed. N. Pirrotta, *The Music of Fourteenth-Century Italy*, CMM 8, vol. 1. HAM nos. 50, 51.

Grenon, Nicolas: selected works ed. J. Marix, *Les Musiciens de la Cour de Bourgogne*.

Guillaume de Machaut (ca 1300–1377): *Musikalische Werke*, ed. F. Ludwig, PAM, Jg.1:1; Jg.3:1; Jg.4:2 (Leipzig 1926).

L. Schrade, *Polyphonic Music of the Fourteenth Century*, vols. 2–3. *S'il estoit nulz* (motet): HAM no. 44; HAM nos. 45, 46.

R. Hoppin, *An Unrecognized Polyphonic Lai of Machaut*, MD 12 (1958), 93–104.

Jacopo da Bologna: works ed. N. Pirrotta, *The Music of Fourteenth-Century Italy*, CMM 8, vol. 4. HAM no. 49.

Johannes de Muris: Strunk, SR, 172–179.

Landini, Francesco (ca 1335–1397): works ed. L. Schrade, *Polyphonic Music of the Fourteenth Century*, vol. 4. HAM nos. 53, 54; MM no. 14.

Machaut: see Guillaume.

Mass of Tournai: L. Schrade, *Polyphonic Music of the Fourteenth Century*, vol. 1, p. 110; Ch. Van Den Borren, *Missa Tornacensis*, CMM 13 (1957).

Matheus de Perusio: *Pour Dieu*

vous pri (rondeau), and other works, ed. W. Apel, *French Secular Music* (no. 18).

Ma trédol rosignol (virelai-motet): W. Apel, *French Secular Music,* no. 68.

Muris: *see* Johannes.

Musica ficta: E. Lowinsky, *The Function of Conflicting Signatures in Early Polyphonic Music,* MQ 31 (1945), 227–260.
R. Hoppin, *Conflicting Signatures Reviewed,* JAMS 9 (1956), 97–117.

Or sus vous dormez trop (virelai): W. Apel, *French Secular Music,* no. 70.

Perusio: *see* Matheus.

Philippe de Vitry (1291–1361): works ed. L. Schrade, *Polyphonic Music of the Fourteenth Century,* vol. 1. The treatise *Ars nova,* ascribed to Philippe de Vitry, is trans. L. Plantinga, JMT 5 (1961), 204–223.

Piero: works ed. N. Pirrotta, *Music of Fourteenth-Century Italy,* CMM 8, vol. 2.

Roman de Fauvel: polyphonic works ed. L. Schrade, *Polyphonic Music of the Fourteenth Century,* vol. 1.

Senleches: selected works ed. W. Apel, *French Secular Music,* nos. 47–51.
HAM no. 47.

Solage: selected works ed. W. Apel, *French Secular Music: Corps femenin* (ballade), no. 32; *S'aincy estoit* (ballade), no. 34.

Virelai: *Par maintes foy, Onques ne fut:* W. Apel, *French Secular Music,* nos. 69, 71; see also nos. 72, 73, 67, and 50.

Vitry: *see* Philippe.

French and English Developments

Arnold de Lantins: mass ed. Ch. Van den Borren, *Polyphonia sacra,* p. 1.

Chansons ed. Ch. Van den Borren, *Pièces polyphoniques profanes de provenance liégeoise. Flores musicales belgicae,* vol. 1 (Brussels 1950).
HAM no. 71.

Billart: *Salve virgo–Vita, via-*SALVE REGINA (motet), ed. Ch. Van den Borren, *Polyphonia sacra,* p. 159.

Binchois, Gilles (ca 1400–1460): selected works ed. J. Marix, *Les Musiciens de la Cour de Bourgogne: Te Deum,* p. 219; *Je loe amours,* p. 52; *Pour prison,* p. 69. *Credo* ed. Ch. Van den Borren, *Polyphonia sacra,* p. 63.
HAM nos. 69, 70; MM no. 16.

Carmen: works ed. G. Reaney, *Early Fifteenth-Century Music,* CMM 11, vol. 1.

Cesaris: works ed. G. Reaney, *Early Fifteenth-Century Music,* CMM 11, vol. 1.

Dufay, Guillaume (ca 1400–1474): motets ed. G. de Van, *Guglielmi Dufay opera omnia,* CMM 1, vol. 1 (1947). Masses ed. H. Besseler, *Guglielmi Dufay opera omnia,* CMM 1, vols. 2–4 (1960).
Adieu m'amour (rondeau): HAM no. 68; *Mon chier amy* (ballade): HAM no. 67; HAM nos. 65, 66; MM no. 15.

Dunstable, John (ca 1385–1453): *Complete Works,* ed. M. F. Bukofzer, MB 8 (London 1953). HAM nos. 61, 62.

Faburden and Fauxbourdon: B. Trowell, *Faburden and Faux-bourdon,* MD 13 (1959), 43–78. H. Besseler, *Bourdon und Faux-bourdon* (Leipzig 1950).

Frye, Walter: *Collected Works,* ed. S. W. Kenney, CMM 19 (1960). S. W. Kenney, *Walter Frye and the Contenance Angloise. Yale Studies in the History of Music,* 3 (New Haven 1964).

Hugo de Lantins: chansons ed. Ch. Van den Borren, *Pièces polyphoniques profanes de provenance*

liégeoise. Flores musicales belgicae, vol. 1. HAM no. 72.

Lantins: *see* Arnold, Hugo.

Legrant, Guillaume: *Gloria-Credo* ed. Ch. Van den Borren, *Polyphonia sacra,* p. 123.
HAM no. 56.

Old Hall Manuscript: A. Ramsbotham (with H. B. Collins and Dom A. Hughes), *The Old Hall Manuscript,* 3 vols. (Nashdom Abbey, Burnham, Bucks 1933–1938).
M. F. Bukofzer, *The Music of the Old Hall Manuscript,* MQ 34 (1948), 512–532; 35 (1949), 36–59. HAM nos. 63, 64.

Tapissier: works ed. G. Reaney, *Early Fifteenth-Century Music,* CMM 11, vol. 1.

Tinctoris, Johannes (ca 1436–1511): Strunk, SR, 193–199.

CHAPTER 6 FRANCO-FLEMISH MASS AND MOTET 1450–1500

GENERAL

The starting point for further work in this period, as in the following one, is the splendid handbook by G. Reese, *Music in the Renaissance* (New York 1954). Useful especially for the cyclic mass, but also for individual composers, is E. H. Sparks, *Cantus Firmus in Mass and Motet, 1420–1520* (Berkeley 1963).

* * *

Agricola, Alexander (1446?–1506): *Opera omnia,* ed. E. R. Lerner, CMM 22 (1961–).

Brumel, Antoine: *Opera omnia,* ed. A. Carapetyan, CMM 5 (1951–); a mass, ed. H. Expert, MMRF vol. 9 (1898).

Busnois, Antoine: C. V. Brooks, *Antoine Busnois, Chanson Composer,* JAMS 6 (1953), 111–135.

Chanson: *Trois Chansonniers francais du XVe siècle,* ed. E. Droz, G. Thibault, and Y. Rokseth, *Documents artistiques du XVe siècle,* vol. 4 (Paris 1927).

Compere, Loyset (died 1518):
Opera omnia, ed. L. Finscher,
CMM 15 (1958–).

L. Finscher, *Loyset Compere and
His Works*, MD 12 (1958), 105–
143; 13 (1959), 123–154; 14
(1960), 131–157; 16 (1962), 93–
113.

HAM no. 79.

de La Rue, *see* La Rue

Des Pres: *see* Josquin.

Dufay, Guillaume (ca 1400–1474):
masses ed. H. Besseler, *Opera
omnia*, CMM 1, vols. 2–4 (1960).
Ave Regina coelorum (motet),
ed. H. Besseler, *Capella: Meister-
werke mittelalterliche Musik* I
(Kassel 1950).

Faugues, Guillaume: *Collected
Works*, ed. G. C. Schuetze
(Brooklyn 1960).

Gaspar van Weerbecke: GMB no.
58.

Isaac, Heinrich (ca 1450–1517):
Choralis Constantinus Book III,
ed. L. Cuyler, *University of
Michigan Publications. Fine Arts*,
vol. 2 (Ann Arbor 1950).
Introiten . . . zu 6 Stimmen, ed.
M. Just, *Das Chorwerk* 81 (1960).
Five Polyphonic Masses, ed. L.
Cuyler (Ann Arbor 1956).
Messe, ed. F. Fano, *Archivum
musices metropolitanum Medio-
lanense*, vol. 10 (Milan 1962).
HAM nos. 87–88.

Josquin Des Pres (1440/1450–
1521): *Werken*, ed. A. Smijers,
49 vols. (Leipzig, Amsterdam
1925–1962).

J. Mattfeld, *Some Relationships
between Texts and Cantus Firmi
in the Liturgical Motets of Josquin Des Pres*, JAMS 14 (1961),
159–183.

HAM nos. 89, 90, 91; MM no. 19.
In a forthcoming article, E. H.
Sparks will show that the *Missa
Da pacem*, long attributed to Jos-
quin, is probably not by him.

La Rue, Pierre de: *Liber missarum*,
ed. A. Tirabassi (Malines 1941);

Requiem, ed. F. Blume, *Das
Chorwerk*, vol. 11 (1931); *Drie
Missen*, ed. R. B. Lenaerts and
Jozef Robjins, MMB vol. 8
(1960); *Vier Motetten*, ed. N.
Davison, *Das Chorwerk*, vol. 91
(1964).

HAM no. 92.

Meantone temperament: J. M. Bar-
bour, *Tuning and Temperament,
A Historical Survey* (East Lan-
sing 1951).

Obrecht, Jacob (1450?–1505): *Op-
era omnia*, ed. A. Smijers, and
M. Van Crevel (Amsterdam 1953).
HAM nos. 76, 77, 78; MM no. 18.

Ockeghem, Johannes (ca 1424–ca
1495): *Collected Works*, ed. D.
Plamenac (2nd corrected ed. New
York 1950–).
Alma redemptoris (motet), ed.
H. Besseler, *Altniederländische
Motetten* (Kassel 1929).
Ma bouche rit (virelai), HAM
no. 75; also HAM nos. 73, 74;
MM no. 17.

Petrucci, Ottaviano (1466–1539):
O. Sartori, *Bibliografia delle opere
musicali stampate de Ottaviano
Petrucci* (Florence 1948).
Harmonice musices odhecaton A,
ed. H. Hewitt (Cambridge, Mass.
1942).
(From the *Bossinensis tablature*)
B. Disertori, *20 Ricercari da
sonar nel lauto* (Milan 1954).

Regis, Johannes (ca 1430–ca 1485):
Opera omnia, ed. C. Lindenburg,
CMM 9 (1956).

Weerbecke: *see* Gaspar.

CHAPTER 7 DIFFUSION OF FRANCO-FLEMISH STYLE 1500–1600

GENERAL

For this period, G. Reese, *Music in
the Renaissance* (New York 1954)
continues to be the basic handbook.
The classic study by A. Einstein,
The Italian Madrigal, 3 vols., trans.

A. H. Krappe, R. H. Sessions, and
O. Strunk (Princeton 1949), takes
up many aspects of the 1500s beside
the madrigal. Einstein's *The Golden
Age of the Madrigal* (New York
1942) is an important collection of
madrigals.

Since musical materials are generally published nowadays by composer, rather than by source (as has
been the case for previous periods),
they are listed here by composer.
During the 1500s, however, music
still appeared in large anthologies,
whose makeup is important for
tracing stylistic development. Such
anthologies can be studied in R.
Eitner, *Bibliographie der Musik-
Sammelwerke des XVI und XVII
Jahrhunderts* (Berlin 1877), and in
*Recueils Imprimés, XVIe–XVIIe
siècles*, ed. F. Lesure, *Répertoire
International des Sources Musicales*
(Munich 1960). Another important
tool is the output of a publisher, as
described, for example, in Sartori's
study of Petrucci (see Chapter 6).
Sartori's *Bibliografia della musica
strumentale italiana stampata in
Italia fino al 1700* (Florence 1952)
is also useful. The new series,
Monuments of Renaissance Music,
ed. E. E. Lowinsky, is specifically
designed to reflect original collections; *see also* Attaingnant.

*   *   *

Air de cour: *Chansons au luth et
airs de cour français du XVIe
siècle*, ed. A. Mairy, *Publications
de la Société française de musicologie*, series 1, vols. 3–4 (Paris
1934).

Antoine de Fevin, *see* Fevin

Antonio de Cabezón, *see* Cabezón

Attaingnant, Pierre (1495?–1551):
*Treize livres de motets parus chez
Pierre Attaingnant en 1534 et
1535*, ed. A. Smijers and A. Till-
man Merritt, 13 vols. (Paris
1934–1963).
See also Chanson, Ricercar.

Arcadelt, Jacques (ca 1405?–before

1472): *Chansons*, ed. E. Helm, SCMA vol. 5 (1942).

Einstein, *Golden Age*, no. 1; HAM no. 130; GMB no. 100.

Aria di Ruggiero: C. Palisca, *Vincenzo Galilei and Some Links Between "Pseudo-Monody" and Monody*, MQ 46 (1960), 344–360.

Bermudo, Juan: *Declaración de Instrumentos musicales*, 1555, facs., ed. M. S. Kastner, DM series 1, vol. 11 (1957).

R. Stevenson, *Juan Bermudo* (The Hague 1960).

Bourgeois, Louis: *37 Psalmen in Vierstemmige Bewerking van Louis Bourgeois vit 1547*, ed. K. Ph. Bernet Kempers (Delft 194–?).

HAM no. 132.

Bull, John (ca 1562–1628): *Keyboard Music*, ed. J. Steele and F. Cameron, MB vols. 14, 19 (1960, 1963).

HAM no. 178.

Byrd, William (1543?–1623): *Collected Works*, ed. E. H. Fellowes, 20 vols. (London 1937–1950).

HAM nos. 150, 151; MM no. 25. J. Kerman, *On William Byrd's Emendemus in melius*, MQ 49 (1963), 431–449.

J. Jackman, *Liturgical Aspects of Byrd's Gradualia*, MQ 49 (1963), 17–37.

Cabezón, Antonio de (ca 1500–1566): selected works ed. F. Pedrell, *Hispaniae schola musica sacra*, vols. 3–4, 7–8 (Barcelona 1894–1898).

W. Apel, *Early Spanish Music for Lute and Keyboard Instruments*, MQ 20 (1934), 289–301. HAM nos. 133, 134.

Capirola, Vincenzo (1474–?): *Compositione. Lute-book (circa 1517)*, ed. O. Gombosi, *Publications de la Société de musique d'autrefois. Textes musicaux*, vol. 1 (Neuilly-sur-Seine 1955).

Cavazzoni, Girolamo: *Musica sacra, ricercari e canzoni*, ed. G. Ben-

venuti, *I Classici della musica italiana*, vol. 6 (Milan 1919). HAM nos. 116, 117, 118.

Cavazzoni, Marc Antonio (ca 1490?–after 1559): *Ricercari, motetti, canzoni*, ed. G. Benvenuti, CMI vol. 1 (1941).

K. Jeppesen, *Die italienische Orgelmusik am Anfang des Cinquecento*, 2 vols. (2nd ed., Copenhagen 1960).

Chanson: *Anthologie de la chanson parisienne au XVIe siècle*, ed. F. Lesure (Monaco 1953).

Thirty Chansons for 3 and 4 Voices from Attaingnant's Collections, ed. A. Seay, CM vol. 2 (1960).

W. H. Rubsamen, D. Heartz, H. Brown, *Chanson and Madrigal, 1480–1530; Studies in Comparison and Contrast*, ed. J. Haar, *Isham Library Papers*, vol. 2 (Cambridge, Mass. 1964).

Cipriano de Rore (1516–1565): *Opera omnia*, ed. B. Meier, CMM 14, 3 vols. (1959–1963).

The Madrigals of Cipriano de Rore for 3 and 4 Voices, ed. G. P. Smith, SCMA vol. 6 (1943). HAM no. 131.

Costeley, Guillaume (ca 1531–1606): *Musique (1570)*, ed. H. Expert, MMRF vols. 4–6 (1896–1905).

HAM no. 147.

Clement, Jacques (ca 1510–1556/1558): *Opera omnia*, ed. K. Ph. Bernet Kempers, CMM 4, 11 vols. (1951–1964).

HAM no. 125.

Conforto, Giovanni Luca: *Breve et facile maniera d'essercitarsi a far passaggi, Roma 1593*, facs. ed. J. Wolf, *Veröffentlichungen der Musik-bibliothek Paul Hirsch*, vol. 2 (Berlin 1922).

Cori spezzati: H. Zenck, *Adrian Willaert's "Salmi Spezzati" (1550)*, MF 2 (1949), 97–107.

G. d'Alessi, *Precursors of Adriano Willaert in the Practice of Coro*

Spezzato, JAMS 5 (1952), 187–210.

Dalza, Joan Ambrosio: HAM no. 99a.

De Monte, Philippe (1521–1603): *Opera*, ed. Ch. Van den Borren, 26 vols. (Düsseldorf 1927–1935). HAM no. 146b.

Diminutions: I. Horsley, *The 16th Century Variation: A New Historical Survey*, JAMS 12 (1959), 118–132; *The Solo Ricercar in Diminution Manuals: New Light on Early Wind and String Techniques*, Acta musicologica 33 (1961), 29–40.

Dowland, John (1562–1625/1626): *Ayres for Four Voices*, ed. E. H. Fellowes (with Th. Dart and N. Fortune), MB vol. 6 (1953).

E. H. Fellowes, *The English School of Lutenist Song-Writers*, 32 nos. (London 1921–1925). HAM no. 163.

English Madrigal: E. H. Fellowes, *The English Madrigal School*, 36 vols. (London 1913–1924).

J. Kerman, *The Elizabethan Madrigal; a Comparative Study* (New York 1962).

English sacred music: *Tudor Church Music* (London 1923–1929); F. Ll. Harrison, *Eton Choirbook*, MB vols. 10–11.

Fevin, Antoine de (ca 1470–1511/1512): *Missa Mente tota*, ed. H. Expert, MMRF vol. 10 (1899). HAM no. 106.

Festa, Costanza (died 1545): *Opera omnia*, ed. A. Main, CMM 25 (1962).

Hymni per totum annum, ed. G. Haydon, MPI vol. 3 (1958). HAM no. 129.

Fitzwilliam Virginal Book: ed. J. Fuller Maitland and W. Barclay Squire, 2 vols. (1899, reprinted 1949, 1963).

Fogliano, Giacomo (1468–1548): *see* Cavazzoni, Marc Antonio.

Frottola: Ottaviano Petrucci, *Frottole*, Buch I und IV, ed. R.

Schwartz, PAM, vol. 8 (Leipzig 1935).
HAM no. 95.

Gabrieli, Andrea (ca 1515–1586): *Andrea e Giovanni Gabrieli e la music astrumentale in San Marco*, ed. G. Benvenuti, IMAMI vols. 1–2 (1931, 1932).
Einstein, *Golden Age*, no. 4.
L. Schrade, *La Représentation d'Edipo tiranno au Teatro Olimpico (Vicenza 1585). Collection le choeur des muses* (Paris 1960).
P. Pidoux, *Canzonen und Ricercari ariosi, für Orgel* (Kassel 1952).
L. Torchi, *L'Arte musicale in Italia*, vol. 2 (Milan 1897).
HAM nos. 135, 136.

Gabrieli, Giovanni (ca 1555–1612): *Opera omnia*, ed. D. Arnold, CMM 12, 3 vols. (1956–1962).
HAM nos. 157, 173.
See Gabrieli, Andrea.

Gesualdo, Carlo (ca 1560–1613): *Sämtliche Madrigale für fünf Stimmen*, ed. W. Weismann, 6 vols. (Hamburg 1957–1962).
HAM no. 161.

Giaches de Wert, *see* Wert

Gombert, Nicolas (ca 1500–ca 1556): *Opera omnia*, ed. J. Schmidt-Görg, CMM 6 (1951–).
HAM no. 114.

Goudimel, Claude (ca 1514–1572): *Les Cent cinquante psaumes de David (1580)*, ed. H. Expert, MMRF vols. 1–3 (1895–1897).
HAM no. 126.

Intermedii: F. Ghisi, *Feste musicali della Firenze Medicea (1480–1589)* (Florence 1939).
D. Heartz, *A Spanish "Masque of Cupid,"* MQ (1963), 59–74.

Jannequin, Clement (1485–ca 1560): selected chansons ed. A. Seay, *Das Chorwerk*, vol. 73 (1959).
HAM no. 107.

Kerle, Jacobus (1531/1532–1591): *Die "Preces speciales etc.,"* ed. O. Ursprung, DDT series 2, Jg. 26 (1926).

HAM no. 148.

Lasso, Orlando di (1532–1594): *Sämtliche Werke*, ed. F. X. Haberl and A. Sandberger, 21 vols. (Leipzig 1894–1926); *Neue reihe*, (Kassel 1956).
HAM nos. 143, 144, 145; MM no. 23.

Lejeune, Claude (ca 1530–1600): *Le Printemps*, ed. H. Expert, MMRF vols. 13–15 (1900); *Revecy venir du printans*, no. 2.
HAM no. 138.

Luzzaschi, Luzzascho (1545–1607): A. Einstein, *Golden Age*, no. 7; GMB no. 166.
O. Kinkeldey, *Orgel und Klavier in der Musik des 16. Jahrhunderts* (Leipzig 1910).

Macque, Giovanni (ca 1550–1614): *Charles Guillet, Giovanni (de) Macque, Carolus Luython*, ed. J. Watelet, MMB vol. 4 (1938).
HAM no. 174.

Malvezzi, Cristofano (1547–1597): *Musique des intermèdes de la Pellegrina*, ed. F. Ghisi et al., *Les fêtes du mariage de Ferdinand de Medicis et de Christine de Lorraine, Florence 1589*, I (Paris 1963).

Marenzio, Luca (1553/1554–1599): *Sämtliche Werke*, ed. A. Einstein, PAM Jg. 4:1; Jg. 6 (Leipzig 1929–1931). MM no. 27.

Merulo, Claudio (1533–1604): *Toccate per organo*, ed. S. Della Libera, 2 vols. (Milan 1959).
HAM no. 153.

Milán, Luys (ca 1500–after 1561): *Libro de musica de vihuela de mano intitulado El maestro*, compuesto por Luys Milan, ed. L. Schrade, PAM vol. 2 (1927).
HAM no. 121.

Monte, *see* De Monte

Mouton, Jean (1459?–1522): *Fünf motetten, zu 4 und 6 Stimmen*, ed. P. Kast, *Das Chorwerk*, vol. 76 (1959).
GMB no. 66.
See Attaingnant.

Musica ficta: E. Lowinsky, *Adrian Willaert's Chromatic Duo Reexamined, Tijdschrift voor muziekwetenschap*, vol. 18. E. Lowinsky, *Matthaeus Greiter's Fortuna*, MQ 42 (1956), 500–519.
K. J. Levy, *Costeley's Chromatic Chanson*, AM 3 (1955), 213–263.

Ortiz, Diego: *Tratado de glosas sobre clausulas y otros generos de puntos en la musica de violones, Roma 1553*, ed. M. Schneider (3rd ed., Kassel 1961).

Parody mass: R. B. Lenaerts, *The 16th Century Parody Mass in the Netherlands*, MQ 36 (1950), 410–421.

Palestrina, Giovanni Pierluigi da (ca 1525–1594): *Le Opere complete*, ed. R. Casimiri, 30 vols. (Rome 1939–1962). K. Jeppesen, *The Style of Palestrina and the Dissonance* (2nd ed., Copenhagen 1946).
See the important table of masses by O. Strunk, published in Reese, *Music in the Renaissance*, pp. 470–472.
HAM nos. 140, 141, 142; MM no. 24.

Parthenia, or The Maydenhead of the First Musicke that was ever printed for the Virginalls, composed by William Byrd, Dr. John Bull, and Orlando Gibbons, ed. K. Stone (New York 1951).

Ricercar: See the summary in *Preludes, Chansons, and Dances for Lute (Attaingnant, 1529–1530)*, ed. D. Heartz, *Publications de la Société de musique d'autrefois. Textes musicaux*, vol. 2 (Neuilly-sur-Seine 1964).
Musica nova, ed. H. C. Slim, MRM vol. 1 (Chicago 1964).

Rore: *see* Cipriano.

Senfl, Ludwig (ca 1492–1555): *Werke*, ed. Th. Kroyer, DDT series 2, Jg. 3:2 (1903).
Das Erbe deutscher Musik, series 1: *Sieben Messen*, ed. E. Löhrer and O. Ursprung, vol. 5 (1936);

Deutsche lieder, ed. A. Geering, vol. 10 (1938); *Motetten,* ed. W. Gerstenberg, vol. 13 (1939). *Sämtliche Werke,* ed. Schweizerischen Musikforschenden Gesellschaft (Wolfenbüttel 1937). HAM nos. 109, 110.

Spinaccino, Francesco: HAM no. 99b; GMB no. 63.

Sweelinck, Jan Pieterszn (1562–1621): *Werken voor Orgel en Clavecimbel,* ed. M. Seiffert, in *Werken van Jan Pieterszn Sweelinck,* vol. 1 and supplement (Amsterdam 1943–1958). Fantasia no. 3 of *Werken,* vol. 1 = *Fitzwilliam Virginal Book,* vol. 2, p. 297.

Verdelot, Philippe (died before 1552): GMB nos. 97, 98.

Vicentino, Nicola (ca 1511–1572): *Jerusalem convertere ad Dominum* (motet), ed. L. Torchi, *L'Arte musicale in Italia,* vol. 1 (Milan 1897), p. 145. H. Kaufmann, *Vicentino and the Greek Genera,* JAMS 16 (1963), 325–346.

Victoria, Tomás Luis de (ca 1548–1611): *Opera omnia,* ed. F. Pedrell, 8 vols. (1902–1913). HAM no. 149.

Walther, Johann (1496–1570): *Sämtliche Werke,* ed. O. Schröder, (Kassel 1953–1961); *Geistliches Gesangbüchlein,* vols. 1–2. HAM no. 111.

Wert, Giaches de (1535–1596): *Collected Works,* ed. C. MacClintock, CMM 24 (1961–). HAM no. 146a.

Willaert, Adrian (ca 1490–1562): *Opera omnia,* ed. H. Zenck, CMM 3 (1950–). W. Wiora, *Italienische Madrigale zu 4–5 Stimmen, Das Chorwerk,* vol. 5 (195–?). HAM nos. 113, 115.

Zacconi, Ludovico (1555–1627): F. Chrysander, *Lodovico Zacconi als Lehrer des Kunstgesanges,* VfMW 10 (1894), 531–567; see espe-cially pp. 542–543. See also Pietro Cerone, Strunk, SR, 263–273.

Zarlino, Gioseffe (1517–1590): Strunk, SR, 229–261. R. L. Crocker, *Discant, Counterpoint, and Harmony,* JAMS 15 (1962), 1–21.

PART III   Part Music on a Triadic Basis   1600–1750

GENERAL

A standard work in English on this period is M. F. Bukofzer, *Music in the Baroque Era* (New York 1947). A. Loewenberg, *Annals of Opera 1597–1940* (2nd ed., Geneva 1955), is an extremely informative listing of new operas produced throughout the period (and up to the present). Equally useful is the listing of instrumental publications in C. Sartori, *Bibliografia della musica strumentale italiana stampata in Italia fino al 1700* (Florence 1952). Other important works covering the whole period are W. S. Newman, *The Sonata in the Baroque Era* (Chapel Hill 1959); F. T. Arnold, *The Art of Accompaniment from a Thorough-Bass as Practised in the XVIIth and XVIIIth Centuries* (London 1931).

*   *   *

CHAPTER 8   NEW ITALIAN DRAMATIC STYLES   1600–1650

GENERAL

Early music-drama is discussed, with many examples, in A. A. Abert, *Claudio Monteverdi und das musikalische Drama* (Lippstadt 1954); for an informative summary, see the review by L. Schrade, JAMS 9 (1956, 31–37). Early monody is described in N. Fortune, *Italian Secular Monody from 1600 to 1635: An Introductory Survey,* MQ 39 (1953), 171–195. See the general works listed under Part III.

*   *   *

Italy

Caccini, Giulio (ca 1550–1610): *Le Nuove musiche,* preface trans. Strunk, SR, 377–392. GMB nos. 172, 173. HAM no. 184.

Frescobaldi, Girolamo (1583–1643): *Orgel-und Klavierwerke,* ed. P. Pidoux, 5 vols. (Kassel 1949–1954).

Marini, Biagio (1597–1665): selected works ed. J. W. von Wasielewski, *Instrumentalsätze vom Ende des XVI. bis Ende des XVII. Jh.* Supplement to *Die Violine im XVII Jahrhundert* (Berlin 1905). GMB nos. 182, 183.

Merula, Tarquinio (ca 1595–1665): *Composizioni per organo e cembalo,* ed. A. Curtis, *Monumenti di musica italiana,* series 1, vol. 1 (Brescia 1961). GMB no. 184.

Monteverdi, Claudio (1562–1643): *Tutte le opere,* ed. G. F. Malipiero, 16 vols. (Asolo 1926–1942).

Peri, Jacopo (1561–1633): *L'Euridice,* ed. L. Torchi, *L'Arte musicale in Italia,* vol. 6. GMB no. 171. HAM no. 182.

North of the Alps

Hammerschmidt, Andreas (1611–1675): *Dialogi; oder, Gespräche einer gläubigen Seele mit Gott. 1. Theil,* ed. A. W. Schmidt, DTOe Jg.8:1 (1901).

Scheidemann, Heinrich (ca 1596–1663): *Fifteen Preludes and Fugues for Organ,* ed. M. Seiffert, *Organum,* Reihe 4, no. 1 (Lippstadt 1925); *46 Choräle für Orgel, von J. P. Sweelinck und seinen deutschen Schülern,* ed. G. Gerdes, *Musikalische Denkmäler,* vol. 3 (Mainz 1957).

Scheidt, Samuel (1587–1654):

Werke, ed. G. Harms, C. Mahrenholz, and A. Adrio (Hamburg 1928–).

Schein, Johann Hermann (1586–1630): *Sämtliche Werke,* ed. A. Prüfer (Leipzig 1901–).

Schütz, Heinrich (1585–1672): *Sämtliche Werke,* ed. P. Spitta (Leipzig 1885–1894); *Neue Ausgabe sämtlicher Werke* (Kassel 1955–).

CHAPTER 9 TRENDS TOWARD CLARITY 1640–1690

GENERAL

H. C. Wolff, *Die venezianische Oper in der zweiten Hälfte des 17. Jahrhunderts* (Berlin 1937), takes up much important material and includes many examples. E. J. Dent, *Foundations of English Opera* (Cambridge 1928), is a standard work.

*   *   *

Italy

Bononcini, Giovanni Maria (1642–1678): W. Klenz, *Giovanni Maria Bononcini of Modena* (Durham 1962).

Cantata: K. Jeppesen, *La Flora, arie &c. antiche italiane,* 3 vols. (Copenhagen 1949).

Carissimi, Giovanni Giacomo (1605–1674): *Opere complete,* ed. L. Bianchi, *Istituto italiano per la storia della musica, Monumenti 3,* vols. 1–8 (Rome 1951–). G. Rose, *The Cantatas of Giacomo Carissimi,* MQ 48 (1962), 204–215.

Cavalli, Francesco Bruni (1602–1676): *Il Giasone,* ed. R. Eitner (Act I only), PAPTM vol. 12 (1883). GMB nos. 200, 201. HAM no. 206.

Cesti, Marc Antonio (1623–1669): *Il Pomo d'oro,* DTOe Bd. 3:2 and Bd. 4:2 (1896); *La Dori,* ed. R. Eitner (Act I only), PAPTM vol. 12 (1883); selected cantatas ed.

D. L. Burrows, *The Italian Cantata,* vol. 1, *The Wellesley Edition,* no. 5 (Wellesley 1963).

Vitali, Giovanni Battista (ca 1644–1692): *Artifici musicali, opus XIII,* ed. L. Rood and G. P. Smith, SCMA no. 14 (1959). HAM no. 245.

North of the Alps

Biber, Heinrich (1644–1704): *Sechzehn Violinsonaten,* ed. E. Luntz, DTOe Jg. 12:2 (1905).

Buxtehude, Dietrich (1637?–1707): *Werke,* ed. W. Gurlitt, G. Harms, and H. Trede, 7 vols. (Hamburg 1925–1937); *Sämtliche Orgelwerke,* ed. J. Hedar, 4 vols. (Copenhagen 1952).

Cambert, Robert (1628–1677): *Pomone* (Act I only) and *Les peines et les plaisirs de l'amour* (Act I only), ed. J.-B. Wekerlin, *Chefs-d'oeuvre de l'opéra français* (Paris, 188–?).

Chambonnières, Jacques Champion de (1602?–1672?): *Oeuvres complètes,* ed. P. Brunold and A. Tessier (Paris 1925).

Charpentier, Marc-Antoine (1634–1704): H. W. Hitchcock, *The Latin Oratorios of Marc-Antoine Charpentier,* MQ 41 (1955), 41–65.

H. W. Hitchcock, *Marc-Antoine Charpentier, Judicium Salomonis. Recent Researches in the Music of the Baroque Era,* vol. 1 (New Haven 1964). HAM no. 226.

Couperin, Louis (ca 1626–1661): *Oeuvres complètes,* ed. P. Brunold (Paris 1936).

Froberger, Johann Jakob (1616–1667): *Werke für Orgel und Klavier,* ed. G. Adler, DTOe Jg. 4:1, Bd. 8; Jg. 6:2, Bd. 13; Jg. 10:2, Bd. 21 (1897–1903).

Gaultier, Denis (ca 1600–1672): *La Rhétorique des dieux et autres pièces de luth. Publications de la Société française de musicologie,*

series 1, vols. 6–7 (Paris 1932).

Lully, Jean Baptiste (1632–1687): *Oeuvres complètes de J.-B. Lully,* ed. H. Prunières (Paris 1930–1939). GMB nos. 232, 233, 234.

Masque: E. J. Dent, *Cupid and Death, Matthew Locke and Christopher Gibbons,* MB vol. 2 (1951).

Pachelbel, Johann (1653–1706): *Klavierwerke,* ed. M. Seiffert, DDT series 2, Jg. 2:1 (1901); *Ausgewählte Orgelwerke,* ed. K. Matthaei, 3 vols. (Kassel 1931–1934).

CHAPTER 10 INTERNATIONAL STYLE AND NATIONAL TASTES 1680–1750

GENERAL

An unusual and fascinating account of Italian opera of this period is to be found in Vernon Lee, *Studies of the Eighteenth Century in Italy* (London 1887). Recent studies, sometimes entailing basic revisions in traditional ideas, are W. J. Weichlein, *Problems of Nomenclature in 18th Century Italian Opera,* JAMS 12 (1959), 265–266; N. Burt, *Opera in Arcadia,* MQ 41 (1955), 145–170; and two papers on *The Neapolitan Tradition in Opera* by H. Hucke (in German) and E. Downes, International Musicological Society, *Report of the Eighth Congress,* ed. J. Larue (Kassel 1961), vol. 1, pp. 253–277, 277–284. E. J. Dent, *Alessandro Scarlatti* (London 1905, 1960), with many examples, and R. Kirkpatrick, *Domenico Scarlatti* (Princeton 1953) are both extremely valuable for musical style. Introductory articles to the new research on J. S. Bach are given under his name.

*   *   *

Italy

Corelli, Arcangelo (1653–1713): *Les Oeuvres de Arcangelo Corelli,* ed.

F. Chrysander, 4 vols. (London 1890).

Pallavicino, Carlo (ca 1630–1688): *La Gerusalemme liberata,* ed. H. Abert, DDT series 1, Bd. 55 (1916).

Scarlatti, Alessandro (1660–1725): *La Rosaura* (Acts I and II), ed. R. Eitner, PAPTM vol. 14:2 (1885); *Il Trionfo dell'onore,* rev. V. Mortari (Milan 1941); A. Lorenz, *Alessandro Scarlatti's Jugendoper,* 2 vols. (Augsburg 1927). GMB nos. 258, 259, 260.

Steffani, Agostino (1654–1728): *Ausgewählte Werke,* ed. A. Einstein, A. Sandberger, and H. Riemann, DDT series 2, Jg. 6:2; Jg. 11:2; Jg. 12:2 (1902–1912).

Torelli, Giuseppe (1658?–1709?): *Concerto, C minor, for Violin and String Orchestra, Op. 8 No. 8,* rev. E. Praetorius (London 1950); *Concerto, Mi minore, Op. 8 No. 9, per violino concertante e orchestra d'archi,* rev. B. Paumgartner (Zürich 1950). GMB no. 257.

Vivaldi, Antonio (ca 1678–1741): *Works,* ed. Istituto Italiano Antonio Vivaldi (Milan 1947–), with a corresponding thematic catalog, *Antonio Vivaldi, Indice tematico di 200 opere strumentali* (1955). (Other thematic catalogs by M. Pincherle, *Antonio Vivaldi et la musique instrumentale,* vol. 2, *Inventaire-thématique,* Paris 1948, and M. Rinaldi, *Catalogo numerico tematico delle compositioni di Antonio Vivaldi,* Rome 1945.) Concertos from Op. 3 in *Chamber Suites and Concerti Grossi,* ed. A. E. Wier (New York 1940).

North of the Alps

Bach, Johann Sebastian (1685– 1750): *Werke,* ed. Bach-Gesellschaft, 46 vols. (Leipzig 1851– 1899); *Neue Ausgabe sämtlicher Werke,* ed. Johann-Sebastian-Bach-Institut Göttingen, and Bach-Archiv Leipzig (1954–). A. Dürr, *Studien über die frühen Kantaten J. S. Bachs* (Leipzig 1951); F. Blume, *Outlines of a New Picture of Bach* in *Music and Letters* 44 (1963), 214–227; H. T. David and A. Mendel, *The Bach Reader* (New York 1945). W. Schmieder, *Thematisch-Systematisches Verzeichnis der musikalischen Werke von Johann Sebastian Bach* (= Bach Werke-Verzeichnis, or BWV, Leipzig 1950).

Couperin, François (1688–1733): *Oeuvres complètes,* ed. M. Cauchie, 12 vols. (Paris 1932).

Fischer, Johann Kaspar Ferdinand (ca 1650–1746): *Sämtliche Werke für Klavier und Orgel,* ed. E.v. Werra (Leipzig 1901); *Ariadne musica,* ed. E. Kaller, *Liber organi,* Bd. 7:2 (1931).

Fux, Johann Joseph (1660–1741): *Sämtliche Werke,* ed. Johann Joseph Fux Gesellschaft (Kassel 1959–); *Costanza e fortezza,* ed. E. Wellesz, DTOe Jg. 17, Bd. 34–35 (1910); *Steps to Parnassus,* trans. A. Mann (New York 1943).

Graupner, Christoph (1683–1760): *Ausgewählte Kantaten,* ed. F. Noack, DDT series 1, Bd. 51–52 (1926).

Handel, Georg Frideric (1685– 1759): *Werke,* ed. F. Chrysander (Leipzig 1858–1885); *Hallische Händel-Ausgabe,* ed. M. Schneider and R. Steglich (Kassel 1955–); W. Dean, *Handel's Dramatic Oratorios and Masques* (London 1959).

Keiser, Reinhard (1674–1739): *Croesus,* ed. M. Schneider, DDT series 1, Bd. 37–38 (1912).

Krieger, Johann (1651–1735): *Präludien und Fugen,* ed. F. W. Reide, *Die Orgel,* Reihe 2, no. 3 (Lippstadt 1957); Johann Krieger, Franz Xaver Anton Mursch-hauser und Johann Philipp Krieger, *Gesammelte Werke für Klavier und Orgel,* ed. M. Seiffert, DDT series 2, Jg. 18 (1917).

Krieger, Johann Philipp (1649– 1725): *21 ausgewählte Kirchenkompositionen,* ed. M. Seiffert, DDT series 1, Bd. 53–54 (1916).

Kuhnau, Johann (1660–1722): *Klavierwerke,* ed. K. Päsler, DDT series 1, Bd. 4 (1901); *Six Biblical Sonatas for Keyboard (1700),* ed. K. Stone (New York 1953).

Purcell, Henry (1659–1695): *Works* (London 1878–). F. B. Zimmermann, *Henry Purcell . . . An Analytical Catalogue of His Music* (London 1963); R. E. Moore, *Henry Purcell and the Restoration Theatre* (Cambridge, Mass. 1961).

Zachow, Friedrich Wilhelm (1663– 1712): *Gesammelte Werke,* ed. M. Seiffert, DDT series 1, Bd. 21–22 (1905).

Italy and the European Scene

Gasparini, Francesco (1668–1727): *The Practical Harmonist at the Harpsichord,* trans. F. S. Stillings, ed. D. L. Burrows (New Haven 1963).

Hasse, Johann Adolf (1699–1783): *Arminio,* ed. R. Gerber, *Das Erbe deutscher Musik,* vol. 27 (Mainz 1957).

Heinichen, Johann David (1683– 1729): G. Buelow, *Heinichen's Treatment of Dissonance,* JMT 6 (1962), 216–274.

Jomelli, Nicolò (1714–1774): *Fetonte,* ed. H. Abert, DDT series 1, Bd. 32–33 (1907).

Pergolesi, Giovanni Battista (1710– 1736): *Opera omnia,* ed. F. Caffarelli, 24 vols. (Rome 1942); *Olimpiade,* ed. M. Zanon, *Associazione dei musicologi italiani. Publicazioni,* vol. 1 (Florence? 1915); *Lo Frate 'nnamorato,* ed. E. Gerelli (Milan 1961).

Rameau, Jean-Philippe 1683–1764) : *Oeuvres complètes,* ed. C. Saint-Saëns, 8 vols. (Paris 1895–1913); J. Ferris, *The Evolution of Rameau's Harmonic Theories,* JMT 3 (1959), 231–256.

Scarlatti, Domenico (1685–1757) : *Sixty Sonatas,* ed. R. Kirkpatrick, 2 vols. (New York 1953).

Tartini, Giuseppe (1692–1770) : *Concertos in A minor and F major,* ed. G. Ross, SCMA no. 9 1947); *Concerto in G minor,* ed. M. Rostal (London 1941); *Concerto, E major,* ed. H. Scherchen (Zürich 1947); *Concerto in D major,* ed. G. Ross (New York 1953). M. Dounias, *Die Violinkonzerte Giuseppe Tartinis* (Wolfenbüttel 1935).

PART IV Extension of Triadic Forms 1750–1900

GENERAL

From this point on, every major composer (and most minor ones) have received at least one biography; many of these are in English or in English translation. These works tend to be more useful for the "life" than for the "works" of the composer they treat. Easily accessible through other listings, biographies are not given here, unless they are the best source for a catalog of the composer's works, or unless—like E. J. Dent's *Mozart's Operas*—they contain a truly remarkable discussion of the composer's style as well as that of his contemporaries.

The bibliography of opera from 1750 on is problematic. Much of the standard repertory (to say nothing of works no longer performed) is not available in modern critical editions. There are, on the other hand, numerous piano-vocal scores dating from the 1800s. Even though such scores frequently provide the only

access to a work, their sporadic distribution in modern libraries seemed to render useless the type of listing attempted here. Similarly, instrumental works have been listed here only in standard editions, except where those are unavailable.

* * *

CHAPTER 11 GERMAN SYMPHONY AND INTERNATIONAL OPERA 1750–1780

GENERAL

A convenient summary of opera during this period is available in D. J. Grout, *A Short History of Opera* (New York 1947); valuable glimpses of the same repertory can be found in A. Einstein, *Gluck,* trans. E. Blom (London 1936). A. Lowenberg, *Annals of Opera 1597–1940* (2nd ed., Geneva 1955), continues to be extremely useful. W. S. Newman, *The Sonata in the Classic Era* (Chapel Hill 1963) is a guide to instrumental music.

* * *

Bach, Philipp Emanuel (1714–1788) : *Konzert, D-dur, für Cembalo,* ed. L. Landshoff (Berlin 1932).
Concerto in D minor, in *Instrumental Konzerte deutscher Meister,* ed. A. Schering, DDT series 1, Bd. 29–30 (1906).
4 Orchester-Sinfonien, nach der Königliche Bibliothek zu Berlin befindlichen Original-Handschrift des Componisten (Leipzig 1860).
Die Preussischen Sonaten für Klavier, ed. R. Steglich (Kassel 1927–1928).
Die Württembergischen Sonaten für Klavier, ed. R. Steglich (Celle 1928).
Die sechs Sammlungen von Sonaten, freien Fantasien und Rondos für Kenner und Liebhaber, ed. C. Krebs (Leipzig 1953).
Essay on the True Art of Playing

Keyboard Instruments, trans. and ed. W. J. Mitchell (New York 1949).
Thematisches Verzeichnis der Werke von Carl Philipp Emanuel Bach, ed. A. Wotquenne (Leipzig 1905).

Bach, Johann Christian (1735–1782) : *Fünf Sinfonien,* ed. F. Stein, *Das Erbe deutscher Musik,* Bd. 30 (Wiesbaden 1956).
Zehn Klavier-Sonaten, ed. L. Landshoff (Leipzig 1925).
HAM no. 303.
C. S. Terry, *John Christian Bach* (London 1929), includes a thematic catalog.

Bach, Wilhelm Friedemann (1710–1784) : *Sinfonie F-dur,* in *Mittel- und Norddeutsche Kammersinfonien,* vol. 3 (Leipzig 1957?).
Sämtliche Klaviersonaten, ed. F. Blume, 3 vols. (Kassel 1955–1959).
Concerto C-moll, ed. W. Eickemeger, *Antiqua; eine Sammlung alter Musik* (Mainz 1931).
Konzert für Cembalo, ed. W. Upmeyer, *Musikschätze der Vergangenheit* (Berlin 1931).
HAM nos. 288, 289.

Dittersdorf, Karl Ditters von (1739–1799) : *Doctor und Apotheker,* ed. H. Burkard (Vienna 1961).
HAM no. 305.

Eckard, Johann (1735–1809) : *Oeuvres complètes pour le clavecin,* ed. J. Ligtelijn (Amsterdam 1956).

Galuppi, Baldassare (1706–1785) : *Il Filosofo di campagna,* ed. F. Malipiero, *I Classici della musica italiana,* vol. 13 (Milan 1919).
HAM no. 285.

Gassmann, Florian (1729–1774) : *La Contessina,* ed. R. Haas, DTOe Jg. 21 (1914).

Gluck, Christoph (1714–1787) : *Sämtliche Werke,* ed. A. A. Abert and L. Finscher (Kassel 1963–).

Haydn, Joseph (1732–1809) : The

state of modern publication of Haydn's works is complex. In addition to numerous miniature scores (especially by Eulenburg) and practical editions of varying degrees of reliability, four collected editions have been started. Two of these have ceased, incomplete; the other two are continuing simultaneously. All four are listed here, with special indications for the symphonies.

Werke (Leipzig: Breitkopf & Härtel, 1907–1922); includes Symphonies nos. 1–49.

Complete Works, ed. J. P. Larsen, Haydn Society, Boston (Leipzig: Breitkopf & Härtel, 1950–1957); includes Symphonies nos. 50–57, 82–92, ed. H. Schultz.

Werke, ed. J. P. Larsen, Joseph Haydn-Institut, Köln (Munich: G. Henle, 1958–); includes Symphonies nos. 21–31, ed. H. Walter; nos. 102–104, ed. H. Unverricht; String Quartets op. 9, 17, ed. G. Feder.

The Symphonies of Joseph Haydn. Collected Edition, to include (1) Symphonies nos. 1–49, ed. H. C. Robbins-Landon (Vienna: Döblinger 1962–); (2) Symphonies nos. 50–104, ed. H. Schultz and H. C. Robbins-Landon (Salzburg: Haydn-Mozart Presse 1962–).

A. van Hoboken, *Joseph Haydn, Thematisch - bibliographisches Werkverzeichnis* (Mainz 1957).

H. C. Robbins-Landon, *The Symphonies of Joseph Haydn* (London 1955), includes a thematic catalog.

The complete string quartets are so far available for study only in miniature scores (Eulenburg).

Hiller, Johann Adam (1728–1804): *Die Jagd*, ed. R. Kleinmichel (Wien 1915?).

Holzbauer, Ignaz (1711–1783):

Günther von Schwarzburg, ed. H. Kretzschmar, DDT series 1, Bd. 8–9 (1902).

Piccini, Nicola (1728–1800): HAM no. 300.

Schobert, Johann Christoph (d. 1767): *Sechs Sinfonien für Cembalo mit begleitung von Violine und Hörnern ad Libitum, Op. 9 und Op. 10*, ed. W. Kramolisch, *Das Erbe deutscher Musik*, Sonderreihe Bd. 4 (Kassel 1960).

Stamitz, Johann (1717–1757): *Sinfonien der pfalzbayerischen Schule (Mannheimer Symphoniker)*, ed. H. Riemann, DDT series 2, Bd. 3:1, 7:2, 8:2 (Leipzig 1902–1907). HAM no. 294.

Wagenseil, Georg Christoph (1715–1777): *Wiener Instrumentalmusik vor und um 1750*, ed. K. Horwitz, K. Riedel, and W. Fischer, DTOe Jg. 15, 19 (Leipzig 1908–1912). *Sinfonie in D dur für Streicher, Flöten und Hörner*, ed. R. Sondheimer (Berlin 1927).

The description of Philipp Emanuel Bach at the clavichord is taken from Charles Burney, *The Present State of Music in Germany, The Netherlands, and United Provinces*, vol. 2 (London 1773), p. 269.

CHAPTER 12 HAYDN AND MOZART 1770–1800

Cimarosa, Domenico (1749–1801): *Il Matrimonio segreto* (New York 1959).

Haydn, Joseph (1732–1809): see Chapter 11.

Mozart, Wolfgang Amadeus (1756–1791): *Werke. Kritisch durchgesehene Gesamtausgabe*, 40 vols. (Leipzig 1877–1887; Ann Arbor 1951–1955).
Neue Ausgabe sämtlicher Werke, ed. Internationalen Stiftung Mozarteum, Salzburg (Kassel, 1955–).

The Ten Celebrated String Quartets, ed. A. Einstein (London 1945).
Sonatas and Fantasies for the Piano, ed. N. Broder (Bryn Mawr 1956).
Chronologisch-thematisches Verzeichnis sämtlicher Tonwerke Wolfgang Amadé Mozarts (3rd ed., A. Einstein, Leipzig 1937; 6th ed., F. Giegling, A. Weinmann, G. Sievers, Wiesbaden 1964).
Mozart Handbuch, ed. O. Schneider and A. Algatzy (Vienna 1962).
E. J. Dent, *Mozart's Operas: a Critical Study* (2nd ed., London 1947).
E. J. Simon, *The Double Exposition in the Classic Concerto*, JAMS 10 (1957), 111–118.
Paisiello, Giovanni (1740–1816): *Il Barbiere di Siviglia*, ed. M. Parenti (Milan 1961).

CHAPTER 13 EXPANSION OF THE SYMPHONY 1800–1830

Beethoven, Ludwig van (1770–1827): *Werke. Vollständige kritisch durchgesehene . . . Ausgabe*, 25 vols. (Leipzig 1862–1949).
Supplement, ed. W. Hess (Wiesbaden 1959–).
Werke, ed. J. Schmidt-Görg, Beethoven-Archiv, Bonn (Munich 1961–).
G. Kinsky, *Das Werk Beethovens, Thematisch - bibliographisches Verzeichnis*, ed. H. Halm (Munich 1955).
Cherubini, Luigi (1760–1842): *Medea* (Milan 19–?).
Schubert, Franz (1797–1828): *Werke. Kritisch durchgesehene Gesammtausgabe*, 21 vols. (Leipzig 1885–1897).
O. E. Deutsch and D. R. Wakeling, *Schubert, Thematic Catalogue* (London 1951).

CHAPTER 14 SYMPHONIC DERIVATIVES AND OTHER MUSIC 1830–1850

GENERAL

A. Einstein, *Music in the Romantic Era* (New York 1947), is useful for this period.

*   *   *

Bellini, Vincenzo (1801–1835): *Norma* (Milan 1915).

Berlioz, Hector (1803–1869): *Werke*, ed. Ch. Malherbe and F. Weingartner, 20 vols. (Leipzig 1900–1907).

C. Hopkinson, *A Bibliography of the Musical and Literary Works of Hector Berlioz* (Edinburgh 1951).

Chopin, Fryderyk (1810–1849): *Complete Works*, ed. I. J. Paderewski, Fryderyk Chopin Institute (Warsaw 1949–).

M. J. E. Brown, *Chopin, An Index of His Works in Chronological Order* (London 1960).

Donizetti, Gaetano (1797–1848): *L'Elisir d'amore* (Milan 1962).

Liszt, Franz (1811–1886): *Musikalische Werke*, ed. F. Busoni et al., Franz Liszt-Stiftung, 31 vols. (Leipzig 1908–1936).

Liszt Society Publications, 4 vols. (London 1950–1959).

H. Searle, *The Music of Liszt* (London 1954).

Mendelssohn, Felix (1809–1847): *Werke. Kritisch durchgesehene Ausgabe*, ed. J. Rietz, 18 vols. (Leipzig 1874–).

Schumann, Robert (1810–1856): *Werke*, ed. Clara Schumann, 13 vols. (Leipzig 1881–1893).

Weber, Carl Maria von (1786–1826): *Der Freischütz*, ed. H. Abert (Leipzig 1933).

CHAPTER 15 BETWEEN BRAHMS AND WAGNER; DEBUSSY 1850–1900

GENERAL

Provocative discussions of operas of Verdi and Wagner (and others) can be found in J. Kerman, *Opera as Drama* (New York 1956).

For Debussy (as for the following chapter), works are cited by their first edition, where known.

*   *   *

Brahms, Johannes (1833–1897): *Sämtliche Werke*, ed. Gesellschaft der Musikfreunde in Wien, 26 vols. (Leipzig 1926; Ann Arbor 1949).

Bruckner, Anton (1824–1896): *Sämtliche Werke. Kritische Gesamtausgabe*, ed. L. Nowak, Österreichischen Nationalbibliothek and the Internationalen Bruckner-Gesellschaft (Wien 1951–), miniature score.

Debussy, Claude (1862–1918): Premier Quatœur (Paris: Durand 1894)

Pelléas et Mélisande, drame lyrique (Paris: Fromont 1902)

Estampes (Paris: Durand 1903)

La Mer, three symphonic sketches (Paris: Durand 1905)

Images (Paris: Durand 1905)

Twelve Preludes, for piano (Paris: Durand 1910, 1913)

Twelve Etudes, for piano (Paris: Durand 1916)

Sonata for violin and piano (Paris: Durand 1917).

List of works in *Catalogue de l'oeuvre de Claude Debussy* (Paris: Durand 1962).

Dvořák, Antonín (1841–1904): *Complete Edition* (Prague 1955–).

Franck, César (1822–1890): *Symphony in D minor* (Paris 189–?).

Mahler, Gustav (1860–1911): *Sämtliche Werke. Kritische Gesamtausgabe*, ed. Internationalen Gustav Mahler-Gesellschaft, (Vienna 1960–).

Mussorgsky, Modest (1839–1881): *Boris Godunov* . . . ("complete, original text") . . . , ed. P. Lamm (Moscow 1928).

Pictures at an Exhibition, ed. P. Lamm (New York 1952).

Saint-Saëns, Camille (1835–1921): *Danse macabre*, Op. 40 (Paris 1875?).

Strauss, Richard (1864–1949): Symphonic poems ed. in miniature score, Wiener Philharmonischer Verlag (Vienna 1904–1923).

Tchaikovsky, Peter Ilyitch (1840–1893): complete works (Moscow 1946–).

Verdi, Giuseppe (1813–1901): operas ed. in miniature score, Ricordi (Milan).

Wagner, Richard (1813–1883): operas and music-dramas ed. in miniature score, B. Schott's Söhne (Mainz).

Prose Works, trans. W. A. Ellis, 8 vols. (London 1893–1899).

J. M. Stein, *Richard Wagner and the Synthesis of the Arts* (Detroit 1960).

CHAPTER 16 NEW MUSIC AFTER 1900

GENERAL

One of the most useful books for this chapter is N. Slonimsky, *Music Since 1900*, 3rd ed. (New York 1949), a chronicle. Especially good for modern times are *Baker's Biographical Dictionary of Musicians*, 5th ed., N. Slonimsky (New York 1958), and *International Cyclopedia of Music and Musicians*, 9th ed., R. Sabin (New York 1964). G. Perle, *Serial Composition and Atonality* (Berkeley 1962), is a technical survey. There are many publications of chronicle, biography, analysis, theory, and opinion about music in the 1900s, but as yet few stylistic histories.

There are, of course, no collected editions; listed here are first editions, unless the first edition could not be determined or was inaccessible. Publishers are included for music and for other publications where this information may be necessary. It has not been possible in this book to list recordings; but most of the music mentioned here has been recorded. In fact, very recent works are more likely to be recorded than published.

*   *   *

Antheil, George (1900–): *Ballet mécanique* (Delaware Gap: Shawnee 1959—rev. ed.)

Babbitt, Milton (1916–): String Quartet no. 2 (New York: Independent Music Publishers 1954)

Bartók, Béla (1881–1945): (Vienna: Universal Edition, except as noted)
The Miraculous Mandarin (1925 —piano score)
First String Quartet (Budapest 191–?)
Second String Quartet (1920)
Third String Quartet (1929)
Fourth String Quartet (1929)
Fifth String Quartet (1936)
Sixth String Quartet (New York: Boosey and Hawkes 1941)
Concerto no. 1, for piano and orchestra (1929)
Concerto no. 2, for piano and orchestra (1932)
Music for Strings, Percussion, and Celesta (1937)
Sonata for Two Pianos and Percussion (New York: Boosey and Hawkes 1942)
Violin Concerto (New York: Boosey and Hawkes 1946)
List of works in H. Stevens, *The Life and Music of Béla Bartók* (New York 1953)

Berg, Alban (1885–1935): (Vienna: Universal Edition)
Wozzeck, opera in 3 acts (1926— piano score; 1954—full score)
Lyric Suite, for String quartet (1927)
Violin Concerto (1936)
List of works in H. F. Redlich, *Alban Berg* (1957)

Boulez, Pierre (1925–): *Le Marteau*

sans maître (Vienna: Universal Edition 1954)

Cage, John (1912–): list of works in *John Cage* (New York: Peters 1962)

Carter, Elliot (1908–): String Quartet (New York: Associated Music Publishers 1956)
String Quartet no. 2 (New York: Associated Music Publishers 1961)

Copland, Aaron (1900–): Concerto, for piano and orchestra (New York: Cos Cob 1929)

Dallapiccola, Luigi (1904–): *Canti di prigionia* (Milano: Carisch 1941)

Fine, Irving (1914–1962): String Quartet (New York: C. Fischer 1955)

Goehr, Alexander (1932–): *Little Symphony* (New York: Associated Music Publishers 1964)

Honegger, Arthur (1892–1955): *Le Roi David* (Lausanne: Foetisch Frères 1924)
Pacific 231 (Vienna: Universal Edition 1924)

Imbrie, Andrew (1921–): Second String Quartet, Third String Quartet (Delaware Gap: Shawnee 1960)

Ives, Charles (1874–1954): Second Pianoforte Sonata, "Concord, Mass., 1840–1860" (New York: Arrow 1947—2nd ed.)

Kirchner, Leon (1919–): String Quartet (New York: Mercury 1950)
String Quartet no. 2 (New York: Associated Music Publishers 1963)

Milhaud, Darius (1892–): *La Création du monde* (Paris: Eschig 1929)

Riegger, Wallingford (1885–1961): Symphony no. 3 (New York: Associated Music Publishers 1949)

Russolo, Luigi (1885–1942): an account of the 1914 concert in N. Slonimsky, *Music Since 1900*, pp. 147–148.

Satie, Erik (1866–1925): *Parade, ballet réaliste* (Paris: Rouart, Lerolle 1917)

Schoenberg, Arnold (1874–1951): (Vienna: Universal Edition, except as noted)
Verklärte Nacht, op. 4 (Berlin: Dreililien 1905?)
Chamber Symphony for Fifteen Instruments, Op. 9 (1912)
Second String Quartet, Op. 10 (1919)
Three Piano Pieces, Op. 11 (1910)
Five Pieces for Orchestra, Op. 16 (Leipzig: C. F. Peters 1912)
Erwartung, monodrama, Op. 17 (1922—piano score; 1950)
Pierrot lunaire, Op. 21 (1914)
Serenade, Op. 24 (Copenhagen: Wilhelm Hansen 1924)
Suite for Piano, Op. 25 (1925)
Third String Quartet, Op. 30 (1927)
Variations for Orchestra, Op. 31 (1929)
Concerto for Violin and Orchestra, Op. 36 (1939)
Fourth String Quartet, Op. 37 (New York: G. Schirmer 1939)
Concerto for Piano and Orchestra, Op. 42 (New York: G. Schirmer 1944)
String Trio, Op. 45 (Hillsdale: Boelke-Bomart 1950)
Moses und Aron, opera in 3 acts (Mainz: B. Schott's Söhne 1958)
List of works in J. Rufer, *The Works of Arnold Schoenberg* trans. D. Newlin (London 1962)

Sessions, Roger (1896–): Symphony no. 2 (New York: G. Schirmer 1949)
Symphony no. 3 (New York: Marks 1962)

Stockhausen, Karlheinz (1928–): *Nr. 7: Klavierstücke XI* (London: Universal Edition 1957)

Stravinsky, Igor (1882–): *Petrouchka*, burlesque in four scenes (Berlin: Edition Russe de Musique 1911)
Le Sacre du printemps, pictures

of pagan Russia (Berlin: Edition Russe de Musique 1913)

Les Noces, Russian dance scenes (London: J. & W. Chester 1922)

L'Histoire du Soldat (London: J. & W. Chester 1924)

Octet for Wind Instruments (Berlin: Edition Russe de Musique 1924)

Symphony of Psalms (Berlin: Edition Russe de Musique 1931)

Symphony in C (Mainz: B. Schott's Söhne 1948)

Orpheus (New York: Boosey and Hawkes 1948)

The Rake's Progress, Opera in three acts, text by W. H. Auden and Chester Kallman (New York: Boosey and Hawkes 1951—piano score)

Agon, ballet for twelve dancers (New York: Boosey and Hawkes 1957)

Threni (New York: Boosey and Hawkes 1958)

Movements for Piano and Orchestra (New York: Boosey and Hawkes 1960)

List of works in *Igor Strawinsky, Complete Catalogue* (London: Boosey and Hawkes 1957)

Varèse, Edgar (1885–1965): *Octandre, Intégrales* (New York: G. Ricordi 1956)

Webern, Anton (1883–1945): (Vienna: Universal Edition, except as noted)

Five Pieces for String Quartet, Op. 5 (1922)

Six Bagatelles for String Quartet, Op. 9 (1924)

Five Pieces for Orchestra, Op. 10 (1923)

Symphony, Op. 21 (1929)

Quartet, for Violin, Clarinet, Tenor Saxophone, and Piano, Op. 22 (1932)

Concerto for Nine Instruments, Op. 24 (Liège: Dynamo Editions 1948)

String Quartet, Op. 28 (1939)

First Cantata, Op. 29 (1957)

Variations for Orchestra, Op. 30 (1956)

Second Cantata, Op. 31 (1956)

List of Works in *The Complete Music of Anton Webern,* R. Craft (Columbia K4L-232)

₰   ₰   ₰   ₰

SELECTED READINGS

The following list is suggested as supplementary reading for a shorter survey. Being excerpts, these selections do not by themselves provide a continuous account, but will need explanatory comment from the teacher.

Gregorian chant
1–3, 6–10, 14–18

Medieval chant
25–26, 34–38, 40–43, 47–49, 54–57

Polyphony in the 1200s
71–72, 73–80, 84, 87–90, 91–92, 103–105

Polyphony in the 1300s
106–107, 119–121, 123, 126–129, 129–134

Polyphony in the 1400s; Josquin
143–151, 154–156, 172–180, 181

Polyphony in the 1500s
182–190, 204–206, 206–220

Dramatic music 1600–1750
223–231, 234, 241–243, 248–253, 255–265, 286–289, 306–312, 340–342

Corelli and Vivaldi
302–306, 312–313

Bach and Handel
326, 330–337, 340

German music after 1750
355–360, 363–364, 368–369

Haydn's early works
372–380

Mozart's early works
386–392

Haydn and Mozart
392–411

Beethoven
415–417, 419–424

After Beethoven to 1850
426–430, 434–437, 437–455

Wagner to 1900
456–480

After 1900
483–494, 501–507, 507–513, 515–526

INDEX

A CATALOG OF SELECTED

DOVER BOOKS

IN ALL FIELDS OF INTEREST

A CATALOG OF SELECTED DOVER BOOKS IN ALL FIELDS OF INTEREST

CONCERNING THE SPIRITUAL IN ART, Wassily Kandinsky. Pioneering work by father of abstract art. Thoughts on color theory, nature of art. Analysis of earlier masters. 12 illustrations. 80pp. of text. 5⅜ × 8½. 23411-8 Pa. $2.25

LEONARDO ON THE HUMAN BODY, Leonardo da Vinci. More than 1200 of Leonardo's anatomical drawings on 215 plates. Leonardo's text, which accompanies the drawings, has been translated into English. 506pp. 8⅜ × 11¾. 24483-0 Pa. $10.95

GOBLIN MARKET, Christina Rossetti. Best-known work by poet comparable to Emily Dickinson, Alfred Tennyson. With 46 delightfully grotesque illustrations by Laurence Housman. 64pp. 4 × 6¾. 24516-0 Pa. $2.50

THE HEART OF THOREAU'S JOURNALS, edited by Odell Shepard. Selections from *Journal*, ranging over full gamut of interests. 228pp. 5⅜ × 8½. 20741-2 Pa. $4.00

MR. LINCOLN'S CAMERA MAN: MATHEW B. BRADY, Roy Meredith. Over 300 Brady photos reproduced directly from original negatives, photos. Lively commentary. 368pp. 8⅜ × 11¼. 23021-X Pa. $11.95

PHOTOGRAPHIC VIEWS OF SHERMAN'S CAMPAIGN, George N. Barnard. Reprint of landmark 1866 volume with 61 plates: battlefield of New Hope Church, the Etawah Bridge, the capture of Atlanta, etc. 80pp. 9 × 12. 23445-2 Pa. $6.00

A SHORT HISTORY OF ANATOMY AND PHYSIOLOGY FROM THE GREEKS TO HARVEY, Dr. Charles Singer. Thoroughly engrossing non-technical survey. 270 illustrations. 211pp. 5⅜ × 8½. 20389-1 Pa. $4.50

REDOUTE ROSES IRON-ON TRANSFER PATTERNS, Barbara Christopher. Redouté was botanical painter to the Empress Josephine; transfer his famous roses onto fabric with these 24 transfer patterns. 80pp. 8¼ × 10⅞. 24292-7 Pa. $3.50

THE FIVE BOOKS OF ARCHITECTURE, Sebastiano Serlio. Architectural milestone, first (1611) English translation of Renaissance classic. Unabridged reproduction of original edition includes over 300 woodcut illustrations. 416pp. 9⅜ × 12¼. 24349-4 Pa. $14.95

CARLSON'S GUIDE TO LANDSCAPE PAINTING, John F. Carlson. Authoritative, comprehensive guide covers, every aspect of landscape painting. 34 reproductions of paintings by author; 58 explanatory diagrams. 144pp. 8⅜ × 11. 22927-0 Pa. $4.95

101 PUZZLES IN THOUGHT AND LOGIC, C.R. Wylie, Jr. Solve murders, robberies, see which fishermen are liars—purely by reasoning! 107pp. 5⅜ × 8½. 20367-0 Pa. $2.00

TEST YOUR LOGIC, George J. Summers. 50 more truly new puzzles with new turns of thought, new subtleties of inference. 100pp. 5⅜ × 8½. 22877-0 Pa. $2.25

THE GUIDE FOR THE PERPLEXED, Moses Maimonides. Great classic of medieval Judaism attempts to reconcile revealed religion (Pentateuch, commentaries) with Aristotelian philosophy. 473pp. 5⅜ × 8½. 20351-4 Pa. $6.95

SMOCKING: TECHNIQUE, PROJECTS, AND DESIGNS, Dianne Durand. Foremost smocking designer provides complete instructions on how to smock. Over 10 projects, over 100 illustrations. 56pp. 8¼ × 11. 23788-5 Pa. $2.00

AUDUBON'S BIRDS IN COLOR FOR DECOUPAGE, edited by Eleanor H. Rawlings. 24 sheets, 37 most decorative birds, full color, on one side of paper. Instructions, including work under glass. 56pp. 8¼ × 11. 23492-4 Pa. $3.50

THE COMPLETE BOOK OF SILK SCREEN PRINTING PRODUCTION, J.I. Biegeleisen. For commercial user, teacher in advanced classes, serious hobbyist. Most modern techniques, materials, equipment for optimal results. 124 illustrations. 253pp. 5⅜ × 8½. 21100-2 Pa. $4.50

A TREASURY OF ART NOUVEAU DESIGN AND ORNAMENT, edited by Carol Belanger Grafton. 577 designs for the practicing artist. Full-page, spots, borders, bookplates by Klimt, Bradley, others. 144pp. 8⅜ × 11¼. 24001-0 Pa. $5.00

ART NOUVEAU TYPOGRAPHIC ORNAMENTS, Dan X. Solo. Over 800 Art Nouveau florals, swirls, women, animals, borders, scrolls, wreaths, spots and dingbats, copyright-free. 100pp. 8⅛ × 11. 24366-4 Pa. $4.00

HAND SHADOWS TO BE THROWN UPON THE WALL, Henry Bursill. Wonderful Victorian novelty tells how to make flying birds, dog, goose, deer, and 14 others, each explained by a full-page illustration. 32pp. 6½ × 9¼. 21779-5 Pa. $1.50

AUDUBON'S BIRDS OF AMERICA COLORING BOOK, John James Audubon. Rendered for coloring by Paul Kennedy. 46 of Audubon's noted illustrations: red-winged black-bird, cardinal, etc. Original plates reproduced in full-color on the covers. Captions. 48pp. 8¼ × 11. 23049-X Pa. $2.25

SILK SCREEN TECHNIQUES, J.I. Biegeleisen, M.A. Cohn. Clear, practical, modern, economical. Minimal equipment (self-built), materials, easy methods. For amateur, hobbyist, 1st book. 141 illustrations. 185pp. 6⅛ × 9¼. 20433-2 Pa. $3.95

101 PATCHWORK PATTERNS, Ruby S. McKim. 101 beautiful, immediately useable patterns, full-size, modern and traditional. Also general information, estimating, quilt lore. 140 illustrations. 124pp. 7⅞ × 10¾. 20773-0 Pa. $3.50

READY-TO-USE FLORAL DESIGNS, Ed Sibbett, Jr. Over 100 floral designs (most in three sizes) of popular individual blossoms as well as bouquets, sprays, garlands. 64pp. 8¼ × 11. 23976-4 Pa. $2.95

AMERICAN WILD FLOWERS COLORING BOOK, Paul Kennedy. Planned coverage of 46 most important wildflowers, from Rickett's collection; instructive as well as entertaining. Color versions on covers. Captions. 48pp. 8¼ × 11. 20095-7 Pa. $2.25

CARVING DUCK DECOYS, Harry V. Shourds and Anthony Hillman. Detailed instructions and full-size templates for constructing 16 beautiful, marvelously practical decoys according to time-honored South Jersey method. 70pp. 9¼ × 12¼. 24083-5 Pa. $4.95

TRADITIONAL PATCHWORK PATTERNS, Carol Belanger Grafton. Cardboard cut-out pieces for use as templates to make 12 quilts: Buttercup, Ribbon Border, Tree of Paradise, nine more. Full instructions. 57pp. 8¼ × 11. 23015-5 Pa. $3.50

25 KITES THAT FLY, Leslie Hunt. Full, easy-to-follow instructions for kites made from inexpensive materials. Many novelties. 70 illustrations. 110pp. 5⅜ × 8½.
22550-X Pa. $1.95

PIANO TUNING, J. Cree Fischer. Clearest, best book for beginner, amateur. Simple repairs, raising dropped notes, tuning by easy method of flattened fifths. No previous skills needed. 4 illustrations. 201pp. 5⅜ × 8½.
23267-0 Pa. $3.50

EARLY AMERICAN IRON-ON TRANSFER PATTERNS, edited by Rita Weiss. 75 designs, borders, alphabets, from traditional American sources. 48pp. 8¼ × 11.
23162-3 Pa. $1.95

CROCHETING EDGINGS, edited by Rita Weiss. Over 100 of the best designs for these lovely trims for a host of household items. Complete instructions, illustrations. 48pp. 8¼ × 11.
24031-2 Pa. $2.00

FINGER PLAYS FOR NURSERY AND KINDERGARTEN, Emilie Poulsson. 18 finger plays with music (voice and piano); entertaining, instructive. Counting, nature lore, etc. Victorian classic. 53 illustrations. 80pp. 6½ × 9¼. 22588-7 Pa. $1.95

BOSTON THEN AND NOW, Peter Vanderwarker. Here in 59 side-by-side views are photographic documentations of the city's past and present. 119 photographs. Full captions. 122pp. 8¼ × 11.
24312-5 Pa. $6.95

CROCHETING BEDSPREADS, edited by Rita Weiss. 22 patterns, originally published in three instruction books 1939-41. 39 photos, 8 charts. Instructions. 48pp. 8¼ × 11.
23610-2 Pa. $2.00

HAWTHORNE ON PAINTING, Charles W. Hawthorne. Collected from notes taken by students at famous Cape Cod School; hundreds of direct, personal *apercus*, ideas, suggestions. 91pp. 5⅜ × 8½.
20653-X Pa. $2.50

THERMODYNAMICS, Enrico Fermi. A classic of modern science. Clear, organized treatment of systems, first and second laws, entropy, thermodynamic potentials, etc. Calculus required. 160pp. 5⅜ × 8½.
60361-X Pa. $4.00

TEN BOOKS ON ARCHITECTURE, Vitruvius. The most important book ever written on architecture. Early Roman aesthetics, technology, classical orders, site selection, all other aspects. Morgan translation. 331pp. 5⅜ × 8½. 20645-9 Pa. $5.50

THE CORNELL BREAD BOOK, Clive M. McCay and Jeanette B. McCay. Famed high-protein recipe incorporated into breads, rolls, buns, coffee cakes, pizza, pie crusts, more. Nearly 50 illustrations. 48pp. 8¼ × 11.
23995-0 Pa. $2.00

THE CRAFTSMAN'S HANDBOOK, Cennino Cennini. 15th-century handbook, school of Giotto, explains applying gold, silver leaf; gesso; fresco painting, grinding pigments, etc. 142pp. 6⅛ × 9¼.
20054-X Pa. $3.50

FRANK LLOYD WRIGHT'S FALLINGWATER, Donald Hoffmann. Full story of Wright's masterwork at Bear Run, Pa. 100 photographs of site, construction, and details of completed structure. 112pp. 9¼ × 10.
23671-4 Pa. $6.50

OVAL STAINED GLASS PATTERN BOOK, C. Eaton. 60 new designs framed in shape of an oval. Greater complexity, challenge with sinuous cats, birds, mandalas framed in antique shape. 64pp. 8¼ × 11.
24519-5 Pa. $3.50

CHILDREN'S BOOKPLATES AND LABELS, Ed Sibbett, Jr. 6 each of 12 types based on *Wizard of Oz, Alice,* nursery rhymes, fairy tales. Perforated; full color. 24pp. 8¼ × 11. 23538-6 Pa. $2.95

READY-TO-USE VICTORIAN COLOR STICKERS: 96 Pressure-Sensitive Seals, Carol Belanger Grafton. Drawn from authentic period sources. Motifs include heads of men, women, children, plus florals, animals, birds, more. Will adhere to any clean surface. 8pp. 8½ × 11. 24551-9 Pa. $2.95

CUT AND FOLD PAPER SPACESHIPS THAT FLY, Michael Grater. 16 colorful, easy-to-build spaceships that really fly. Star Shuttle, Lunar Freighter, Star Probe, 13 others. 32pp. 8¼ × 11. 23978-0 Pa. $2.50

CUT AND ASSEMBLE PAPER AIRPLANES THAT FLY, Arthur Baker. 8 aerodynamically sound, ready-to-build paper airplanes, designed with latest techniques. Fly *Pegasus, Daedalus, Songbird,* 5 other aircraft. Instructions. 32pp. 9¼ × 11¼. 24302-8 Pa. $3.95

SIDELIGHTS ON RELATIVITY, Albert Einstein. Two lectures delivered in 1920-21: *Ether and Relativity* and *Geometry and Experience.* Elegant ideas in non-mathematical form. 56pp. 5⅜ × 8½. 24511-X Pa. $2.25

FADS AND FALLACIES IN THE NAME OF SCIENCE, Martin Gardner. Fair, witty appraisal of cranks and quacks of science: Velikovsky, orgone energy, Bridey Murphy, medical fads, etc. 373pp. 5⅜ × 8½. 20394-8 Pa. $5.50

VACATION HOMES AND CABINS, U.S. Dept. of Agriculture. Complete plans for 16 cabins, vacation homes and other shelters. 105pp. 9 × 12. 23631-5 Pa. $4.50

HOW TO BUILD A WOOD-FRAME HOUSE, L.O. Anderson. Placement, foundations, framing, sheathing, roof, insulation, plaster, finishing—almost everything else. 179 illustrations. 223pp. 7⅞ × 10¾. 22954-8 Pa. $5.50

THE MYSTERY OF A HANSOM CAB, Fergus W. Hume. Bizarre murder in a hansom cab leads to engrossing investigation. Memorable characters, rich atmosphere. 19th-century bestseller, still enjoyable, exciting. 256pp. 5⅜ × 8. 21956-9 Pa. $4.00

MANUAL OF TRADITIONAL WOOD CARVING, edited by Paul N. Hasluck. Possibly the best book in English on the craft of wood carving. Practical instructions, along with 1,146 working drawings and photographic illustrations. 576pp. 6½ × 9¼. 23489-4 Pa. $8.95

WHITTLING AND WOODCARVING, E.J Tangerman. Best book on market; clear, full. If you can cut a potato, you can carve toys, puzzles, chains, etc. Over 464 illustrations. 293pp. 5⅜ × 8½. 20965-2 Pa. $4.95

AMERICAN TRADEMARK DESIGNS, Barbara Baer Capitman. 732 marks, logos and corporate-identity symbols. Categories include entertainment, heavy industry, food and beverage. All black-and-white in standard forms. 160pp. 8⅛ × 11. 23259-X Pa. $6.00

DECORATIVE FRAMES AND BORDERS, edited by Edmund V. Gillon, Jr. Largest collection of borders and frames ever compiled for use of artists and designers. Renaissance, neo-Greek, Art Nouveau, Art Deco, to mention only a few styles. 396 illustrations. 192pp. 8⅜ × 11¼. 22928-9 Pa. $6.00

THE MURDER BOOK OF J.G. REEDER, Edgar Wallace. Eight suspenseful stories by bestselling mystery writer of 20s and 30s. Features the donnish Mr. J.G. Reeder of Public Prosecutor's Office. 128pp. 5⅜ × 8½. (Available in U.S. only)

24374-5 Pa. $3.50

ANNE ORR'S CHARTED DESIGNS, Anne Orr. Best designs by premier needlework designer, all on charts: flowers, borders, birds, children, alphabets, etc. Over 100 charts, 10 in color. Total of 40pp. 8¼ × 11.   23704-4 Pa. $2.25

BASIC CONSTRUCTION TECHNIQUES FOR HOUSES AND SMALL BUILDINGS SIMPLY EXPLAINED, U.S. Bureau of Naval Personnel. Grading, masonry, woodworking, floor and wall framing, roof framing, plastering, tile setting, much more. Over 675 illustrations. 568pp. 6½ × 9¼.   20242-9 Pa. $8.95

MATISSE LINE DRAWINGS AND PRINTS, Henri Matisse. Representative collection of female nudes, faces, still lifes, experimental works, etc., from 1898 to 1948. 50 illustrations. 48pp. 8⅜ × 11¼.   23877-6 Pa. $2.50

HOW TO PLAY THE CHESS OPENINGS, Eugene Znosko-Borovsky. Clear, profound examinations of just what each opening is intended to do and how opponent can counter. Many sample games. 147pp. 5⅜ × 8½.   22795-2 Pa. $2.95

DUPLICATE BRIDGE, Alfred Sheinwold. Clear, thorough, easily followed account: rules, etiquette, scoring, strategy, bidding; Goren's point-count system, Blackwood and Gerber conventions, etc. 158pp. 5⅜ × 8½.   22741-3 Pa. $3.00

SARGENT PORTRAIT DRAWINGS, J.S. Sargent. Collection of 42 portraits reveals technical skill and intuitive eye of noted American portrait painter, John Singer Sargent. 48pp. 8¼ × 11⅛.   24524-1 Pa. $2.95

ENTERTAINING SCIENCE EXPERIMENTS WITH EVERYDAY OBJECTS, Martin Gardner. Over 100 experiments for youngsters. Will amuse, astonish, teach, and entertain. Over 100 illustrations. 127pp. 5⅜ × 8½.   24201-3 Pa. $2.50

TEDDY BEAR PAPER DOLLS IN FULL COLOR: A Family of Four Bears and Their Costumes, Crystal Collins. A family of four Teddy Bear paper dolls and nearly 60 cut-out costumes. Full color, printed one side only. 32pp. 9¼ × 12¼.

24550-0 Pa. $3.50

NEW CALLIGRAPHIC ORNAMENTS AND FLOURISHES, Arthur Baker. Unusual, multi-useable material: arrows, pointing hands, brackets and frames, ovals, swirls, birds, etc. Nearly 700 illustrations. 80pp. 8⅜ × 11¼.

24095-9 Pa. $3.50

DINOSAUR DIORAMAS TO CUT & ASSEMBLE, M. Kalmenoff. Two complete three-dimensional scenes in full color, with 31 cut-out animals and plants. Excellent educational toy for youngsters. Instructions; 2 assembly diagrams. 32pp. 9¼ × 12¼.   24541-1 Pa. $3.95

SILHOUETTES: A PICTORIAL ARCHIVE OF VARIED ILLUSTRATIONS, edited by Carol Belanger Grafton. Over 600 silhouettes from the 18th to 20th centuries. Profiles and full figures of men, women, children, birds, animals, groups and scenes, nature, ships, an alphabet. 144pp. 8⅜ × 11¼.   23781-8 Pa. $4.50

SURREAL STICKERS AND UNREAL STAMPS, William Rowe. 224 haunting, hilarious stamps on gummed, perforated stock, with images of elephants, geisha girls, George Washington, etc. 16pp. one side. 8¼ × 11. 24371-0 Pa. $3.50

GOURMET KITCHEN LABELS, Ed Sibbett, Jr. 112 full-color labels (4 copies each of 28 designs). Fruit, bread, other culinary motifs. Gummed and perforated. 16pp. 8¼ × 11. 24087-8 Pa. $2.95

PATTERNS AND INSTRUCTIONS FOR CARVING AUTHENTIC BIRDS, H.D. Green. Detailed instructions, 27 diagrams, 85 photographs for carving 15 species of birds so life-like, they'll seem ready to fly! 8¼ × 11. 24222-6 Pa. $2.75

FLATLAND, E.A. Abbott. Science-fiction classic explores life of 2-D being in 3-D world. 16 illustrations. 103pp. 5⅜ × 8. 20001-9 Pa. $2.00

DRIED FLOWERS, Sarah Whitlock and Martha Rankin. Concise, clear, practical guide to dehydration, glycerinizing, pressing plant material, and more. Covers use of silica gel. 12 drawings. 32pp. 5⅜ × 8½. 21802-3 Pa. $1.00

EASY-TO-MAKE CANDLES, Gary V. Guy. Learn how easy it is to make all kinds of decorative candles. Step-by-step instructions. 82 illustrations. 48pp. 8¼ × 11. 23881-4 Pa. $2.50

SUPER STICKERS FOR KIDS, Carolyn Bracken. 128 gummed and perforated full-color stickers: GIRL WANTED, KEEP OUT, BORED OF EDUCATION, X-RATED, COMBAT ZONE, many others. 16pp. 8¼ × 11. 24092-4 Pa. $2.50

CUT AND COLOR PAPER MASKS, Michael Grater. Clowns, animals, funny faces...simply color them in, cut them out, and put them together, and you have 9 paper masks to play with and enjoy. 32pp. 8¼ × 11. 23171-2 Pa. $2.25

A CHRISTMAS CAROL: THE ORIGINAL MANUSCRIPT, Charles Dickens. Clear facsimile of Dickens manuscript, on facing pages with final printed text. 8 illustrations by John Leech, 4 in color on covers. 144pp. 8⅜ × 11¼. 20980-6 Pa. $5.95

CARVING SHOREBIRDS, Harry V. Shourds & Anthony Hillman. 16 full-size patterns (all double-page spreads) for 19 North American shorebirds with step-by-step instructions. 72pp. 9¼ × 12¼. 24287-0 Pa. $4.95

THE GENTLE ART OF MATHEMATICS, Dan Pedoe. Mathematical games, probability, the question of infinity, topology, how the laws of algebra work, problems of irrational numbers, and more. 42 figures. 143pp. 5⅜ × 8½. (EBE) 22949-1 Pa. $3.00

READY-TO-USE DOLLHOUSE WALLPAPER, Katzenbach & Warren, Inc. Stripe, 2 floral stripes, 2 allover florals, polka dot; all in full color. 4 sheets (350 sq. in.) of each, enough for average room. 48pp. 8¼ × 11. 23495-9 Pa. $2.95

MINIATURE IRON-ON TRANSFER PATTERNS FOR DOLLHOUSES, DOLLS, AND SMALL PROJECTS, Rita Weiss and Frank Fontana. Over 100 miniature patterns: rugs, bedspreads, quilts, chair seats, etc. In standard dollhouse size. 48pp. 8¼ × 11. 23741-9 Pa. $1.95

THE DINOSAUR COLORING BOOK, Anthony Rao. 45 renderings of dinosaurs, fossil birds, turtles, other creatures of Mesozoic Era. Scientifically accurate. Captions. 48pp. 8¼ × 11. 24022-3 Pa. $2.25

JAPANESE DESIGN MOTIFS, Matsuya Co. Mon, or heraldic designs. Over 4000 typical, beautiful designs: birds, animals, flowers, swords, fans, geometrics; all beautifully stylized. 213pp. 11⅜ × 8¼. 22874-6 Pa. $6.95

THE TALE OF BENJAMIN BUNNY, Beatrix Potter. Peter Rabbit's cousin coaxes him back into Mr. McGregor's garden for a whole new set of adventures. All 27 full-color illustrations. 59pp. 4¼ × 5½. (Available in U.S. only) 21102-9 Pa. $1.50

THE TALE OF PETER RABBIT AND OTHER FAVORITE STORIES BOXED SET, Beatrix Potter. Seven of Beatrix Potter's best-loved tales including Peter Rabbit in a specially designed, durable boxed set. 4¼ × 5½. Total of 447pp. 158 color illustrations. (Available in U.S. only) 23903-9 Pa. $10.50

PRACTICAL MENTAL MAGIC, Theodore Annemann. Nearly 200 astonishing feats of mental magic revealed in step-by-step detail. Complete advice on staging, patter, etc. Illustrated. 320pp. 5⅜ × 8½. 24426-1 Pa. $5.95

CELEBRATED CASES OF JUDGE DEE (DEE GOONG AN), translated by Robert Van Gulik. Authentic 18th-century Chinese detective novel; Dee and associates solve three interlocked cases. Led to van Gulik's own stories with same characters. Extensive introduction. 9 illustrations. 237pp. 5⅜ × 8½.

23337-5 Pa. $4.50

CUT & FOLD EXTRATERRESTRIAL INVADERS THAT FLY, M. Grater. Stage your own lilliputian space battles. By following the step-by-step instructions and explanatory diagrams you can launch 22 full-color fliers into space. 36pp. 8¼ × 11. 24478-4 Pa. $2.95

CUT & ASSEMBLE VICTORIAN HOUSES, Edmund V. Gillon, Jr. Printed in full color on heavy cardboard stock, 4 authentic Victorian houses in H-O scale: Italian-style Villa, Octagon, Second Empire, Stick Style. 48pp. 9¼ × 12¼.

23849-0 Pa. $3.95

BEST SCIENCE FICTION STORIES OF H.G. WELLS, H.G. Wells. Full novel *The Invisible Man*, plus 17 short stories: "The Crystal Egg," "Aepyornis Island," "The Strange Orchid," etc. 303pp. 5⅜ × 8½. (Available in U.S. only)

21531-8 Pa. $3.95

TRADEMARK DESIGNS OF THE WORLD, Yusaku Kamekura. A lavish collection of nearly 700 trademarks, the work of Wright, Loewy, Klee, Binder, hundreds of others. 160pp. 8¾ × 8. (Available in U.S. only) 24191-2 Pa. $5.00

THE ARTIST'S AND CRAFTSMAN'S GUIDE TO REDUCING, ENLARGING AND TRANSFERRING DESIGNS, Rita Weiss. Discover, reduce, enlarge, transfer designs from any objects to any craft project. 12pp. plus 16 sheets special graph paper. 8¼ × 11. 24142-4 Pa. $3.25

TREASURY OF JAPANESE DESIGNS AND MOTIFS FOR ARTISTS AND CRAFTSMEN, edited by Carol Belanger Grafton. Indispensable collection of 360 traditional Japanese designs and motifs redrawn in clean, crisp black-and-white, copyright-free illustrations. 96pp. 8¼ × 11. 24435-0 Pa. $3.95

TWENTY-FOUR ART NOUVEAU POSTCARDS IN FULL COLOR FROM CLASSIC POSTERS, Hayward and Blanche Cirker. Ready-to-mail postcards reproduced from rare set of poster art. Works by Toulouse-Lautrec, Parrish, Steinlen, Mucha, Cheret, others. 12pp. 8¼× 11. 24389-3 Pa. $2.95

READY-TO-USE ART NOUVEAU BOOKMARKS IN FULL COLOR, Carol Belanger Grafton. 30 elegant bookmarks featuring graceful, flowing lines, foliate motifs, sensuous women characteristic of Art Nouveau. Perforated for easy detaching. 16pp. 8¼ × 11. 24305-2 Pa. $2.95

FRUIT KEY AND TWIG KEY TO TREES AND SHRUBS, William M. Harlow. Fruit key covers 120 deciduous and evergreen species; twig key covers 160 deciduous species. Easily used. Over 300 photographs. 126pp. 5⅜ × 8½. 20511-8 Pa. $2.25

LEONARDO DRAWINGS, Leonardo da Vinci. Plants, landscapes, human face and figure, etc., plus studies for Sforza monument, *Last Supper*, more. 60 illustrations. 64pp. 8¼ × 11⅛. 23951-9 Pa. $2.75

CLASSIC BASEBALL CARDS, edited by Bert R. Sugar. 98 classic cards on heavy stock, full color, perforated for detaching. Ruth, Cobb, Durocher, DiMaggio, H. Wagner, 99 others. Rare originals cost hundreds. 16pp. 8¼ × 11. 23498-3 Pa. $2.95

TREES OF THE EASTERN AND CENTRAL UNITED STATES AND CANADA, William M. Harlow. Best one-volume guide to 140 trees. Full descriptions, woodlore, range, etc. Over 600 illustrations. Handy size. 288pp. 4½ × 6⅜. 20395-6 Pa. $3.50

JUDY GARLAND PAPER DOLLS IN FULL COLOR, Tom Tierney. 3 Judy Garland paper dolls (teenager, grown-up, and mature woman) and 30 gorgeous costumes highlighting memorable career. Captions. 32pp. 9¼ × 12¼. 24404-0 Pa. $3.50

GREAT FASHION DESIGNS OF THE BELLE EPOQUE PAPER DOLLS IN FULL COLOR, Tom Tierney. Two dolls and 30 costumes meticulously rendered. Haute couture by Worth, Lanvin, Paquin, other greats late Victorian to WWI. 32pp. 9¼ × 12¼. 24425-3 Pa. $3.50

FASHION PAPER DOLLS FROM GODEY'S LADY'S BOOK, 1840-1854, Susan Johnston. In full color: 7 female fashion dolls with 50 costumes. Little girl's, bridal, riding, bathing, wedding, evening, everyday, etc. 32pp. 9¼ × 12¼. 23511-4 Pa. $3.50

THE BOOK OF THE SACRED MAGIC OF ABRAMELIN THE MAGE, translated by S. MacGregor Mathers. Medieval manuscript of ceremonial magic. Basic document in Aleister Crowley, Golden Dawn groups. 268pp. 5⅜ × 8½. 23211-5 Pa. $5.00

PETER RABBIT POSTCARDS IN FULL COLOR: 24 Ready-to-Mail Cards, Susan Whited LaBelle. Bunnies ice-skating, coloring Easter eggs, making valentines, many other charming scenes. 24 perforated full-color postcards, each measuring 4¼ × 6, on coated stock. 12pp. 9 × 12. 24617-5 Pa. $2.95

CELTIC HAND STROKE BY STROKE, A. Baker. Complete guide creating each letter of the alphabet in distinctive Celtic manner. Covers hand position, strokes, pens, inks, paper, more. Illustrated. 48pp. 8¼ × 11. 24336-2 Pa. $2.50

KEYBOARD WORKS FOR SOLO INSTRUMENTS, G.F. Handel. 35 neglected works from Handel's vast oeuvre, originally jotted down as improvisations. Includes Eight Great Suites, others. New sequence. 174pp. 9⅜ × 12¼.

24338-9 Pa. $7.50

AMERICAN LEAGUE BASEBALL CARD CLASSICS, Bert Randolph Sugar. 82 stars from 1900s to 60s on facsimile cards. Ruth, Cobb, Mantle, Williams, plus advertising, info, no duplications. Perforated, detachable. 16pp. 8¼ × 11.

24286-2 Pa. $2.95

A TREASURY OF CHARTED DESIGNS FOR NEEDLEWORKERS, Georgia Gorham and Jeanne Warth. 141 charted designs: owl, cat with yarn, tulips, piano, spinning wheel, covered bridge, Victorian house and many others. 48pp. 8¼ × 11.

23558-0 Pa. $1.95

DANISH FLORAL CHARTED DESIGNS, Gerda Bengtsson. Exquisite collection of over 40 different florals: anemone, Iceland poppy, wild fruit, pansies, many others. 45 illustrations. 48pp. 8¼ × 11.

23957-8 Pa. $1.75

OLD PHILADELPHIA IN EARLY PHOTOGRAPHS 1839-1914, Robert F. Looney. 215 photographs: panoramas, street scenes, landmarks, President-elect Lincoln's visit, 1876 Centennial Exposition, much more. 230pp. 8⅞ × 11¾.

23345-6 Pa. $9.95

PRELUDE TO MATHEMATICS, W.W. Sawyer. Noted mathematician's lively, stimulating account of non-Euclidean geometry, matrices, determinants, group theory, other topics. Emphasis on novel, striking aspects. 224pp. 5⅜ × 8½.

24401-6 Pa. $4.50

ADVENTURES WITH A MICROSCOPE, Richard Headstrom. 59 adventures with clothing fibers, protozoa, ferns and lichens, roots and leaves, much more. 142 illustrations. 232pp. 5⅜ × 8½.

23471-1 Pa. $3.50

IDENTIFYING ANIMAL TRACKS: MAMMALS, BIRDS, AND OTHER ANIMALS OF THE EASTERN UNITED STATES, Richard Headstrom. For hunters, naturalists, scouts, nature-lovers. Diagrams of tracks, tips on identification. 128pp. 5⅜ × 8.

24442-3 Pa. $3.50

VICTORIAN FASHIONS AND COSTUMES FROM HARPER'S BAZAR, 1867-1898, edited by Stella Blum. Day costumes, evening wear, sports clothes, shoes, hats, other accessories in over 1,000 detailed engravings. 320pp. 9⅜ × 12¼.

22990-4 Pa. $9.95

EVERYDAY FASHIONS OF THE TWENTIES AS PICTURED IN SEARS AND OTHER CATALOGS, edited by Stella Blum. Actual dress of the Roaring Twenties, with text by Stella Blum. Over 750 illustrations, captions. 156pp. 9 × 12.

24134-3 Pa. $7.95

HALL OF FAME BASEBALL CARDS, edited by Bert Randolph Sugar. Cy Young, Ted Williams, Lou Gehrig, and many other Hall of Fame greats on 92 full-color, detachable reprints of early baseball cards. No duplication of cards with *Classic Baseball Cards.* 16pp. 8¼ × 11.

23624-2 Pa. $2.95

THE ART OF HAND LETTERING, Helm Wotzkow. Course in hand lettering, Roman, Gothic, Italic, Block, Script. Tools, proportions, optical aspects, individual variation. Very quality conscious. Hundreds of specimens. 320pp. 5⅜ × 8½.

21797-3 Pa. $4.95

HOW THE OTHER HALF LIVES, Jacob A. Riis. Journalistic record of filth, degradation, upward drive in New York immigrant slums, shops, around 1900. New edition includes 100 original Riis photos, monuments of early photography. 233pp. 10 × 7⅞. 22012-5 Pa. $7.95

CHINA AND ITS PEOPLE IN EARLY PHOTOGRAPHS, John Thomson. In 200 black-and-white photographs of exceptional quality photographic pioneer Thomson captures the mountains, dwellings, monuments and people of 19th-century China. 272pp. 9⅜ × 12¼. 24393-1 Pa. $12.95

GODEY COSTUME PLATES IN COLOR FOR DECOUPAGE AND FRAMING, edited by Eleanor Hasbrouk Rawlings. 24 full-color engravings depicting 19th-century Parisian haute couture. Printed on one side only. 56pp. 8¼ × 11. 23879-2 Pa. $3.95

ART NOUVEAU STAINED GLASS PATTERN BOOK, Ed Sibbett, Jr. 104 projects using well-known themes of Art Nouveau: swirling forms, florals, peacocks, and sensuous women. 60pp. 8¼ × 11. 23577-7 Pa. $3.00

QUICK AND EASY PATCHWORK ON THE SEWING MACHINE: Susan Aylsworth Murwin and Suzzy Payne. Instructions, diagrams show exactly how to machine sew 12 quilts. 48pp. of templates. 50 figures. 80pp. 8¼ × 11. 23770-2 Pa. $3.50

THE STANDARD BOOK OF QUILT MAKING AND COLLECTING, Marguerite Ickis. Full information, full-sized patterns for making 46 traditional quilts, also 150 other patterns. 483 illustrations. 273pp. 6⅞ × 9⅝. 20582-7 Pa. $5.95

LETTERING AND ALPHABETS, J. Albert Cavanagh. 85 complete alphabets lettered in various styles; instructions for spacing, roughs, brushwork. 121pp. 8¾ × 8. 20053-1 Pa. $3.75

LETTER FORMS: 110 COMPLETE ALPHABETS, Frederick Lambert. 110 sets of capital letters; 16 lower case alphabets; 70 sets of numbers and other symbols. 110pp. 8⅛ × 11. 22872-X Pa. $4.50

ORCHIDS AS HOUSE PLANTS, Rebecca Tyson Northen. Grow cattleyas and many other kinds of orchids—in a window, in a case, or under artificial light. 63 illustrations. 148pp. 5⅜ × 8½. 23261-1 Pa. $2.95

THE MUSHROOM HANDBOOK, Louis C.C. Krieger. Still the best popular handbook. Full descriptions of 259 species, extremely thorough text, poisons, folklore, etc. 32 color plates; 126 other illustrations. 560pp. 5⅜ × 8½. 21861-9 Pa. $8.50

THE DORÉ BIBLE ILLUSTRATIONS, Gustave Doré. All wonderful, detailed plates: Adam and Eve, Flood, Babylon, life of Jesus, etc. Brief King James text with each plate. 241 plates. 241pp. 9 × 12. 23004-X Pa. $6.95

THE BOOK OF KELLS: Selected Plates in Full Color, edited by Blanche Cirker. 32 full-page plates from greatest manuscript-icon of early Middle Ages. Fantastic, mysterious. Publisher's Note. Captions. 32pp. 9¾ × 12¼. 24345-1 Pa. $4.50

THE PERFECT WAGNERITE, George Bernard Shaw. Brilliant criticism of the Ring Cycle, with provocative interpretation of politics, economic theories behind the Ring. 136pp. 5⅜ × 8½. (Available in U.S. only) 21707-8 Pa. $3.00

THE RIME OF THE ANCIENT MARINER, Gustave Doré, S.T. Coleridge. Doré's finest work, 34 plates capture moods, subtleties of poem. Full text. 77pp. 9¼ × 12.
22305-1 Pa. $4.95

SONGS OF INNOCENCE, William Blake. The first and most popular of Blake's famous "Illuminated Books," in a facsimile edition reproducing all 31 brightly colored plates. Additional printed text of each poem. 64pp. 5¼ × 7.
22764-2 Pa. $3.00

AN INTRODUCTION TO INFORMATION THEORY, J.R. Pierce. Second (1980) edition of most impressive non-technical account available. Encoding, entropy, noisy channel, related areas, etc. 320pp. 5⅜ × 8½.
24061-4 Pa. $4.95

THE DIVINE PROPORTION: A STUDY IN MATHEMATICAL BEAUTY, H.E. Huntley. "Divine proportion" or "golden ratio" in poetry, Pascal's triangle, philosophy, psychology, music, mathematical figures, etc. Excellent bridge between science and art. 58 figures. 185pp. 5⅜ × 8½.
22254-3 Pa. $3.95

THE DOVER NEW YORK WALKING GUIDE: From the Battery to Wall Street, Mary J. Shapiro. Superb inexpensive guide to historic buildings and locales in lower Manhattan: Trinity Church, Bowling Green, more. Complete Text; maps. 36 illustrations. 48pp. 3⅞ × 9¼.
24225-0 Pa. $1.75

NEW YORK THEN AND NOW, Edward B. Watson, Edmund V. Gillon, Jr. 83 important Manhattan sites: on facing pages early photographs (1875-1925) and 1976 photos by Gillon. 172 illustrations. 171pp. 9¼ × 10.
23361-8 Pa. $7.95

HISTORIC COSTUME IN PICTURES, Braun & Schneider. Over 1450 costumed figures from dawn of civilization to end of 19th century. English captions. 125 plates. 256pp. 8⅜ × 11¼.
23150-X Pa. $7.50

VICTORIAN AND EDWARDIAN FASHION: A Photographic Survey, Alison Gernsheim. First fashion history completely illustrated by contemporary photographs. Full text plus 235 photos, 1840-1914, in which many celebrities appear. 240pp. 6½ × 9¼.
24205-6 Pa. $6.00

CHARTED CHRISTMAS DESIGNS FOR COUNTED CROSS-STITCH AND OTHER NEEDLECRAFTS, Lindberg Press. Charted designs for 45 beautiful needlecraft projects with many yuletide and wintertime motifs. 48pp. 8¼ × 11.
24356-7 Pa. $1.95

101 FOLK DESIGNS FOR COUNTED CROSS-STITCH AND OTHER NEEDLE-CRAFTS, Carter Houck. 101 authentic charted folk designs in a wide array of lovely representations with many suggestions for effective use. 48pp. 8¼ × 11.
24369-9 Pa. $1.95

FIVE ACRES AND INDEPENDENCE, Maurice G. Kains. Great back-to-the-land classic explains basics of self-sufficient farming. The one book to get. 95 illustrations. 397pp. 5⅜ × 8½.
20974-1 Pa. $4.95

A MODERN HERBAL, Margaret Grieve. Much the fullest, most exact, most useful compilation of herbal material. Gigantic alphabetical encyclopedia, from aconite to zedoary, gives botanical information, medical properties, folklore, economic uses, and much else. Indispensable to serious reader. 161 illustrations. 888pp. 6½ × 9¼. (Available in U.S. only)
22798-7, 22799-5 Pa., Two-vol. set $16.45

REASON IN ART, George Santayana. Renowned philosopher's provocative, seminal treatment of basis of art in instinct and experience. Volume Four of *The Life of Reason.* 230pp. 5⅜ × 8.
24358-3 Pa. $4.50

LANGUAGE, TRUTH AND LOGIC, Alfred J. Ayer. Famous, clear introduction to Vienna, Cambridge schools of Logical Positivism. Role of philosophy, elimination of metaphysics, nature of analysis, etc. 160pp. 5⅜ × 8½. (USCO)
20010-8 Pa. $2.75

BASIC ELECTRONICS, U.S. Bureau of Naval Personnel. Electron tubes, circuits, antennas, AM, FM, and CW transmission and receiving, etc. 560 illustrations. 567pp. 6½ × 9¼.
21076-6 Pa. $8.95

THE ART DECO STYLE, edited by Theodore Menten. Furniture, jewelry, metalwork, ceramics, fabrics, lighting fixtures, interior decors, exteriors, graphics from pure French sources. Over 400 photographs. 183pp. 8⅜ × 11¼.
22824-X Pa. $6.95

THE FOUR BOOKS OF ARCHITECTURE, Andrea Palladio. 16th-century classic covers classical architectural remains, Renaissance revivals, classical orders, etc. 1738 Ware English edition. 216 plates. 110pp. of text. 9½ × 12¾.
21308-0 Pa. $10.00

THE WIT AND HUMOR OF OSCAR WILDE, edited by Alvin Redman. More than 1000 ripostes, paradoxes, wisecracks: Work is the curse of the drinking classes, I can resist everything except temptations, etc. 258pp. 5⅜ × 8½. (USCO)
20602-5 Pa. $3.50

THE DEVIL'S DICTIONARY, Ambrose Bierce. Barbed, bitter, brilliant witticisms in the form of a dictionary. Best, most ferocious satire America has produced. 145pp. 5⅜ × 8½.
20487-1 Pa. $2.50

ERTÉ'S FASHION DESIGNS, Erté. 210 black-and-white inventions from *Harper's Bazar*, 1918-32, plus 8pp. full-color covers. Captions. 88pp. 9 × 12.
24203-X Pa. $6.50

ERTÉ GRAPHICS, Erté. Collection of striking color graphics: *Seasons, Alphabet, Numerals, Aces* and *Precious Stones.* 50 plates, including 4 on covers. 48pp. 9⅜ × 12¼.
23580-7 Pa. $6.95

PAPER FOLDING FOR BEGINNERS, William D. Murray and Francis J. Rigney. Clearest book for making origami sail boats, roosters, frogs that move legs, etc. 40 projects. More than 275 illustrations. 94pp. 5⅜ × 8½.
20713-7 Pa. $1.95

ORIGAMI FOR THE ENTHUSIAST, John Montroll. Fish, ostrich, peacock, squirrel, rhinoceros, Pegasus, 19 other intricate subjects. Instructions. Diagrams. 128pp. 9 × 12.
23799-0 Pa. $4.95

CROCHETING NOVELTY POT HOLDERS, edited by Linda Macho. 64 useful, whimsical pot holders feature kitchen themes, animals, flowers, other novelties. Surprisingly easy to crochet. Complete instructions. 48pp. 8¼ × 11.
24296-X Pa. $1.95

CROCHETING DOILIES, edited by Rita Weiss. Irish Crochet, Jewel, Star Wheel, Vanity Fair and more. Also luncheon and console sets, runners and centerpieces. 51 illustrations. 48pp. 8¼ × 11.
23424-X Pa. $2.00

TOLL HOUSE TRIED AND TRUE RECIPES, Ruth Graves Wakefield. Pop-overs, veal and ham loaf, baked beans, much more from the famous Mass. restaurant. Nearly 700 recipes. 376pp. 5⅜ × 8½. 23560-2 Pa. $4.95

FAVORITE CHRISTMAS CAROLS, selected and arranged by Charles J.F. Cofone. Title, music, first verse and refrain of 34 traditional carols in handsome calligraphy; also subsequent verses and other information in type. 79pp. 8⅜ × 11. 20445-6 Pa. $3.00

CAMERA WORK: A PICTORIAL GUIDE, Alfred Stieglitz. All 559 illustrations from most important periodical in history of art photography. Reduced in size but still clear, in strict chronological order, with complete captions. 176pp. 8⅜ × 11¼. 23591-2 Pa. $6.95

FAVORITE SONGS OF THE NINETIES, edited by Robert Fremont. 88 favorites: "Ta-Ra-Ra-Boom-De-Aye," "The Band Played On," "Bird in a Gilded Cage," etc. 401pp. 9 × 12. 21536-9 Pa. $10.95

STRING FIGURES AND HOW TO MAKE THEM, Caroline F. Jayne. Fullest, clearest instructions on string figures from around world: Eskimo, Navajo, Lapp, Europe, more. Cat's cradle, moving spear, lightning, stars. 950 illustrations. 407pp. 5⅜ × 8½. 20152-X Pa. $4.95

LIFE IN ANCIENT EGYPT, Adolf Erman. Detailed older account, with much not in more recent books: domestic life, religion, magic, medicine, commerce, and whatever else needed for complete picture. Many illustrations. 597pp. 5⅜ × 8½. 22632-8 Pa. $7.95

ANCIENT EGYPT: ITS CULTURE AND HISTORY, J.E. Manchip White. From pre-dynastics through Ptolemies: scoiety, history, political structure, religion, daily life, literature, cultural heritage. 48 plates. 217pp. 5⅜ × 8½. (EBE) 22548-8 Pa. $4.95

KEPT IN THE DARK, Anthony Trollope. Unusual short novel about Victorian morality and abnormal psychology by the great English author. Probably the first American publication. Frontispiece by Sir John Millais. 92pp. 6½ × 9¼. 23609-9 Pa. $2.95

MAN AND WIFE, Wilkie Collins. Nineteenth-century master launches an attack on out-moded Scottish marital laws and Victorian cult of athleticism. Artfully plotted. 35 illustrations. 239pp. 6⅛ × 9¼. 24451-2 Pa. $5.95

RELATIVITY AND COMMON SENSE, Herman Bondi. Radically reoriented presentation of Einstein's Special Theory and one of most valuable popular accounts available. 60 illustrations. 177pp. 5⅜ × 8. (EUK) 24021-5 Pa. $3.50

THE EGYPTIAN BOOK OF THE DEAD, E.A. Wallis Budge. Complete reproduction of Ani's papyrus, finest ever found. Full hieroglyphic text, interlinear transliteration, word-for-word translation, smooth translation. 533pp. 6½ × 9¼. (USO) 21866-X Pa. $8.50

COUNTRY AND SUBURBAN HOMES OF THE PRAIRIE SCHOOL PERIOD, H.V. von Holst. Over 400 photographs floor plans, elevations, detailed drawings (exteriors and interiors) for over 100 structures. Text. Important primary source. 128pp. 8⅜ × 11¼. 24373-7 Pa. $5.95